COLOUR LIBRARY BOOK OF

GREAT BRITISH WRITERS

COLOUR LIBRARY BOOK OF

GREAT BRITISH WRITERS

Colour Library Books

CLB 2238
This edition published 1993 by Colour Library Books Ltd
Godalming Business Centre, Woolsack Way,
Godalming, Surrey GU7 1XW

Prepared by Marshall Cavendish Books Ltd
58 Old Compton Street, London W1V 5PA

Typeset by Litho Link Ltd, Welshpool, Powys, Wales
Printed in Hong Kong

ISBN 0 86283 678 6

Contents

Introduction

The desire to curl up with a good book and escape – through the marvellous and unmatched powers of the human imagination – into other people's lives, loves and adventures is a strong one. The explosion in forms of communication has given us satellite television and videos, car phones and word processors, but all singularly lack the comfort and satisfaction of reading a good book.

Now, incredibly, about 60,000 new books are published in English every year. Yet men and women, boys and girls, turn again and again to the classics. Those well-loved volumes have peopled our lives in a very real way with a gallery of vibrant and diverse characters such as Jane Eyre, Hamlet, Long John Silver, Miss Havisham, Sherlock Holmes, Lady Macbeth, Cathy and Heathcliff, Mr Pickwick, Frankenstein, the Mad Hatter, and Romeo and Juliet, who live and breath in scenes of unforgettable brilliance.

What then of the lives of the writers who have made such an impact on English language and literature for ordinary readers? It is undeniably fascinating to trace the people, places and experience of the writer's young life, so often mirrored in many ways in his or her writing. We can picture the 12-year-old Dickens working in the shoe blacking factory, probably the most traumatic experience of his life, later to become the inspiration for scenes in *David Copperfield;* the 22-year-old Darwin keeping his notebooks during *Beagle's* five-year voyage, 20 years before the revolutionary *Origin of Species* was published; the girl Emily Brontë at one in solitude and intensity with the Yorkshire moors, where she later placed *Wuthering Heights;* the Reverend Charles Dodgson first meeting with the four-year-old Alice Liddell, for whom he wrote *Alice's Adventures in Wonderland.* This is compulsive reading. And images and scenes that fired the writer's imagination are here too in an abundance of beautiful illustrations which recall his or her family, home and life.

Who can define literary genius? Whatever it is, it cuts across sex, class, experience, generations – every barrier – to strike chords of essential truths in the hearts and minds of millions of readers. This genius, in stirring the imagination of the reader with intense colour, emotion and detail is such that, when a famous novel is made into a film, no matter how good the production, there is always a vague sense of disappointment that it 'did not live up to the book'.

While the classics have proven themselves to critics and ordinary people alike, it is the judgement of the latter that ensures their greatness and survival. *Great British Writers* is part of an exchange of experience and understanding which brings the household of the famous writer into the household of the appreciative reader.

P. M. Pierce

Fotomas

GEOFFREY CHAUCER

c.1340-1400

Chaucer's mental energies must have been phenomenal, his character full of contradictory virtues. He was a diplomat, tactful and discreet, yet he was called on to entertain the Court with songs and poems; he was a civil servant entrusted with important missions abroad, yet he found time to educate himself in every field of study. And all the while he was writing poetry of originality and vigour which would set his name at the very foundation of English literature.

The Perfect Courtier

As a 14th-century courtier, Chaucer was steward, statesman, soldier, poet and politician; literary genius in no way freed him from his duties to a succession of powerful masters.

It was not unusual in the Middle Ages for men to combine different strands of occupation in their lives, yet Geoffrey Chaucer's achievements, not only as the first great English poet, but as scholar, courtier, civil servant and diplomat, prove him an unusual and exceptionally gifted man. Sadly, we know a good deal about his career as a servant of the king, but virtually nothing of his personal life and character.

He was born in the early 1340s, at a time when England, with Edward III on the throne, was more stable and settled than it had been for half a century. Within a few years of his birth, England had achieved a glorious and devastating victory over the knighthood of France at the Battle of Crecy, and Edward's court was beginning to emerge as one of the most brilliant and colourful in Europe.

Chaucer's family were part of the newly rising merchant class. His great-grandfather had a tavern in Ipswich, in the county of Suffolk. But his grandfather Robert Malin le Chaucer set up a wine wholesale business in London, and made such a success of it that Chaucer's father John was able to marry a wealthy heiress, Agnes Copton, niece and ward of a 'moneyer' at the Royal Mint. The flamboyant John Chaucer had been outlawed as a ringleader of a rebel troop in the 1320s, but in 1338 went to the wars in France as a member of the King's retinue.

A PAGE AT COURT

Whole villages were wiped out by wars or by that other wholesale slaughter – the Plague or Black Death. Yet some bitter comfort was to be derived from it: shortage of labour in the country freed many serfs from their bondage, while the sudden loss of many courtiers gave the sons of ordinary merchants like Chaucer the chance to rise in the King's service. As a boy Chaucer probably went to one of London's three grammar schools, where the pupils were taught Latin grammar, and learned Latin poetry. At this time, French (the language of court) was spoken by people of any social pretension, and Chaucer would have learned it alongside his native English. He must have done well at school, for by the time he was 14 or so, he was a page in the service of the illustrious Elizabeth, Countess of Ulster, and then her husband, Prince Lionel, son of Edward III. A document dated 4 April 1357 shows that Elizabeth bought 'Galfridus Chaucer' shoes, black and red breeches and a 'paltok' (short cloak).

By 1359, he had 'received arms' and become a squire, an apprentice knight, well versed in all the arts of chivalry – fighting, paying court and Christian duty. Perhaps the picture of the squire in *The Canterbury Tales*, "a lover and a lusty bachelor", recalls Chaucer's own days as a squire. It may be that Chaucer actually fought in the French wars, for he was certainly captured by the French for a while, and released only when a ransom was paid; King Edward contributed £16.

As Lionel's squire, Chaucer witnessed the splendour and sophistication of Edward III's court at first hand, following its grand progress around the country. He must have heard fashionable French poets recite and sing their elegant romances to the

Edward III
Crowned in 1327, Edward III (above) reigned for 50 years and had six sons. He was a warrior king, but had a highly cultured court.

New wealth
John Chaucer, Geoffrey's father, returned from outlawry to inherit a new family fortune made from wine trading (below).

Key Dates

c.1340 born in London

1357 page to the Countess of Ulster

1359 captured in France and ransomed

1366 marries Philippa Roet

1367 joins the King's household

1372-3 first journey to Italy

1374-86 Controller of Wool Customs

1378 second journey to Italy

c.1387 begins *The Canterbury Tales*

1389 becomes Clerk of the King's Works

1391 moves to Somerset as forester

1399 returns to London

1400 dies at Westminster

AN INFLUENTIAL MARRIAGE

About three years after marrying Chaucer, both Philippa and her sister Katherine Swynford were taken on as ladies-in-waiting in John of Gaunt's household. Katherine soon became John's mistress. Some speculate that Philippa did, too, for he often gave her money. But the union between John and Kate was less than casual, for he married her in 1396 – much to the horror of the court. Their great-great-grandson laid claim to the Crown and became Henry VII.

court, and perhaps he began to copy them then.

In the early 1360s, Chaucer is thought to have withdrawn from court to study for a while, perhaps at Oxford or Cambridge, perhaps at London's Inner Temple. But by 1365, he was back in royal service, and soon to be part of the King's own household.

A document from 22 February 1365 shows him on important diplomatic business in Aquitaine, south-west France, where the alliance between England and the Spanish kingdom of Castile was causing alarm. It seems likely that he was working for the Black Prince, Edward III's eldest son.

Over the next 20 or so years, Chaucer was to make many trips abroad in the King's service, and it is clear that he was held in high regard and considered capable and discreet. He was also valued as a man of letters and a linguist, well-versed in Italian and the dialects of northern and southern France.

But a yeoman like Chaucer did not only go on important diplomatic missions. He was also expected to make beds, hold torches and serve food at the King's table. He had to entertain the court by telling stories or giving out the latest political news, or with music and songs. Perhaps the young Chaucer now wrote his first verses, romances in the French style. His fellow poet John Gower relates that, 'in the flower of his youth, in various ways', Chaucer filled the country with his 'ditties and glad songs'.

At about the time he entered the King's service, Chaucer married Philippa Roet, a lady-in-waiting to Queen Philippa. The young French poet Froissart wrote of Philippa Chaucer that she had a fine sense of protocol (which she was to need later). The marriage brought Chaucer into closer contact with John of Gaunt, the Duke of Lancaster, Edward's third son and – next to the King – the most powerful man in the kingdom. Philippa became a lady-in-waiting to John's second wife.

Chaucer had known John for some time before Philippa had joined his household, and it was as a memorial to John's first wife, the lovely Blanche who died in 1368, that Chaucer wrote his first major poem, *The Book of the Duchess*.

After the outbreak of the plague that carried off

Born Londoner
Chaucer's father's house was near the Thames quays where the wine tuns were unloaded. Within a few square miles lived nobility, merchants, beggars, craftsmen, whores, politicians and churchmen: his boyhood was crowded with every class and type. Crown work kept him in touch with London (above) all life long.

Latin education
Geoffrey probably attended, until the age of 12 or 13, a grammar school (left) where the prevailing language was Latin. He was to become a versatile and fluent linguist, translating not just the Latin poets, such as Ovid and Virgil whom he had studied at school, but French and Italian works as well.

The Customs man
As Controller of Wool Customs, Chaucer was well placed to know, and make literary use of, the double-dealing that went on in an international port (left) such as London. The Merchant in The Canterbury Tales *is manipulating foreign currency, for instance.*

Hundred Years' War
Begun by Edward III in 1337 as he laid claim to the French throne, the string of major battles and inconclusive skirmishes known as the Hundred Years' War (below) dragged on, draining the economies of Europe and occupying men at a time when Plague had already devastated the population.

Fact or Fiction

BLACK DEATH

In 1348 the Black Death struck. A contemporary wrote, 'This great pestilence . . . raged for a whole year in England so terribly that it cleared many country villages entirely.' On one estimate, more than a third of the population died. It became common to personify Death in art and poetry, and in the Pardoner's Tale three drunks swear that they will seek out and murder the dread Grim Reaper.

Blanche and Edward's Queen Philippa too, the atmosphere at court began to turn sour. The war with France was resumed, disastrously for England. French raids on South Coast ports were frequent, trade was disrupted, and taxes to pay for the war became increasingly burdensome for a population ravaged by the plague. Edward III was slipping into senility, and doted on his rapacious mistress Alice Perrers.

Twice during the 1370s, Chaucer braved the dangers of war to travel to Italy on diplomatic missions, first to Genoa, then to Florence. In Italy he was able to buy copies of poems by the great Italian poets Dante, Petrarch and Boccaccio. He may even have met the latter two. Dante's profound and philosophical work, *Divine Comedy*, proved that poems could encompass a range of ideas and feelings far beyond the scope of the light French court romances. Boccaccio, inspired by the poets of ancient Rome, proclaimed that the poet was not simply an entertainer but also a scholar and philosopher.

COURT CIRCULARS

Chaucer himself became increasingly learned. He collected 'sixty bokes olde and newe' and read voraciously both at home and in London's many libraries, applying both an acute intelligence and scepticism. In this way, he became a highly accomplished scholar, well versed in a variety of subjects from classical literature to the latest scientific and astrological studies of the day.

At the same time, he continued writing poetry in his native language, English – poems achieving a richness far beyond anything in the vernacular

Peasants' Revolt
The boy-king Richard II was manipulated by rival court factions. He promised mercy to the peasant Wat Tyler and his rebellious followers (left), but later took bloody reprisals, probably on the counsel of his cynical advisors.

Powerful patron
Son of Edward III and uncle of Richard II, John of Gaunt, Duke of Lancaster (below left), was the second most powerful man in England. He sired a dynasty of kings, and was an invaluable patron and contact for Chaucer.

A prized poet
Clearly Chaucer had risen to a position of great status as a poet by the time he was pictured (below) reading a manuscript (probably his narrative poem Troilus and Criseyde) *to the assembled court including Richard and his Queen Anne. Only when plots against the King became rife did Chaucer withdraw to the relative peace of Somerset.*

before. These poems, from *The House of Fame* (c.1374) to *Troilus and Criseyde* (c.1385), were written down and circulated, unlike his early works which were simply recited at court.

All this scholarship and writing occupied him in his spare time, after a long day at work. On 8 June 1374, he was appointed by royal warrant as Controller of the Wool Custom and Wool Subsidy, a very important post, for taxes on exports of wool were the biggest peacetime source of revenue.

The wool taxes were paid to two collectors at the Port of London, and as controller it was Chaucer's job to keep a counter-roll against which the accounts of the collectors could be checked. Before wool was exported, it had to have a licence, sealed by a stamp one half of which was retained by the controller, and the other by the collectors.

Chaucer was given an apartment, rent-free, above the Aldgate, ten minutes' walk from the Port. But it was not an easy job, for the collectors were often wealthy and powerful merchants with a vested interest in slipping wool through untaxed, and Chaucer was frequently absent on diplomatic missions. Still he remained controller until the end of 1386.

A MYSTERIOUS CASE

These years were, on the whole, prosperous, but his life was not without troubles. A curious document dated 1 May 1380 in the name of Cecily Chaumpaigne releases Geoffrey Chaucer from any action over 'both my rape and other cause'. Could Chaucer have sexually assaulted Mistress Chaumpaigne, or abducted her (which the word 'rape'

also meant then)? One theory is that it was an attempt by London merchants to frame him, but there is no evidence either way.

Whatever the truth there is no doubt that by 1386 he was a man of some substance and status. The year before, he had become a Justice of the Peace and, in October, he entered Parliament as one of the two Knights of the Shire for Kent, where he was now living. But trouble was brewing.

TROUBLE AT COURT

Ever since the death of Edward III in 1377, there had been bitter infighting at court for control of the boy-king Richard II, between the courtiers and aristocrats closest to the boy, the Lancastrians, around John of Gaunt, and the barons. In 1386, the barons gained the upper hand, and began purging the royal household of opponents. A few went to the block and Chaucer, closely associated with both the court party and the Lancastrians, must have felt his position, if not his life, threatened.

Perhaps he was ousted, perhaps he resigned. At all events, he disappeared from royal service for the next few years, and took the chance to begin writing *The Canterbury Tales*.

"God save King Henry, unking'd Richard says"
Hated and envied by many, Richard II was forced to abdicate in favour of Henry Bolingbroke (son of John of Gaunt) at Flint Castle in 1399 (left). He was imprisoned and probably murdered the following year – the same year in which Chaucer himself died. Four months after his coronation, Henry IV renewed Chaucer's annuity of £20 and a barrel of wine, so the poet's last months were comfortable.

Clerk of the Works
Once Richard II was of age, Chaucer found himself in royal favour again. His new post meant that he was wage-master, foreman and administrator, overseeing maintenance (above) of the royal palaces.

Robbed!
Twice in one week Chaucer was set upon by footpads and robbed of wages intended for the building workers (below). What he objected to a great deal more, however, was having his horse stolen each time.

In July 1389, two months after Richard II came of age and began to assert his power, Chaucer was back at work again, this time as Clerk of the Works. This job was, if anything, more arduous than that of controller, for it entailed overseeing the construction and maintenance of many important buildings, such as the Palace of Westminster. In 1390, Chaucer had to organize the restoration of St George's Chapel, Windsor.

As Clerk of the Works, Chaucer had hundreds of men to manage and direct, from master-craftsmen to simple labourers, besides keeping detailed accounts and a check on materials and equipment. It could be dangerous, too: in 1390, Chaucer was attacked and robbed twice in a week.

In 1391 he accepted – perhaps with relief – a job as forester of the King's park in North Petherton,

Italian visits
As yeoman in the King's household, Chaucer made frequent trips abroad on business. He spent the winter of 1372-73 in Italy (left) and it is known he went to Florence. Did he meet his contemporary, Petrarch? Or Boccaccio, author of The Decameron *(the so-called 'Italian Canterbury Tales')? Did he acquire, while he was there, books for his great collection? He certainly admired Italian writers, especially Dante, read Italian with ease and spoke it well enough to negotiate loans for Edward III's wars. He returned to Italy in 1378, to Lombardy.*

Somerset. He then had time to continue writing *The Canterbury Tales* – and he was out of the way of the political intrigues building up against the cruel, increasingly tyrannical King Richard.

In February 1399, John of Gaunt died, and Richard, desperate for money to fight wars in France and Ireland, confiscated the Lancastrian estates. Later that year, while Richard was in Ireland, John's son Henry Bolingbroke returned from exile to reclaim his inheritance, and received such ardent support that he soon laid claim to the Crown. Richard was imprisoned, and probably murdered, and Bolingbroke was crowned Henry IV.

Chaucer moved back to London and rented a house in the garden of Westminster Abbey. He seems to have begun to wonder if his poetry was actually a self-indulgence. A text of the time complained that 'demons feed on the songs of the poets, the vanity of worldly wisdom, the pomp of rhetorical language', and Chaucer may have started to feel this was true. At the end of The Parson's Tale, the poet begs forgiveness for his poems, his 'endytinges of worldly vanitee', and describes his regret at writing 'many a song and many a lecherous lay'.

On 25 October 1400, Chaucer died. He was buried in Westminster Abbey, leaving behind him poetry of a richness and depth never before achieved in English, and not to be equalled for 200 years.

Last resting place
Chaucer's last house stood within the grounds of Westminster Abbey (below), and after his death in October 1400 he was buried there – esteemed as a writer, translator and loyal servant of the Crown. It was a rare honour for a commoner, and set a precedent establishing the present 'Poets' Corner'.

Saints and Sinners

Chaucer's world was a mere province of Christendom. Every aspect of life, every member of society, good and bad – all were enfolded by the powerful presence of Mother Church.

Chaucer's pilgrims represent a vivid cross-section of medieval society, reminding us that religion was a subject of universal concern in the Middle Ages. It played a central part in everyone's life – from kings to peasants – and although England was in many ways separate from the Continent, it was also part of Christendom under the dominion of the Pope.

His supreme authority stemmed from being part of a line that stretched back to St Peter (the first pope), who had been invested by Christ himself. During the 13th century, Popes tried to use their religious authority to claim political supremacy over secular rulers. The result was conflict between Popes and monarchs, which, in part, was the cause of the 'Great Schism' (1378-1417), during which two, and sometimes three, Popes claimed to be the true head of the Church.

Few, however, questioned the truth of the Church's teachings, and religion was pre-eminent in everyday life, from the cradle to the grave. On the day of birth, a child was baptized in church. Walter Hilton, a priest writing in Chaucer's day, explains: 'A soul of a child that is born but not christened . . . hath no likeness of God; he is nought but an image of the fiend and a brand of hell – but as soon as he is christened, he is reformed to the image of God.'

As children grew, they would join the crowd standing in church each Sunday morning to hear the mass celebrated and to listen to the sermon. All around them were vivid wall-paintings depicting Bible stories or scenes of Judgement Day. And in front of them, hiding the ritual of the mass which proceeded out of sight up by the high altar, was the rood screen with a huge central crucifix. Only once a year, at Easter, could lay people participate in the communion.

LEARNING THE BIBLE

Whether the worshippers were instructed by their own parish priest, by a paid substitute, or by a friar (a member of a monastic order dependent on charity), they learned the teachings of the Church. There were mystery plays, too, which took place each year, when Bible stories were acted out; so people were familiar with the Bible

The old, old stories
There was a widespread, thorough knowledge of Bible stories such as Jonah and the Whale (above) and Noah's Ark (above right). Teaching was reinforced by religious paintings, drama and simple word of mouth, passed on from one generation to the next.

Preaching the word
Such instruction as the common man and woman received came from the pulpit (left). The only educated men (apart from the nobility) were men of the Church. The substance of what they taught was religious. Knowledge and religious truth were therefore virtually synonymous. The only 'outside' influence would have been dimly understood, centuries-old pagan folklore, much of it accommodated into Christian festivals and theology. God was an unquestioned, everyday reality, while the clergy enjoyed an assumed superiority.

even when they could not read it for themselves.

For unsophisticated people, moral instruction had to be put in simple terms, so cautionary tales featuring the Seven Deadly Sins – Pride, Covetousness, Lust, Envy, Gluttony, Anger and Sloth – were popular with preachers. Unfavourable weather conditions were pointed to as signs of divine displeasure, and it was commonly held that the Black Death was a punishment for sins.

From the many grotesque church frescoes, manuscript illuminations and paintings, it would be easy to conclude that the medieval Church played unremittingly on the pains of Hell and Purgatory and so held the people in thrall. There is, however, also ample evidence of medieval religion portraying a tender, generous manifestation of God's love, available to all, rich or poor, with or without intervention of the clergy. But there is no doubt that death was an everyday preoccupation for English men and women in the 14th century, even before successive epidemics of plague had devastated the population.

Key-holder of Heaven
Pope Gregory XI (above) conducted a long-drawn-out war of wits with Edward III over the proportion of church taxes hived off to Rome, and the appointment of Ministers.

INVESTMENT IN HEAVEN

The fear of death (and what would come after it) made people give large amounts of money to the Church. One benefactor of a monastery sums up his motive: 'I fear for the pains of hell, and I desire to come to the joys of paradise, and for the love of God and his glorious mother, and for the salvation of my soul and those of my parents, I give to God, St Mary and all the saints my whole inheritance.' To the medieval mind this was a straightforward bargain. Masses could 'pay off' a debt of sin, and if enough could not be sung in a lifetime, someone must be paid to sing them after one's death. This careful provision for the afterlife helped to build up the extraordinary wealth of the Church.

'Jacob's ladder'
The Church hierarchy (below) provided almost the only career ladder for an intelligent young man born without rank. A tonsure (shaved head), therefore, was not necessarily an indication of religious calling.

Christendom
A contemporary map of the Christian world (left) shows how deep-seated was the concept of Christendom. Jerusalem was at the centre (just as, at the time, Earth was seen as the centre of the Universe). Strictly speaking, however, the Pope was the focal point of Christendom. Even while war split Christian nation from nation, nationalistic feelings never dented Europe's allegiance to the Roman Church.

An increasingly common feature of 14th-century church life was the chantry, an endowment by a wealthy patron for the saying of daily masses for his soul and the souls of his family. The chantries could be comfortable sinecures which left a cleric plenty of time free to curry favour with rich patrons and 'drum up' further trade. Especially in London, where many of the wealthiest people in the country congregated, this could be highly lucrative. The clamour of bells was to be heard there every morning, signifying the celebration of masses – a sort of 14th-century status symbol.

PROFESSIONAL CONNECTIONS

The Church not only served the rich, it also helped to *make* men rich. In medieval England, it offered the one real chance of rising above the social class of one's birth. The disadvantage of humble beginnings could be flung off by studying at one of the church schools and progressing to Oxford or Cambridge. All students were in minor holy orders and most proceeded to the priesthood. A trained clerk might become an estate manager for some great monastery or for a nobleman. The Law recruited solely from among university students. And of course the Civil Services of both the royal court and the papal administration were staffed by trained priests. Once a successful young student found himself a rich patron, humble birth was no bar to advancement. The richest Englishman of his time, William of Wykeham, who was King Edward III's Chancellor (1367-1371) and Bishop of Winchester, was the son of a 'villein' – that is, a farm worker tied to the land of his overlord. And William of Wykeham's annual income was £875 at a time when one was thought well off on £5 a year.

English society in Chaucer's day, although passionately religious, was almost as fervently anticlerical. As people began to understand more of the Gospel, so they began to judge the clerics by the standards they taught. And some did not stand up to close inspection. As Langland put it in his poem *Piers Plowman*: 'Covetousness has overcome the priests and all clergy/And the unlettered are led (unless our Lord helps them)/By such incompetent clergy to incurable agonies.' The English Church in the 14th century no longer demanded the rejection of all worldly goods. The great monastic houses had become (as shown in Chaucer's fictional Monk and Prioress) comfortable places for well-born but landless men and women. Thus the hunting monk became a common target of criticism. He was not perceived as wicked, but people objected to his lifestyle which was remarkably similar to that of the landed gentry rather than being governed by monastic rule.

And the friars (monks dependent on charity), who had found their special niche in schools and universities, invited criticism for chasing wealthy patronage: 'Friars follow after rich folk/And put little price upon poor people.'

Officers of the Church were empowered to

Divine retribution *The Black Death was looked upon as a punishment visited on Mankind by God (above), and increased the sense of need for strict religious observance and obedience of God's laws.*

Sin personified *Sin and temptation took on a very vivid reality by being portrayed as imps and demons (right).*

Monkish mischief

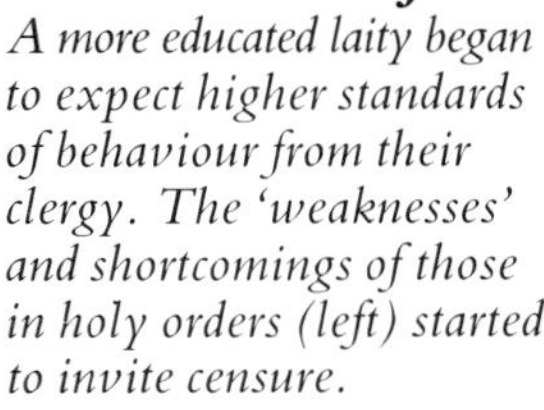

A more educated laity began to expect higher standards of behaviour from their clergy. The 'weaknesses' and shortcomings of those in holy orders (left) started to invite censure.

Treasures in heaven *Indulgences were granted by a pardoner (right) to 'exempt' people from time in Purgatory. It was a system that could be, and was, easily abused.*

grant indulgences – dispensations from the Pope allowing 'days off' torment in Purgatory. The sale of such indulgences for money was a growing practice; and although originally not intended as a swindle, it was fast becoming exactly that: a cynical exploitation of people's fear. And the Pope did little to stamp it out. The Pardoner in *The Canterbury Tales* claims he can absolve sin completely with his indulgences. He also carries phoney relics – supposed possessions or bodily remains of the saints – promising blessings to those who paid to touch them. It is easy to understand why such shameless confidence tricksters should incense men like Chaucer who saw rogues in clerical garb taking advantage of the ignorant and frightened.

Absentee priests drew salaries from parishes they never visited; chantry priests fawned on rich patrons who would ensure rich livings for their friends and families; bishops were obliged to toady to both King and Pope. Yet despite these abuses and corruptions, it would be wrong to assume that the whole spiritual fabric of the kingdom was rotten. The records teem with intelligent, conscientious ministers who were witty, perceptive, lively and well-informed. Richard Rolle, a mystic hermit who preached abstinence, meditation, prayer and spirituality by his own example, and the visionary Mother Julian were just two such examples. Capable and educated ministers challenged the less educated in matters of faith. Humble parsons, like the one in *The Canterbury Tales*, whose ministry is unobtrusive and selfless, were equally typical.

The loudest critics of the favoured few were often those trained priests who had *not* managed to attract the favour of a patron or were perhaps saddled with a wretchedly paid curacy for an absentee rector. William Langland, for example, most virulent of critics, was himself a clerk in minor orders,

Cult of the Virgin
Hail Mary full of wynne [grace]/The Holy Ghost is thee within/Blessed be thou over all women/And be the fruit of thy womb. Amen.

There was a very great emphasis placed on the role of the Virgin Mary (above) as intercessor for sinners. The downfall of Man was blamed on Eve; but salvation was possible through the second Eve – the mother of Jesus.

John Wyclif
The famed radical theologian Wyclif (above right) instigated the first translation of the Bible into the language of the people. And when he argued against the extent of papal taxes (from the cloistered seclusion of Oxford University), his arguments suited the King's purposes. Later Wyclif became more extreme, less 'acceptable' – and was consequently shunned.

who failed to rise through the Church's hierarchy.

Some have seen a similar bitterness and envy at the root of John Wyclif's radical theology. John Wyclif spent most of his life at Oxford University, and his theological discussions were conducted in Latin along traditional lines. But he fervently believed that Christians should be able to hear and read the Bible in everyday English. He translated the New Testament himself – the whole Bible was ready by 1388. He attacked the growing secular power of the Pope and condemned the priesthood for trying to monopolize Christ's mercy.

Wyclif enjoyed the patronage of John of Gaunt, the third son of Edward III, and proved a useful tool to Edward III. As early as 1343, Edward encouraged Parliament to write to the Pope and protest against his demands for revenue from the English Church. This was just one tactical move in Edward's game-like political struggle with the Pope. He had no intention of denying the Pope's right to tax the Church, and he was certainly not making a bid to free England from the grip of Rome. Wyclif's scholarly arguments and refutations were wagged at the Pope only until rival claimants to the papal throne were rendering the papacy too weak to oppose the English king. Once the challenge had gone out of the 'game', the propaganda campaign was dropped, and as Wyclif's ideas became more and more extreme, he was abandoned by his noble patrons. Only the wildest of his followers, though, went as far as to reject papal authority altogether, and preached Christian socialism. Independent of Wyclif, John Ball preached a classless society. He was imprisoned and excommunicated, but freed from gaol by the mob during the Peasants' Revolt. He urged the execution of all lords, prelates and monks, but was hanged after the defeat of the uprising. His efforts had only served (by unjust association) to discredit John Wyclif with the landed classes, and many more besides.

Despite the dissent and the abuses of the time, it was a pious, believing age. Chaucer's pilgrims are as varied a collection of saints and sinners as could be found: yet they all devote time and money to travel to Canterbury to honour the most famous English saint of the time. They would all have seen themselves as members of the all-pervasive Church. All education, literacy, law and managerial skills stemmed from it. The Church provided for the care of each individual soul throughout life and after. Although flawed in practice, it was a Church which no-one would have been able to ignore.

The pilgrim way
Pilgrimages (above) were a popular religious observance of the time. And the most important saint of all in the 14th century, to English pilgrims, was Thomas à Becket, whose shrine stood in Canterbury Cathedral.

Hellfire and mercy
Because so much art survives showing souls in torment (left), Hell, demons and the Devil, it is widely assumed that the laity of the Middle Ages cowered in fear of the after-life, their anxieties fuelled by a cynical, power-hungry clergy. But there is just as much proof of a caring, tender, merciful religion portraying a Saviour (right) extending a democratic redemption towards rich and poor, serf and nobleman alike.

WILLIAM SHAKESPEARE

1564-1616

The greatest and most famous of English writers, Shakespeare reigned supreme in the theatre at a particularly fertile period of English drama. His career as actor/playwright took him from Stratford to London, where he wrote his celebrated tragedies in the first decade of the 16th century. Unmatched in his gift for language, he created legendary characters and dramatic moments which have inspired audiences and artists down to the present day.

Immortal Bard

Shakespeare's dazzling theatrical career was based in London; but he regarded Stratford as his true home, his fellow playwright Ben Jonson dubbing him 'Sweet Swan of Avon'.

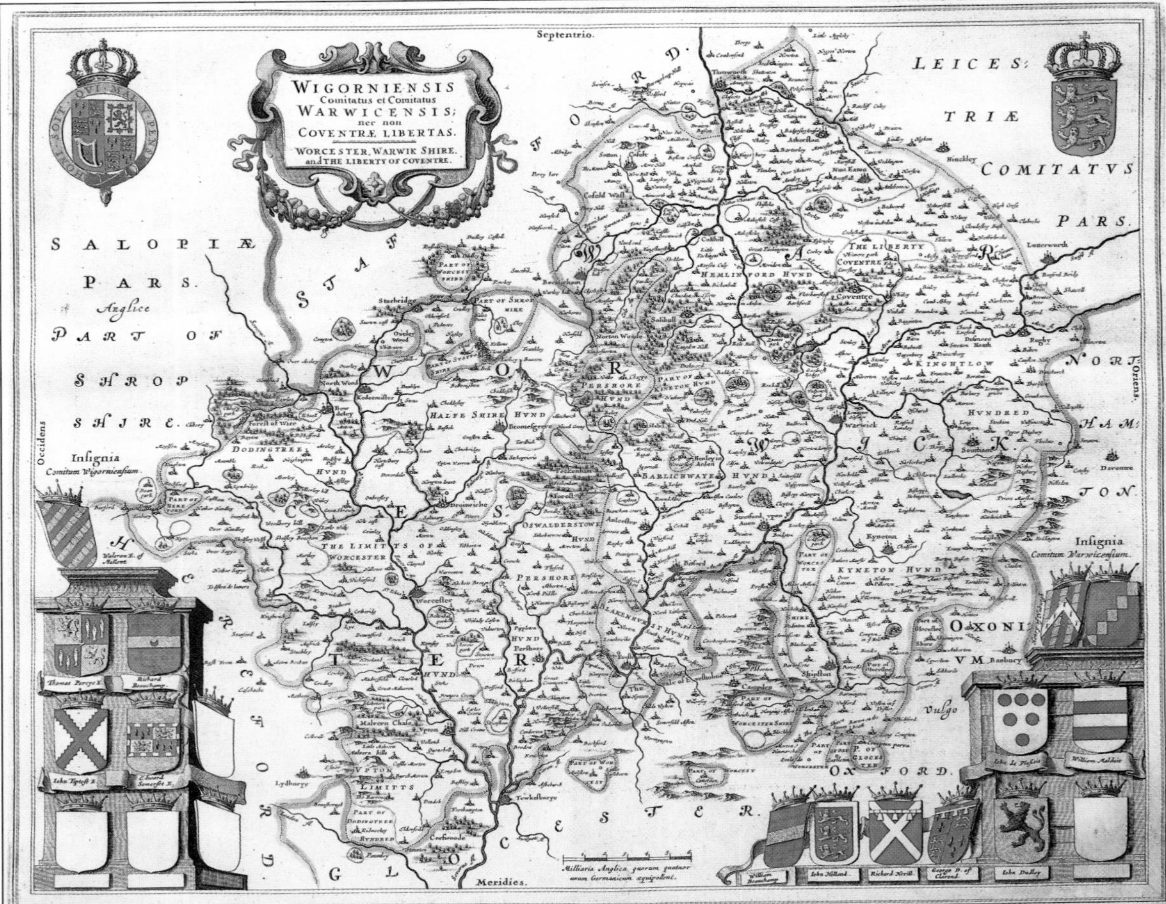

Heart of England
(left) The area of Warwickshire where Shakespeare grew up is noted for its beauty and historical richness – a fertile background for his work.

Family home
(below) Shakespeare is said to have been born in this house in Stratford's Henley Street. When his father died in 1601, Shakespeare inherited the property.

Unlike his plays, William Shakespeare's career was singularly undramatic, for he lived the life of a cautiously successful middle-class businessman. As far as we know, he never went abroad, and his life revolved around two towns: his native Stratford-upon-Avon in Warwickshire, with which he kept in touch all his life; and London, about 90 miles away, where he achieved a leading position as a man of the theatre – playwright, actor, and part-owner of the country's foremost theatrical company.

William Shakespeare was baptized in the parish church of Holy Trinity, Stratford, on 26 April 1564. We do not know exactly when he was born, but it is unlikely to have been more than a few days before this, and patriotic sentiment has settled on 23 April – St George's Day – as the most fitting date for the birth of England's greatest

Schooldays
Shakespeare probably began his education at a petty (elementary) school, then spent about five or six years at Stratford grammar school (above), where he mastered Latin.

writer. He was the third child of John and Mary Shakespeare; two older sisters died in childhood, and later he had two more sisters and three brothers, about whom very little is known.

John Shakespeare was a glover, and he also traded in timber, wood and other commodities. The first record of him dates from 1552, when he was fined by the Stratford authorities for having an unlicensed dunghill or refuse heap in Henley Street, rather than using the 'comyn mukhyll'. This lapse was soon forgotten, however, and John prospered in his business and personal life. In 1556 he bought two houses in Henley Street and the following year he married Mary Arden, who was of a rather higher social class.

John Shakespeare came to own a considerable amount of property in Stratford and was one of the town's most respected citizens, holding a succession of public offices, including that of bailiff (mayor). Stratford at this time was, in the words of the contemporary antiquarian William Camden, a 'handsome small market town'. Its population was about 1500 when William Shakespeare was born, but in that very year the plague struck and 237 burials were recorded from July to December – roughly one in six of the inhabitants died.

Baby William was no doubt fortunate to survive his plague-ridden first year, but nothing is documented of this or the rest of his childhood. However, as the eldest son of one of the town's leading citizens, he would have received the best education available locally, and it is likely that he attended Stratford grammar school.

Shakespeare probably started at the school aged seven or eight, and would have been thoroughly steeped in Latin, doing little else for about eight hours a day, six days a week. It was probably during his schooldays that he first became stage-struck. Stratford had no theatre, but travelling players often performed there, and Shakespeare's father as bailiff had the duty of licensing them. It was no doubt in the Guildhall, immediately below his schoolroom, that young William saw his first plays.

Pupils usually attended the grammar school until they were about 15, but Shakespeare may have left earlier in order to help his father, who had run into financial difficulties. The next firm date we have in Shakespeare's life, however, is 1582, when, at the age of 18, he married Anne Hathaway, who was eight years his senior and three-months pregnant. She came from a land-owning family at a nearby village, but nothing is known about her personally.

The ceremony took place in November and a daughter, Susanna, was born in May 1583; two more children – the twins Hamnet and Judith – followed in 1585. Because the marriage was evidently made in haste and because Shakespeare spent much of his later life away from his family in London, it has been surmised that the union was an unhappy one. However, there is no real evidence for this and Shakespeare certainly regarded Stratford as his permanent home.

Between the birth of his twins in 1585 and the first mention of him as a playwright in London in

Key Dates

1564 born in Stratford
1582 marries Anne Hathaway
1583 birth of daughter Susanna
1585 birth of twins Hamnet and Judith
1592 first mentioned as dramatist in London
c.1595 *Romeo and Juliet*
1596 death of son Hamnet
1597 buys New Place, Stratford
c.1600 *Hamlet*
1601 death of father
c.1605 *King Lear*
1608 mother dies
c.1610 retires to Stratford
1616 dies in Stratford
1623 publication of First Folio – earliest collected edition of his work

Anne Hathaway's Cottage
(left) Shakespeare's wife came from Shottery, just outside Stratford. Although known as Anne Hathaway's cottage, this house was her father's.

Royal patron
(above) Elizabeth I was an enthusiastic patron of the theatre. She had her own troupe of actors (the Queen's Men) and Shakespeare's company often performed for her.

Stratford-upon-Avon
Shakespeare's home town was fairly small, but it had a splendid church and was the prosperous centre of a rich agricultural region. By the time of the 300th anniversary of Shakespeare's birth (above) it was becoming important for tourism.

1592 there is no documentary evidence as to what Shakespeare was doing, and consequently this period has been called 'the missing years'. Predictably, there has been no shortage of theories to fill the gap, and because Shakespeare's work covers such a vast range of human experiences, it has been suggested he was a soldier, a sailor, a lawyer, and many other things. The 17th-century antiquary John Aubrey, however, wrote on good authority that Shakespeare 'had been in his younger years a Schoolmaster in the Countrey'.

Two of the most popular legends about Shakespeare refer to 'the missing years'. The first tells how he is supposed to have poached deer from the estate of Sir Thomas Lucy at Charlecote, near Stratford, was whipped, wrote an abusive ballad in revenge, and fled home to escape Sir Thomas' wrath. The second tells how Shakespeare gained his entry to the theatrical profession by looking after the horses of rich theatregoers whilst they watched the performance.

A JEALOUS RIVAL

Both claims go back a long way, but modern research has cast grave doubts on their authenticity. All we know for certain about the missing years is that at some point after 1585 Shakespeare left home, went to London, joined a theatrical company, and began writing for the stage – although not necessarily in that order.

By 1592, when he was 28, Shakespeare must have been well known in his profession, for in that year the playwright Robert Greene wrote a pamphlet called *Greenes Groats-worth of Witte* in which he refers enviously to an 'upstart Crow' who fancies himself 'the onely Shake-scene in the country'. Greene parodied a line from *Henry VI* Part 3, so we know that Shakespeare had written at least part of this trilogy (generally regarded as his first surviving work) by this date.

Shakespeare's blossoming theatrical career was interrupted, however, by the plague, which closed down London's playhouses virtually completely

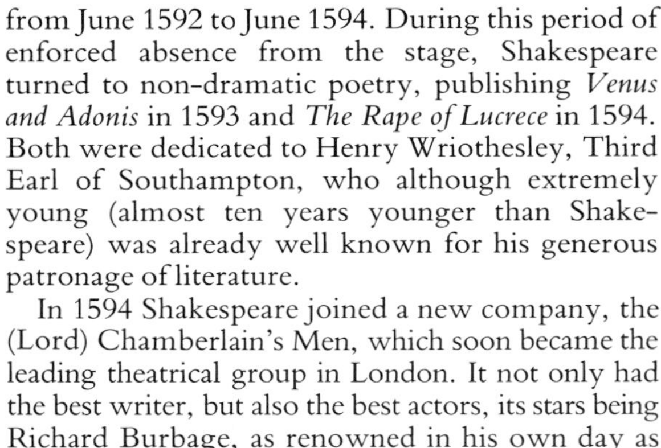

from June 1592 to June 1594. During this period of enforced absence from the stage, Shakespeare turned to non-dramatic poetry, publishing *Venus and Adonis* in 1593 and *The Rape of Lucrece* in 1594. Both were dedicated to Henry Wriothesley, Third Earl of Southampton, who although extremely young (almost ten years younger than Shakespeare) was already well known for his generous patronage of literature.

In 1594 Shakespeare joined a new company, the (Lord) Chamberlain's Men, which soon became the leading theatrical group in London. It not only had the best writer, but also the best actors, its stars being Richard Burbage, as renowned in his own day as David Garrick or John Gielgud were to later ages, and Will Kempe, famous as a low comedian and dancer (in 1600 he morris-danced from London to Norwich for a bet).

The Chamberlain's Men made their first appearance at court at Christmas 1594, and payment was made jointly to Burbage, Kempe and Shakespeare – an indication of their prominence in the company. Shakespeare remained with the Chamberlain's Men (renamed the King's Men after the accession of James I in 1603) for the rest of his career. He was the only major writer of the time to have a permanent, prominent position with a team of first-class actors, and he often wrote parts with particular members of the company in mind. His own acting skills were valued by his colleagues (among the parts he is said to have played is the Ghost in *Hamlet*), but as he became busier as a writer and manager he had less time for acting, and

New Place
By 1597 Shakespeare was affluent enough to buy New Place (below), the second largest house in Stratford. Standing in about an acre of ground, it had two barns and two orchards. The property was demolished in the 18th century and a garden (right) now occupies the site of the house.

Shakespeare's London
London in Elizabethan times was a thriving cosmopolitan city. The theatrical district was in the area of Southwark called Bankside (foreground in the engraving above).

his last recorded performance was in a production of Ben Jonson's *Sejanus* in 1603.

By this time, Shakespeare, now approaching 40, had achieved great professional and financial success. In 1597 (a year after the death of his son Hamnet) he bought New Place, one of the finest houses in Stratford, and in 1602 (a year after the death of his father) he bought 127 acres of land there. The clearest indication of the reputation he enjoyed in the theatrical world is a passage in a literary handbook called *Palladis Tamia: Wit's Treasury* by Francis Meres, published in 1598: 'As Plautus and Seneca are accounted the best for Comedy and Tragedy among the Latines, so Shakespeare among the English is the most excellent in both kinds for the stage.'

EARLY RETIREMENT

In about 1610 Shakespeare left London and settled at his house in Stratford, where he lived the life of a retired gentleman. No-one knows why Shakespeare decided to leave the stage when he was still only in his mid-40s, but it has been suggested that he had suffered a severe illness. His first biographer, Nicholas Rowe, in his *Life* of 1709, wrote that Shakespeare spent his final years 'in ease, retirement, and the conversation of his friends'. He had family as well as friends to occupy him. His mother had died in 1608, but his wife and two daughters were still living. Susanna, the elder, married in 1607 and gave birth to a daughter the following year; Judith, the younger, married in February 1616.

Shakespeare was very dubious about his second son-in-law, Thomas Quiney, and with good reason. Not long before his marriage Quiney had made another woman pregnant, and a month after the wedding there was an unsavoury scandal when that woman died in childbirth. Two weeks later Shakespeare revised his will to try to ensure Judith a stable income if her feckless husband should leave her. A month later, on 23 April 1616 (on or about his 52nd birthday), Shakespeare died, and two days afterwards was buried in the church in which he had been baptized. The cause of death is unknown, but John Ward, vicar of Stratford half a century later, wrote that 'Shakespear, Drayton [another playwright], and Ben Jhonson had a merry meeting, and itt seems drank too hard, for Shakespear died of a feavour there contracted.'

A memorial bust, showing the writer with pen and paper, was soon erected in the church, but the real monument to Shakespeare came a little later, with the publication of the first collected edition of his plays in 1623. Of the many tributes paid to Shakespeare, the one that his friend Ben Jonson wrote for this volume has never been bettered:

. . . I confesse thy writings to be such,
As neither Man, nor Muse, can praise too much . . .
He was not of an age, but for all time!

Tribute in stone
The memorial bust of Shakespeare in Stratford church is shown being made in this later, romanticized painting (below).

Myths and Follies

Shakespeare has inspired a huge amount of biographical research, but wild speculation has often taken over from sober interpretation, leading to outlandish fantasies about his life and work.

It is often said that little is known of Shakespeare's life, but the assertion is only partly true. For a man of his time, in his profession, the amount of solid information that has survived about Shakespeare is fairly substantial. Most, however, is contained in colourless official documents (baptismal records, papers relating to the sale of property, and so on) – sources that tell us nothing about the man's personality.

Biographers have naturally been keen to flesh out the figure of Shakespeare, drawing on local traditions about him and also on inferences about his life or personality contained in his work, but these practices are fraught with difficulty. Certainly Shakespeare sometimes alluded to contemporary events, and it is often tempting to connect passages in his work to his own life (for example Prospero's beautiful final speeches in *The Tempest*, which sound like the author's farewell to the stage). But Shakespeare's writing is so many-sided that this kind of link can never be more than intriguing speculation.

THE BACONIAN HERETICS

Some admirers of Shakespeare's works, however, have been so unsatisfied with the prosaic biographical outlines, that they have come to the wayward conclusion that the lad from Stratford cannot have grown into one of the world's greatest writers, and that someone else must have penned the immortal works for him. The evidence that Shakespeare did in fact write the plays and poems that bear his name is so abundant, unambiguous, consistent and cogent that it seems astonishing that any rational person could doubt it, but the arguments of the 'anti-Stratfordians' have more to do with snobbery and misplaced imagination than with common sense.

As far as is known, nobody seriously doubted the orthodox opinion – that Shakespeare wrote Shakespeare – until the late 18th century, and it was not until the mid-19th century that a movement to discredit Shakespeare began. The book that started it off was written by an American

Many-sided genius
Philosopher, statesman and essayist, Francis Bacon (right) was one of the intellectual giants of his age. Some misguided admirers think he was also the true author of the plays bearing Shakespeare's name (inset).

called Joseph C. Hart and bore the unlikely title of *The Romance of Yachting* (1848). His ideas were taken up by his fellow countrywoman Delia Bacon, who was convinced that her namesake Francis Bacon, one of the most eminent public figures of Shakespeare's day, was the mastermind behind the plays, directing a group of authors to express his ideas.

Miss Bacon thought that the 'Stratford poacher' was a 'vulgar, illiterate man', a member of a 'dirty, doggish group of players', and therefore could not have written the great works attributed to him. She died insane in 1859, but her work was carried on by a host of followers, maintaining her line that the author of the supreme masterpieces of English literature must be a highly educated, cultured man, not a country bumpkin.

The 'proof' of these sceptics consisted mainly in pointing out verbal correspondences (most of them so commonplace as to be inconsequential) between the works that went under the name of Shakespeare and the undoubted works of Bacon, and in finding concealed 'messages' in these writings. The height of absurdity was reached in 1910 when one of the most distinguished of all Baconians, Sir Edwin Durning-Lawrence, published *Bacon is Shakespeare*. In this book, Sir Edwin – otherwise a sane man – claimed to have discovered a coded message in the First Folio edition of Shakespeare's works (1623) which proved not only that Bacon wrote it, but also that he intended this message to be unveiled in 1910, the very year in which *Bacon is Shakespeare* was published.

Digging for the truth
In 1909 Orville Ward Owen, a Detroit physician and dedicated Baconian, thought he had decoded a message revealing that manuscripts were buried near the River Wye which would prove that Bacon wrote Shakespeare. He excavated for years (above), but found nothing.

Professional code-breakers have shown that using Baconian methods one can find virtually any message one wants to find in virtually any book, and other Baconian 'evidence' is just as worthless. Nevertheless, the Baconians still keep going, and they are not the only 'disbelievers', for there is now a host of other 'claimants'. Chief among them is Edward de Vere, 17th Earl of Oxford, a courtier, literary patron and amateur poet. His claims were first put forward by a Gateshead schoolteacher called J. Thomas Looney in a book published in 1920 (recognizing that the author's name would be a gift to sarcastic reviewers the publishers tried to persuade Looney to adopt a pseudonym, but he bravely resisted).

MESSAGES FROM THE SPIRIT WORLD

One of Looney's followers in the Oxfordian camp, Percy Allen, had the bright idea of engaging a medium 'of unimpeachable integrity' through whom he talked to Shakespeare, Bacon and Oxford. Their heavenly testimony, recorded in *Talks with Elizabethans* (1947), was that the plays were works of collaboration, with Oxford the major contributor. Even without the support of messages from beyond the grave, Oxford is a slightly more plausible claimant than Bacon, but an objection that none of his supporters has been able to get round is that he died in 1604, when several of Shakespeare's most celebrated plays were still to be written.

Other candidates (of varying degrees of absurdity) who have been put forward as claimants to Shakespeare's laurels include the actor Richard Burbage, assorted poets and playwrights of the period – including Ben Jonson, Christopher Marlowe and Edmund Spenser – a team of Jesuits, Elizabeth I and Mary Queen of Scots.

Apart from the authorship question, the lunatic fringe has been more often attracted to the sonnets than to any other aspect of Shakespearean studies. Fortunately these wonderful poems have also fos-

Bizarre theories
The numerous unlikely candidates proposed as the 'real' author of Shakespeare include Mary Queen of Scots (above), who died before any of the plays were written, and a team of Jesuits (below). In Did the Jesuits Write Shakespeare? *(1910), Harold Johnson suggested that 'Shakespeare' was a pseudonym adopted to honour Adrian IV (born Nicolas Breakspear), the only English pope.*

tered much serious and ingenious scholarship, for they pose many fascinating questions, to some of which definitive answers are unlikely ever to be found. The sonnets – 154 of them – do not form a strict sequence (and they may not have been printed in the order Shakespeare intended), but a story of sorts emerges. It involves three people: the poet; his friend, a handsome young nobleman (to whom most of the sonnets are addressed); and a dark-haired woman, the poet's mistress, who is stolen from him by his friend.

William Wordsworth, wrote of the sonnets that 'With this key Shakespeare unlocked his heart', and many other critics share his view that the poems are autobiographical. If this is so (which is by no means certain), then the identities of the young man and the 'Dark Lady' become major issues in Shakespeare's biography.

The Dark Lady?
Of all the women who have been proposed as the original of the 'Dark Lady' of Shakespeare's sonnets, Mary Fitton (left) has found the most support. Born in about 1578, she became one of Queen Elizabeth's maids of honour in 1596, and several courtiers became besotted with her. She was free with her sexual favours, but there is no evidence that Shakespeare was one of her conquests.

A possible clue to the identity of the young man is contained in the enigmatic dedication of the 1609 book: 'To the onlie begetter of these insuing sonnets Mr. W. H. . . .' The dedication is signed (or initialled) by the printer, Thomas Thorpe, rather than by Shakespeare, and it may be that Thorpe is thanking a contact who obtained the poet's manuscript for him to print (another printer, called William Hall, has been suggested as a candidate). However, many critics assume that 'Mr. W. H.' is the young man of Shakespeare's poem, and much ingenuity has been expended in finding names to fit the initials.

Two young aristocrats have found more support than any other candidates: Henry Wriothesley, Third Earl of Southampton (whose initials must be reversed to make him 'W.H.'); and William Herbert, Third Earl of Pembroke. Southampton was a notable patron of literature, and Shakespeare dedicated his poems *Venus and Adonis* and *The Rape of Lucrece* to him (they are his only works to have such dedications).

Herbert was the holder of several important offices during the reign of James I, and it was to him and his brother, Philip, Earl of Montgomery, that Shakespeare's friends dedicated the First Folio edition of his works, published in 1623. Both men seem reasonably plausible candidates, then, but there is no real evidence to support their claims, and objections can easily be raised to them, not least that neither was a 'Mr', since they both had noble titles.

Shakespeare's sonnets also mention another poet, 'a worthier pen' to whom he is 'inferior far' and who is a rival for the favour of his patron. There has been much speculation about his identity. Christopher Marlowe is the favourite choice, and other contenders include George Chapman (author of a famous translation of Homer), Ben Jonson and Edmund Spenser, as well as several lesser known figures.

Even more than the Rival Poet, however, it is the Dark Lady who has caught the imagination,

Aristocratic links
William Herbert, 3rd Earl of Pembroke (above), came from a noted literary family. His mother, the sister of Sir Philip Sidney, was the finest woman poet of her age. The family home, Wilton House (above) in Wiltshire, was a meeting place for writers, and Shakespeare's company performed there in 1603, when the plague had closed the theatres in London. The circumstantial evidence that William Herbert was the 'Mr W.H.' of Shakespeare's sonnets is intriguing, but there is no firm documentary link between the two men.

and much energy has been devoted to trying to unmask this mysterious temptress who bewitches the poet and seduces his adored young friend. From the sonnets we learn that she was dark-haired, dark-eyed and dark-skinned (although how dark is uncertain – some scholars have looked for a negress to fit the bill), that she was musical and younger than the poet, and that although she was not conventionally beautiful, she was highly seductive and promiscuous.

The first person to tackle the problem was an antiquarian called George Chalmers, who, in two fat volumes published in the 1790s, attempted to show that the sonnets were addressed to Elizabeth I (even though she must have been about 60 when they were written). Like many of his successors in the Victorian age, Chalmers refused to admit the obvious fact that the sonnets have a very powerful sexual charge, and declared that Shakespeare – 'a husband, a father, a moral man' – would not have written erotic verses to a young man and a woman of easy virtue.

Of the many other women who have more plausibly been put forward as candidates for the Dark Lady, the best known is Mary Fitton, one of Queen Elizabeth's maids of honour and a notoriously promiscuous woman (in 1601 there was a scandal when she gave birth to a stillborn illegitimate child, whose father was William Herbert – possibly the Mr. W. H. of the sonnets). Mary is a strong contender in some ways, but portraits show that she had a fair complexion, and there is no evidence that she even met Shakespeare, let alone had an affair with him.

ANOTHER DARK LADY

The search therefore continues, the latest major candidate to emerge being Emilia Lanier, née Bassano, the daughter of an Italian musician. She was put forward in 1973 by the eminent but controversial Elizabethan historian A. L. Rowse, who found references to her in the manuscripts of Shakespeare's contemporary Simon Forman, a physician, astrologer, playgoer and lecher.

It appears from Forman's notes that Emilia was promiscuous, and Rowse points out that she is described in them as 'very brown in youth' and that she was married to a man called William, whose name (together with that of Shakespeare himself) figures in the many 'will' puns of the sonnets. Further investigation, however, showed that Rowse had misread Forman's notes, where Emilia is described as 'very brave' (that is 'splendid' or 'showy') not 'very brown', and that her husband was called not William, but Alfonso – a name on which even Shakespeare would have found difficulty making puns. Thus Emilia too joined the ranks of 'possibles' rather than 'probables'.

All the fervent convictions and painstaking scholarship that have gone into investigating Mr. W. H., the Rival Poet and the Dark Lady may, indeed, be nothing more than contributions to one of the greatest wild-goose chases in history, for it is quite possible that the sonnets were written as a literary exercise (such collections were highly popular), rather than as an outpouring of the soul.

There is sometimes scope for biographical speculation not only in Shakespeare's work, but also in the documents relating to him. The best-known instance is the clause in his will in which he leaves his wife (the only bequest named to her) 'my second best bed'. This has led to the conjecture that Shakespeare cared little for his wife, but according to the law of the time a widow automatically received a good share of her late husband's estate, so there was no need to specify it. The 'second best bed' was no doubt an additional, highly personal bequest – a touching remembrance rather than an indication of neglect or indifference. The best bed would normally be reserved for guests, so the bed Shakespeare left his wife was probably the one in which they slept together.

Shakespeare himself is said to have composed the inscription on his gravestone in Stratford church:

Good friend for Jesus sake forbear
To dig the dust enclosed here.
Blessed be the man that spares these stones
And cursed be he that moves my bones.

In spite of theories that the grave contains material that would shed light on the poet's life, it has never been opened. Shakespeare's personal life remains – and is ever likely to remain – a closed book.

Enigmatic dedication *(below) The publisher of Shakespeare's sonnets, Thomas Thorpe, prefaced the book with this perplexing note, with its mysterious full stop after every word. Identifying 'Mr W.H.' has become one of the most famous pursuits in literary detection, yet it is still uncertain whether the 'onlie begetter' is the inspiration of Shakespeare's poems or the procurer of the manuscript for Thorpe.*

TO.THE.ONLIE.BEGETTER.OF.
THESE.INSVING.SONNETS.
Mr.W.H. ALL.HAPPINESSE.
AND.THAT.ETERNITIE.
PROMISED.
BY.
OVR.EVER-LIVING.POET.
WISHETH.
THE.WELL-WISHING.
ADVENTVRER.IN.
SETTING.
FORTH.

T. T.

Shakespeare's patron *Henry Wriothesley, 3rd Earl of Southampton, was the young nobleman to whom Shakespeare dedicated his poems* Venus and Adonis *and* The Rape of Lucrece, *and he is a favourite candidate for the role of the friend addressed by the poet in the sonnets. However, we do not know how close their relationship was. Shakespeare's first biographer Nicholas Rowe (1709) said that Southampton gave Shakespeare a gift of £1000 (then a huge sum), but this seems unlikely, even for so generous a lover of literature.*

The Elizabethan Theatre

During Shakespeare's lifetime some actors advanced from being mere 'strolling players' – little better than vagabonds – to respected professionals who even performed at court.

The theatrical environment that nourished Shakespeare's genius had all the vigour and freshness of youth, for it had begun within his own lifetime. Throughout the Middle Ages, plays had normally been local and amateur productions – often of considerable artistry – which dealt with biblical subjects and were performed to celebrate saints' days and other holy days. When, with the 16th-century Protestant Reformation, the saints' days disappeared, the old plays were suppressed as religiously and politically suspect. Religious topics were officially banned from the stage. As a result the Elizabethan – and Shakespearean – drama became strikingly secular, with love, lust, ambition and murder becoming the dramatist's chief preoccupations.

THE FIRST THEATRE

The suppression of the amateur tradition gave the professionals their opportunity. Troupes of 'players' had already been in existence for a century or more. Until the 1570s they worked as 'strolling players', continually on the move and performing in places such as guildhalls and inn courtyards. Their status was not far removed from that of vagrants. The players' only protection was to attach themselves to a noble patron who would allow them to become his 'men' and wear his livery, thus guaranteeing them an income as well as ridding them of the stigma of being 'masterless'. If the noble was a royal favourite, like the Earl of Leicester, his 'men' might be given the opportunity to appear before the court; but at other times their patron was only too pleased if the players continued to 'stroll' rather than be entirely dependent on his bounty. Powerful patronage remained essential even after the players built their own theatres, and all the great Elizabethan companies were somebody's men – the Lord Chamberlain's, the Lord High Admiral's, the Earl of Worcester's, for example.

Companies of players are known to have hired halls in London early in Elizabeth I's reign, but their conquest of the city did not begin until 1574, when Shakespeare was already 10 years old. In this year the Queen allowed Leicester's Men to perform regularly in the city on weekdays. Two years later their leader, James Burbage, took a 21-year lease on some ground at Shoreditch and built England's first playhouse, known simply as the Theatre. Almost simultaneously an enterprising schoolmaster started a rather different venture in Blackfriars, using his pupils as performers. And in Shoreditch the Theatre soon had a rival and neighbour in the Curtain.

Playhouses obviously satisfied a demand, but there were never more than a handful in London and one or two in the provinces, since drama had powerful enemies. Puritanism was already at work in English life, and its influence made the City fathers hostile to plays and players – so much so that Elizabethan theatres were built in places where the authorities had no jurisdiction: in 'liberties' such as London's Shoreditch, or just across the Thames on Bankside in Southwark, among the bear gardens (where the popular pastime of bear-baiting took place), and in brothels.

It was to Bankside that James Burbage's son, Richard, moved the Theatre in 1599, when its lease ran out. The building was dismantled, timber by timber, reassembled on the other side of the river, and renamed the Globe. This is where most of Shakespeare's greatest works received their first performance.

The City fathers closed the playhouses whenever they could find an excuse. During outbreaks of plague they claimed, not unreasonably, that playhouses constituted health hazards. The worst outbreak closed the theatres for two years from 1592 to 1594.

The court and the aristocracy were generally more sympathetic to the players than the City

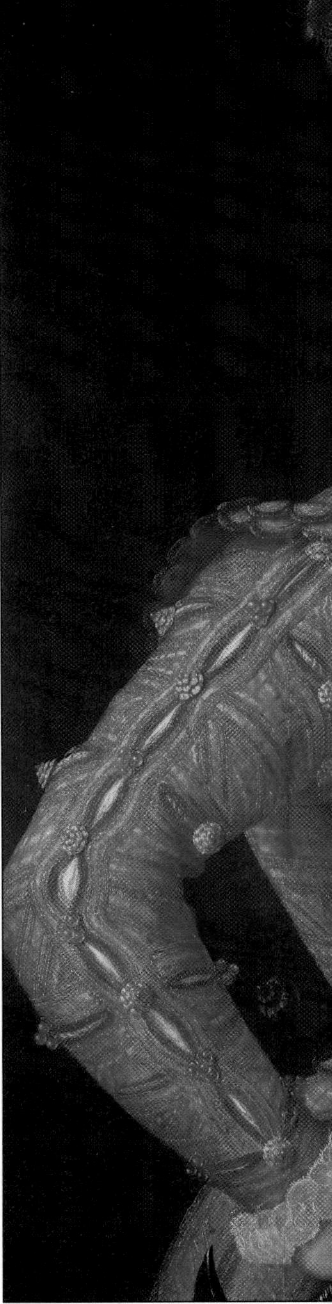

Noble patron
Robert Dudley (above), Earl of Leicester, a favourite of Elizabeth I, had his own company of actors.

Bloody entertainment
Bear-baiting (left), bull-baiting and cock-fighting were immensely popular in the 16th century. Acting was initially part of the same disreputable world.

fathers, but tight control was still exercised over the plays. Every script had to be submitted to a court official, the Master of the Revels, for vetting, and in 1605 the unlicensed performance of *Eastward Hoe!*, a comedy containing uncomplimentary remarks about the Scots, led to a wholesale shake-up of the player companies, which were forcibly amalgamated into three and put under the patronage (and control) of the Privy Council.

Despite all these hazards, there was money to be made in the theatre by those leading members owning shares in the companies. The most successful were the Lord Chamberlain's Men, run by the Burbages, and the Admiral's Men, effectively controlled by Philip Henslowe. Henslowe was a

Inn-yard drama
(above and right) Before the establishment of permanent theatres in London, plays were acted in public halls and private houses, but above all in inn-yards. The typical layout of the yards provided a ready-made arena and galleries for spectators, and landlords welcomed the additional trade.

The Swan Theatre
(left) This drawing, a copy of one made by Johannes de Witt, a Dutchman who visited London in 1596, is the only known contemporary view of the interior of an Elizabethan theatre. De Witt described the Swan (which was newly opened at the time) as 'the largest and most magnificent' of London's theatres, 'for it accommodates in its seats three thousand persons, and is built of a mass of flint stones . . . and supported by wooden columns painted in such excellent imitation of marble that it is able to deceive even the most cunning'. More commonly theatres were made entirely of wood. This was a fire hazard – and indeed the Globe burned down in 1613

hard-as-nails businessman whose diverse interests included pawnbroking, bear-baiting and brothels. Shakespeare worked for the Lord Chamberlain's Men, where Richard Burbage established himself as a great actor in such roles as Richard III, Hamlet, King Lear and Othello. Burbage's only rival on the Elizabethan stage was the Admiral's Edward Alleyn, who took the lead in the plays of their own outstanding writer, Christopher Marlowe. Alleyn was shrewd enough to marry Henslowe's step-daughter, thus joining the management. He became very rich and respectable, founding the famous school Dulwich College.

Competition between these leading companies was fierce. When Shakespeare wrote a play featuring a rascally fat knight named Sir John Oldcastle, objections from the descendents of Oldcastle – a real person – forced him to change the character's name to Falstaff. Henslowe and the Admiral's men quickly jumped into the fray, commissioning a new piece, *Sir John Oldcastle,* to give a 'true and honourable history' of the knight as a counter to Shakespeare's 'forged invention'. An alternative method of dealing with a rival's successful play was to pirate it – a possibility that deterred companies from publishing their plays, often for years. Only 18 of Shakespeare's dramatic works were published during his lifetime, half a dozen of them probably without the owner's consent.

The owner of the text was not the dramatist but the company, which normally paid between £5 and £10 outright for a play. Authors did not make large sums of money. Most seem to have led a hand-to-mouth, bohemian existence, ending their lives in penury. Shakespeare was the exception – not because of the quality of his work, but because he was a shareholder in the Chamberlain's Men, later the King's Men, entitled to wear the royal livery and playing in two theatres.

The Globe, described by the Chorus in *Henry V* as 'this wooden O', was more or less circular, although this was not necessarily true of all Elizabethan theatres. The building was open to the sky, and performances were given, weather permitting, by the natural afternoon light. The stage projected right into the open area at the centre of the building, so that it was faced on three sides by the audience.

Actor friends
The page from the First Folio of Shakespeare's plays (right) lists the main actors who appeared in them. The greatest among them was Richard Burbage (below), who was lionized by the public and much admired by his colleagues. Shakespeare remembered him in his will.

The Workes of William Shakeſpeare,
containing all his Comedies, Hiſtories, and
Tragedies: Truely ſet forth, according to their firſt
ORJGJNALL.

The Names of the Principall Actors
in all theſe Playes.

William Shakeſpeare.	Samuel Gilburne.
Richard Burbadge.	Robert Armin.
John Hemmings.	William Oſtler.
Auguſtine Phillips.	Nathan Field.
William Kempt.	John Underwood.
Thomas Poope.	Nicholas Tooley.
George Bryan.	William Eccleſtone.
Henry Condell.	Joſeph Taylor.
William Slye.	Robert Benfield.
Richard Cowly.	Robert Goughe.
John Lowine.	Richard Robinſon.
Samuell Croſſe.	Iohn Shancke.
Alexander Cooke.	Iohn Rice.

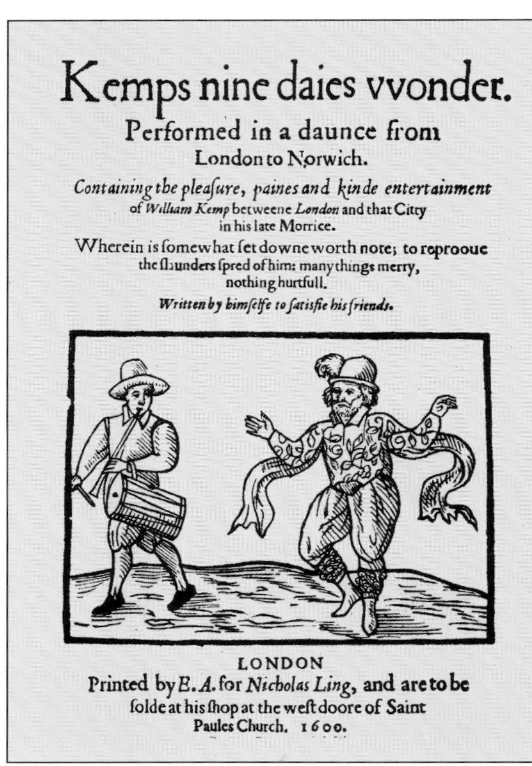

Kemps nine daies vvonder.
Performed in a daunce from London to Norwich.
Containing the pleaſure, paines and kinde entertainment of William Kemp betweene London and that Citty in his late Morrice.
Wherein is ſomewhat ſet downe worth note; to reproove the ſlaunders ſpred of him: many things merry, nothing hurtfull.
Written by himſelfe to ſatisfie his friends.

LONDON
Printed by E. A. for Nicholas Ling, and are to be ſolde at his ſhop at the weſt doore of Saint Paules Church. 1600.

Prince of clowns
Will Kempe, shown left performing his famous dance from London to Norwich, was the star low comedian of Shakespeare's company.

Deadly enemy
(below) The plague closed down theatres during Shakespeare's career both in 1592-94 and 1603.

At the back of the stage lay the changing room, known as the 'tiring house', which also served as scenery, representing a house, a castle or a hill. The actors made their entrances and exits through two doors in the tiring house, which also seems to have been equipped with windows and some sort of upper gallery serving as castle battlements, for example, and doubtless as a balcony in Romeo and Juliet's legendary love scene.

At the level of the stage, probably between the doors, an alcove provided an extra acting area where discoveries or concealments could be effected by drawing or closing curtains in front of it. In the stage itself, a trapdoor served as the gateway to the infernal regions: '*Ghost cries under the stage*' reads one of the stage directions in *Hamlet*. Finally, a part of the acting area was covered by a star-decorated canopy, called the 'heavens', which protected the players from the elements.

In these conditions – acting in natural light, almost surrounded by the audience, with a fixed background and a relatively small number of 'props' – an Elizabethan performance cannot have been realistic in the modern sense. There were non-realistic acting conventions such as the soliloquy – a speech in which a character speaks alone to himself or addresses the audience, commenting on the action or revealing his thoughts. And all the female parts were played by boy apprentices; some of these youths must have been excellent actors, since Shakespeare went to the trouble of creating great (and difficult) female parts. He frequently devised plots, however, which involved women disguised as boys – a neat solution to problems of credibility.

A TASTE FOR SPECTACLE

Strenuous efforts were made to satisfy the Elizabethan taste for spectacle, surprise and horror – pigs' blood stored in a bladder and splashed about in the more gory scenes, splendid costumes, and the roar of a real cannon fired at some dramatic moment from the 'hut' at the top of the building. The best authorities advised actors to be 'natural', although standards of naturalness have changed so much over the centuries that it is hard to be sure what this means. In his famous speech to the players, Hamlet instructs them not to 'tear a passion to tatters' (over-act).

Since an Elizabethan actor must have relied heavily on the dialogue he spoke to create a sense of place and sustain the dramatic illusion, intelligent and intelligible delivery of his lines must have been one of his essential qualities. Elizabethans wrote of 'hearing' – not seeing – a performance. The emotional response achieved was evidently intense, and at the end of the proceedings, the tension was relaxed with a 'jig' involving slapstick clowning.

Elaborate staging can hardly have been possible for a small, busy company which put on a different play every afternoon for six days a week. In the course of a year the Chamberlain's Men performed some 40 plays, perhaps half of them new; there was no such thing as a theatrical 'run', although popular plays would come round quickly and often.

The spectators usually paid a penny to enter the building, and were entitled to stand as 'groundlings' in the 'yard' around the stage. The better-off paid up to sixpence to go into the boxes next to the stage or the three galleries running round the walls. References to the groundlings in Elizabethan literature tend to be uncomplimentary; they were also known as 'stinkards', and Hamlet describes them as 'capable of nothing but inexplicable dumb shows and noise'. They were certainly capable of 'mewing' (cat-calling) bad

The Globe Theatre
The most famous of the Elizabethan theatres, the Globe (below) was the home of Shakespeare's company from 1599. In 1613 it was destroyed by fire (although it was during a performance, no-one was killed and 'only one man had his breeches set on fire'). It was rebuilt and reopened in 1614.

acting, but a penny was no small sum for a poor man to spend on entertainment, and the groundlings doubtless took the performance seriously. They may well have been less of a nuisance than the gallants who paid to sit on a stool right on the stage, where they smoked and gossiped and generally tried to attract attention away from the players to themselves.

The Elizabethan theatre matured with astonishing speed. Only a few years after the opening of the playhouse, great works of art were being written and new dramatic genres developed. Thomas Kyd introduced the revenge tragedy, popular for half a century. It contained elements which might seem faintly familiar: a noble young avenger, usually dressed in black, pausing frequently for set-piece soliloquies and real or feigned bouts of madness, is generally corrupted by his mission, before going down in a welter of blood in the final scene. *Hamlet* was no theatrical novelty.

INFLUENCE OF THE MASQUE

Chronicle plays also enjoyed an extraordinary boom. They frequently left history in a better state than the playwright found it, supplying interpretation of historical events in a way guaranteed to please the audience and the monarch. Shakespeare's history plays were the zenith of this playform, too.

Command performance
Falstaff (above) is Shakespeare's greatest comic character. Shakespeare's first biographer, Nicholas Rowe (1709), said that Queen Elizabeth was so delighted with Falstaff in Henry IV *that she commanded Shakespeare to 'show him in love'. The result was* The Merry Wives of Windsor *(below).*

Shakespeare also emerged as master of romantic comedy, thus bringing to perfection all the genres which had gone before. He created in his last years great plays which defy classification. Written after the accession of James I in 1603, these late 'romances', in which dramatic realism gives place to fantasy and lyricism, show the growing influence of the masque.

The masque, a courtly entertainment involving music, dance and poetry, had seen one age of splendour during the reign of Henry VIII, but reached its ultimate glory under King James. The collaboration of playwright Ben Jonson and architect Inigo Jones resulted in entertainments of quite breathtaking extravagance, ingenuity and pomp. Massively complex stage machinery worked miraculous special effects; costumes and sets aspired to dream-like magnificence; and Jonson in particular brought a lyricism to the verse which leaves a worthwhile relic of an art form quite beyond replication these days. A modern audience might well find masques slow-moving, but there is no doubting the influence they had on playwrights of the time.

The 'Elizabethan' theatre lived on until 1642, when Puritans and Parliamentarians (who saw the playhouses as dens of iniquity) closed them down. Shakespeare's style of theatre, although certainly not his plays, had gone for good.

SIR WALTER SCOTT

1771-1832

A romantic as well as a realist, Sir Walter Scott had a lifelong passion for Scotland's dramatic history, which he poured into his poetry and prose. His seemingly effortless ability to relive the past made him – almost by accident – a pioneer of the historical novel, and a writer of incalculable influence on such diverse novelists as the Brontës, George Eliot and Leo Tolstoy. His literary fame was coupled with immense personal popularity, and at his death he was designated by the historian Thomas Carlyle as the 'pride of all Scotchmen'.

'Wizard of the North'

The most famous and revered Scotsman of his time, Scott acquired a renown for his extraordinary literary achievements that reached far beyond the borders of his native country.

In Princes Street, the main thoroughfare of Edinburgh, stands a monument to Sir Walter Scott, towering 200 feet high. Few British writers have been so conspicuously honoured in their native city. But the tribute is not excessive – it is a testimony to the enormous influence Scott exerted, both as a writer and as a popularizer of his country's history, traditions and landscape.

Walter Scott was born in Edinburgh on 15 August 1771. On both sides of the family he was descended from ancient Border yeoman families. His father, also named Walter Scott, was the first member of his family to live in a town and adopt a profession – he was a respected solicitor. Scott's mother, Anne Rutherford, was the daughter of a professor of medicine at Edinburgh University. From his father, a stern but fair man, Walter inherited his disciplined attitude to work, and from his cultured mother he took his imaginative gifts.

CRIPPLED IN CHILDHOOD

Walter was the fourth of six surviving children. When he was a baby the family moved from Edinburgh's picturesque but dirty Old Town to the much healthier New Town – an area of splendid contemporary Georgian buildings. Despite the beneficial move, Walter, while still a toddler, was struck by an illness (probably poliomyelitis) that left his right leg permanently lame. He was therefore sent to live at his paternal grandfather's farmhouse at Sandy-Knowe in the country air of the Border moorlands. Various remedies were tried to cure his lameness, and one of his earliest memories was of lying on his grandfather's parlour floor, wrapped in the skin of a newly killed sheep.

His disability remained, but young Walter grew up strong and vigorous in all other ways. One of his greatest pleasures was listening to the tales of Border history and legend that the old folks told. His memory for these tales was phenomenal, and this early period at his grandfather's house had a strong influence in nurturing his vivid historical imagination.

In 1778, Walter entered the High School in Edinburgh, where he acquired a proficiency in Latin and modern languages that was directly inspired by his desire to read stories and poems in these languages. Naturally high-spirited and outgoing, he quickly made himself popular with the other boys with his inexhaustible gift for storytelling. This popularity was to last throughout his life – indeed, he came to be loved and admired by virtually everyone he met, from royalty to peasants.

Walter spent six months at Kelso Grammar School before proceeding to Edinburgh University at the age of 12 – then not unusually young. Like many students, he did not read for a degree, but simply attended classes in which he was interested. However, his studies were interrupted by a serious illness, described by his later son-in-law and biographer, John Gibson Lockhart, as 'the bursting of a blood vessel in the lower bowels'.

After his convalescence (during which he was forbidden to speak), young Scott embarked on a five-year legal apprenticeship to his father. He later said he would have become a soldier if he had not been lame; instead he submitted to 'the dry and barren wilderness of forms and conveyances'. Unlike his father, he decided to become an advocate (barrister) and in 1792 was admitted to the Bar.

Although Scott's heart was not in the Law, he made a living at it, and found that life as a young advocate had many pleasant aspects. He travelled considerably around his native countryside and so added to his knowledge of Scottish history, folklore and traditions. When he was 24 he became curator of the Advocates' Library, where he spent many happy hours in the study

Old Town, New Town
(right) Edinburgh in the late 18th and early 19th centuries was one of the most cultivated cities in Europe, and many splendid buildings were constructed in Scott's lifetime. This view shows Princes Street in 1825 (where Scott's monument now stands). On the right is the Old Town with its tightly packed buildings; on the left the regular facades of Princes Street mark the edge of the spaciously laid out Georgian New Town.

A varied childhood
(above and right) Scott was born in this street of rather ramshackle houses, but by the time he was six (when the portrait above was painted) he had moved several times – first to the New Town, then to his grandfather's Border farmhouse, and then to Bath, where he spent a year with an aunt in the hope – which unfortunately was not realized – of curing his lameness. When Scott was six, the writer Alicia Cockburn called him 'the most extraordinary genius of a boy I ever saw'.

Key Dates

1771 born in Edinburgh

1773 becomes lame

1783 enters Edinburgh University

1787 studies law

1792 qualifies as lawyer

1797 marries Charlotte Carpenter

1805 publishes *The Lay of the Last Minstrel*; partnership with James Ballantyne

1810 publishes *The Lady of the Lake*

1811 buys property at Abbotsford

1814 *Waverley* published anonymously

1819 *Ivanhoe* published

1820 becomes baronet

1822 supervises George IV's visit to Scotland

1826 goes bankrupt; wife dies

1831 Mediterranean cruise for health

1832 returns to Scotland; dies at Abbotsford

of old documents. His busy social life included membership of literary and debating societies, and in 1792 he joined a German class in order to read German Romantic literature. His enthusiasm bore fruit in his first book, a translation of some German poems which was published anonymously in 1796.

A HAPPY MARRIAGE

At this time, Scott was also experiencing the pleasures and pains of love. In the early 1790s he was smitten by Williamina Belsches, who was from a higher social class than he, but seemed to return his affections. In 1796, however, she married a rich young banker, and Scott said that although he could put together the pieces of his broken heart, 'the crack will remain to my dying day'. He did, indeed, remember his first love all his life, but the next year he not only fell for another woman, but married her. She was Charlotte Carpenter or Charpentier, who had been born in France but brought to England as a girl. Their relationship was companionable rather than passionate – 'it was something short of love in all its fervour', he wrote – but it apparently made for a very happy marriage.

In 1799 Scott's father died, leaving a sizeable legacy to each of his children, and the same year Scott was appointed Sheriff-Depute of Selkirkshire, a post which paid £300 a year in return for fairly light duties. The improvement in his financial circumstances allowed

Parental influence
Scott's solicitor father was a formal and temperate man, but he was also kind-hearted and extraordinarily scrupulous in his business dealings. Scott, who inherited his father's integrity and concern for others, said 'He had a zeal for his clients which was almost ludicrous'. Scott's mother was privately educated to be 'well-bred in society', and her son also grew up to be at ease in any company.

Laird of Abbotsford
(above and right) Scott loved his life as a country gentleman at his beautiful Abbotsford estate (above). A most generous host to his many guests, he was also extremely popular with the local people. In this painting (right) by the leading Scottish artist Sir David Wilkie, Scott has had himself and his family depicted as a group of peasants. Scott was devoted to his dogs, and frequently, as here, they appear in portraits with him.

him to devote more time to writing, and in 1802-3 he published to great acclaim his first major work, the three-volume *Minstrelsy of the Scottish Border.*

Meanwhile, the war with Napoleon's France had sparked off fears of an invasion, and in 1797 Scott joined the Royal Edinburgh Volunteer Light Dragoons. He became 'Paymaster, Quartermaster and Secretary' and took part in drilling and exercises, for although he was lame, his strength was such that he could walk 30 miles a day and he was an excellent horseman.

His military exploits, however, were not appreciated by the Lord Lieutenant of Selkirkshire, who thought that Scott was devoting too much of his time to soldiering and invoked an old rule that the Sheriff-Depute of the county should live within the area of his jurisdiction for at least four months of the year. So in 1804 Scott rented a house called Ashestiel, a few miles from Selkirk and pleasantly situated on the Tweed. By this time he had two daughters and a son; a second son, born in the following year, completed the family.

Scott's work in editing medieval romances encouraged him to try a similar type of composition himself, and in 1805 he published a long narrative poem, *The Lay of the Last Minstrel*, set in the 16th century and based on a Border legend of a goblin. This, his first important original literary work, was an immediate success, running to five editions in a year. In the next few years Scott published several other best-selling poems in the same vein, notably *Marmion* and *The Lady of the Lake.* The latter engendered a rush of interest in Loch Katrine, the setting of the poem.

Scott was prospering in other ways. In 1804 an uncle left him some property which he sold for £5000, and in 1806 he was appointed a Clerk of Session, an important official in Scotland's supreme civil court. The duties

Scotland's tourist image
(right) Virtually single-handed, Scott created the glamorous public image of Scotland's history and landscape, and in so doing he gave birth to Scotland's tourist industry. The Edinburgh publisher Robert Cadell described the 'extraordinary sensation' caused by Scott's poem The Lady of the Lake *(1810), which is set at Loch Katrine (right). 'The whole country rang with the praises of the poet – crowds set off to the scenery of Loch Katrine, till then comparatively unknown; and as the book came out just before the season for excursions, every home in that neighbourhood was crammed with a constant succession of visitors.'*

carried a salary of £1300 a year but were not too arduous, and Scott often used his time in court to catch up with correspondence (he was even accused of writing his books in court, but he denied this).

In 1811, Scott bought a farmhouse on the Tweed. The site was originally called Clarty Hole, but he renamed it, more romantically, Abbotsford. This was to be his home for the rest of his life, although he had to spend a good part of the year in Edinburgh because of his court duties. He bought neighbouring land to create an estate and built up a palatial country house, complete with a large library. Scott realized that, even with his sheriffship and clerkship, he needed to keep up a prolific literary output to finance Abbotsford, and he continued to pour out narrative verse. In 1813 he was offered, but declined, the poet laureateship.

Companion and wife
Charlotte Carpenter or Charpentier married Scott in 1797. He said that their love increased with the years, but he never forgot his first, lost love, and his marriage 'was something short of love in all its fervour which I suspect people only feel once *in their lives'.*

A CHANGE OF DIRECTION

That same year, quite by chance, the direction of his career changed completely. According to Scott's own account, he was searching for some fishing tackle in a drawer when he came across the manuscript of a novel he had begun eight years earlier. He had laid it aside then, because of adverse comments by a friend whose judgement he valued. But Scott decided to complete it, and, warming to his task, he wrote the last two-thirds during the evenings of three weeks. The book was *Waverley*, which on its publication in 1814 proved even more successful than *The Lady of the Lake*, and marked the beginning of one of the most remarkable sequences of novels in English literature.

The book was published anonymously, and its successors always carried on the title page the words 'by the author of Waverley'. Various explanations have been suggested as to why Scott wanted to keep his authorship secret – one being that the novelist's 'lowly' status conflicted with his dignity as an important legal official. Another factor is that speculation about the identity of 'the Great Unknown' kept interest in the books alive and boosted sales. In literary circles Scott's secret was an open one. In the year that *Waverley* was published, Jane Austen wrote: 'Walter Scott has no business to write novels, especially good ones. It is not fair. He has Fame and Profit enough as a Poet . . .' Yet to outsiders it seemed scarcely credible that someone who already had an extraordinarily full business and social life could find time to write substantial novels at a rate of almost two a year.

Scott's method was to rise early in the morning and do several hours' work at his desk while the rest of the household slept. His many guests at Abbotsford, to whom he was the perfect host, never suspected the labours he accomplished before they came down to breakfast. Most of the 'Waverley Novels' dealt with Scottish history, so Scott already had much of the material in his head and wrote with astonishing

Fact or Fiction

ROBIN HOOD

The first recorded mention of Robin Hood is in a 14th-century poem; later he became a popular figure in ballads. There is no firm evidence that such a man ever lived, but there is almost certainly some historical basis for the stories. In Scott's *Ivanhoe*, he appears as the honourable outlaw, Locksley, who opposes the upstart Norman Prince John.

Son-in-law biographer
The writer John Gibson Lockhart who, like Scott, was a lawyer by training, married Scott's daughter Sophia in 1820. This portrait of them was painted much later, in fact after Sophia was dead. Lockhart knew his father-in-law intimately and his extremely long, minutely detailed Life of Sir Walter Scott *is one of the classics of literary biography. Many critics rank it next to Boswell's* Life of Johnson.

fluency. An exception is *Ivanhoe*, the first of his novels with a purely English setting. Although he did not publicly acknowledge his authorship of the Waverley novels until 1827, Scott was by now the most famous living Scotsman. In 1820 he was made a baronet and in 1822 he supervised George IV's visit to Scotland.

Scott enjoyed his busy and energetic life to the full, and his happiness reached a peak in 1825 when his beloved elder son, also called Walter, married a pretty young heiress, Jane Jobson. 'There is gold in her garters', wrote Scott, and although his attitude was not really as mercenary as it sounds (he had a deep affection for her), the subject of money was always at the forefront of his mind. As 1825 drew to a close it was an increasing source of worry. His fortune was, in fact, built on very shaky foundations, and the next year it was to topple like a house of cards.

FINANCIAL RUIN

This extraordinary downfall can be explained by the complex nature of his literary dealings at a time when publishing was becoming 'big business' and fortunes could be made or lost overnight. Since 1805, Scott had been involved in publishing as more than an author, for he had gone into partnership with the printer James Ballantyne, an old school friend. Four years later he founded the firm of John Ballantyne and Company, booksellers and publishers, with James and his brother John. Both the printing and publishing sides of the business ran into financial trouble. Scott was able to steer business their way, but he also lost money for them by getting them to produce unsaleable antiquarian texts. They were rescued by another Edinburgh publisher, Archibald Constable, who from 1818 onwards issued Scott's novels.

The financial arrangements linking the Ballantynes, Constable and Scott became extremely involved, and Scott often spent money that he did not really have. He borrowed large sums and was in the habit of getting advances from Constable in the form of post-dated bills of exchange, which he would immediately sell at a discount for cash. In December 1825 Constable's London agents, Hurst Robinson & Co., went bankrupt, and in a chain reaction Constable and Ballantyne (and thus Scott himself) followed suit.

Scott had kept secret his involvement in publishing and when it suddenly became known that he was

ROBERT BURNS

Scott's greatest contemporary Scottish writer was Robert Burns (1759-96), who also had a great love for his country's heritage. They met only once, when Scott was 15. This painting records an earlier incident with young Scott gazing at Burns in an Edinburgh bookshop.

Royal pageantry
(left) Scott was one of the guests at the coronation of George IV in London on 19 July 1821. He wrote that it was 'impossible to conceive a ceremony more august and imposing in all its parts, and more calculated to make the deepest impression both on the eye and the feelings'. In the following year Scott was given the honour of organizing the ceremonials for the King's visit to Scotland.

A nation mourns
(below) Scott was so popular that his death caused widespread grief. His son-in-law Lockhart recorded that at his funeral at Dryburgh Abbey 'when the coffin was taken from the hearse, and again laid on the shoulders of the afflicted serving-men, one deep sob burst from a thousand lips.'

ruined – with personal debts of over £100,000 – his friends were shocked and dismayed. A group of them offered to lend him money, but with a magnificent resolve that would have done credit to any of his fictional heroes, Scott refused, saying 'No, this right hand shall work it all off!' He was allowed to keep Abbotsford and he settled down to a regime of work that was gruelling even by his standards. The death of his wife in 1826 was another bitter blow, but he worked on indomitably, and in the space of two years his writing paid off nearly £40,000 of his debts. His astonishing output included not only novels, but also a nine-volume biography of Napoleon.

As a result of the strain of such a workload, the quality of Scott's writing declined and his health began to give way. He had a stroke in 1831 and, in the hope of recovery, made an eight-month voyage to the Mediterranean. It is a mark of the esteem in which he was held that his ship was provided by the Government.

Scott had further strokes on the voyage and, realizing he was dying, could think of nothing but getting back to his beloved Scotland. His son-in-law Lockhart has movingly described the long journey home – how Scott, bemused and feeble though he was, rose in spirits as he recognized places he knew and murmured their names. He arrived back at Abbotsford on 11 July and died on 21 September 1832, with all his children at his bedside. 'It was so quiet a day', wrote Lockhart, 'that the sound he best loved, the gentle ripple of the Tweed over its pebbles, was distinctly audible as we knelt round the bed and his eldest son kissed and closed his eyes.'

Sir Walter Scott was buried at Dryburgh Abbey, a few miles from his home, and Lockhart records that the newspapers 'had the signs of mourning usual on the demise of a king'. His copyrights and remaining liabilities were taken over by the publisher Robert Cadell, who made a fortune from them. His beloved home, Abbotsford, however, passed to Scott's eldest son and still belongs to his direct descendants.

The Age of Chivalry

Some of Scott's finest works were inspired by the romance of the Middle Ages, and were themselves a key factor in the 19th-century revival of chivalric ideals.

One of Sir Walter Scott's lesser known literary works is an article on chivalry he wrote for the *Encyclopaedia Britannica* in 1818, one year before the publication of *Ivanhoe*. He was regarded as an authority on the subject because of the vast store of antiquarian knowledge he had built up from studying the ancient ballads of Scotland. In his learned essay Scott described 'the total decay of the chivalrous principle' and tells how 'men learned to despise its fantastic refinements'; yet chivalry underwent a remarkable revival in Scott's lifetime, and he himself played a leading role in this.

Ivanhoe is set in the 1190s when chivalry was at its most active. The word was originally a collective term for knights or other mounted soldiers, then came to refer to the system of ethical values observed by this group. The Crusades (the series of wars undertaken by Christian nations of Europe against the Muslims) were chiefly responsible for the development of these ideals. Indeed, the first organized Orders of chivalry – dedicated to the care and protection of pilgrims to Jerusalem – were founded in the Holy Land in the early 12th century.

Courtly love
(below left) During the 12th century, poets in France developed a concept of courtly love that became an enduring theme in medieval literature. Central to it was the idea that the love of the knight for his lady should be a kind of ennobling religious devotion rather than a physical passion, and so convention established that she was in some way unattainable. In this exquisite 15th-century tapestry the lover offers his heart to his lady.

They were the Knights of the Order of the Hospital of St John of Jerusalem (Hospitallers) and the Poor Knights of Christ and of the Temple of Solomon (Templars). Both organizations became rich, international brotherhoods. The Templars, feared as a powerful secret society, were eventually suppressed by papal decree in 1312, and the Grand Master of the Order and several other members were burned at the stake as heretics. In *Ivanhoe*, the formidable Sir Brian de Bois-Guilbert is a Templar.

A knight owed loyalty to his spiritual master, God; to his temporal master, usually the king; and to the mistress of his heart, who in medieval literary romance was usually a woman married to someone else or otherwise unattainable (so that the love was 'pure'). But vital to the concept of chivalry was military glory. In *Ivanhoe*, when the hero is prevented by his wounds from taking part in the assault on Torquilstone Castle, he explains to his nurse Rebecca how he longs to be in the fray:

'The love of the battle is the food upon which we live – the dust of the mêlée is the breath of our nostrils! We live not – we wish not to live – longer than while we are victorious and renowned – Such, maiden, are the laws of chivalry to which we are sworn, and to which we offer all that we hold dear.'

The high-minded and kind-hearted Rebecca remonstrates with Ivanhoe: 'What remains to you as

The crusading spirit
(above) The Crusades were crucial to the development of chivalry, but the high ideals that led thousands of Christian soldiers to travel to the Holy Land to recapture Jerusalem from the Muslims all too easily degenerated into bloodlust. The First Crusade began in 1095, and Jerusalem was taken by siege (above) in 1099, after which the Crusaders carried out a horrible massacre of the Muslim and Jewish inhabitants. Jerusalem was recaptured by the Muslims in 1187, and Ivanhoe and Richard the Lionheart were part of the Third Crusade, which began in 1189 and failed to regain the Holy City.

Lionhearted king
(right) Richard I, who throughout most of Ivanhoe *is disguised as 'the Black Knight', represented the chivalric ideal of martial valour more completely than any other man of his day. He was an awesome warrior and his prowess made him a favourite topic for poets, as well as popular with his subjects. However, he was a failure as a king, with more interest in fighting than in governing his country. Here he is shown with his barons, but during his ten-year reign he spent no more than a few months in England.*

the prize of all the blood you have spilled – of all the travail and pain you have endured – of all the tears which your deeds have caused, when death has broken the strong man's spear, and overtaken the speed of his war-horse?' Ivanhoe cries, 'Glory, maiden! Glory!'

Ivanhoe tells her, 'Thou art no Christian, Rebecca; and to thee are unknown those high feelings'. In so doing he reveals one of the great flaws in the chivalric ideal, for the fine sentiments to which a knight laid claim extended only to those of his own class and beliefs. Rebecca is the noblest character in the novel, but because she is a Jewess she is treated with contempt. In practice, also, pious martial valour could descend into bloodlust, and refined courtly love into sordid adultery.

Although chivalry continued to be an enormously popular element in literature, in reality it was in decline by the 15th century. This was partly because the armoured horseman was no longer the dominant force on the battlefield. The English longbowmen who slaughtered the flower of French knighthood at the battles of Crecy (1346), Poitiers (1356) and Agincourt (1415) showed that war was now a matter of ruthless professionalism and technique.

Vivid pageantry
(below) The tournament represented chivalry at its most colourful and its popularity continued long after the knight had lost his pre-eminence in battle. But in spite of the pageantry, the fighting was often grimly real and fatalities were common. In the tournament in Ivanhoe *four knights are killed and "upwards of thirty were desperately wounded".*

CHIVALRY'S LONG SLUMBER

The pageantry of knighthood still continued on ceremonial occasions, however, and in the tournament – Henry VIII of England was a renowned combatant. In the reign of Elizabeth I there was an Indian summer of chivalry, centred on a cult of the Queen herself. One of Elizabeth's courtiers, the poet and soldier Sir Philip Sidney, was a real-life chivalric hero – renowned for his bravery and honour. As he lay fatally wounded on the battlefield of Zutphen in the Netherlands, he handed a proffered cup of water to an injured comrade with the words 'Thy necessity is yet greater than mine'. But in spite of such men, chivalry was by this time largely a matter of romantic nostalgia rather than a code for living. In the early years of the 17th century, Cervantes' immortal novel *Don Quixote* satirized the chivalric conventions as his ageing hero, whose mind has been unbalanced by reading too many chivalric romances, tilts at windmills and other imagined combatants.

Chivalry's long slumber lasted until the late 18th century, although elements of its code and trappings always survived – in heraldry, for example, and in certain traditions of manners and etiquette. The 18th century is known as the Age of Enlightenment, a time

Renaissance chivalry
Soldier, statesman, poet, courtier and patron of the arts, Sir Philip Sidney was regarded as the ideal of chivalric courtesy. He died valiantly from battle wounds when he was only 31.

Regal rivalry
In 1520 Henry VIII of England and Francis I of France had a diplomatic meeting near Calais. The occasion was so splendid it was known as the Field of the Cloth of Gold. Jousting was part of the lavish entertainment.

when civilized citizens strove to free themselves from superstition and championed the cause of human reason. In such an intellectual climate the ideals of chivalry seemed ridiculous rather than noble, and in his *History of Great Britain*, David Hume, one of the leading philosophers of the Enlightenment, called the Crusades 'the most signal and durable monument of human folly that has yet appeared in any age or nation'.

Paradoxically, however, the rational spirit that guided Hume helped to create a new interest in all aspects of medieval life, including chivalry. Historians of the time approached the past in a new, objective fashion, and began to study medieval documents and artifacts with scientific curiosity. Whereas the rationalists of the Enlightenment showed a scholarly attitude to the distant past, it was the very distance and mystery of the Middle Ages which appealed to the Romantics of the late 18th and early 19th century.

Since chivalry appealed to the emotions rather than the intellect, it stirred the imagination of Romantic poets. Scott was too level-headed to be called a true Romantic, but he was so deeply steeped in the literature and history of the Middle Ages that he handled medieval subjects with effortless flair.

About a third of Scott's novels are devoted to medieval themes. Apart from *Ivanhoe*, the best known are *Quentin Durward* and *The Talisman*; and the narrative poems which made him famous are very much concerned with chivalry and romance. Both poems and novels reached an astonishingly wide audience – and not just in Britain. In 1811, for example, Louis Simond, a French traveller visiting England, compared Windsor Castle to 'a castle of Sir Walter Scott's own building'. And Sir Adam Ferguson read aloud a stirring battle description from Scott's *The Lady of the Lake* to encourage his troops when they were under attack during the war against Napoleon in Portugal. *Ivanhoe* achieved unprecedented heights of popularity, for in the year after it was published no fewer than five dramatized versions of the chivalric tale were being shown in London.

Scott's influence can also be seen in the visual arts of the time. After the success of *Ivanhoe*, it was unusual for the Royal Academy summer exhibition not to include at least one picture illustrating a scene from the book; and Scott's house at Abbotsford initiated the style called Scots Baronial that became all the rage in mid-19th century Scotland. Scott wanted his house to be like an 'old English hall such as a squire of yore dwelt in'.

DAZZLING PAGEANTRY

The revival of the chivalrous spirit manifested itself most clearly and colourfully, however, in the field of pageantry. From the early years of the 19th century, the monarchy seized on every opportunity to dress up the Court in the most magnificent anachronistic fashion. One instance was the great installation ceremony for Knights of the Garter held at Windsor Castle on St George's day in 1805. The breathtaking ceremonial was followed by superb banquets, and a contemporary chronicler wrote, 'It was his majesty's [George III's] particular wish, that as many of the old customs should be kept up as possible.' At a time when Britain was locked in a mighty struggle with Napoleon (this was the year of the Battle of Trafalgar) it made sound sense, as the chronicler put it, 'to cherish that chivalrous spirit . . . which burned in the breasts of our ancestors' and 'to fan the flame of loyalty and patriotism'.

The pomp and magnificence was even greater at George IV's coronation in 1821. Scott was a guest at the ceremony, and said that foreign dignitaries present were 'utterly astonished and delighted to see the revival of feudal dresses and feudal grandeur when the occasion demanded it, and that in a degree of splendour which, they averred, they had never seen paralleled in Europe'. The following year, the new King George visited Edin-

burgh, and Scott was chosen to direct the pageantry that accompanied his regal progress.

When Queen Victoria was crowned in 1838, however, pageantry was severely curtailed. The Prime Minister, Lord Melbourne, thought conspicuous display would be inappropriate at a time of economic depression. Melbourne was a Whig (a member of the party that favoured political and social reform) and his Tory opponents were outraged by the 'Penny Coronation', which they felt was an attack on the monarchy, not just on tradition.

This feeling led to the most famous and most farcical display of chivalric revival – the Eglinton Tournament. Lord Eglinton, a rich young Tory, decided to hold a tournament to flaunt the values that had been spurned by the Government. The tournament was arranged for 28 August 1839 at Eglinton Castle in Scotland, and the interest it aroused was enormous, requests for tickets even coming from India and South America.

Scott's account of the tournament in *Ivanhoe* was a major source of inspiration to Lord Eglinton. A huge amount of preparation was involved in organizing the

The Black Prince wins his spurs
(above) At the Battle of Crecy in 1346 Edward III's son, Edward the Black Prince, then only 16, conducted himself with conspicuous gallantry. He was one of the original Knights of the Garter, a British Order of chivalry.

The tournament revived
(right) The Eglinton Tournament of 1839 was the most spectacular event in the Victorian revival of chivalry, but it was ruined by the rain. One participant said he had never seen 'the disagreeable and the ridiculous so completely mixed together'. Another said 'the rain began, and the knights threw down their lances, and put up their umbrellas.' When the weather cleared they salvaged some pride and jousted successfully.

Medieval inspiration
(above) Many 19th-century artists were inspired by chivalric romance. This tapestry designed by Sir Edward Burne-Jones shows an episode from Arthurian legend.

Nostalgic fancy dress
(below) In 1842 Queen Victoria gave a costume ball at Buckingham Palace. Most guests wore medieval costume and some dressed as characters from Scott's novels.

armour (most of it hired from a London dealer), costumes and marquees, and in practising the lost art of jousting. It proved particularly difficult for the young noblemen taking part in the tournament to persuade their horses to gallop close enough to the barrier that separated the charging knights, but a dress rehearsal went off very well.

When the great day arrived, spirits were high and the audience 100,000 strong. The tournament opened with a procession, but just as it got under way a clap of thunder announced a torrential rainstorm that lasted throughout the day. Soon participants and spectators were drenched, the horses slithered in the mud, and the whole affair degenerated into a fiasco. However, Lord Eglinton refused to be downcast, and when the weather cheered up a couple of days later, he arranged jousting and banqueting with some success. But it was the farcical element that was to be remembered. Whig newspapers had a field day, and a knight with an umbrella came to symbolize the tournament.

Despite the ludicrous aspects of the Eglinton Tournament, the chivalric ideal became part of Victorian culture. Victoria's consort, Prince Albert, seemed to the Queen to be the embodiment of knightly virtue and she loved to see him in armour. In 1842 she held a lavish costume ball in which she and her husband went dressed as Edward III and his wife Queen Philippa. This delight in medieval trappings also featured in a revival of interest in Arthurian legend which affected both literature and art (for example, the poems of Alfred, Lord Tennyson and the paintings of the Pre-Raphaelites).

A 'GENTLEMANLY' IDEAL

The chivalric ideal also coloured the whole notion of what it was to be a 'gentleman' – someone who was loyal to Queen and country, who treated women with reverence, who preferred death to dishonour and stood up for truth and fair play. It was an ideal which characterized such men as Sir Arthur Conan Doyle – whose preoccupations with honour and patriotism imbued his literature, and his life in the army and on the cricket-field. Indeed, sport was seen almost entirely in chivalric terms, and the popular magazine *Punch* described the qualities of a good sportsman thus:

'He is one who has not merely braced his muscles and developed his endurance by the exercise of some great sport, but has . . . learnt to control his anger, to be considerate to his fellow men . . . to bear aloft a cheerful countenance under disappointment, and never own himself defeated until the last breath is out of his body.'

These ideals continued into the 20th century – Sir Robert Baden-Powell's *Scouting for Boys*, published in 1908, the year in which he founded the Boy Scouts movement, is full of chivalric imagery. Significantly, *Ivanhoe* was one of the books he recommended scouts to read. It was the First World War that sounded the death knell of chivalry. St George figured prominently in wartime propaganda, but after millions had been slaughtered it was impossible to pretend that war was a glorious adventure. As Scott put it in his essay on chivalry, 'We can now only look back on it as a beautiful and fantastic piece of frostwork, which has dissolved in the beams of the sun!'

WILLIAM WORDSWORTH
1770–1850

SAMUEL TAYLOR COLERIDGE
1772–1834

LORD BYRON
1788–1824

PERCY BYSSHE SHELLEY
1792–1822

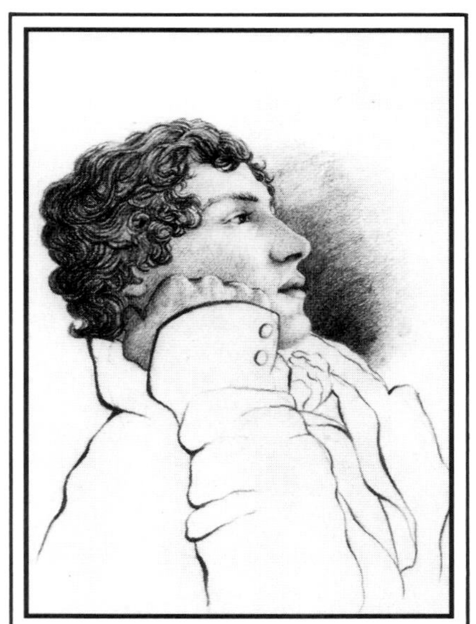

JOHN KEATS
1795–1821

THE ROMANTIC POETS

Reacting against the formal, rational elements of 18th-century verse, five writers emerged who, within decades, changed the face of English poetry. Wordsworth, with his belief in the inspiration of Nature, and Coleridge, who was fascinated by the supernatural, were 'first-generation' Romantics. Byron, Shelley and Keats, who followed, were tragically short-lived – but not so their art. They created some of the most angry and most lyrical of English poems, and revolutionized ideas on beauty, truth and imagination.

William Wordsworth

In the course of his long life Wordsworth changed from a young rebel to a pillar of the Establishment. His literary eminence made the Lake District – where he spent most of his life – a place of pilgrimage.

The aged poet
(right) Ironically, as Wordsworth's imaginative powers declined, his popularity soared. Passionate youth gave way to sober middle age in his poetry and personality alike, but the public lionized him. However, his younger contemporaries Byron and Shelley mocked the simplicity of his poetry, and deplored him as a reactionary.

Wordsworth was of the first generation of Romantic poets. His life was a model of artistic dedication and persistence – most of it spent quietly, frugally and laboriously in the Lake District, while metropolitan critics savagely abused his work. But he lived to achieve universal recognition, and in his old age became Poet Laureate.

William Wordsworth was born on 7 April 1770 at Cockermouth, a little Cumbrian market town on the edge of the Lake District. He lost his mother when he was seven, but his schooldays at Hawkshead were happy. However, when his father died in 1783, the five young Wordsworths found themselves impoverished and dependent on the charity of relatives. William was sent to St John's College, Cambridge, but, rapidly disillusioned by university life, deliberately neglected his studies. Despite his slender resources, he refused to take up a conventional career, dedicating himself to poetry and adopting radical opinions.

On a visit to France and Switzerland in 1790, he was fired by popular enthusiasm for the French Revolution. Returning to France in 1791, Wordsworth had a love affair, at Orléans, with a girl named Annette Vallon, who bore him a daughter. Later in 1792 he left for England to raise money, possibly intending to go back and marry Annette; but war broke out between Britain and France, ending the relationship by cutting off all communications for years. This episode in the poet's life remained a closely guarded secret until the 1920s.

A CHANGE OF FORTUNES

Wordsworth's early publications had aroused little interest, but a turning point in his fortunes occurred in 1795, when a young admirer died and left him £900 – enough for the 'plain living and high thinking' that appealed so strongly to Wordsworth. It was also enough to support his sister Dorothy, who could now share his home and become his closest companion. Dorothy Wordsworth proved to be a remarkable observer, and her journals – works of literature in their own right – often serve as source-books for the background of such famous poems as William's *Daffodils.*

At about this time, the poet Samuel Taylor Coleridge also entered Wordsworth's life. William and Dorothy became the Coleridges' neighbours at Nether Stowey in Somerset, and the two poets stimulated each other to an intense pitch of creativity. Local antagonism to their bohemian lifestyle and radical friends eventually persuaded them to move on.

To finance a trip to Germany, Wordsworth and Coleridge published *Lyrical Ballads* (1798), a selection of their work now recognized as a landmark in English poetry. Nineteen out of the 23 poems were by Wordsworth, although the volume appeared anonymously. ('Wordsworth's name is nothing', Coleridge explained, 'and mine stinks.') Wordsworth's intention was 'to choose incidents and situations from common life, and to relate or describe them, throughout, as far as possible in a selection of language really used by men'. But although the collection contained masterpieces such as *Tintern Abbey*, it received just three reviews and sold only a handful of copies.

A devoted sister
(left) One year younger than William, Dorothy Wordsworth lived with her brother from 1795 until his death 55 years later. Coleridge described himself, Dorothy and William as 'three people with one soul'.

The German trip was also a failure, and William and Dorothy returned to England in February 1799. They settled in the Lake District, and rented – for £8 a year – the most famous of all their homes, Dove Cottage in Grasmere. The years at Dove Cottage (1800–08) saw

Love and loyalty
(above) Wordsworth first met his wife Mary when they were at infants' school together. They were married for almost 50 years, and had five children – two of whom died tragically in the same year, 1812.

Rydal Mount
(below) Wordworth's move to his grand home, Rydal Mount, coincided with his assumption of the government post of Distributor of Stamps for Westmorland. He lived in this 'modest mansion of sober hue' until his death in 1850.

Wordsworth at his creative peak. Many great poems from this period, such as *Intimations of Immortality*, chronicle moments of almost mystical rapture that were to become increasingly rare with the years.

Time made Wordsworth a more staid, less inspiring figure. In 1802 he married Mary Hutchinson, a woman he had known since childhood, and fathered five children. He became a political reactionary, now attacked as a turncoat by younger radicals such as Byron and Shelley. In 1813 he accepted a post – from the Government he had once detested – as Distributor of Stamps for Westmorland, and moved into his last and grandest home, Rydal Mount. The government post brought him the healthy sum of £400 a year, and in his later life he was a wealthy man; in 1827 his friend Sir George Beaumont, a noted patron of the arts, left him a legacy, and in 1842 he was awarded a pension of £300 a year.

Walking tour
In 1799 Wordsworth and Coleridge walked from County Durham to the Lakes – crossing Greta Bridge (below) on the way. Wordsworth shared with his friend the scenes described in The Prelude.

FAME AND HONOURS

By this time Wordsworth had become one of the most famous and honoured of English writers, for the critics had started eating their words and hailing him as a great poet in about 1820. Thomas de Quincey, author of *Recollections of the Lake Poets* (1834-39), summed up his friend's change of fortunes when he wrote: 'Up to 1820 the name of Wordsworth was trampled underfoot; from 1820 to 1830 it was militant; from 1830 to 1835 it has been triumphant.' An increasingly venerated figure, Wordsworth composed a *Guide to the Lakes* (1822) and in old age became one of the district's chief tourist attractions. He outlived all his great contemporaries to become Poet Laureate in 1843, seven years before his death on 23 April 1850.

A few months later, Mary Wordsworth published the most ambitious of all her husband's works – *The Prelude* – completed years before but reserved for posterity. This record of 'the Growth of a Poet's Mind' made a fitting climax to the whole of the English Romantic movement.

Samuel Taylor Coleridge

Eloquent, idealistic and with wide-ranging talents, Coleridge nevertheless failed to find the love and fulfilment he craved – except, perhaps, in his inspiring friendship with the Wordsworths.

Coleridge's brilliant mind and eloquent tongue fascinated almost everyone who met him. Wordsworth, though often impatient with his friend's weaknesses, described him as 'the most wonderful man I have ever known'. Although Coleridge's splendid genius began to flag early in life, undermined by opium and unhappiness, he left a handful of magical, incantatory poems that place him among the greatest spirits of English literature.

Samuel Taylor Coleridge was born on 21 October 1772 at Ottery St Mary in Devon. On the death of his father, the village vicar and schoolmaster, he was sent to Christ's Hospital, a London school where he rapidly attracted attention as a prodigious scholar, omnivorous reader and spellbinding conversationalist. At Jesus College, Cambridge, he seemed certain of a great future, until events revealed the flaws in his curiously helpless, childlike character. In debt and rejected by Mary Evans, the girl he loved, Coleridge ran away and joined a regiment of dragoons under the fanciful name Silas Tomkyn Comerbacke. Although discovered and bought out by his elder brother, he failed to settle down again at Cambridge and left without taking a degree.

Another curious episode occurred shortly afterwards, at Bristol, when Coleridge fell in with another poet, Robert Southey. These two idealistic young men planned to set up a utopian community in the wilds of America. Since there would have to be women in the community, they rather hastily became engaged to two sisters, Sara and Edith Fricker. Coleridge evidently had qualms about the arrangement, drifted off to London and even proposed again – without success – to Mary Evans. But when Southey tracked him down, Coleridge tamely allowed himself to be taken back and wedded to Sara Fricker. The utopian community never materialized, and Coleridge soon discovered that he and his wife were hopelessly mismatched.

The couple settled close to the Quantock Hills, at Nether Stowey in Somerset. By now, Coleridge had produced a political journal, *The Watchman*, and toyed

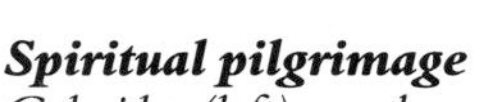

Spiritual pilgrimage
Coleridge (left) was the son of the vicar of Ottery St Mary in Devon (below) and seemed destined to follow in his father's clerical footsteps. But with his new friend Robert Southey, the 21-year-old Coleridge was captivated by the idea of a utopian community, one of whose main precepts was complete religious freedom. Later in life, however, Coleridge reappraised his unorthodox views and spent his last years studying the Bible and writing extensive commentaries on it.

Wordsworth's sister-in-law. But Coleridge's unfulfilled relationship with her gave him little happiness, and it was to her that he addressed *Dejection: An Ode*, which has been called the saddest poem in the language. It was also to be his last major poem.

Racked by illness and hopelessly addicted to opium, Coleridge seemed to be deteriorating fast. In 1804 he went to Malta for three years as secretary to the governor, but returned in no better health and spirits. He separated from his wife, and for two years lived with the Wordsworths at Dove Cottage – a relatively stable episode during which he regularly brought out a periodical, *The Friend*, dictated to Sara Hutchinson.

When Sara left the Lake District, Coleridge moved to London. He was to be deeply wounded by Wordsworth's reported remarks about his trying domestic habits, and the ensuing breach between the two poets was never fully healed. Despite his apparent decline, Coleridge was to live for many years, mainly thanks to Dr James Gillman, who in 1816 took him into his own family and looked after him until the poet's death on 25 July 1834.

In his later years, Coleridge had made a new reputation as a lecturer and produced much distinguished philosophical and critical writing, including a famous literary autobiography, *Biographia Literaria* (1817). His poetic output was tiny compared with his fellow-Romantic Wordsworth, yet it includes at least two of the most famous and most frequently anthologized poems in the English language.

Fruitful friendship
In 1797 the Wordsworths rented Alfoxden Park (left) near Nether Stowey in Somerset in order to be near Coleridge. The two poets talked, walked and wrote, roaming the Quantock Hills for inspiration.

Wife and daughter
Against his better judgement, Coleridge married Sara Fricker (below left) in 1795. He separated from her some years later, having fathered three sons and Sara (below), who grew into a great beauty and intellectual.

with the idea of becoming a Unitarian minister. His association with William and Dorothy Wordsworth, however, reaffirmed and revitalized his poetic vocation. Coleridge contributed only four poems to *Lyrical Ballads*, of which 'it was agreed, that my endeavours should be directed to persons and characters supernatural, or at least romantic'. But one of these poems was an awesome parable-like story of unsurpassed potency, *The Rime of the Ancient Mariner*.

In 1797, Coleridge stayed for a time at a farm near Porlock in Somerset. There, according to a note he wrote in 1816, suffering from 'a slight indisposition' for which he had taken laudanum (opium in liquid form), he fell into a reverie or drugged dream in which he 'read' a long poem about the Khan Kubla. On waking, he began to write it down but, according to his own account, he was interrupted by 'a person from Porlock' and lost the thread. Wildly beautiful, exotic and enigmatic, *Kubla Khan* remained a fragment – but, nevertheless, an imperishable masterpiece.

In 1800 Coleridge and his family moved to Keswick in order to be closer to the Wordsworths. Another strong attraction of Grasmere was Sara Hutchinson,

Lord Byron

Byron was both famous and infamous for his audacious poetry, his scandalous love life and his devotion to liberal ideals. Ostracized by English society, he died fighting for Greek independence.

The family seat
(above) Newstead Abbey in Nottinghamshire came into Byron's possession when, at the age of ten, he inherited the title and estate of his great-uncle, the 5th Lord Byron. The building, which had originally been presented to the Byrons by Henry VIII in the 16th century, was in a semi-ruined state, but the young Byron fell in love with its romantic atmosphere. In 1818, however, he sold Newstead for almost £100,000 to pay off his debts.

Byron made a unique impression on 19th-century Europe, not only as a poet but as a legendary personality: a great lover and solitary brooding outsider, set against a landscape of wild romantic scenery. The real Byron was more complex, alternating his romantic role with that of a fashionable society man, and writing sustained masterpieces of comic and satirical verse.

George Gordon Byron was born on 22 January 1788 in a furnished room in London. His mother, a Scottish heiress, had seen most of her money spent by her wild, fortune-hunting husband, Captain John Byron. The young family fled from its creditors to Aberdeen, and the Captain soon decamped to France, where he died.

Until he was ten, Byron was sent to school in Aberdeen, and meanwhile a succession of doctors tried in vain to correct his deformed right foot, of which he was always to be morbidly conscious. Byron's lameness may account for his need to prove himself in love and action, and it became an important element of his romantic image.

An unexpected death promoted Byron to the ranks of the aristocracy as Baron Byron of Rochdale, with Newstead Abbey as his family seat. He was sent to Harrow, and went on to Trinity College, Cambridge, graduating in 1808. He appeared to be a typical Regency buck, deep in debt and prone to reckless dissipation, but he was also publishing a good deal of verse. When the *Edinburgh Review* dismissed it with scorn, he lashed out at the criticism in a long, immensely funny poem entitled *English Bards and Scotch Reviewers* (1809).

In July 1809, Byron left England on a Mediterranean tour which lasted for two years. He was delighted with the exotic, untamed Balkans, and above all with Greece. 'If I am a poet,' he said, 'the air of Greece has made me one.' Back in England, he spoke out in the House of Lords against government repression of working-class discontent. Then in March 1812 he published the first two cantos of *Childe Harold's Pilgrimage*, which narrates the travels and adventures of the first distinctive 'Byronic' hero – whom contemporaries rightly assumed to be a disguised self-portrait. *Childe Harold* made Byron famous virtually overnight, and gave added allure to his extraordinary good looks and mercurial character. One of the many women who pursued him was the unstable Lady Caroline Lamb. Despite her famous description of him as 'mad, bad,

Indiscreet passions
(right and below) Byron insisted that he was the victim, rather than the seducer, of women, but his stormy love life shocked his contemporaries. His most famous affair was with Lady Caroline Lamb (below), and he is rumoured to have had an incestuous relationship with his adored step-sister Augusta (right), and to have had a child with her.

meanwhile, had given birth to Byron's daughter, Allegra. Mother and child travelled to Italy with the Shelleys in 1818, and Byron took on responsibility for Allegra's care. He put the little girl in a convent. But she died of typhus at the age of five.

In 1819 Byron met Teresa, the 19-year-old wife of the elderly Count Guiccioli. They became lovers, and Teresa eventually left her husband. For several years Byron led a relatively settled life with Teresa. But in 1823 he answered appeals to help the Greek revolt against Turkish rule. He was financing and training troops at Missolonghi when he fell ill with a fever. After ten days' illness, on 19 April 1824, a clap of thunder rang out and the Greeks in the streets of the town looked at one another and said, "The great man is gone." Byron had died, but in that moment a legend was born.

An exotic image
(left) Byron had a fascination with the colour and romance of the East and of the more remote areas of Europe, and he delighted in having himself painted in exotic costume. He was proud of his remarkable good looks, but he was also highly self-conscious about his club-foot, which is here artfully concealed by the draperies among which he reclines.

Greece's sufferings
(below) Byron was not the only celebrity who felt compassion for the Greeks in their fight for freedom against the Turks; artists and intellectuals all over Europe sympathized with their plight. The great French Romantic painter Eugène Delacroix painted this picture of the victims of a Turkish massacre in 1824, the year in which Byron died in Greece.

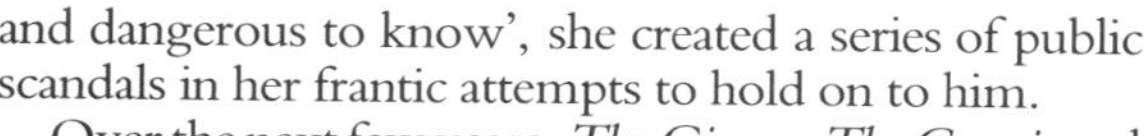

and dangerous to know', she created a series of public scandals in her frantic attempts to hold on to him.

Over the next few years, *The Giaour*, *The Corsair* and similar narrative poems, with eastern settings and mysterious, tormented heroes, reinforced the Byronic image. Yet Byron himself was trying to settle down, and in January 1815 he married Annabella Milbanke. She bore him a daughter but the marriage broke down within 15 months. Annabella, a rather solemn intellectual woman, had no idea how to handle Byron's moods and erratic behaviour.

Stung by the campaign of innuendo and insult that followed his separation from Annabella, Byron left England – as it proved, for ever – on 24 April 1816. He had already succumbed to the determined attentions of Claire Clairmont, who renewed their relationship in Switzerland and introduced Byron to her step-sister Mary, and Percy Bysshe Shelley. The poets struck up a friendship, living as neighbours at Lake Geneva.

After Shelley returned to England, Byron settled in Italy. The sale of Newstead Abbey cleared his debts, and his prolific literary output brought in huge sums. Everyone was reading Byron, though his reputation was such that a lady novelist fainted with fright in a salon when his name was announced. In the summer of 1818 he began *Don Juan*, a long, rollicking novel-like poem in which he perfected a discursive conversational style that enabled him to treat every subject under the sun. This, rather than his gloomy romantic narratives, is now regarded as Byron's master-work. Claire,

Percy Bysshe Shelley

An atheist and radical, Shelley spent his life in virtual exile for his beliefs. Before his early death, he had stamped his unique intelligence and optimistic political vision on a series of pamphlets, essays and poems.

Shelley was above all an idealist, and in his restless, complicated private life, ideals and realities constantly clashed. His poetry is a reflection of this conflict – exalting personal and political freedom but also mirroring Shelley's own struggles with failure and disillusion.

Percy Bysshe Shelley was born on 4 August 1792 at Field Place in Sussex. His family were wealthy members of the gentry, and Shelley was sent to Eton and Oxford where he became a fine classical scholar. But he was a rebel and misfit even at school, where he was bullied mercilessly. As one schoolmate reported, 'I have seen him surrounded, hooted, baited like a maddened bull, and at this distance of time I seem to hear ringing in my ears the cry which Shelley was wont to utter in his paroxysm of revengeful anger.'

At Oxford, Shelley published a pamphlet entitled *The Necessity of Atheism*, for which he was sent down. At 18, the future poet was already a political radical, a vegetarian, an apostle of free love, and an atheist. He was also a tousled eccentric, subject to hallucinations and fits of sleep-walking, but his transparent sincerity and enthusiasm won over most of the people he met.

In London, Shelley encountered Harriet Westbrook, who attended the same boarding school as his sisters. They eloped and were married in Edinburgh on 28 August 1811. Shelley was 19, and Harriet 16. From this time, Shelley led a wandering life, rarely staying in the same place for more than a few months. Having quarrelled with his father, he was often short of money and deep in debt.

During a stay in Dublin, Shelley wrote pamphlets denouncing English rule in Ireland and discrimination against Catholics. He and Harriet lived variously in Wales, England and Scotland, while Shelley composed *Queen Mab*, his first sustained poetic statement.

Meanwhile, the incompatibility between Shelley and Harriet had become increasingly obvious – to Shelley, at least. Though Harriet was pregnant with their second child, he left her for Mary Godwin, the daughter of two people Shelley admired intensely: the radical philosopher William Godwin and his long-dead wife, the feminist Mary Wollstonecraft. In July 1814, Shelley and Mary eloped to the Continent, accompanied by Claire Clairmont, daughter of Godwin's second wife. Shelley had already displayed a taste for group living, and Claire was to stay with him and Mary for years.

Lack of money brought Shelley and his companions back to England within six weeks, but in 1816 they set out again for Switzerland. Claire Clairmont steered them to Lake Geneva, where she hoped to resume her affair with Lord Byron (she was already pregnant by

Florentine vistas
Enamoured of Italy, Shelley composed 'Ode to the West Wind' near the banks of the river Arno (above). And when his only surviving son was born there in November 1819, he and Mary named him Percy Florence to commemorate the place of his birth – which Shelley designated 'the most beautiful city I ever saw.'

Romantic impression
(left) This image of Shelley captures the essence of Romanticism – at one with Nature, a solitary figure, windswept, gaunt, deep in thought, with gnarled trees in the background. On the title page are the mythical figures of Shelley's imagination.

Eton schooldays
Shelley's time at Eton (above) was not happy – his fellow students ostracized him for his studiousness, and his tutors were outraged by his interest in black magic, finding him on several occasions surrounded by fire, apparently intent on 'raising the Devil'.

him). The two poets met and formed an important, stimulating friendship. A tour of the lake with Byron inspired Shelley to compose his first unmistakably great poem, *Hymn to Intellectual Beauty*.

In September 1816 Shelley returned to England. Three months later the unlucky Harriet, pregnant by an army officer, drowned herself. Shelley and Mary were married a few days later, but this gesture towards respectability failed to procure Shelley the custody of his children by Harriet.

After a year in England, Shelley was in poor health, stifled and discouraged by the atmosphere of political repression. In March 1818 the Shelleys, their children and Claire Clairmont left for Italy, where renewed contact with Byron inspired Shelley's *Julian and Maddalo*, a vivid verse portrait of the two men. Shelley was now at the height of his powers, and *Prometheus Unbound*, *The Cenci*, *Ode to the West Wind* and *The Mask of Anarchy* were all composed in 1818-19. Much of his late verse was political, but in May 1821 the news of Keats' death prompted the elegaic *Adonais*.

THE FINAL JOURNEY

By this time, Shelley's relations with Mary were often strained. All but one of their children died, and Shelley continued to find inspiration in other women, the last one being Jane Williams to whom he wrote many poems, including 'When the lamp is shattered'.

Edward and Jane Williams were new friends who moved in with the Shelleys in April 1822 and shared their home at Lerici, on the Bay of Spezia. Although unable to swim, Shelley had a life-long passion for the water, and he intended spending the summer sailing with Edward Williams and Byron. But on 8 July, on a trip from Livorno to Lerici, Shelley's boat disappeared. Ten days later, the bodies of Shelley, Williams and their boat boy were washed ashore. Shelley was identified by the copy of Keats' poems in his pocket. Byron was one of the small party that was present when the remains of his friend were cremated on the beach. At his death, Shelley was not quite 30.

Jane Williams
(below) Shelley was one of Jane Williams' many admirers, writing poems to her such as 'When the lamp is shattered'. Later, when both he and her husband had lost their lives, Mary Shelley seems also to have fallen under Jane's extraordinary spell.

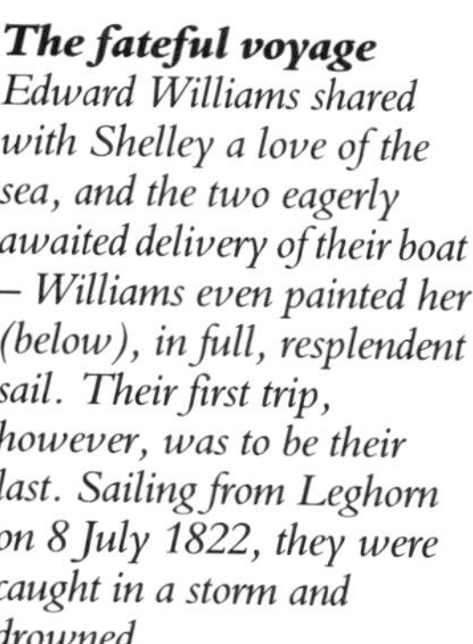

The fateful voyage
Edward Williams shared with Shelley a love of the sea, and the two eagerly awaited delivery of their boat – Williams even painted her (below), in full, resplendent sail. Their first trip, however, was to be their last. Sailing from Leghorn on 8 July 1822, they were caught in a storm and drowned.

John Keats

Although his life was tragically short, Keats was blessed with a "teeming" poetic gift which triumphed over both his personal suffering and savage criticism.

Keats was the youngest of the great Romantics, and the first to die. Yet because of his precociously mature genius, he left a substantial body of work, including poems whose sensuous loveliness demonstrates his cherished belief that Beauty and Truth are one and the same.

John Keats was born in London on 31 October 1795. His father ran a prosperous livery stable in the parish of Moorfields, and at the age of seven Keats was sent to a good private school at Enfield. But both his parents died by the time he was 14, and in 1810 his guardian apprenticed him to a surgeon and apothecary at Edmonton, Middlesex. Although he qualified in 1816 and spent a few months studying surgery at Guy's Hospital, the lure of poetry proved too strong for Keats. For the rest of his brief life he lived precariously as a professional writer, sometimes desperately short of money and working with great intensity while his health lasted.

A PRECOCIOUS GENIUS

As a teenager Keats steeped himself in English poetry, and his first efforts at verse – probably made at about 18 – were predictably lush and imitative. But by 1816 he was maturing fast. In April, Leigh Hunt's magazine *The Examiner* published Keats' sonnet *To Solitude*. By the end of the year he had shown further skill and subtlety with *On First Looking into Chapman's Homer* (a poem about a poem – George Chapman's early 17th-century translation of the *Iliad* and the *Odyssey*), and Hunt was confidently prophesying greatness for him.

Joseph Severn
A true friend to Keats, Joseph Severn (right) was a frequent visitor at his house, and the only one of their circle who was prepared to leave England for Italy when Keats' health failed. In Rome, Severn tended him night and day, cooking, reading to him, and trying to make his final days as comfortable as possible. He even reputedly stopped Keats from committing suicide on one particularly bleak occasion. Severn painted Keats in this sensitive pose (far right) during happier days together.

Leigh Hunt, himself a distinguished essayist and journalist, gave Keats invaluable encouragement, introducing the inexperienced young poet to his literary circle, which included Shelley and the critic William Hazlitt. However, most of these men were regarded as dangerous radicals by powerful establishment periodicals such as *Blackwood's*, and Keats was later to suffer for his association with what they sneeringly labelled 'the Cockney school of poetry'.

When his first collection of poems appeared in March 1817, it was ignored rather than abused. Not discouraged, Keats moved out of London to Hampstead – then a country village – and worked for months on an epic poem, *Endymion*. The result was flawed in parts, but the disciplined effort involved seems to have brought Keats to the verge of his astonishingly early artistic maturity. In the spring of 1818, he completed another long narrative poem, *Isabella; or, the Pot of Basil*.

That summer, Keats and a friend embarked on a 42-day walking tour of the Lake District, Ulster and Scotland which overtaxed the poet's strength. When he reached Inverness, a local physician insisted that he

Hampstead Heath
During the winter of 1816-17, Keats left London and joined his brothers in the village of Hampstead (left), to be near his friend and fellow-writer Leigh Hunt. The Heath was his back garden, and he delighted in strolling across it, watching the wind ruffling great fields of barley like the motion of "the inland sea".

Roman requiem
With books and a piano to distract him, Keats spent his final weeks in a corner room beside the Spanish Steps in Rome's Piazza di Spagna.

return home at once. This ominous incident was followed by the death of Keats' brother Tom, whom he nursed devotedly through the last stages of consumption – the disease that was, in the space of three short years, to take the poet's own life.

Meanwhile, the Tory reviewers had begun to single out Keats for attack. *Blackwood's* snobbishly derided the poetic efforts of footmen, farm-servants and apothecaries, sardonically lamenting 'the calm, settled, imperturbable drivelling idiocy of *Endymion*'. It advised, 'It is a better and wiser thing to be a starved apothecary than a starved poet; so back to the shop Mr John, back to the "plasters, pills and ointment boxes".'

Shelley's *Adonais* implies, and legend has it, that such savagery broke Keats' heart and killed him. In reality, the reviews appeared just when he was entering his 'Great Year', 1818-19, when he produced one masterpiece after another, including *Hyperion*, *The Eve of St Agnes*, all his great Odes, such as *Ode to a Nightingale*, and *La Belle Dame Sans Merci*.

After this supreme creative output, Keats was unwell in the winter of 1819-20, and in February 1820 began to cough blood. He immediately recognized this as his 'death warrant'. The blow was all the more cruel because he had met and become engaged to a young neighbour named Fanny Brawne. Their relationship was stormy, since Keats, realizing he was to die, suffered agonies of jealousy. But it was among the Brawne family that he spent his last weeks in England.

Keats' love
Fanny Brawne (left), who met Keats in November 1818, was five years younger than the poet. Keats was immediately and completely enthralled by her, expressing his passion in many poems and letters. She was the "sweet home of all my fears,/ And hopes, and joys, and panting miseries . . ." They became secretly engaged in 1819, but his illness marred what happiness they might have had. She wore mourning for several years after his death, but finally married in 1833.

A PAINFUL DEATH

By September 1820 Keats' condition was desperately serious, and his friends believed that only the Southern sun might cure him. A close friend, the painter Joseph Severn, travelled with him to Rome, and the two men took rooms on the Piazza di Spagna, at the bottom of the Spanish Steps. Here, after terrible suffering, Keats died in Severn's arms on 23 February 1821. He was buried in Rome's Protestant cemetery, where his tombstone was inscribed, as he had instructed, with the gloomy words 'Here lies one whose name was writ in water.' But his name has not disappeared – posterity has endorsed his defiant response to the reviewers: 'I think I shall be among the English poets after my death.'

Romanticism

Poets of vision and revolution, the Romantics rejected the values of 18th-century rationalists and revelled in the power of the Imagination – their key to the mysteries of the universe.

Many of the revolutionary characteristics of Romanticism are taken for granted today; and, like most historical phenomena, the Romantic Movement can only be understood in terms of what came before. It represented a violent reaction to the political, social, intellectual and artistic climate of the 18th century, and occurred – by no coincidence – against the setting of the French Revolution. It was a parallel idealistic bid for freedom (in language) and represented a parallel shift in concerns and values. These concerns particularly affected the extraordinary group of poets who gave the Romantic Movement in England its substance and direction.

The French Revolution itself was a primary source of inspiration for the 'first generation' of Romantic poets: Wordsworth, Coleridge and Blake. It seemed to signal the victory of liberty over tyranny, and triggered a time of change when accepted norms were being questioned and tested.

While these poets were fired by political and social changes, the 'second generation' of Romantics – Byron, Shelley and Keats – reacted against the absence of them. They grew up in a society in which privilege and oppression had been reasserted by a series of Tory governments. Shelley and Byron in particular applied their art to satirizing leading political figures, and expressing their outrage at the state of the Nation.

Apart from responding to external, political changes, Romanticism reflected an even more fundamental, internal revolution – a radical change in attitude towards the value of personal human experience. The 17th and early 18th centuries had been a time of scientific discovery, an age when investigation and analysis were seen as the tools of enlightenment, and when human beings were primarily valued as citizens who played their 'correct' roles in society.

If the 18th century saw itself as the Age of Reason, the Romantic era was the Age of Emotion. The Romantics were interested in feelings, not facts. They emphasized passion and atmosphere over precision and argument. All good poetry, wrote Wordsworth, 'is the spontaneous overflow of personal feelings'. The Romantic era was an age of grand gestures and rhetorical flourishes, an age when defiance was more fashionable than decorum.

There were three major areas in which Romantic writers differed markedly from their immediate predecessors: in their attitudes to the Individual, to Imagination, and to Nature.

Human beings were seen by the Romantics as individuals rather than members of society – individuals whose emotional responses were more important than their rational ones. Their real links were with Nature rather than the artificiality of urban, social existence, and they did not accept that established religious ideas and social rules were necessarily 'the truth'. Instead they sought a freer concept of truth based on individual experience and – most importantly – the Imagination.

Revolutionary inspiration
(left) The French Revolution focused some of the radical ideas and ideals of the Romantic movement. It represented an attempt to overthrow a system of oppression and feudal privilege and allow the common people their freedom and dignity.

Return to Nature
(left) For the Romantics, cities spelt confusion, corruption and false values, and it was only in Nature – in its various moods, from gentle to wild and sublime – that Truth and Inspiration could be found. A magnificent mountain scene (below) could bring about an ecstatic vision, such as Wordsworth described in The Prelude*: "And I have felt/A presence that disturbs me with the joy/Of elevated thoughts; a sense sublime . . ."*

Supernatural images
The Romantics were intent on capturing fleeting images, which might have been inspired by dreams, drugs or simply unrestrained reverie. In writing The Rime of the Ancient Mariner *(left), Coleridge maintained that his rational mind was held in abeyance, allowing his psyche to conjure up obsessions, forebodings and hallucinations that lie just below the surface of consciousness.*

'I am certain of nothing but the holiness of the Heart's affections, and the truth of Imagination', wrote Keats. And indeed, despite their individual differences, all the Romantic poets (except, perhaps, for Byron) shared this belief in the importance of Imagination. It was the key to their poetry, to their understanding of the meaning of things, and to their very existence. Without Imagination, they were nothing; with it they could glimpse the innermost secrets of the Universe.

In his *Prophetic Books,* William Blake talked of the need to 'cast aside from Poetry all that is not Inspiration'. His chief complaint about his Royal Academy training was that 'copying nature deadened the force of my imagination'; it is noticeable that his own drawings are nearly always symbolic and very rarely strictly representational. And in Coleridge's *The Ancient Mariner, Christabel* and *Kubla Khan,* the poetic utterance seems to belong less to the domain of reason than to that of dream or nightmare.

A dream-like atmosphere is common to a number of great works of Romanticism. Coleridge's particular poetic visions were undoubtedly stimulated by his addiction to opium – a drug that seemed for a while to free the mind from its chains. The hallucinatory effect of opium and laudanum (which were taken medicinally in the 19th century) can often be glimpsed in the imagery of Romantic poems such as Keats' *Ode to a Nightingale* and *Ode on Melancholy.* Thomas De Quincey's book *Confessions of an English Opium Eater* was partly the self-apology of an addict, and partly a glorification of the powers of the Imagination.

The Romantics' fascination with Imagination might also account for another of their concerns – the world of childhood. To them, children had the capacity to see things more

Key Dates

1757 William Blake born in London

1770 William Wordsworth born at Cockermouth, Cumbria

1772 Samuel Taylor Coleridge born at Ottery St Mary, Devon

1783 Britain defeated in American War of Independence

1788 George Gordon Byron born in London

1789 French Revolution begins. Blake's *Songs of Innocence* published

1790 Wordsworth in France

1792 Percy Bysshe Shelley born at Field Place, Sussex. France becomes a republic

1793 Britain at war with France (1793-1802; 1803-15)

1794 Blake's *Songs of Experience* published

1795 John Keats born in London

1797 Coleridge writes *Kubla Khan*

1797-98 Wordsworth and Coleridge working together in Somerset

1798 *Lyrical Ballads* published

1800-08 Wordsworth at Dove Cottage

1802 Wordsworth marries Mary Hutchinson

1804 Napoleon becomes Emperor of France

1805 Nelson victorious at Trafalgar, Napoleon at Austerlitz. Wordsworth finishes *The Prelude*

1809 Byron's *English Bards and Scotch Reviewers*

1811 Shelley's *The Necessity of Atheism.* Shelley sent down from Oxford

1812 *Childe Harold* makes Byron famous

1813 Wordsworth becomes Distributor of Stamps and moves to Rydal Mount. Jane Austen's *Pride and Prejudice* published

1814 Fall of Napoleon. Shelley elopes with Mary Godwin. Scott's *Waverley* published

1815 Napoleon returns from Elba and is defeated at Waterloo. Byron marries Annabella Milbanke

1816 Byron separates from his wife and leaves England. Friendship with Shelley begins

1817 Coleridge's *Biographia Literaria* published

1818 Mary Shelley's *Frankenstein,* and Keats' *Endymion* published

1818-19 Keats' 'Great Year' of creativity

1819 Byron meets Countess Guiccioli; first two cantos of *Don Juan* published. Shelley writes *The Mask of Anarchy*

1821 Keats dies in Rome. Shelley writes *Adonais* in his memory. Napoleon dies on St Helena

1822 Wordsworth's *Guide to the Lakes.* Shelley drowned in the Bay of Spezia

1824 Death of Byron at Missolonghi

1827 Death of Blake

1829 Greece wins independence

1834 Coleridge dies

1843 Wordsworth becomes Poet Laureate

1850 Death of Wordsworth. *The Prelude* published

English Romantic art
Like the Romantic poets, Romantic painters set out to experience the variety of Nature. Joseph Turner once had himself tied to a ship's mast in order to be able to paint the full onslaught of a storm.

clearly than adults did. As Coleridge once stated, 'The Poet is the one who carries the simplicity of childhood into the powers of manhood; who, with a soul unsubdued by habit, unshackled by custom, contemplates all things with the freshness and wonder of a child.' Certainly Blake's *Songs of Innocence* and Wordsworth's poems *The Prelude* and *Tintern Abbey* value the freshness and immediacy of child-like intuition over the clumsier results of adult reasoning and experience.

A favourite subject of Romantic poetry was the poet himself. It was not a period of impersonal commentary, but was characterized by epics of either overt or disguised autobiography, such as Wordsworth's *The Prelude* or Byron's *Don Juan* or Odes such as those of Shelley and Keats. In these, the poetry distilled and expressed the mystical links the poet felt with the world as he experienced it. The Romantic period also included expression of obscure personal mythology, as in the later works of Blake.

For the Romantic artist, the individual was a being of infinite potential. Yet the artist also had a vision of himself as an outsider. Wordsworth's and Coleridge's most memorable poems are about solitude, and their most memorable characters, such as Coleridge's Ancient Mariner and Byron's Childe Harold, are isolated figures who seem not to have a natural place in the realm of ordinary society.

The Romantics saw themselves as rebels against established modes of thought, both artistic and political. Blake was not merely contemptuous of the traditional training he received at the Royal Academy of Arts; politically, his ideas were so extreme that on one occasion they were thought to be treasonable. Shelley was expelled from University College, Oxford, for his co-authorship of a deliberately provocative pamphlet, *The Necessity of Atheism*. And Byron's scandalous and allegedly incestuous private life shocked the conventional moral standards of the time and forced him into exile.

INSPIRATION IN NATURE

One of the qualities which set the Romantics apart from earlier poets was their attitude to Nature. In Nature they saw beauty, and out of beauty came inspiration. They undoubtedly reacted against an increasingly industrialized age and rejected the degrading and dehumanizing aspects of mechanization.

The Romantics' attitude to Nature was also a reaction against what they saw as the arrogant rationality of the previous age, and an attempt on their part to restore a sense of magic and wonder to human responses. Coleridge states this view when he describes Wordsworth's poetic aims in his *Biographia Literaria*. These were 'to excite a feeling analogous to the supernatural, by awakening the Mind's attention from the lethargy of custom and directing it to the loveliness and the wonders of the world before us.' Wordsworth's own lines in his poem *The Tables Turned* perfectly captures the Romantic attitude to the mysterious beauty of Nature:

Sweet is the lore which Nature brings;
Our meddling intellect
Misshapes the beauteous form of things:
We murder to dissect.

Each Romantic poet tended to have his own individual views on Nature. For Wordsworth, Nature's inspiration provided sufficient subject-matter in itself. Coleridge habitually equated Nature with moral qualities. In *The Ancient Mariner,* Nature behaves throughout as a moral force, with drought, for example, symbolizing the Mariner's spiritual aridity, the rain his regeneration, the sun acting as an agent of punishment and the moon as one of redemption.

Other Romantics used Nature as a means of discussing their personal crises. For example, Keats' *Ode to a Nightingale* and Shelley's *Ode to the West Wind* are both as much about the problems of artistic creativity as about the wonders of Nature.

A significant fact is that the term 'Romantic' was not applied to any of these poets during their lifetime, either by others or by themselves. The importance of this is that they were not consciously following any school of thought and certainly not concerned to prove any particular theory. None of the famous critical texts of the period – Wordsworth's *Advertisement and Preface* to the *Lyrical Ballads,* Coleridge's *Biographia Literaria,* Shelley's *Defence of Poetry* – can really be seen as manifestoes of the Romantic movement. The essence of Romanticism is in the eloquence and fervour of the poems themselves.

JANE AUSTEN

1775-1817

The six most polished, controlled and elegant social comedies to be found in English literature were written by a woman whose personal life remains an enigma. Observing her own leisured social circles, Jane Austen's cool judgement, ironic detachment and refined sentiments give her novels a unique depth and compelling charm. Her 'exquisite touch' earned her the immediate admiration of the greatest writers of her day and her popularity remains undimmed. But many agree with the poet, Alfred Lord Tennyson — who ranked Jane Austen alongside Shakespeare — when he 'thanked God Almighty with his whole heart that he knew nothing, and that the world knew nothing of Jane Austen'. Her delightful novels are almost all we know for certain.

A Charming Enigma

The 'real' Jane Austen seems always to elude her readers. Her life appears to have been a picture of tranquillity, untouched by the traumas engulfing Europe, but it gave her ample material for her art.

Jane Austen's novels have been immensely popular since the early decades of the 19th century, yet even now there are many aspects of the author's life that remain completely unknown. We know almost nothing of her emotional life and very little about her thoughts, opinions, tastes, prejudices and personality. What we do know derives largely from three sources: her nephew's memoirs written more than 50 years after her death; her own letters written to her sister Cassandra (who destroyed most of them in her old age); and gossip.

Consequently the portrait that has come to be accepted as the 'real' Jane Austen is essentially a view of her created by her family. Yet that view presents a picture that seems strangely at odds with the author of six of the most polished, ironically witty and perceptive novels in the English language.

Jane Austen was born on 16 December 1775 in the rectory of Steventon in Hampshire, where her father was vicar. The Reverend George Austen was a distinguished classical scholar, spending as much time with his books as his parish duties permitted him. Jane's mother, Cassandra, was a keen gardener, mother of eight children and inordinately proud of her aristocratic relations and heritage – particularly her aristocratic nose. There is little to suggest that she had a close understanding or relationship with her second daughter, Jane.

Jane was the sixth child, two years younger than her sister Cassandra. All the sons – James, Edward, Henry, Francis and Charles – distinguished themselves in later life, though Jane's favourite, Henry was thought to lack application. There was one other brother, 'poor George', the second son, who was fostered out to a family in the neighbouring village of Dean. He is believed to have suffered fits, and was never spoken of and never met any of his brothers or sisters.

The Austens were a happy, lively family, reputedly good-natured and sweet-tempered, and family squabbles were almost unknown. According to the custom

A privileged brother
(right) Jane's brother Edward was adopted by the rich but childless Thomas Knight and his wife. As a wealthy landowner, Edward proved to be 'quite a man of business' and was to support his mother and sisters in later life.

Close confidante
(right) Cassandra remained Jane's lifelong friend and confidante. Mrs Austen said of her daughters, 'If Cassandra were going to have her head cut off, Jane would insist on sharing her fate.'

Key Dates

1775 born 16 December, Steventon

1782 attends Mrs Cawley's school. Nearly dies of fever

1784 attends Mrs Latournelle's Abbey School, Reading

1801 moves to Bath. Probable romance in South Devon

1802 Harris Bigg-Wither proposes

1805 father dies

1806 moves to Clifton, then Southampton

1809 moves to Chawton, Hampshire

1811 *Sense and Sensibility* published

1813 *Pride and Prejudice* published

1814 *Mansfield Park* published

1816 *Emma* published. Health deteriorates

1817 moves to Winchester, 24 May. Dies, 18 July.

of their class and time Jane and Cassandra – 'Jenny' and 'Cassie' to the family – led quite different lives from their brothers. While the boys received a classical education and went riding, hunting and shooting, the girls were schooled in household management and taught the 'feminine arts' of singing, dancing and drawing. Jane in addition learned the piano. At the age of seven she and her sister were packed off to a small school run by a relative, Mrs Cawley – a forbidding, stiff and formal personality. But the school was not a success – possibly because of Mrs Cawley – and in due course moved from Oxford to Southampton. Here, very soon after arriving, both girls fell victim to putrid fever, and had it not been for Jane's hasty despatch home she might well have died.

HAMPSHIRE SOCIAL CIRCLES

Her stay at home, however, was short, for in 1784 she and Cassandra were sent to Mrs Latournelle's Abbey School at Reading. Here Jane spent two pleasant years. Having acquired the rudiments of a young lady's education, she and Cassandra returned to Steventon in 1785. They helped their mother make preserves, syrups, home-made wine and beer, and in the afternoons received instruction from their father. In later life Jane Austen was misleadingly modest about her education, declaring, 'I think I can boast myself with all possible vanity, the most unlearned and uninformed being that ever dared to be an authoress'. In fact she received a thorough grounding in English language and literature, read fluently in French and had, in addition, a passing acquaintance with Italian.

When the daily duties were done, evenings with the family were spent playing charades round the candle-lit table and then – while the girls and Mrs Austen sewed, darned or embroidered – George, James or Henry Austen would read aloud from their favourite authors; Shakespeare, Dr Johnson, Addison and Steele and the contemporary poet, William Cowper. Sometimes they would read a play with each member of the family taking a part. Occasionally, especially at Christmas, plays would be performed.

As Jane grew into her teens, her closest companion and confidante remained Cassandra. They shared the same interests, enthusiasms and sense of humour. And when household duties permitted, they walked together in the nearby woods or through the pretty Hampshire countryside – the sort of countryside Jane had in mind when she later said, 'The beauties of nature must for me be one of the joys of Heaven'. There were also visits to relatives and family friends. In 1788 she and Cassandra visited their great-uncle in Sevenoaks, Kent where they met their cousin Philadelphia Walters, remembered for her unflattering description of Jane: 'not very pretty and very prim, unlike a girl of twelve'.

Whatever the physical charms of the young Jane Austen, her writings of the time were far from being prim. Before the age of 16 she had filled three notebooks with stories, poems and plays bearing such

Presenting a son
(left) This silhouette shows Jane's father, the Reverend George Austen, presenting his son Edward to Mr and Mrs Thomas Knight. The Knights were a wealthy landowning family; Edward became heir to the family seat at Godmersham Park in Kent and to Chawton Manor, Hampshire.

Steventon Rectory
(below) Jane Austen's home for the first 25 years of her life was in the wooded chalkland of Hampshire.

'The beauties of nature'
(left) Jane Austen loved the quiet beauty of her native Hampshire countryside: "It was a sweet view – sweet to the eye and the mind, English verdure, English culture, English comfort seen under a sun bright without being oppressive."

titles as *The Mystery, Kitty,* or *The Bower, Love and Freindship* – misspelt throughout. Each was dedicated to a different member of the family, and each was a comic burlesque of some contemporary tale.

In common with girls of her class, at the age of 16 Jane was launched into society. This consisted, for the most part, in visiting other families belonging to the same social class – gentry and minor aristocracy; the Jervoices, Terrys, Boltons, Portsmouths, Digwoods and Harrods. Slightly further afield lived the Bigg-Wither family at Manydown House, near Basingstoke, where Jane and Cassandra stayed when attending nearby balls.

Dancing formed a large part of these Hampshire social gatherings, as Jane revealed to Cassandra in a letter of September 1796, 'We dined at Goodestone', she wrote, 'and in the Evening danced two Country Dances and the Boulangeries. I opened the Ball with Edwd Bridges . . .'. Her letters also hint at a number of flirtations which she related to Cassandra in jest. 'At length the day is come', she wrote in one, 'on which I am to flirt my last with Tom Lefroy, and when you receive this it will be over. My tears flow as I write at the melancholy idea'.

There were also visits to Godmersham Park in Kent, where her brother Edward lived. Here, and later at Stoneleigh Abbey in Warwickshire and at Bath, she had a taste of the aristocratic life which was to form the background material for her later novels. While Bath was not the brilliant place it had been earlier in the century, it was still nevertheless a favourite spot for the fashionable, now denied their visits to the Continent because of war with Napoleon. Certainly for Jane there were many distractions and novelties attended by the rich and famous – masquerades, firework displays and fancy dress balls.

COMING OF AGE

Throughout this period Jane Austen continued to write. By 1796 she had completed '*Elinor and Marianne*' (an early version of *Sense and Sensibility*), '*First Impressions*' (the first version of *Pride and Prejudice*) and in 1798 '*Susan*' (later to be called *Northanger Abbey*, set in and around Bath). Unlike the view of her held later, Jane Austen was not at this time a shy and retiring author. Her work was read and appreciated by all the family and was thought sufficiently good by her father for him to offer *First Impressions* to a London publisher. He received no reply. And within the family at least, Jane was not a victim of the false modesty that was said to have afflicted her later in life.

In 1801 the easy, elegant life at Steventon suddenly ended with her father's announcement that on his retirement the family was moving to Bath. Long after her death it was said that Jane fainted on hearing the news. Of the five years spent there we know very little, and only three letters from this period survive, all written to Cassandra. These rare details, together with several critical remarks made later, have led to an assumption that Jane's years at Bath were unhappy. Her unhappiness is thought to have been deepened by an event that might have occurred in the summer of 1801 while holidaying with her parents in South Devon. There she is said to have met and fallen in

The Knights
(left) Mr Thomas Knight and his wife Catherine were continuing a family tradition of patronage to the Austens when they adopted Jane's brother Edward. In 1761, Thomas Knight's father had presented Jane's father with the living of Steventon. Edward was to develop the relationship; he changed his name to Knight in 1812.

Thomas Lefroy
(right) Jane's only 'affair' was with the 'very gentlemanlike, good-looking' Thomas Lefroy. But Lefroy was ambitious and moneyless, and forced to seek a fortune in marriage. The equally moneyless Jane Austen was not suitable.

Chawton Manor
(left) When the widowed Mrs Austen and her daughters decided to leave Southampton, Edward came to their aid. He offered them a house near his own Chawton Manor in Hampshire, which they accepted. They were keen to return to the familiarity of their native locality, and proud to call themselves 'Hampshire-born Austens'.

Madame de Feuillide
(left) Jane's cousin Eliza shared the Austen's love of theatre, encouraging their family play-acting. Her French husband, the Comte de Feuillide, died on the guillotine after an unsuccessful attempt to save his estates. Despite her knowledge of her cousin's tragedy, Jane Austen's novels never refer to the conflict sweeping Europe.

love with a man whose sudden subsequent death dealt her a blow from which she never fully recovered.

Whatever the truth of this – and there is little to substantiate it – the three letters that do survive do not betray any great unhappiness or dissatisfaction: Jane seems to have continued to join in the general social life of the town. What they do show, however, is a sense of time passing as she approached her thirtieth birthday – as in a letter of 1805: '. . . seven years are enough to change every pore of one's skin and every feeling of one's mind'.

DISRUPTIONS

Certainly there had been changes. She was no longer a young girl. She had been made at least one serious proposal of marriage – by Harris Bigg-Wither, six years her junior, in 1802. After initially accepting the offer, she changed her mind and declined the very next morning. Furthermore, after moving to Bath the family income had been dramatically reduced – with the death of her father in January 1805, financial worries became a constant problem.

Mrs Austen and her two daughters stayed on in Bath another year, though life was now far less agreeable. When they left early in 1806, it was with a feeling of escape, first to Clifton, then to Southampton where they were to live for the next two years. Here, close to brother Frank – now married and pursuing a career in the Royal Navy – life went on as before, with occasional visits to Henry in London and Edward at Godmersham. But Jane's essentially unproductive years continued – no-one quite knows why – until 1809 when she moved to Chawton with her mother and sister, to a cottage provided by Edward close to his Hampshire estate.

Most biographers are agreed that with this move to Chawton, nothing more of significance happened to Jane Austen. By this they mean that there was no major upheaval or event or move to distract her from

THE LOST LOVER?

Suggestions that Jane Austen met and fell in love with a man in either Sidmouth or Teignmouth in 1801 are as veiled and obscure as everything else in her personal life. They are based on a story told by Jane's sister Cassie to her niece Anna – but recollected by Anna's daughter, Mrs Bellas. Neither the age, name or appearance of the young man – if such he was – is known. Nevertheless, the inevitable speculation has ranged from the suggestion that he was a clergyman, to the more colourful suggestion that he was none other than Captain John Wordsworth – the brother of William, the celebrated Lakeland poet – who drowned at sea. It is unlikely that the truth of the matter will ever be known, and we can only guess at the effect it had on the character, and the novels, of Jane Austen.

A rare holiday in Sidmouth, Devon *may have led to Jane Austen's only love affair.*

Fact or Fiction

WOMEN, MARRIAGE AND MEN

In Jane Austen's circles, women were almost wholly dependent on men for their survival. Estates were passed from male to male, and only widowed women – who could be bequeathed their husbands' estates – owned property.

Marriage was the only sure way for a woman to gain financial security if, like the Bennets in *Pride and Prejudice,* there were no brothers to inherit the family money. In their case, the estate could *only* be inherited by a male; thus Mrs Bennet is anxious to marry off her daughters.

A man lacking a fortune likewise looked for a suitable marriage, and a prospective wife was more attractive if her husband was to inherit 'her' fortune. The themes in Jane Austen's novels were no different to the realities of her own life – her youthful flirtation with Thomas Lefroy ended when it became known that neither had a fortune. Lefroy's relatives packed him off to Ireland where, after only one year, he became engaged to 'a considerable fortune'. He went on to become Lord Chief Justice of Ireland.

Fortunes changed hands, *(right) in Jane Austen's world, when the wedding vows were made.*

her chosen path: to remain single and to devote herself to her writing. For whatever the outward events of Jane Austen's life, the real life that she led – the only thing that in the end helped create her art – was that of the imagination. And at Chawton for the seven remaining years of her life, Jane Austen's art suddenly blossomed and reached full maturity.

To all outward appearances she seemed no more than just another refined spinster gentlewoman living with her mother and sister in the country. She dressed in the style of an older woman, generally wearing a cap, symbol of middle-age. All thoughts of an active social life, let alone marriage, seem to have been abandoned. With no carriage at their disposal there was in any case no opportunity to join in the social life of the district. And there was no-one, other than Edward and his family, within walking distance with whom she could have met and spoken as an equal. At Chawton, the Austens kept themselves to themselves.

A QUIET ROUTINE

It was a simple, but fulfilling life, founded on regularity and routine, punctuated by the change of seasons and visits to or from relatives. Mrs Austen spent much of her time in the kitchen garden or at her embroidery, leaving the running of the house to Cassandra. Before breakfast each day, which invariably she prepared, Jane practised at her piano. Until lunch at twelve, she wrote, read or revised her work. After a light lunch, the afternoon was spent in the garden or in walking or shopping at nearby Alton. After an early dinner, the rest of the day was spent playing cards, spillikins, or cup and ball.

The Pump Room, Bath *(above) Before moving to Bath in 1801, the Austens had enjoyed several visits to the famous spa resort. Though it was no longer the pinnacle of fashionable high life, Bath still attracted many visitors who now came for health rather than gaiety. Mrs Austen and Jane had accompanied Edward and his family to Bath the previous year, primarily because Edward and his mother were hypochondriacs. According to Jane, 'My mother continues hearty, her appetite & nights are very good, but her Bowels are not entirely settled, & she sometimes complains of an Asthma, a Dropsy, Water in her Chest & a Liver Disorder.' Yet she outlived Jane.*

Prince Regent *(right) The Prince admired Jane Austen's works, and kept a set of them in each of his royal houses.* Emma *was dedicated to him.*

To her nieces and nephews, Jane was an amusing, interesting and animated speaker, subject to fits of laughter. She enjoyed the company of children, and with so many nieces and nephews she was able to enjoy this pleasure to the full.

Hers was a tranquil world, far removed from the traumas engulfing much of Europe. But it was conducive to her art, for in 1811 she published her first book, *Sense and Sensibility*, "by a lady", to be followed by *Pride and Prejudice* (1813), *Mansfield Park* (1814), and in 1816, in the shadow of Waterloo, *Emma*, which received a glowing review from Walter Scott.

But the effort of composition took its toll. She began to suffer from back pains and fits of utter fatigue and weariness. Though undiagnosed at the time, she was suffering from the early stages of Addison's Disease, at that time fatal. The doctors were baffled, and her decline continued. In May 1817 she was advised to move to Winchester to consult a Dr Lyford. Lodgings were found for her in College Street, where she was looked after by the ever-devoted Cassandra. She remained cheerful to the end, joking, writing letters and saying she expected to recover. It was a forlorn hope. Attended by Cassandra night and day, her condition gradually deteriorated. In the third week of July she was told she had not long to live. Calmly she took her leave of each of her relatives in turn. On the evening of 17 July she fell unconscious. At 4.30 in the morning of 18 July 1817, Jane Austen died, her head pillowed on Cassandra's shoulder. She was 41.

Chawton House
(left) Enjoying frequent visits from her beloved nieces and nephews, Jane – with Cassie and Mrs Austen – lived here until 1817.

College Street, Winchester
(below) When it became obvious that Jane was dying, she moved here to receive medical care. She died in Cassandra's arms.

Taking the Waters

In Jane Austen's day, the spas and sea-bathing resorts of England were exciting, fashionable places, where the leisured classes could take care of their health and indulge their pleasures.

For the English gentry at home – that class so brilliantly satirized in her books – Jane Austen's era was a time of unrivalled pleasure and civilized indulgence. London in 1800 was the most opulent, wealthy capital in the world, and English country houses, set amid acres of landscaped parkland and groves of mature trees, were among the most beautiful in Europe. Providing he did not gamble his money away – which happened all too often – the English gentleman faced only two real problems in life: maintaining his health, and staving off boredom. Both these burdens might be lightened at once by a visit to one of the fashionable health resorts to take the waters.

The fashion among the gentry for taking the waters dated back to the reign of Charles II, when the Cavaliers made the spa towns of Epsom, Tunbridge Wells and Bath the liveliest places in the kingdom. But the later years of the 18th century, and the heady days of the Regency, saw the fashion at a peak. With war-torn Europe effectively closed, more people than ever before were discovering the pleasures of elegant resorts such as Cheltenham, Scarborough and, especially, Bath – Jane Austen's home for five years, and the setting of much of *Northanger Abbey* and *Persuasion*. And every year a new resort seemed to spring up.

Each summer, fashionable society would leave behind the noise of London or the tranquillity of the country houses, and bowl along the new roads to spend a few invigorating months at the resort then in vogue (or most accessible). Entire families, often accompanied by friends, rented a large house in one of the graceful new terraces and crescents in the resort, leaving their homes empty of all but a few servants for months on end.

'THIS BOASTED SYSTEM'

From a purely medical point of view, taking the waters – whether bathing in them or drinking them – made as much sense as any other health cure then available. It certainly seemed as beneficial as the attentions of a money-minded quack doctor peddling bizarre, and often dangerous, remedies. It also had a pedigree dating back to the Romans and, according to the 18th-century Dr William Falconer of Bath, there were already 1000 treatises prepared to prove its merits beyond doubt.

Jane Austen's hero, Dr Johnson, was sceptical: 'There is nothing in all this boasted system: No, sir; medicated baths can be no better than warm water: their only effect can be that of tepid moisture'. But few shared his doubts; numerous local men of science could show incontrovertibly just how effective the waters of

A stroll on the crescent *(right) Among the greatest pleasures of the fashionable health resort were the regular promenades along the gracious new crescents and streets. As Jane Austen observed in* Northanger Abbey, *". . . a fine Sunday in Bath empties every house of its inhabitants, and all the world appears on such an occasion to walk about and tell their acquaintance what a charming day it is." There were friends to meet, acquaintances to renew – and, perhaps, the chance to follow up an encounter at the previous night's ball.*

Leaving London
(above) At the height of the season dozens of coaches would leave London each day to bowl along the new turnpike roads to Bath and other resorts. But the journey was long and arduous; one coach company boasted 'a flying machine to London from Bath, at eleven o'clock every night, which arrives at seven in the evening of next day in London'.

Sydney Gardens, 1805
(left) When she was in Bath, from 1801 to 1806, Jane Austen lived in a handsome new house opposite Sydney Gardens, 'a wide and extensive hexagonal plantation'. These pleasant gardens provided some relief from the bustle of the streets.

'Doctored to death'
(right) When the alternative was the dubious attentions of the quack doctor, taking the waters must have seemed an attractive – and safe – form of medical treatment. But for those not satisfied with water alone, there were always plenty of quacks on hand in the resorts to proffer advice – though in the contemporary Poetical Bath Guide, *a sick man's nurse 'Declared she was shocked that so many should come To be doctored to death such a distance from home; At a place where they tell you that water alone Can cure all distempers that ever were known'.*

their own town were at curing all manner of illnesses. Taking the waters was at least relatively harmless.

Besides, fashionable society was more than willing to advocate the health value of taking the waters when it was mixed with the delightful round of social activities offered by the leading resorts. Indeed, for most people who went to the spas, taking the waters meant merely sipping a small glass in the Pump Room every now and then. Only the genuinely infirm or the reckless would actually plunge into the pools or drink their contents in any quantity.

For the rest, the attractions of the resorts were primarily social rather than medical. They went for the chance to mingle with the best possible company in pleasant surroundings and indulge in all kinds of fashionable pursuits. Kept away from Europe, there could be few more delightful ways of whiling away the summer months than staying in a resort and getting swept along in the tide of social activities carefully orchestrated by the resort's master of ceremonies.

THE GLITTERING ROUND

Each resort laid on a glittering round of balls, dinners, concerts, and theatrical performances. And there were dinner parties to attend, evening sessions of whist and faro to play, expeditions to local beauty spots to be made and numerous other occasions to keep social diaries permanently full. In between, ladies would fill the day pleasantly, promenading through the elegant streets, dropping into their favourite shops, chatting about the latest novels and exchanging gossip, while the men often went out hunting on their magnificent thoroughbred horses, returning in the evening to tell of their daring leaps and reckless pursuits.

In all the fashionable resorts, every day's activities followed the same regular routine. Early morning would see people taking turns (circulating) around the Pump Room, meeting acquaintances and perhaps sampling the waters. Then there was breakfast, usually in private, but sometimes in the Assembly Rooms or coffee houses where gentlemen would adjourn to read the newspapers. After the morning church service, ladies and gentlemen were free to go shopping, visit the Circulating Library, take a stroll, go for a drive or canter on the downs.

Dinner was taken between two and three-thirty, then everyone dressed up for a gentle promenade until tea-time in the Assembly Rooms. A little time relaxing at home then prepared them for the variety of entertainments on offer.

Glamour, and the possibility of romantic encounters, was an essential part of the appeal of these resorts – which made them a perfect setting for many scenes in Jane Austen's work. *Ruff's History and Guide to Cheltenham* (1803) paints an exotic picture of morning in the Pump Room. 'The sun has no sooner begun to absorb the cool dews of the morning, and the whole sky to be animated with its warmth and influence . . . than the "busy hum" commences at the well. Between six and seven the walks begin to be filled. From seven till nine they are crowded. Here may be seen a galaxy of beauty, which overpowers even Aurora herself. Here, the sparkling eye – the bewitching mien – the elegant costume, which fascinated all beholders at the evening ball – assumes an altered character. The warm glow of the midnight dance is exchanged for the fresh tint of the morning. The brilliant robe, the necklace, the ear drop, and the head-dress, are transformed into an easier, a simpler, and more becoming attire.'

Sometimes introductions to beauties seen in the Pump Room or the Assembly Rooms were made through mutual friends; sometimes they were effected by the master of ceremonies – such as that of Henry Tilney to Catherine Morland in *Northanger Abbey*. But the regular routine, and the constant round of social engagements, meant there were many opportunities for young people to meet and for romances to blossom – routines which were crucial to the eventual reconciliation of Anne Eliot and Captain Wentworth in *Persuasion*. The more staid resorts became places for respectable families to come and find husbands for their daughters, and young men to find wives.

'FIVE AND THIRTY FRIGHTS'

Many men who frequented the resorts regarded themselves as connoisseurs of female beauty, and were apt to express disappointment at the lack of pretty faces on view, like Sir Walter in *Persuasion*. In a brilliantly satirical passage, Sir Walter's own comments damn him and his type: "The worst of Bath was the number of its plain women . . . He had frequently observed, as he walked, that one handsome face would be followed by thirty, or five and thirty frights; and once, as he stood in a shop in Bond-street, he had counted eighty-seven women go by, one after another, without there being a tolerable face among them."

Yet there was an element of truth in Sir Walter's comments, for the most glamorous young women,

Out in the phaeton
(below) Afternoon drives in the best resorts were like fashion parades. Young ladies and gentlemen vied with each other to be seen wearing the very latest London styles.

The portrait sitting
(above) Like Thomas Gainsborough, who worked in Bath from 1759 to 1774, many portrait painters set up studios in the health resorts to take advantage of wealthy patrons with time on their hands, and during the day a string of friends and relatives would drop in at the studio to watch the artist transform their gouty old uncle into a debonair squire; it was, of course, the artists who created the most flattering pictures – not the most life-like – who received the lucrative commissions.

Bathing at Ramsgate
(above) When the fashion for sea bathing caught on in the late 18th century, men and women bathed naked together. But soon the more respectable resorts introduced bathing wagons where women could bathe 'Safe from the ken Of those impudent men Who wander about on the shore'. Many people still bathed nude, though, which led one writer to complain that Ramsgate attracted visitors who 'seem to have no more sense of decency than South-Sea islanders!'

A view of Cheltenham
(left) Many of the fashionable resorts were set amid beautiful scenery.

and the most fashionable young men would always head for the resort that was in vogue. By Jane Austen's time Bath was no longer 'in'.

In the mid 18th century, Bath had been the queen of the resorts, with a glamour barely matched by London. The social whirl and excitement promoted and directed by Beau Nash had drawn everyone who was anyone to the city. In Smollett's *Humphrey Clinker* (1770), Squire Bramble complains, "Every upstart of fortune, harnessed to the trappings of mode, presents himself at Bath".

But by the time Jane Austen moved there in 1801, the glamour was beginning to fade, and the city was slipping into respectability. Infirm dowagers were now seen more often than bright young things, and it was now bath chairs, not sedan chairs that pulled up outside the Assembly Rooms. It became a place for solid, comfortable country families to frequent and meet other equally solid, well-to-do country families – the kind of society that Jane Austen portrays so sharply in her novels.

For young girls used only to the narrow world of country society, Bath still seemed an exciting place even in Jane Austen's time. In *Northanger Abbey* Jane Austen recalls the thrill of her own first visit to the city in that of the 17-year-old Catherine Morland: "They arrived at Bath. Catherine was all eager delight; – her eyes were here, there, everywhere, as they approached its fine and striking environs, and afterwards drove through those streets which conducted them to the hotel. She was come to be happy, and she felt happy already". The nights at the theatre, balls and concerts in the Assembly Rooms, and all the other activities for which Bath was famed – combined with the frisson of meeting handsome men – seemed to make Bath a delightful place for the innocent.

But the fashionably bored had seen it all before and soon tired of the city. As Isabella says in *Northanger Abbey*, "'Do you know I get so immoderately sick of Bath . . . though it is vastly well to be here for a few weeks, we would not live here for millions.' " Jane Austen was merciless in her satire of people like these who sneered at innocent pleasure simply because it was *à la mode* to do so. She came to dislike Bath precisely because it was full of people like Isabella.

Just as Bath's fashionableness declined, so the fortunes of other resorts rose and fell. Cheltenham was the favourite around the turn of the century, but Brighton soon outshone it. Brighton became to the opulent days of the Regency what Bath had been to the mid 18th century – glamorous, glittering, fashionable and scandalous.

THE RUSH TO THE SEA

Brighton was part of a new trend in health resorts. It was not a spa but a place to bathe in the sea. Ever since Dr Richard Russell published his book on *The Use of Sea-Water in Diseases of the Glands* in 1754, the idea that sea-bathing was good for you had been gaining more and more adherents, and received a particular boost from royal endorsement. King George III plunged into the sea at Weymouth in 1789, while it was his son George IV, as Prince of Wales and Prince Regent, whose fondness for sea bathing transformed the little village of Brighthelmstone into Brighton – described by Thackeray as 'London plus prawns for breakfast and sea air'.

The idea of sea bathing caught on to such an extent that the seaside resorts soon all but eclipsed the spas.

The Austens' favourite contemporary poet, William Cowper captured the mood in his poem *Retirement*, telling how spas were now abandoned and all 'Fly to the coast for daily, nightly joys, And all impatient of dry land, agree, With one consent to rush into the sea.' Jane Austen visited the seaside herself at Lyme and Sidmouth on many occasions, and many scenes in *Persuasion* are set in Lyme.

At first, men and women bathed naked, but as it became more and more popular – and men brought telescopes to spy on the bathing beauties – resorts with any pretensions to respectability began to use bathing machines to ensure modesty. These were wagons with covered steps that allowed bathers to descend into the sea unseen. After the advent of bathing costumes, most resorts had on hand 'dippers' to encourage the more timid to take the plunge, of which the most famous was Brighton's formidable Martha Gunn. Dippers were strong, tough women who took female bathers 'in their parti-coloured dresses, and gently held them to the breakers, which not so gently passed over them'.

In Jane Austen's time, though, most people went to the sea not to bathe but to enjoy the same company and activities they did in the spas or, in the smaller resorts, the fresh sea-air alone. Mr Musgrove is the only character in *Persuasion* to take the plunge at Lyme; Anne and Henrietta are content to stroll to the sea: "They went to the sands, to watch the flowing of the tide, which a fine south-easterly breeze was bringing in with all the grandeur which so flat a shore admitted. They praised the morning; gloried in the sea; sympathized in the delight of the fresh-feeling breeze . . ."

Like the spas, the seaside resorts provided a wealth of opportunities for Jane Austen to observe the kind of society and people she portrays so accurately. Like the spas, too, they were ripe for the romantic encounters that are so important in her novels – Jane herself may even have fallen in love in Sidmouth in 1801.

But their fashionableness was to survive barely two decades longer than Jane Austen herself, for the coming of the railways in the 1830s enabled millions of people of all classes to visit the seaside. With the beaches overcrowded, and the tone of resorts lowered, fashionable society abandoned them. Sometimes they returned to the English spas, but following Napoleon's defeat and the prospect of safe passage in Europe, they soon began to patronize the even more exclusive spas of Germany. The days of the fashionable English health resort – and the society that frequented them – were all but ended.

Big Dippers
(above) At the large sea bathing resorts, big, strong women 'dippers' were on hand to plunge the more timid bathers – both male and female – under the waves.

'The Folly at Brighton'
(below) Although much ridiculed, the Prince Regent's oriental-style Pavilion at Brighton was the centrepiece of the resort that had become the fashionable playground of Europe.

Beau Brummell
(above) From 1800 to 1810, Beau Brummell, described by Hazlitt as 'the greatest of small wits' and by Carlyle as 'a clothes-wearing man', was the arbiter of fashion in resorts such as Brighton, and his style set the tone for the age.

MARY SHELLEY

1797-1851

Remembered today as the daughter of illustrious parents and the wife of a famous poet, Mary Shelley shrank from any form of publicity and contributed to the obscurity that still clouds her name. Many people are astonished to learn that as a quiet, intellectual girl of 19, she wrote one of the most imaginative and horrific novels of the time – *Frankenstein*. Mary's eight years with Shelley were marked by tragedy, trauma and exile, but they were also years of inspiration for her own distinctive imagination.

The Shadow of Fame

Drawn into an illustrious circle and a life of extraordinary intensity, Mary Shelley suffered more than her fair share of tragedy. Within a few years of a teenage elopement, she was widowed and alone.

Mary Shelley's life was overshadowed by her famous parents and husband. It was also overshadowed by the deaths of those she loved. She was born on 30 August 1797 to the pioneer feminist Mary Wollstonecraft and the political philosopher William Godwin. But Mary was never to know her mother. She died of septicaemia just 10 days after the birth, leaving Mary forever deprived of a secure, loving relationship.

Although Mary adored her father, he had little time to spend with her. He remarried a few years later and Mary took an immediate (and understandable) dislike to her new mother, Mrs Mary Jane Clairmont, an unremarkable but pretentious widow with two children, Charles and Jane. As she grew up, Mary Godwin took refuge in the studies which were to serve as a great consolation throughout her life.

Mary Shelley
A supposed portrait of the writer when she was 19. By now Mary had enjoyed a passionate, clandestine love affair with Shelley, who was married to another; had eloped with him against her father's and his family's wishes; had travelled to Switzerland and back with him; had watched him go into hiding to avoid imprisonment for debt; had given birth to a baby daughter by him and suffered the anguish of seeing her baby die just two weeks later.

SECRET AFFAIR

In 1812, when Mary was staying with a family friend near Dundee, a young and fervent admirer of Mary's father began to frequent the Godwin household. The visitor was Percy Bysshe Shelley, aristocrat, political revolutionary and poet, who was also highly imaginative, somewhat unstable and, to many women, irresistible. He had married at 19 and had a daughter, Eliza Ianthe. These details, however, did not stop him from falling for the 16-year-old Mary when she finally returned from Scotland in the spring of 1814. Mary was not strikingly attractive, but, according to a friend, she was 'agreeable, vivacious and sparkling, very pretty with fair hair and complexion and clear bright white skin' – and she was an intellectual.

For Shelley, now disillusioned with his young wife Harriet, Mary's attraction was all the greater because her parents were the remarkable William Godwin and Mary Wollstonecraft. By the end of June – after a clandestine courtship at Mary Wollstonecraft's grave – Shelley and Mary had declared their mutual love.

Godwin was horrified. He tried to persuade Shelley to patch up his relationship with Harriet, who was pregnant again, and insisted that he stopped seeing Mary. But he could not keep the lovers apart and at the end of July they decided to elope to the Continent. At the last moment they agreed that Mary's stepsister Jane – soon to adopt the name Claire – should come with them. Claire, with her dark hair, olive skin, exuberant and demanding nature, was in many ways the opposite of Mary, and Mary would soon regret the invitation.

The three young people fled to France and embarked on a journey through a country ravaged by war and starvation. Their high spirits carried them through but by the time they reached Switzerland, these, as well as their finances, had begun to wane. Mary was pregnant, unwell and irritated by Claire's company. Des-

Illustrious father
(above) William Godwin was a radical intellectual who attracted a coterie of distinguished admirers. He had published a seminal work entitled An Enquiry Concerning Political Justice *and challenged contemporary thinking on politics and religion, as well as marriage. Despite his emancipated ideas, he was a distinctly selfish man who caused incalculable distress to his daughter.*

River Tay, Scotland
Frail and unwell, Mary, aged 14, was despatched to her father's friend William Baxter, near Dundee. She spent two happy years there, going for long walks on the Sidlaw hills and along the river Tay (left). As she wrote in her introduction to Frankenstein, *'It was beneath the trees of the grounds belonging to our [the Baxters'] house . . . that my true compositions, the airy flights of my imagination, were born and fostered.'*

perately short of money, the three decided, quite suddenly, to return home.

The problems, however, continued in England. Despite constant visits to banks, lawyers and money-lenders, Shelley had to go into hiding to avoid the bailiffs and the dreaded debtors' prison, leaving a pregnant Mary, terrified and alone. Eventually, Shelley succeeded in securing a loan, whereupon Mary's father, who was still hostile to the couple, made the first of a series of demands for money which were to plague Mary and Shelley throughout their life together.

In February 1815, when she was not quite seven months pregnant, Mary gave birth to a tiny, fragile daughter. Two weeks later she awoke to find that her baby had died. She desperately needed Shelley's support, but he was now more interested in her stepsister Claire, and left Mary to be comforted by an old university friend of his, Thomas Hogg. An entry in her journal reflects the anguish she felt over her loss: 'Dream that my little baby came to life again; that it had only been cold, and that we rubbed it before the fire and it lived.'

Gradually, Mary began to recover her good spirits, helped no doubt by Shelley's agreement that Claire should leave their household and by a financial settlement which guaranteed Shelley an annual income of £1000. They moved into a house on Bishopsgate Heath, at the edge of Windsor Forest, and Mary, who was pregnant again, happily settled into a private life with Shelley, in which they studied, wrote, walked and rowed on the Thames with friends. She developed from an ill, anxious girl into a confident young woman, and in January 1816 she gave birth to a strong, healthy son whom they named William after her father.

Childhood home
(above) Mary grew up in the modest surroundings of London's Skinner Street in Holborn. It was here, over a shop at number 41, that her parents lived, and here that she first set eyes on the ardent young poet and radical, Percy Bysshe Shelley.

Key Dates

1797 born in London

1814 elopes with Shelley

1816 William born; Fanny and Harriet commit suicide

1817 Clara born

1818 *Frankenstein* published; Clara dies

1819 William dies; Percy Florence born

1822 Shelley dies

1826 *The Last Man* published

1839 Shelley's *Poetical Works* published

1845 son Percy inherits

1851 dies in London

Graveside romance
(above) In order to escape the constant wranglings at home, and also to conduct her courtship in secret, Mary began meeting Shelley by her mother's grave in St Pancras Churchyard. It was here that, united in hearts and spirit, they pledged their troth to one another.

Meanwhile, Claire had succeeded in 'capturing' no less a figure than the poet Lord Byron. It was a brief affair, but by the time Byron departed for Switzerland, Claire was pregnant. Shelley and Mary, distressed by Godwin's continual demands for money, the public's indifference to Shelley's poems and their own rejection by society, were contemplating a return to the Continent, and Claire easily persuaded them to take her with them to Switzerland. Mary had been introduced to Byron and, while repelled by his excesses, had found him fascinating, and was happy to meet him again. Once more, the threesome travelled across the Continent and joined Byron, in May 1816, on the shores of Lake Geneva. Here they rented two adjacent villas and spent much time together, going on boating trips and talking long into the night at Byron's Villa Diodati. The conversation frequently turned to subjects of horror and one night they decided to make up ghost stories. This was the starting-point of Mary's first novel, *Frankenstein*.

Relations between the two households were strained, Byron having long lost interest in Claire. And as the summer came to an end, Mary and Shelley decided it was time to leave, and in September they arrived back in England.

UNFORESEEN TRAGEDIES

They settled in Bath, in happy domesticity, until they received the news that Mary's half-sister Fanny had committed suicide. Mary, stricken with guilt and grief, was almost expecting the next blow when in December they heard that Shelley's wife Harriet had also committed suicide, by drowning herself in the Serpentine in Hyde Park. Shelley immediately set off for London to claim custody of his two children, Ianthe and Charles, and decided that he would have a better chance of doing so if he and Mary married. It was against his principles, but the ceremony duly took place in December 1816.

In January Claire, who was again living with the Shelleys, gave birth to a daughter, Allegra, and the chancery suit for custody of Shelley's children began. The following month, Mary realized she was pregnant again and they moved to Marlow in Buckinghamshire where she settled down to finishing *Frankenstein*.

In September she gave birth to a baby daughter Clara, but immediately succumbed to post-natal depression. At the same time Shelley's health – frequently bad – deteriorated drastically. In the meantime, there was a flurry of local speculation about Allegra's origins. Claire had never publicly explained her daughter's parentage but had always hoped that Byron would give his daughter a privileged upbringing. Gossip now put the Shelleys under pressure to help her.

In March 1818, they set off for Italy. The lively, affectionate Allegra was sent with their nursemaid, Elise, to Venice, and the rest of the party travelled to Tuscany. Meanwhile *Frankenstein* had been published anonymously and an excited Mary was beginning to get favourable reports about it.

In August, Shelley and Claire set out to see Allegra and ten days later Mary received a letter asking her to join them. Her daughter Clara, not yet one year old, was ill, but Mary felt that she must go. So began a

nightmare journey across Italy in which Mary had to watch her small daughter visibly failing in her arms. On arrival in Venice the baby died. In her anguish, Mary blamed Shelley for Clara's death and never fully forgave him.

A BLEAK WINTER

Mary, Shelley and Claire soon embarked on another period of travel, this time to Rome and Naples. Here they immersed themselves in the study of Italian and classical literature, but it was a bleak winter in which they all felt depressed and homesick. In February 1819, the birth of a girl named Elena Adelaide Shelley was registered in Naples. Her official parents were Mary and Shelley. But her true parentage has remained a source of speculation to this day. There have been claims that she was the daughter of Shelley and Claire, but more probably her parents were Allegra's nursemaid Elise and Byron. Whoever they were, Elena was left with foster parents when the Shelleys once more returned to Rome.

Rome was Mary's favourite city, but she could not shake off a sense of gloom. Then, her beloved son William succumbed to a bout of dysentery. He seemed to rally, but suddenly, just two weeks after the first signs of illness, he died before Mary and Shelley's despairing and disbelieving eyes.

William's death was a blow which was to mark Mary for life. Quite unconsoled by the knowledge that she was pregnant again, she left Rome as quickly as she could and returned with the others to Tuscany. After five years of trouble and tragedy, Mary was in the

MARY WOLLSTONECRAFT

Born in London in 1759, Mary Shelley's mother, Mary Wollstonecraft, experienced a difficult childhood. One of three daughters, she had little formal education and often witnessed her drunken father beating her mother. These scenes planted in her a determination to fight for the cause of women, to ensure, among other things, that girls received a decent education, that they had the possibility of supporting themselves and that they were not always physically and economically at the mercy of men. She wrote a book called *Thoughts on the Education of Daughters* and gradually found herself part of a distinguished and radical social circle. In 1792 she published *A Vindication of the Rights of Woman,* a pioneering feminist work which has recently been reprinted.

Her private life was less successful. At 32 she became infatuated with the painter Henry Fuseli and, reeling from that hopeless relationship, she travelled alone to France where she soon became involved with an American adventurer, Gilbert Imlay, and found herself pregnant by him. By the time their daughter Fanny was born in 1794, Imlay had already begun to tire of her. Mary attempted suicide, first in Paris, then in London, and it was not until she formed a friendship with William Godwin that she found genuine happiness. In March 1797 they married – Mary was pregnant. But their joy was to be short-lived – on 10 September 1797 Mary died a few days after giving birth to a daughter, Mary.

Alpine travels
Claire Clairmont (inset left), Mary's stepsister, joined the young lovers when they eloped to Switzerland and became increasingly unwelcome as their journey progressed. At a certain point Shelley invested in a donkey to help transport Mary and some of their belongings along the way. But the animal was tiny, ill and feeble and Shelley ended up by carrying it clasped to his bosom, with Mary and Claire following, exhausted, at the rear.

Percy Bysshe Shelley
(right) Poet, free-thinker and political revolutionary, Shelley swiftly captured Mary's heart. At 16, months after meeting him, she wrote the verse: 'But ah! I feel in this was given/ A blessing never meant for me,/ Thou art too like a dream from heaven/ For earthly love to merit thee!'

Fact or Fiction

ANOTHER WILLIAM

An alert and happy child, little William (named after Mary's father) was his parents' pride and joy. Mary felt a special closeness to him, but always had a sense of impending doom.

On one occasion, as her son lay sleeping in his cot, she wrote of another – fictional – William "with sweet laughing blue eyes" whose life is cruelly cut short. Her dark imagination pictured this boy "rosy with health" strangled by Frankenstein's monster. Her vision of death was prophetic. Three years later her own William fell ill with dysentery and died.

Field House
(right) Situated in the village of Warnham, near Horsham, Sussex, Shelley's family home reflected the luxury into which he was born. Quarrels with his father, however, kept Shelley away from the house for much of his life. Even when his grandfather died, Sir Timothy would not let him in to hear the reading of the will; Shelley reputedly sat on the steps in front of the house reading Milton's Comus.

In 1844, after old Sir Timothy's death, Mary's son Percy inherited the baronetcy and moved into the family residence, reclaiming what his father had been denied.

throes of an emotional breakdown. Shelley offered her love and care, but she felt incapable of responding.

A son, Percy Florence, was born in November 1819, but Mary doubted that he would flourish and live. It was a difficult time for her. Godwin was demanding money again; Byron was refusing all Claire's pleas to let Allegra spend some time with her; and things were reaching breaking point between the two sisters. On top of this, Paolo Foggi, an ex-servant and husband of Elise, was attempting to blackmail them over little Elena Adelaide Shelley, who had recently died.

The only alleviation in Mary's difficulties came when Claire departed from the household and Mary was able to establish a happy working routine, writing her third novel *Valperga*. At the end of October 1820 the Shelleys moved to Pisa and made a number of new friends, including Edward and Jane Williams. Byron joined them a year later, having left Allegra behind in a convent, and shortly afterwards Edward John Trelawny, a swashbuckling adventurer, also arrived. He fuelled Shelley's love of water and boats with his tales of adventures at sea.

'EXPECTATION OF EVIL'

In some ways it was a happy time for Mary, until news came of Allegra's death from typhus. A distraught Claire joined them as they and the Williamses moved to a house on the Bay of Spezia. Mary was pregnant again and unwell, and while Shelley and Edward Williams threw themselves into the enjoyment of sailing their new boat, she began to feel depressed and inexplicably anxious.

In June she suffered a miscarriage. She was still weak from it when Shelley announced that he and Williams were going to sail up the coast to Leghorn. Years later she wrote that 'a vague expectation of evil shook me to agony' and she tearfully begged him not to go.

Both she and Jane Williams, with whom Shelley was now in love, received letters describing his and Will-

Funeral pyre
Edward Trelawny, deeply moved by the death of his friends, Shelley and Edward Williams, battled with the Italian authorities for permission to cremate Shelley in the style of his beloved Greeks. Having seemingly moved heaven and earth to do so, he finally won his concession and accordingly set up a funeral pyre in a wild and beautiful spot on the shores close to Via Reggio, near Florence. In classical Greek fashion, Trelawny procured salt and frankincense to fan the flames and poured wine and oil over the body. A copy of Keats' last book, which had washed ashore with Shelley, had been placed beside his body – so that the souls of the two great poets might, at some level, be merged together.

As the flames lapped Shelley's body, Trelawny plunged his hand into the fire and pulled out his friend's heart, struck by all that it symbolized. At Mary's request, the poet's ashes were buried at the English cemetery in Rome beside the body of her and Shelley's beloved young son William.

Byron's Allegra
Born to Claire Clairmont and Byron, Allegra was soon caught in a bitter tug-of-war between them. Byron would not allow Claire to see her and eventually put her into a convent. Tragically, when Allegra was just 5, she caught typhoid and died before either Claire or Byron could reach her.

iams' safe arrival in Leghorn. There was a terrible thunderstorm which they thought would have delayed the two men's departure for home. But then they waited – and waited – for their return.

Mary later wrote, 'To tell you all the agony we endured during those 12 days would be to make you conceive a universe of pain – each moment intolerable and giving place to one still worse.' Their worst fears were finally confirmed when Shelley's and Williams' bodies were washed up on the shore on 18 June 1822.

LIFE WITHOUT SHELLEY

In the days that followed, Mary was overwhelmed with despair. She longed to die, but the future of her son depended on her. So she unwillingly pulled herself together and made plans to stay in Italy and work, in the hope that she would be helped by an allowance from Shelley's family. But when his father wrote that he would maintain her son, Percy, only if she gave him up, she refused and returned reluctantly to England. Here she met up with Jane Williams again and felt the beginnings of a love which was not to be reciprocated, although the two women were to spend much time together.

Faced with lack of money and dismal lodgings, she struggled to write her next novel *The Last Man*. It was then that she heard of Byron's death and more than ever saw herself as the 'last man', "girded, walled in, vaulted over, by seven-fold barriers of loneliness".

In 1827 Jane Williams went to live with Hogg, with whom she had been having a love affair for some years. Away from Mary she began to gossip about the Shelleys' relationship, trampling on Mary's precious memories. Many of Mary's other old friends were to turn against her in later years. They regarded her as a cold, unemotional, conventional woman who disappointingly rejected the radical beliefs of her husband in favour of society's approval.

Meanwhile little Percy was fast becoming the only male to whom she could give her love. He was never to show any signs of genius, but he was an affectionate, easy-going boy and, eager to give him a good education, she sent him as a day boy to Harrow at the age of 12. Her life was now poverty-stricken and solitary.

LESS TROUBLED DAYS

Mary eventually began to enjoy a middle age in which she travelled to the Continent with Percy and wrote various pieces of non-fiction. And in 1844, when Shelley's father, Sir Timothy, died, leaving his estate and baronetcy to his grandson, her money worries were over. Unfortunately her new status made her vulnerable to blackmail attempts . She fought them but the attacks on her privacy took their toll on her health.

Mary had tired of life by the time she met her son's wife-to-be, Jane St John, in early 1848. Jane was a young widow who quickly became a devoted friend. She contributed much to what happiness Mary enjoyed in the last years of her life. In the winter of 1850, Mary became increasingly paralyzed and, knowing she was dying, passed on to Jane the care of Shelley's papers and reputation. On 1 February 1851, Mary Shelley died.

Gothic Horror

The sensational, the supernatural and the macabre were essential elements of the 'new' kind of novel that thrilled readers of all kinds and classes and made them thirsty for more.

Yet tales of terror are her dear delight,
All in the wintry storm to read at night.

So wrote the poet George Crabbe, describing the fashion for the Gothic novel – a type of story of the macabre and supernatural that had immense popularity during the late 18th and early 19th centuries. The craze for such books was particularly strong in England, but they also flourished on the Continent, especially in Germany, where they were known as *Schauerromane* ('Shudder Novels'). There is much more to Mary Shelley's *Frankenstein* than horror, but all the contemporary reviews treated it as a Gothic romance, and it does indeed use many of the trappings and themes typical of this kind of book – "vaults and charnel-houses" and the "decay and corruption of the human body".

Horror and the supernatural in literature were, even then, part of a long tradition. Some of the standard constituents of the ghost story, for example, go back almost 2000 years, to the Roman writer Pliny the Younger, who told a tale about a large sinister house haunted by a spectre that moaned and rattled its chains at dead of night.

But the Gothic novel broke new ground in its use of situations and props that have since become the stock-in-trade of horror movies: bleak castles, lightning, cobwebbed rooms lit by guttering candles, skeletons dressed in monks' cowls, torture chambers, dungeons, graveyards, gargoyles. The term 'Gothic' originally referred to the medieval settings typical of such stories, but during the late 18th century the meaning changed to suggest a more general notion of remoteness, strangeness and mystery.

IRRATIONAL FEAR

The Gothic novel was one aspect of the very broad movement known as Romanticism, which marked a reaction from the prevailing 'Age of Enlightenment'. Much European thought in the 18th century was characterized by rationalism – asserting the value of reason over imagination. But such a sensible, intellectual stance left unsatisfied a deep-seated human need –

Romantic gloom
(below) When writers in the 18th century invented their tales of horror, they gave the stories such eerie settings as ruined Gothic monasteries and bleak, comfortless castles. The term 'Gothic' orginated from the architectural style of the Middle Ages, but came to describe the dark, terrifying tales that achieved such popularity.

The appeal of ghosts
'All were alive to the solemn and terrible graces of the appalling spectre', wrote a commentator, assessing the public's obsession with stories of the supernatural. The Mysteries of Udolpho *(below) gave a rational explanation to every outlandish incident, which irked some of Mrs Radcliffe's readers. Homely and shy of publicity, Mrs Radcliffe had no experience of the places she described.*

Sex and violence
Matthew Lewis' book The Monk *is charged with all the adolescent sexual intensity of the 19-year-old who wrote it. Its heroine Mathilda (above) is captivated by the eloquence of Abbot Ambrosio and enters the abbey disguised as a monk. Her passion for the Abbot arouses his, and devastates these two chaste lives. Because of its explicit violence and sex, there were demands for the book to be banned.*

Horror upon horror
Walpole's Castle of Otranto *(spelt wrongly above!) is no literary masterpiece, but its supernatural mystery makes use of elements which were to become the established conventions of the Gothic novel.*

Fuseli's 'Nightmare'
(left) This is one of two versions of a painting by the great Anglo-Swiss artist Henry Fuseli, depicting a woman in the grip of an erotic nightmare. Remarkable for its daring subject matter, it represents not just the outward show of terror but also suggests the dark recesses of the mind.

a need which horror stories could partly satisfy without involving the reader in any personal risk. In 1798, the physician Dr Nathan Drake commented 'Of all the various kinds of superstition which have in any age influenced the human mind, none appear to have operated with so much effect as the Gothic . . . even the most enlightened mind, the mind free from all taint of superstitition, involuntarily acknowledges its power.'

The most popular phase of the Gothic novel was from 1765 to 1820. It affected America as well as Europe, and attracted readers of all social classes, from rich intellectuals to poor servants. Some novels were published in sumptuous three-volume editions, others as cheap throw-aways.

THE GRAVESIDE MANNER

Acknowledged forerunners of the Gothic novelists were the 'Graveyard Poets' who wrote reflective, melancholy works dealing largely with human mortality. The best known of these is Thomas Gray, author of *Elegy written in a Country Churchyard* (1751). But the very first Gothic novel is generally held to be *The Castle of Otranto* (1764) by Horace Walpole. Walpole, the 4th Earl of Orford, was a son of Sir Robert Walpole (Britain's first Prime Minister). He was a connoisseur of works of art, as well as a writer, and had an extremely varied career as a man of letters. *The Castle of Otranto* was written at his home, Strawberry Hill at Twickenham (a pioneering work of the Gothic Revival in architecture) and was inspired by a dream: 'I thought myself in an ancient castle . . . and that on the upper bannister of the staircase I saw a gigantic hand in armour.'

Walpole, who wrote the book in under two months, published it anonymously, offering it as a translation 'From the Original Italian of Onuphrio Muralto, Canon of the Church of St Nicholas at Otranto', a 13th-century cleric. Walpole feared ridicule, and to a literary public accustomed to novels of domestic sentiment, his tale must have seemed outlandish. The plot was as labyrinthine as the castle's gloomy passages and vaults. It featured ghosts, giants, and statues that came to life, while its human characters gave unrestrained vent to their emotions. Sensation rather than subtlety was Walpole's strong point – and the public loved it. A second edition was called for within a year, and ten more followed, as well as French and Italian translations.

To modern readers, the book seems convoluted, artificial and not very well written. Certainly it is now hard to credit that after reading it, the poet Thomas Gray (an old schoolfriend of Walpole) was 'afraid to go to bed o' nights'. Walpole himself did not try to follow up *The Castle of Otranto* – and in spite of its success it was some time before imitations appeared. The next Gothic novel with a claim to fame was *Vathek* (1786) by William Beckford.

Beckford came from a family that had made a vast fortune from sugar plantations in the West Indies (Lord Byron referred to him as 'England's wealthiest son'). He grew into a beautiful young man, but it was rumoured that he was involved in black magic, and one of his female cousins described him as 'a second Lucifer'. In 1784 Beckford was caught in the bedrom of a 13-year-old boy – a nobleman's son for whom he had conceived a passion – and the ensuing scandal caused him to leave England with his wife and daughter.

He returned ten years later, a widower, and lived in eccentric seclusion at Fonthill in Wiltshire. There he built, at frantic speed, an enormous Gothic house – Fonthill Abbey – which was soon regarded as one of the architectural wonders of the age. He collected vast numbers of books and works of art, but in 1822 he was forced by financial pressures to sell the house. Three years later the 280 foot high tower collapsed and crashed through the building.

ORIENTAL ALLURE

Beckford's novel, *Vathek,* was written in French but translated into English. Subtitled 'An Arabian Tale', it is a prime example of the 'Oriental' type of Gothic story, which took the exotic Middle or Far East as its setting. Vathek is a cruel caliph who, in his thirst for power and forbidden knowledge, becomes a servant of Eblis (the Devil). The story is fast-moving and full of dramatic incident, as ghastly crime follows ghastly crime. It sustains the sense of fantasy more effectively than Walpole's book, and ends powerfully with Vathek condemned to eternal torment. Beckford claimed to have written it in three days and two nights while in a kind of trance, inspired partly by the engravings of the 18th-century Italian artist Giambattista Piranesi, who produced a famous series of powerful etchings with a nightmarish quality, entitled *Imaginary Prisons.*

William Beckford
(above) He had everything money could buy, plus looks and intelligence, but he dabbled in the occult and disgraced himself with a sexual scandal. Forced to leave England, he travelled in Europe and wrote his oriental fantasy Vathek.

'Imaginary prisons'
The engraving below, made by Giambattista Piranesi as one of a series of nightmarish interiors, was an inspiration to William Beckford and shows a similar concern with the grim and terrifying.

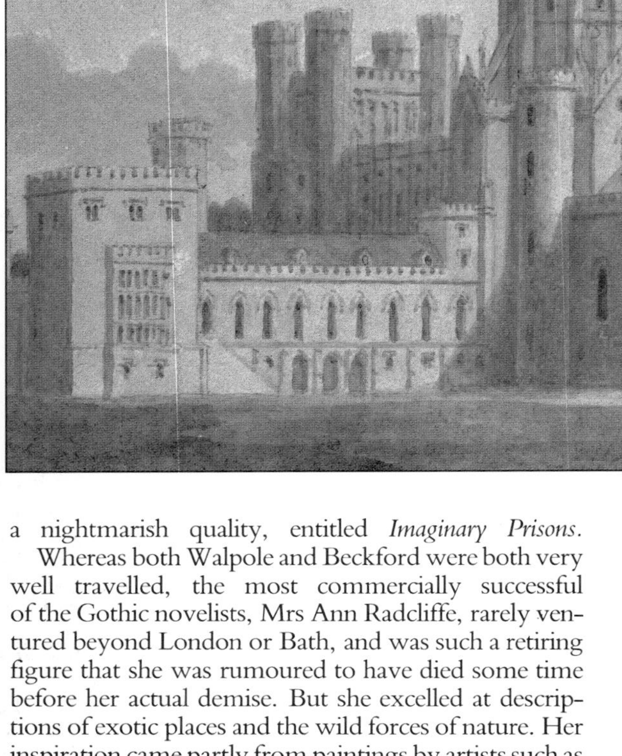

Whereas both Walpole and Beckford were both very well travelled, the most commercially successful of the Gothic novelists, Mrs Ann Radcliffe, rarely ventured beyond London or Bath, and was such a retiring figure that she was rumoured to have died some time before her actual demise. But she excelled at descriptions of exotic places and the wild forces of nature. Her inspiration came partly from paintings by artists such as the popular 17th-century Neapolitan Salvator Rosa.

Mrs Radcliffe wrote half a dozen Gothic romances, the best known of which is *The Mysteries of Udolpho* (1794). An indication of her popularity is that she was paid a publisher's advance of £500 for this book, then an unprecedented sum. Mrs Radcliffe's tale is set in a gloomy castle in the mountains of Italy, to which the beautiful heroine is abducted by her villainous uncle. Various inexplicable horrors beset her, which are all eventually shown to have human origin. Mrs Radcliffe was the chief representative of this 'rational' approach, and in spite of her popularity, some readers felt cheated when apparently supernatural events were ultimately given a prosaic explanation.

EXPLICIT TREATMENT

In *The Mysteries of Udolpho* the heroine's honour as well as her life is threatened, but the sexual element is veiled and timorous compared with its treatment in *The Monk* (1796). Matthew Lewis wrote *The Monk* at the age of 19, when he was attaché at the British Embassy in The Hague. Set in Spain, it is a lurid tale of a once-worthy monk who becomes sexually obsessed, uses supernatural aid to pursue the object of his desires, and finally rapes and murders the unfortunate girl. After being discovered and tortured by the Inquisition, he is hurled to damnation by the Devil, with whom he has attempted to make a pact.

Not surprisingly, this heady mixture of sex and violence caused a sensation, and there were calls for the book to be suppressed. It was excitingly and skilfully written, however, and Lewis was befriended by leading literary figures such as Scott and Byron (Byron called him 'Wonder-working Lewis'). To the public at large he became known as 'Monk Lewis'; he never again wrote anything of the quality of his masterpiece.

Fonthill Abbey
(above) Beckford's home after he returned from Europe to Wiltshire, was inspired by his intense, flamboyant imagination. It was a folly, a grandiose statement in stone, and it won the same kind of fame as did the Gothic writings of the time. But, having been built at great speed, the central tower of Fonthill collapsed quite suddenly – rather like the vogue for weird and wonderful Gothic.

Pleasure in pain
Agony and torment, inflicted either by human torturers (such as the Spanish Inquisition above left), or by the fires of Hell, often occur in Gothic literature. The voyeuristic sado-masochistic implications are obvious. Readers of such books as The Monk, Vathek *and* Udolpho *were invited to witness the most lurid extremes of human behaviour for their dubious pleasure.*

Sympathetic elements
(above) Scenes of fictional horror were almost always accompanied by dramatic weather – illuminated by lightning or lashed by pitiless rain – so as to heighten the atmosphere. Science had been making efforts to analyze lightning's cause and harness its energies. Electricity was held in awe and some people even believed that it could imbue the inanimate with life.

SHOCKING IMAGES

The fascination with the mysterious, horrific and erotic found in Gothic novels is paralleled in contemporary painting, most notably in the work of Henry Fuseli, for whom Mary Shelley's mother had an obsessive infatuation. Fuseli was Swiss-born (his original name was Johann Heinrich Füssli) and settled permanently in England in 1779. A writer as well as a painter, he was much respected in intellectual circles, and the great poet-painter William Blake described him as:

The only man that e'er I knew
Who did not make me almost spew.

Fuseli's most celebrated painting is *The Nightmare*, (1781) an unforgettable image of a woman in the throes of a violently erotic dream. Like Lewis, he shocked his public, but overcame their moral scruples by force of his genius.

SATIRE AND PARODY

By the time Mary Shelley's *Frankenstein* appeared in 1818, the heyday of the Gothic novel had passed. Indeed, in the same year two books appeared ridiculing its conventions – *Northanger Abbey* by Jane Austen and Thomas Love Peacock's *Nightmare Abbey*. Jane Austen is subtle in her satire, but Peacock is gleefully mocking, his characters having names like Diggery Deathshead and Mr Toobad. At the end of the book Scythrop Glowry (a character based on Shelley) thinks of killing himself, but decides instead to open a bottle of Madeira.

The end of the great period of the Gothic novel is marked by the publication of Charles Maturin's *Melmoth the Wanderer* in 1820. It is the only one of Maturin's works which is still remembered, and is perhaps the most powerful of all Gothic novels – one of the few whose reputation has not decreased.

At the outset of the novel, Melmoth is already over 100 years old, having sold his soul to the Devil in return for prolonged life. He can escape from his dreadful pact only by finding someone to take over his part in it, and the plot involves his attempts to persuade a succession of characters to do this. They include a prisoner in the hands of the Inquisition and a man whose children are dying of hunger, but none of the unfortunates will buy freedom at the price Melmoth asks, and he is condemned to eternal torment.

The plot is involved and potentially repetitive, but the pace never flags and Maturin handles the story with magnificent bravura. Professed admirers of the book have included William Makepeace Thackeray and the painter Dante Gabriel Rossetti. Oscar Wilde called himself 'Sebastian Melmoth' after his release from prison, finding the name of the doomed wanderer appropriate to his plight as a social outcast.

The joy of fear
There is no modern literary equivalent for the massive cult following Gothic books enjoyed. Their appeal overstepped the bounds of class, and the most respectable, refined and genteel of ladies (above) were gripped by the taste for gore, rape and supernatural terror. The absurd extremes to which some novelists went gave rise to Gothic parodies by such wry observers as Jane Austen.

LATER CREATIONS

The Gothic novel did not disappear overnight after *Melmoth the Wanderer*, but it had run its course as the most popular literary form of the day, to be succeeded by the historical novel, of which Sir Walter Scott was the great pioneer. Echoes of the Gothic tradition recur in Victorian literature, however (for example, in Dickens' novels). And the most celebrated of vampire stories, *Dracula* by Bram Stoker, was not published until 1897.

The chilling tale of Dracula's relentless pursuit of his victims has inspired a multitude of horror movies, which tend to highlight the lurid and sensational elements of the tale, rather than its imaginative power. *Frankenstein*, like *Dracula*, has been widely interpreted and promoted on film. Indeed, perhaps the most moving recreation of Mary Shelley's story is the 1931 cinema classic. Boris Karloff's monster, like the original, is not merely bestial – he is a pathetic creature who suffers because of his creator's presumption in trying to usurp the power of God.

Twentieth-century Gothic
Although Gothic literature burned itself out and largely disappeared during the 19th century, its elements survive today in horror movies and 'pulp novels'. Some motion pictures based on the best of the literature (right) have created legends of their own.

CHARLES DARWIN

1809-1882

From the secluded calm of his country home, the reclusive semi-invalid Charles Darwin unleashed upon the world ideas that rocked Victorian society and shook the very foundations of the Christian church – ideas that provoked some of the most bitter scientific debates ever heard. Even today, the storm of controversy raised by the publication of *The Origin of Species* and Darwin's theory of evolution by natural selection is far from over. The germ of this revolutionary theory had been sown 20 years before – during a voyage around the world he had made as a young naturalist.

The Quiet Revolutionary

After an adventurous youth, Darwin devoted his life to his family and to research. Unwittingly, this gentle scientist became the focus of the greatest controversy of all time.

A more unlikely revolutionary than Charles Darwin is hard to imagine. Humble, kindly and thoroughly respectable, Darwin's only real passion in life was for natural history. As a young man, he embarked on what was to be a momentous voyage round the world, but then, a few years after his return, he retreated to a secluded house in the Kent countryside. There he remained almost continuously until his death 40 years later, living quietly with his large, adoring family, tending to his plants, carrying out research, and writing.

There was hardly a hint of the battles to come in the easy tranquillity of Darwin's childhood. Born on 12 February 1809 in a house called The Mount, overlooking the River Severn near Shrewsbury, Charles was the fifth of six children. His mother Susannah was the accomplished daughter of the great pottery magnate Josiah Wedgwood. Darwin remembered little of her, for she died when he was barely eight, but his family remained close to her brother, also called Josiah – the association was to be significant. But it was his father Robert Darwin who dominated The Mount.

A dour but widely respected and wealthy physician, Dr Robert Darwin was a gigantic man, like his famous naturalist and philosopher father Erasmus Darwin, weighing almost 24 stone. His children, who loved him dearly, used to say that when he came home in the evening it was like the tide coming in. The Darwin children's chatter always abated when their father rolled in, and the atmosphere at The Mount tended to be a little restrained. But it was a happy home, and Charles' childhood there was comfortable and secure, with ample time to indulge his passion for collecting pebbles, plants and birds' eggs.

As a boy, Charles had a tendency to fib – an odd contrast to his unimpeachable integrity in later years. For example, he once claimed that he could grow different coloured crocuses by watering them with coloured water. But his exaggerations were no more than youthful exuberance. His particular obsession was for hunting beetles, and he and his second cousin William Darwin Fox went to great lengths to capture unusual species. Once, he later recalled, 'I saw two rare beetles and seized one in each hand; then I saw a third and new kind, which I could not bear to lose, so I popped the one which I held in my right hand into my mouth. Alas it ejected some intensely acrid fluid, which burnt my tongue so that I was forced to spit the beetle out.'

Charles was a healthy, affable youth, always out walking, riding or hunting with his cousins, and dashing up to Staffordshire to see Uncle Josiah and his daughters Emma and Fanny in their home at Maer Hall. But there were few signs of academic distinction. Determined that his son should follow a career, Robert Darwin sent Charles to Edinburgh University to study medicine in 1825. But Charles was not cut out to be a doctor. Anaesthetics had yet to be invented, and the two operations that he witnessed – one an amputation on a child – made him feel so sick that he had to rush out. The lectures he liked little better, remembering only 'cold breakfastless hours on the properties of rhubarb'. So he occupied his 18 months in Edinburgh looking for shellfish in the Forth, learning to stuff animals, and shooting.

Key Dates

1809 Born near Shrewsbury
1825 Goes to Edinburgh University
1827 Enters Christ's College, Cambridge
1831 Joins *HMS Beagle*
1839 Marries Emma Wedgwood
1842 Moves to Down House, Kent
1858 Ideas of Wallace and Darwin presented at Linnaean Society
1859 *Origin of Species*
1871 *Descent of Man* published
1882 Dies at Down House

Dr Eramus Darwin
Charles' grandfather (top) in his book Zoonomia *(65 years predating the* Origin*), had asked whether 'all warm-blooded animals have arisen from one living filament?'*

Brother and sister
(above) Charles (aged six) pictured with his younger sister, Catherine.

LOOKING FOR A CAREER

If Charles was not to be a doctor, Robert proposed that he should become a clergyman and, in autumn 1827, the 18-year-old Darwin was sent off to Cambridge. But he was no more keen on his studies here than he had been in Edinburgh and, in his own words, 'continued to collect insects, hunt, shoot & be *quite* idle'. He enjoyed himself in Cambridge and his warm, outgoing nature made him many friends, notably Adam Sedgwick, Professor of Geology at Cambridge, and John Henslow, the Professor of Botany. Indeed Darwin's friendship with Henslow grew so close that he became known as 'the man who walks with Henslow' Both Henslow and Sedgwick encouraged his interest in natural history, and introduced him to the work of the geologists William Paley and Charles Lyell, and the great scientist-explorer Alexander von Humboldt. While still an undergraduate, Darwin gained a reputa-

Mother and family
(above) Seated on horseback is Susannah, with her parents Sarah and Josiah Wedgwood on the right.

Country life
(below) Darwin's father told his son: 'You care for nothing but shooting, dogs and rat-catching, and you will be a disgrace to yourself and all your family.'

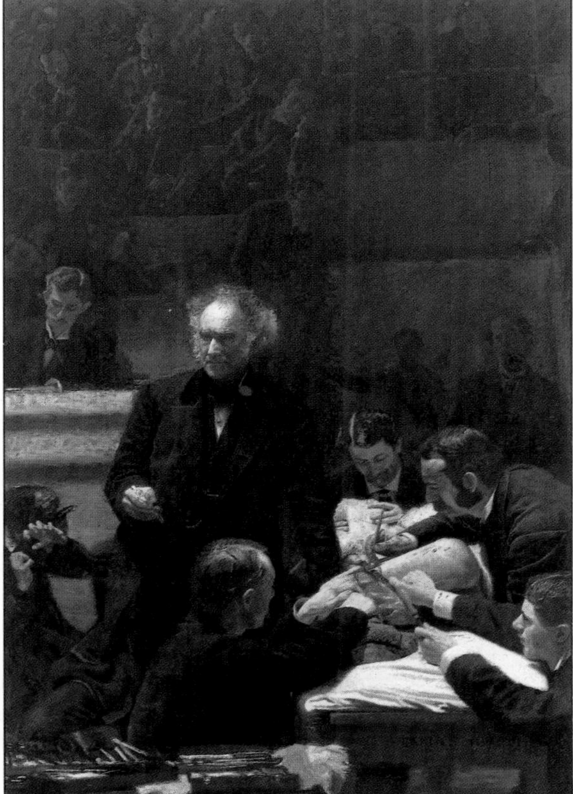

tion as one of the leading British amateur naturalists.

When he graduated from Cambridge in 1831 Adam Sedgwick took him on a surveying trip in North Wales. On his return to The Mount at the end of August, he found awaiting him an invitation from the navy to join *HMS Beagle* as naturalist on a survey trip around the world. Darwin was only 22 – it was the chance of a lifetime.

VOYAGE ON THE 'BEAGLE'

His father was at first reluctant to let him go, but was persuaded by Charles' uncle Josiah Wedgwood, a man for whom both father and son had developed an unbounded respect. By the end of the year, Darwin was sailing southwards in the *Beagle*, equipped with all the naturalist's standard gear and a large library that included Charles Lyell's recently published *Principles of Geology* – a classic book that laid the groundwork for Darwin's theories by establishing that the world is much, much older than the Church of the time stated.

The voyage lasted almost five years, and the experience was priceless. As the *Beagle* sailed on round the world, Darwin collected thousands of wonderful speci-

An abandoned career
Charles was expected to become a doctor, following in both his father's and his grandfather's footsteps. But witnessing operations carried out without anaesthetics (left) convinced Darwin that a career in medicine was not for him.

mens and sent them back to Henslow along with detailed explanatory letters. Henslow publicized the contents of these remarkable letters and by the time Darwin arrived back home in October 1836, his name was well known. More importantly, it was the observations made on this trip, especially on the Galapagos Islands, 500 or so miles off the west coast of South America, that were eventually to lead him to his theory of evolution by natural selection.

He returned to England a changed man. Gone was the old frivolity and carelessness. He was now a deeply thoughtful young academic – quite sober-minded enough for his father to provide him with an income which ensured that he would never have to look for a career again.

NATURAL SELECTION

Immediately he got back, Darwin settled in London to sort out his collection and write up his journal for the voyage. As he worked diligently away, he became more and more convinced that the different species had not been fixed once and for all, as was widely believed, but were continually changing. He was not alone in this belief, but he was alone in his determination to prove it. Established in a flat in Great Marlborough Street, he began by sending out questionnaires to horse breeders, cabbage-growers, zoologists – anyone who could provide him with clues.

Gradually, he began to build up a mountain of evidence in support of the transmutation of species (that is, evolution). He continued to write up his journal of the *Beagle* voyage, but devoted more and more time to the species problem.

By the middle of 1838, he was beginning to show signs of the ill-health that was to dominate his remaining 40 years, and may have been the reason for his reclusive life. Many people in his lifetime accused him of malingering and hypochondria – an accusation he vehemently denied – but he was probably suffering from Chagas' disease, a debilitating tropical illness he caught when bitten by a Pampas bug during the *Beagle* voyage. But his work went on and, early in 1839, the *Beagle* journal was published. It was beautifully written, captivating the non-specialist reader as well as the scientist.

Even before the publication of the *Beagle* journals, Darwin had become a popular figure in London academic circles, sought after by eminent men like the geologist Charles Lyell and the botanist Joseph Hooker. But there was something he disliked about London. He longed for Shropshire and the countryside. He longed for something else, too, and in July he sat in his room carefully weighing up the pros and cons of marriage: 'Imagine living all one's day solitarily in smoky, dirty London – only picture to yourself a nice soft wife on a sofa with good fire, and books and music perhaps . . . Marry – Marry – Marry: Q.E.D.'

He probably knew already who he wanted to marry: Emma Wedgwood, his cousin and childhood friend from Maer Hall. But it took him a long while to pluck up courage to ask, and it was not until November that he finally made his proposal. According to his daughter Henrietta, 'He was far from hopeful, partly because of his looks, for he had the strange idea that his delightful face, so full of power and sweetness, was repellently plain.' Emma had no such doubts. Nor did her father Josiah Wedgwood, who wept for joy when told. They were married in January 1839.

The marriage was an extremely happy one, and they had ten children all of whom Darwin treasured unreservedly. Emma Darwin never accepted the ultimate implication of Darwin's work – the unreality of the biblical Creation story – but the difference seemed to cause no friction between them, and she was happy to spend her life with him and raise their family.

It was about the time of their marriage that Darwin's belief that species survived by adaptation began to crystallize, and it may have been in the library at Maer Hall that he read Malthus' treatise on population. Malthus' proposal that population growth was self-limiting

Emma Darwin
Emma Wedgwood Darwin was Charles' cousin, friend, and then wife. Although sceptical about his ideas on evolution, which challenged her religious beliefs, she nevertheless loved and supported her husband throughout his life.

The 'Beagle'
The five years Darwin spent on the 'Beagle' were to change his life, and to lead to his theory of evolution. The 'Beagle' docked in Sydney harbour (right) on 12 January 1836, towards the end of its epic round-the-world voyage.

Down House
(above) Painted by Darwin's niece, Julia Wedgwood in 1886, Darwin lived here from 1842 until his death over 40 years later. Down House was situated 19 miles from London and formed an ideal base, despite the fact that it had neither bathroom nor running water. It gave him the seclusion he cherished and allowed him to continue his writing and research undisturbed.

suggested to Darwin the idea of natural checks and balances on the growth of species numbers – checks which meant that those individuals poorly adapted to their environment would not survive to pass on their characteristics to their offspring. Over the next 20 years he was to refine and clarify this idea of natural selection and build up an incontrovertible weight of evidence which he finally published in *The Origin of Species*.

In 1842, Darwin and his wife moved to the large, secluded house in Downe, Kent, that was to be their home for more than 40 years. Down House was a rambling, tranquil place, set in 18 acres of ground, where Darwin could work in peace surrounded by his wife, his children, numerous cats, dogs, squirrels, horses and pigeons. He rarely left Down House, except to make trips back to Shrewsbury, to London's scientific societies, or to take a water cure – for he was frequently unwell – but scientist friends like Hooker and Lyell and Thomas Huxley often came to visit.

For 14 years after he moved to Downe, he continued to build up the evidence for his theories, making a special, exhaustive study of barnacles. But he decided not to make his findings public until the evidence could not be disputed. Then in 1855 came the news that someone else, the botanist Alfred Wallace, was also working on an evolutionary theory. Darwin's friends encouraged him to make his work public soon. Slowly and reluctantly, he started to write his great book, sending a letter to Asa Gray at the Linnaean Society to inform him of his ideas. He was only a fraction of the way through his book when, in June 1858, Wallace wrote him a letter from the Moluccas Islands outlining a theory of evolution by natural selection almost identical to Darwin's own.

Darwin was thunderstruck, admitting to Lyell, 'all my originality . . . will be smashed', and asked what he should do. The outcome was a brilliantly productive

THE WEDGWOOD CONNECTION

Charles Darwin's marriage to his cousin Emma Wedgwood in 1839 saw the continuation of a close bond between two remarkable families that lasted for well over a century. The Wedgwoods were one of the great liberal families of the early Industrial era. Emma's grandfather, Josiah Wedgwood I, is best known for creating the world-famous Wedgwood potteries in Staffordshire, while his youngest son Thomas was the first person successfully to record a camera image.

This Wedgwood cameo *illustrates the family's campaign against slavery.*

Josiah Wedgwood II
'Uncle Jos' was instrumental in young Charles sailing on the 'Beagle'. He achieved fame by campaigning for the abolition of slavery and in setting up the Royal Horticultural Society at Kew.

Charles and Emma
Although Charles had been a robust youth, in later years he suffered constant ill-health, spending much of his life as a semi-invalid. He kept a diary of his condition, often 'not able to do anything one day out of three'. But he was not unproductive when ill. Emma tended lovingly to his needs and Darwin continued to write and work prodigiously, writing an autobiography as well as consolidating his work on natural selection.

compromise. At Lyell's suggestion, Wallace's paper and Darwin's letter outlining his ideas to Asa Gray were presented together at a meeting of the Linnaean Society in July.

Though the papers attracted surprisingly little attention, Darwin immediately set to work writing an account of his ideas. Originally intended as an 'abstract' – or synopsis – it was soon extended to make an entire book. This book, completed in over a year, was *The Origin of Species*.

The study at Down House
Because of Darwin's continuing poor health and lack of energy, he would move around his study at Down House with the help of his chair on wheels. Despite his weakness he was easily persuaded to play with his children. Darwin's books, journals and research materials are now on view at Down House, which has been opened to the public as a museum.

THEORY OF EVOLUTION

The first edition of the *Origin* sold out on the day it was published. It created a furore in academic and religious circles and was soon the talk of middle-class Victorian parlours all over England. Soon every thinker in England was debating the case for or against evolution. In his *The Origin of Species,* Darwin studiously avoided anything more than a hint that Man might be implicated in the evolutionary process. But the hint was enough; people inferred that Darwin was suggesting Man had descended from the apes, and before long, furious debates were raging up and down the land.

Throughout the 1860s, as the evidence in favour of evolution by natural selection began to pile up, Darwin continued to work away quietly on a variety of projects, including a treatise on orchids. Then, in 1868, he decided the time was ripe to include Man in his scheme of things, and began work on his third major book *The Descent of Man*. He argued, 'Man in his arrogance thinks himself a great work worthy the interposition of a deity. More humble & I think truer to consider him created from animals.' By August 1870, the manuscript was at the publishers, and early in the following year, it was published.

As Darwin predicted, the book caused as great a stir as *The Origin of Species*. But Darwin, having presented his carefully measured argument, refused to be drawn into the public affray, and remained at Down House working – this time on the study of the expression of emotions in man and animals and on the power of movement in plants. But he was getting old now, and frail, and he felt time begin to drag. On one occasion, he is said to have gone into the drawing room saying, 'The clocks go so dreadfully slowly, I have come in here to see if this one gets over the hours any quicker than the study one does.'

On 18 April 1882, he suffered the most severe of a series of heart attacks. Recovering consciousness, he whispered calmly 'I am not in the least afraid to die'. He died the following afternoon and was buried in Westminster Abbey on 26 April. After the funeral, the eulogies flowed and many agreed with Huxley who mourned the loss of Darwin's 'intense and almost passionate honesty by which all his thoughts and actions were irradiated, as by a central fire.'

THE GREAT DEBATE

When *The Origin of Species* was published in 1859, most people still believed that the Creation was a factual account, and that God really had created Man and every species of animal once and for all in the Garden of Eden (below). The words of the Bible were taken literally. By trying to show that species were not fixed but had evolved gradually from a single source, Darwin plunged into a storm of controversy and started a battle of science versus religion that, even today, is unresolved.

One of the most spectacular clashes was that between Darwin's champions, Thomas Huxley and Joseph Hooker, and his vehement critic, Bishop Wilberforce at a meeting of the British Association in Oxford in 1860. The high point of the Debate was when Wilberforce asked Huxley, 'was it through his grandfather or his grandmother that he claimed descent from a monkey?' 'I would rather be the offspring of two apes than be a man afraid to face the truth,' Huxley is believed to have replied.

The then Vice-Admiral Fitz Roy (the captain of the *Beagle*) attended the debate, and tried to denounce his former colleague, but was shouted down by Darwin's supporters, and walked out in bewildered fury. To him, and many others, Darwin's theory was an affront to his most sacred beliefs.

'Soapy Sam' versus 'Darwin's bulldog'
Bishop Samuel Wilberforce, known as 'Soapy Sam' because of his glib eloquence, proclaimed before the Oxford Debate that he was out to 'smash Darwin'. He asked Thomas Huxley (known as 'Darwin's bulldog', below) whether it was through his grandmother or grandfather that he was descended from apes, only to be demolished by Huxley's witty riposte.

Natural Delights

From pond-dipping to eating rhino pie in the bush, ardent Victorian amateur naturalists seemed willing to go to any length in search of new species and new experiences.

When Darwin was a child scouring the Shropshire countryside for beetles and birds, an interest in natural history was regarded as a little odd. A naturalist was someone who 'went "bug-hunting" simply because he had not the spirit to follow a fox' (although this was hardly true of the young Charles Darwin). But by the time Darwin had finished writing his journal of the *Beagle* voyage in 1838, natural history was well on the way to becoming the most popular of all Victorian pastimes, attracting thousands of ardent enthusiasts up and down the country.

Summer weekends would see many a Victorian gentleman – and some ladies too – donning sensible shoes, picking up a good, stout walking stick and strolling out in the countryside to 'botanize' and observe the wonders of nature. It was not unusual to catch sight of an elderly clergyman bending his arthritic back for a closer look at humble woodspurge or an unfamiliar beetle. Seashores became an especially popular destination for amateur naturalists, possibly due to Philip Gosse, whose exuberant explorations of rockpools and beaches near his Minehead home attracted many an enthusiastic disciple.

ZOOS AND GARDENS

Observation, though, was rarely enough. To capture the experience, and for the sake of 'science', specimens had to be collected. Wildflowers, fungi and ferns were uprooted from the ground and taken home for examination under the microscope or for display in the study. Butterflies were netted and many an unfortunate bird and wild animal ended up stuffed and mounted in a fine glass and mahogany case. It was a time when naturalists went out armed with a gun, not a camera, and the art of taxidermy was a thriving business. Countless Victorian homes were adorned with natural history specimens, which were as much a feature of some parlours as the displays of expensive porcelain, and tinted prints. Aquaria and ferns were especially popular – although every couple of years a new kind of plant or creature became the focus of attention.

Exotic species excited the Victorian natural historian, and the general public, as much as, if not more than local wildlife. The first half of the century saw zoological and botanical gardens established in towns and cities all over Britain to house and display some of the weird and wonderful specimens brought back from the tropics by intrepid adventurers such as Darwin himself. Of all the gardens, none was more famous than the Royal Botanic Gardens at Kew in Surrey. The original plant collection dated from the end of the 17th century, but the real work of establishing the nine-acre plot began in 1759 under the eye of George III. The first official director was Sir William Hooker, and his son, Joseph, who held the post for 47 years, travelled as far as Tibet in search of rare specimens. Joseph Hooker was both a friend and champion of Darwin's. Kew and the new Regent's Park Zoo were kept constantly in the headlines by the *Field* columnist Frank Buckland.

Buckland was a national figure – though with a rather strange penchant, surprisingly common at the

Botanists botanizing *(right) were a familiar sight in the lanes, fields and woodlands of Victorian England.*

me if I cared for him as he cared for
did not hesitate to tell him that
heart I felt that I never would
we were engaged I struggled
was only to draw the web m
for how could I treat him
ed, he said very sadly: but

Margaret Fountaine *had a strict Victorian upbringing, but broke a great many conventions travelling the world collecting butterflies. Her diaries (above) record as much about her encounters with men as with butterflies: her adventurous spirit did not stop short at lepidoptery. She is pictured right collecting in the United States where she once earned a living gathering spiders' nests at four dollars a dozen.*

Alfred Wallace
(above) sent Darwin, in 1858, his latest paper to read. The paper reached the selfsame conclusions Darwin had spent 20 painstaking years compiling. "I never saw a more striking coincidence," wrote Darwin. But the 'coincidence' only really indicates the great preoccupation with natural sciences at that time.

'glowing accounts'
Alexander von Humboldt (above) travelled the equinoctial regions of America between 1799 and 1804. His Personal Narrative *of his travels was one of the few books Darwin took on his famous voyage. For Darwin, as for others, Humboldt's narrative fired the imagination and revealed the secrets of Nature: 'he like another Sun illuminates everything I behold'. The compliment was returned – Humboldt read Darwin's accounts of tropical nature with deep interest and was lavish in his praise of Darwin's powers of observation.*

time, for 'zoophagy' (eating wild creatures). Beginning as a schoolboy with squirrel and mice in batter, he graduated to rhino pie (which he cooked before his lecture audiences), giraffe cooked 'on the hoof' (when the giraffe house at the zoo caught fire), panther (already dead and buried three days before he dug it up for the pot), elephant's trunk soup and virtually every British species of wild bird.

BATS AND BALONEY

Often, the study of natural history became hugely competitive, and it was soon every natural historian's dream to discover a new species, or identify a particularly rare example. Sometimes, species hunting went to quite ridiculous extremes. The famous American bird-illustrator Jean Jacques Audubon claimed that his rival William Swainson 'never goes to bed without describing some new species' – a tendency he and many others were equally prone to.

The eccentric Audubon was once visited by the even more eccentric Constantine Rafinesque-Schmaltz. He woke one night to find his guest running round the house naked, clutching Audubon's valuable Cremona violin and beating it violently against the walls in his attempts to down a bat of a species he claimed to be new. Audubon's revenge for the destruction of his fiddle was to keep slipping into Rafinesque's notes illustrations of invented species, such as the Devil-Jack Diamond fish which had bullet-proof scales. Rafinesque included these species in his book with the addendum, 'This genus rests altogether on the authority of Mr Audubon who presented me with a drawing of the only species belonging to it.'

GLOBE-TROTTING BOTANISTS

In their desire to find new species, naturalists would go literally to the ends of the Earth. Darwin, who voyaged round the world in that capacity on the *Beagle,* was just one of the many who journeyed far and wide in the early 19th century in search of new species, either as official naturalists on naval voyages of exploration, or as independent travellers. The German scientist-explorer, Alexander von Humboldt, was by far the most famous, and was much admired by Darwin, but there were numerous others.

South America in particular seemed to draw the intrepid naturalist-explorer like a magnet. Humboldt voyaged up the Orinoco and scaled Chimborazo, then thought to be the highest mountain in the world, while Charles Waterton voyaged up the Essequibo again and again between 1812 and 1825, bringing back numerous birds and animals each time – once wrestling with an alligator to ensure its capture.

In the 1840s, Henry Bates and Alfred Wallace (the naturalist whose theory of natural selection was announced along with Darwin's in 1858) made many dangerous expeditions through the Amazon basin to discover new species. In his 11 years in South America, Bates – who threw up his job as brewery clerk in Buxton to go exploring – collected 14,000 specimens, of which 8,000 were of previously unknown species. Later in the century, women, typically as illustrators, made equally brave voyages, and Marianne North came back with a wealth of beautiful paintings showing the plants she had seen on her trips everywhere from Brazil (1873) to Borneo (1876).

Margaret Fountaine, a clergyman's daughter born in 1862, travelled all over the world in search of butterflies, men and adventure. She voyaged from South Acre near Norwich to Budapest, Turkey, the United States, Africa, India and to the borders of Tibet, dying eventually on the island of Trinidad 78 years later, with a butterfly net at her side. She bequeathed to the world ten handsome mahogany display cases containing no less than 22,000 butterflies, her 'diurnal lepidoptera', and twelve volumes of diaries spanning her life from the age of 15 to a few months before her death. These, she wrote in her will, were not to be opened until 100 years after her first entry, and accordingly we did not discover about the loves and exploits of this extraordinary woman until April 1978.

Some idea of the huge interest in natural history in mid-Victorian England is given by the wealth of literature on the subject. All the daily newspapers had a natural history column. So too did many of the general interest periodicals. Popular natural history journals like the *Field* had large circulations among the middle classes, while the *Entomologist's Weekly Intelligencer* was bought and read avidly by thousands of working-class men and women every week.

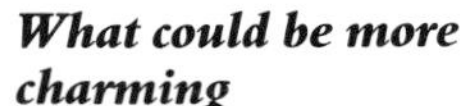

What could be more charming

and edifying than a family ramble (right), studying the wonders of God's creation? So thought pious Victorians — until Darwin drew their attention to some unfortunate fundamentals in Nature: kill or be killed; only the fittest survive. The romance paled. No longer could quaint human characteristics be attributed to animals: easier to attribute bestial characteristics to people.

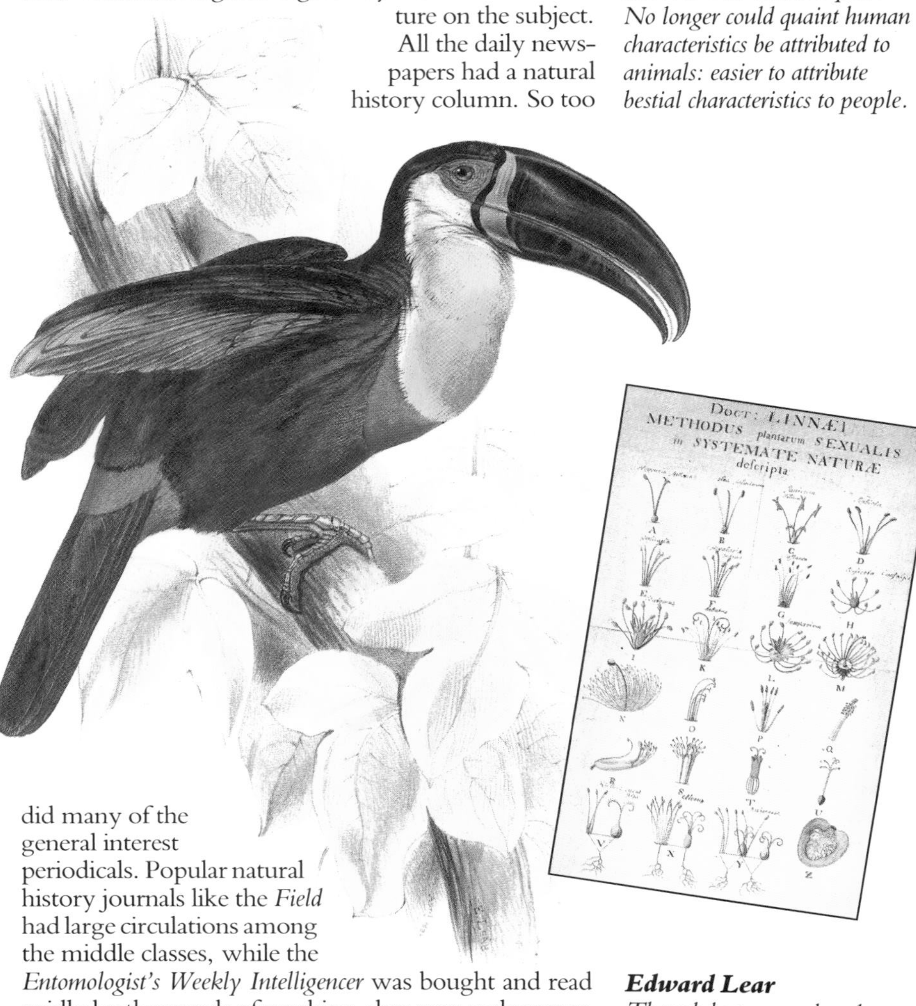

Edward Lear

Though best remembered for his nonsense verses, Lear was primarily a painter of natural studies, such as the Toucan, above left. Collectors commissioned him to immortalise their menageries. Precise, perfect illustrations were vital for systematic classification of plant and animal life. Naming and categorizing were the rage, largely thanks to the Linnaean System (example above) developed in the 18th century by Carolus Linnaeus.

BEST-SELLERS

But surprisingly it was books which fed most Victorians' fascination for the subject. Natural history books were second only to novels in popularity, and when a Victorian gentleman wandered into the drawing room for a quiet read, he was as likely to pick up something like *The Marvels of Pond Life* as the latest Charles Dickens story. Books on natural history sold in huge numbers and successes like the Reverend J.G. Wood's *Common Objects of the Country* which sold 100,000 copies in a week were by no means unusual.

Forerunners of these books were the perennially popular journals of the 18th-century Hampshire vicar, Gilbert White, and his *Natural History of Selborne* (1789) went through numerous editions in the early Victorian

A dangerous pursuit
The aged clergyman strolling through the countryside could furnish only so much information for the new sciences. Some dedicated naturalists exposed themselves to enormous risks in pursuit of knowledge. Charles Waterton, for example climbed treacherously dangerous cliffs to gather birds' nests (right) and even wrestled with an alligator in South America.

Lost explorers
Grisly perils awaited those who went abroad in search of uncharted, unrecorded wonders. But this was the age of the heroic exploit. It took little to justify an expedition of exploration, and the various scientific societies were eager to finance such trips. The Royal Society of Victoria, for example, sponsored the disastrous Great Northern exploration of Australia. Despite the despatch of equally heroic rescue parties (below) all but one of the explorers died.

period. After reading *Selborne* as a child, Charles Darwin could not understand why every gentleman did not become a naturalist. Dozens more such books appeared, including Darwin's three major works, the *Beagle* journals (1839), *The Origin of Species* (1859) and *The Descent of Man* (1871). Indeed, it seemed that nearly every country vicar and reasonably literate lady (and some not so literate) wanted to write a nature book and kept meticulous diaries to that end.

Many of the authors of the day were well-informed and could back up their claims with considerable experience in the field. Others, however, were more inclined to rely on flowery prose, or anecdotes, which inevitably led to certain myths becoming popular. One famous 'fact' averred in many natural history books was the supposed ability of toads to live forever when encased in rock – at the Great Exhibition of 1862 a toad was on show which was believed to have emerged from a lump of coal. And Mrs Loudon gave the follow-

ing advice in her book the *Entertaining Naturalist:* 'When in danger of being attacked by a Bull, the best course is to stand still, and open an umbrella, or flap a shawl, or something of that kind, in the Bull's face; as with all his fierceness he is a great coward and only pursues those who fly from him.'

NO CUDDLY ANIMALS

Even the best-informed authors, such as Darwin, could not refrain from using anecdotes to illustrate their work occasionally. Nor could they avoid the equally universal tendency to credit wild creatures and plants with human qualities, emotions and even morals. In her book *The Herb of the Field,* Charlotte M. Yonge describes the polypody moss as 'one of those cheerful, humble things, that seems to have a kindness for what is venerable and excellent, even in decay.' But this sentimental view of Nature was completely overturned by Darwin's *The Origin of Species* and the seemingly brutal idea of the 'survival of the fittest'.

Darwin had been reluctant to publish his findings on natural selection because of the cataclysmic repercussions they were bound to have. They challenged the accepted beliefs about God and Creation – in the late 17th century the Archbishop Ussher had calculated that God's six-day creation of the world and every creature on it began at 9am on 23 October, 4004 BC. And although in Darwin's day this view was beginning to lose ground, his contemporaries were still aeons away from allowing the possibility that the world and all its inhabitants could be in a state of flux, constantly changing and adapting.

But Darwin did eventually reveal his ideas to the public. And the furore that his writing produced was even greater than the gentle naturalist had ever anticipated.

Ironically, his success led to a decline in popularity of natural history for the lay person. Evolutionary theory and the suggestion of the supremacy of Nature over Creation made the study of Nature the province of the specialist scientist rather than the amateur natural historian. Professional biologists and zoologists were taking over, and by the 1880s the familiar collections of butterflies and birds began to gather dust in attics – forgotten symbols of a previous generation's strange and rather quaint obsession.

Flora and fauna
In 1876, Marianne North went to Ceylon. Hence the addition to her collection of 'Foliage and flowers of a Red Cotton Tree (Bombax malabaricum) *and a pair of Common Paradise Flycatchers* (Terpsiphone paradisi)*' (below).*

Darwin's kindred spirit
The extraordinary Marianne North (above) spent 16 years travelling to remote corners of the world alone, painting superb detailed studies of places and plants. A gallery at Kew Gardens, which she herself endowed, houses her work. It attracted the praise of Darwin who became her friend and advisor – it was he who suggested a further expedition to Australia.

ELIZABETH GASKELL

1810-1865

From a witty, talkative, vivacious beauty, Elizabeth Gaskell matured into a woman of astounding energy and hard-won experience. The poverty and injustice she witnessed set her writing, but she never let literature outweigh the other aspects of her busy life. Given her sociable nature and social conscience, her time was already full. But, beset by demands for her work, she laboured on, despite her over-taxed health, to preserve in the words and images of fiction a disappearing world she valued for its charm and innocence.

Faith, Hope and Charity

Principled, humorous and strong in her Unitarian belief, Mrs Gaskell took action in words and deeds to redress social wrongs and overcome seemingly insurmountable barriers.

Elizabeth Gaskell's character and talent were the product of a fostered childhood, of a stimulating and free-thinking religion, of rural peace and urban suffering, of domestic routine and poignant personal loss. The woman who emerged was energetic and positive, an observant, cultured artist, a classless friend to the famous and unknown alike, and above all a devoted wife and mother.

In her early 30s she wrote, on receiving some of her dead mother's letters from a family friend: 'I think no-one but one so unfortunate as to be early motherless can enter into the craving one has after the lost mother.' Yet despite her own early loss, Elizabeth's childhood was a very contented one. She was born Elizabeth Cleghorn Stevenson on 29 September 1810 in Chelsea. Her mother, worn out by giving birth to eight children – of whom only Elizabeth and her brother John survived – died 13 months later. Elizabeth's father, William, a Unitarian and the Keeper of the Treasury Records, was overwhelmed by the prospect of caring for such a small child on his own, and gratefully seized on his sister-in-law's suggestion that Elizabeth should go and live with her in Knutsford, Cheshire.

Until she was 14, Elizabeth lived a happy and sheltered life in her aunt Hannah Lumb's large red-brick house, on the edge of the common in Knutsford. The house was really a little farm, with pigs, poultry, geese and a vegetable garden, and here Elizabeth learned the arts of housekeeping and cooking.

When her domestic duties were done, she spent hours reading or sewing in some nook or cranny of the house, or in the shade of an old fir tree on the front lawn. Often she joined the host of cousins who lived in nearby Sandlebridge, for a picnic or an outing. She also went with her uncle on his doctor's rounds of the local villages, and taught at Sunday school, as well as attending the Unitarian chapel. It was a peaceful, predictable atmosphere of provincial life.

Her visits to her father in London were in sharp contrast to this country idyll. William Stevenson remarried

Key Dates

1810 born in Chelsea

1811 moves to Aunt Lumb's in Cheshire

1832 marries William Gaskell

1840 first writing published by William Howitt

1848 *Mary Barton*

1850 commissioned by Dickens; meets Charlotte Brontë

1853 *Cranford*

1857 meets Charles Eliot Norton

1865 dies at Alton, Hampshire

A London birthplace
(far left) Elizabeth was born at fashionable Cheyne Walk, Chelsea (then Lindsey Row), overlooking the Thames.

Benevolent influences
Hannah Lumb (right) and Dr Peter Holland (far right), her mother's sister and brother, were devoted surrogate parents to 'Lily', as they called her. She was often to be seen accompanying her uncle, the local surgeon, on his neighbourhood rounds.

A country girl
(left) On her mother's death, Elizabeth (aged one year) was sent to live with her aunt at Knutsford, Cheshire. She thrived on the wholesome, tranquil atmosphere, and here established her life-long love of literature and of the countryside.

'Cranford'
This picture (below), taken in 1865, shows the High Street of Mrs Gaskell's home town of Knutsford, which was the inspiration for her most famous novel.

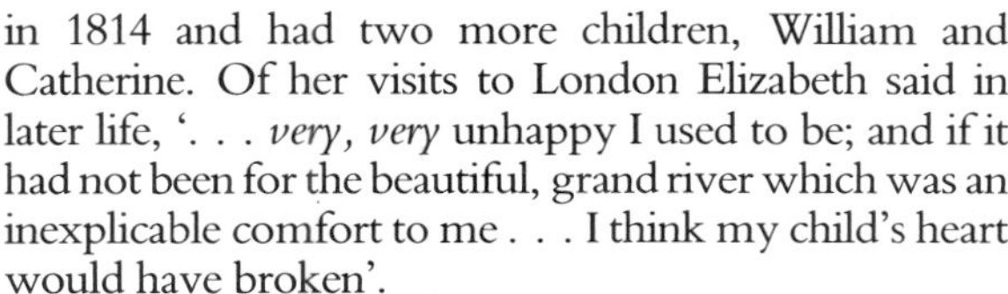

in 1814 and had two more children, William and Catherine. Of her visits to London Elizabeth said in later life, '. . . *very, very* unhappy I used to be; and if it had not been for the beautiful, grand river which was an inexplicable comfort to me . . . I think my child's heart would have broken'.

At the age of 13, Elizabeth went as a boarder to Avonbank school in Stratford-upon-Avon, which was run by her stepmother's relatives, the Misses Byerley. Here she stayed for three years without returning to Knutsford, and seems to have been perfectly happy learning languages, deportment and etiquette – the traditional subjects for a young lady of her day.

In 1827 Elizabeth returned to Knutsford – but not for long. In August 1828, she received a letter from her brother John, a mariner with the East India Company. He wrote that he was setting sail for a new life in India, and concluded, 'Should we never meet again, accept my very best wishes for your welfare through life and may every blessing attend you'. Shortly afterwards he was reported missing, presumed drowned at sea.

This news devastated Elizabeth's father and he requested her company immediately. For the next two years, Elizabeth was part of the Stevenson household and nursed her father through failing health and a stroke, until he died in 1829. After this she seems to have broken almost entirely with her stepfamily, not seeing them again for 25 years.

A COMPASSIONATE NATURE

Elizabeth spent the next two winters in Newcastle, at the home of a distant family connection, a Unitarian minister and teacher, William Turner. He was greatly revered in the town for his commitment to cultural and philanthropic improvements. The Unitarian faith in principle stood for freedom of thought and action, and these ideals infused Elizabeth's philosophy all her life. William Turner's brand of active, charitable religion formed a blueprint for Elizabeth's own. She was compassionate by nature, and her religion was always motivated by an unaffected desire to help others. Neither dogmatic nor censorious, her zeal was never at odds with her irrepressible sense of fun and gaiety.

An outbreak of cholera in Newcastle sent Elizabeth and William Turner's daughter, Anne, to seek the safety of Edinburgh, where Elizabeth's beauty and vivacity attracted attention. On her return to Knutsford in 1831, 21-year-old Elizabeth visited William Turner's daughter Mary, who lived in Manchester. Mary's hus-

An attraction of opposites
Elizabeth (below right) is shown here at the age of 21, the time at which she met her future husband, William Gaskell, a Unitarian minister (below). Despite their contrasting personalities (he was shy and scholarly, she 'giddy and thoughtless'), they fell deeply in love and married after a courtship of months. An unusually liberal Victorian husband, William encouraged Elizabeth to write her first novel, Mary Barton, *and helped her to weather the storm of criticism that her candid, pioneering brand of writing aroused.*

band was the senior minister at the Unitarian Cross Street Chapel. His junior minister, William Gaskell, was a serious and learned man who was to make his name as a German scholar, a Professor of English History and Literature, an authority on Lancastrian dialect and a writer of hymns.

Elizabeth and William felt a swift mutual attraction, despite a seemingly radical difference in character which caused Aunt Lumb to say jokingly, 'How could the man ever take a fancy to such a little, giddy, thoughtless thing as you?' Elizabeth's 'wonderful' incessant conversation was later described by one of her husband's pupils as 'like the gleaming ripple and rush of a clear deep stream in sunshine'.

The couple were married in Knutsford Parish Church on 30 August 1832. Following the local custom, the villagers sprinkled red sand outside their houses and decorated this with flowers of white sand, in their honour. After a month's blissful honeymoon in Wales, the Gaskells settled in Manchester at 14 Dover Street.

Now Elizabeth had to draw on all her resources to cope – emotionally and practically – with the desperate privations she witnessed among her husband's mill-worker parishioners. As a minister's wife – and as the woman she was – she could not but be deeply involved in attempts to help them. But she was faced with poverty that could not be alleviated by simple charity. At this time, a mill-worker might have an income of 1/6d per week with which to feed, house and clothe his family. Most lived in one-room hovels and watched their babies die one by one.

Mrs Gaskell's own first child was still-born, but in September 1834 she bore a daughter, baptized Marianne but always known as Ma or Minnie. Meta, the Gaskells' second daughter, was born in February 1837. In May of the same year, her beloved Aunt Lumb died, leaving a sudden void in Elizabeth's life – 'Oh there never will be one like her'. But Aunt Lumb left her a legacy of £80 a year – a great help to the Gaskells' finances.

FIRST WRITING

At about this time, Mrs Gaskell made a tentative start on her writing career. She wrote to William Howitt, a famous contemporary author, after reading about a book he and his wife were compiling: *Visits to Remarkable Places*. She asked him if one of her favourite school-day haunts, Old Clopton Hall, was to be included, and vividly described it. Indeed, it *was* included, and in her own words.

William Howitt insisted that she should devote herself to writing full-time – an impracticable suggestion for the hard-working wife of a minister. However, the correspondence between the two started a lasting friendship. This was consolidated when, in 1841, the Gaskells' circumstances improved sufficiently to allow them to visit the Rhine, where the Howitts had settled. Mrs Gaskell was so impressed by the Howitts' splendid residence in Heidelberg, that she wrote to a friend, 'My word! authorship brings them in a pretty penny'.

In 1842 another daughter, Florence Elizabeth (Flossy), was born and the Gaskells moved to 121 Upper Rumford Street to accommodate the growing family. A baby boy, William, was born in 1844 and Mrs Gaskell's days followed a tranquil ritual of domestic routine. William was especially dear to her, and she later wrote, '. . . so affectionate and *reasonable* a baby I never saw'.

The following year, however, while the family was

Fact or Fiction

Lost At Sea

Mrs Gaskell's older brother, John Stevenson, disappeared on a sea voyage to India in 1828. This tragedy is often reflected in her writing, notably in the similar disappearance of Peter Jenkyns that casts a shadow over Miss Matty's life in *Cranford*, and adds to the poignancy of her solitary suffering.

A twist was added to Mrs Gaskell's own loss in that her brother was rumoured to have survived and landed at Calcutta. And in her fiction – for instance, *Sylvia's Lovers* – Mrs Gaskell devised a happy ending to the incident, perhaps willing that her own beloved brother might one day reappear in England, safe and sound. But despite this element of wish-fulfilment in her writing, her nautical characters have a freshness and authenticity that come from first-hand experience.

on holiday in Wales, 10-month-old William died of scarlet fever. Mrs Gaskell was so overcome that her own life was thought to be in jeopardy, and her husband searched desperately for some means of rousing her from her grief and depression. He suggested she write a book, and so it was that her personal sorrow became interwoven with the extreme poverty she saw daily in Manchester. The novel that evolved was *Mary Barton*. Although flawed in some respects, it owes much of its power to a bereft woman's urgent need to ease her own anguish, and to her compassionate insight into the conditions of the working class.

The birth of her fourth daughter, Julia Bradford, in September 1846, was a further comfort but, when moving house four years later, Elizabeth was still referring to the memories evoked by their previous home – 'the precious perfume lingering of my darling's short presence in this life'.

Meanwhile, with her novel awaiting publication, Mrs Gaskell published three short stories in William Howitt's journal, under the pen-name Cotton Mather Mills, Esq. This attempt to protect her identity was partly to avoid causing trouble to her husband, who preached to the wealthy mill-owners she criticized, as

Marianne, Meta and Flossie

This drawing (below) shows Mrs Gaskell's three eldest daughters in 1845. In that year, Mrs Gaskell was devastated by the death of her baby William, her only son. She later said, 'one evil of this bustling life [is] that one never has time calmly and bravely to face a great grief'.

The plight of the poor

In the 'Hungry Forties', Manchester was the heart of the industrial north; people flooded into the city from the surrounding countryside (left), in search of work. They found only squalor, unemployment and high levels of infant mortality. The Gaskells worked daily with the city's poor, teaching, feeding and clothing them. These experiences gave direction and insight to Mrs Gaskell's early novels, and a contemporary critic wrote: 'Do they [the rich] want to know why poor men . . . learn to hate law and order . . . to hate the rich, in short? Then let them read Mary Barton.*'*

City of contrasts
'Rightly understood, Manchester is as great a human exploit as Athens', wrote Disraeli, and for many it seemed a city of opportunities. But another contemporary account pointed out, 'there is no town in the world where the distance between the rich and the poor is so great'. Mrs Gaskell knew both sides intimately.

well as the poor mill-workers she championed. Mrs Gaskell was pleasantly surprised, however, when one manufacturer actually thanked her for portraying him so faithfully!

The success of her first novel brought Mrs Gaskell to social prominence, and she found herself in London, dining with Dickens and meeting Thackeray, as well as corresponding with Carlyle. Dickens was keen for Mrs Gaskell to contribute to his new journal, *Household Words*. And so, *Cranford* was born.

Mrs Gaskell and Charlotte Brontë met for the first time shortly before *Cranford*'s success, at the house of a mutual acquaintance. Elizabeth described Charlotte – in mourning for Emily, Anne and Branwell – as 'the little lady in the black silk gown', while Charlotte thought Mrs Gaskell was 'a woman of the most genuine talent — of cheerful, pleasing and cordial manners and — I believe — of a kind and good heart'.

Their lifestyles were in marked contrast. Mrs Gaskell ran a large, bustling household with children and several servants. Charlotte Brontë, the unmarried daughter of a most difficult father, lived a life of seclusion in the wild setting of Haworth. Yet even though Charlotte and Mrs Gaskell seem never to have been on first-name terms, they became good friends, visiting each other and maintaining a regular correspondence, at least until Charlotte's marriage in 1854. And when Charlotte died in 1855, it was Mrs Gaskell whom Mr Brontë asked to write his daughter's biography.

Mrs Gaskell's *Life of Charlotte Brontë* was published in

FLORENCE NIGHTINGALE

'The lady with the lamp', Florence Nightingale, forged the modern concept of nursing in the field hospitals of the Crimea. Mrs Gaskell met her in 1854 and found her 'like a saint'. 'She has no friend – she wants none. She stands perfectly alone, halfway between God and his creatures.' But Mrs Gaskell disagreed with her ideas on child-rearing (that it should not be done by the mother), and once related how they 'had a grand quarrel one day. She is, I think, too much for institutions . . .'

The Nightingale family were kind to Mrs Gaskell, inviting her to their Derbyshire home to write *North and South* in the seclusion of a 'turret . . . a quarter of a mile of stair cases . . . away from everyone in the house'. She enjoyed this quiet time, calling it 'my happy, happy pause of life'.

Roman spring
One of Mrs Gaskell's most memorable holidays was her visit to Rome (left) with her daughters, when she met Charles Eliot Norton, an American intellectual. He was 16 years her junior, but the rapport between them was immediate and lasting.

A fellow writer
Mrs Gaskell met Charlotte Brontë (right) in 1850, and they formed a friendship based on mutual liking and respect. The biography which Mrs Gaskell wrote after Charlotte's death stirred up a 'hornets' nest' of controversy – but has borne out Mr Brontë's opinion that it would be 'in the first rank of Biographies till the end of time . . .'

1857 and is considered by some to be one of the finest biographies in English literature. George Eliot found it 'as poetic as one of her [Mrs Gaskell's] own novels', and there does seem to have been a certain amount of creative licence involved in its writing. The first edition had to be withdrawn so that various offending passages relating to Mr Brontë, Rev. Nicholls (Charlotte's husband), the servants and a widow who may have had an affair with Branwell Brontë, could be removed.

Initially, Mrs Gaskell was blissfully unaware of the uproar caused by her book, as she was holidaying in Rome with two of her daughters. Here she met Charles Eliot Norton, a young Unitarian intellectual from America, on a European tour. He was a great admirer of Mrs Gaskell's work, and they spent several happy weeks of a magical spring in Rome. In this short time, a deep and intense friendship grew up between them, and they exchanged little notes daily in addition to their meetings. All too soon the idyllic interlude was over. Mrs Gaskell returned to England to face a barrage of correspondence about *The Life of Charlotte Brontë*. Norton returned to America, where he eventually married, but the two maintained a regular correspondence until Mrs Gaskell's death.

LATER LIFE

As her children grew up, Mrs Gaskell was able to allow herself the luxury of time devoted solely to writing. She was invited by Florence Nightingale's family, for example, to seclude herself at their house, Lea Hurst in Derbyshire, to work on *North and South*.

Travel was to be a feature of Elizabeth's later life, and a long sojourn in Whitby furnished the material for *Sylvia's Lovers*. Most of her travels were undertaken without her husband, who refused to be parted from his work, except for the occasional solitary holiday abroad. Mrs Gaskell herself went abroad frequently, often with her daughters, visiting France and Germany. Much of *Wives and Daughters* was written while visiting the eccentric Parisian hostess, Mme Mohl.

But she still spent much time on her arduous duties as a minister's wife. In 1862, after tireless work among the famine-struck mill-workers, she and her daughters spent a short period of recuperation at Eastbourne. She suffered increasingly from fatigue and strain, but she cheered herself up by purchasing a large house and four acres of land at Alton in Hampshire. This was initially to be a secret from William Gaskell, for she hoped to be able to persuade him to retire there. Sadly, she was never to live in her country home. Nor was she ever to finish her final novel, *Wives and Daughters*. The last lines she wrote for its serialization in *Cornhill Magazine* were, 'and now cover me up close and let me go to sleep, and dream about my dear Cynthia and my new shawl'.

On 12 November 1865, while visiting her new house with her son-in-law and two daughters, Mrs Gaskell died suddenly but peacefully, while taking tea in the afternoon.

A final home
'The house is large, . . . in a very pretty garden . . . and in the middle of a pretty rural village', wrote Mrs Gaskell of 'The Lawn', at Alton in Hampshire (below). She bought the house – from the proceeds of her writing – as a surprise for her husband, and hoped to retire there. But her plan was never to be realized. She died suddenly, on her first visit to the house, during Sunday tea by the drawing-room fire.

The Poor Man's Charter

The appalling poverty that Mrs Gaskell encountered in the slums of Manchester inspired her early industrial novels – and resulted in the first political organization by the working class.

A bitter choice
Instead of improving conditions and pay, British politicians urged the starving poor to emigrate, with promises of impossible luxury abroad. This 1819 cartoon (below) highlights the hypocrisy of MPs by contrasting an image of violent repression of the working classes at Peterloo with a propagandist depiction of happy people at the Cape of Good Hope.

The world of Cranford looks stable and secure at first sight. In their young days, the Cranford ladies were those described by Jane Austen, whirling on the Regency dance-floors of Royal Bath. But the 40 years which have made Miss Jenkyns "grey, withered and wrinkled", and Miss Matty too old to wear an Indian muslin shawl, have also changed the England in which they live.

When Elizabeth Gaskell published *Mary Barton* in 1848, she wrote to inform the prosperous middle classes of just what was happening in their own country. Reviewing it, *Fraser's Magazine* wrote, 'People on Turkey carpets, with their three meat meals a day, are wondering, forsooth, why working men turn Chartists and Communists. Do they want to know why? Then let them read *Mary Barton*.' Hers was not an isolated voice. In that year, newspapers and literature alike were obsessed with the 'Condition of England' question. The strains and stresses at work on the fabric of society were threatening to tear it asunder.

THE PETERLOO MASSACRE

When Elizabeth Stevenson was nine years old, living with her Aunt Lumb in Knutsford, a crowd of unemployed weavers and their families – 60,000 of them – gathered on St Peter's Fields, near Manchester, to listen to Henry 'Orator' Hunt declaim the cause of their misfortunes. The police ordered that the speaker be arrested, but as it was impossible to reach him, the Hussars were commanded to charge a way through the

defenceless crowd. Eleven people were killed and more than 400 injured. The Government's reputation was destroyed. And the horror of Peterloo lasted long after.

It made a strong impact on the historian Thomas Carlyle, whose writings were, in turn, to influence Mrs Gaskell. He wrote, 'A million of hungry operative men rose all up, came all out into the streets and – stood there. What other could they do? Their wrongs and griefs were bitter, insupportable, their rage against their fate was just.' Peterloo took place in 1819. During the next 30 years, the problems caused by industrial growth, and the grinding poverty of the working man only increased.

The birthplace of Chartism
Manchester, caught up in the industrial boom of the early 19th century, was a source of great affluence for some – such as the owners of the Bridgewater Canal (right) – but many of its people were homeless and hungry (above). Chartism seemed to be the answer.

BOOMING MANCHESTER

Manchester in the 1830s and 1840s was the pride and the shame of England, the best and worst of places to live. Mrs Gaskell was the friend of many educated and well-intentioned, middle-class Mancunians. But her charity work also took her into poor homes of unimaginable squalor.

The centre of the textile industry, Manchester was making a whole new class rich. Not all achieved their wealth at the expense of their fellow men. Some factory owners organized a shorter (11-hour) day; some ran factory schools for the children working there. The factories themselves were modern, and even critics such as Carlyle acknowledged the thrill of the new:

'Has thou heard with sound ears the awakening of Manchester on Monday morning at half-past five by the clock? The rushing off of its thousand mills, like the boom of an Atlantic tide, ten thousand times ten thousand spools and spindles all set humming there.'

Manchester was at the hub of the new and expanding

Petitioning Parliament
A huge procession supported the second Chartist petition in 1842 (above); six years later, Feargus O'Connor (right) presented a third petition. Both failed.

railway system. It enjoyed an efficient public supply of gas from 1802, and was manifestly at the forefront of industrial growth.

That same Manchester was, however, the scene of intense suffering for the factory labourers, and of something worse for the unemployed. In the first 40 years of the 19th century, the town had trebled in size. Much of the new housing thrown up was appalling. In 1842 an official report to Parliament compared industrial Manchester with agricultural Rutland: though a labourer's average wages were twice as high in Manchester, the cost of living ate up the extra money and the living conditions in the city were far worse. At a time when an agricultural labourer had a life-expectancy of 38 years, that of a Manchester labourer was just 17. Well over half the children of Manchester labourers died before the age of five. In one area, 380 people shared one privy.

GRINDING POVERTY

In other areas, notably 'Little Ireland', there were no water supplies or sewerage at all, and refuse of all kinds was thrown into unpaved streets built narrow so as to crowd in the maximum number of back-to-back dwellings. Many families had no furniture at all. 'Frequently several families occupied different corners of the same chamber and there was no separation of the sexes, save the distances between beds of straw.'

When the weavers were in work, there was just enough to eat. In the years of slump (which often coincided with bad harvests and a high price for bread) their destitution was complete. Mrs Gaskell recounted to a friend how a father took hold of her arm and, grasping it tightly, said with tears in his eyes, 'Ay, ma'am, but have ye ever seen a child clemmed [starved] to death?' The Rev. R. Parkinson summarized life in Manchester in 1842 saying, 'There is no town in the world where the distance between the rich and the poor is so great, or the barrier between them so difficult to be crossed.'

THE CHARTISTS

The 1832 Reform Act extended the right to vote to most middle-class men. The labouring classes, however, were still without a voice in Parliament. By the 1830s, a feeling was growing that 'the government should do something'. If only working men could be elected to Parliament, surely their grievances would get a fair hearing. Mrs Gaskell's fictional hero, John Barton, expresses their profound anger and sense of injustice: "We're their [the employers'] slaves as long as we can work; we pile up their fortunes with the sweat of our brows, and yet we are to live as separate as if we were in two worlds."

In 1839, the London Working Men's Association drew up the Charter which gave them their name. It attracted support from Manchester, Birmingham and Wales. That year the Charter was presented to the House of Commons by Thomas Attwood, a sympathetic Member of Parliament. The demands were:

'That it might please their Honourable House to take the petition into their most serious consideration, and to use their utmost endeavour to pass a law granting to every man of lawful age, sound mind and uncontaminated by crime, the right to vote by ballot; that the duration of Parliament should in no case be of greater

Kennington Common
On 10 April 1848, a large and angry crowd gathered at Kennington Common, London (below), to support O'Connor when he presented the third Chartist petition. Events like this terrified the propertied classes, who remembered the forced abdication in February 1848 of the King of France, Louis-Philippe (above).

Privileged patriots
The 150,000 'noblemen, gentlemen and other patriots' who rallied to suppress the 1848 rising were lauded by the frightened middle and upper classes. A contemporary song-sheet (right) lionizes these brave defenders of privilege.

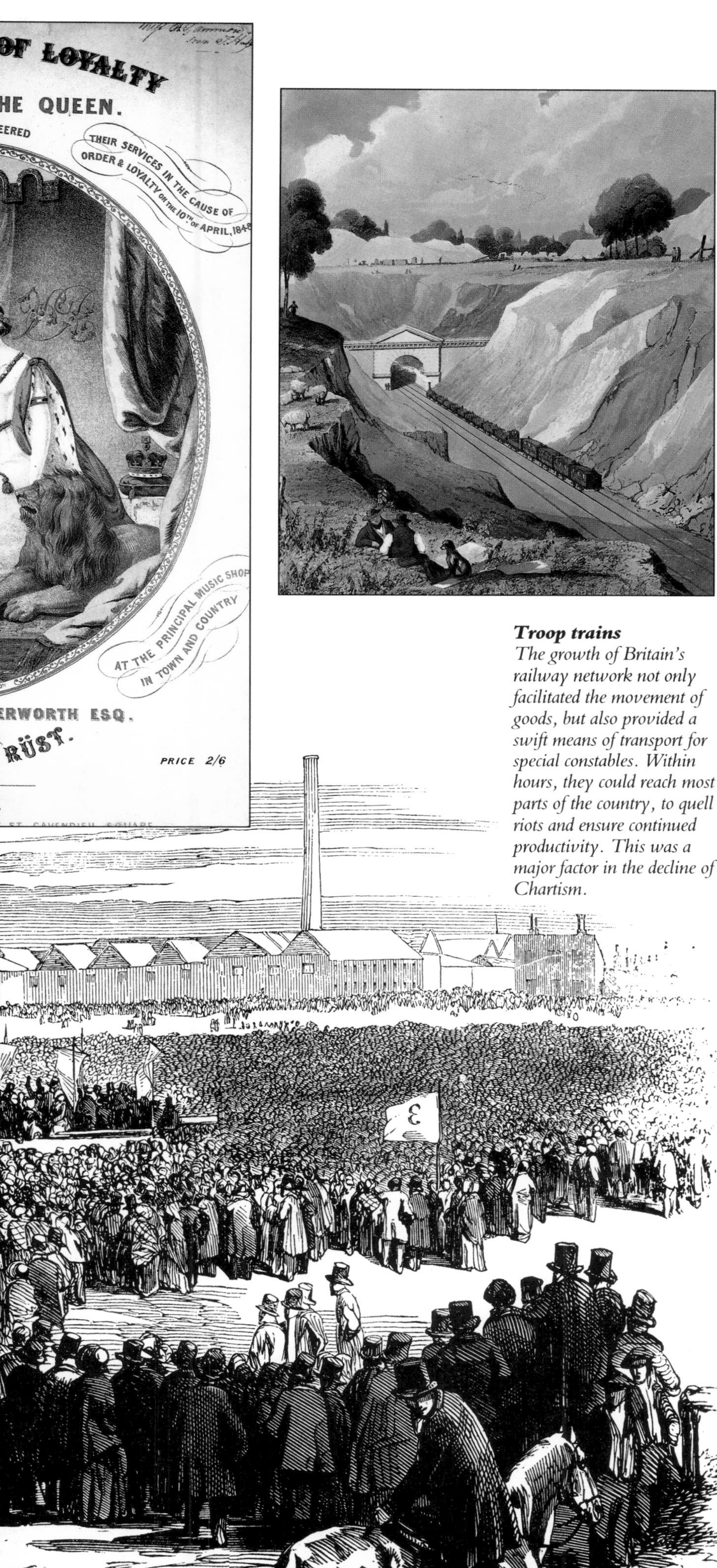

Troop trains
The growth of Britain's railway network not only facilitated the movement of goods, but also provided a swift means of transport for special constables. Within hours, they could reach most parts of the country, to quell riots and ensure continued productivity. This was a major factor in the decline of Chartism.

duration than a year; that they would abolish all property qualifications to entitle persons to sit in their Honourable House, and that all Members elected should be paid for their service.' Attwood summed up the needs of the petitioners as 'A fair day's wages for a fair day's work'.

The Charter was greeted with howls of derision by MPs, and the House refused to receive the petition. It was refused again three years later. Meanwhile, bad harvests had forced up the price of bread, a slump threw 10,000 weavers out of work in Manchester alone, and the disastrous Irish potato blight sent thousands of emigrants into the North-West of England.

The revised Poor Law gave out no 'relief' (assistance) except in return for forced labour and the break-up of families. 'Bitter discontent grown fierce and mad' was how Thomas Carlyle described the state of mind of the Chartists.

1848 was a decisive year not only in England but all over Europe. A wave of revolts broke out from the Austro-Hungarian Empire to Paris. And the National Chartist Convention prepared to present its petition for the third time to Parliament.

FEARGUS O'CONNOR

The Chartists had by now just one Member of Parliament – Feargus O'Connor, elected in Nottingham. He was to present the Charter on 10 April. In support of him, a vast crowd of the unemployed, students, strikers, and Chartist sympathizers, estimated at between 15,000 and 100,000 converged on London. This 'Convention' was addressed by speakers who promised to force the Government to accede to their demands. Wild promises of nationalization and redistribution of land struck terror into the property-owners who heard about them. London prepared itself for revolution, with barricades and an army of special constables. One of these special constables was Louis-Napoleon Bonaparte, nephew of the great Napoleon and soon to become the ruler of France.

Palmerston sat in the Foreign Office, his windows blocked with copies of *The Times*. London's defence was put in the hands of the Duke of Wellington. After the Convention, the Duke wrote:

'God knows how many people did attend, but the effect was to place all the inhabitants of the metropolis under alarm, paralysing all trade and business of all description and driving individuals to seek safety by arming themselves for the protection of their lives and those of their neighbours and of their property.'

On the night before, the Chancellor of the Duchy of Lancaster wrote to his brother, 'This may be the last time I write to you before the Republic is established.'

At the last moment, Feargus O'Connor was warned by the Commissioner of Police of the plans to protect London. He faltered then and there. After a long and rambling speech to his supporters, he left the great crowd on Kennington Common and went, with just a small delegation in three cabs, to the House of Commons. The crowd, bewildered, waited for something to happen. Scuffles broke out between enthusiastic special constables and the more zealous of the demonstrators.

Then the rain poured down, and after getting soaked

through, the great Chartist army drifted, cold and wet, to a hundred different refuges. Meanwhile, O'Connor was presenting the Charter, claiming there were 5,000,000 signatures on it. Within a very short time – much too short a time for a proper count to be made, said O'Connor – the petition was declared to have only 1,250,000 signatures, many of them bogus: Queen Victoria and Mr Punch were just two names challenged. The Charter was rejected for the third and last time.

In many cities in the North, rioting and strikes followed, but the action was unco-ordinated and the Chartists' political framework had been shattered. Troop-trains full of special constables were quickly despatched to put down any unrest. The leadership of the Chartists, never outstanding, collapsed. Within a month of his failure, Feargus O'Connor was seen shambling round Covent Garden, his mind broken. Ernest Jones, O'Connor's second-in-command, accused his followers of spending time and money in the 'gin-palace' instead of on the Chartist Movement. In fact grass-roots Chartism survived long after the leadership had withered away.

CHARTISM IN DECLINE

Two changes sealed the fate of the Chartist cause: a slight relief in suffering, combined with the working man's loss of faith that a political Charter would ever improve his life. Trade Unions were beginning to provide a more direct weapon of change. A succession of better harvests brought down the price of bread. The Manchester-based Anti-Corn-Law League organized the import of cheaper corn from abroad in time of bad harvests in England. The Government gradually took steps to improve water, sewage and town-planning. And in 1851, Prince Albert's Great Exhibition convinced all but the poorest classes of the advantages of industrialization.

No way in
The horror that greeted the presentation of the Charter to the House of Commons is well illustrated by this satirical drawing (above) – as is the despair of the working men promoting it.

A new life
After the failure of the third Charter, many people abandoned hopes of political reform in England. Thousands left to seek a better life in America or Australia (below left).

The great downfall of the Chartists lay in their isolation from the middle class. The middle class had organizational ability and some political influence, but the working class, on its own, had none. The middle class did not support Chartism, nor did the successful artisans, and the very poorest members of society were simply unable to sustain a nationwide campaign.

Many of the Chartists found an escape route in the years that followed. At the end of *Mary Barton*, Jem Wilson and Mary turn their backs on the smoke and filth of the cities and emigrate to America. Others left for Australia. In 1848 alone, 250,000 people, most of them from the poorest class, left England for a fresh start. In California, gold was discovered and thousands headed West.

Events in England in 1848 had been influenced by events in Europe. The English upheaval, in its turn, had an impact on Europe. Louis-Napoleon went back to take power in France. Prince von Metternich, who had also taken refuge in London, returned to his former influence in Germany. Karl Marx and Friedrich Engels published the *Communist Manifesto* in 1848 and cited the examples of Manchester factories to encourage German working-class uprisings. It would take some time, however, for those in power to realize that the poor could no longer be ignored.

W. M. THACKERAY

1811-1863

William Makepeace Thackeray wrote some of the finest satirical novels in the English language. And his ebullient personality matched his most colourful creations. His own life was as chequered and as beset by loss and adversity, as any work of fiction. Intimate with the fashionable world, sucked into its unsavoury undertow, he rose above it to become a grand old man of letters. When he died of an overstrained heart, the greatest writers of his day lamented, for he told 'the truth in spite of himself'.

Larger Than Life

The public image of the young Thackeray – gambler and rake – concealed a man with a generous heart. Private tragedy was to transform him into a devoted father and man of letters.

Thackeray's life reads like a novel – a Thackeray novel. It was propelled by sudden changes of fortune, none more significant than that following the publication of *Vanity Fair* in 1847. It was his greatest work, and the only English novel of the time to rival Tolstoy's *War and Peace*. At the age of 36, it brought him immense and immediate literary and social success and status. But it did not make his fortune. And having lost his inheritance through gambling and a banking crisis, he spent the rest of his life striving to regain his fortune through writing.

William Makepeace Thackeray was born in India on 18 July 1811, the only son of Richmond Thackeray, a wealthy official of the East India Company, and his 18 year-old wife, Anne. Living in Calcutta, in a mansion serviced by a large staff, the first few years of Thackeray's life were luxurious and exotic: he later recalled his visions of 'great saloons and people dancing in them, enormous idols and fireworks, riders on elephants or in gigs, and fogs clearing away and pagodas appearing over the trees'.

This sort of lifestyle was not to last. One day, his father invited a colleague, Henry Carmichael-Smyth, to dinner – unaware that Henry was his wife's ex-lover. Three years earlier, in England, the couple had been separated by Anne's devious grandmother. She had told Anne that Henry had died of fever, and then packed her off to India. Henry and Anne could not conceal their feelings from each other or from Richmond. When Richmond died three years later, young Thackeray was sent to school in England, and the following year his mother became Mrs Carmichael-Smyth. Thackeray never saw India again.

From 1817, he attended a private school in Southampton – 'a school of which our deluded parents had heard a favourable report, but which was governed by a horrible little tyrant'. For six year-old Thackeray, it meant dreadful food, beatings, cold – and nightly prayers that 'I may dream of my mother'. His mother returned to England with her new husband in 1820: Thackeray recalled their emotional reunion some 30 years later when he wrote of Henry Esmond's meeting with his mother: "The soul of the boy was full of love, and he had longed . . . for someone on whom he could bestow it."

At the age of ten, 'a pretty, gentle, and rather timid boy', Thackeray entered one of the most prestigious public schools in England – Charterhouse. Despite its reputation, the teaching was poor, and fagging and flogging were normal practice. In one particularly unpleasant incident, some senior boys arranged an entertainment in which Thackeray had to fight another pupil. His nose was shattered, disfiguring him for life. Paradoxically, when Thackeray was older, he spoke well of Charterhouse and its system – which he thought had an improving effect. But for Thackeray the schoolboy, Charterhouse deserved a harsher name: he called it 'Slaughter House'.

An only child
(above) For three years, young William enjoyed the retinue of a prince and the undivided attention of his parents. This portrait of Anne, Richmond and their child was made by Calcutta's most renowned artist.

Exotic early years
(left) Though his memories of India were scanty, they were powerful. Thackeray 'could just remember' his late father – along with 'crocodiles floating on the Ganges'.

'Slaughter House'
(right) Thackeray began his 'education as a gentleman' at Charterhouse in 1822.

A threatened future
(above) Young Thackeray had no clear idea of his future. His sociable and open nature led him into financially perilous activities. He was to squander his inheritance.

Isabella Shawe
(above right) The couple met in London in 1835, married, and for four years were blissfully happy. Thackeray sketched her many times.

Key Dates

1811 born in Calcutta
1815 father dies
1816 sent to England for his education
1817 mother remarries
1829 goes up to Cambridge
1830 leaves without taking his degree
1836 marries Isabella Shawe
1840 onset of Isabella's insanity
1845 Isabella committed to permanent care. Begins *Vanity Fair*
1855 lectures on *The Four Georges*
1857 loses Oxford by-election
1860 edits *Cornhill* magazine
1863 dies on Xmas eve

His gentleman's education continued at Trinity College, Cambridge, which he entered in 1829. Initially, he had high hopes of academic success, but instead of leaving with a degree, he took away with him two lifelong passions – for banqueting and for the theatre. He also acquired a dangerous taste for gambling. One evening, he was set up by a group of professional card-sharps, to whom he lost £1,500 – a sum he was not even due to inherit until he came of age in 1832.

COMING OF AGE

Thackeray abandoned his university career in June 1830, and within a month, he was preparing for a prolonged visit to Germany – in particular to Weimar, the country's cultural capital. For six months, he attended balls and dinners, flirted, met Goethe, and in mid-winter, hired sedan chairs to carry him through the snow to court. He was becoming a rake.

Back in England in 1831, Thackeray began training for the law. He applied himself for some months, but within a year he had given up his studies – informing his mother that 'this lawyers preparatory education is certainly one of the most cold-blooded prejudiced pieces of invention that ever a man was slave to'. He kept on his chambers in the Middle Temple as a *pied à terre*, and squandered his time and money lounging about London, drinking, fencing, womanizing and gambling at cards and dice. He was becoming a compulsive gambler, and his diary shows him to have been full of self-reproach at his idleness, and desperate to free himself from his urge to gamble.

In July 1832, Thackeray came of age, and celebrated with a trip to France, visiting galleries and theatres, reading French literature, frequenting the best restaurants – and gambling. In November, he returned to London and resolved to settle down and behave like a model young gentleman. He tried 'bill discounting' (a kind of money lending) for a short while, and then became involved in the less shady enterprise of buying and editing an arts-oriented newspaper, *The National Standard*. The paper lasted only a year, but by the end of that time, Thackeray had made his entry into London's literary scene.

Yet at this time he was more inclined to think of himself as an artist than as a writer. In 1833, he was painting in Paris – able to indulge his drawing ability, with no fear of having to make a living from it. But at the end of that year, his fortune – some of which he had already gambled away – disappeared almost completely with the collapse of the India banks in which his inheritance was invested.

Apparently undeterred, Thackeray continued his art studies – in London, and then in Paris. Lack of money seemed to free him rather than oppress him, and he enjoyed the Bohemian lifestyle of a Parisian artist: 'I was as poor as Job: and sketched away most abominably, but pretty contented: and we used to meet in each others little rooms and talk about Art and smoke pipes and drink bad brandy and water.'

It was not among the Parisian Bohemians, but among the English middle-classes in Paris that he met the young woman who was to become his wife. Isabella Shawe was small, shy, red-haired, naïve – and poor. They fell in love in 1835, and despite parental discouragement, married the following year.

At first they were blissfully happy, living in a tiny Parisian apartment, enjoying their new domestic routine. Thackeray was earning eight guineas a week for writing one or two articles for the *Constitutional and Public Ledger*, a paper which his step-father had bought. In 1837, the young couple returned to London, where their three daughters were born: Anne (born in 1837); Jane (born in 1838 but died in 1839), and Harriet (born in 1840). Thackeray was enchanted by his children, and deeply attached to his wife. In 1838, he wrote that they had 'been nearly 2 years married and not a single unhappy day'. He had no idea that their happiness was soon to be shattered.

Three months after Harriet's birth, he set off alone for Belgium's art galleries, against Isabella's wishes. She had been depressed since before her confinement and was now probably suffering from post-natal depression. Thackeray, on the other hand, thrived. He had 'a delightful trip, pleasure and sunshine the whole way'. But when he returned he was so alarmed by Isabella's mental state that he took her to visit her mother and sister in Ireland.

The journey was 'three days and four nights of hell', during which Isabella plunged into 'absolute insanity'.

Cambridge days
(above) Thackeray entered Trinity College, Cambridge half-way through the academic year, and left after only two years — with mixed feelings; 'three years industrious waste of time might obtain for me mediocre honors which I did not value a straw'.

Fact or Fiction

THE HAZARDS OF GAMBLING

Most of the gambling casinos of Europe were squalid places with an atmosphere of hysteria that concealed the financial tragedies enacted there. Thackeray himself gambled away his own inheritance, and used his experiences in *Vanity Fair*. Ironically, he found it a relief; 'My golden time was when I had no gold'.

Gambling hysteria
The English were reputed to be cold-blooded enough to stick to a system, but many privileged young men lost their fortunes.

My dearest Nanny. Your letter was so pleasant to me that I hope you will send me many many more. Why not one every week to tell me what you and my dearest Minny are doing? If you go on writing better and better one day you shall come and be my little Secretary – my secretary and housekeeper. How I should like to have you to make breakfast for me! Mamma is very well and lives with Mrs. Gloyne's mother at a very pretty house not very far from this. I go to see her and dine with her every other day. I should like to

Letters *to his daughters reveal his devotion.*

Minny and Anny *(left) While he pursued his career in London, Thackeray was forced to leave his growing daughters in care, and near their disturbed mother, in Paris. Later, they were to give his life its only real focus of affection. Despite the many obstacles, he was an ideal and devoted father who succeeded in making them feel secure through, as Anny observed, 'certainty of love far beyond our deserts'. Both daughters were to nurse him through his many illnesses.*

A Parisian artist *(below) Reminding his mother that 'At twenty . . . we all thought I was a genius at drawing', Thackeray settled in Paris with his grandmother and 'made believe to be a painter'. Studying and copying old masters in the Louvre, 'It was a very jolly time'.*

She attempted suicide by leaping into the sea where for 20 minutes she floated before being located. She had to be continually watched at her mother's, and was never left in sole charge of the children. At nights, Thackeray tied a ribbon linking their waists lest she made any further suicide attempts.

Thackeray was under enormous pressure, not least from his mother-in-law whom he had always disliked (whenever he wrote about an unhappy marriage there was always a pestering mother-in-law in the background doing her worst). Just as she was instructing him to put Isabella into an asylum, he took the family and fled to the safety of Paris.

His own mother took care of the children from 1840-45 at her home in Paris, while he divided his time between lodgings in London and Paris. From here Thackeray took Isabella round Continental clinics, vainly seeking a cure. In 1845 he gave up. He brought Isabella back to England and consigned her to the care of a Mrs Bakewell. The pressure began to tell; he visited her less and less until, at last he concluded, 'I think it best not to see her'. Nevertheless, her welfare remained of prime importance to him. Insane, Isabella was to outlive him by 30 years.

COMING TO TERMS

Thackeray had been forced to earn his living since he was 22. He worked as a freelance journalist during the early years of his marriage, writing reviews, comic sketches and art criticism for a variety of publications including *The Times* and *Punch*. Writing under pseudonyms, he used the name Michael Angelo Titmarsh (Michelangelo also had a broken nose); it was not until he was 32 that he wrote under his own name.

In 1845, the same year that he settled Isabella's future, Thackeray began *Vanity Fair* – his first major novel. It was published in 20 monthly parts in 1847-8, and was an instant critical success. But the Victorian reading public did not like its cynical attitude to society. And although *Vanity Fair* made Thackeray's literary reputation, it did not make him a vast amount of money. He received £60 for each instalment and £2,000 from the sales of bound editions, which was more than he had ever earned before, but by no means a fortune. Importantly, though, it did mean that as a great novelist, he could now command higher rates than he had previously received.

As a literary celebrity, Thackeray was much in demand by high society. He wrote that he spent his time reeling 'from dinner party to dinner party – I wallow in turtle and swim in claret and Shampang'. But apart from being a larger-than-life public figure, Thackeray was also a devoted and conscientious father to his daughters. At home in Young Street, Kensington, he provided Anny and Minny with 'the best learning of all, love and usefulness . . . and the faith of home, its peaceful rest and helpful strength'.

This initial period of literary fame was also dominated by unrequited love. In 1842, Thackeray's friend from university days, William Brookfield, had introduced him to his wife, Jane. Thackeray's allegiance gradually swayed from husband to wife. It was a relationship in which Thackeray demanded more than Jane was ever prepared to give. She flirted with and confided in him, particularly when she had marriage problems, but they were never lovers. The end came in 1851 when her husband demanded that she finish with Thackeray.

It was in that year that Thackeray hit upon a new way of making money. He undertook a lecture series entitled *The English Humourists of the Eighteenth Century*. The readings in Willis's Rooms, St James's in London

were given on six successive Thursdays at three in the afternoon. They were so successful that the streets outside were packed with the carriages of aristocrats and writers. His enthusiastic audiences would have been shocked to discover that the self-conscious Thackeray thought his lectures worthless 'humbug' and 'quackery'. Nonetheless, they were both profitable and good experience for future lecture tours.

He lectured in America in 1852. The audiences, often numbering 1,200 a night, were as impressed by his appearance – he was six foot, three inches tall, approximately 16 stone, and had a huge head with a fine mop of silvery hair – as by his lectures. Returning home in 1853, aged 42, he was uncertain whether to continue lecturing or writing. He settled for writing *The Newcomes* and set off for Europe with his daughters, to gather source material. On their return to London in 1854 they moved into 36 Onslow Square, Kensington.

Thackeray's life was becoming increasingly punctuated by punishing bouts of illness. They were aggravated by a urethral problem – probably the result of a venereal disease contracted in his youth – and his excessive eating and drinking. While his body was slowly dying on him, his imagination – which he thought had also had its day and become an 'unexploded squib' – suddenly burst back into life.

Outraged by the suffering and injustice of the Crimean war, he lectured on *The Four Georges* in 1855,

Alfred, Lord Tennyson
(above) Thackeray enjoyed the admiration of the greatest writers of his day. Of Pendennis, *Tennyson said, 'It was quite delicious . . . a produce of the Man's Wit & Experience of the World'. He befriended the family.*

Jane Brookfield
(above left) Condemned, in his own words, to a life as a 'grass widower', Thackeray sought comfort from the wife of an old university friend. Her own unhappy marriage led her to welcome his circumspect advances.

Palace Green, Kensington
(right) 'it is one of the nicest houses I have ever seen', enthused Thackeray when buying his last house. The spacious rooms of the 'Palazzo', as the family called it, enchanted him.

saving his finest invective for an attack on George IV and the aristocracy. He was so scathing that London society more or less outlawed him for the next 18 months. Having discharged his radical fury, Thackeray returned to the profitable life of giving lecture tours and sailed for America.

The success of *The Four Georges* and of his standing as a lecturer prompted Thackeray to try for Parliament. He declined to stand at Edinburgh because his liberal views, advocating Sunday entertainment, would have been political suicide in Scotland, but he did fight the

Oxford by-election in 1857. However, the grand literary celebrity found the rough and tumble of street electioneering quite different from lecturing and lost, albeit by 1,005 votes to 1,070.

Thackeray was continually ill at this time. He retched so violently that he was often left 'half dead'. However, illness did not prevent him from editing and writing for the *Cornhill Magazine*, and enjoying the company of his two daughters. And since he was now financially secure, he lent money to his many friends.

In 1862 the Thackerays moved to 2 Palace Green, in Kensington. It became one of London's showpieces with its antique paintings, Corinthian pillars, marble hall and vast fireplaces. He set about a new novel, *Denis Duval*, and visited Rye and Winchelsea in Sussex for background information.

On 21 December, 1863, he dined with Charles Dickens, announcing that he had now completed the first four instalments of his novel. On Tuesday, he attended a funeral at Kensal Green, returning home 'very gentle and sad and cold'. On Wednesday he was ill again – his daughter Anny said that he just 'lay very still with large eyes . . . and said it can't be helped darling'. The following morning, just after she had got up, she heard a 'strange crying sound'. She found him 'lying back with his arms over his head, as if he tried to take one more breath'. He was buried at Kensal Green near his baby daughter Jane who had been brought there 25 years before. Two thousand people attended.

Portrait of an old man
(left) The recurring illnesses of old age kept Thackeray 'squeamish & ill' and confined to his rooms, intensifying the 'deep, steady melancholy of his nature'.

THE WRITER AS ARTIST

Thackeray's early promise lay not in writing but in drawing and painting. In the summer of 1833, he resolved to set up in Paris as an artist. Having left Cambridge without a degree, he felt obliged to assure his mother that in Paris an artist was 'by far a more distinguished personage than a lawyer & a great deal more so than a clergyman'. She was easily persuaded – 'we all thought I was a genius at drawing' – and he had already sold some caricatures.

For three years he studied and copied old masters, generally having a 'jolly time' but growing increasingly disappointed with his 'mean little efforts'. Marriage, and the attendant financial responsibilities, finally ended his artistic aspirations – in 1836 he took a job as Paris correspondent with the *Constitutional and Public Ledger.* Yet art remained an interest throughout his life. He often illustrated his letters, and continued to take pleasure in sketching his family.

A facility for comic drawing
Despite advice from George Cruikshank (Dickens' illustrator), Thackeray could not rise above caricature.

The Shadow of Napoleon

The French Revolution unleashed energies and passions that swept all Europe into war. One figure rose above the tumult to personify the threat, the power and the nameless fears.

The year Thackeray was born, 1811, saw Britain and much of the Continent of Europe engaged in a desperate war with the armies of Revolutionary France – a war that had already raged for 16 years and was to continue for a further six. Although as an infant Thackeray lived in India, remote from war, it fascinated him in later years, and was to play a central role in his masterpiece *Vanity Fair*. In the novel, the great events of the closing years of the wars with Napoleon, from the Battle of Leipzig to Wellington's triumph at Waterloo, are linked with the personal histories of Becky Sharp and Amelia Sedley.

On the whole, the English gentry and bourgeoisie were remarkably untroubled by the war – although a few, like old Mr Sedley in *Vanity Fair*, were financially ruined (or made) by the turn of events, and young aristocrats in their dashing uniforms would set young ladies' hearts aflutter thinking of the dangers their paramours might face. Yet it was a war both Britain and France, the two main protagonists, threw themselves into with great ferocity. Unusual for modern warfare, neither side would settle for less than total victory. It was to be, the British Prime Minister, William Pitt informed the House of Commons early in the war 'a war of extermination'.

'OLD BONEY'

At the centre of the conflict was the figure – small in stature but vast in power and influence – of Napoleon Bonaparte. Napoleon was, some have argued, 'the most powerful genius who ever lived'. A brilliant soldier, his remarkable military victories made many believe he was utterly invincible, as Joe Sedley echoes fearfully on the eve of Waterloo in *Vanity Fair*: "Napoleon! What warrior was there, however famous and skilful, that could fight at odds with him?"

In the minds of many English men and women, though, Napoleon was an evil, ruthless tyrant. To old Mr Sedley, ruined by Napoleon's 'comeback', he was the 'Corsican scoundrel from Elba', while a generation of English nursemaids terrorized naughty children with dire threats of 'Old Boney'. When Thackeray was six, the ship bearing him from India to England stopped at the lonely island of St Helena where Napoleon was

Napoleon Bonaparte
(right) In this magnificent painting, the French painter Jacques-Louis David portrayed Napoleon heroically as the great war leader – a warrior fit to rank with Charlemagne.

Josephine Beauharnais
(left) Soon after he first became famous in 1796, Napoleon married Josephine, the widow of a French aristocrat executed by the Revolution. She bore him two daughters and became his Empress in 1804. But when she failed to give him a son, he annulled their marriage and married the daughter of the Austrian Emperor.

Napoleon at bay
(right) The allies' view of Napoleon, 'the Corsican ogre' was considerably less than heroic – especially after his defeat at Liepzig.

The Battle of the Pyramids
(above) In 1798, Napoleon's expeditionary force swept through Egypt and into Syria. But the defeat of the French fleet at the Battle of the Nile ended the campaign.

in exile after the war. After a long trek across the island, Thackeray's servant pointed out a man walking and whispered to the young boy: 'That is he, that is Bonaparte! He eats three sheep every day, and all the little children he can lay hands on!'

Like his military tactics, Napoleon's career was marked by breathtaking speed. In 1791, at the age of 22, he was a lieutenant in the Revolutionary Army. A year later, he was captain. A year after that he was a national hero. That year, 1793, as Louis XVI went to the guillotine and the Revolution turned increasingly bloody, France was torn by internal rebellion even as she threw down the gauntlet to the world. It was Napoleon who engineered an artillery siege that ensured the capture of the rebellious port of Toulon for the Revolutionary Army.

Further successes elevated him to the command of the French Army of Italy in 1796. In a lightning campaign across northern Italy, he scored a dozen resounding victories in as many months and brought Austria to its knees with an army of less than 30,000 men.

Given command of the French Army of England, he set about planning the downfall of France's greatest enemy. After careful study, Napoleon concluded that a direct assault across the English Channel would fail, so he chose an audacious attack – through Egypt to India, which would devastate Britain's economy.

The French expeditionary force which set sail in May 1798 met with initial success: first Malta, then Alexandria and the Nile delta falling before it. But a crushing defeat at the hands of Horatio Nelson in the Battle of the Nile on 1 August ruined Napoleon's grand design, stranded the army and left him to escape back to France alone.

The failure in Egypt did nothing to diminish his ambitions, nor to harm his prospects. Within a month, he had conspired in a successful *coup d'état* and emerged as First Consul. He went on to become First Consul for Life in 1802 and finally crown himself Emperor in 1804. But from the moment of the *coup d'état* in November 1799, he was effectively master of France.

Revolutionary hero
Though his enemies feared and despised him, there is little doubt that his soldiers – and the risen but leaderless masses of post-Revolutionary France – revered him. His part in the popular uprising that had swept France – to the accompaniment of the guillotine – and his dazzling military successes gave a focus to the enormous energies that had been released. Even Thackeray felt compelled to speak in the Cambridge Union on the subject of 'Napoleon as a Captain, a Lawgiver, and a King merited & received the esteem & gratitude & affection of the French Nation'.

There was only the briefest of pauses while Napoleon consolidated his power. Then, in spring 1800, he struck at the Austrians again, in northern Italy. After struggling through the snow-covered St Bernard Pass, the French fell upon the Austrians and defeated them at Marengo on 14 June. With the Austrians out of the war, Britain and France glared at each other in hatred across the Channel, but it was stalemate – thunder as they might against 'Boney', the British could not challenge him on the Continent, while Napoleon could not bring down 'this nation of shop-keepers' with the British fleet still controlling the seas. In mutual frustration, the two nations signed a peace treaty at Amiens on 25 March 1802.

The peace of Amiens could not last; it was no more than an armed truce between two irreconcilable enemies. A year later, the war resumed, and resumed in such a way as to give the British a real fright. With no-one left on the Continent who dared to fight him, Napoleon concentrated his entire military might on a cross-channel invasion. Over the next two years, a Grand Army was assembled at the Channel ports, and some 2,000 flat-bottomed boats were built to transport 10,000 soldiers across to England.

But to invade England, the French had to control the English Channel. Napoleon's strategy was to lure the British fleet into the Atlantic, so that a combined French and Spanish fleet could sweep unopposed up the Channel to rendezvous with the invasion flotilla. What happened, in fact, was that the French fleet under Admiral Villeneuve was hounded back and forth by Nelson and finally driven to take refuge in Cadiz. On 19 October 1805 Villeneuve ventured forth to do battle – against his better judgement, but on the express orders of an incensed Napoleon. Two days later, his fleet was annihilated off Cape Trafalgar, and the great invasion scare was lifted.

On the Continent the war raged on. Crushing victories over the Austrians at Ülm, and over combined Austrian and Russian forces at Austerlitz on 2 December 1805, made it plain that on land France was still invincible. Prussia entered the fray belatedly in 1806, only to have her armies destroyed at Jena and Auerstadt. And if there was still any doubt as to who was master of Europe, it was settled in the summer of 1807, at Friedland, where the Grand Army inflicted 25,000 casualties on the Russians.

Trafalgar had destroyed Napoleon's hopes of invading Britain, but he might still beat her by wrecking her trade – by totally excluding her from Europe. To do this, he first had to seal off Britain's entry to the west. And so it was that Napoleon turned his gaze on the Iberian peninsular and Portugal, Britain's old ally.

THE PENINSULAR WAR

Within a year, the French had occupied Lisbon; within two, Napoleon's brother Joseph was on the throne of Spain. But then Napoleon encountered a new problem: the Spanish and Portuguese people rose up against the French. The years of savage guerilla warfare that ensued allowed the British to establish a bridgehead on the Continent and made the name of Sir Arthur Wellesley, later the Duke of Wellington, as Commander of the British army in the Peninsular.

Britain's other entry to the Continent was via Russia, where the Tsar, despite the earlier Treaty of Tilsit, turned a blind eye to his merchants' evasion of the trade ban. But if Napoleon's attempt to subjugate Spain and Portugal was a mistake, his move against Russia was a disaster.

Retreat from Moscow
(below) The turning point in Napoleon's career was the terrible retreat from Moscow in 1812, when the Grand Army was decimated by their struggle home in bitter cold and without food.

In Spring 1812, Napoleon amassed a force of half a million men and struck out for Moscow. Seventy five miles short of the goal, on 7 September 1812, one of the goriest engagements of the war was fought to a standstill – the Battle of Borodino. Technically a French victory, since the Russians withdrew leaving Moscow deserted and blazing, it cost Napoleon as dear as any defeat. He held Moscow, it was true, but the Russian capital was a ruin, the Russian army had not come to terms, and worst of all, they had left behind a land ravaged and bereft of food. Napoleon had no alternative but to retreat before the onslaught of the Russian winter. So began one of the most ghastly episodes in the history of war. Starving, freezing, stumbling through blinding snowstorms, harassed on all sides by Russian snipers and decimated by the icy torrents of the river Beresina, the tattered remnants of the Grand Army straggled back to Poland. Of the 600,000 who entered Russia, barely 100,000 returned.

The retreat from Moscow shattered the myth of Napoleon's invincibility, and soon Britain and her allies were closing on his battered army. At the Battle of Leipzig, in October 1813, the Grand Army was smashed; in November, Wellington crossed the Pyrenees; in December, the Prussians crossed the Rhine. Twist and turn as Napoleon might, in a dazzling series of defensive manoeuvres, there was no escape. On 31 March 1814, the victorious allies entered Paris, Napoleon was sent into exile on the isle of Elba, and the powers of Europe sat down in Vienna to divide up the spoils of war.

The myth shattered
(above) The disastrous flight from Russia 'snuffed out' the myth that Napoleon was invincible on land – though he was still yet to be beaten in battle – and opened the way for a renewed allied assault on his decimated army, an assault that was to drive him to exile in Elba.

The Duchess's Ball
(above right) On the eve of Waterloo, while Napoleon's army was launching its first attack on the allies, barely 20 miles away in Brussels, the English were fighting for tickets to the Duchess of Richmond's glittering ball and, in Vanity Fair, *Becky was flirting with George. In the early hours of the morning, many soldiers left the ball for the battle.*

The Congress of Vienna was still sitting ten months later when the news came 'like a bombshell' that Bonaparte had escaped from Elba: "In the month of March, Anno Domini 1815, Napoleon landed at Cannes, Louis XVIII fled, and all Europe was in alarm, and the funds fell, and old John Sedley was ruined." For 100 days, the Napoleonic legend lived again, as the former Emperor gathered an army of peasants and soldiers large enough to "disturb the peace of Europe".

News from Waterloo
(left) When they read of the victory at Waterloo in the Gazette, *'all England thrilled with triumph and fear'. Only later came 'the sickening dismay when the lists of the regimental losses were gone through', naming the dead. Thackeray himself visited the famous battlefield years later – it was a sight that moved him deeply: 'A man of peace has no right to be dazzled by that red-coat glory, and to intoxicate his vanity with . . . carnage and triumph'.*

Wellington boot
(below) The Duke of Wellington was hailed as England's saviour after the victory at Waterloo, and became a hero to many. He also gave his name to a new style of footwear, modelled on his riding boots.

Immediately, the British and Prussians began to remobilize, while Napoleon went on to the offensive, marching his Old Guard into Belgium to confront the armies marshalling against him. Few expected him to move quite so fast and, in Brussels, the British Army, along with the George Osbornes, the Rawdon Crawleys and all of Vanity Fair, were having a ball. "There never was . . . such a brilliant train of camp-followers as hung around the Duke of Wellington's army in the Low Countries in 1815; and led it dancing and feasting, as it were, up to the brink of battle."

On 15 June, while English society revelled at the Duchess of Richmond's ball in Brussels, Napoleon advanced within 25 miles of the city and had already engaged an English troop. The next day, the Prussian army under Blücher was sent scurrying from Ligny while Wellington clung desperately to Quatre Bras. On the 18th, the final confrontation took place at Waterloo, not far from Brussels.

WATERLOO FIELD

"All day long, whilst the women were playing ten miles away, the lines of the dauntless English infantry were receiving and repelling the furious charges of the French horsemen." Then just as all seemed lost, the English were reinforced by the Prussians, and Napoleon's Guard turned and fled.

30 years after the battle, William Thackeray visited Waterloo before starting work on *Vanity Fair*. 'Let an Englishman go and see that field,' he wrote in *Fraser's Magazine*, 'and he *never forgets it*.' Yet Thackeray felt it was wrong to wallow in false glory, condemning it as 'egotistical, savage, unchristian'. 'A man of peace has no right to be dazzled by that red-coat glory, and to intoxicate his vanity with those remembrances of carnage and triumph . . .'

As for Napoleon, he was taken under armed guard aboard *HMS Bellerophon* to the remote isle of St Helena, where the infant Thackeray saw him little more than a year later. Bonaparte died in 1821, a sad embittered man, maintaining to the end that 'If the English had let me, I would have lived in peace.'

CHARLES DICKENS

1812-1870

Charles Dickens was the greatest novelist of his time and is regarded by many as the greatest English writer after Shakespeare. The 'Dickensian' world is entirely his own, peopled with characters larger than life – Mr Micawber, Samuel Pickwick, Ebenezer Scrooge and a host of others. But Dickens was more than just a creator of memorable and colourful characters – he was essentially a subversive writer. He made his readers think and feel and *act* in a way that was new. Though he came to be embraced by the Establishment of his own time, Dickens spent his life fighting its tyranny and injustice. When he died, a cabman's testimonial summed him up: 'Ah, Mr Dickens was a great man and a true friend of the poor'.

Tragedy and Triumph

Dickens achieved immense literary success and public acclaim, but his private life was haunted by traumatic childhood experiences and an unsatisfied quest for emotional fulfilment.

Few writers have written so movingly about, or captured so completely the inner workings of the child's mind as Charles Dickens. Dickens never lost the feeling of what it was like to be a child or to see as a child. And the memory of childhood – 'the best and purest link between this world and a better' – is recollected and retold again and again in his novels and short stories.

Dickens' own childhood began in a tiny terraced house in Landport, near Portsmouth, on 7 February 1812, a few hours after his mother, Elizabeth, had returned from a dance. His father, John Dickens was verbose, kind-hearted, hospitable and generous. He worked as a clerk at the Navy pay office, but he was chronically incapable of living within his means.

The second of seven children, Charles – as he himself said – was 'a very little . . . very sickly boy', subject to violent 'spasms'. These spasms recurred at times of unhappiness and stress throughout his life.

A HAPPY BEGINNING

When Charles was two years old, his father was transferred to London, where the family lived in lodgings in Norfolk Street. Three years later, they settled at Chatham in Kent. Here, Charles spent some of the happiest days of his life. Later, he was to recall those far-off days with almost bitter nostalgia.

But Dickens was no sentimentalist when it came to depicting childhood. He knew from his own experience that fear – fear of the unknown and fear of being ridiculed and of not being understood – plays a large part in the life of a child. Young Charles, an unusually imaginative and sensitive boy, suffered more than most. Nightly, his nurse Mary Weller fed his fertile

A pastoral idyll
(above) In the heart of the Kent countryside that so delighted Dickens as a boy, Rochester and Chatham provide settings for both Great Expectations *and* David Copperfield. *Inclined to be nostalgic, Dickens was to comment later, 'everything wore a richer and more brilliant hue than it is ever dressed in now'. Fond memories of those days led him to buy a second home there.*

Dickens' parents
(right) John and Elizabeth, taken from contemporary engravings. Young Charles accompanied his father to inns and public houses where he sang songs and recited stories, to be tipped with meals and drink. In later life, his parents unashamedly lived on Dickens' credit, even selling scraps of his discarded manuscripts. 'It is a melancholy truth that even great men have their poor relations.'

Marshalsea Prison
(above) Dickens' family was imprisoned here for debt – a trauma he never forgot.

The Blacking Factory
(right) The bitter experience of working here as a boy was to scar Dickens for life.

imagination with ghoulish tales of the occult and of the horrors told her by the midwife and undertaker.

But at this time it seemed as if 'everything was happy'. Not even Dickens' first school – kept by a 'grim and unsympathetic old personage, flavoured with musty dry lavender and dressed in black crape', who 'ruled the world with the birch' – could cloud these idyllic days.

Unable to join in the games of his companions because of his frail physique, Dickens found happiness in reading. 'When I think of it, the picture always arises in my mind of a summer evening, the boys playing in the churchyard, and I sitting on my bed, reading as if for life.'

Together with a love of reading, Dickens delighted in singing, mimicry and recitation. He began performing at home to selected guests, then his proud and boastful father took him to local inns, where, standing on a stool or table, he sang comic songs, or recited short stories learned by heart, for which he would 'be tipped' and treated to a dinner of 'salmon and fowl'.

Acting and entertaining certainly seemed to come more easily to him than scholarship. Dickens disliked school. And the type of school to which he was sent became the subject of his lashing satire, instilling in him a lingering revulsion for the Bible-thumping, kill-joy views of the puritans of his day. To him they were selfish, vain, spiteful and ill-tempered – qualities that he despised above all others.

But school made less of a lasting impression on him than the Kent countryside, the Kent coast and the towns of Rochester and Chatham. Like young Pip in *Great Expectations*, he explored the Kent marshes – that "dark flat wilderness beyond the church" – and at Chatham docks saw prisoners from the prison hulks manacled together.

PAIN AND POVERTY

In 1822, when Charles was ten, the Dickens family moved yet again – to 16 Bayham Street, Camden Town, in London. John Dickens' debts had become so severe that all the household goods were sold, and reduced circumstances and the demands of a growing family left no money to educate Charles.

The family's fortunes plummeted to still greater depths. Mrs Dickens had the desperate and somewhat impractical idea of bolstering their income by starting a school, and so rented a house at 4 Gower Street North, in the more fashionable – and expensive – area of Bloomsbury. The brass plate '*Mrs Dickens' Establishment*' adorned the door, but Dickens later recorded that 'Nobody ever came to the school, nor do I recollect that anybody ever prepared to come . . .'

Unable to pay his debts, John Dickens was taken to the Marshalsea, the debtors' prison, where he was later joined by his wife and children. Two weeks earlier, two days after his twelfth birthday, Dickens had begun work at Warren's Blacking Factory – wrapping shoe-blacking bottles for six shillings a week. It was

Key Dates

1812 born at Landport, near Portsmouth
1817 moves to Chatham, Kent
1822 moves to London
1824 works at Warren's Blacking Warehouse
1828 enters journalism
1830 falls in love with Maria Beadnell
1833 first story published. Breaks with Maria Beadnell
1836 *Sketches by Boz* published. Marries Catherine Hogarth
1837 first child born. Moves to Doughty Street. Mary Hogarth dies
1839 moves to Devonshire Terrace
1842 visits America
1851 father dies. Moves to Tavistock House
1856 buys Gad's Hill
1857 meets Ellen Ternan
1858 first public reading. Separation from Catherine Dickens
1863 mother dies
1865 visits France with Ellen and Mrs Ternan
1867 American reading tour
1870 dies at Gad's Hill

possibly the most traumatic event of his life, and certainly he felt that it was the most shameful. Virtually nobody knew, until his death in 1870, that Dickens had worked at Warren's, an experience he called 'the secret agony of my soul'.

Some six months later, the family's fortunes revived – a small inheritance paid off most of the debts – and the Dickens family emerged from prison. Charles' father removed him from Warren's, although his mother felt that it might be better for him to stay on. Charles never forgave her.

The awful experience at Warren's had a profound effect on Dickens. His obsessive determination never to be short of money, and his stringent attitude to household management (he partly blamed his mother's mismanagement for his father's imprisonment) had their roots in his response to this experience of 'shameful' poverty. His compassion for poor, abused, abandoned children probably originated here, too.

SCHOOLDAYS AND YOUTH

Having removed his son from the warehouse, John Dickens sent him to a nearby private school, Wellington House Academy ('Salem House' in his fictionalized autobiography, *David Copperfield*). A fellow pupil said of him, 'My recollection . . . is of a rather short, jolly-looking youth, very fresh-coloured, and full of fun, and given to laugh immoderately without any apparent reason . . . He was not particularly studious, nor did he show any special signs of ability.'

Three years later, aged 15, Dickens left Wellington House and, through his mother, was found a job as office boy to a firm of solicitors (Ellis & Blackmore) in Gray's Inn. The work was dull and undemanding, but the pay was enough for him to become acquainted with London life. In the music-halls and theatres of the 1820s, Dickens saw at first-hand the young bloods, pimps, prostitutes, drunkards and other examples of low life that were to people his first attempts at fiction.

But he was not happy with the law and had no intention of remaining a clerk all his life, so with a copy of Gurney's *Brachygraphy,* he began teaching him-

48 Doughty Street *(left) Now a Dickens Museum, this was the author's home from 1837-9, where he enjoyed both public acclaim and domestic contentment, and wrote* The Pickwick Papers, Oliver Twist *and* Nicholas Nickleby. *His sister-in-law Mary formed part of the household soon after Dickens' marriage to Catherine Hogarth; she was his ardent admirer and companion until her tragically early death in 1837.*

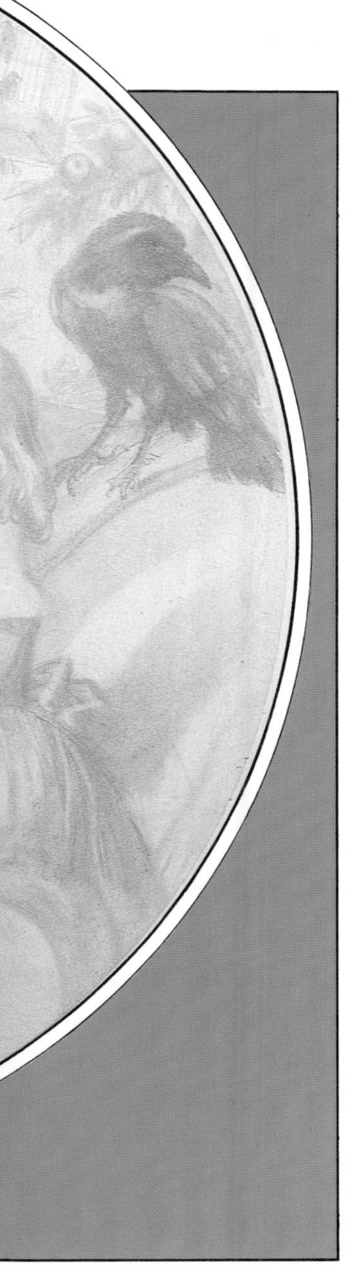

self shorthand, thinking of journalism as a career. He quickly mastered the discipline.

After a brief period with another solicitor, Charles Molloy in Lincoln's Inn, Dickens started work as a freelance reporter in Doctor's Commons – the court where church and nautical cases were heard, and marriage licences to 'love-sick couples and divorces from unfaithful ones', were granted. His contempt for the law was confirmed but, with a ticket to the Reading Room of the British Museum, he set about educating himself. The time spent here, he was later to say, was the most useful of his life.

FIRST LOVE

Now 18, Dickens fell in love with Maria Beadnell, the pretty, bright-eyed daughter of a Lombard Street banker. For four years he courted her, while she, though enjoying his attention, flirted and gossiped and toyed with him, finally snubbing him at his twenty-first birthday party (which he paid for himself), by calling him 'boy' and then leaving early. Heart-broken, Dickens returned her letters.

Few were to know of the pain the affair caused him. Only in middle-age, when he met her again, 'toothless, fat, old and ugly', did he finally exorcise her ghost – though he remained resentful and disillusioned.

Although this event damaged his pride and self-esteem, he had already become one of the foremost reporters of his day. Joining the *Mirror of Parliament* – which reported verbatim on the daily proceedings of Parliament – in 1832, he also contributed to an evening paper, the *True Sun*.

But, just as familiarity with the law had bred contempt, so insights into the workings of the House of Commons and 'honourable' Members of Parliament led to a profound detestation. In his experience, most MPs were 'pompous', with only 'a tolerable command of sentences with no meaning in them'.

Joining the liberal *Morning Chronicle* (second only to *The Times* in circulation), Dickens reported on the nationwide meetings that led to the great Reform Act of 1832. In the days before railways and the telephone, Dickens had to take his copy to London by coach, and it was always a race to see whether he or *The Times* man would file his story first. It was an exciting and heady experience, but though journalism was to remain a lasting passion, it was an anonymous short story that started Dickens' rise to fame.

THE ORIGINS OF MISS HAVISHAM

Miss Havisham, in *Great Expectations*, seems a rather far-fetched figure but Dickens may well have based her on real characters. When Dickens was a boy, a weird old lady, dressed in white, was often to be seen wandering aimlessly near London's Oxford Street. This potent image was reinforced by a report published in *Household Words* in 1850. This told the story of Martha Joaquim, whose lover blew his brains out while sitting next to her: 'From that instant she lost her reason . . . led the life of a recluse, dressed in white and never going out'.

Wilkie Collins' novel, *The Woman in White* – 'the very title of titles', said Dickens – was published just three months before *Great Expectations*. Evidently, the conundrum of these mad women, arrested in time by the traumatic loss of a lover, and dressed in white caught and held Dickens' imagination.

Wilkie Collins
(above) A lengthy correspondence between Dickens and his fellow-author led to the choice of Collins' most famous title, The Woman in White.

The jilted bride
(left) Victims of dashed hopes and unrequited love, real-life women in white haunted Dickens' imagination and inspired the creation of the weird Miss Havisham.

Dickens' children
(above) Kate, Walter, Charles and Mary – shown here in 1841 – were the first four of nine surviving children.

Catherine Dickens
(left) Cruelly rejected by Maria Beadnell, Dickens later courted and married Kate Hogarth, whom he often affectionately addressed in his letters as 'dearest darling Pig'. The match met with approval on all sides, especially since Catherine's father, a journalist himself, recognized and appreciated the young Dickens' talents.

Gad's Hill
(above) John Dickens pointed out this house to young Charles, saying that it might one day be his. Dickens bought it in 1856.

A tribute to success
(right) Spy's sketch of Dickens was made in 1870 – the year of his death – from memory.

Entitled by the publishers 'A Dinner at Poplar Walk', Dickens' first published story appeared in the *Monthly Magazine* in 1833. Though he received no payment for the piece, he was asked to contribute more. Seizing the opportunity, Dickens wrote a series of 'sketches' under the pen-name of 'Boz' (his youngest brother Augustus' nickname). Under the same name, he also contributed short pieces of fiction and reviews to the *Morning Chronicle* and the *Evening Chronicle*, for which he received two guineas a piece in addition to his salary. From these modest beginnings, Dickens' career as a writer took off rapidly. His collected stories were published on his twenty-fourth birthday, in 1836 – under the title *Sketches by Boz*.

SUCCESS AND MARRIAGE

With the money he made from *Sketches by Boz*, and a commission to write 20 monthly instalments of 12,000 words (*The Pickwick Papers*), Dickens felt financially able to marry. On 2 April, 1836, he married Catherine Hogarth, the placid, voluptuous daughter of George Hogarth, the editor of the *Evening Chronicle*.

The marriage lasted until 1858 (when the couple separated) and produced 10 children (one of whom died). It had all the outward signs of happiness and contentment, but was not what Dickens had hoped for.

But in 1837, with the birth of his first son and the publication of *The Pickwick Papers*, which sold 40,000 copies a week, the future looked bright. The young author was fêted everywhere. He commanded a large income, from both his fiction and his journalism.

At his new home, 48 Doughty Street, he lived the life of a gentleman in a household that included his brother, Fred, and his wife's sister, Mary, who at the age of 16 came to keep house.

Dickens developed a strong attachment for Mary, and she for him. To him, she seemed everything that his wife was not – quick, intelligent, and interested in all that he did. When, in May 1837, Mary became ill and died (in his arms), Dickens felt that he had been dealt a blow from which he would never recover. She, or an idealized vision of her, was to remain with him. appearing in his novels as Rose Maylie (*Oliver Twist*),

WIFE AND MISTRESS

Secret guilt tormented Dickens' later years. His wife, Catherine, was a placid and amiable woman but her disorganization and vacuity infuriated him. Agonizing over marital responsibilities and his own ingratitude, his health began to fail.

Dickens' life changed when he met Ellen Ternan, a well-born actress, in 1857. His passion for her led him to re-evaluate his jaded marriage, finding it 'a dismal failure'. At the inevitable separation, he claimed that Catherine was an unfit wife and mother which led to an acrimonious public row. But when Catherine left, her sister Georgiana remained in the marital home, confusing the gossips. Surprisingly, the scandal did little to harm Dickens' popularity.

Dickens never openly declared his love for Ellen but she was a frequent visitor to Gad's Hill. She accompanied him to France – with her mother – and he rented a house for her, with lodgings for himself nearby. It was Ellen who was called to his deathbed and named first in his will.

Mrs Catherine Dickens *in later life. She and Charles separated in 1858.*

Ellen Ternan, *the young actress whose friendship with Dickens lasted until his death.*

Poet's Corner *(right Despite Dickens' contempt for pomp, his grandiose tomb at Westminster Abbey places him among the titans of literature.*

Little Nell (*The Old Curiosity Shop*) and Little Dorrit. His sense of loss led Dickens to view the love between brother and sister as the perfect kind.

ILLNESS AND NOSTALGIA

During the long years spent with Catherine (1836–1858), Dickens achieved the status of the greatest living writer of his day. Despite being plagued by ill-health – suffering from rheumatism of the face, a congenital kidney complaint and a weak heart – his creative energy was boundless. In addition to 10 major novels written during these years and numerous short stories (including the celebrated *A Christmas Carol*), he edited a popular weekly (*Household Words*), started a new national daily newspaper and worked in various charities.

In 1856, Dickens took a step that reunited him with the past. Gad's Hill Place in Kent was a house his father had pointed out to him when he was a boy, saying that it might one day be his when he was rich and famous. Now, rich and famous, he bought the house. After separation from Catherine in 1858, he lived there until his death in 1870.

A year before leaving his wife, Dickens fell in love with a mysterious young actress, Ellen Ternan – mysterious because even now little is known of her or of her life with Dickens. However, the extraordinary lengths to which the couple went to hide their relationship would seem to indicate that they were lovers.

From 1858 onwards, despite recurrent bouts of illness, Dickens threw himself into a series of remarkable public readings of his works to rapturous audiences. He toured England, Scotland, Ireland and the United States, to which he returned in 1867–8.

Prompted partly by financial necessity, the readings gave Dickens the thrill of the footlights, of acting, and of being able to move an audience to both laughter and tears, but it was a punishing programme.

Prematurely aged, and unable to pronounce even the name 'Pickwick', Dickens returned to Gad's Hill Place in 1870. On 8 June he spent the day working on his latest novel, *Edwin Drood*. That evening he collapsed, and the next day he died.

Dickens left a fortune of £93,000 – more than half of which came from the proceeds of his public readings. He was buried, against his wishes, in Westminster Abbey, amid the pomp and ceremony of a system he had spent his life attacking. Two days after his death, Queen Victoria voiced the feelings of many. 'He is a very great loss', she confided to her diary. 'He had a large loving mind and the strongest sympathy for the poorer classes.'

Dickens' London

The noisy, bustling, crowded streets of 19th-century London — to which Dickens felt the 'attraction of repulsion' — were at the heart of his world and a constant source of inspiration.

The London of Dickens' imagination, the London recreated and described in his major novels, is essentially the London of the 1820s – the scene of his childhood and early manhood. It is the portrait of a city not yet hidden under the smog of Victorian prudery – a city brimming with life.

Already the largest city in Europe when Dickens was born in 1812, London was to become the first city in the world by the time of his death. Into this melting-pot poured the rural poor of England and poverty-stricken Ireland, in search of plentiful work building London's railways and the great institutions of the wealthy Empire.

AN EXPLODING POPULATION

Increasing from one to three million in Dickens' lifetime, London's population spread out from the centre, northwards – to Hampstead, Highgate and Kentish Town – and southwards to Clapham, Brixton, Wandsworth and Walworth ("a collection of back lanes, ditches, and little gardens" where Wemmick in *Great Expectations* keeps an eccentric household). Only a generation earlier – the time of the French Revolution – sheep had grazed in Soho Square, and open fields bordered north Oxford Street.

But Dickens' London was essentially the subterranean world of the poor. Huddled together in what came to be known as 'Rookeries' – the poor banded together in large numbers, like rooks – the vast class of London's down-and-outs scratched a living. It was a world of vice and squalor that few of London's respectable classes even knew existed – places like Jacob's Island, a rotting, reeking, rabbit-warren of courtyards and alleyways in Bermondsey where barefoot and half-naked infants splashed about in excrement and slime. It is the London seen by the ragged orphan Oliver Twist.

The ways were foul and narrow; the shops and houses wretched; and people half-naked, drunken, slipshod and ugly. Alleys and arches, like so many cesspools, disgorged their offences of smell and dirt, and life upon the streets; and the whole quarter reeked with crime, and filth and misery.

And festering in the heart of London was the most notorious 'Rookery' of all, Seven Dials – the area at the top of St Martin's, close to Covent Garden – where Dickens witnessed 'wild visions of wickedness, want and beggary'. Here over 3,000 people were packed into fewer than a hundred houses. When on one occasion a house caught fire, 37 men, women and children were found occupying a single room – with just one shilling between them all. It was conditions like these, as Dickens recognized, that provided an ideal breeding ground for crime and prostitution.

Not surprisingly in a city overpopulated and poorly housed, disease was rife. Infant mortality was common – a fact noted in many of Dickens' novels – and the city suffered from periodic epidemics of typhus, cholera and smallpox. The major cause of disease was bad drainage and inadequate sanitation. Between Putney

Public executions
(right) The 'wickedness and levity' of the crowds gathering at these events appalled Dickens. Street hangings were a common feature of London until 1869.

High society
(below) The elegance of Regent Street, built in Dickens' youth, testified to the wealth of the largest city in the world. Running north from Piccadilly Circus, Regent Street was one of the thoroughfares separating fashionable London from the more squalid suburbs.

On the streets
(above) 'Costermongers', street traders, pick-pocket and child crossing-sweepers were all part of the shifting population of London's changing streets.

'The Rookeries'
(left) Wild Court, Seven Dials – where up to 40 people occupied a single room, and Dickens witnessed 'wild visions of wickedness'.

Waifs and strays
(below) Pathetic, destitute, abandoned children were, Dickens said, 'one of the worst sights in London'.

and Blackwall, 369 sewers discharged their effluent into the River Thames, together with waste from tar and tanning factories and slaughterhouses.

Yet at low tide, the scummy mud banks of the pestilent Thames provided a 'living' of sorts for one of the many species of scavengers infesting London – the so-called 'Mudlarks', mainly young children who sifted the sewer exits for saleable items, or stole pieces of coal from barges.

THE UNDERWORLD

The 'low girls' who plied their trade at Seven Dials were just a few of the vast army of prostitutes that walked the streets of London in Dickens' time. Writing in 1851, Dickens' contemporary, Henry Mayhew, in his *London Labour and London Poor,* calculated that there were some 80,000 'board lodgers', 'sailors' women', or 'dolly mops' (some barely in their teens) in London alone. These women were not confined to the poorer parts, either. The greatest number was to be found in 'the brilliant gaiety of Regent Street and the Haymarket' where streetwalkers catered for all pockets and tastes, while private establishments conducted their business in a more leisurely manner.

While Dickens avoided any specific portrayal of prostitutes in his writing, their plight – caught as they were in a web of poverty, destitution and disease – prompted him to act. In 1846 he helped the wealthy philanthropist Angela Burdett Coutts to establish a home for fallen women (known as Urania Cottage) in Shepherd's Bush. Dickens had few illusions about what could be done, but he hoped that care, sympathy and understanding would encourage them to start a new life in Australia or to marry and settle down.

Prostitution was by no means the only social problem endemic in the poorer parts of the city. Thieves, burglars, forgers, card-sharps and con-men abounded. Mayhew did not even attempt to number them, though Dickens was to chronicle their activities and describe their haunts in his radical journalism of the 1850s and in short pieces such as *A Night Scene in London* (1856). There were, according to police estimates, some 3,000 houses of 'bad character' which were likely to receive stolen goods. The 'Rookeries' served as refuges for many gangs (such as that run by the malevolent Fagin in *Oliver Twist*), who could elude pursuit in the sunless labyrinths and enjoy the hospitality of 'flash houses' – establishments that combined the appeal of the public house and the brothel as well as providing exits for customers on the run.

In Dickens' youth, the 'Robin Redbreasts', red-waistcoated Bow Street runners, failed to stem the London crime wave. However, matters improved somewhat with the introduction, in 1829, of 'bobbies' or 'peelers' (so-called after the Home Secretary of the day, Sir Robert Peel).

Those who fell into the arms of the law received little mercy – harsh retribution was the stock-in-trade of a perverse, tyrannical and unforgiving legal system. Jaggers' character and the nature of 'Little Britain' in *Great Expectations* was no exaggeration. Britain's prisons were among the worst in Europe, and London's Newgate (to which Dickens was a frequent visitor) was one of the worst in Britain. These centres of human degradation were specifically designed to deter the would-be criminal and were made so appalling that no-one could tolerate a return visit. It was a policy that Dickens, surprisingly, endorsed – though he did campaign vigorously against capital punishment and the popular public hangings, then a feature of London life. When George Manning and his wife were 'topped' at Horsemonger Lane in 1849, Dickens was just one of 30,000 Londoners who witnessed the scene. 'The conduct of the people', he wrote in a letter to *The Times,* 'was so indescribably frightful, that I felt for some time afterwards almost as if I were living in a city of devils.'

"AN AMAZING PLACE"

The Londoners who people the pages of Dickens' fiction – from Sam Weller, the cheerful cockney in *The Pickwick Papers* (1837), to John Jasper, who visits the opium dens of the Docklands in *The Mystery of Edwin Drood* (1870) – were observed by Dickens at first hand on his energetic walks through the city. He would think nothing of covering eight to ten miles a night, northwards to Highgate or westwards to Fulham, to clear his mind after a day's writing and to gather fresh impressions which were later woven into his novels.

Life in all its shapes and forms crowded the noisy, bustling, streets of London. Some 30,000 'costermongers' engaged in the sale of fruit, vegetables, and fish. Notoriously a turbulent tribe, politically radical, and sworn enemies of the police, they kept themselves to themselves, separate even from other street folk.

Jostling with the 'costers' for custom were traders and hawkers selling their wares. Beggars were also a

The railway boom
(below) The railways changed the face of Dickens' London – thousands of homes were swept aside to make way for them.

common sight, and they would often fake afflictions to gain sympathy – and a few pennies.

London, as David Copperfield observed, was "an amazing place", richer in wonderment "than all the cities of the earth". The sights that had delighted the young Dickens in his youth – the street entertainers, musicians, dancers, clowns and acrobats, as well as showmen with mini-theatres such as Punch and Judy and the marionettes of the Fantoccini Man – were still a feature of the Victorian City.

The noise that bombarded the pedestrian was deafening. Coaches, private carriages, hackney cabs, carts and wagons clattered through thoroughfares, many still narrow and winding. Congestion was frequent, and lack of regulation often led to chaos as omnibuses crossed from the left-hand side to the right, obligingly dropping passengers at their doorsteps.

London's entertainments *(left and below) Dickens loved the theatre – a passion shared by high-brow and low-life alike. With London's theatre, the two worlds could collide: young bloods would mingle with prostitutes and drunks in the coffee-houses close to the theatres, such as this one near the Olympic.*

It was all, as Dickens said, like a marvellous magic lantern – a stimulus to his work that he found difficult to do without when abroad or even when staying in the country for any length of time. 'Put me down to Waterloo Bridge at eight o'clock in the evening,' he wrote to his friend John Forster from Italy, 'and I would come home . . . panting to go on. I am sadly strange as it is, and can't settle.'

CITY OF CHANGE

With success, Dickens left the back streets of Camden Town – where he had lived as a boy – far behind. After writing *Pickwick Papers* and *Oliver Twist* he moved first to 1 Devonshire Terrace, a splendid Nash building near to Regent's Park. In 1851 he moved to the larger Tavistock House in Tavistock Square, on the borders of Bloomsbury. But the life that he led here and in fashionable society – riding in the new hansom cabs, and shopping at Fortnum and Mason's – seems not to have stirred his imagination at all. It was the poorer, but more colourful, districts which repelled but also attracted him, to which he returned time and again for inspiration.

In the 58 years of Dickens' life, London underwent drastic changes. Many of London's landmarks were new, or of very recent vintage, when Dickens was young: Regent Street, Regent's Park with its spacious terraces, Buckingham Palace, the Haymarket, Trafalgar Square and Nelson's Column (erected in 1843) and the new House of Commons – built on the ashes of the old (where Dickens had been a reporter) in 1834.

Reforms and improvements urged upon a reluctant government by Dickens and other humanitarian reformers – slum clearance, decent sanitation, adequate street lighting and proper policing – had been carried out. There were still great stretches of slums, but some of the worst were knocked down to make way for

Covent Garden *(above) "when it was market morning was wonderful company." (*Uncommercial Traveller*).*

new thoroughfares – and the first 'model' housing developments were laid out. After the 'Great Stink' of 1858, when an exceptionally hot dry summer forced a mass evacuation from the Thames – and the Houses of Parliament – a new and effective main drainage system was devised. Respectable opinion finally put an end to public executions in 1869. The Victoria, Albert and Chelsea Embankments were constructed and more and more bridges spanned the Thames. The great London railway termini were built, and the new suburban lines and the Underground Railway (opened in 1863) advanced the revolution in communications.

Consequently, Dickens' Londoners lived in a world more exciting but also more precarious than their ancestors'. In the commercial and financial heart of the first-ever industrial nation, there were opportunities galore for the energetic or rich. But there were also new insecurities as booms and slumps alternately created business empires and bankruptcies, good wages followed by unemployment – reversals of fortune that play so large a part in Dickens' novels. Thousands lost their homes as those new thoroughfares and housing developments were laid out, and many more thousands were dispossessed when whole communities were destroyed to make way for London's railway system. Existence in London was taking on the rootless, anonymous quality now associated with big cities everywhere.

Dickens was the first novelist to chronicle the life of London. For millions of readers he charted a strange and unknown land full of mystery and terror. 'Life in London as revealed in the pages of Boz,' wrote Richard Ford of the influential *Quarterly Review*, 'opens a new world to thousands bred and born in the same city. . .for the one half of mankind lives without knowing how the other half dies'. And Dickens' popularity (his publishers Chapman and Hall sold 4,239,000 volumes in the first twelve years after his death) ensured that his view of the city became familiar to the whole nation. As his contemporary Walter Bagehot wrote, 'Dickens describes London like a special correspondent for posterity'.

Newgate prison
(above) The most notorious of London's prisons, Newgate both fascinated and revolted Dickens. In Great Expectations, *the "grim stone building" near Jaggers' office is one of Pip's first sights of the City. "This was horrible, and gave me a sickening idea of London."*

DICKENS' LONDON TODAY
1: 48 Doughty Street. Dickens' home from 1837-9 is now a museum.
2: Seven Dials. The dense labyrinth of slums was a focus of Dickens' interest in crime.
3: Adelphi Theatre. Dickens' love of the theatre inspired his public readings. The Adelphi is mentioned in *The Pickwick Papers.*
4: Lincoln's Inn. The heart of the English legal system in *Bleak House.*
5: St Dunstan's, Fleet Street. The church that inspired *The Chimes* also occurs in *David Copperfield.*
6: St Paul's Cathedral occurs in many of the novels.
7: The Guildhall houses the City Giants, Gog and Magog, in *Pickwick Papers.*
8: The George Inn. A galleried inn of the type visited by Mr Pickwick.

ANTHONY TROLLOPE

1815-1882

Convinced, with good reason, that he was unloved and unregarded, Anthony Trollope struggled long and hard for a foothold in the world. But his vast resources of energy and dogged hard work broke down the barriers to success and found him loved, fêted and avidly read. His labours were Herculean. He pitted himself against Time to produce a library of books about credible people and their credible foibles. His readers responded by recognizing Trollope as a shrewd, honest, wry portrayer of English life.

'A Good Roaring Fellow'

Disregarded and undervalued, Trollope suffered a childhood of neglect and poverty. By sheer hard work, he achieved personal happiness and literary success, earning the accolade 'a Trojan of a man'.

The life of Anthony Trollope might have been written by a novelist, or conceived by a writer of fairy tales. Neglected and unloved by his parents, he survived a childhood of unrelieved misery. At school he suffered almost every form of injustice which small boys are capable of perpetrating against one another. In his youth and early manhood he felt himself to be a failure, his life not worth living. Then suddenly and dramatically, his fortunes changed. In a few short years he found wealth, a wife, happiness and a creative energy almost unique in the history of literature.

Anthony Trollope was born in Keppel Street, Bloomsbury, London, on 24 April 1815, the fourth child in a family of six. Thomas, the eldest, was born in 1810 and was his mother's favourite. Only he and Anthony survived past maturity.

Their father, Thomas Trollope, was a conscientious and serious barrister, but with an extraordinarily difficult temperament. His hectoring, arrogant manner proved a severe handicap to his career – so much so that his practice failed totally. Rather in the manner of Dickens' character Pip, he had 'great expectations'. In this, as in almost everything, he was to be disappointed. The inheritance he believed to be his slipped through his fingers when his childless benefactor remarried unexpectedly at the age of 60 and fathered six children. The disappointment deepened a constitutional gloom such that it was said of him by his eldest son that he induced a state of acute anxiety in all those who were thrust into his company.

After a series of unsuccessful attempts to revive the family fortunes, Thomas Trollope retreated into a solitary and unreal world, writing a monumental encyclopedia of all known ecclesiastical terms. When he died at the age of 61 he had just reached the letter 'D'.

A FORMIDABLE MOTHER

Anthony's mother, Mrs Frances Trollope, was another formidable personality. She was devoted to her husband, energetic, pretty, strong-willed and hopelessly extravagant. Unable to live within her means, it was her recklessness with money, as much as her husband's ineptitude, that caused their financial ruin. And although she was devoted to Tom, her eldest son, to Anthony she showed an indifference bordering on negligence.

With such parents it is scarcely surprising that Trollope's early years were disturbed. Tired of his failing career, Mr Trollope rented a tract of farm land near Harrow on which he built a large house, 'Julians'. From here all three Trollope boys (Tom, the second son Henry and Anthony) were sent to Harrow, the fashionable public school. As day-boys they paid no fees, and were looked down upon by the other boys. To make matters worse, they were badly clothed, with

Key Dates

1815 born London

1822-34 educated at Harrow and Winchester

1834 joins Post Office

1841 sent to Ireland

1844 marries Rose Heseltine

1857 writes *Barchester Towers*

1861 elected to the Garrick Club

1863 mother dies

1867 resigns from Post Office. Edits *St Paul's Magazine*

1868 stands as Liberal candidate for Beverley

1871 visits Australia

1875-76 writes his *Autobiography*

1880 moves to Harting Grange, Sussex

1882 dies in London

Frances Trollope *(left) This resourceful mother was forced to draw on every ounce of her remarkable stamina. But for Anthony she had little maternal feeling, and later did not even read his books.*

Harrow School *Here Trollope suffered "a daily purgatory". An atmosphere of barbaric violence prevailed (right) and he was despised as a day-boy. A contemporary recalled, 'He gave no sign of promise whatsoever . . . and was regarded by masters and boys as an incorrigible dunce.'*

The Post Office
Trollope escaped the horrors of schooling when he was given a clerk's job at St Martin's-le-Grand in London (above), the administrative heart of the Post Office.

shoes always down at heel. Even in old age neither Tom nor Anthony was able to forget or forgive their father for having sent them there.

When he was 10, Trollope was sent on to Winchester, his father's old school. He fared better there, but not much. His elder brother was a prefect at the school and his mother had urged him to watch over Anthony. This he did with a vengeance. Anthony was to write years later in his *Autobiography*, 'in those school-days he [Tom] was, of all my foes, the worst . . . Hang a little boy for stealing apples, he used to say, and other little boys will not steal apples . . . The result was that, as part of his daily exercise, he thrashed me . . .'

OVERSEAS FOLLIES

Anthony was still at Winchester when his mother conceived the idea of opening an emporium in Cincinnati in the United States. She travelled there, and her husband and her children followed – except Anthony. He was left behind to fend for himself. From the age of 12 to 15, he never saw his mother. After two years the Trollopes returned to England, having lost what little money they had. But the time had been considerably worse for Anthony.

While the family was away, Anthony's school fees were not paid; local tradesmen ceased to give him credit and his pocket money was stopped. He had no home to go to during the school holidays, and spent one summer vacation wandering about the deserted law buildings of Lincoln's Inn, his father's old chambers. Suicide seemed a possible escape: 'how well I remember all the agonies of my young heart; how I considered whether I should always be alone; whether I could not find my way to the top of that college tower, and from thence put an end to everything?'

Clerical drudgery
(right) Office work did not suit his temperament. He found it very hard to "live in London, keep up my character as a gentleman, and be happy" on £90 a year. With his family abroad, he eked out a seedy, listless existence in lodgings. At this low point, he wrote nothing, convinced of his worthlessness.

On the family's return, Anthony was removed from Winchester, penniless and in disgrace, and sent once more to the much-hated Harrow. From 'home', a small, derelict farmhouse, he walked to school every day in battered boots and mud-stained clothes. 'Poor Trollope was tabooed', recalled a classmate. 'He gave no sign of promise whatever . . . I avoided him for he was rude and uncouth.'

Back at home in England, Frances Trollope wrote *Domestic Manners of the Americans,* and on the strength of its great success, 'Julian's Hill', a larger, more comfortable house, was acquired. But within two years, the accumulated debts of a lifetime caught up with the Trollopes. Fearing imprisonment in the Marshalsea – the debtors' prison in London known intimately to Dickens' parents – the family escaped to Bruges in Belgium before the bailiffs arrived. Anthony remained in England, alone.

Oxford would have been open to Trollope had his schooling not been bungled. Instead, when he was 19, his mother obtained a commission in the Austrian cavalry for him, and also used her influence to arrange an interview for him at the General Post Office in St Martin's-le-Grand, London. Anthony chose the Post Office position although his education had done very little to equip him for any career. Asked to produce a sample of his handwriting, Trollope managed only a smudged, blotted scrawl. Totally ignorant of even simple arithmetic, he was relieved when told that he would not be tested until the following day, and even more relieved when on returning the next day he was informed that the test had been waived.

GOING TO WASTE

After ten years of schooling, Trollope had acquired only a shaky grasp of Latin and Greek; no other subject had been included in the curriculum. At 19, however, he joined the Post Office. He was to remain in its service for the next 33 years.

Little was expected of him, although even that he found difficult. Being polite and obsequious – the only qualities demanded of a very junior clerk – did not come naturally to him. The work was dull and repetitive, and he loathed it. Alone in London, living in miserable digs off the Marylebone Road, he felt his life wasting away.

Outside office hours he went for long walks (sometimes covering as much as 30 miles a day), got drunk on gin, and read. But it was no life for someone of his energies and talents. At 24, feeling his life to be not worth living, he suffered an illness which nearly killed him. What the illness was, no-one knew, but it was probably connected with his state of mind at the time. Apart from the circumstances of his daily life, he had much to be depressed about. His brother Henry had died a lingering, painful death from consumption in Bruges, and his father had fallen ill and died shortly afterwards. Negligent as ever, so far as Anthony was concerned, his mother did not think of summoning him to either his father's or his brother's funeral.

At 26 it seemed that Anthony Trollope was destined to follow in his father's footsteps – to be a disappointed and frustrated man. But then a vacancy for a Post Office Surveyor's clerk occurred in the south of Ireland, and to his astonishment he was given the job.

Ireland was to be the making of Trollope. As luck would have it, he was asked to carry out many of the duties of the Surveyor, whose job it was to travel the region on horseback inspecting post offices, investigate complaints and chart new postal routes. Trollope loved almost every aspect of the work: the open air, the people he encountered and the handsome salary he was paid. It was here too that he was introduced to hunting – a passion that was to remain with him for the rest of his life.

In Ireland, all Trollope's longings and latent powers

A HOUSEHOLD NAME

The daughter of an eccentric country parson, Frances 'Fanny' Trollope was an unusually free-thinking woman for her time. She emigrated to America with her children (except Anthony) to join an idealistic community. She found conditions there "vividly dreadful", but was determined to open a general store in Cincinnati. It failed. Returning to England aged 52, she wrote, in sheer desperation, a first book: *Domestic Manners of the Americans*. The Americans hated her for it, and years later, when Anthony visited the States, they were still smarting at her insults. But it was a best-seller in Britain and was followed by 40 more books. Her novels annoyed the Establishment, for they made outspoken attacks on child labour and the New Poor Law. In later years she lived in Florence with her eldest son, Tom, at the Villino Trollope.

'The Factory Boy'
(left) Social injustice was a favourite target for Fanny's writing. She wrote vigorous, hard-hitting books with plenty of violence and pathos. Most were illustrated by her companion in Cincinnati, Auguste Hervieu.

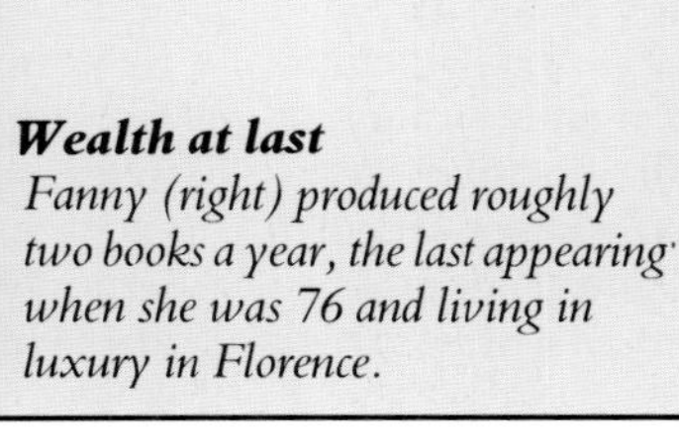

Wealth at last
Fanny (right) produced roughly two books a year, the last appearing when she was 76 and living in luxury in Florence.

Travels abroad
Post Office business took Trollope to many far-flung places. When sent to Egypt (left) he took the opportunity of making a private excursion to the Holy City, Jerusalem.

Rose Heseltine
(above) Trollope met his future wife, the daughter of a bank manager, while living in Ireland. Their marriage produced two children and lasted the rest of Trollope's life.

Riding to hounds
(above) While in Ireland, Trollope took up hunting, and came to "love it with an affection which I cannot myself fathom". Despite his being heavy, short-sighted and often short of funds, "Nothing has ever been allowed to stand in the way of hunting".

were realized. He was a changed man. In place of the shy, retiring, nervous youth, unsure of himself and of his place in the world, a big, blustering man appeared, exuding energy and self-confidence. He began to enjoy life to the full.

Within months of his arrival, he met his future wife. Little is known of Rose Heseltine, the daughter of a Rotherham bank manager. Several years his junior, she was small, attractive, shrewd and witty. Whether they continued to be happy or contented together is not known, but their marriage lasted from 1844 to Trollope's death. They had two sons, Henry, born in 1846 and Frederick, in 1847.

Trollope always claimed that before September 1843 he had never put pen to paper. By the time of his marriage, however, he was more than half-way through his first novel, *The Macdermots of Ballycloran.* His mother arranged for its publication, but did not bother to read his work.

A NEW DEPARTURE

If literary success was not instant, Trollope's career at the Post Office prospered. In 1851, he was given the job of reorganizing the postal service in south-west England, and in 1854 was promoted to Surveyor. It was while visiting Salisbury that the idea of 'Barchester' was first formed. With the publication of the first of the Barchester novels *The Warden*, in 1855, his name began to be noted in the literary world. And with *Barchester Towers* (1857) he became more widely known to the reading public.

In old age, Trollope claimed that from his youth his life had been unusually happy, although there is little evidence to support this. He did have a rare talent for enjoying himself, but his ceaseless activity and obsession with work may have fulfilled a psychological need. It was as if he feared idleness, or that too much time on his hands would plunge him into feelings of insecurity or depression.

Appointed Chief Surveyor in charge of the eastern counties, he moved, in 1859, to Waltham House in Waltham Cross, Hertfordshire. Here he enjoyed the best years of his life. His daily timetable was gruelling in the extreme, yet he thrived on it. It began at 5am with a cup of coffee. At 5.30 he was at his desk reading and revising the previous day's work. At 9.30 he stopped writing, having completed 2500 words. After a substantial breakfast, he took the train to London,

Love and approbation
Trollope craved affection and, in mid-life (left), won it in plenty. One friend called him 'a good roaring fellow', another 'crusty, quarrelsome, wrong-headed, prejudiced, obstinate, kind-hearted and thoroughly honest'. "The Garrick Club [right] was the first assembly of men at which I felt myself popular," wrote Trollope (standing fourth from left). His illustrator, John Everett Millais, leans on his cue, far right.

arriving at his office at 11.30. Working to 5.00pm he then retired to the Garrick Club for tea and a rubber of whist, returning home for dinner at 8.00pm.

Trollope entertained lavishly, and enjoyed eating and drinking. When a guest once remarked that he seemed to enjoy a healthy appetite, he replied in typically bluff manner, 'Not at all, madam, but, thank God I am very greedy.'

Two days a week he forgot the cares of the Post Office, and hunted in the company he enjoyed best – farmers and country gentlemen. He also found time to travel extensively, combining official business with pleasure. Often accompanied by his wife, he would go armed with a commission to write a travel book. He visited Egypt, the West Indies, America (twice), Australia (twice, staying with his son Frederick, a sheep farmer) and South Africa. In addition, he was a regular visitor to his mother and brother Tom at the family villa (Villino Trollope) in Florence, where in 1860 he met Kate Field, a young, rich and cultured American.

A CHOSEN FRIEND

In his *Autobiography*, he described her as 'one of the chief pleasures . . . of my later years.' To him she was 'my most chosen friend . . . a ray of light'. At the time of their meeting Kate was 21, he 45. Their relationship was almost certainly platonic. But they wrote to each other frequently. They met seldom – when he visited America, or she London or together at the 'Villino Trollope' in Florence. He assumed the role of teacher and advisor to her. She never married, but continued to intrigue and court the attention of famous men, and women, throughout her life.

In his career, things went well but not to the extent he might have wished. Promotion to the highest level at the Post Office eluded Trollope, and he never made as much money from his books as Dickens and Wilkie Collins had. But he seemed satisfied with his lot, as

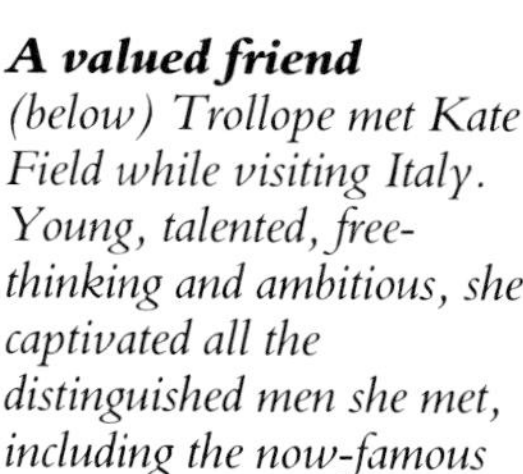

A valued friend
(below) Trollope met Kate Field while visiting Italy. Young, talented, free-thinking and ambitious, she captivated all the distinguished men she met, including the now-famous novelist.

Visit to Australia
(above) Anthony's son Fred emigrated to Australia to run a sheep farm. He was notably unsuccessful, and lost his father a lot of money. Two visits by Anthony and Rose, however, were cheerful excursions and gave rise to a travel book and two novels, the best of which was John Caldigate.

Parliament [should be] the highest . . . ambition of every educated Englishman'). He lost badly, coming bottom of the poll.

Having retired early, Trollope forfeited his pension. He sold Waltham House and moved to Montague Square in London. From here he continued to write, to attend his clubs – the Garrick and Athenaeum – for tea, whist and conversation. But as his health deteriorated, he was advised to move to the country. He took a renovated farm-house. 'Harting Grange', near the Hampshire/Sussex border. But away from his beloved clubs and the noise and bustle of London, he became bored. With few visitors and little to do, he aged rapidly. He continued writing, but in his heart felt that life was slipping away.

NO MORE WORDS

His wife arranged for him to stay for a while at Garlands Hotel in the West End of London, hoping that back in the city his spirits would revive. He visited his clubs again and dined out, but at Alexander Macmillan's, the publisher's, he suddenly fell off his chair, one evening, paralyzed down his right side. Rushed to hospital, he lingered there for a month, unable to speak a word – dying on 6 December 1882. For a man who gloried in language, it was a painfully silent death.

A tribute in the magazine *Vanity Fair* during his life paid him a grudging compliment which Trollope may have prized above any other: 'His manners are a little rough, as is his voice, but he is nevertheless extremely popular among his personal friends'. All his life, Trollope had wanted just that.

novels continued to pour from his pen at a remarkably regular rate. He rode with the hunt well into his 60s, and loved the activity "with an affection which I cannot myself fathom".

In 1867 Trollope resigned from the Post Office. Resentment at having been passed over in promotion may have been part of the reason, but a more practical one was the offer of the editorship of the *St Paul's Magazine*. It proved to be a false step. Trollope lacked the necessary qualities to make a good editor, and the magazine failed. He then stood as a Liberal candidate for Parliament ('I have always thought that to sit in . . .

Fact or Fiction

THE REAL BARCHESTER

In 1852 Trollope visited Salisbury and, "wandering there one midsummer evening . . . I conceived the story of *The Warden* . . . stood for an hour on the little bridge and . . . made out the spot on which Hiram's Hospital should stand". But in the book, he likens Barchester to "Wells or Salisbury, Exeter, Hereford or Gloucester". There is no real Barchester. It was invented by a man who "never lived in any cathedral city – except London".

Look-alikes

The Bishop of Clifton declared he knew Barchester to be Wells in reality, for it had two towers. Trollope retorted that it was not Wells at all, but Winchester (below).

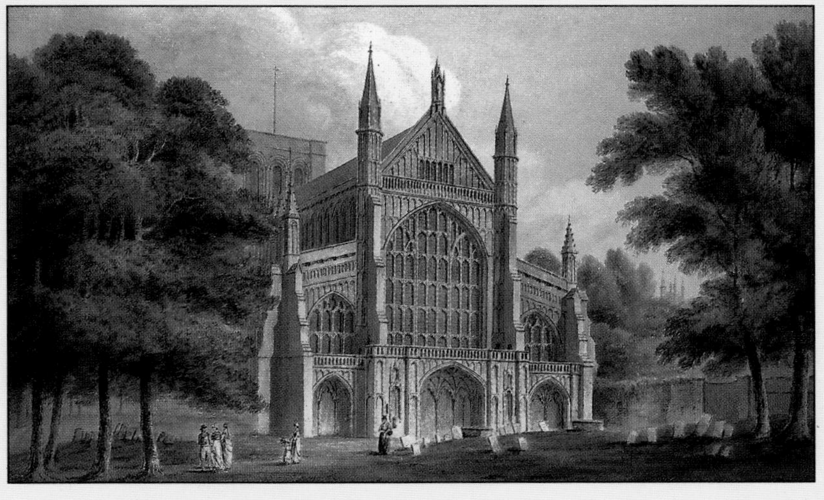

The Postal Boom

The postal reforms of the 1840s and 50s ushered in a new era for the Post Office – postage was cheaper, services became more efficient and the number of letters mailed virtually tripled.

Trollope's energies were, for most of his life, divided between writing and his work for the Post Office. Despite a clash of personalities with his renowned but dour boss, Rowland Hill, he undoubtedly made great contributions to the organization of the national and international postal system. He is even reputed to have invented the pillar box. His lifetime spanned the single most vital period in the development of postal services, and although something of this was due to the calibre of such men as Trollope and Hill, advances came also in response to social change. During Trollope's life, Britain and its Empire were transformed from a group of isolated communities into an interdependent whole.

The news of Anthony Trollope's birth in 1815 would have been learned by relatives around the county by letter. The letters would have travelled by stage-coaches which sped night and day along Britain's great post-roads. The 17th century had seen the creation of the General Post Office – a public service under government control. The 18th century had seen a vastly improved road network and the system of 'post boys' on horseback replaced by stage-coaches. Every night, at exactly 8 o'clock, mail coaches left London for all parts of Britain. They were kept to schedule with the aid of time-pieces which could only be unlocked by supervisors at the various staging posts along their routes.

By 1797, 42 such routes were in operation. Journey times were kept to a minimum: 27 hours from London to Holyhead and 43 hours from London to Edinburgh. Everything was done to minimize delay. Teams of horses could be changed in two minutes. Village mail was dropped off and taken aboard without the coach even stopping. And despite this being the era of the highway robber, the mail coaches had a well-deserved reputation for efficiency, punctuality and reliability. There were still many grounds for complaint and aspects which cried out for improvement. Letters were paid for at the receiving end, and charged according to the number of sheets and the mileage that had been covered, which often proved to be uneconomic. Postage could cost less on a short letter going from London to Edinburgh than for a long one going from London to Kent. Additionally, letters might be refused by their recipients, much as a reverse-charge phonecall might be refused today: then the letter had to be returned to sender without any recompense to the Post Office. The postal system did not seem to be keeping up with the needs of a modern, industrial economy. Another problem was that it favoured the weal-

The pillar box
(above) Based on an idea by Trollope, the pillar box was instituted in the 1850s. Prior to that, letters had to be taken to receiving stations or to 'bellmen' – roving, bell-ringing postmen.

Sir Rowland Hill
Disliked by Trollope, Hill (left), was an impassioned reformer whose commitment to improving the postal system bordered on an obsession.

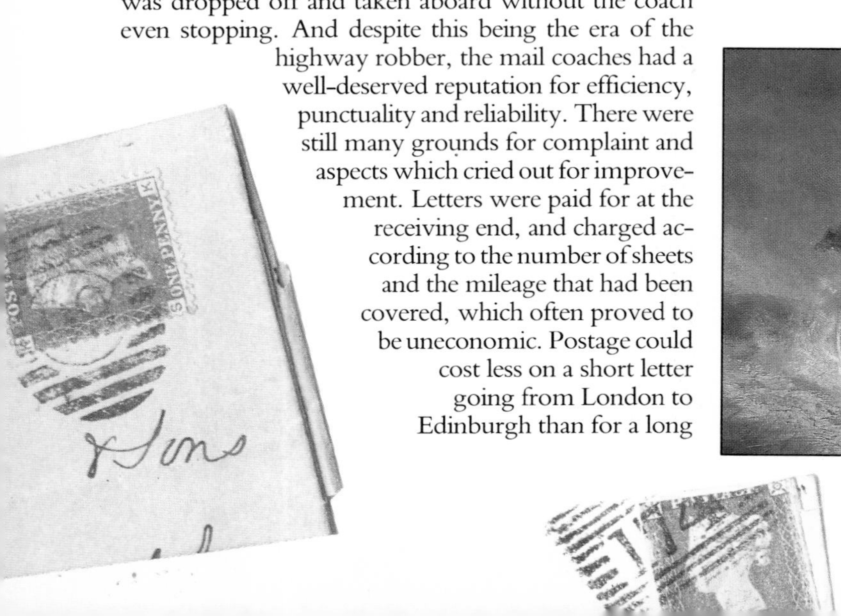

The General Post Office
This crowded scene (above) shows the range of Londoners who rushed to catch the post just before closing time at 6 o'clock.

Post boys
(left) In the early 18th century letters were carried across the land on horseback. Progress was slow, riders were unarmed and robbery was commonplace. A Parliamentary Act of 1765 insisted that post boys should not loiter on the roads, nor 'wilfully misspend' their time, nor cover less than 6 miles an hour.

The Royal Mail
John Palmer, born in Bath in 1742, first suggested the use of stage-coaches for transporting mail. Mail coaches were duly tested in 1784 and proved an immediate success. With a team of four horses and an armed guard, the post was conveyed to its destination in safety and what seemed at the time remarkable speed.

thy. By reducing and standardizing postal rates, Hill envisaged social benefits as well as financial ones. The working class would be encouraged to keep in touch with friends and relatives by letter and consequently greater literacy would be fostered.

ROWLAND HILL

The man who mobilized public opinion and the government was (Sir) Rowland Hill. He was one of those extraordinary Victorian supermen, with interests including printing, astronomy, mathematics, transportation and taxation. In 1837 he privately issued a little book entitled *Post Office Reform: its Importance and Practicability* (officially published the following year). In it he suggested a blindingly simple system. Postage should be pre-paid, and letters should be charged by weight only. For a flat rate of one penny, letters of less than half an ounce should be carried anywhere inland. Such a cheap, uniform rate would mean more people would use the service, which would be cheaper to administer and so, in the long run, would not operate at a loss.

The Post Office should provide pre-paid envelopes and wrappers. But for those wishing to use their own stationery, he proposed 'a bit of paper just large enough to bear the stamp' (meaning the official Post Office hand-stamp) 'and covered at the back with a glutinous wash, which might, by applying a little moisture, attach to the back of the letter . . .' This was the origin of the Penny Black, the world's first adhesive postage stamp.

Backed by public enthusiasm, Rowland Hill was asked by the government to revamp the General Post Office. There he was much resented by the other officials (among them Anthony Trollope) who saw him as an outsider, a new broom whose appointment implied criticism of them. The tensions betweeen Hill and Trollope were particularly marked, for the novelist was by character as 'bluff and boisterous' as the reformer was 'calm and freezing'.

In his *Autobiography* Trollope discussed his relationship to Hill with characteristic frankness, 'With him I never had any sympathy, nor he with me . . . I was always an anti-Hillite, acknowledging indeed the great thing which Sir Rowland Hill had done for the country, but believing him entirely unfit to manage men or to arrange labour.'

Hill's reforms began to take effect. By May 1840 stamps, wrappers and envelopes were available to the public. Until the invention of an envelope-making machine in the 1850s, envelopes were an expensive lux-

ury. Nevertheless, contrary to expectation, it was the glutinous stamps bearing the young Queen Victoria's portrait which sold best. Printers worked night and day to keep pace with sales of the Penny Black: 66 million were produced before the colour was changed to red a year later.

Hill's trust in the popularity of a cheaper postal system was immediately vindicated. The number of letters posted in 1840 was double that of the year before. Government revenue fell, however, not to be redeemed for several decades.

By 1855 pillar boxes dotted the country, replacing the more expensive 'letter-receiving' offices which did the job first. If the pillar box was indeed Trollope's invention, it indicates how sincerely he did work for Rowland Hill's 'great thing' despite his dislike of the man. In 1870 the postcard – an innovation pioneered by the Austrians – was introduced, incorporating a half-penny stamp. It proved particularly popular in Scotland.

TRAINS AND SCHOOLS

Vital to the take-off of the new postal system was the integration of the Royal Mail with the expanding railway network. The last mail stage-coach left London in 1846, but letters had been carried on trains before the Penny Post – even as early as 1830. And the Penny Post coincided with Britain's 'railway mania'. By 1855, 8000 miles of track were in operation. Not only were trains faster than stage-coaches, they also afforded facilities for sorting the mail in transit.

In Trollope's Britain the very word 'railway' smacked of a new, ultra-modern way of life. The fact that the railways ran to a published timetable led to a nationwide synchronization of pocket watches: they could be set by station clocks which told the same time from one end of the country to the other.

WRITING HOME

The ability to communicate by letter became more important as Britain was transformed from a rural to an urban, industrial society. By the 1851 census, the urban population had overtaken the rural, and it was no longer common to die in the parish of your birth. Prime Minister William Gladstone considered that the Penny Post had a part to play in easing the pain of such migration as families separated in the search for work: 'Think what softening of domestic exile, what an aid in keeping warm the feel of family affection, in mitigating the rude breach in the circle of the hearth.'

As the postal system expanded, another major breakthrough in communication came with the telegraph. William Cooke and Charles Wheatstone had patented their method in the very year of Rowland Hill's influential book on Post Office reform. But it was an American, Samuel Morse, who gave his name to the most successful code. A British Electric Telegraph Company was set up in 1845, but by 1870 the Post Office had taken exclusive control of all the telegraph offices. The first cable between Britain and France was laid in 1850, between Britain and America in 1866, and

Envelope-making machine
(right) The advent of stamps and the reform of postal rates, led to another popular innovation – the envelope.

American links
(below right) In 1868 Trollope went to America to negotiate an international postal treaty. By 1881, 25 per cent of Britain's overseas mail came from there.

Sea mail
Overseas letters were transported in two ways – on private vessels and on government or Post Office ships. The picture right shows a post office aboard a private vessel, the steamer 'Pekin'.

The iron horse
(below) The building of an efficient rail network presented another opportunity for the Post Office. Letters began to be carried by train in 1830 and by 1838 mail trains were equipped with travelling post offices on board. Travel times were approximately 20 miles an hour.

between Britain and Australia, via Singapore, in 1871.

Women were associated with telegraphy from the outset. When the Post Office took over, it was decided to permit women telegraphists. This had nothing to do with emancipation. It simply reflected the fact that the GPO could not do without them. The story goes that the Chairman of the London Electric Telegraph Company heard of a stationmaster's daughter who had been ably carrying out all of her father's telegraph duties for several years. Soon the Company found that 'the girls are not only more teachable, more attentive, and quicker-eyed than the men clerks', but also 'sooner satisfied with lower wages'.

These female telegraphists underwent far more rigorous scrutiny of their abilities and characters than the young Anthony Trollope had done in 1834. The age of patronage, old-boy networks and class snobbery died with the introduction in 1870 of competitive examinations. for recruitment to the Civil Service in general. The same decade saw 'gentlewomen of limited means' employed as Post Office clerks for the first time. Fears about the impropriety of 'the admixture of the sexes' proved unfounded. On the contrary, it was seen to raise 'the tone of the male staff by confining them during many hours of the day to a decency of conversation and demeanour which is not always to be found where men alone are employed'.

OVERSEAS MAIL

The Penny Post, the telegraph and the railways shrank Britain, and the rest of the world was shrinking too. Railways wound their way across continents, and steam ships ploughed the oceans. Other governments were quick to imitate Britain's cheap, pre-paid system of postage. In the spring of 1868, Trollope went on a special mission to America to negotiate a postal treaty. Although a 'far from agreeable' mission, on account of the offhand inefficiency of one American official who offended the novelist 'grievously', it was successful. The year 1874 saw the setting up of an International Postal Union whose members agreed to place their inland postal systems at the disposal of all others, and to pool information about improvements.

The colonies, in particular, enjoyed excellent com-

munication facilities, so that administrators and armies could be quickly contacted by the motherland, and emigrants could keep in touch with families at home.

Trollope had retired before the next round of revolutionary advances in the Post Office. These can largely be attributed to Henry Fawcett who, in four short years as Postmaster General (1880-1884), made the Post Office counter central to daily life. He introduced six major new services: the parcel post, postal orders, sixpenny telegrams, savings stamps, and annuity and insurance schemes. (The habit of thrift he encouraged had a social effect. Urban workers tended to marry rather than cohabit, since a post-office nest-egg could not be left to a common-law spouse.)

In 1885, the postman (a word coined only in Fawcett's time) traded his penny-farthing for a 'safety bicycle'. He must have cut a figure rather akin to the lone and long-gone 'post boy'. But behind him now towered a monumental organization of a vast labour force, technology and bureaucracy – a General Post Office indispensable to the social and economic maintenance of country and Empire.

Cheap labour
The Post Office was a pioneer in the employment of women, but it was for economic motives rather than progressive ones. Women could be paid less than men, and tended to be more efficient and better educated than their male counterparts. In 1897, 33 per cent of telegraphists and over half the counter clerks were female, and there was an agreement that one-third of the staff at the Central Telegraph Office (above) would be female. A condition of employment was that the women would resign on marriage. This served to keep their salaries low since they would rarely stay long enough to be promoted.

'Hen and Chickens'
Aptly nicknamed, this bicycle (left) was introduced in 1881 to help with parcel deliveries, but did not catch on. Bicycle postmen, in general, were expected to cover between 26 and 28 miles a day.

CHARLOTTE BRONTË

1816-1855

Sole surviving sister of a tragic and talented family, Charlotte Brontë was the only one to receive public acclaim before she, too, died prematurely. In early adulthood she shared the precarious lot of Victorian women, forced to live a 'walking nightmare of poverty and self-suppression'. Only literary success gained her some independence, ironically achieved by adopting a sexless pseudonym. Fittingly, it is the injustice of Victorian attitudes to women, and a woman's struggle to establish her own identity in a man's world that are her great themes. Drawing on her remarkable family and her own woefully circumscribed experiences for inspiration, she explored her themes with startling passion and clarity. Only now is she recognized as a truly revolutionary writer.

A Passionate Individual

Living in a remote Yorkshire parsonage, Charlotte Brontë's few real experiences were blighted by family deaths, social stigma and unrequited love. But she found an escape through fantasy.

Like Jane Eyre, Charlotte Brontë was a small, plain woman, who was fiercely independent, passionate in spirit and had little interest in the conventional life to which Victorian women were expected to aspire. Yet her life was a sacrifice to duty – despite her yearning for greater things, she played out the roles of dutiful daughter and accommodating wife.

She was born on 21 April 1816 at Thornton vicarage in Yorkshire, the third daughter of Patrick Brontë, the Irish curate of the parish, and his gentle, Cornish wife Maria. Around the time of Charlotte's fourth birthday, her father was appointed perpetual curate of nearby Haworth, and the family made the ten-mile journey there in a wagon and seven carts. By now, three more children had been born – Branwell, Emily and Anne.

The austere parsonage which became their lifelong home, the steep hill-village with its dark cobbled streets, and the bleak beauty of the surrounding moors were formative influences on the children.

MOTHERLESS CHILDREN

The year after the family's arrival at Haworth, Maria Brontë died of cancer. Her sister, Elizabeth Branwell, was persuaded to leave sunny Penzance to look after the six motherless children in damp, windy Yorkshire. Though conscientious in her duties, 'Aunt' showed little affection for her charges, and even less for the wild countryside they so loved.

In 1824, Patrick Brontë managed to find a school for the four older girls. For only £14 a year, the Rev. Carus Wilson would board and educate the daughters of the clergy at Cowan Bridge. But unknown to Mr Brontë, the size of the fee reflected the neglect and undernourishment suffered by the girls.

A wealthy evangelical clergyman, the Rev. Wilson

The family home
The Brontë family – the Reverend, his wife and their six children – moved to Haworth parsonage when Charlotte was four, and it remained their lifelong home. Papa Brontë outlived all his children and died there.

Mother and aunt
Charlotte's warm-hearted mother Maria (inset, far right) died the year after the family's arrival at Haworth. Her place was taken by her austere sister, 'Aunt Branwell' (inset, right).

aimed to prepare the daughters of poorer clergymen for a life of self-denial and submission by breaking their spirit with severe frugality, continuous punishment and repression. Such treatment had the opposite effect on the eight-year-old Charlotte: it instilled in her a deep, bitter and lasting resentment which she expressed some 20 years later in *Jane Eyre*.

In the novel, Carus Wilson becomes the harsh "black marble clergyman" Mr Brocklehurst, and Cowan Bridge becomes the hateful institution Lowood, Charlotte's gentle, submissive (and untidy) eldest sister Maria becomes the fictional Helen Burns. Like Helen, Maria died of consumption (tuberculosis), which she contracted at school. A month later, in June 1825, the second sister, Elizabeth, died of the same illness. Charlotte and Emily were brought home.

For the next six years, Charlotte settled into the enclosed life of the parsonage. The remaining children were left very much to their own devices: 'Aunt' kept a certain distance from them, and 'Papa' was a still remoter figure behind his study walls, and took his meals alone. So the young Brontës drew closer together and soon became immersed in telling, then writing stories about fantasy worlds they created.

IMAGINARY GLASS TOWN

The story-telling began in 1826, when Papa brought home a box of wooden soldiers. All four children had a soldier, each with its own imaginary kingdom, which together formed the 'Great Glass Town Confederacy'. Soon Charlotte and Branwell introduced an imaginary counterpart of their great hero the Duke of Wellington into the fantasies, then invented a special kingdom called Angria for his imaginary son Arthur Wellesley. In Charlotte's romantic fantasies about Arthur, he becomes the charismatic Duke of Zamorna, with two wives and several mistresses.

In 1830, Mr Brontë suffered a serious illness. It brought home to him the fact that – lacking any conventional training – his children would become paupers if he died. So, with financial help from her godparents, Charlotte was sent to school again – to Miss Wooler's establishment in an elegant country house at Roe Head.

Mary Taylor, who was to become her lifelong friend, records her arrival one cold January morning in 1831: 'in very old-fashioned clothes, and looking very cold and miserable . . . She looked like a little old woman, so short sighted that she always appeared to be seeking something, and moving her head from side to side to catch a sight of it. She was very shy and nervous, and spoke with a strong Irish accent'. When invited to join in game-playing, 'she said that she had never played and could not play'.

Despite Charlotte's shyness, her sharp intellect soon took her to the top of the school, and she made a second lifelong friend – Ellen Nussey. Within 18 months, having absorbed all Roe Head had to teach, she returned home to Haworth.

Deaths at school
Charlotte and three of her sisters were sent to Cowan Bridge in 1824. Only two survived.

A friend for life
(below) Charlotte met Ellen Nussey at Roe Head school, and they became faithful friends.

Key Dates

1816 born at Thornton
1820 family moves to Haworth parsonage
1824-5 pupil at Cowan Bridge; two sisters die
1831 goes to Roe Head
1835-8 teacher at Roe Head
1839 first post as a governess
1842 pupil at Pensionnat Heger, Brussels. Falls in love with M. Heger
1843-4 teacher at the Pensionnat
1847 *Jane Eyre* published
1848-49 Branwell, Emily and Anne die
1854 marries Rev Arthur Bell Nicholls
1855 dies at Haworth

The next three years were spent in domestic quietude, or absorbed in writing romantic Angrian dramas. Then, when Charlotte was 19, Miss Wooler offered her a post as assistant teacher at Roe Head, with a tiny salary and free schooling for one of her sisters. Despite her limited experience of normal childhood, the opportunity to help the family was too good to miss.

Charlotte felt oppressed – understandably – by the enforced sociability of school life: 'Stupidity the atmosphere, school-books the employment, asses the society', she noted bitterly in her journal. After almost three years of depression, her health failed and she returned to the quiet intensity of the family home.

Her next venture into the world was equally unhappy. In May 1839 – two months after turning down a proposal from Ellen's brother, the Rev. Henry Nussey – Charlotte became a temporary governess to the Sidgwicks of Stonegappe near Skipton. She left in July. The little Sidgwicks were 'devils incarnate' – 'more riotous, perverse, unmanageable cubs never grew'.

A month after her return, she received and rejected another proposal – this time from an impetuous young Irish curate who had been captivated by her during a single visit to her father.

Two years passed at Haworth before Charlotte found another position, again as a governess – this time with the Whites of Rawdon, Leeds. The Whites were more agreeable than the Sidgwicks, but Charlotte was peculiarly ill-equipped for such employment. To the already difficult lot of a governess she brought a shyness, a social awkwardness and a proud consciousness of her personal superiority.

ADVENTURE IN BELGIUM

Charlotte finally hit upon a plan that seemed to offer a decent future for herself and her sisters – they would open their own school. Amazingly, the obstacles were overcome. 'Aunt Branwell' was persuaded that a school would be a good investment for her capital, and even agreed to finance the necessary preliminary: a course of study that would give the girls a proper command of French and German. In 1842, a French school in Brussels, the Pensionnat Heger, accepted Charlotte and Emily's application.

The Pensionnat Heger was a spacious and well-run school for girls, presided over by Madame Claire Heger. Charlotte worked there with her accustomed zeal, and made rapid progress, although she and Emily had little or nothing to do with their fellow pupils. Charlotte found them 'singularly cold, selfish, animal and inferior', making no allowance for the fact that they were just schoolgirls. Their easy-going Roman Catholicism outraged her puritanical notions.

One Catholic was excepted from these strictures. Monsieur Constantin Heger spent most of his time teaching at a neighbouring boys' school, but he lived at his wife's establishment and gave some lessons there. A volatile, black-moustachioed figure in his early thirties, Heger was a passionate, exacting teacher who often reduced Charlotte to tears; whereupon 'Monsieur' became contrite and proffered handkerchieves and bonbons to repair the damage. Perhaps Heger, her 'Black Swan', reminded Charlotte of her dark Angrian heroes. In any event, she fell in love with him.

Cloistered creativity
After the deaths of their eldest sisters, the four remaining Brontë children spent their childhood and early teenage years at Haworth in virtual isolation from the outside world – with little contact even with the adults of the family. 'Aunt Branwell' spent much of her time in her room, while Papa shut himself up in the study, leaving the children to amuse themselves in the parlour (left). With no outsiders to play with, the young Brontës turned to each other for stimulation and created an imaginary world together. Later, it was during evenings in the parlour that Charlotte, Emily and Anne (shown above, right to left, in a painting by Branwell) wrote the novels which finally won for them the attentions of the literary world.

In November 1842, following the death of 'Aunt Branwell', Charlotte and Emily returned to Haworth. Charlotte soon went back to Brussels as a teacher. Without Emily she was isolated: 'I get on here from day to day in a Robinson-Crusoe-like sort of way; very lonely, but that does not signify', and was still at odds with her Catholic colleagues and pupils. But she had the joy of giving lessons to Monsieur who had decided to learn English.

Inevitably, Madame noticed the little Englishwoman's adoration of her husband and, without the slightest fuss, took measures to reduce their contact to a minimum. Soon Charlotte felt spied on, although it is impossible to say how much of this was in her own guilty imagination. In January 1844, after a year as a teacher, she left the Pensionnat with a diploma, the warm good wishes of Monsieur and Madame, and an intense unrequited passion.

Returning to Haworth from her Belgian adventures, Charlotte found her father near-blinded by cataracts, and realized that it would be impossible to leave him: her plans for a school would come to nothing. In her loneliness, she wrote Monsieur letters that, while falling just short of an open declaration of devotion, were embarrassingly ardent.

DESPERATE LETTERS

As she waited in vain for a letter from Monsieur, her desperation increased. In November 1845, nearly two years after she had seen him, she wrote: 'To forbid me to write to you, to refuse to answer me, would be to tear from me my only joy on earth . . . when day by day I await a letter, and when day by day disappointment comes . . . I lose appetite and sleep – I pine away.'

Charlotte had renounced Angria in 1839, and had written little since. But her misery over Heger prompted her to compose a good deal of verse. Then, in the autumn of 1845, she discovered some of Emily's poems and realized their exceptional quality. This

THE FAMILY FAILURE

Patrick Branwell Brontë was a year younger than Charlotte, and her chief collaborator in their mighty childhood epics. As the only son, the hopes of the family fell on him, but he was never able to escape the fantasy world of childhood.

Branwell boasted about his talents, but drank them away at the Black Bull, failing miserably to make anything of his early artistic ability, and not even managing to hold down a job as a railway clerk. In 1843, he was taken on as a tutor, but was sacked two years later. He declared that this was because of his passionate relationship with the mistress of the house.

Returning to Haworth, Branwell's drinking increased and he became addicted to opium, begging it from the chemist while the rest of the family was at church. 'He thought of nothing but stunning or drowning his agony of mind', Charlotte wrote, 'No one in the house could have rest'. Branwell's alternating stupor and delirium ended in 1848, when he died suddenly of consumption.

The only brother
(left) In this teenage portrait of himself and his sisters Branwell shows himself in an upright, 'manly' pose with his gun. But the realistic demands of manhood proved too much for him to cope with. While his sisters escaped their narrow lot through writing, Branwell found his escape in delirium induced by drugs and alcohol.

Fantasy lands
(above) It is thought that Charlotte painted this watercolour of the imaginary 'Bay of Glass Town'. For six years, she and Branwell worked together on the Glass Town sagas that they based in the fictional kingdom of 'Angria': Charlotte wrote the tales of romance, and Branwell created charismatic, warring heroes that he could never live up to.

seems to have awakened her powers of leadership. Though she had no illusions about her own poetic talent, she mobilized her sisters, and the three women put together a volume of poems. Charlotte found a publisher of religious books who was willing to produce it – at the authors' expense.

CURRER, ELLIS AND ACTON BELL

When the slim volume appeared, the authors were named as Currer (Charlotte), Ellis (Emily) and Acton (Anne) Bell. The pseudonyms were chosen because they were sexually ambiguous, leaving it open to question whether the versifiers were male or female; 'Bell' was taken, as a joke, from the middle name of the Rev. Brontë's new curate, Arthur Bell Nicholls.

Poems was not a success – only two copies were sold – but all three sisters were now writing hard. Charlotte finished *The Professor*; Emily's *Wuthering Heights* and Anne's *Agnes Grey* were written at about the same time. For several months Charlotte patiently sent them off, only to receive them back, rejected.

In July 1847 she eventually found a publisher for her sisters, but not for *The Professor*. The publishing firm of Smith, Elder also returned her novel, but intimated that a three-volume novel by Currer Bell would merit their careful attention. Charlotte sent off *Jane Eyre* which she had recently completed, and the miracle occurred: it was accepted and published within six weeks. And its reception was rapturous.

'Currer Bell' was famous, and his/her sex and identity were the subjects of wide speculation. The publisher of Emily's and Anne's books, T.C. Newby even attempted to cash in by implying that they might be Currer Bell's works. When he stated that Anne's

Curate's daughter
Charlotte's father (above), the Rev. Patrick Brontë was a constant but remote figure in her life. Born an Irish peasant, he climbed the social scale to become a Cambridge graduate and changed his name from Brunty to Brontë before settling into the curacy at Haworth. He outlived his wife and all his children.

Curate's wife
The Rev. Arthur Bell Nicholls (right) was curate to Charlotte's father for five years before he plucked up enough courage to ask for her hand. She was initially unimpressed, but his passion persuaded her.

Passion rejected
When Charlotte was 26, she and Emily travelled to Belgium to complete their education at the Pensionnat Heger in Brussels (right). Charlotte was impressed by the beauty of the city, but an even stronger impression was made by her teacher Monsieur Heger (below). Charlotte became desperately infatuated with her 'master', but he was married, and showed no sign of returning her love. This unrequited passion found expression in her last novel Villette.

Tenant of Wildfell Hall was by 'Currer', Charlotte and Anne decided to prove their separate existences.

They walked through a thunderstorm to Keighley, caught trains to Leeds and London, and presented themselves to George Smith of Smith, Elder. When Charlotte showed him one of the firm's letters addressed to Currer Bell Esq., he said sharply, 'Where did you get this?'. But he was soon convinced that the two little ladies in quaint old-fashioned dresses were indeed Currer and Acton Bell, and gallantly escorted them to the opera that evening.

Meanwhile, Branwell had proved unable to apply himself to any one thing, and had begun a rapid decline – wandering around in a drunken stupor, begging money from the sexton to buy more alcohol. Charlotte had little sympathy for her brother's weaknesses: 'he will never be fit for much', she told Ellen Nussey.

FAMILY DEATHS

On 24 September 1848, Branwell died of consumption. Emily and Anne caught the disease and were carried off within a few months. By spring 1849, Charlotte had lost all her family except Papa. She was condemned to a strange dual existence: for most of the year she lived in the lonely parsonage, the sole prop of a father who nonetheless continued to take his meals apart from her. But the solitude was broken by forays into the great world, where her reputation won her invitations to meet famous people. One such acquaintance, who became a close friend, was the novelist Elizabeth (Mrs) Gaskell – her *Life of Charlotte Brontë* is the definitive biography.

It seems likely that she hoped for a proposal from her publisher George Smith, but he never advanced beyond effusive friendship. Another member of his firm, James Taylor, did court her. Although she wavered, she could not overcome a fundamental physical revulsion: when he came near her, her 'veins ran ice'.

In December 1852, shortly after finishing *Villette*, the novel in which she evoked – and perhaps exorcised – the spell of Monsieur Heger, Charlotte received another offer of marriage from an unexpected quarter. The stammered proposal came from her father's curate of five years' standing, Arthur Bell Nicholls. Charlotte considered Nicholls a narrow-minded, boring high-churchman, nothing like her intellectual equal. But his scarcely bridled passion affected her.

Her father vehemently opposed the match. Nicholls responded dramatically – he broke down during a Communion service, refused to eat and drink, and volunteered to be a missionary in Australia (but took another curacy in Yorkshire). He wrote to Charlotte again and again – and eventually she secretly replied. In 1854 she promised to become his wife.

Charlotte and Arthur were married on 29 June 1854. Patrick Brontë refused to attend, and her old headmistress, Miss Wooler, gave her away. Ellen Nussey was the only guest. The couple spent their honeymoon in Arthur's native Ireland, then returned to Haworth where Charlotte settled into parish activity – 'my time is not my own now'.

She was soon pregnant, but morning sickness, endless nausea and vomiting proved too much for her frail body. On her deathbed she said to Arthur, 'I am not going to die, am I? He will not separate us — we have been so happy'. But she did die, on the night of 31 March 1855, leaving her husband, 'sitting desolate and alone in the old grey house'.

Fact or Fiction

THE MAD WOMAN IN THE ATTIC

The chilling image of mad Mrs Rochester locked in the attic of Thornfield Hall seems too horrific to be anything but the creation of Charlotte Brontë's imagination – yet it had a factual basis. When Charlotte was a governess, she visited Norton Conyers Hall near Ripon. The old house still stands today – an atmospheric place, strongly echoing Thornfield, and, tellingly, associated with an 18th-century legend of a madwoman locked away upstairs. Moreover, in 1845, Charlotte went to North Lees Hall near Sheffield, an old farm belonging to a family called *Eyre*. Here too there was a legend of a madwoman (this one perished in a fire). In an age when good asylums were few and far between, many caring families chose to keep their mad relatives at home.

Closeted madwoman
When his attempts to marry Jane Eyre bigamously are foiled, Rochester is forced to reveal his lunatic wife – whom he has kept locked in the attic. Charlotte may have drawn her inspiration for this savage figure from the legend of Norton Conyers Hall (left).

The Impoverished Gentlewoman

A woman with gentility but no money was out of place in Victorian society. She had to work to survive, but most of the ladylike options open to her were ill-paid and humiliating.

Along with thousands of other women, Charlotte Brontë and her sisters were the victims of a characteristic 19th-century dilemma. They were too poor to live without working, yet they were also ladies, a fact that severely limited what decent society would allow them to do without loss of caste. Paradoxically, almost all ladylike employments were ill-paid, stressful and humiliating.

In theory, gentility and wealth went hand in hand, but in reality there were many women who were obviously genteel and yet lacked money of their own or a man to maintain them. Often ladies came down in the world because the family fortunes collapsed in the still-unstable circumstances of early Victorian enterprise, characterized by alternating speculative manias and bank failures, booms and slumps. Victorian novels are full of financial catastrophes. In *Agnes Grey*, by Charlotte Brontë's sister Anne, speculations ruin the heroine's father and force her out into the world as a governess.

Less sensationally, the children of more poorly paid professional men – such as Charlotte's Cambridge-educated clergyman father – were faced with poverty if the breadwinner became incapable or died. Cramped as the early lives of the Brontë sisters were, their prospects must have seemed even more alarming. If Mr Brontë died, the parsonage would be taken over by another man and the sisters would face destitution. It must have been clear at an early date that drunken, erratic Branwell Brontë would never be able to support any of his sisters.

The fact that Patrick Brontë – already 60 when Charlotte reached the age of 21 – outlived every one of his children could not have been predicted, and made no difference to the way they viewed their prospects when girls. Haworth parsonage remained a refuge for them all their lives.

One obvious option for the impoverished gentlewoman was to live with relatives. Sometimes she was welcome and wanted, but the impoverished single relative might also become the family drudge, made humiliatingly aware of her dependency, as little Jane Eyre is by her bullying cousin John Reed: "You are a dependant, Mamma says, you have no money; your father left you none; you ought to beg, and not to live here with gentlemen's children like us."

The trials of teaching
(above left) Many educated but poor gentlewomen earned a pitiful salary teaching in charity schools as did Jane Eyre. Like her, many must often have felt "degraded" and "dismayed".

The poor seamstress
(above right) Dressmaking seemed a 'genteel' occupation for a respectable woman but, in reality, it was desperately unrewarding work – employment was insecure, the hours dreadful and the wages minimal.

Marriage prospects
(right) One of the few ways a poor gentlewoman could escape the trap of poverty and degradation was through marriage. Any caring father would scrutinize the financial standing of a prospective husband very carefully.

Nineteenth-century writers were quite certain that marriage was the norm, and the proper goal for any healthy woman. They also recognized that genteel poverty was an evil. Yet, inconsistently, they scorned husband-hungry girls and their man-trapping mothers. One of the most famous examples in 19th-century literature is the foolish Mrs Bennet in Jane Austen's *Pride and Prejudice,* who can think of nothing except finding husbands for her five daughters. Yet her marital scheming could just as easily have been presented as caring and commonsense. To the impoverished gentlewoman, marriage meant release from the threat of poverty or, at worst, a sharing of burdens.

ESCAPE INTO MARRIAGE

Although most marriages were no longer 'arranged' by families, many were negotiated with at least half an eye on practicalities – hence Mr Rochester's unfortunate contract with Bertha Mason in *Jane Eyre.* A poor gentlewoman might have chances if she was prepared to ignore personal inclination. When Charlotte Brontë received a proposal from Henry Nussey, the curate told her plainly that he was about to take in pupils and needed a wife to look after them. When St John Rivers proposes to Jane Eyre, he wants a loyal helper in his missionary work. Both the fictional and the real offers were refused, but there were plenty of girls who were more down-to-earth in their expectations. Henry Nussey soon found a wife to fulfil his needs.

Marriage had severe drawbacks for a woman of independent spirit, whether impoverished or not. A husband became the master of her person, and

The abandoned mother

(above) Solitary women were prey to 'adventurers' who played upon their need to find security through marriage. Seamstresses for rich households were especially vulnerable – there were countless untold tragedies of seduced women abandoned with an illegitimate child.

Elizabeth Gaskell

(above) Charlotte Brontë's friend and biographer, the novelist Mrs Gaskell, was one of the fortunate few women whose literary talents allowed them to earn a living respectably – but even she was obliged to work at the dining room table so that her husband could occupy the study.

also of her property and income – a situation only remedied by Married Women's Property Acts from 1870 onwards. A wife was expected to submit to her husband's will, adopt his opinions and run the household in such a way that he remained free from its worries. Although Charlotte's friend and biographer Mrs Gaskell was a celebrated novelist, it was her husband who occupied the study – she wrote her novels on the dining room table, from which she could monitor the servants and children.

Charlotte Brontë, already a famous writer when she married, allowed Arthur Bell Nicholls to interfere in her correspondence with Ellen Nussey, and in the last few months of her life spent more time on her husband's parish duties than in her creative writing. Real life was rather different from the fictitious world of *Jane Eyre,* where it is the man who becomes a helpless dependant, or of *The Professor* and *Villette,* where the heroines retain their independence as teachers to the very last page.

Accomplished ladies
(below, left and right) Young ladies were expected to play the piano and sketch prettily. Jane Eyre can play "like any other English schoolgirl" but, as Rochester recognizes, she is an artist of rare talent. Yet neither Jane nor any other lady could respectably exploit her talent – the best she could hope for was to teach.

A WOMAN'S PLACE

'The female sphere' – a woman's proper place – was the home, whether she ruled as its mistress or laboured in it as a servant. Genteel work outside the home was almost non-existent: public office, the professions and the universities were all closed to women, while commerce and manual labour were simply not respectable.

If 'reduced ladies driven to obtain a maintenance' wished to retain their gentility, they had to do 'women's work' in a setting as domestic as possible. Of employments now thought of as 'traditionally' feminine and respectable, even nursing was out of the question; nurses were working-class women with bad reputations until Florence Nightingale's reforms took effect in the 1860s.

Some gentlewomen worked as seamstresses, although the profession was mainly recruited from girls who belonged to a lower social class (like Mrs Gaskell's Mary Barton) and were attracted by the seeming gentility of dressmaking. In reality, the seamstress was pitifully paid and overworked.

In London and other cities the demand for her services was tremendous but concentrated: during 'the season' she sewed for an average of 18 hours a day, whereas her working day during the rest of the year was only 12 hours. The hardship and penury – contrasted with the often glamorous contacts they made – quite often led to seduction, followed by a rapid descent into prostitution.

The murky moral and economic facts about dressmaking were repeatedly exposed by Victorian writers such as Thomas Hood, whose poem 'The Song of a Shirt' had a tremendous vogue. Such exposés did little to improve the seamstress's lot,

A solitary life
(above) Life for the governess was often intensely lonely, lived in a limbo between master and servants, excluded from friendship with either. Jane Eyre's experience at Thornfield Hall is typical – the governess hears all the fun, but cannot join in: " . . . light steps ascended the stairs; and there was a tripping through the gallery, and soft cheerful laughs, and opening and closing doors and, for a time, hush".

Women together
(left) Although working class women were often much worse off materially than even the impoverished gentlewoman, many at least had the fellowship of other women. This contemporary picture shows women millworkers in Wigan together during a break.

but they effectively discouraged gentlewomen, who rarely took up this kind of work.

At the other extreme, literature held out the possibility of an extraordinary advance in affluence and status, if only for the lucky and talented few. Not all men approved: when Charlotte Brontë turned to the poet Robert Southey for advice, he told her that 'Literature cannot be the business of a woman's life, and it ought not to be', and that her household duties should take up all her time. Charlotte's beloved teacher, 'Monsieur', was equally negative about a writing career.

But these were rather old-fashioned views. Women had long been accepted as novelists, partly because the novel itself was originally regarded as a lightweight literary form requiring no great knowledge or talent. Writing continued to be a respectable profession for ladies, partly because it could be carried out at home – though by the 19th century, great restrictions had been placed on the language and subject matter permitted to writers of both sexes, and to women in particular. One good reason for the Brontë's pseudonyms was given by Mary Ann Evans, who herself wrote as 'George Eliot': 'The object of anonymity was to get the book judged on its own merits, and not prejudged as the work of a woman'.

THE VICTORIAN GOVERNESS

Although Charlotte eventually joined the ranks of the famous – and potentially rich – her earlier work experience was identical to that of most other impoverished gentlewomen: she was engaged as governess. Governesses included what we now call teachers; women who worked in charity or boarding schools. Standards in these institutions varied greatly. Charlotte and Emily Brontë taught at Yorkshire schools in the mid 1830s, but the work was virtually slave labour.

To obtain a decent position – or better still, to run a school of one's own – required a more systematic education than most gentlewomen acquired. This was why Charlotte and Emily studied at the Pensionnat Heger in Brussels – its value was proved by the fact that a large Manchester boarding school later offered Charlotte the post of 'first governess' for the magnificent sum of £100 per annum. Because of her father's ill-health, Charlotte refused; but her novel, *Villette,* ends on a note of wish-fulfilment, with Lucy Snowe as an independent professional woman in charge of her own school.

By contrast, Charlotte's salary as the White family's 'private governess' – that is, live-in teacher and child minder – was a mere £20 a year, with £4 deducted for laundry. She was not cut out for the work. She did not care for small children, liking only Mr White because 'He never asks me to wipe the children's smutty noses or tie their shoes or fetch their pinafores or set them a chair'. And she complained that Mrs White 'cares nothing in the world about me except to contrive how the greatest quantity of labour may be squeezed out of me, and to that end she overwhelms me with oceans of needlework, yards of cambric to hem, muslin

Nursing the sick
Surprisingly perhaps, even nursing the sick was not considered suitable work for a respectable lady. In Charlotte Brontë's day, nurses generally had a rather dubious reputation. It took the efforts of Florence Nightingale – shown here tending the wounded in the Crimea, 1856 – to elevate the status of nursing.

nightcaps to make, and, above all things, dolls to dress'. Others were similarly treated.

As well as being underpaid and overworked, the governess suffered from the contradictions inherent in her position. She was a lady, admitted to the drawing and dining rooms when her employees wanted to show her off, and too good to eat or associate with even the upper servants (whose salaries were nonetheless at least as large as hers). But she was also an employee, and as such must be prepared to endure brusque treatment and severe rebukes. She had to make herself unobtrusive so that her mistress should not feel rivalled.

CONTINUAL SLIGHTS

Even the governess's authority over the children was insecure, since she had no power to discipline them without the mistress's consent; and even if they were 'riotous, perverse, unmanageable cubs', like the little Sidgwicks who Charlotte Brontë was employed to tame, their mother was too often inclined to make excuses for them while resenting the trouble she was being caused.

Charlotte's resentment of the slights she endured as a governess are reflected in *Jane Eyre* – for example when Mr Rochester's beautiful 'fiancée' Blanche Ingram recounts (in Jane's hearing) the cruel fun that she and her brother had at their governess's expense:

But poor Madame Joubert! I see her yet in her raging passions, when we had driven her to extremities – spilt our tea, crumbled our bread and butter, tossed our books up to the ceiling, and played a charivari with the ruler and the desk, the fender and the fire irons. Theodore, do you remember those merry days?'

'Yaas, to be sure I do,' drawled Lord Ingram; 'and the poor old stick used to cry out, "Oh you villains childs!" and then we sermonized her on the presumption of attempting to teach such clever blades as we were, when she was herself so ignorant.'

This catalogue of woes does not just come from Charlotte Brontë's writing. Her sister Anne, who worked as a governess for seven years, gives a similar account in *Agnes Grey*. And non-fictional evidence proves that the governess's life was singularly isolated and stressful.

The low salaries received by governesses ensured that those who outlived their usefulness would save little or nothing, and end their days in the workhouse. However, Victorian novels and reports did encourage public concern, and in 1843 the Governesses' Benevolent Institution was founded. It set up a Home for those in temporary difficulties, awarded annuities to aged governesses, and kept a register of available employment. But more important in the long run was the founding of Queen's College in London.

This was intended to give governesses a proper training, but it was soon flooded with women eager to improve themselves, including some of the future pioneers of education for women. Their work, and the wider job opportunities provided by social change and intelligent agitation, began the transformation of impoverished gentlewomen into educated, efficient women.

A sign of improvement
(below) Towards the end of the 19th century, the lot of the poor gentlewoman began to improve, with the establishment of institutions such as Queen's College in London. This was set up to give governesses a proper training, but many others took advantage of it.

EMILY BRONTË

1818-1848

Emily Brontë's life was intensely solitary. Her gifted brother and sisters were her only real human contact, and with her younger sister Anne (above, left) she created a world of childhood fantasy which remained essential to her in adult life. Only happy when roaming her native moors alone, she acquired not one single friend. But the strength of her personality inspired the deep admiration and love of all her sisters – but especially Anne's. Emily's extraordinary courage and inability to compromise resulted in one of the most passionate, violent and controversial books of the 19th century, and a unique body of poetry, all published shortly before her early death. As D. H. Lawrence wrote, '. . . life does not mean length of days. Poor old Queen Victoria had length of days. But Emily Brontë had life. She died of it.'

'No Coward Soul'

Life was never easy for Emily Brontë. Only alone on the moors, surrounded by the familiar sights of her private world, could she find peace and inspiration.

The life of Emily Brontë was short, intense and led in almost total seclusion. All that we know of her is what she reveals in her poems, and her single novel, *Wuthering Heights*, and what has been left in the recorded memoirs of the few who knew her. Her sister Charlotte is a major source of information, but for some reason she destroyed many of Emily's papers after her death and suppressed the most significant aspect of her – that she was a mystic who drew inspiration not from what she called 'the World without', but from visions and moments of intense emotion when she felt a oneness with Nature and the immaterial Universe. These fleeting moments were to provide her greatest happiness and were what gave shape to her life, her thought, and her work.

Emily Jane Brontë was born on 30 July 1818 at Thornton parsonage in the parish of Bradford in Yorkshire. Two years younger than Charlotte, and a year younger than her brother Branwell, Emily was closest to her younger sister Anne, who was to be her dearest friend and confidante.

In character and temperament, she seems to have had much in common with her father, Patrick Brontë, a Celt with a vivid imagination, strong literary tastes and a forceful, unbending personality. Of her mother, Emily knew or remembered nothing, being only three when she died of cancer at the age of 38, leaving six children. The family's 'mother-figure' was to become their Aunt Branwell, a well-meaning, but nevertheless stern and undemonstrative woman.

In 1824, Emily joined her sisters Charlotte, Maria and Elizabeth at Cowan Bridge school. Though Maria and Elizabeth were to die of tuberculosis, and Charlotte was marred for life by the experience, Emily seems to have been surprisingly unaffected. As the youngest pupil, she was seen as 'a darling child', 'quite the pet nursling of the school', and was protected from the grim, miserable reality of the place.

Returning to Haworth after an absence of six months, Emily remained at home for the next ten years. Though tutored by her father, from whom she acquired a passion for poetry, she grew up free from

The Reverend Brontë *(right) Of all the children, Emily was the most similar to her father in temperament. He, too, was intensely private and an awesome personality. Throughout his long life he ate his meals alone, engendering equal stoicism and detachment in his children.*

Yorkshire landscape *(below) In her cherished Haworth, Emily could escape to the moors. They were her refuge and her playground, and she loved the windy heights, the soft heathers and the inexorable flow of the seasons.*

Pastoral quietude
The beautiful setting of Thornton was just 8 miles from Haworth, where the Brontës moved to in 1820. Of all the influences on Emily's life, the landscape of her childhood was to have the most profound effect on her art.

Emily's birthplace
All six Brontë children were born at the Thornton vicarage in the parish of Bradford. Emily Jane Brontë was the fifth, born on 30 July 1818. Anne, who was to become her lifelong friend and confidante, was born there 18 months later.

many of the restrictions normally placed on children.

Under the watchful eye of Tabitha Aykroyd, 'Tabby', a widow of 56 employed at the parsonage as housekeeper, Emily would roam up to 20 miles a day over the moors, returning home at night to the austere little parsonage and the bed she shared with Charlotte. During these walks, her imagination was fed with tales of the supernatural told by Tabby whose memory stretched back to the turbulent times of the old century.

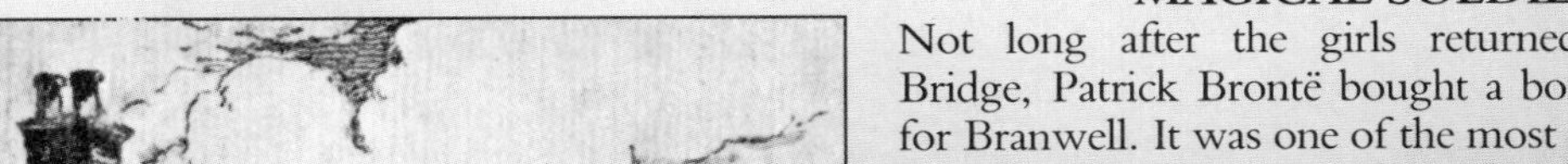

MAGICAL SOLDIERS

Not long after the girls returned from Cowan Bridge, Patrick Brontë bought a box of toy soldiers for Branwell. It was one of the most important events of the children's lives. Each sister chose a soldier. According to Charlotte, Emily's was dubbed 'Gravey' because the face of the little soldier was so very grave. But Branwell wrote that Emily called him 'Parry', after the Arctic explorer Captain Edward Parry. Certainly Emily was later to weave tales around 'Parrysland', a never-never land bearing a marked resemblance to Yorkshire.

Soon the Brontë children were writing stories based on the adventures of their adopted characters, jointly in the 'Glass Town' epic. Charlotte and Branwell later paired off to produce the sagas of 'Angria', while Emily and Anne created the 'Gondal' chronicles. First formulated at the age of 12, the Gondals were to sustain Emily for the rest of her life. Indeed, as the years went by, Emily increasingly inhabited the fantasy world created by her own imagination.

Excruciatingly shy in public, she rarely uttered a

Key Dates

1818 born at Thornton, Yorkshire

1820 family moves to Haworth parsonage

1821 death of mother

1824 attends Cowan Bridge school

1825 death of sisters Maria and Elizabeth

1826 Patrick Brontë brings home 12 wooden soldiers

1831 begins 'Gondal'

1835 pupil at Roe Head school

1837 governess at Law Hill school, Halifax

1842 pupil at Pensionnat Heger, Brussels

1846 *Poems by Currer, Ellis and Acton Bell*, published

1847 *Wuthering Heights* published

1848 Branwell's death, followed by Emily's

ANNE BRONTË

The youngest of the Brontë children, Anne has tended to be neglected, overshadowed by her more forceful sisters and brother. Yet her two novels *Agnes Grey* and *The Tenant of Wildfell Hall*, show her to have been a frank, independent and forthright personality. "Such talents as God has given me", she wrote, "I will endeavour to put to their greatest to use."

Forced to live a life she loathed – that of governess – she nevertheless suffered it in silence. But her experience led her to become a feminist at a time when the word was unknown, claiming equal rights for women.

Under her reticent exterior, Anne hid a deeply passionate nature. The love that she formed for her father's curate, Willie Weightman, she could only express after his death. She was to mourn her loss until her own death, from consumption, five months after Emily's in 1849.

Talented sisters
Last but not least in the Brontë family, Anne was the subject of Charlotte's portrait (above) and collaborated with Emily on her diaries (left).

word to strangers or even to those to whom she had been introduced. On the rare occasions when Emily was thrown into the company of people outside the family circle, Charlotte's constant anxious question was, 'How did Emily behave?' Often she remained totally silent when spoken to.

DESPERATELY HOMESICK

Charlotte, and even the timid Anne, adapted sufficiently to become governesses and live (albeit unhappily) away from home. Not so Emily. When, at the age of 17, she went as a pupil to Roe Head school, at which Charlotte was a teacher, it proved virtually impossible for her. Writing 15 years after the event, Charlotte said of her sister, 'Liberty was the breath of Emily's nostrils, without it, she perished . . . Every morning when she woke, the vision of home and the moors rushed on her . . . her health was quickly broken . . . I felt in my heart she would die if she did not go home . . .' After an absence of only three months, Emily returned to Haworth – where she revived in spirit and in health.

But gradually and relentlessly the shadows began to darken and close in on Emily and her family. At home, feeling herself to be a failure, she was thrown almost exclusively into the company of Branwell, a failure of Byronic intensity. Inevitably, the two drew closer together.

Increasingly she herself withdrew further from the world, despising its cruelty and meaningless social conventions. Only in the world of Nature, in the silent, seemingly self-contained world of animals, did she feel any sense of affinity. Not surprisingly, she sought companionship and solace from her ever-increasing band of pets – pigeons, pheasants, geese, her dogs Grasper and Keeper, her Merlin hawk Hero, together with numerous cats.

When Aunt Branwell threatened to expel Keeper unless he was properly house-trained, Emily beat the obstinate beast about the head with her bare hands until, bloody and bruised, his spirit broke and he obeyed his mistress. Her own spirit and strength of will were indomitable, her physical courage phenomenal. Bitten by a suspected rabid dog she cauterized the wound with red-hot tongs.

Apart from her household duties – cooking, baking bread and managing household affairs – she taught herself German, played the piano and wrote her poetry. It was a quiet, simple, secluded life, 'all tight and right' as she described it in a Diary Paper of 1837. Yet there was a dark side to her nature, a feeling of inadequacy coupled with her feeling of separateness. 'Terrifically

Pensionnat Heger
(below) In 1842 Charlotte and Emily enrolled at the Pensionnat Heger in Brussels. Both girls worked hard: Charlotte because of her hunger for knowledge; Emily because she refused to fail. M. Heger was to say of her that her head for logic and her capability for argument were extraordinary – particularly in a woman.

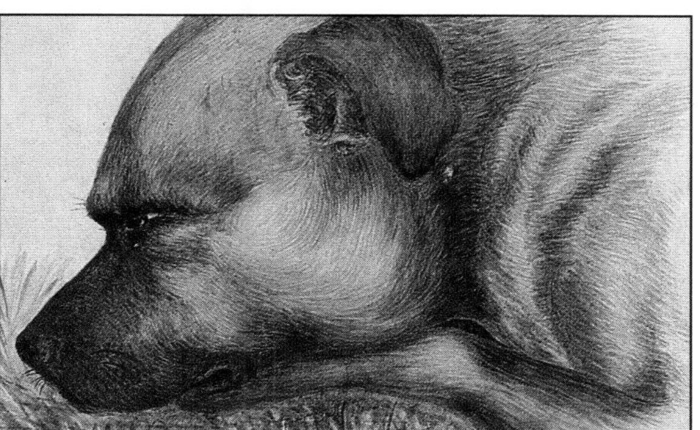

Haworth parsonage
(above) From 1820, the Brontë home was a Georgian house, finely proportioned but small for such a large household. The five bedrooms had to serve the Rev. and Mrs Brontë, their six children, two servants and, until her death, Mrs Brontë's nurse. The four eldest girls slept together in a room that was barely sufficient for one.

Devoted friend
Emily drew her beloved dog Keeper on the day she returned to Haworth in April 1838. Fiercely protective of his mistress, he tended to terrorize visitors and accepted dominion only from Emily.

Merlin hawk
Emily always seemed more comfortable in the company of animals than people, and by 1841 her 'family' included not just dogs but also a cat, two tame geese and a hawk. Clearly sensing an affinity with the bird, she spent long hours studying and sketching it, and honoured it in verse: "And like myself lone, wholly lone, It sees the day's long sunshine glow; And like myself it makes its moan In unexhausted woe."

and idiotically and brutally STUPID', is the harsh judgement she passed on herself. In a poem written in the same year, when she was 18, which begins:

I am the only being whose doom
No tongue would ask, no eye would mourn;

she wrote:

'Twas grief enough to find mankind
All hollow, servile, insincere;
But worse to trust to my own mind
And find the same corruption there.

It was in that same year, 1837, that Emily made another attempt at living in the world. She went as governess to the Law Hill school, Halifax. It was a desperate, unhappy attempt. To her friend Ellen Nussey, Charlotte wrote 'I have had one letter from her [Emily] since her departure . . . it gives an appalling account of her duties – hard labour from six in the morning until near eleven at night, with only one half-hour of exercise between. This is slavery. I fear she will never stand it'.

Returning to Haworth on 24 April 1838, Emily remained at home for the next four years. Although Charlotte and Anne were to take up appointments as governesses and Branwell attempted to stave off his accelerating decline, Emily followed the old routine becoming more indispensable around the house as Tabby grew less active.

Alone in the tiny old nursery room she created her own world. The room was simply furnished, with a low armchair in which she wrote, and a camp-bed pushed across the window from which at night she could gaze at the moon and the stars. There was no fireplace in the room or any form of heating. Comfort or physical ease were things she disregarded.

With the declining health of Patrick Brontë and the loneliness and isolation felt by both Charlotte and Anne, who were both living as governesses, a plan was conceived that would help the family fortunes and unite the sisters under one roof. They would set up a school of their own. Aunt Branwell agreed to finance the venture, and it was decided that Charlotte and Emily should attend a school on the Continent to perfect their French and improve their German. Their choice fell on the Pensionnat Heger in Brussels.

STUDYING ABROAD

What Emily Brontë made of it all we do not know. She left no record of her journey from the Yorkshire moors to London, the Channel crossing and arrival at Brussels. We know nothing from her own pen of her impressions of the Roman Catholic school into which she was plunged, her view of the school's proprietors, Monsieur and Madame Heger, or of the giggling girls with whom she was thrown into contact. All we have are the recollections of Charlotte as told to her biographer Mrs Gaskell, the testimony of M. Heger himself and a memoir of a former pupil, Laetitia Wheelwright.

From Mrs Gaskell we learn that 'Emily had taken a fancy to the fashion, ugly and preposterous even during its reign, of gigot sleeves, and persisting in wearing them long after they were 'gone out'. Her petticoats, too, had not a curve or wave in them, but hung straight and long, clinging to her lank figure.' To Mrs Gaskell we also owe M. Heger's opinion of Emily as 'egotistical and exacting', exercising 'a kind of unconscious tyranny over' Charlotte. And from Laetitia Wheelwright we are told that Emily was a 'tallish, ungainly ill-dressed figure . . . always answering our jokes with "I wish to be as God made me". . .'.

These are unflattering, humourless portraits. One can only guess from the evidence of the poems and comments from Charlotte's letters at Emily's unhappiness, but utter determination not to fail this time. 'Emily works like a horse' noted Charlotte in a letter to Ellen Nussey, and we know that M. Heger had the highest opinion of Emily's intellectual powers.

PASSIONATELY PRIVATE

Emily had been in Brussels nine months when Aunt Branwell died. She returned to Haworth immediately to look after her father, now almost totally blind. With Anne and Charlotte away, she was mistress of the house, free to come and go as she pleased. Her poetic powers reached new heights of expression.

In 1845 her self-contained life at home was invaded by the return of Branwell. And for the next three years, Emily witnessed his daily disintegration, unable to help, incapable of averting his inevitable end. Anne returned home that same year, as did the unhappy Charlotte, suffering the pangs of an unrequited love for M. Heger.

In September or October 1845 Charlotte happened to find two rather scruffy note-books, one bearing the heading, 'Emily Jane Brontë, GONDAL POEMS'. The other also consisted of flimsy, poor-quality paper, on which were written poems of a more personal nature. Charlotte was immediately struck by their quality. These were 'not at all like the poetry women generally wrote. I thought them condensed and terse, vigorous and genuine.'

This 'discovery' of Charlotte's was something that Emily found almost unbearable. Flying into a violent

Fact or Fiction

A SIMILAR STORY

While at Law Hill, Emily heard a story remarkably like *Wuthering Heights*. It concerned an orphan, Jack Sharp, who was adopted by Mr Walker of Walterclough Hall. The boy grew up arrogant and cunning, gradually taking over the Walker business.

On Mr Walker's death in 1771, the eldest son John, egged on by his wife, claimed his rights as heir. Reluctantly, Sharp left, promising revenge. Building Law Hill a mile away, he enticed the easy-going John into gambling and ruined him. He also corrupted Sam Stead, a relative of Walker's, who later disrupted the Walker household, teaching their children foul language.

Also, Jack Sharp's manservant was called Joseph, and the Walker children's nurse, like Ellen Dean, had frequent clashes with Sharp.

High Withens, Haworth Moor *is thought to be the original Wuthering Heights.*

Shibden Hall *(right) In 1837, Emily took a post as governess at Law Hill, a girls' boarding school on one of the Pennine hills surrounding Halifax. Although it was not a happy time for her, it was not without its distractions. She was within walking distance of the magnificent Shibden Hall, and almost certainly spent time there and drew inspiration from it for her image of Thrushcross Grange in* Wuthering Heights.

Branwell *Talented in music, art and writing, Branwell was not to live up to his family's expectations. Ill-equipped for life, he gave way to alcohol and drugs and died tragically.*

rage, she accused Charlotte of betrayal and having destroyed the one thing that meant so much to her: the secret, private world of her innermost thoughts and feelings. But somehow, with Anne's assistance, the storm abated, Emily eventually consenting to Charlotte's proposal that the three of them each contribute some of their poems for a joint volume of verse.

Although *Poems by Currer, Ellis and Acton Bell* failed commercially, the three sisters each embarked on the writing of a novel. Writing under her nom-de-plume of 'Ellis Bell', Emily wrote *Wuthering Heights* between the autumn of 1845 and her 28th birthday in July 1846. It met with a favourable public response, though the literary establishment condemned it variously as 'disgusting', 'inhuman', 'evil', 'uncivilized', 'artistically immature'. To Emily, their response was entirely predictable and of little consequence.

Within a year of the publication of *Wuthering Heights* Branwell was dead, succumbing to the ravages of consumption, alcohol and drugs. At his funeral in October 1848 Emily caught a cold. Suffering from pains in the chest, shortness of breath and a hacking cough, she nevertheless refused to rest, take medicine or permit the attendance of a doctor. Painfully thin and white, she continued to perform her daily tasks – rising at seven in the morning, feeding her animals, returning to her cold bed at ten o'clock at night.

On the morning of 19 December when she rose as usual at seven, the death-rattle could be heard distinctly as she dragged herself downstairs. Charlotte gave her a last sprig of heather gathered from the moor. She was too far gone to recognize it. Lying on the horsehair sofa in the sitting-room, she made a last concession to her sisters. 'If you'll send for a doctor I'll see him now', she whispered, dying moments later. She was buried at Haworth Church on 22 December. Keeper, her devoted dog, howled outside her bedroom door for weeks after her departure.

Charlotte Brontë
(left) Emily did not have an easy relationship with her elder sister. But whatever their differences, Charlotte never failed to be impressed by her sister's strength of will and sharp, penetrating mind.

Sir Walter Scott
(right) Charlotte wrote to a friend 'For fiction, read Scott alone; all novels after him are worthless.' And a young Emily named him as one of the three men she would wish to be with her on a dream island. His novels presented to her a prototype of ideal womanhood – independent and daring, and scornful of lesser minds. That was how she envisioned her heroines, and how she herself wished to be.

Yorkshire Life

The steely strengths of Yorkshire character were put to the test by the Industrial Revolution. It starved and subjugated the majority, but created a new breed of Yorkshireman: the self-made capitalist.

The pale, tough grass and dun heather, the tumbling becks and black rock of the wild, windswept moors around Haworth are as much a part of *Wuthering Heights* as Cathy and Heathcliff themselves. Yet Emily Brontë drew her inspiration not only from the fells and dales of Yorkshire, but also from the hardy, proud breed of people who lived among them.

Emily rarely left the Parsonage in Haworth except to go to church or stride out alone across the moors, and had little direct contact with local people. And yet, according to her sister Charlotte, 'she knew them: knew their ways, their language, their family histories; she could hear of them with interest, and talk of them with detail, minute, graphic, and accurate'.

The pages of *Wuthering Heights* are filled with echoes of the distinctive character of Yorkshire folk, their rugged independence contrasting with the bland softness of 'offcomers' like the narrator Mr Lockwood. Indeed, Emily may have found the basic idea for the plot locally, in the sad story of the Walkers, a Halifax family of farmers and manufacturers, whose fortunes were bedevilled by an adopted son.

PROUD CRAFTSMEN

At the time Emily Brontë was writing, the distinctive Yorkshire character was already a byword: dour and pragmatic, cautious but blunt, suspicious of strangers yet warm-hearted and proudly independent – a character moulded by centuries of wresting a living from a harsh landscape, often on remote hill farms. But the three decades of Emily's life saw Yorkshire and Yorkshire lives changing dramatically as the Industrial Revolution stormed through the West Riding.

Perched high on the bleak moors, Haworth seems far removed from the great centres of industry today. Yet it was not so when the Brontës first went to live there in 1820. Haworth was not a remote farming community then, but one of a dense cluster of bustling manufacturing villages that ran all the way down the steep valleys of the Aire and Calder to Bradford and Halifax. In the solid, grey stone cottages of these villages worked thousands of independent master clothiers – 'little makers' – and weavers and woolcombers who had helped make the West Riding of Yorkshire the focus of the English fine woollen and worsted industry. The wool came from Yorkshire sheep.

It was the small master clothiers, more than anyone, who created the Yorkshire reputation for bluntness and bluff pride – their way of life fostered a sense of independence. Half a century previously, the small master clothier would ride over to the Yorkshire Wolds to buy his own raw wool. He would weave the wool himself on a hand-loom, perhaps employing a few journeyman weavers to help him, and then ride over to Halifax or Leeds to sell the cloth independently in the great Cloth Hall. By 1800, he had come to rely on merchants to buy and sell wool, but he was still free to work as and when he pleased.

Writing of Cleckheaton in the 1830s, Frank Peel described the character of the small master clothier:

Hunting with gundogs *(above) Hunting and shooting were the prime leisure pursuits of the gentleman farmer, the rugged landscapes providing excellent sport.*

The cottage weaver *(left) Weavers had a secure, if limited, income and a proud independence – until the mills opened and made craftsmanship defunct almost overnight.*

'dark, satanic mills'
(left) Yorkshire became the centre of the textile world. Some mill-owners adopted a fatherly role, providing schooling, housing and health care for their workers. For the majority, however, work in the mills meant squalor, malnutrition and an early death.

The Victorian family
(below) The traditional image of the large Victorian family was a reality, but only the children of the well-to-do (most of whom belonged to a new class) had a better-than-even chance of surviving infancy.

God's estate
A strict and austere piety governed all aspects of Yorkshire life. The Methodist movement thrived in town and country, encouraging thrift, hard work and suspicions as deep-rooted as the colourful folklore.

'The little makers were men who doffed their caps to no one, and recognized no right in either squire or parson to question, or meddle with them . . . Their brusqueness and plain speaking might at times be offensive . . . If the little maker rose in the world high enough to employ a few of his neighbours, he did not therefore cease to labour with his own hands, but worked as hard or perhaps harder than anyone he employed. In speech and in dress he claimed no superiority'. An admirable race.

Towards the end of the 18th century, with demand for fine woollens rising and prices high, woolcombers and croppers, and even journeyman weavers, earned a good enough income to infect them with a similar sense of independence – good enough for them to barely notice the loss of control over their lives.

No one who came to Yorkshire around the turn of the century could fail to appreciate the bluff pride and down-to-earth manner of the wool craftsmen of the West Riding and their families. Emily Brontë must have seen such folk, for well into the 20s there were something like a thousand small master clothiers and weavers working away in the cramped cottages of Haworth, and their frequent comings and goings on business must have made the tiny, cluttered village into a bustling, active place.

Yorkshire collieries
Steel furnaces and the railways sent the demand for Yorkshire coal rocketing. But there was no shortage of hands ready to work in the pits – men, women and children. The picture above, entitled 'Pitmen at Play' almost achieves the impossible in sentimentalizing the harsh life these miners led – Yorkshire pits were notoriously unsafe.

DECLINE AND FALL

By then, however, the fortunes of the woolcraftsman were sinking fast beneath the rising tide of the Industrial Revolution, as factory after factory went up in the big cities of the West Riding to manufacture wool on a massive scale. The affluent independence of the woolcraftsmen was reduced to abject poverty almost overnight, for they stood no chance against the great factories. The factories employed hundreds of workers at starvation wages to operate steam-powered machines and monopolized both the supply of raw wool and the sale of finished cloth.

The wool croppers – once the aristocrats of the wool trade – had already gone under. They had fought desperately against the introduction of the cropping frames in factories which threw thousands of them out of work, but to no avail – one of the worst of the 'Luddite' riots against the new machines was in Patrick Brontë's own parish of Hartshead in 1812, and Emily's father must have been aware of the ruthless way the rioters were dealt with. In the 1820s and 30s, when Emily was living in Haworth, it was the weavers who were plunged into beggary by the extension of the factory system, and the introduction of the 'labour-saving' Jacquard power-loom.

Robbed of their trade, and indeed of any work, the woolcraftsmen of Haworth and the other villages of the West Riding sank into terrible poverty. Shrugging off their traditional pride, they trekked into Bradford and Leeds to beg for work in the factories. There they met with thousands of other destitute migrants, from the Yorkshire countryside and beyond, forced off the land by the enclosure movement (in the interests of more efficient farming techniques). To Bradford in the 1820s, 'they came from Kendal, North Yorkshire, Leicester, Devonshire, and even the Emerald Isle; so that to spend an hour in a public-house . . . one might have heard a perfect babble of different dialects.' Outsiders, even immigrants from overseas – Jews, Germans and, especially after the Great Famine of the 1840s, Irish – flooded in to swell the population of the cities of the West Riding and subtly alter the character of urban Yorkshire.

Heathcliff's origin is unknown, and in the course of *Wuthering Heights*, he is showered with all sorts of

epithets: he is a vagrant, a gypsy, "a little Lascar, or an Armenian or Spanish castaway". But his character may well have been suggested by the Irish children who arrived with their starving families at Liverpool, where Mr Earnshaw finds the little child – and where, in reality, Branwell Brontë must have seen them dying in the streets when he visited the city in 1845.

Few of the immigrants were as lucky as Heathcliff; most faced conditions as bad, if not worse, than those they had fled. With so many willing hands, the factories were able to pay workers less than a pittance, and lay them off at will. A bitter strike of 20,000 woolcombers and weavers in Bradford in 1825 for better conditions ended in disaster – partly because when the strike became a struggle for union recognition, the employers sacked all the children whose parents supported the idea of a trade union.

Men, women and children were forced to work long hours in exhausting, dangerous jobs for abysmal wages in the factories, and in the new coal mines which were covering the landscape of the West Riding with slag heaps and soot. Crawling on all fours, far underground in a choking atmosphere, girls and boys of all ages from 7 to 21 would work in the mines virtually naked, dragging coal along with 'belts round their waists and a chain passing between their legs'.

Up at the big house
Life was good among the merchant classes. Great status was to be won by sheer financial success. A man had absolute power within his own home, and might achieve advantageous 'mergers' by means of his children's marriages. In many respects, his life resembled the privilege of the landed gentry, though the aristocracy liked to look down on those in 'trade' as jumped-up nouveaux riches.

Urban sprawl
Canals and railways brought raw materials to the factory door. And the workforce, too, had to move close to their only hope of employment. Families drifted in from the countryside – many made homeless by the notorious 'Enclosures Act' – to rows of bleak, back-to-back houses. The blight of such housing still scars many Yorkshire towns today.

The conditions these folk lived in were equally terrible. Most ex-weavers and their families dressed in rags, slept fitfully in sheds completely bare of any furniture but a stool or two, and, according to the Bradford social reformer Richard Oastler, 'they do not know what it is to taste flesh meat'. Worse still, the cities were unbelievably filthy and unhealthy, and working men died, on average, at only 19-20 years old while almost half the children died before the age of six. Back in the villages, conditions were little better, though the air was clean, and a report in 1840 showed that Haworth was one of the filthiest, most disease-ridden towns in England.

UNREST AND PROTEST

Naturally, the working class people protested every now and then about their conditions, and it is hardly surprising that the Chartist movement had widespread support in Yorkshire – though their activities were dealt with brutally and 'efficiently' by the army. 'Trouble at t'mill' became an all too familiar phrase for the Yorkshire mill-owner. There were philanthropic mill-owners, such as the grand textile baron, Sir Titus Salt, who set up a 'model' mill, away from the smoke of Bradford, at Saltaire. But such enlightened men were all too rare.

Some mill-owners, like Salt, were self-made men in the traditional Yorkshire mould – master clothiers and craftsmen who had built up their businesses from humble beginnings. Living in large, lavishly decorated

The grand hunts
Down South, and in the refinement of the cities, the Yorkshire squires were written off as coarse country bumpkins. Within the Ridings, however, a man's worth was often judged by his horsemanship and the calibre of his dogs. The Yorkshire calendar was marked out in terms of the traditional hunting days and the annual hunt balls.

houses, and adopting the aristocracy's taste for art and for hunting, they still retained their blunt manner and, often, their Yorkshire dialect. Despite their wealth, and their often genuine refinement, they were frequently shunned by the traditional land-owning aristocracy – unless, of course, hard times encouraged a prudent match. Brought up in genteel poverty, the Brontë sisters too tended to scorn the virtues of the wealthy self-made man, regarding him as rather coarse.

For a generation or two, the mill-owners were not regarded as wholly acceptable to polite society. Then the influence of public school was brought to bear on their sons, producing an upper class in which squires and manufacturers shared identical manners, morals and tastes and were hard to tell apart.

LIVES OF QUALITY

The self-made manufacturers, however, were always in the minority, for it was the landowners who had the capital and influence to set up an industrial enterprise. They built their houses in town at first, it is true, often on the hill overlooking their factory. But when the towns became too dirty, they readily moved out to country estates and joined in – and even monopolized – the old rural pursuits.

Of all the rural pursuits, none was more popular than hunting, and the Yorkshire squires were renowned for their enthusiasm for chasing foxes – though few could match the ardour of Lord Darlington, leader of the famous Raby Hunt, who was in the saddle nearly every day of his life for over 50 years. The ladies, meanwhile, and the less energetic gentlemen, would resort to the quiet elegance of spa towns such as Harrogate and Skipton to take the waters for their health and join the sophisticated social round.

Without a doubt, the land itself influenced the Brontës as much as the people it bred. The bleak, uncomprising wildness of the moors, consorting with the almost domestic gentleness of the Dale Valley farms maintain a presence in Emily's novel as powerful as any male-female entanglement. The extreme climate, particularly winter, held a far greater significance than modern town-dwellers can easily appreciate. The cold, wind and wet were life-threatening adversaries. Indeed, they only could be said to have triumphed over those daughters of Yorkshire, the Brontë sisters.

The Peterloo Massacre
(below) In August 1819, 11 people died and over 400 were injured when troops charged a peaceful protest meeting at St Peter's Fields, Manchester. (The carnage was compared to that on the battlefield of Waterloo.) Such protests were met with similar brutality in Yorkshire.

GEORGE ELIOT

1819-1880

Mary Ann Evans – better known as George Eliot – would have been an extraordinary woman in any age, but in her own she challenged the norms of Victorian social convention and extended the boundaries of fiction. In a period renowned for its strict moral and religious values, she lived openly with a married man and rejected Christianity. In her novels she replaced orthodox Christianity with a 'religion of Humanity'. The compassion and insight with which she shows her characters growing and developing marks her out as one of the most sensitive and intelligent novelists in the English language. Her exceptional qualities as a writer finally gained her – if not complete social acceptance – her rightful position as a great English woman of letters.

The Estranged Intellectual

Mary Ann Evans spent much of her life as a social outcast and wrote her novels under the pseudonym of George Eliot. It was only her formidable gifts that stemmed the relentless tide of public opinion

Warwickshire birthplace
(left) Mary Ann Evans was born in 1819 at South Farm on the Warwickshire estate of Arbury which her father managed for more than 30 years.

Mary Ann's father
(above) Robert Evans – perhaps the inspiration for Adam Bede – was a highly respected practical man. Despite their religious differences, Mary Ann was very close to him.

Of all the million or more words written by Mary Ann Evans, no two were more carefully chosen than those which were to carry her literary reputation: George Eliot – George, she explained later, because it was her 'husband's' name; Eliot because it was easy to pronounce. She carefully chose a male pseudonym to secure for herself 'all the advantages without the disagreeables of reputation'. Yet she divorced herself from many of those advantages, not by her writing but by her choice of a 'husband'. For by daring to live openly with a married man, Mary Ann Evans put herself beyond the pale of Victorian respectability.

Mary Ann was born in Arbury, Warwickshire on 22 November 1819. Her father, Robert Evans, was the estate manager at Arbury Hall, a self-taught man who had started out as a carpenter.

Shortly after Mary Ann's birth, the family, consist-

Coventry background
(right) Mary Ann spent three years at school in Coventry, and lived there for eight years from the age of 21. The town and the countryside around made a deep impression on her and years later, when writing her novels, she was to draw on her memories of the area again and again. 'Middlemarch', the town at the centre of her greatest novel, may be a portrait of the Coventry of her youth – when it was still a quiet, provincial town.

ing of Robert's second wife Christiana and their children Chrissey and Isaac, moved into the comfortable, rambling farmhouse called Griff, which was to be her home for 20 years.

Mary Ann's father and brother were to have an indelible influence on her personality. Her father took her on his inspections of the estate, holding her firmly on the saddle of his large grey horse. Isaac played marbles with her, showed her how to spin humming tops, and took her fishing by the local canal.

At the age of five she was sent to a local boarding school – while Isaac was sent to school in Coventry. The parting from Isaac hurt her deeply, and she hated her time at Miss Lathom's. Four years later, she went on to the Elms School in Nuneaton, where she became firm friends with the governess, Maria Lewis. Under Maria's guidance, Mary Ann became sternly Christian, renouncing her vanity by cutting off her curls and wearing a prim cap. She completed her formal education with a three-year spell at the Misses Franklin's school in Coventry. By the age of 16, she played the piano with refinement, was well read and had completely lost her provincial accent.

A LEARNED 'OWL'

In February 1836, Mary Ann's mother died. When her elder sister Chrissey married the following year, Mary Ann became her father's housekeeper and companion. But she did not neglect her education and took private tuition in German, French, Italian, Greek and Latin, and, in her own words, 'used to go about like an owl, to the great disgust of my brother'. She was rapidly becoming such a formidable paragon of learning that her father feared she would never find husband.

At the age of almost 70, Robert Evans left Griff to Isaac and retired to Coventry where he hoped his 21 year-old daughter would meet potential husbands. Ironically, although he rented a villa in Foleshill, a highly respectable neighbourhood, his choice of house set Mary Ann on the path to social disgrace.

Their next-door neighbour, Mrs Abijah Pears, was the sister of Charles Bray, an enthusiastic social reformer and the most notorious freethinker in Coventry. Mary Ann met him and his wife Cara in November 1841, and they soon became firm friends. Mary Ann had long since believed that it was perfectly possible to be a Christian without being moral, and vice versa; the Brays convinced her that she was right.

On 2 January 1842, Robert Evans' diary notes: 'Went to Trinity Church in the forenoon. . . Mary Ann did not go.' Those two short sentences do not reveal the outrage that shook the family. Robert's daughter had suddenly, she informed him, 'lost her faith in Church doctrine'. And so fierce was his anger that she fled to stay with her sister Chrissey and then Isaac.

Four months passed before her father reluctantly allowed her to return, and Mary Ann agreed to go to church with him. The eruption subsided but the change in her beliefs was irreversible. At the Brays' house she continued to meet influential thinkers such as Robert Owen, the socialist factory owner and, in 1848, Ralph Waldo Emerson, the American philosopher-poet.

In 1844, Cara Bray's brother Charles Hennell gave

Mary Ann at 27
(right) One of the earliest known likenesses of the future George Eliot, this sketch was made from a silhouette by Sara Hennell, who also painted the view of Coventry (below left). Sara, Cara Bray's sister, was Mary Ann's best friend for many years, and in her letters Mary Ann often addresses her as cara sposa *('dear wife'). Later she wrote to Sara, 'How many sweet laughs – how much serious pleasure . . . you and I have had together in a past islet of time that remains very sunny in my remembrance'.*

Bird Grove, Foleshill
(right) Robert Evans moved with Mary Ann to this big old house in Coventry in 1841, and it was here she came into contact for the first time with the radical religious ideas that were to become so important to her. Living in the adjoining house were Mr Abijah Pears and his wife Elizabeth, the sister of the freethinker Charles Bray. Charles Bray was an important early influence on the young Mary Ann.

Key Dates

1819 born 22 November at Arbury, Warwickshire

1841 to Coventry; meets the Brays

1844 translates a Life of Jesus from German

1849 father dies. Travels in Europe

1854 elopes with Lewes to Germany

1855-78 lives with Lewes

1856 writes fiction

1860 *Mill on the Floss*

1871 *Middlemarch*

1876 moves to Witley

1878 Lewes dies

1880 marries John Cross. Dies 20 December, aged 61

Charles Bray
(left) Mary Ann met Charles Bray and his wife Cara soon after she moved to Coventry, and they became life-long friends. Both held advanced views on religion and education, and at their house Mary Ann was able to exchange ideas with such important radical thinkers as Robert Owen and Ralph Waldo Emerson.

George Henry Lewes
(left) Mary Ann and Lewes lived openly together for more than two decades, and they were profoundly happy; on the manuscript to her collected poems she wrote, 'To my beloved Husband, George Henry Lewes, whose cherishing tenderness for 20 years has alone made my work possible to me.' But Lewes was married to another, and Mary Ann became a social outcast.

Mary Ann her first writing commission – a translation of a German *Life of Jesus,* which was published two years later by John Chapman in London. And when Bray bought the *Coventry Herald,* she wrote several learned reviews of books on Christianity and philosophy.

To Bray, she was 'the most delightful companion I have ever known; she knew everything. . . But there were two sides; . . . she was frequently very depressed – and often very provoking, as much so as she could be agreeable – and we had violent quarrels'. He also noted her profound need for emotional support, 'always requiring someone to lean on'. In a prophetic analysis of her character made in 1844, the famous phrenologist George Combe noted, 'she was not fitted to stand alone'.

Robert Evans died in May 1849. Mary Ann had nursed him for months, sleeping night after night on the sofa in his bedroom. Now she inherited a modest income of £100 a year – and five days after the funeral left England with the Brays for a journey through France, Italy and Switzerland. Despite her depression, the trip gave her a lasting taste for travel, and when she reached Geneva she decided to remain there for the winter – staying in a lodging house run by the charming D'Albert Durades. M. D'Albert Durade, a four-foot tall hump-backed painter, was especially endearing to Mary Ann, and may have provided the inspiration for Philip Wakem in *The Mill on the Floss.*

Mary Ann's future was uncertain. Despite one marriage proposal in 1845, which she had rejected, there were no more likely offers for the 30 year-old spinster. Neither Isaac nor Chrissey wanted a permanent guest in their homes; nor did she relish the prospect. Instead, she took the courageous step of moving to London to lodge at John Chapman's house on the Strand in January 1851.

Chapman, who had just bought the *Westminster Review* (a leading literary paper), took on Mary Ann, now calling herself Marian, as his unpaid assistant editor. She wrote a series of learned articles and, at Chapman's 'open evenings', met numerous influential thinkers including Giuseppe Mazzini, T.H. Huxley, Florence Nightingale, Wilkie Collins, Charles Dickens, Charles Babbage and Herbert Spencer. But her two-year stay in Chapman's house was not easy. Chapman lived there with his wife, two children, and mistress. The two women did not take kindly to another rival and joined forces to drive her out of the Strand for six months from March 1851.

Marian's experience of this unconventional house-

hold prepared her for the greatest crisis of her life. In 1853, after an unhappy liaison with Herbert Spencer, she fell in love with George Henry Lewes, an actor, novelist, journalist and, later, the author of two highly successful books explaining science to the layman. He was small, lively and so bristling with facial hair that the famous philosopher Thomas Carlyle nicknamed him 'the Ape'.

Lewes' lifestyle was as unconventional as Chapman's. He openly accepted his wife's relationship with their close friend Thornton Hunt and his family. Agnes had had four children by Lewes, and two more by Hunt. Consequently Lewes no longer regarded her as his wife, but having condoned her infidelity, had forfeited the right to sue for divorce.

LONDON OUTRAGE

There could not have been a more unlikely partner for Marian Evans than Lewes. He was as renowned for his sexual laxity as she for her moral probity, yet the attraction between 'the Ape' and the 'great horse-faced blue-stocking' – as Henry James once admiringly called her – was immediate and intense. In October 1853, Marian left Chapman's house for private lodgings; the following July the lovers eloped to Germany, escaping the storm of outrage and condemnation that they had aroused in London. One of their fiercest critics, the sculptor Thomas Woolner – who later became a friend – described them as 'hideous satyrs and

SOCIAL OUTCAST

By living 'in sin' with Lewes, a married man, Marian Evans affronted 'decent' Victorian society. When they eloped abroad, vicious stories circulated back home and, on their return, she was shunned everywhere. Women in particular risked social disgrace if they associated with such a pariah. What hurt Marian most was the hypocrisy. Men could keep mistresses with little embarrassment, but any woman who lived 'in sin' became a social outcast. And adultery was condoned as long as it was kept behind closed doors. It was only because Marian's deeply moral nature would not allow such subterfuge that she was condemned.

Double standards
Victorian society was not as straight-laced as is often portrayed – for men. Men had so much sexual freedom that Dickens once remarked that if his son was not *promiscuous he might worry about his health. But for women any hint of sexual scandal was enough to provoke social condemnation.*

The shores of Lake Geneva
(left) After her father died in 1849, the Brays took Mary Ann travelling on the Continent – leaving her for five happy months with the D'Albert Durades in Geneva. She fell in love with Monsieur D'Albert as 'father and brother both', and fell in love with travelling too.

Arbury Estate
(left) The tranquillity of the Arbury estate where Mary Ann spent her childhood provided the background for much of her earlier fiction, such as Scenes of Clerical Life *(1858) and* Adam Bede *(1859). But the estate was not all peace and quiet; coal had been found on the estate, and production increased throughout Mary Ann's lifetime. In the first tale in* Scenes of Clerical Life, Amos Barton, *she recalls a dismal district of roads 'black with coal-dust' and rows of dark houses 'dingy with smoke.'*

Fact or Fiction

THE ORIGINAL MILL ON THE FLOSS

Many of the settings in George Eliot's novels draw on childhood memories, but the mill on the Floss was an unusual mixture. There is an element of the old mill at Arbury. But she also had to find a location where sudden flooding was possible, and detailed research for the book in 1860 reminded her of the tidal surges she had seen on the Trent 15 years earlier. She combined these memories with close observation of a watermill near Weymouth to create Dorlcote Mill.

Realistic idyll
In Dorlcote Mill, George Eliot paints an idyllic picture of an old watermill: "The rush of the water, and the booming of the mill, bring a dreamy deafness, which seems to heighten the peacefulness of the scene. And now there is the thunder of the huge covered wagon coming home with sacks of grain . . . and the unresting wheel sending out its diamond jets of water." Yet though the scene is idyllic, Eliot placed a high value on realism, and researched her subject thoroughly.

Berlin 'honeymoon'
(right) When Mary Ann eloped with Lewes in 1854, they spent three months in Weimar, which they both loved, and four in Berlin, which they found dismal.

Isaac Evans
(far right) Stern and pious, Mary Ann's beloved brother Isaac cut her off completely when she lived with Lewes. Only when she married Cross did he acknowledge her again.

smirking moralists . . . stinkpots of humanity'.

Though the sharpest barbs were launched at Lewes for deserting his wife, Marian left herself open to attack as a hypocrite – her translation of Feuerbach's *The Essence of Christianity* had been published that month, under her own name. But as she bitterly remarked in later years, it was her integrity that brought down society's wrath. If she had secretly become Lewes' mistress, all would have been well. Victorian society was more offended by her daring to openly flout its moral laws – Marian was well aware of the hypocrisy.

In April 1855, Lewes and Marian returned to London and soon moved into lodgings in Richmond. At first they had few visitors and even fewer invitations. Her brother Isaac, who still lived in Warwickshire, was so shocked by their setting up house together that he disowned her. A further problem was that since Lewes was still supporting Agnes and their sons, and her children by Hunt, their finances were limited. But gradually the barriers lifted. First Chapman, then Bray, visited Richmond, and Marian began writing again for the *Westminster Review*.

EARLY FICTION

Without such enforced isolation and with Lewes' encouragement, Marian might never have turned to fiction. Her first three stories – *Scenes of Clerical Life* – were published under her pseudonym in January 1858. Her first full-length novel, *Adam Bede*, 'a country story – full of the breath of cows and the scent of hay', for which she drew heavily on her childhood memories, was published the following year. The central character was based on her father, Robert Evans.

While she was writing *Adam Bede*, her publisher, John Blackwood, visited Richmond. He guessed that Marian was the mysterious George Eliot, and agreed to keep the secret. When the book was published in February 1859, it attracted tremendous interest and

Richmond Hill
(below) Soon after their return to London in 1855 Mary Ann and Lewes moved to Richmond. Shunned by society, they had few visitors and often went walking alone on Richmond Hill.

speculation about the real identity of its author.

Her brother Isaac realized at once that his sister had written *Adam Bede*, but kept it a secret. Other local readers also recognized the characters and background detail, but decided that the real author was a former curate, Joseph Liggins, who had fallen on hard times. To Marian's astonishment, Liggins not only claimed authorship, but also declared that Blackwood had not paid him a penny! This farce turned perilously close to fraud when a group of readers organized a fund-raising committee to compensate Liggins. By mid 1859 Marian was forced to admit her authorship publicly.

The 40 year-old Marian Lewes, as she now called herself, had become famous as the novelist George Eliot. With *Adam Bede's* success – it sold over 5,000 copies in a fortnight – she and Lewes were able to buy a house in Wandsworth.

THE GREAT AUTHOR

The domestic lives of the couple continued almost unchanged for the next 20 years. Marian produced a steady flow of best-sellers from *The Mill on the Floss* to *Daniel Deronda*. The consequent improvement in their financial position (Marian's income rose from £800 for *Adam Bede* to £8,000 for *Middlemarch*) meant that they could afford to take a bigger house, the Priory near Regent's Park, and travel widely in Europe.

But despite her success, she was never entirely socially accepted. Lewes received the invitations, not her. And when people visited the Regent's Park house they often left their wives behind; it tended to be only the more 'emancipated' women who dared the social barbs. But the range of visitors to George Eliot's Sunday afternoons reads like a cultural Who's Who, including Tennyson, Rossetti, Henry James, Edward Burne-Jones and many more.

The success of *Middlemarch* made George Eliot much more socially acceptable as perhaps the country's greatest living writer. Now a grand dame, she often drove around London in her own carriage, wearing a hat with a giant ostrich feather.

In the mid 1870s, the Leweses began looking for a country house, and enlisted the aid of John Cross, a young stockbroker friend. After two years he found the ideal location – a large red-brick house at Witley in Surrey. But Marian's joy at being back in the countryside was short-lived. Lewes had developed a serious stomach illness, and his health slowly grew worse. By the end of November 1878 he was dead.

For a week, Marian was inconsolable. She remained in her room, and would talk to no-one. Then she began work again, doggedly completing Lewes' final book, then correcting proofs for her own *Impressions of Theophrastus Such*, published in May. Johnny Cross became such a regular visitor that, by the end of the summer, this strangely matched couple, with 20 years difference in their ages, had fallen in love.

They married in 1880 and sailed for a honeymoon to the Continent. While in Milan, they received a letter of congratulation from Isaac, who, for the first time in 23 years, now acknowledged his sister. In December, Mr and Mrs Cross moved into a new home in Cheyne Walk, Chelsea, and began enjoying London life, going to the theatre and concerts. But two weeks later Marian was struck down by a severe kidney infection and after three days of extreme pain collapsed into unconsciousness. She died on 22 December 1880.

The consequences of Marian's social transgression pursued her to the grave – she was denied a funeral at Westminster Abbey as befitted a writer of her undoubted greatness. But her family ties had been fully restored. Isaac Evans was a mourner at her burial, beside Lewes' grave in Highgate Cemetary – so too were many famous men and, significantly, many women, deeply mourning the death of such an inspiring fellow woman.

Questioning the Faith

The spiritual crisis experienced by George Eliot was symptomatic of the Victorian age, and – paradoxically – provided much of the intellectual and emotional energy of her novels.

For most educated Victorians, religion lay at the very centre of life. The people who believed were in deadly earnest – but so were those who, like George Eliot, doubted or denied the supernatural, and worked out their own purely secular creed. The age was one in which sects and parties multiplied within the churches, while, almost simultaneously, new ideas and scientific advances undermined the very foundations of religion. For all their energy and self-confidence, the Victorians were oppressed by doubts, and George Eliot herself experienced an acute religious conflict difficult to imagine today.

During the 18th century, the Christian churches in England lost a good deal of their vitality. The Church of England, in particular, became as much a social institution as a religious organization, teaching its parishioners to chant,

Bless the squire and his relations
And keep us in our proper stations.

Many families were like the Dodsons and Tullivers in *The Mill on the Floss* – "they didn't know there was any other religion, except that of chapel-goers, which appeared to run in families, like asthma". And the clergy resembled their vicar, who "was not a controversialist, but a good hand at whist, and one who had a joke always ready for a blooming female parishioner".

The Evangelical movement developed as a reaction to this state of affairs. It was not a new sect, but a powerful general impulse that was felt within almost all the Protestant churches, and was essentially a revival of Protestant values. Evangelicalism stressed the importance of the individual's experience of conversion and replaced the Church's authority with a personal interpretation of the Scriptures. The movement was responsible for the creation of one new breakaway sect – the Methodists, followers of the Anglican clergyman John Wesley, whose willingness to preach in the fields or market-place angered his superiors. As a result, Methodism reached many thousands of working men and women in the great new industrial towns, who were virtually ignored by the Church of England.

However, the Evangelical wing of the Anglican Church was also active – and influential in changing social conditions. Its ranks included such outstanding figures as the anti-slavery campaigner William Wilber-

A materialistic clergy
(above) During the 19th century clergymen were becoming increasingly conscious of social status, like Mr Stelling in The Mill on the Floss, *who "had a true British determination to push his way in the world".*

The persuasive Methodist
(left) Women as well as men taught the doctrines of Methodism, following the example of John Wesley, who preached in the open to working people. George Eliot's aunt was one such preacher, the model for Dinah Morris in Adam Bede.

force, and Lord Shaftesbury, who was responsible for the earliest legislation regulating hours and conditions of work in Britain's factories.

The Evangelicals were devotees of preaching and lectures, and poured much energy into philanthropic societies, and raising money for foreign missions. They dressed soberly, observed the sanctity of the Sabbath and tended at the slightest provocation to proclaim their allegiance in the universal battle between sin and salvation. At best, the Evangelical was heroic; at worst, pompous, sanctimonious or even hyprocritical, like Mr Bulstrode in George Eliot's *Middlemarch*, who had "an immense need of being something important and predominating".

THE OXFORD MOVEMENT

George Eliot knew Evangelicalism from the inside. Under the influence of her teacher, Miss Maria Lewis, she held strict Evangelical beliefs until she was 22. She refused to go to such a sinful place as the theatre with her brother Isaac (although she later regretted the impulse to deny him 'what I now see to have been quite lawful amusements'), and her first publication was a religious poem in Evangelical vein.

Evangelicalism remained the dominant religious 'style' for most of George Eliot's lifetime, although a substantial minority of Anglicans, including her brother Isaac, were drawn in the diametrically opposite direction – towards the Tractarian or Oxford movement led by the High Church intellectual, John Henry Newman who was to exert such an influence over the young Oscar Wilde. Newman and his followers reasserted the importance of ritual and the sacraments, rejected the individualism of the Evangelical tradition and made the Church rather than conscience the basis of theological authority and the means of salvation. They even went so far as to argue that the Church of England was not Protestant at all, but a purified form of the Catholic Church and should have no truck with Protestant 'heretics'.

The publication of the 'Tracts for the Times', which set out the movement's principles, caused a furore almost inconceivable today. Hostility towards Roman Catholicism was still widespread, and to most Protestant Englishmen the doctrines of the Oxford movement seemed bent on 'Romanizing' the Church of England. Such fears were strengthened by defections to Rome, the most sensational being that of Newman himself, who later became a Cardinal.

Pomp and circumstance
(left) At one extreme of the fermenting religious controversy lay High Anglicanism, which made full use of ritual and its trappings. Buildings and services alike were lavish and splendid, indicating the wealth invested in this branch of the Church.

Looking towards Rome
(right) The most influential man behind the Church's movement towards Rome was the Oxford vicar, John Henry Newman. He persuaded as much by his personal devoutness as by his powerful writings. But his later conversion added fuel to the widespread Protestant hostility to the Catholic 'threat'.

In the early 19th century, those in authority had no doubt that the function of religion was to uphold the social order, and that atheists and deists (people who believed in God but dispensed with all dogma and ecclesiastical authority) were likely to be dangerous revolutionaries. One such was the poet Shelley (also a radical, a vegetarian, and an apostle of free love), who was sent down from University College, Oxford, in 1811 for his pamphlet 'The Necessity of Atheism', the first advocacy of complete unbelief to be published in English. Later, Shelley was beaten up at Keswick, probably because of his religious opinions.

Attempts to convert the working class to atheism and radicalism were continued by agitators like George Holyoake, the last man in England to be imprisoned for professing atheism. However, secularist propaganda touched only a small section of the working class, although working people long remained vaguely anti-clerical because of the presumed alliance between the Churches and the propertied class.

This assumption was weakened by the rise of a socially concerned group, the Christian Socialists, in the middle of the century, but neither they nor the 'slum parsons' and energetic church-builders of the late Victorian period managed to reverse the trend towards mass irreligion. Its sympton was the decline in church- and chapel-going, and it signified indifference rather than any positive commitment to secular beliefs.

By contrast, writers, scientists and intellectuals experienced serious religious crises and conflicts throughout the Victorian period. If their numbers were not great, their influence was widely felt, and George Eliot's circle included many men who had refused to take holy orders or abandoned them as a matter of conscience. For some, loss of faith was experienced as a liberation from the gloom of Original Sin and the threat of hell-fire. George Eliot herself cast off Evangelical Christianity with a 'feeling of exultation and strong hope', her soul 'liberated from the wretched giant's bed of dogmas on which it has been racked and stretched ever since it began to think'.

Others, like Thomas Carlyle, were overwhelmed by the meaninglessness of a universe without God, although 'From suicide a certain aftershine . . . of

The Romantic atheist
(above) One of the earliest advocates of atheism was the Romantic poet Percy Bysshe Shelley, whose radical views clashed alarmingly with the Victorian establishment, and drove him to settle in Italy. Shelley's dramatic life ended prematurely when he drowned in a summer squall at sea. His body was burned on the shore, in keeping with ancient Greek custom and his own unorthodox views.

Herbert Spencer
(below left) One of the great Victorian liberal philosphers, Spencer elevated science into a religion, and was a vigorous advocate of Darwin's theory of evolution. His progressive views were of great interest to George Eliot and gave intellectual stimulus to their friendship.

Slavery and the Church
(right) An Evangelical convert, William Wilberforce, was among the first to denounce the evils of the slave trade, and to campaign against it. The Emancipation Act – which abolished slavery in Britain and its colonies – was finally passed in 1834.

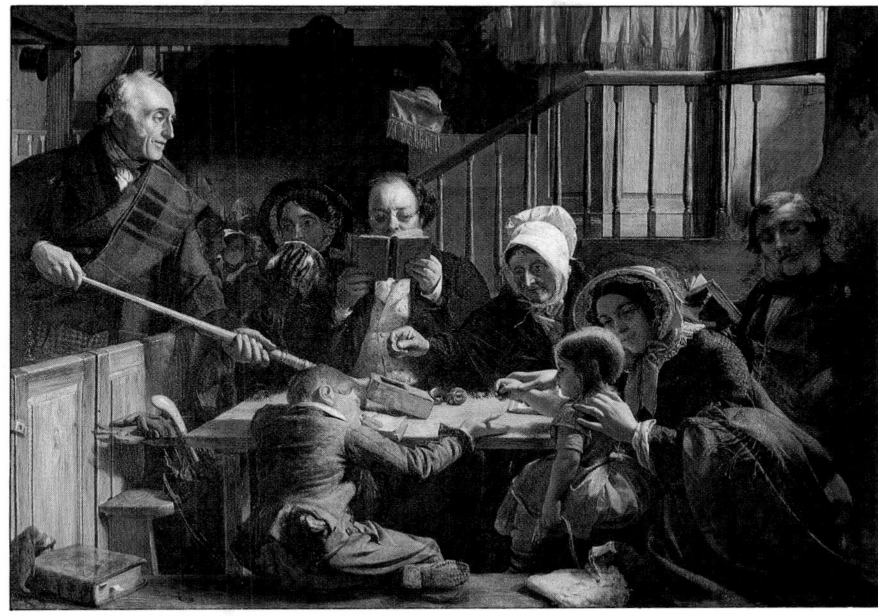

Christianity withheld me.' The note of doubt and melancholy is strong in Victorian literature. It was given its classic expression in Matthew Arnold's poem 'Dover Beach', where only the 'melancholy, long, withdrawing roar' of the Sea of Faith is heard.

BROKEN FAMILY TIES

As well as private agonies, the Victorian doubter had to endure the disruption of personal relationships. Religious differences broke friendships and – even more important in a family-centred age – divided parents and children, brothers and sisters. George Eliot's experiences in this respect had many parallels. When she refused to go to church, her father moved away and their differences were only patched up when she agreed to conform outwardly. Her Methodist uncle Sam, less easily placated by conventional gestures, broke off all contact with her. And religious differences created a distance between George Eliot and her beloved brother Isaac, although it was her liaison with George Henry Lewes that occasioned the final break. As late as 1869 she noted sadly that 'I cling strongly to kith and kin, even though they reject *me*.'

The chief cause of this turmoil was the impact of science, particularly on the credibility of the Bible. Every advance in knowledge broadened the picture of a universe governed by general laws and working through the logic of cause and effect. The area in which miracles might plausibly occur grew continually smaller, whereas the 'miracles' of technology – that is, applied science – multiplied. More specifically, the Higher Criticism, which was mainly a product of German universities, applied scholarly method and rules of historical evidence to sacred texts, and drew devastating conclusions as to their truth and reliability. George Eliot was profoundly influenced by this sort of Biblical criticism, and translated into English David Friedrich Strauss's *Das Leben Jesu*, which stripped the life of Christ of all its supernatural elements.

Victorian orthodoxy sustained one shock after another, but the severest came from what George Eliot called 'The Doctrine of Development': the concept of evolution, which undermined belief in a single Creation and in fixed moral standards – and much

Evangelical practice
(above) Evangelicalism was responsible for the founding of numerous religious societies and foreign missions, and to this end was indefatigable in its fund-raising activities.

Transforming society
(below) The appalling working conditions in Britain's mines and factories were seen as a matter of Christian – as well as political – concern by certain leading church figures. The most notable was Lord Shaftesbury, who had the power to effect radical social changes.

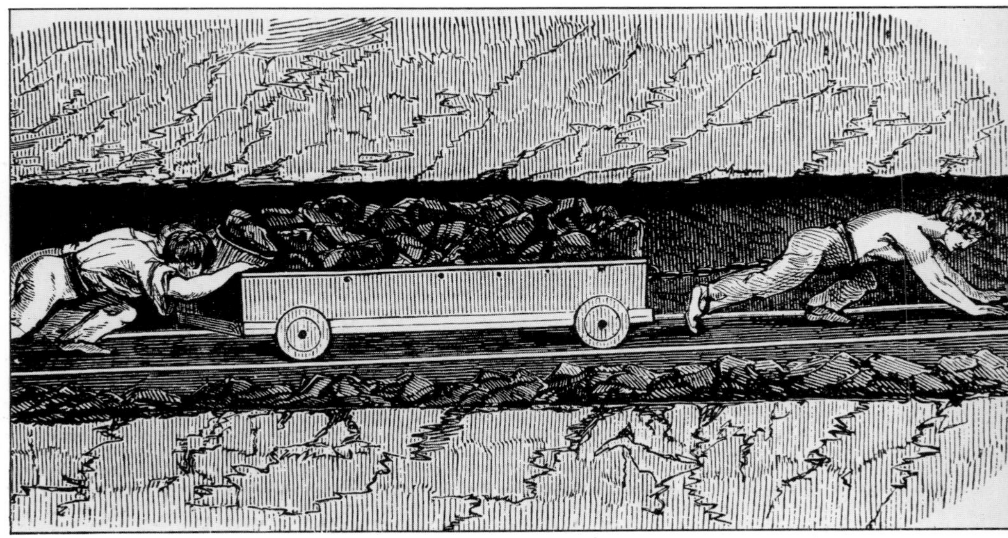

else. George Eliot's friend Herbert Spencer applied the concept of evolution to human society. Charles Darwin's *Origin of Species* substituted biological evolution for a single act of creation which left species forever fixed. The process of natural selection – 'the survival of the fittest' – was also at variance with the idea of a benevolent creation. Instead, as the poet Tennyson lamented, there was 'Nature, red in tooth and claw'.

THE DESCENT OF MAN

Darwin's book appeared in November 1859, while George Eliot was working on *The Mill on the Floss*. Though judging it 'ill-written', she recognized at once that 'it makes an epoch', and she and Lewes became convinced Darwinians. Darwin himself was anxious to avoid trouble, and omitted almost all mention of the most controversial issue – human development – from *Origin of Species*. But orthodox critics were quick to realize that natural selection implied the descent of man from some ape-like creature – an intolerable insult to a being 'created in God's image', and an implicit subversion of the moral framework of existence. Denounced by many, Darwin's theories found an able defender in the brilliant scientist T.H. Huxley, who tirelessly publicized and debated them. In the course of one such debate at Oxford, the glib Bishop Samuel ('Soapy Sam') Wilberforce enquired on which side of his family Huxley claimed to be descended from an ape. Darwinism survived and ultimately forced the churches to rethink and restate their orthodoxies.

Avowed atheists also achieved public acceptance, although many preferred to call themselves 'agnostic'. This term was coined by Huxley, and he thereby discreetly stressed his lack of certain knowledge concerning the existence of God, rather than his disbelief. By 1888, after an epic series of elections and ejections, Charles Bradlaugh had established the atheist's right to become an MP, and to give evidence in a court of law, without swearing by a deity he believed to be non-existent. Nonetheless, in 1878, a British court decided that Bradlaugh's colleague Annie Besant, who had published *The Gospel of Atheism* the year before, was not a fit person to have custody of her daughter.

In reality, the Victorian atheist was a morally earnest person. George Eliot was therefore in many respects a representative figure, like the philosophers who influenced her. She translated Ludwig Feuerbach's *Essence of Christianity*, which argued that the splendid qualities, hitherto projected on to God, must be found among the mutual relationships of humans. And she admired the Positivism of Auguste Comte for its would-be scientific approach to society and its 'religion of humanity', though she was evidently well aware of its slightly absurd side.

Neither Feuerbach nor Comte was crude enough to denounce Christianity. Their view of it as a necessary phase in human development appealed to George Eliot's strong feeling for the past and the old ways, expressed in the gallery of sympathetic portraits of clergymen and pious folk that occur in her works. For George Eliot herself, unbelief was no easy option. In a now famous passage, F.W.H. Myers has recorded how she, 'taking as her text the three words which have been used so often as the inspiring trumpet-calls of men, – the words *God, Immortality, Duty* – , pronounced, with terrible earnestness, how inconceivable was the *first*, how unbelievable the *second*, and yet how peremptory and absolute the *third*.'

A shocking theory
(above) In 1859, the naturalist Charles Darwin published his monumental work, Origin of Species, *and rocked the very foundations of Church and society. To the theory that species survive and develop by a process of natural selection, Darwin brought a body of scientific evidence based on his researches in South America, the South Seas and the Antipodes. The ensuing row between science and religion reached a peak in a famous debate at Oxford between Bishop Samuel Wilberforce and the biologist T. H. Huxley (above left). On this occasion science emerged triumphant, and Huxley continued to be the most tireless champion and exponent of Darwin's theory, saying in 1881 that if the idea of evolution had not existed, they 'would have had to invent it'.*

WILKIE COLLINS

1824-1889

When Wilkie Collins paused in the telling of his latest thriller, Victorian England held its breath. His heroines were the talk of every parlour, and success drew a cloak around the celebrity's highly unconventional private life. A colossus, twinned with Dickens, his was the art not of caricature but of intricate plot, plausible villain, spine-chilling encounter, heart-stopping shock. But perhaps the brooding fears which menace his characters convince his readers because such torments surrounded Collins himself.

Runaway Success

Wilkie Collins wrote prodigiously, took on two common-law wives, fathered three illegitimate children, and made a fortune. In his life as in his work he was a 'Master of Sensation'.

William Wilkie Collins was the firstborn son of William Collins, a successful landscape artist and Royal Academician. Like his father, Wilkie was to be a part of the circle of writers and painters of his day, but that was where the similarity ended. The elder William Collins was a blinkered, tight-fisted Victorian, espousing the beliefs and morality of the Church of England and the Tory party. The younger William Collins was a radical freethinker, and brazenly flaunted his disdain for the conventions of the day throughout his life.

Wilkie was born on 8 January 1824 in a small house in Hampstead, north London. Probably due to some accident at birth, Wilkie's left temple was depressed while his right one bulged. As an adult this, together with a disproportionately large head, short stature (5 feet 6 inches), acute short-sightedness and unusually small hands and feet, gave him an extremely odd appearance.

When Wilkie was six, the family moved to more spacious accommodation in Bayswater from where Wilkie, three years later, was sent to Maida Hill Academy, an exclusive private school. Here, though not far from home, he boarded. Like many imaginative and intelligent boys, he hated school.

TOUR OF ITALY

Already possessed of a strong will, Wilkie was 'perpetually getting punished as a bad boy'. Yet his proficiency led to accusations of being a teacher's pet, and he was frequently bullied and thrashed by the bigger boys. But at the age of 14 his father took him, together with the rest of the family, to Italy. They stayed six months, and the experience for Wilkie was decisive. 'I learnt more which has since been of use to me among the pictures, the scenery, and the people', he recalled later, 'than I ever learnt at school.'

At the age of 17 he left Maida Hill with no clear idea of what he was going to do. Oxford was considered by his father but, to Wilkie's relief, rejected when the cost was calculated. While the family debated what he should do, Wilkie spent his first summer of freedom roaming round the countryside that then bordered north London. As recalled in the semi-autobiographical *A Rogue's Life,* he met 'horsemen in hunting fields', chatted 'amicably with tinkers in ditches. . .pedlars, tramps and labourers. . .all. . .were alike to [his] cosmopolitan sympathies'.

What Wilkie wanted was a life of excitement and adventure, 'a good berth in the merchant navy. . .or an exploring expedition to Australia'. But after rows with his father and empty threats to run away, he settled for a desk job at Antrobus & Co., the London tea brokers.

William Collins, RA
Charles Collins captured the image of his father (left) on paper in 1846; his brother Wilkie was to do the same two years later in a celebrated biography.

THE LIFE
WILLIAM COLLINS, ESQ. R.A.
BY HIS SON.

Boyhood portrait
An early portrait of Wilkie by his father. William Collins named his son after his friend and colleague Sir David Wilkie. It is perhaps ironic that it was his second son, Charles, who was to achieve fame as an artist rather than Wilkie.

His sole diversion during this time was the 'brilliant land of glitter and glass' of London's West End. It was a vicarious pleasure he enjoyed, too poor on a clerk's pay to buy anything more than an occasional cheap cigar. Walking home after his 'nine hours of the most ungrateful daily labour' he sat in his bedroom almost every night and wrote.

Exactly when he formed the ambition to become a writer is not known. But by the age of 19 he was turning out romantic and melodramatic stories for the penny-novel journals. None of these early efforts of his seem to have survived, but as Professor Nuel Davis, Collins' biographer, suggests, they were undoubtedly 'trash'.

Increasingly, writing became his real interest. In the imagined scenes he created night after night he lived a life denied him at Antrobus & Co. Utterly determined, ignoring countless rejections, he finally wrote a story in 1843, *The Last Stagecoachman*, worthy of the pages of *The Illuminated Journal*. Encouraged by its editor Douglas Jerrold, Collins began a novel. Set in Tahiti, it was an improbable story of love and intrigue. Undaunted by its failure to find a publisher, he began another, a story of ancient Rome called *Antonina*.

It took Collins some seven years to complete *Antonina*. In 1846, on seeing just a part of it his father was sufficiently impressed by Wilkie's intellectual ability to release him from Antrobus & Co. and enter his name on to the rolls of Lincoln's Inn.

The law held no more interest for Wilkie as an occupation than did tea, and there is no evidence that he ever studied it with a view to practising. Content to live at home and write, he ate the required number of dinners and in due course was called to the Bar.

But it was his father's death in 1847 that was to change his life. One of the last requests of William Collins was that his eldest son should write his biography. Despite the hostility that had existed between them, Wilkie accepted the commission and wrote a dutiful, competent, *Memoir*. 'An author I was to be,' he said, 'and an author I became in 1848.'

Though not a commercial success, the book brought Wilkie to the attention of the critics – mainly family friends – who wrote encouragingly of his abilities as an author. With £100 pocketed from sales of the book he went to Paris where, apart from completing *Antonina*, he discovered an appetite for dry champagne, French cuisine and prostitutes.

Hampstead Heath
(left) Wilkie's first home made a lasting impression on him. In The Woman in White *it forms the dramatic backdrop to the equally dramatic encounter.*

Courtroom drama
Wilkie never practised as a barrister, but he studied Law and was fascinated by the subject. He based The Woman in White *on an earlier French lawsuit.*

Key Dates

1824 born in London

1847 father dies

1848 first book, *The Memoirs of William Collins RA* published

1851 meets Charles Dickens

1854 encounter with Caroline Graves

1860 *The Woman in White* published

1868 mother dies. Caroline Graves marries. Becomes involved with Martha Rudd. *The Moonstone* published

1870 Dickens dies

1871 reunited with Caroline Graves

1873 reading tour of the United States

1889 dies in London

Home was now 38 Blandford Square, London, to which his mother had moved after the death of her husband. Here with his younger brother Charley, already a recognized artist, he met publishers, writers and the two leading pre-Raphaelite painters, William Holman Hunt and John Everett Millais. With the publication of *Antonina* (1850), through the efforts of John Ruskin, Collins became an accepted author leading a comfortable, sheltered life in his mother's house.

Seeing himself as a producer of saleable commodities for a commercial market, books followed in swift succession. *Rambles Beyond Railways* was written after trudging 238 miles around Cornwall accompanied by an artist named Blandling who illustrated the book. A second novel, *Basil,* was begun, and a play, *A Court Duel,* written and produced at Miss Kelly's Theatre, Soho. His short stories appeared in Bentley's *Miscellany* – one of the leading periodicals of the day.

Still only 27, Collins had good reason to appear confidently pleased with himself. But it was his meeting with Charles Dickens on 12 March 1851 in the rooms of John Forster, that was to prove the most important encounter of his life, both as a writer and as a man.

Dickens was 12 years his senior. In him Collins recognized a tireless nervous energy that matched his own, an inexhaustible and stimulating creativity, and a man who at the age of 40 had a similar penchant for the seamy side of life. Together they formed a friendship which, if lacking in emotional warmth – Collins himself was an undemonstrative, rather tepid man – gave each the confidence to flout the conventions of a society they both, at heart, despised.

Wining and dining at fashionable West End restau-

Fact or Fiction

THE WOMAN IN WHITE

It was after a dinner party in July 1854 that an event took place which was to change the course of Wilkie's life and inspire his greatest work. Wilkie was accompanying the painter Millais back to his studio when, according to Millais' son, they suddenly heard 'a piercing scream coming from the garden of a villa. . . . While pausing to consider what to do, the iron gate leading to the garden was dashed open, and from it came the figure of a young and very beautiful woman dressed in flowing white robes that shone in the moonlight.'

The mysterious woman was 20-year-old Caroline Graves. From this strange beginning, she was to fall in love with Collins and live with him for most of his life.

John Everett Millais
(above) The artist was with Collins and his brother Charles on the fateful summer's evening when they encountered the 'Woman in White'. Wilkie was so moved by this that he charged after her, into the night, to discover her secret.

Venetian travels
In 1853 Wilkie embarked on a two-month tour of Italy with Dickens and Augustus Egg. They took in all the major sights and of his stay in Venice he wrote to his mother 'We lead the most luxurious, dandy-dilettante sort of life here. Our gondola . . . waits on us wherever we go. We live among pictures and palaces all day, and among Operas, Ballets and Cafes more than half the night.'

'Master of Sensation'
Wilkie once complained that Nature had got him 'all out of drawing' and this somewhat cruel cartoon by Adriano Cecioni captures his disproportionately large head in relation to his small body and spindly legs. It appeared in Vanity Fair *in 1872 when the author would have been just 48 and shows how gout and illness had prematurely aged him.*

rants, they shared a passion for the theatre which resulted in many joint private performances, attended music halls and planned nights of 'dissipation', behaving in each other's company, 'like Don Giovanni' as Dickens described it. Whether this included visits to brothels in London is unknown, but they certainly frequented such establishments when travelling together on the Continent.

Impressed by the younger man's literary abilities, Dickens took Collins under his wing. Commissioning articles and short stories for his own weekly *Household Words,* he advised the less experienced Wilkie on how to handle wily publishers in that most delicate of matters, money. A willing and accomplished pupil, Collins soon mastered this art and was able to command a handsome return for his work.

TRAVELS WITH DICKENS

In October 1853, Dickens and Collins made their first trip abroad together with the artist Augustus Egg. The 'holiday' was a gruelling itinerary taking in almost every city and sight between Boulogne and Rome and back. Always physically weak, Collins could not keep up with Dickens. He sprained an ankle early in the trip, and rode on a donkey while Dickens strode ahead on foot. Collins' purse also proved unequal to Dickens' inexhaustible extravagance. Staying only at the best hotels and consuming nothing but the choicest food and wine, Collins returned to London in debt.

The debts, however, were short-lived. Under the patronage of Dickens, Collins prospered to a degree that was to equal and eventually exceed that of the master himself. Financial independence also set him free from the stifling conventions he so despised. A radical freethinker, his sympathy for the casualties of Victorian England took on an increasingly socialistic hue as he grew older. And in his personal life he went even further in his defiance of accepted social mores than Dickens ever dared.

From 1854, after his dramatic encounter one July evening with the beautiful Mrs Câroline Graves, he set up house with her and her baby daughter Lizzie, though he retained a nominal address at his mother's.

Whatever view society took of Collins' relationship with Caroline Graves, it was one which was to last until the end of his life. He missed her terribly in the periods when they were separated and, as he wrote in *The Queen of Hearts,* he was "a man bewitched". In *The Frozen Deep* he described how on their very first meeting "when she embraced me, her arms folded round me like the wings of an angel".

Caroline would have been happy to marry Collins. He, however, never showed the slightest inclination to do so. When his mother died in 1868 (she was always thought to be a barrier to their marriage), Caroline issued Wilkie with an ultimatum, in effect, 'marry me or I'll marry Mr Clow' (a plumber whom she had met when he carried out some work in their home).

'Wilkie's affairs defy all prediction,' Dickens wrote to his sister-in-law Georgina, 'For anything one knows, the whole matrimonial pretence may be a lie of that woman's.' It was not, however, and on 4 October 1868 Caroline married Mr Clow with Wilkie in attendance.

CHARITABLE ACTS

Among the many affinities that Wilkie Collins and Dickens shared was a love of theatre. Together they saw performances, planned and wrote plays, and ultimately acted side-by-side in their own creations.

In 1851 Dickens formed the Guild of Art and Literature, an organization which put on plays to raise money for needy authors and artists. Its aims were 'to render such assistance to both as shall never compromise their independence; and to found a few Institutions where honourable rest from arduous labour shall still be associated with the discharge of congenial duties.'

Not so Bad as We Seem by Bulwer-Lytton was their first comedy, and Dickens subsequently wrote to its author that 'Wilkie fell upon his new part with great alacrity and heartiness', and to his wife Dickens wrote 'Collins was *admirable* — got up excellently, played throughly well, and missed nothing.' The production, which had its debut in London before touring the provinces, raised a staggering £4,000 for the Guild.

The Frozen Deep *by Wilkie was a stirring play about heroism, sex and sacrifice set in the North Pole. Starring Dickens (below) and Wilkie – each sporting nine months' growth of beard – it was a brilliant vehicle for their talents.*

One reason for Collins' apparent indifference to Caroline's marriage was that he had taken up with the "fine-fleshy beef-fed English girl" (as he describes her in *The Fallen Leaves*), Martha Rudd. Nine months to the very day after Caroline's wedding, Martha gave birth to a daughter, Marian. But with Caroline's marriage failing, she was back with Wilkie in the summer of 1871, soon after the birth of Wilkie's second daughter by Martha Rudd. From then on Collins' visits to Martha became very infrequent, although a third child, a boy, was born in 1875.

Collins' unusual private life did nothing to diminish his popularity. His earnings for the time were phenomenal. For a novel of which he had not written a word he was paid an advance of 5000 guineas in 1862. And in the year ending September 1863 his earnings topped £10,000 – probably more than any other writer earned in a single year in the 19th century.

RACKED WITH PAIN

But behind the appearance of a successful, self-assured author, Wilkie Collins suffered torments in mind and body. He could be a tiresome hypochondriac, and fussy about his personal comfort and well being. But from the age of 30, he suffered from what was medically defined as 'rheumatic gout'. It first attacked his eyes so that, as one observer remarked, they became 'bags of blood'. The disease spread to his knees and feet, and he was a virtual invalid for the last 20 years of his life, spending long periods confined to bed. There, surrounded by bottles, potions and tablets, he continued to work indefatigably.

To the gout was added neuralgia, rheumatism, arthritis and insomnia. There is a tendency to think that these afflictions were psychosomatic in origin, and it seems that each attack was preceded by a bout of intense

New York harbour
(above right) Wilkie sailed into New York on 25 Sept 1873 at the start of his American lecture tour. He enjoyed it but complained of autograph hunters and female reporters. Although he must have taken some pleasure in his fame, he felt that he could well have done without the embraces of 'the oldest and ugliest' of the female reporters.

'Divine laundanum'
(left) Prescribed laudanum as a painkiller, Collins took it in ever-increasing doses, occasionally seeing a green woman with tusk teeth lying in wait for him. Apparently when his manservant George Hellow consumed just half of his master's dose, he died almost instantly.

Kensal Rise Cemetery
Collins' burial in Sept 1889 was a simple affair in accordance with his wishes. Caroline Graves was buried at his side in 1895 and Martha Rudd, his other 'wife', tended the grave until her own death a year later.

morbid depression. But the origins of the illness did nothing to diminish the appalling pain Collins had to contend with almost daily. Trying almost every known remedy (principally colchicum and morphine) and engaging a succession of eminent physicians and quacks, he eventually found relief in 'divine laudanum'.

Of the many novels, short stories and plays he continued to pour out with unceasing application, none show quite so clearly his addiction to laudanum as *The Moonstone*. Serialized in Dickens' literary magazine *All the Year Round,* its strange, eerie effect was undoubtedly drug-induced. It was written while his mother lay dying in an adjacent room suffering from the last stages of senile dementia, while he himself suffered the ravages of gout. 'In the intervals of grief, in the intermissions of pain', he said of this time, 'I dictated from my bed. . . *The Moonstone.*'

This novel marked the high point of Collins' literary career. Though he continued to publish novels, short stories and plays at an extraordinary rate, his reputation

among the critics, never high at the best of times, slumped. Even his loyal supporter Dickens became disenchanted with him for a while, commenting on *The Moonstone* that 'the construction was beyond endurance'. But by 1868 the two men had re-established friendly relations and Dickens' death in 1870 lost Collins his closest friend, one who had in many ways mirrored his own view of literature and society.

In 1873-4, Collins embarked on a reading tour of the United States, following once again in Dickens' footsteps. Although it was greeted with warmth and kindness it was not the financial success he had hoped for, due almost entirely to his poor reading ability.

Now an overweight, wheezing, stooped little man with round spectacles and a flowing white beard, the last 15 years of his life were spent with Caroline and her daughter Lizzie (who became his secretary), writing and fighting daily against pain and drug addiction.

Still popular with the public – the only yardstick he considered worthwhile – he was almost entirely forgotten and neglected by the literary establishment. Few critics even knew he was still alive, and for years Collins worried about reading of his death in a newspaper.

Alone in his gas-lit study writing serials, he gradually sank into delirium, believing himself to be pursued by a green woman with tusk teeth. On mounting the staircase on his way to bed, he imagined her biting a chunk out of his shoulder.

On 23 September 1889, after suffering a heart attack, Wilkie Collins wrote a last note to his long-suffering physician Frank Beard, 'I am dying – come if you can'. At 10.35 that morning, aged 65, he died. Following his instructions, he was buried without ceremony in a common plot at Kensal Green Cemetery, London. When Caroline Graves died six years later in 1895, she was buried beside him.

Fear of the Madhouse

The image of the asylum in *The Woman in White* found an audience embarrassed by the phenomenon of madness. Conflicting interests all too often concealed a wretchedly inhumane treatment of the insane.

At the time when Wilkie Collins wrote *The Woman in White,* the mentally ill were feared and shunned by respectable society. The relatives of the insane tended to be ashamed of them, and most 'normal' people were glad to see lunatics put out of the way in special institutions.

Yet madhouses, and the 'mad doctors' associated with them, had a distinctly sinister reputation. In the public mind, an asylum was a place where, for questionable reasons, a person was shut up against her or his will, neglected and mistreated by brutal keepers, and often kept in confinement long after 'sanity' had been restored.

The unsavoury reputation of madhouses was based on a long history of real scandals and abuses, and although many reforms had been introduced by the mid-19th century, shocking facts about the treatment of the insane still came to light. In 1858, the year before Collins began work on *The Woman in White,* patients at two private madhouses were declared sane after an investigation. And one of them, a Mrs Turner, charged that the proprietor, as well as improperly detaining her, had sexually assaulted her.

Although Collins nowhere implies that there is anything amiss with the "prettily laid out" madhouse in *The Woman in White,* where Anne Catherick and Laura, Lady Glyde, are incarcerated, the horrors associated with such places certainly reinforced its emotional impact on Victorian readers.

Earlier attitudes to mental affliction were more open. Idiots and lunatics, although liable to be mocked and provoked, were tolerated within the community, and the 'village idiot' was a familiar figure. The tendency to segregate mad people by putting them in institutions became marked in the 18th century, but the notion that lunacy was a comic phenomenon lingered on.

The oldest public hospital specializing in the treatment of insanity was London's Bethlehem Hospital, whose origins dated back to the 14th century. Its name was soon contracted to Bethlem, which became in familiar speech the notorious 'Bedlam'. Here the unfortunate pauper inmates were put on show for the benefit of spectators who paid twopence a head to watch them, while hucksters sold fruit and nuts, and obliging keepers brought in beer for a small consideration. Public feeling changed slowly, and it was only in 1770 that the first restrictions were placed on visitors to Bedlam. But the hospital's infamous image – influencing attitudes to its inmates – continued well into the 19th century, and was reflected in popular ballads.

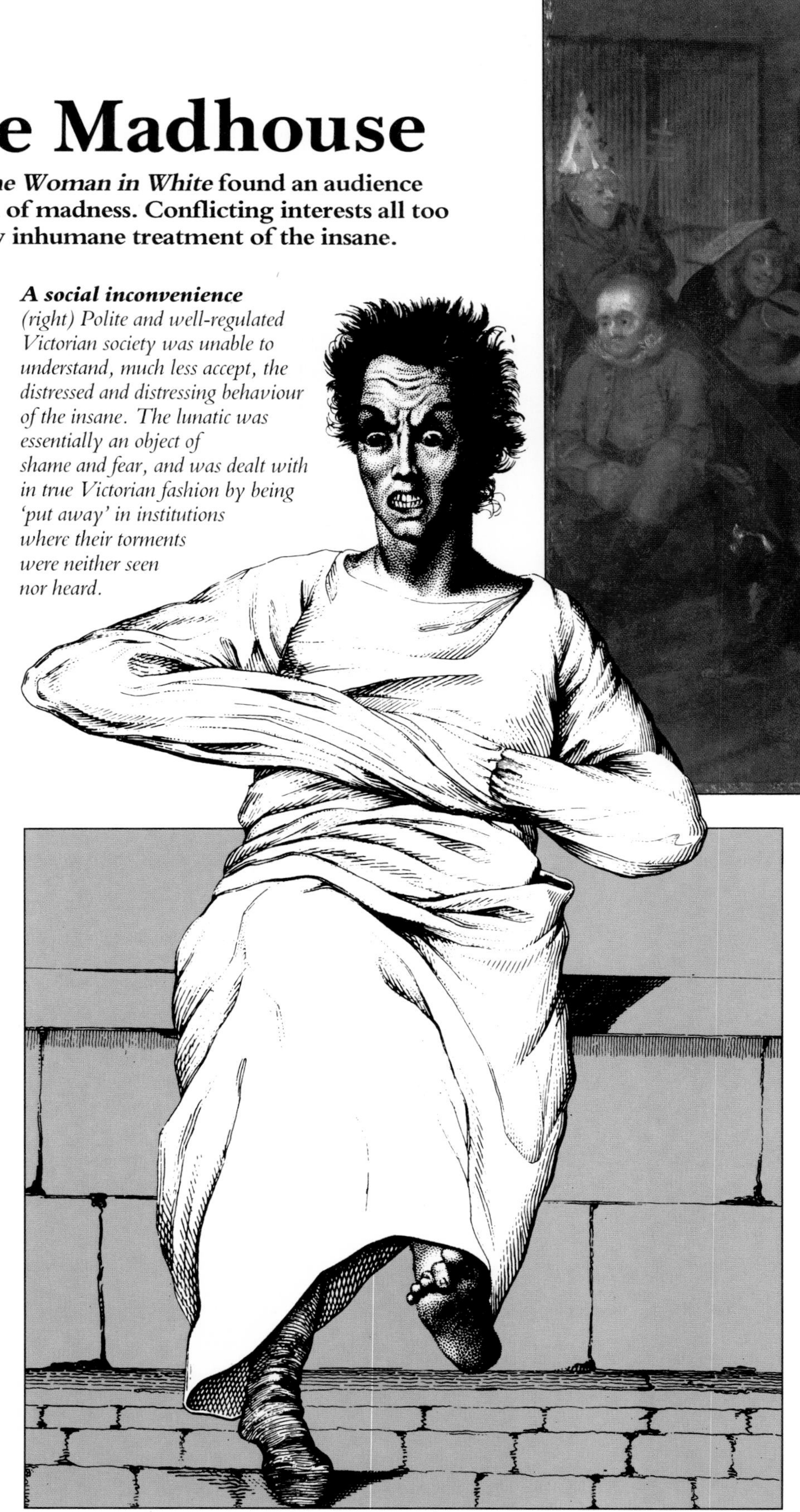

A social inconvenience
(right) Polite and well-regulated Victorian society was unable to understand, much less accept, the distressed and distressing behaviour of the insane. The lunatic was essentially an object of shame and fear, and was dealt with in true Victorian fashion by being 'put away' in institutions where their torments were neither seen nor heard.

Madhouse entertainment
(left and inset) The first lunatic asylum in England was the notorious Bethlehem or 'Bedlam' hospital. Here inmates not only suffered brutal ill-treatment, but, until long into the 18th century, were put on show for the amusement of fashionable ladies and gentlemen and for the profit of the proprietors.

Still I sing bonnie boys, bonnie mad boys,
Bedlam boys are bonnie.
For they all go there,
And they live on the air,
And they want no drink nor money.

Several other institutions were established by public subscription in the course of the 18th century, notably St Luke's in London and the York Asylum. But demand was fast outrunning supply, and more and more private madhouses were opened, catering to rich patients who could afford to pay fees, and pauper inmates whose board was funded from the rates. From 1774, the proprietors of private madhouses could not operate without a licence granted by a magistrate, but they were not obliged to possess qualifications of any kind. Given the bizarre nature of the professional treatment usually meted out to mental patients, this was not necessarily a drawback.

The mad wife
(right) Mr Rochester's tragically demented wife in Jane Eyre *was more than just a character of fiction. Charlotte Brontë herself knew of instances where a mad woman was looked after at home by her family, rather than be placed in an institution. But she did not know that the novelist Thackeray, to whom she dedicated the second edition of* Jane Eyre, *himself had an insane wife who was kept in care. Like other compassionate individuals at the time, he was concerned that his wife should have the kindness and attention she needed – and that an institution for the treatment of the insane would not provide it.*

DOUBLE STANDARDS

Public and private institutions varied greatly, and there were compassionate and professional figures associated with both. But if the public asylums were too often neglectful and brutal, the private madhouse proprietor – whose sole intention was to make a profit – faced a double temptation: to spend as little time and money as could be on poor patients, and to keep rich ones interred, regardless of their actual mental state. As in so many other matters, rich and poor people in the 19th century were treated quite differently in the madhouse.

Since paupers were a charge on the rates, local authorities tried to maintain them as cheaply as possible. But apart from Bethlem and a few other urban institutions, there were no public places available for Britain's poor who were mentally ill. Poor people who became ill in any way usually ended up dependent on charity and were simply placed in the workhouse, alongside the old, infirm and unemployed.

Some were, however, boarded out with local people who were prepared to take them in for a small payment. In these circumstances, the care of the insane was rudimentary, and treatment was non-existent. Even in Collins' day, when legislation had outlawed the practice, dangerous and violent lunatics were still sometimes kept in workhouses on the orders of negligent or penny-pinching magistrates.

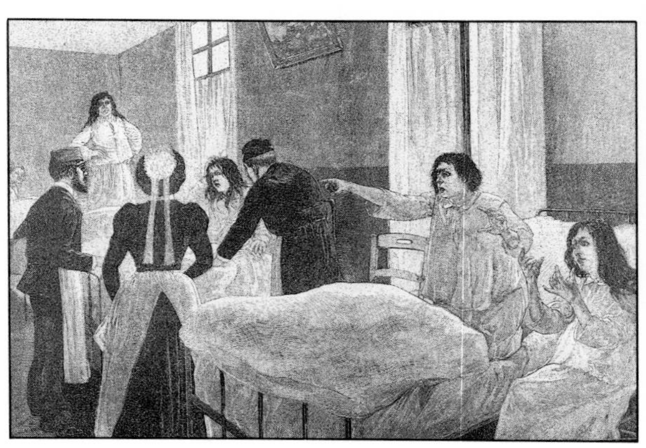

Home and abroad
(above and top) In England, the many forms of madness and the complexity of its causes went virtually unrecognized; and treatment made no attempt to study the individual's case and domestic circumstances (top). Contemporary French doctors were, however, relatively enlightened, and the most famous founded asylums where their methods were put into practice. One of the most celebrated was Jeanne Esquirol's Maison de Santé *(above), where Thackeray's wife was a short-term patient. Thackeray was disturbed by the sight of 'wild fierce women rambling about in the garden' but considered it 'the very best place' in terms of compassionate treatment of the insane.*

From the late 18th century, private madhouses were increasingly used as dumping grounds for pauper lunatics, and in some areas there was furious competition between rival houses for the custom of local authorities. The 'price-cutting wars' that ensued meant favourable terms for the authorities, but were rather less advantageous for the paupers. With only a few shillings a week to spend on each pauper inmate, the proprietors inevitably employed poorly paid, brutal keepers, and crowded their patients into filthy, unventilated sheds and outhouses, where they were chained up if they caused any trouble.

Such abuses most often came to light when a lunatic escaped or was removed from 'care', such as the inmate taken from Gate Helmsley in Yorkshire in 1847, who was dying 'in a filthy condition and with running wounds'. Official indifference was underlined by the 'improved' legislation, which until 1828 specifically excluded parish paupers from regulations about commitments and the inspection of premises.

APPALLING CONDITIONS

In terms of care and conditions, the poor got the worst of things in both private and public institutions. At York Asylum, despite its public character, rich patients were accepted and the pauper inmates were appallingly housed and neglected – so much so that, when an investigation began in 1815, an 'accidental' fire was started to burn down some of the most suspect buildings, and members of the staff destroyed incriminating records.

The polite term 'mechanical restraint' was used to describe the most economical method of controlling patients who were violent or simply obstreperous or restless. In reality, the term meant chains, manacles and a virtual Chamber of Horrors of contraptions which were found by 19th century investigators.

One of them, Edward Wakefield, created a sensation by his description of the conditions in which James Norris had been confined at Bethlem for 14 years. He had 'a stout iron ring. . .riveted round his neck' and chained to an iron bar on the wall. His arms were pinioned, his right leg was chained to the trough in which he slept, and additional chains, only twelve inches long, made it impossible for him to do much more than either stand or lie down in one position, on his back.

Class, much more than sex, determined attitudes to the mentally disturbed, and dictated the treatment that was received. To the 'mad doctor', the rich were a different species from the poor. The Physician to Bethlem, Dr Thomas Monro, declared before a public enquiry that chains were 'fit only for the pauper lunatics: if a gentleman was put in irons he would not like it. I am not accustomed to gentlemen in irons; I never saw anything of the kind; it is a thing so totally abhorrent to my feelings that I never considered it necessary to put a gentleman in irons.'

He might have added that gentlemen and women (or their relations) could afford to pay for kindly individual attention, and were more likely to be listened to if they complained of being neglected or ill-treated. And if their families were compassionate, they had more chance of being looked after by a keeper than of being placed in an institution.

Some relatives might be the reverse of caring, however. In the 18th century it was not unknown for men and women to be put away because they were an embarrassment, had fallen in love with someone 'unsuitable', or were just in the way. As early as 1728, Daniel Defoe, the author of *Robinson Crusoe,* complained of 'the vile Practice so much in vogue among

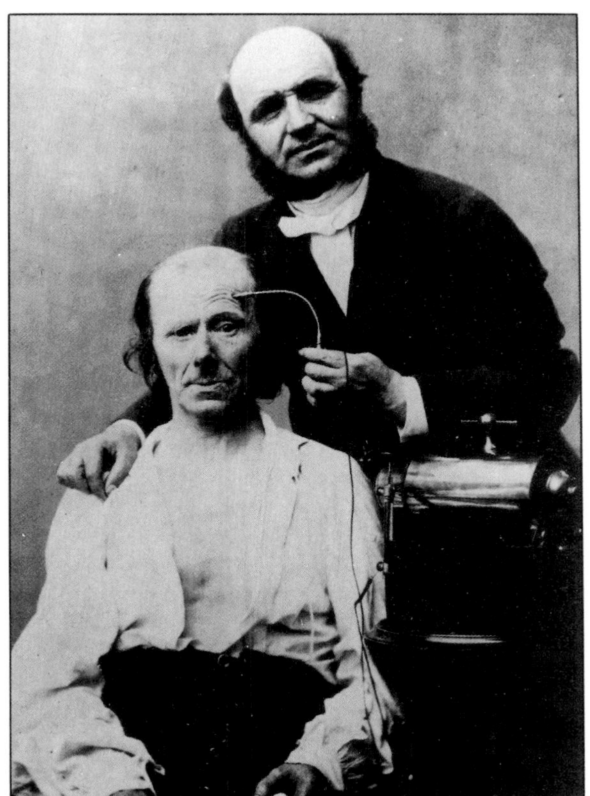

The plight of the poor
(above) The poor who became mentally ill were treated in the same way as those who were homeless, destitute, unemployed or physically sick. They were placed in the workhouse, where their illness, aggravated if not partly engendered by deprivation, received no attention at all.

The 'victim patient'
(left) Mental patients were acutely vulnerable to vicious medical practices, as the activities of the French doctor, M.G.B. Duchenne reveal. This photograph, taken in 1862, shows him with a patient he has electrocuted to achieve what he called 'electro-physiognomy'. This perverse practice he termed an 'art form'.

the better Sort. . .namely, the sending their wives to Mad-Houses at every Whim or Dislike, that they may be more secure and undisturb'd in their Debaucheries.'

Another motive was to secure an inheritance or to gain control of an estate, as in *The Woman in White*. Collins' story was based on a French case some 50 years earlier, and by Victorian times such schemes could only be executed through the ingenuity of a Count Fosco. Even so, an eminent medical man, John Conolly, warned in 1830, 'Let no one imagine that even now it is impossible or difficult to effect the seclusion of an eccentric man; or easy for him, when once confined, to regain his liberty.'

PROFITABLE CONFINEMENT

It was particularly difficult for gentlefolk to be released once confined in a private madhouse, for a wealthy patient's recovery threatened the place's profits. John Perceval, the son of the Prime Minister, Spencer Perceval, wrote two indignant volumes about his own incarceration during the early 1830s. 'I had to fight my way for two years,' he complains, 'wringing from my friends a gradual but tardy assent to the most urgent expostulations; not from the physicians. . .their maxim [is] to clutch and hold fast.'

Perceval was embittered by his family's attitude. They had put him away against his will, and thereafter abided by the self-interested opinions of 'experts', who were even allowed to oversee his letters to his mother.

And the shame attached to insanity was such that Perceval's relations regarded it as proof of his unsound mind that he wished to make public his past history by prosecuting the madhouse proprietors for their treatment of him.

Among Perceval's many grievances was the fact that no attempt was made to reason with him or explain what was being done. As a member of the upper class, he was outraged by the violation of his 'English liberties' and 'insulted and injured by the enforced use of the shower-bath and cold bath'. As far as medical treatment was concerned, pauper patients might well have felt thankful for neglect – for normal medical practice was little short of barbaric.

ALTERNATIVE REMEDIES

A gentleman may not have been manacled, but he was certainly bled, blistered, purged, dosed with bark, forced to vomit and plunged into hot and cold baths by responsible and attentive physicians. Much the same regime was imposed on King George III, whose protracted fits of madness between 1789 and his death in 1820 helped to make the subject an urgent public issue. Within a few decades, mainly due to men such as John Conolly, treatments were gradually becoming more humane and committed to understanding and coping with the patient's malady.

The new attitudes were backed up by changes in the law. From 1774, no person could be committed without a certificate signed by an apothecary, surgeon or physician, and proprietors of private madhouses needed to obtain a licence and submit to regular (if not very effective) inspection. Further progress was slow because so many vested interests were involved in private madhouses. It was not only the proprietors and physicians who resisted change, but the House of Lords also tended to defend the interests of the investors above those of the inmates.

Only in 1845 were magistrates compelled to set up county asylums, which at last removed paupers from private madhouses. In the same year, a Board of Commissioners in Lunacy was established, with powers to inspect all public and private asylums, and to monitor the situation of all patients under restraint. Certification of insanity was also tightened up, although it was not until 1890 that a magistrate's order was required before a patient could be committed against his or her will.

The new system of public asylums had defects of its own. But the reform movement represented a significant advance in care and humanity in the treatment of the insane, which helped to combat those fearful images evoked for Victorian readers by the madhouse in *The Woman in White*.

Both ends of the scale
The case of James Norris (above left) typified the inhuman methods used to 'restrain' pauper patients. An inmate of the Bethlem Hospital, he was manacled and chained by the neck and limbs, making him unable to sit or lie in comfort. Such indignities were not inflicted on well-born patients – such as George III (above) – only the poor underwent the painful and gruelling treatments which were automatically meted out, whatever the illness. George III was incurably and violently insane for the last 30 years of his life, and his condition contributed to an awakening of public concern about the problem of insanity.

Lewis Carroll

1832-1898

The Reverend Charles Lutwidge Dodgson, alias Lewis Carroll, was an extraordinary man who led three lives. One was as a shy, unsociable mathematics don. The second was as a renowned child photographer. And that for which he is best remembered.is as the author of the brilliantly inventive *Alice* stories, inspired by and written for two little girls named Alice. Only at home in the company of children such as these, he died a 'lonely bachelor' at 65.

Childhood's Captive

University undergraduates found him humourless and dry, a scholar living in an ivory tower. But with children the Oxford don turned into a spinner of tales, and a friend on the journey through childhood.

On 4 July 1862, a 30-year-old Oxford don, the Reverend Charles Dodgson, accompanied by his clerical friend Robinson Duckworth, took out a boat and rowed the three daughters of the Dean of Christ Church to Godstow, taking tea on the river bank before returning. Not an unusual event in itself, but one which was to become part of the mythology of English literature. For it was during this journey that the shy, thin, Victorian don first told a story that so interested one of the little girls, Alice Liddell, that she begged Dodgson to write it down for her.

Thus Dodgson created one of the best loved and most influential of children's books, *Alice's Adventures in Wonderland*. Like Dodgson himself, Alice is 'loving and gentle...ready to accept the wildest impossibilities with all that utter trust that only dreamers know...and with eager enjoyment of Life that comes only in the happy hours of childhood.'

Charles Lutwidge Dodgson was born on 27 January 1832 at Daresbury Parsonage in Cheshire where his father, Charles Dodgson senior, was rector. Charles was the eldest in a family of eleven children: four boys and seven girls. As a boy and a young man he was unusually attached to his mother whose kindness and sympathy he was to treasure always. His father, though strict, was by no means tyrannical and the boy grew up in a well-ordered, stable and comfortable environment.

IDYLLIC CHILDHOOD

In 1843, the family moved to Croft on the Yorkshire/Durham border. Here, in a vast house equipped with bake-house, brewery and laundry, managed by plentiful servants, Dodgson spent what he was later to regard as an idyllic childhood. With the rectory went enough livestock to provide all the dairy produce, eggs and bacon that the Dodgsons needed. The family lived an almost entirely self-contained, tribal existence, making few contacts with the world outside the vicarage gardens. But like other boys of his class Dodgson was sent away to school. At Richmond, where he boarded despite the fact that it was only ten miles from home, he soon showed his academic brilliance. He possessed 'a very uncommon share of genius' reported his headmaster at the end of his first term.

From Richmond, Dodgson went on to Rugby. Four years after the death of its illustrious headmaster Dr Thomas Arnold, the worst excesses of bullying and brutality had been stamped out. But the life of the school came as a shock to the sensitive, sheltered Dodgson. He had a severe stammer, which, together with his studiousness and poor performance at games, marked him out for the classroom tyrants. Nothing, he was to admit years later, would have ever induced

Key Dates

1832 born at Daresbury, Cheshire

1846-9 at Rugby School

1851 enters Christ Church, Oxford. Mother dies

1855 teaches Maths at Oxford; takes up photography

1861 ordained deacon

1862 boat trip in which the *Alice* story unfolds

1865 *Alice's Adventures in Wonderland* published

1868 father dies

1871 *Through the Looking-Glass* published

1898 dies at Guildford, Surrey

All Saints Church
Memorial windows based on Tenniel's illustrations for Alice *honour Daresbury's illustrious father and son. Charles Dodgson senior was vicar here from 1827-43, and it was at the nearby parsonage that the future Lewis Carroll was born.*

Archdeacon Dodgson
Charles Dodgson's father was a classical scholar, author of several books on religion and, like his son, was fascinated by mathematics. He also had a similar sense of fun. Years later his son wrote 'The greatest blow that has ever fallen on my life was the death, nearly thirty years ago, of my own dear father.'

Rugby School
(right) The young Charles Dodgson excelled in his academic work while at Rugby, but was less than enthusiastic about his time there: 'I cannot say that I look back upon my life at Public School with any sensations of pleasure or that any earthly considerations would induce me to go through my three years again.' On leaving, he returned home to Croft.

Croft Rectory
The Dodgsons moved to the spacious rectory at Croft in 1843. Situated on the Yorkshire/Durham border, it had more than enough space for a family of 12 – with four reception rooms, a nursery, a butler's pantry and a housekeeper's room.

him to repeat the three years spent at Rugby. With time he learned to cope with the traumas by day, but he was never to forget what he called the 'annoyance at night' to which he was subjected.

Growing up did not come easily. At the age of 18, on the threshold of manhood, he postponed his expulsion from adolescence – "where Childhood's dreams are twined/In Memory's mystic band" – by returning home to Croft to spend one last year at home before going up to Oxford.

On 24 January 1851 he entered his father's old college of Christ Church. Two days later his dream of childhood ended tragically with the sudden and premature death of his adored mother. He felt the loss keenly and the memory stayed with him throughout his life. Nineteen years after the event he was to write to his sister Mary on the birth of her first son: 'May you be to him what your own dear mother was to *her* eldest son. I can hardly utter for your son a better wish than that.' That tiny boy, christened Stuart Collingwood, was to be Dodgson's biographer 47 years later.

Hard-working, serious-minded, fastidious and devout, Dodgson seemed to embody all the solid virtues of mid-Victorian England, with none of its vices. He committed none of the follies normally associated with youth. He did not get drunk or pursue the less respectable forms of female society available to young men of means at the time. He did not fall in love or even show the least interest in girls of his own age.

UNDERGRADUATE DAYS

As an undergraduate, the pattern of Dodgson's life became set. Remaining aloof from his contemporaries, he nevertheless delighted in the company of children. Only with children did he lose his acute nervousness and stammer, and was light-hearted, witty and imaginative. Dr Thomas Fowler, who accompanied Dodgson on a 'reading party' to Whitby during the Long Vacation of 1854, recalled how Dodgson 'used to sit on a rock on the beach, telling stories to a circle of eager young listeners of both sexes'. He became adept at befriending children, and carried a black bag full of games and puzzles with which to attract their interest.

But even at Whitby, work was a priority. As he wrote to his sister Mary, he was getting on 'very swimmingly' with Integral Calculus. The long years of sustained study were duly rewarded that October with a first class degree in Mathematics. The quiet, 22-year-old Dodgson was now almost fully fledged as an Oxford don.

'I don't think he ever laughed', recalled a former child friend, Ellen Rowell, many years later, 'though his own particular crooked smile, so whimsical, so tender, so ironic, was in and out all the time.' But to the undergraduates he was now obliged to teach he was the quintessential don with a 'singularly unsmiling and perfunctory manner'. Essentially a self-centred man, he lacked all interest in his students and seemed almost oblivious of the college servants who were at his beck and call for almost half a century.

Only during the Long Vacation did he permit himself any relaxation, although long, rigorous walks were a feature of term-time. After savouring the delights of the Isle of Wight for several summers, he settled for the charm of Eastbourne, returning to the same lodgings every year for twenty consecutive summers. A creature of the very strictest habits, Dodgson neither sought nor enjoyed change. Only once did he venture abroad – rather unusually to Russia.

Dodgson the dull Oxford don is, however, only a partial portrait. By his dedication to two separate art forms – literature and photography – he transcended the confines of the university.

It was his uncle Skeffington Lutwidge who first introduced Dodgson to photography. From May 1856 to July 1880, capturing beautiful images became virtually an obsession for him. He pursued it single-mindedly, becoming one of the foremost portrait photographers of his day and, arguably, the best photographer of children in the 19th century.

DISCOVERING PHOTOGRAPHY

In the studio he built for himself above his rooms in Christ Church, Dodgson was a man transformed. He lost his shyness and reserve, becoming almost tyrannical in his pursuit of perfection. Photography was then in its infancy, dominated by the formal portrait, and here, as in his writing, Dodgson challenged the conventions of the time. He encouraged naturalism, placing his subjects in a natural setting and attempting realistic, casual poses. Ruskin, Tennyson, Millais and the actress Ellen Terry (who became a lifelong friend) all sat for him, as did hundreds of children.

Dodgson's first meeting with four-year-old Alice Liddell was when he was invited by the Dean, her father, to photograph her and her two sisters in the gardens of the Deanery one day in April 1856. The photographic session was not a success – 'they were not patient sitters' he noted in his diary – but Dodgson was captivated by Alice. The feeling was to last almost ten years, until soon after the success of *Alice in Wonderland*.

Family portrait
(above left) Dodgson made this photographic study of his sisters and brother Edwin when he was 25.

Ellen Terry
In 1856 Dodgson saw a production of A Winter's Tale *in which a nine-year-old girl made her acting debut. The girl was Ellen Terry, and Dodgson was instantly enraptured. In his mind she became 'the one I have always most wished to meet', but that fateful moment was not to happen for another eight years. However, when they did eventually meet they became fast friends, and two years later he set to work on his first play,* Morning Clouds, *specifically for the great actress.*

The Great Exhibition *(above) The year 1851 marked the opening of the Great Exhibition in the Crystal Palace. Arranged and organized by Prince Albert, it formed a landmark in Victorian history and drew visitors from all over the world. Dodgson was spellbound by it – there were mechanical birds, an amazing crystal fountain, and colossal, lifelike statues. To the master of dream-worlds it looked 'like a sort of fairyland.'*

Fact or Fiction

THE MAD HATTER

It seems that *Alice's* illustrator, Tenniel, following Carroll's wishes, drew his Mad Hatter to resemble a certain Theophilus Carter, a well-known furniture dealer who lived near Oxford. Not only did Carter always wear a top hat, but he was renowned in the area for his eccentric ideas and inventions. In the Great Exhibition of 1851, Carter displayed his 'alarm clock bed', a contraption which woke the sleeper by literally tossing him out of bed at a pre-determined time.

Carroll would certainly have seen the bed at Crystal Palace and would have been familiar with the unusual figure of Carter around the streets of Oxford. The prevalence of furniture, in the Tea-Party episode – the table, the writing-desk, the armchair, and the fascination with time, also point to a strong Theophilus Carter connection.

Few of Dodgson's infatuations with little girls outlasted their puberty. Ellen Terry, aware of this tendency, declared after their friendship had weathered this 'difficult' time, that 'he was as fond of me as he could be of anyone over the age of ten.' 'About nine out of ten...of my child-friendships got shipwrecked at the critical point "where the stream and the river meet"', Dodgson himself admitted years later, 'and the child-friends, once so affectionate, became uninteresting acquaintances, whom I have no wish to see again.'

Today there is a tendency to think that Dodgson's delight in dressing little girls in boys' clothes and in photographing them nude, or as he put it more coyly *'sans habillement'*, indicates some form of sexual deviancy. But there is little to suggest that his interest was primarily or even partially sexual. In the vast library of letters he wrote throughout his life (98,721 by his own calculations), there is no suggestion of anything in the least improper. They testify to a man unusually anxious to avoid the slightest whiff of scandal. When writing to his friend Miss E. Gertrude Thompson, inviting her to Oxford, he was most anxious that she came only with her parents' consent. This is perhaps not surprising in an age when almost all contact between unmarried men and women could only occur in public, but excessively prudish in the case of Miss Thompson who was then in her 30s.

Likewise there is no hint of a sexual interest in little girls in the nine surviving volumes of his diary. Only in *Pillow Problems*, which, despite its suggestive title, is concerned with 72 problems of algebra, plane geometry and trigonometry, does he mention 'unholy thoughts, which torture with their hateful presence the fancy that would fain be pure'. But this is scant evidence of a man unduly tormented by the rule of celibacy to which he was bound as an ordained deacon.

However, Dodgson was only too aware that his interest in nude photography had set tongues wagging. Perhaps it was for this reason that, in a typically cut-and-dried manner, he decided in July 1880 to give up photography for ever.

EARLY WRITINGS

But it was, of course, as a writer that Dodgson, under the pen-name Lewis Carroll, was to achieve fame. His beginning as a writer had not been entirely auspicious. As a child he had shown an unusual interest in words and in his teens had written, illustrated and produced what he called his 'domestic journalism'. This consisted in a series of little magazines with titles such as *The Comet*, *Will-o'-the-Wisp* and *The Rectory Umbrella*. In these Dodgson first developed his talent for nonsense verse and humorous short stories.

While staying at Whitby in 1854 Dodgson had had a poem and story published in the local *Gazette*. His work was also published in the *Oxonian Advertiser*, though consistently turned down by *Punch*. But it was the editor Edmund Yates who encouraged Dodgson's writing and prompted him to adopt a *nom de plume*. From a list of four supplied by Dodgson, Yates chose Lewis Carroll, derived, Dodgson said, by reversing his first two names and latinizing them, 'Ludwidge...Ludovic...Louis...and Charles...'.

Yates was also the first to publish a version of 'Jabberwocky' in 1856, although it was, of course, with *Alice* that Lewis Carroll became famous. It was, after a sluggish start, a phenomenal success, assuring Dodgson of a comfortable income for the rest of his life. But it had been created under trying circumstances. Rarely can a publisher have had a more exacting author than Dodgson. His demand to be involved and check every detail of the production process even went as far as his supplying a diagram showing how the parcels containing copies of the book should be properly packaged and tied.

LITERARY SUCCESS

Alice in Wonderland and *Through the Looking-Glass* were immensely popular. Together, 180,000 copies were sold during Dodgson's lifetime, although literary success and fame did little to change the pattern of Dodgson's life. In term-time he wrote mathematical texts, then spent the holidays in Eastbourne. After the death of his father in 1868 he bought a house called 'The Chestnuts' in Guildford for his unmarried sisters, and spent Christmas there each year. With the extra income provided by his books he was able to resign from his lectureship – always a heavy responsibility – and take on the job of Curator at Christ Church. This

A KINDRED SPIRIT

Born in 1824 in rural Aberdeenshire, the author George MacDonald was a friend of both Alfred, Lord Tennyson and Lewis Carroll. He wrote more than 20 novels in his lifetime but is remembered almost exclusively for his children's fiction, notably *At the Back of the North Wind*.

Unlike other children's fiction at the time, MacDonald's writings was dreamlike and fantastical, comparable possibly to Tolkien who was to write his famous *The Lord of the Rings* trilogy some 80 years later. In Carroll's day, books for children were almost exclusively moralistic; they taught religious ideals and notions of good and evil. Sober, humourless poems formed the staple diet of Victorian children's reading and often had to be learned by heart and recited in front of their 'elders and betters'. The kind of writing MacDonald and Carroll engaged in was revolutionary – it allowed, even encouraged, children to be and think like children.

Carroll took photographs of the MacDonald children, and they inspected the *Alice* manuscript before it was submitted to the publishers. Six-year-old Greville loved it, and declared 60,000 copies of it should be printed!

MacDonald and the North Wind
On the left is a contemporary cartoon of George MacDonald and above is one of the fantasy illustrations from his best-loved children's book, At the Back of the North Wind.

Alice and her sister
On 26 April 1856, Charles Dodgson encountered the four-year-old Alice Liddell (shown seated in the chair) for the first time. He could not have imagined the extent to which she was to transform his life.

Thameside college
(right) This watercolour by J.M.W. Turner shows Dodgson's college, Christ Church, where he spent much of his life as student, lecturer and curator.

Artistic circles
(below) Dodgson mixed with both academics and artists, such as Julia Margaret Cameron, who took this photograph of G.F. Watts.

entailed supplying the College with its groceries, wine and fuel, managing the servants and balancing the budget. As always, he performed his duties with extreme care and punctiliousness.

Fame as an author widened his circle of friends and acquaintances. Lord Salisbury, a future Prime Minister, was one. Invited to Hatfield House, Dodgson entertained the children as ever with stories and games and puzzles. At these and other occasions Carroll showed his instinctive rapport with children: 'Carroll was expected at a children's party, and he arrived crawling on hands and knees, covered with a bear rug, and growling. It was the wrong address – a tremendous shock for the parlourmaid who opened the door.'

But despite the adulation of children and adults alike, he felt himself to be a 'lonely bachelor'. As the years passed he became increasingly concerned with his health, taking up the study of medicine in his usual methodical manner. Though perhaps lonely at times, he was not one given to bemoan his fate. In a letter dated August 1894 he wrote, 'my life is so strangely free from all trial and trouble that I cannot doubt my own happiness is one of the talents entrusted to me . . .'

'DEATH IS OVER'

There were still child-friends, and he even kept up with one former child-friend, Gertrude Chataway, to whom he had dedicated *The Hunting of the Snark.* Now in his sixties, Dodgson suffered increasingly from a condition known as synovitis which affected his knees and prevented him from walking. Sometimes he was bed-ridden for months. In the end, however, it was an attack of bronchitis that proved fatal. On 14 January 1898 Charles Dodgson died at about 2.30 in the afternoon in his sisters' house in Guildford. Some years before he had confided in a letter 'I sometimes think what a grand thing it will be to be able to say to oneself, "Death is *over* now; there is not *that* experience to be faced again."'

'A Moment in Time'

The ability to capture the moment came about with the invention of photography in the mid-19th century. But like much Victorian painting, it was often used to evoke the poetry of bygone days.

On the last page of the original manuscript of *Alice's Adventures in Wonderland* is pasted a tiny photograph of the real Alice: Alice Liddell. Charles Dodgson – alias Lewis Carroll – took the picture himself, and it is just one of many he took of her. Carroll was a dedicated photographer – now regarded as one of the greatest of all Victorian photographers. And during the long, warm summer days of her childhood, Alice and her sisters would often pose for hours for 'Mr Dodgson' while he adjusted his camera and attempted to entrance them with his whimsical, delightful stories. Photography concentrated his imaginative interests in more ways than one.

From 1856 until July 1880 – a period during which photographic principles and techniques made many revolutionary leaps forward – Carroll's fascination with photography deepened. There were times when he would spend many hours every day behind his massive plate camera, or in the darkroom preparing the plates. Like many mid-Victorians with an eye on posterity and the future, he was keen to include his heroes in his photograph album, and many famous people – such as Prince Leopold, the painters John Everett Millais and Dante Gabriel Rossetti, and the scientist Michael Faraday – became his subjects.

PHOTOGRAPHIC ORDEAL

When Carroll bought his first camera, in March 1856, photography was a comparatively young art, still exciting and rather mysterious. It was less than 17 years before, in August 1839, that the details of Louis Daguerre's momentous discovery had been revealed to an excited audience at the French Academie des Sciences. And it was barely 12 years since William Henry Fox Talbot had patented his 'calotype' process, the first practical process to use a negative.

The phenomenon of photography had caught on quickly, and before long thousands of middle-class Victorians were willingly subjecting themselves to the ordeal of posing for a daguerreotype portrait. That it was an ordeal is reflected in the grim faces staring out from daguerreotypes of the 1840s – hardly surprising since exposures could last many minutes, and often the only way the photographer could keep his sitter's head immobile was to clamp the neck rigidly in a vice.

Yet though many people were sitting for photographs, very few in England were actually taking them. The complexity of the process was one obstacle, but so too was the sheer cost. For besides buying very expensive materials, English photographers had to pay Daguerre a high fee for the right to use the process. This put the process beyond the reach of all but a few gifted, but more importantly, wealthy, professionals. Fox Talbot's calotype was cheaper, and had the advantage that multiple copies of a photograph could be made because the process started with a negative –

Carroll the photographer
(left) Lewis Carroll took up photography in 1856, and became one of the best child photographers of the 19th century. The equipment he used is shown below.

Inspired by art
(right) Like many photographers, Carroll was greatly influenced by Pre-Raphaelite portraits of 'other-worldly' young women. He owned this painting – The Lady with Lilacs *by Arthur Hughes – and based an early* Alice *illustration on it.*

unlike the daguerreotype, which was a one-off. But Fox Talbot hedged his patent with so many restrictions that few bothered to take it up.

The breakthrough came in 1851, when Frederick Scott Archer launched the collodion or wet-plate process which, like the calotype, gave a negative. But it was only a lawsuit in February 1855 that persuaded Fox Talbot to relinquish his claim that the process was merely a variation of his. From then on, photography progressed in leaps and bounds, and soon thousands of well-to-do Victorians were, like Lewis Carroll, buying cameras and becoming 'pilgrims of the sun'.

Photography was still by no means simple, for the plate for each picture had to be specially prepared in a darkroom moments before use. The collodion process was messy, for the wet-plate was literally wet, and inky black stains from the chemicals on fingers and clothes earned the wet-plate process the name of 'the black art'. It could be dangerous, too. A visitor calling on the photographer Julia Margaret Cameron found her sons marching her up and down, afraid that deadly potassium cyanide might have invaded a cut on her finger.

As if all this were not enough, taking pictures anywhere but at home meant carrying around a huge photographic outfit: large bottles of chemicals, various dishes, scales, weights and measures, heavy glass plates

Naked innocence
(left) The Red and White Roses *by Julia Margaret Cameron, one of the greatest 19th-century photographers, illustrates the Victorian interest in evocative portraits of naked children who belong to a lost world of purity and innocence.*

In the vice
Having your photograph taken in the mid-19th century was an ordeal. To ensure that the subjects remained still for the duration of the exposure, photographers often locked them in vices – a custom satirized in this contemporary cartoon.

The art of perfection
(left) There was a strong, two-way relationship between painting and photography in the late 19th century. Highly finished paintings such as this beautiful picture of St Mark's Square, Venice by John Bunney reveal an almost photographic realism. At the same time, photographers often emulated narrative painters by making their pictures 'tell a story'.

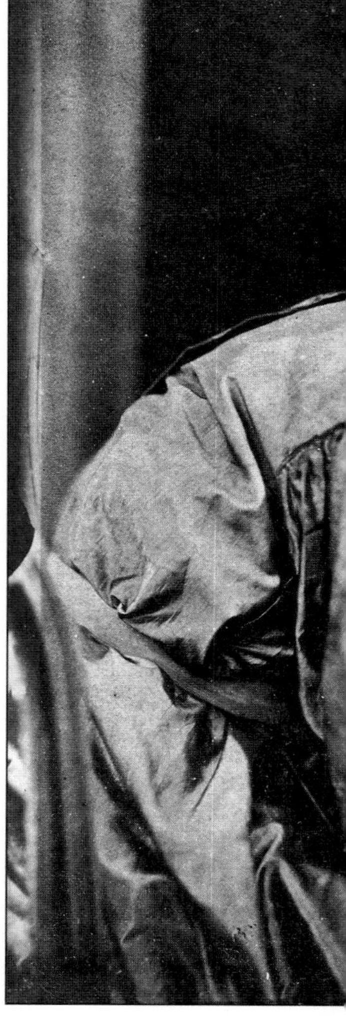

and a vast darkroom tent – not to mention a huge plate camera and a tripod to support it. Photographers and their paraphernalia became the target for many cartoonists, and in his parody of Longfellow's poem *Hiawatha's Photographing* even Carroll pokes fun at the rigmarole of photography:

From his shoulder Hiawatha
Took the camera of rosewood,
Made of sliding, folding rosewood;
Neatly put it all together.
In its case it lay compactly,
Folded into nearly nothing;
But he opened out the hinges,
Pushed and pulled the joints and hinges,
Till it looked all squares and oblongs,
Like a complicated figure
In the Second Book of Euclid.

This he perched upon a tripod -
Crouched beneath its dusty cover –
Stretched his hand, enforcing silence -
Said, "Be motionless, I beg you!"
Mystic, awful was the process.

But none of this complexity deterred the thousands up and down the country who took up photography for business or pleasure. Now that photographs were cheap enough for even the working class to afford, the portrait business boomed. In London, Regent Street alone had 35 'glass houses' where people could have their photographs taken, and in every town in England there were photographers offering to, as *Punch* quipped, 'Take off yer 'ead for sixpence, or yer 'ole body for a shillin!'

The turnover in these portrait studios was phenomenal, and some photographers would pride themselves on the number of clients they could handle, taking as many as 100 negatives in a day for the miniature *carte-de-visite* prints that everyone wanted. Naturally, poses were stereotyped, and pictures were heavily retouched to flatter the sitter. Studios would keep on hand a small range of popular props and backdrops to set the scene, and the results were often bizarre: women in evening dress pose inches from a wild sea-shore or rushing Alpine cataract, or men lean uncertainly against a fake Corinthian column standing alone in an Italianate landscape. Such effects were immensely popular.

Amateur photographers, meanwhile, stood aloof from this hectic business. Indeed, they sneered at it, and photographic journals of the late 1850s are full of complaints about the lamentable standards of contemporary English photography. Amateurs such as Carroll – who took pictures for pleasure, not profit – regarded photography as an art form and took it, and themselves, extremely seriously.

BATTLE OF THE ARTS

One of the many thorny problems for the amateur was that they were not quite sure what direction such an art should take. They were also acutely sensitive to criticism that photography was not an art at all, but merely a mechanical process. Painters were especially likely to make this gibe, for they were equally sensitive to the suggestion that photography made painting redundant – particularly as the invention of photography had actually put hundreds of portrait painters out of business.

Paradoxically, though, both photographers and the young Pre-Raphaelite painters, such as John Everett Millais and William Holman Hunt, had pursued the same ideal in the 1850s: to render Nature in ever more realistic detail. The foxgloves and nettles, ivy and dockleaves that Millais and Hunt painted in exquisite detail, were now photographed with equal sharpness.

The rivalry between painters and photographers was often intense. Photographers crowed that Millais could be 'beat...hollow' by photography and that Francis Bedford's photographs of plants 'would set a Pre-Raphaelite crazy.' The Pre-Raphaelites were equally disparaging about photographers. Indeed, they were extremely touchy about being linked with photo-

Artistic composition
(below and right) Just as paintings could be based on photographs, so photographic compositions could be as carefully planned as an oil painting. The photograph Carolling *by H.P. Robinson was initially composed in a sketch (right), before being set up.*

Pre-Raphaelite models
Both photographers and painters associated with the Pre-Raphaelites created portraits of women with pensive, idealized beauty. Dante Gabriel Rossetti oversaw this photograph (above left) of his adored Jane Morris (wife of William Morris) at a sitting in his Chelsea home in 1865. The portrait, taken by the professional photographer John R. Parsons became the basis of Rossetti's painting Reverie *(above).*

graphy at all, mainly for fear critics might suggest they painted over photographs.

Nevertheless, photographers remained acutely sensitive to the accusation that photography was incapable of high art – an accusation reinforced by the boom in cheap portrait photography. Disillusioned by the struggle to achieve ever greater detail and 'truth to nature', which seemed a purely scientific problem, many photographers sought a way of turning photography into a genuine art form.

In the late 1850s, a number of photographers, such as Oscar Rejlander and Henry Peach Robinson, began to tackle pointedly 'artistic' subjects. They built up elaborate, painterly pictures with a story or moral, by joining together staged photographs of models in costume. Rejlander's vast Renaissance-style tableau called 'The Two Ways of Life' (1857) was a great success, and was purchased by Queen Victoria herself, while Robinson's touching deathbed scene entitled 'Fading Away' became one of the most popular of all Victorian photographs. Such pictures appealed to Victorian taste for morality and melodrama and, for the next 20 years, reproductions of similar 'artistic' photographs sold in considerable numbers. Peter Henry Emerson went one step further – he took his camera into the fields and fens to 'capture' highly stylized naturalistic pictures. But

later, in proclaiming that photography was not Art, he set in motion a debate that raged into the next century. Robinson and others rose to the challenge and sought to develop 'the highest form of art of which photography is capable.'

Lewis Carroll met both Rejlander and Robinson, and was especially drawn to Rejlander's pictures of children in costume. But about the time he was writing *Alice in Wonderland,* in the early 1860s, he began to mix in a circle of people who were creating a new mood in the art world – a circle including such celebrities as the poet Tennyson, the Pre-Raphaelite painters Hunt, Millais, Rossetti and Arthur Hughes, and the photographers David Wilkie Wynfield and Julia Margaret Cameron, perhaps the greatest of all Victorian photographers.

Within this circle, the concern for realism had given way to an obsession with Beauty, and at Little Holland House in London, Sarah Prinsep (like Julia Cameron, one of the famous Pattle sisters) and the painter G.F. Watts created an ambience conducive to the discussion of the Beautiful. There was little sense of time in this house, and young women in loose, flowing dresses and long, wild hair would float in and out, while the men dreamed of bygone ages, painted and photographed.

Neither the painters nor photographers of this circle were now so interested in capturing realistic detail. Julia Margaret Cameron even took pictures out of focus. What they were concerned with was Beauty and 'poetry' and, in particular, inner, spiritual beauty. For many men, dreamy women with long, flowing hair represented the ideal. Their dreaminess suggested spirituality, and young women with a distant look were popular subjects for both painters such as Rossetti and photographers like Julia Margaret Cameron.

Carroll was never very comfortable in the Little Holland House set, or with its ideas. But he shared the wistful concern of the circle for fragile young beauty. He felt that the tender beauty of young girls faded as they left childhood behind them. It was little girls like Alice Liddell and Xie Kitchin – rather than young women – that he sought out as subjects for his photographs. Sometimes, he was content to photograph them as they arrived, dressed in ordinary clothes. But often he felt that these clothes obscured the innocent beauty of his young subjects, and he would dress them in white flannel nightgowns or, occasionally, photograph them without any clothes at all. 'Naked children are so perfectly pure and lovely' he wrote.

He longed to enter the dreamworld of his young friends – a dreamworld like Alice's – and many of his photographs have a dreamy, distant look about them. But he knew that this dreamworld, and along with it the vulnerable beauty, would be lost as the child grew. His photographs, like his books, recaptured a fragment of that lost time.

Fine-art photography
As photography came to be acknowledged as an art form, a vogue arose for 'artistic' photographic prints. One of the most popular prints to adorn Victorian walls was Gathering Waterlilies *by P.H. Emerson (above). Its peaceful atmosphere belies the messy and sometimes hazardous wet-plate or collodion process by which it was produced. Among the chemicals in which the photographic plate was drenched was the deadly potassium cyanide.*

SAMUEL BUTLER

1835-1902

Bitter resentment at an unhappy childhood set Butler against all forms of dogmatism and authority; his witty masterpiece is an autobiographical cry from the heart against parents' inhumanity to children. Despite a personal gentleness and wry sense of humour, his determination to challenge Victorian hypocrisy and religion earned him hostile critics. He shunned marriage, and lived as a semi-recluse, sustained by the love of a few close friends.

Bachelor of Arts

An unorthodox and multi-talented figure, Butler – writer, painter and musician – delighted in controversy. But in spite of his clashes with the Establishment, he led the life of a quiet, eccentric bachelor.

A Victorian rebel, Samuel Butler would have been something of a rarity in any age. In addition to being a writer, he was an artist, photographer and musician, who seemed to enjoy nothing better than taking a recognized theory and showing the experts that they had got it wrong. Whether out of conviction, perversity or the sheer love of debating, Butler tackled religious, scientific and literary theories, repeatedly coming into conflict with the Establishment.

Butler was born in Langar, Nottinghamshire, on 4 December 1835, into a strict, upper-middle-class family. His father, Thomas, was a Reverend (and future Canon) of the Church of England, and his grandfather was a distinguished public-school headmaster and Bishop. Samuel's christening was deferred until this eminent grandfather could perform it, and he later referred drily to the delay as a 'risky business', since 'all those months the devil had the run of me'. His relationship with his father was consistent from the start: 'He never liked me nor I him; from earliest recollections I can call to mind no time when I did not fear and dislike him . . .'

Butler's autobiographical novel *The Way of All Flesh* reveals the atmosphere and some precise details of his formative years. They were joyless and severe, as his heavy-handed, authoritarian and unsympathetic father tried to beat him into conformity. His earliest memories included Latin lessons at the age of four – 'my father thrashed it into me (I mean physically) day after day'. He also remembered a particularly momentous birthday: he had been given a jar of honey as a fourth birthday present, then 'My father came in, told us grandpapa was dead, and took away the honey, saying it would not be good for us.'

When Samuel was seven the gloom was relieved for a short while by a family trip to Italy, which yielded a life-long passion for that country. But his childhood was largely overshadowed by the Victorian public-school system, which he grew to know all too well at Shrewsbury School. Being a 'mere bag of bones' with 'no strength or stamina

Langar Church.

1852

My dear Tar

You have most likely heard that I am now staying at Langar, which is a very pretty pleasant place. The house I am staying in is red, with many windows, like this: Mine has a cross on it. + There are many little children in the village who play about half the day; but some

The Butler clan
The formidable Butler family (below) came of renowned stock. They were steeped in intractable, middle-class ethics and values which Samuel (far left) rejected. The substantial family home is sketched, left, in a letter by a cousin.

'Family Prayers'
Butler painted the above picture in 1864. The figures are not true likenesses of his family, but the room is at Langar. It may have helped to exorcise unhappy memories of his repressively religious upbringing, for Butler referred to it as 'one of the very funniest things . . . I never finished it, but have kept it and hope it will not be destroyed after my death.' In pencil he wrote on the picture, 'if I had gone on doing things out of my own head instead of making copies I should have been all right' – a bitter post mortem on his other career as an artist.

whatsoever . . . useless and ill at ease with football' certainly did not help. According to his fictional hero Ernest in *The Way of All Flesh*, he survived by listening to his 'true self' and ignoring the brutality around him.

Butler's life changed when he went up to Cambridge aged 18. Here, at last, he was 'consciously and continuously happy'. He spent four years studying Classics, finally gaining a first class degree. He began writing and painting and discovered a passion for the music of Handel – 'his music has been the central fact of my life,' he wrote.

While at university, there were few opportunities for Butler to fall out with his father, but when he left Cambridge they did battle in earnest. It had long been assumed that, like his father and grandfather, Samuel would go into the Church. But he had other ideas. He felt no calling to live among the poor and benighted, dispensing goodness, charity and religious certitude. His objections to being ordained centred on a disbelief in infant baptism which he deduced had no effect on human behaviour: it could not turn a bad man into a good one.

Key Dates

1835 born Langar, Nottinghamshire

1854 enters Cambridge

1859 refuses to be ordained. Farms in New Zealand

1864 meets Pauli; returns to England

1867 meets Eliza Savage

1872 *Erewhon* published

1885 Eliza Savage dies

1886 father dies

1892-5 visits Italy, Greece, the Dardanelles

1902 dies in London

1903 *The Way of All Flesh* published

In a series of letters, Thomas Butler implored his son 'to settle on some profession' (by which he meant the Law, now that the Church had been dismissed). Samuel baited him, arguing that he wanted to make 'a fair survey of the prospect to see what may be most advantageous' (by which he meant a career as an artist, teacher, doctor, soldier or anything else his father did not want). He fully expected to be cut off from all financial support, but was not such a malcontent as to want to end all ties with home: 'I should be very sorry to think that any connection other than the money connection should cease.'

LIFE IN NEW ZEALAND

Eventually, aged 23, Butler settled on becoming a New Zealand sheep farmer, provoking his father's wrath – but not to the point at which his allowance would be stopped. Luckily for him, a last-minute shortage of passenger accommodation forced him to change ships – for the one on which he had intented to sail was lost with all hands. During the voyage he read copiously, learned to play the concertina, and organized a choir. On arrival he searched out 8000 acres of land and began life as a farmer.

New Zealand gave Samuel the chance to clarify his ideas and to spend time writing. He wrote in support of Darwin's evolutionary theories and in his letters home he recanted his religious faith entirely: 'A wider circle of idea has resulted from travel, and an entire uprooting of all past habits has been accompanied with a hardly less entire change of opinions'. He also had the satisfaction of making a profit from his farm, nearly doubling his £4400 which Thomas grudgingly sent him. Then in 1864, Butler met Charles Paine Pauli, a man who was to dominate the rest of his life.

A student's vision
While still up at St John's, Cambridge, Butler painted the above study of the town. To him, university was joy unconfined – a place of learning as well as an escape from his family – and he was a brilliant scholar despite having many diverse interests.

'Mr Heatherley's Holiday'
Butler numbered this painting among his best: it was exhibited in the Royal Academy, and depicts Thomas Heatherley, whose school of art Samuel attended. The school's students used to dress up the skeleton (kept for anatomical studies) and dance with it, so Mr Heatherley spent his vacations repairing the damage. The extraordinary debris accumulated by this cultured, eccentric man fills the background. Despite his teasing comments on Heatherley, Butler greatly admired him. Like Butler he was an artist, musician and scholar, and the two remained good friends.

Pauli was everything Samuel was not – socially successful, athletic, suave and handsome. The 20-year-old would-be barrister realized he had made an instant conquest, and persuaded Butler to buy him a ticket back to England. Apparently the best of friends, they now took separate rooms at Clifford's Inn in London, with Butler anxious to finance Pauli's progress to the Bar. Increasingly, Pauli took more than he gave. If Butler could not afford to give him money, Pauli wept. If Butler tried to end the relationship, Pauli 'fell ill'.

Pauli did not hide his boredom at their dinner dates, and when he took new rooms he refused to give Butler his address. Yet he continued his emotional blackmail, regularly picking up a quarterly cheque from Butler long after his student days were over. When Butler wanted an opinion on what he had written and read it aloud to Pauli, he was 'the most freezing critic . . . in so far as he could be got to listen to a passage here and there'. Amazingly, the relationship lasted 30 years. Butler's feelings swung from adoration to wretchedness as he half realized that he was being exploited.

Butler recorded his experiences in New Zealand in *A First Year in the Canterbury Settlement*. The manuscript was lost overboard from a sinking ship and 'fished up from the Indian Ocean so nearly washed out as to have been with some difficulty deciphered'.

Back in London Butler lived 'almost the life of a recluse, seeing very few people.' But in 1867, he made perhaps his most important female friendship. Without the clever, witty Eliza Savage, it is doubtful whether he would have succeeded as a writer. She fired his enthusiasm to write his first novel *Erewhon*, and almost certainly encouraged him to tackle *The Way of All Flesh*, saying, 'it will be a perfect novel or as nearly so as may be'. The relationship could easily have led to marriage; Eliza wanted it, but Butler shunned matrimony.

Even if she had not been 'plain and lame and fat and short', as he crudely put it, Butler may still have preferred to keep his distance. For when he met Isabella Zanetti – the most beautiful woman he had ever seen – he also fled from her. Butler seems to have opted for an undemanding mistress: Lucie Dumas, a Frenchwoman. They met in London in 1872 and he visited her for the next 20 years. It was only after 15 years' acquaintance that he told her his name and address. In his correspondence, he always referred to Lucie as 'Madame'.

PATERNAL FURY

The publication of Butler's religious satire, *The Fair Haven* (1873), infuriated his father, and mortified his mother – something which Samuel was very unhappy to do. She was ill at the time, and told him that it 'tore open the wounds of the Redeemer'. She did not recover from her illness; and Thomas Butler blamed their son's book for her death, while Samuel acidly lamented, 'I had rather It had been my father.'

BUTLER'S FARM

Butler called his New Zealand farmstead 'Mesopotamia' – the Greek for 'lying between two rivers'. Amid wild, uncharted grasslands, he played the piano, painted, read and engaged in bitter wrangles, by mail, with his father, seeking money for such urgent needs as a sheep dip. He recorded the first year in a factual book, and used the landscape in *Erewhon*.

A painful friendship
'Those years were very unhappy as well as very happy ones,' wrote Butler recalling Charles Paine Pauli (left), whom he loved, misguidedly, for 30 years with 'a white heat of devotion'.

Eliza Savage
(right) Witty, shrewd and cultured as she was, Eliza Savage could not capture Butler. After her death he wrote, 'She was too kind, wooed too persistently,/Wrote moving letters to me day by day;/ The more she wrote, the more unmoved was I,/The more she gave, the less could I repay.'

Given such tensions, he did not stay long at Langar after the funeral, escaping to write what he intended to be an uncontroversial novel, 'pure and simple with little purpose'. He did note in passing, however, that he feared 'the cloven hoof will show itself again', and that is precisely what happened with *The Way of All Flesh*, a revenge on his father and on the Establishment which had made him so unhappy.

By his early 40s Samuel's life was stagnating. His painting was good enough to be included in several Royal Academy exhibitions, but his personal and financial life was less successful. His relationship with Pauli dragged on, and the investment of his capital in a Canadian patent steam-engine company was proving a mistake. Both he and Pauli had been made nominal directors in the Canada Tanning Extract Company, and whereas Pauli took no active role, Butler went out to Canada in 1874, 'fighting fraud of every kind' in an endeavour to save the company. Its eventual collapse reduced his capital to £2000, made him once more dependent on his father for an income, and left him feeling horribly guilty towards both Pauli and Pauli's brother whom he had involved in the investment.

Music and journeys to Italy sustained him until, in 1876, he made the second great friendship of his life, with his future biographer Henry Festing Jones, 'far and away the ablest man' he ever met.

When Samuel was 42 he gave up art ('my career . . . fizzled out') to concentrate on writing. He turned his attentions to science, tackling the major issue of the time – evolution. Although he had once been an enthusiastic believer in Darwin's theories, he now challenged the idea of natural selection from 'chance variations', preferring to take the view that species adapted by *active* learning, transmitted from one generation to the next by a kind of 'continuous memory'.

'My second country'
Butler fell in love with Italy as a boy and went back as often as he could, dedicating one book 'to her as a thank-offering for the happiness she has afforded me.' Below is his painting of Chiavenna, which he visited with Festing Jones.

In 1885, Eliza Savage died. Butler wrote, 'It is out of the question I could ever replace her. I never knew any woman to approach her at once for brilliancy and goodness.' He planned an edition of the many letters which had passed between them, but abandoned the idea when he read those he sent, and was appalled at how 'meagre and egotistical they were'. Remorse increased after her

funeral. 'She haunts me, and always will haunt me because I never felt for her the love that if I had been a better man I would have felt.' In despair he abandoned the half-revised *The Way of All Flesh*.

The following year came another death – that of his father. There was to be no such remorse for him, just cynicism: 'One of the greatest feathers in his cap was . . . that he was *my* father.' According to Butler, 'the only person to whom he was ever really attached was the cat . . . me he simply detested.' It was not entirely true. Thomas had always wanted the best for his son and had always stood by him financially. In his will he left Samuel the sizeable income of £1200 a year. He also 'left' his son his clerk, Alfred Emery Cathie, who adopted the role of valet, arranging every little detail of Butler's life.

Alfred Emery Cathie
(above) Despite the amused, paternal tone in which Butler mentions the uneducated simplicity of his 'clerk', Alfred was a devoted servant who for 15 years organized his master's everyday life. He put notes in Butler's pockets reminding him to have his beard trimmed, buy a new hat or go for a walk. Butler tried to teach him music and helped him save up to get married. There was always a message for Alfred in letters home from his travels abroad – from Sicily's classical ruins (below) for instance.

A QUIET DEMEANOUR

Although Butler's life might seem, in retrospect, to have been one long attempt to flout Victorian convention, no-one who met the man found him outrageous or anarchical. A contemporary description of him emphasizes his 'speaking softly and slowly, often with his head a little down' and having the manner of a 'kind old gentleman, prepared to be a little shocked by any disregard of proprieties.' Indeed, Butler balked at the idea of becoming a complete social outcast. 'I have the religious world bitterly hostile; the scientific and literary world are even more hostile than the religious; if to this hostility I am to add that of the respectable world, I may as well shut up shop at once.'

The mention of literary hostility refers to his shocking attempts in the 1880s to prove that *The Odyssey* was not written by Homer but by a Sicilian princess. To do this, he travelled extensively in Sicily and Greece, and made similar journeys to the Dardanelles to check the 'archeological sites' of Homer's *Iliad*, although these did satisfy him as being correct.

His last major literary theory involved the reordering of Shakespeare's sonnets and a commentary which treats them as a series of love letters.

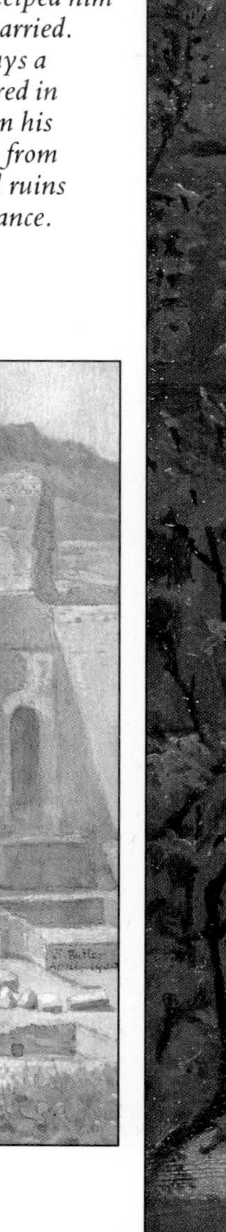

His argument mirrors remarkably his long, wretched affair with Pauli, for he condemns the recipient of the sonnets with such strength of feeling, saying he is 'vain, heartless, and I cannot think that he ever cared two straws for [someone] who no doubt bored him.'

Perhaps Butler was in part helped to come to terms with his feelings towards Pauli by the last important friendship of his life, with a delightful young Swiss, Hans Faesch, whom he called his 'only son'. By contrast with Pauli, Faesch had such a gentle and friendly disposition that Butler named his placid, agreeable horse in the Dardanelles 'Hans' by way of compliment.

In 1897, Pauli died, and Butler was shocked to find that he had been swindling money out of two others as well as himself. He calculated that he had given Pauli £6500. Pauli had lived comfortably all along and left an estate of £9000. So this became a time for reflection for Butler, a time to 'edit his remains' (though he had no reason to think death particularly close). He wrote a detailed account of the Pauli affair, at least two sonnets to Eliza Savage and edited Henry Festing Jones's letters. Two more journeys to Italy followed, on the last of which he fell unexpectedly ill. He hurried home, was diagnosed to be suffering from pernicious anaemia, and appointed an executor to his £33,000 estate.

For the first time in his life, Samuel was gravely ill. Now pitiably 'shrunk, feeble and shockingly pale', he was removed from his old rooms to a nursing home. He died on 18 June 1902, aged 66, purportedly hoping that in the next world he would be among his favourites, Leonardo da Vinci, Homer, Shakespeare and Handel. Ever mindful of his abilities to provoke and annoy, he mischievously looked forward to catching sight of 'the shade of Charles Darwin [gliding] gloomily away when it sees me coming'.

Belated affection
(above) 'Nothing but goodness and kindness ever came out of you . . . I feel as though I had lost an only son with no hope of another,' wrote Butler when his young friend, Hans Faesch, went home to Switzerland showing signs of grave illness.

Clifford's Inn
From the time he returned from New Zealand until his death, Butler lived in the same rather gloomy, spartan rooms, pictured left.

Fact or Fiction

SELF-PORTRAIT

Ernest Pontifex is the young Samuel Butler. *The Way of All Flesh* is so heavily autobiographical that prison and marriage are virtually the only fictions in it. Butler quotes directly from letters, diaries and his music notebooks.

Inevitably, Ernest is musical, for Butler gave as much to music as to writing or art. He said of Handel, 'All day long – whether I am writing or painting or walking . . . I have his music in my head.' The portrait of Butler (right) reflects this. Butler was a competent musician, but perhaps the friend was correct who observed, 'He was too versatile a genius ever to be in the front rank of one particular line.'

Fallen Angels

Victorian morality was rife with hypocrisy – sexual codes were entirely different for men and women, and it was often the innocent who paid 'the price of sin'.

To a generation brought up on sexual liberation and women's rights, the Victorian age presents astonishing contradictions in attitude. For this society, which purported to live by a rigid moral code, and upheld the sanctity of marriage, supported a larger number of prostitutes than at any time before or since.

It was just such hypocrisy that Butler attacked in *The Way of All Flesh*. For middle-class men and women of the Victorian era, sexual repression was the norm within marriage, and resulted in the grossest of double standards. Women were divided into two classes: those to whom sex was an unmentionable indelicacy and those who satisfied men's 'needs'. The extraordinary inconsistencies in the Victorian outlook were magnified as the century progressed, as middle-class attitudes increasingly dominated society.

THE IDEAL OF MARRIAGE

Middle-class morality dictated that sexual intercourse was a dark and evil thing. This notion was ingrained from birth and fuelled by medical and religious opinion. By contrast, marriage was a sacred institution which, although it necessitated the begetting of children, should be based on a pure and noble love.

Marriage was every young woman's goal. It conferred respectability, financial security and status, coupled with the satisfaction of rearing children. Romantic love, pure and unsullied (real or imagined), was eagerly anticipated. (The reality was often different, of course, and divorce extremely difficult, carrying with it a social stigma.) Most women entered marriage ignorant of the realities of sexual intercourse. For some, their wedding night was an experience little short of rape. For others, the intimacy of sex may not have been as traumatic or as disagreeable as they had been led to expect. But pleasure itself could bring guilt, for sex within marriage was considered neither genteel nor moral except for the purpose of conceiving children.

Medical opinion, underlining these attitudes, recommended marital sex no more than once a month, and stated that respectable women had no sexual desire. One distinguished writer, Dr William Acton, maintained: '. . . the majority of women (happily for them) are not very much troubled with sexual feeling of any kind. What

Adultery
The painting below is the first of three (see p. 212) which depict the dissolution of a family. Here the wife's infidelities have just been discovered via an incriminating letter. Her husband grinds her lover's portrait underfoot while the children's house of cards collapses – a darkly symbolic omen.

A royal wedding
Britain's royal family exemplified the double standards inherent in Victorian society. The Prince of Wales' marriage to Alexandra of Denmark (right) was a splendid state occasion. But Edward clearly considered himself above the marriage vows and had a succession of notorious liaisons.

Lily Langtry
Noted for her beauty, the actress Lily (or Lillie) Langtry was Edward the Prince of Wales' most celebrated mistress. Born Emily Charlotte le Breton in 1852, Lily was twice married and had numerous other lovers, including the Crown prince Rudolf of Austria and King Leopold II of Belgium.

men are habitually, women are only exceptionally . . . The best mothers, wives and managers of households know little of sexual indulgences. Love of home, children and domestic duties are the only passions they feel.'

Very many women would have agreed with him, for consciously or unconsciously their sexual feelings were repressed. This repression may have given rise to the many 'nervous' disorders to which Victorian women were prone. One practical disincentive to sex, however, must have been the fear of pregnancy at a time when childbirth was often fatal, and when repeated pregnancies sapped a woman's health and energy.

Men's sexual desires were acknowledged, but it was their moral duty to stifle them. Marriage to a virtuous woman was the one hope of channelling – and eventually dampening – sexual desire. Often men had such an ambivalent attitude to sex that they positively feared marriage. Dr Acton had this advice for them: 'Many men, and particularly young men, form their ideas of women's feelings from what they notice early in life among loose, or at least, low and vulgar women. [But] No nervous or feeble young man need be deterred from marriage by an exaggerated notion of the duties required of him. The married woman has no notion to be treated on the footing of a mistress.'

In these few words, Acton assembled all the unhealthy assumptions governing Victorian life: that both men and women feared marriage; that most Victorian men were presumed to have had a sexually demonstrative prostitute or mistress prior to marriage; and that the respectable wife took no interest or delight in sex. Yet for the many high-minded men who did succeed in stifling or sublimating their sexual desires before the wedding night, marriage could be as traumatic as for their wives.

Such men, before and after marriage, found compensation for their unsatisfied or baffling sexuality in platonic friendships with other men, or even in religion or zealous good works. And for others, unable or unwilling to visit prostitutes, there was a plentiful supply of pornography, catering for all tastes.

PRIVILEGED PROMISCUITY

The morality which came to obsess the middle class did not really extend to either the upper or working classes. Their lives were as 'free' as they had ever been. The poor frequently stopped short of marriage; and the aristocracy modified its promiscuous behaviour only when scandal threatened. Queen Victoria was refreshingly direct about the pleasures of married life with her beloved Albert, and later was remarkably under-

Idealized womanhood
Some men knew about women's bodies only from art. The writer John Ruskin was reputedly appalled to discover his wife had pubic hair.

A moral tale
Continuing the story of the adulterous wife, we are shown her daughters some years later, longing for maternal love (top). Their mother (above) is in more desperate straits, alone and sleeping rough, clutching the child born of her ill-starred, long past affair.

standing about the sexual scandals in which the Prince of Wales was involved. But a handful of intellectuals, such as Samuel Butler, detected and scorned the double standards emerging among their own (middle) class.

There are no reliable statistics, but it has been estimated that in the latter half of the 19th century there were 120,000 prostitutes in London alone. It is unclear whether this includes the vast majority of 'irregulars' (prostitutes who worked only when times were hard), child prostitutes or the many thousands of 'kept' women. It has also been calculated that £8,000,000 was being spent on prostitution each year. The top price paid to a fairly high-class prostitute was one or two pounds, while a few pence bought the pathetic, disease-ridden creatures from the slums of London's East End.

Henry Mayhew, famous for his masterly study *London Labour and the London Poor* (1851-62), divided prostitutes into groups of descending order: kept mistresses and 'prima donnas'; independent women and lodging-house (brothel) women supervised by a madam; low lodging women; sailors' and soldiers' women; park women (dossers); and thieves' women.

The high-class kept women and 'prima donnas' lived a life that was envied not only by their fellow prostitutes but also, perhaps, by the respectable Victorian wife. They lived in fashionable lodgings, were elegantly and expensively dressed, and were seen, with their aristocratic admirers, horse-riding in Hyde Park. Their social status was such that they suffered little from scandal-mongering or ostracism.

ROYAL MISTRESSES

Their attractions often included charm and wit was well as beauty, and they lived in fine style. Catherine Walters (Skittles) and Lily Langtry, both of them friends of the Prince of Wales, were among the most famous. They were not necessarily even single women: the 'Jersey Lily' was married when the Prince met her, and the onus was on her husband to turn a blind eye in the interest of his betters. Harriet Wilson was a courtesan who, in later life when down on her luck, threatened the Duke of Wellington with blackmail – but failed. 'Publish and be damned', he replied when she offered to expunge him from her memoirs for a 'consideration'.

While not attaining this level of fame or infamy, a successful young prostitute could aspire to marriage with one of her clients – a young shopkeeper, say, or a clerk who was not averse to a bride with a few savings. Occasionally they married men of some standing. One fortunate prostitute married a wealthy Norfolk landowner who settled a substantial income on her. His outraged relatives sought a court order declaring him insane, but failed. (He was admittedly a little eccentric and liked to dress up as a minor railway official.) Others, not so lucky as to achieve marriage, were set up in some small suburban house, usually by a member of the professional classes, who visited them regularly while maintaining a wife and children elsewhere.

By far the largest group of prostitutes were the part-timers and street-walkers in the industrial cities, many of whom were driven to prostitution by sheer poverty. However harsh life was in rural areas, the scope for, and rewards of, commercial sex were limited. In the cities, however, there was ample opportunity.

Mayhew describes the plight of a young woman who was a shirt-maker with a small child. She earned two-and-a-half pennies for each shirt – which did not even pay for a roof over her head. Forced into prostitution, she tried, from time to time, to give it up, for the sake of the child. But on one occasion, when she was homeless, her little boy's legs froze to her sides as she carried him. Although she and the boy were saved by an act of kindness, she went back to prostitution subsequently, as the only means of survival. There were many thousands of young women in a similar position, who would have liked to live decently if they had had a choice. Seamstresses, servant girls (dollymops) and milliners' assistants were among those who fell into this poverty trap.

The lives of brothel prostitutes varied according to the class of brothel which housed them. These women at least had a roof over their heads, and some had their food and clothing provided. But a large portion of their earnings was taken by their pimp or madam.

The prostitutes who frequented the dockland slums in London and other ports were in a different class altogether. On Mayhew's list these were the 'lowest of the low'. At any one time, there were thousands of sailors of all nationalities at loose in the dock areas, who had money to spend on drink and sex. Conditions in these areas were indescribably foul. The squat houses and narrow streets were filled with beggars and thieves as well as whores, living many to a room in crumbling and squalid lodging houses.

Here most of the prostitutes were alcoholic or

THE GREAT SOCIAL EVIL.

TIME:—Midnight. A Sketch not a Hundred Miles from the Haymarket.

Bella. "AH! FANNY! HOW LONG HAVE YOU BEEN *GAY*?"

Successful sinner
(above) A high-class prostitute or kept woman could enjoy a life of luxury, pampered and clad in extraordinary finery.

A fallen woman
(left) A poorly dressed woman asks a much smarter companion how long she has been on the game ('gay' was a euphemism for 'immoral'). The scene is London's Haymarket, renowned for its streetwalkers and known at the time as 'Hell Corner'.

Backstage encounters
(right) For women who wanted to climb the social ladder, the stage offered a potential first rung. Those endowed with sufficient charms might discover the key to a better future backstage.

Moral reformers
The Reverend Baptist Noel addresses an assembly of 'fallen women' – Victorian ladies of the night. Having gathered them from the streets at midnight, he dangles the carrot of their eternal salvation in the hope of luring them back into the bosom of society.

disease-ridden – or both – and even the most intrepid reformers never ventured into these areas where crime and violence were a way of life. These prostitutes often supplemented their takings by stealing, since they earned hardly enough to buy gin – and it was among these women that the infamous sex murderer Jack the Ripper found his victims in 1888.

One thing that kept some men 'virtuous' was the fear of venereal disease. It was estimated towards the end of the 19th century that 66 per cent of prostitutes in western Europe had syphilis. The Victorian man was therefore taking a serious risk – if he indulged – of passing on an incurable disease to an innocent wife and to unborn children. One extraordinary example of Victorian attitudes was that for a husband *knowingly and willingly* to infect his wife with venereal disease was not a criminal offence.

Society might turn a blind eye to the habit of visiting prostitutes, but rampant disease was another matter. In an effort to control venereal disease among the armed forces, the Contagious Diseases Acts were passed between 1864 and 1869, which introduced medical check-ups for prostitutes in and around garrison towns.

These Acts aroused a furore. For the first time, prostitution and its consequences were out in the open. Some welcomed the Acts as a practical solution to a major social problem. Others were outraged that the state was seen to condone prostitution, by making it safer, rather than condemning it. Further outrage was caused by the enforcement of the Acts, which permitted the forcible examination of women even suspected of prostitution. Inevitably some women wrongly suspected were subjected to the examination.

Throughout the era there was no shortage of charitable workers and reformers concerned with the plight of the 'fallen woman'. Their motives and mentalities varied. For some there may have been a subconscious sexual thrill to be had from their 'good works'. William Gladstone, the Prime Minister, is well known for his (no doubt) chivalrous attempts to reclaim prostitutes, but was attacked for it by one of his parliamentary colleagues: 'Gladstone manages to combine his missionary meddling with keen appreciation of a pretty face. He has never been known to rescue any of our East End whores, nor for that matter is it easy to contemplate him rescuing an ugly woman.'

IMPASSIONED CRUSADERS

Writers such as Thomas Hardy, Mrs Gaskell and George Bernard Shaw, as well as painters like Dante Gabriel Rossetti and William Holman Hunt, who portrayed the fallen woman in a sympathetic light, were part of a liberal minority.

Mrs Josephine Butler, the aristocratic wife of a clergyman, was largely responsible for the repeal, after 15 years, of the Contagious Diseases Acts. She was outraged that women should be used for men's satisfaction and then treated as offenders. Her agitation for the repeal of the Acts brought the whole issue out into open and honest discussion. One result was the Criminal Law Amendment Act of 1885, which made both procuring and brothel-keeping illegal – and marked the beginning of the end of widespread prostitution in England. Double standards were to be longer in changing, however, and Samuel Butler's incisive criticisms were to be echoed by several major writers of the 20th century.

Poverty and prostitution
For girls born into poverty, life could be unremittingly bleak. Forced to beg for a crust of bread, it was then just a short step to the more lucrative world of prostitution. But the cost was high – syphilis was rampant and a prostitute's life expectancy little more than four years.

THOMAS HARDY

1840-1928

From humble beginnings in rural Dorset, Thomas Hardy rose to achieve the social prominence he craved, but he remained torn between the 'dream country' of his imagination and the world of London's literati. His genius lay in portraying the pastoral life he knew so well – but the honesty with which he wrote about the relationships between men and women outraged Victorian sensibilities. When his last novel was publicly burned in 1896, he withdrew to the country, and devoted himself to poetry.

A Divided Nature

Hardy achieved an elevated social status worlds away from his humble Dorset origins – yet his writing constantly drew him back to the rustic scenes of his boyhood.

The world of Hardy's novels is the world he knew intimately as a child and youth – that of rural Dorset. No subsequent experience gained so strong a hold on his imagination, even though he was to become a figure of outstanding literary fame, and was fêted by London society.

Born on 2 June, 1840, in the small Dorset village of Higher Bockhampton, baby Thomas appeared to be dead at birth, and was almost ignored in the surgeon's concern for his mother. Fortunately, both mother and child survived, and Thomas grew into the fragile, sensitive son of doting parents.

His mother, Jemima, was a youthful, vigorous woman. To young Thomas, she was more of an older sister than a mother, and her vivid personality and ideas were a lasting influence on him.

Hardy's father was a handsome, easy-going man, a stone-mason by trade and a talented amateur musician. Hardy's earliest memory was of being given a small accordian on his fourth birthday, and even at this age he loved to dance to the country tunes his father played. Hardy soon became adept at playing the fiddle himself, and – like his father – was much in demand at country dances and weddings.

At eight, Hardy went to the village school, which was run by the lady of the manor, Mrs Julia Martin. Their unusual fondness for each other probably gave rise to a recurrent theme in Hardy's earlier novels – that of love across class barriers. Years later she still

'a pink-faced youth'
(left) So Hardy described himself in his early twenties, when his innocent appearance reflected his sheltered upbringing.

Hardy's parents
(right) Thomas and Jemima shaped their son's future. From his father young Thomas inherited a talent for music and a love of Nature, while his mother remained a figure of the utmost importance throughout his life. Lively, intelligent and forceful, she was determined her son should be well educated – an ambition he was happy to share.

Architect's apprentice
(above) At the age of 16, Hardy began work for a Dorchester architect. These are his own drawings of capitals in Stinsford Church dating from this time. Hardy found his fellow pupil, Henry Bastow, lively and congenial, and spent much time joking, arguing and reading with him. He also began learning Greek, getting up at dawn to study by his bedroom window, before his walk in to work.

An idyllic birthplace
(left) Hardy was born in this isolated thatched cottage, which had been in the family since his grandfather built it in 1800. His early years were thus spent in the heart of the Dorset countryside, close to the sights, sounds and creatures of nature. He later recalled how in his childhood, he decided he did not want to grow up, or 'to be a man, or to possess things, but to remain as he was, in the same spot'.

called him 'dear little Tommy', while he described his relationship with her as 'almost that of a lover'. Perhaps because of maternal jealousy, Jemima Hardy removed her son from Mrs Martin's school the following year and took him to visit her sister in Hertfordshire.

Hardy's mother was determined he should be well-educated. She encouraged him to read widely and sent him to school in Dorchester where he learned Latin, French and German. Under her watchful eye, Hardy grew into an adolescent who, on his own account, was 'mentally precocious' but with a 'lateness of development in virility'. Despite, or perhaps because of, this he was emotionally susceptible from an early age.

In 1856, when Hardy was 16, he was articled to John Hicks, a Dorchester architect. It was here that Hardy met his close friend and mentor, the scholar and reviewer Horace Moule. Moule was eight years older than Hardy and had been educated at Cambridge. He was a charming and gentle man as well as a brilliant teacher. Together Moule and Hardy studied Greek drama and Moule encouraged his pupil to write poetry.

Teacher and mentor
(above) The brilliant Horace Moule (seen here against the centre window), was Hardy's most influential friend in his early Dorchester days. Moule was an inspiration to Hardy, but was never able to realize his own potential.

Also at this time, Hardy's morbid curiosity led him to witness several hangings – a common sight in the Assize town of Dorchester. The most memorable to Hardy was that of Martha Brown, who killed her husband in a crime of passion. Hardy never forgot 'how the tight black silk gown set off her shape as she wheeled half round and back'. Emotionally and factually, this memory inspired *Tess of the D'Urbervilles.*

In 1862 Hardy moved to London to pursue his career. Here he found work with Arthur Blomfield, specializing in church architecture. The boyish Hardy thus encountered for the first time the sophistication of city life. He also threw himself whole-heartedly into self-education, frequently visiting the theatre, opera and art galleries, and reading voraciously. Meanwhile an article he had written to amuse Arthur Blomfield's pupils – *How I Built Myself a House* – was published, and he began writing poems and submitting them to magazines, although none was accepted.

NEW ATTRACTIONS

On his 25th birthday, Hardy wrote: 'Feel as if I had lived a long time and done very little. Wondered what woman, if any, I should be thinking about in five years' time'. Such thoughts arose from his involvement with two of his cousins, who bore a strong resemblance to his mother – as did their youngest sister.

Hardy's next sweetheart was to be this cousin. Her name was Tryphena Sparks. Striking, dark-haired and independent, Tryphena was a teacher but was quickly promoted to become a headmistress in her twenties. Hardy spent an idyllic summer with her in 1869, but their divergent careers were destined to separate them. Always reticent about personal matters, Hardy's anguish found vent in his poetry, and in *Desperate Remedies*, the novel he was writing at the time. But Tryphena was to remain a type of perfection for him.

The following year, Hardy was sent to St Juliot in Cornwall, to supervise the restoration of the church. Here he met Emma Lavinia Gifford, the rector's sister-in-law. Emma was an energetic and adventurous woman, whose own literary ambitions enabled her to share keenly in the private world of his writing. Hardy's attraction was sharpened by her superior class (she was the daughter of a rich country solicitor). He described their first meeting as 'magic' – taking

Key Dates

1840 born in Higher Bockhampton, Dorset

1856-62 apprenticed to John Hicks, architect. Meets Horace Moule

1862 continues apprenticeship in London

1867 becomes involved with Tryphena Sparks

1870 meets Emma Gifford

1871 first novel, *Desperate Remedies*, published

1873 Moule commits suicide

1874 success of *Far From The Madding Crowd.* Marries Emma

1885 moves into Max Gate

1898 first book of poems published

1907 meets Florence Dugdale

1912 Emma dies. Florence becomes his secretary

1914 marries Florence

1928 dies in Dorset

place as it did against the glorious Cornish landscape.

Hardy's first literary success came with the serialization of *Far From The Madding Crowd* in 1874. Leslie Stephen, Thackeray's son-in-law, was the editor of the *Cornhill Magazine*, which published the story. He was the most influential man of letters in England at the time, and was to take the place of Horace Moule in Hardy's life.

While Hardy had been building a career, Moule had become enmeshed in his own personal tragedy. Incapable of making a success of his life, despite his intellectual gifts, he plunged into increasing bouts of depression, relieved only by drink. Sometimes he even slept with a razor under his pillow. Finally, in 1873, he committed suicide. His death profoundly affected Hardy's writing and darkened his view of fate.

MARRIED LIFE

Happier times were to follow for Hardy. Now established as a man of means, he married Emma Gifford on a lovely autumn day in 1874. None of Hardy's family was present and indeed he had taken pains to keep a distance between his fiancée and his relations. Even the manuscript of *Far From The Madding Crowd* was kept from Emma – it contained too much of his working-class background. Hardy's family were not to meet her for two years.

After several temporary addresses, the couple settled at Sturminster Newton. Hardy remembered their days here as 'Our happiest time'. Delighted with her newly-famous husband, Emma was anxious to please. She made copious notes and copies of quotations for Hardy's use in future novels, and their shared literary interests added a creative sparkle to their marriage. Their idyll did not last, however. Leslie Stephen's sister-in-law had told Hardy that an author should live in London; the couple moved to the city in 1878.

This move marked the beginning of a rift in the marriage. Silent and shy, Hardy was yet avid to observe and absorb the social scene. He loved the theatre – and the actresses – but would sit in his box hiding his face behind his hand, terrified of recognition. But while Thomas went to plays and parties, Emma stayed at home, growing fat and fretful. Nevertheless, she nursed him when he was prostrated for months by a bladder complaint.

Their life became divided between Dorset and London, with occasional visits to the Continent. This gratified Emma's love of Bohemianism, but the London visits also provided her husband with an increasing number of interesting female confidantes.

From about 1890 onwards, Emma was forced to concede victory to a series of society ladies, many of them strikingly attractive, intelligent women who

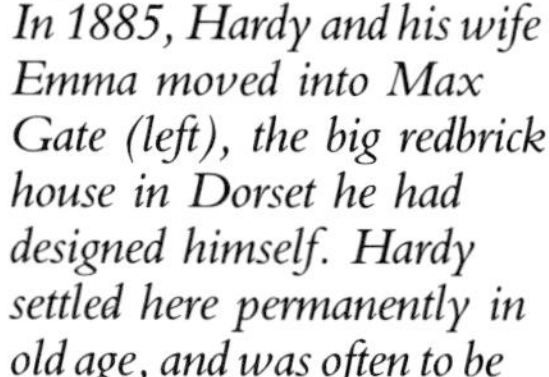

Life in Dorset
In 1885, Hardy and his wife Emma moved into Max Gate (left), the big redbrick house in Dorset he had designed himself. Hardy settled here permanently in old age, and was often to be seen cycling along the winding local lanes, but he frequented nearby Dorchester (below) very little.

The first Mrs Hardy *(left) Hardy married Emma Gifford after an idyllic, if interrupted, courtship. From their first meeting, Hardy was dazzled by Emma's sense of adventure and vitality. Her fearlessness complemented his own physical timidity, while he seemed to her the epitome of a glamorous London intellectual. She, too, was an aspiring writer, so the marriage seemed set fair for success. Sadly, however, their early years of happiness did not last. The more successful and sought-after Hardy became, the less he shared his life with Emma, until she lost what was perhaps dearest to her heart – their shared literary interests. Increasingly bitter and insecure, Emma began denigrating Hardy and his 'peasant origins', and kept a diary which she is said to have entitled 'What I think of my Husband'. Nevertheless, their early relationship was not only vindicated but immortalized after her death, when Hardy wrote some of his most moving and beautiful poems in memory of her.*

epitomized the ideal which Hardy had first glimpsed in Tryphena Sparks. Most galling to Emma was that they often shared her literary ambitions – his associates included the poet Rosamund Tomson, with whom Hardy enjoyed the 'framing of rhymes', and Florence Henniker, a novelist and short-story writer.

These years were, nevertheless, the most successful for Hardy the writer. The publication of *Tess of the d'Urbervilles* finally assured his social status.

'THE END OF PROSE'

In 1892, Hardy's father died. With this further personal tragedy weighing him down, Hardy began work on what was to be his last, darkest and most controversial novel, *Jude the Obscure*.

The publication of the unexpurgated version in 1893 spelt the end of Hardy's novel-writing career, although it sold immensely well – 20,000 copies in the first three months. For Emma – who, again, had not seen the book in manuscript – it proved to be the last straw. Distressed by Hardy's continual neglect, Emma was now moved to fury. One of the main thrusts of the novel was a sustained attack on her deeply-held religious beliefs.

On 17th October, 1896, Hardy wrote that he had reached 'the end of prose'. This decision was only partly the result of the critical outcry at his last book. Hardy had suffered the first of many bouts of rheumatism and felt keenly the physical burden of writing long novels. This kind of writing also tended to become alarmingly self-revelatory. Hardy, a very private man, found personal memories and emotions crowding all too transparently on to the page. Poetry lent itself more readily to obscurity and ambiguity.

Though he had written poetry in almost every phase of his life, Hardy was at first uncertain whether his public would accept him as a poet. He need not have worried – his first published volume in 1898 was an immediate success. Indeed, it was as a poet that he was finally accepted as a scholar and a man of letters.

AN IDEAL WOMAN

Throughout his life, women were a continual and vital inspiration to Hardy. One of his earliest attachments was to his cousin, Tryphena Sparks, who resembled his mother in her dark and decided good looks and independent spirit. Her influence on Hardy continued long after the two had ceased to communicate. Her beauty and character are frequently echoed in Hardy's heroines – notably Sue Bridehead in *Jude the Obscure* – and in the type of society women for whom he often entertained wistful, adolescent infatuations. One of the most striking of these was Florence Henniker. Hardy adored her, calling her a "rare fair woman" in one of the numerous poems referring to her. Hardy often celebrated, or sublimated, his infatuations in poetry, and it says much for Florence's character that his passion was for once transformed into a genuine friendship.

Florence Henniker *– she survived his adoration to become a close friend.*

Tryphena Sparks *– Hardy's early love and an inspiration for his heroines.*

Hardy's main poetic work is a three-part verse epic, *The Dynasts,* set in the Napoleonic Wars. Between the publication of the first and second parts, his mother died. Much of what is known of his life and how such tragedies affected him is drawn from references and implications in the poems. It is, for example, a sad comment on his marriage that his first published volume includes love poems spanning 30 years of his life, of which only one is addressed to his wife.

Yet after Emma's death in 1912, she became for Hardy a "woman much missed", as the memories of their idyllic courtship came flooding back. In the following year, he wrote no fewer than 100 love poems to her – the most moving he ever wrote.

Hardy continued living at Max Gate, the gloomy house in Dorchester he had had built to his own design. The frugal, reclusive life he led earned him the dislike of the very people who had been so vital an inspiration for his novels. They considered him a snob, and children would chant 'Miser Hardy, miser Hardy' around the streets of Dorchester.

Hardy was further protected from the outside world by his second wife, Florence Dugdale. She began work for him as his secretary and they married in 1914. With her he wrote his autobiography, which was published

The hallmark of fame *(right) As an old man, Hardy no longer sought or needed society, but society continually demanded glimpses of him. Among the stream of visitors to Max Gate, his Dorset home, was perhaps the most socially distinguished of all. On 20 July 1923, Edward, Prince of Wales, drove through the streets of Dorchester with Hardy, before lunching at Max Gate with the writer.*

Fact or Fiction

A Model For Bathsheba

Hardy's cousin, Tryphena Sparks, told him the unusual story of a local woman farmer. Catherine Hawkins had been widowed young, but had resolved to run the family farm herself. During the terrible winter of 1865-66 she had been given invaluable help by a shepherd, whose sudden death left her in need. So began the creation of Bathsheba Everdene in *Far From the Madding Crowd.*

A spirited woman *(below) Hardy used a true story to construct Bathsheba's situation, but her strong character was suggested by that of his aunt who had emigrated with an ex-soldier.*

A new wife
(left) Hardy met his second wife, Florence Dugdale, while he was still married to Emma. Like her, Florence considered herself a serious writer, and like Hardy she was Dorset-bred and from a working-class family. To Hardy, now 67, she brought back the "throbbings" of youth, and he typically rewarded her with a series of intense poems. What threatened to become an impossible situation was resolved by a Hardian stroke of fate. Emma died in 1912, and her role passed to Florence.

A last link with Oxford
(above) As a youth greedy for knowledge, Hardy – like his last hero, Jude – had dreamed of the spires of Oxford, which he saw as an ideal world of learning. The publication of his poetry at last brought Hardy unqualified success, and Oxford university was eager to recognize his importance by awarding him an honorary degree. This, together with honours from Cambridge, Aberdeen and St Andrew's, indicated Hardy's total acceptance by the English literary establishment.

after his death in his wife's name. In the process of writing it, they destroyed the personal papers on which it was based. This obsessive concern to conceal his lowly background led to a virtually fictional account of his early life.

Now firmly accepted by the English literary establishment, Hardy was more sought after than ever before. Visitors to Max Gate included Ramsay Macdonald, Virginia Woolf and Augustus John, a troupe of actors who performed *Tess* in the drawing room, American tourists and an Indian who had travelled 10,000 miles to speak to the great man, only to be denied access to him. Yet of those who were admitted, few were able to pierce the guard of Florence's vigilance and Hardy's mixture of silence and determined small talk. But remarkably, his poetry still flowed as effortlessly and beautifully as ever.

When he died on 11 January, 1928, the conflicting demands of nation and family dictated the somewhat unorthodox burial arrangements. His ashes were placed in Poets' Corner in Westminster Abbey, while his heart was buried in Stinsford Church in Dorset, with his first wife and his parents. The gulf between his humble origins and his exalted status remained with him even in death.

Hardy's Wessex

An amalgam of an ancient West Saxon kingdom and his own native Dorset cast the mould for Hardy's 'Wessex'. It both harnessed and released his imagination.

Higher Bockhampton lies three miles east of Dorchester, the county town of Dorset. At the end of a narrow lane, known as Cherry Alley, stands a "long low cottage" with a "hipped roof of thatch", tucked between "a heath and a wood". Built in 1800 by the novelist's great-grandfather, it is known simply as 'Hardy's Cottage'. In the autumn of 1873, Thomas Hardy III, was living here with his parents, helping with the cider-making and immersed in writing *Far From The Madding Crowd*. In the novel, cottages such as this punctuate the 'Weatherbury' landscape like beacons.

Inspired by scenes familiar to him from childhood, Hardy continually drew on the Dorset countryside, his family and neighbours in writing the book. Almost every scene or setting was based on personal experience – incidents of local life recollected and recounted to him by his mother, or on his own close observation of nature and people during this period. His diary entry on 4th November records a thunder-storm at Bockhampton. 'The light is greenish and unnatural . . . A silver fringe hangs from the eaves of the house to the ground.' In Chapter 37 of *Far From The Madding Crowd*, "The Storm – The Two Together", in which Gabriel Oak and Bathsheba Everdene protect the ricks from the storm, the lightning is "emerald" and the rain comes "in liquid spines, unbroken in continuity".

As he matured as a novelist, Hardy came to realize that Dorset was almost his sole source of inspiration. He needed 'to be actually among the people described at the time of describing them'. Away from his roots he felt isolated and ill at ease and his novel-writing became stilted, stale and conventional.

PART REAL, PART DREAM

The first time Hardy uses the term 'Wessex' to describe the area in which his forebears had lived for centuries is in the opening sentence of Chapter 50 in *Far From The Madding Crowd*. In 1895 he described his reasons for adopting the term; 'The series of novels I projected', he wrote, 'being mainly of the kind called local . . . seemed to require a territorial definition of some sort to lend unity to their scene. Finding that the area of a single county did not afford a canvas large enough for this purpose, and that there were objections to an invented name, I disinterred the old one [the ancient kingdom of the West Saxons]. The region designated was known but vaguely'. It is hardly surprising, then, that ancient monuments loom large in his novels or that a strong sense of history pervades every village and landscape.

A familiar landscape
(right) Hardy was unique in creating a semi-fictional world, with a consistent system of place names, and applying it to a real geographical area – his native Dorset. A tourist attraction in his own lifetime, Dorchester ('Casterbridge') was the heart of 'Wessex', but his characters roam over a wider realm of six 'counties' (inset).

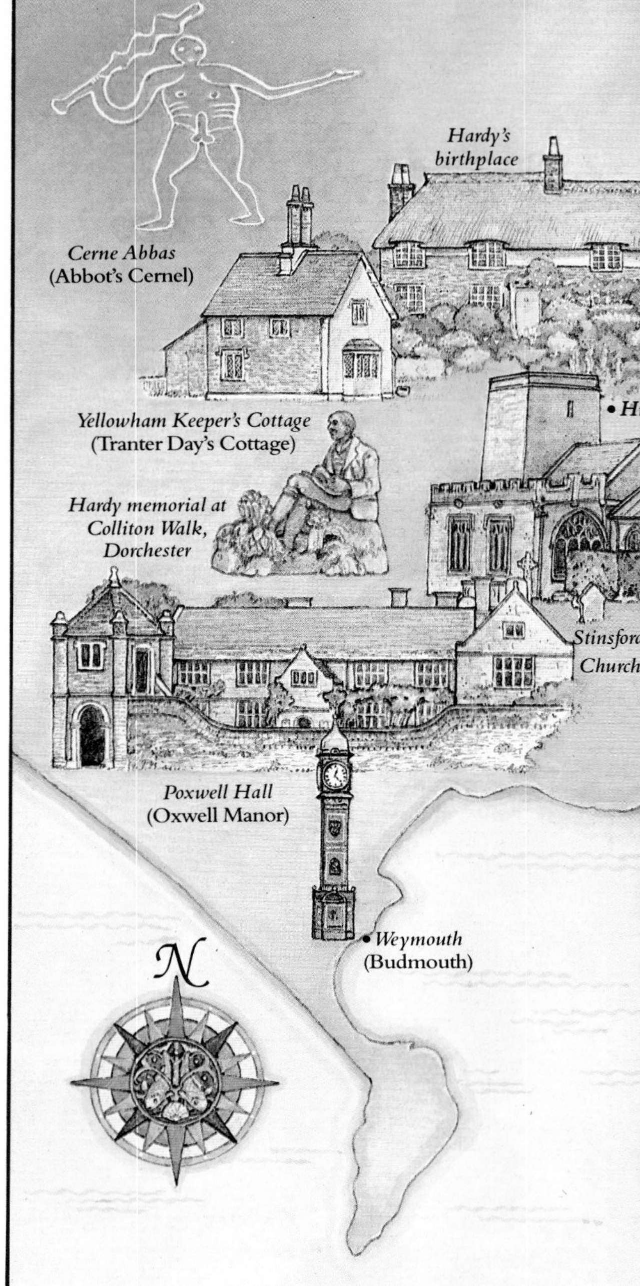

'things were like that'
(below) The novelist drew on scenes familiar to him since childhood and took great pains to ensure authenticity. Intimate observation of agricultural activities and customs gave his descriptions a pungent realism. But the inhabitants 'engaged in certain occupations . . . just as they are shown doing . . .'

The Turberville Window
• Bere Regis
(Kingsbere)
Bockhampton
(Mellstock)
Egdon Heath
Lulworth Cove
(Lulwind/Lulstead)
Durdle Door
Oxford •
• Stonehenge
Shaftesbury •
• Dorchester
• Corfe Castle

An ancient kingdom
(left) In Hardy's time, Dorset was 'known but vaguely' to the outside world, yet the landscape bore all the signs of a history stretching back to pagan times. Stonehenge remains as a monument to it, and appears as a potent symbol in Tess of the D'Urbervilles.

Timeless characters
(above) Many inhabitants of Hardy's Dorset relied upon an orally transmitted knowledge and wisdom, and were resistant to change imposed from the outside world. Time itself takes on a different quality in Hardy's dramas of country life; "Ten generations failed to alter the turn of a single phrase"

Corfe Castle
(left) Though picturesque, Hardy's settings were not sentimentalized – real hardship and abject poverty were too evident during the agricultural depression. At Corfe Castle in 1868, for example, a family of eight lived in an outhouse built for a calf. Hardy called the castle ruins 'Corvsgate'.

This 'partly real, partly dream-country' covered an area larger than that of the county of Dorset and, as Hardy suggests, was closer to ancient Wessex in consisting of six counties: Berkshire ("North Wessex"); Hampshire ("Upper Wessex"); Wiltshire ("Mid-Wessex"); Dorset ("South Wessex"); Somerset ("Outer Wessex"); and Devon ("Lower Wessex"). Cornwall is adjacent and is referred to as "Off Wessex".

Though Hardy draws on this large and, in his day, remote area, all his major novels, with the exception of *Jude the Obscure*, are set in the county of Dorset. And most of these concentrate on the even smaller area immediately surrounding Dorchester.

SEEKING AN IDENTITY

Thomas Hardy applied his own system of place names to a fictional area based in fact. He did so comprehensively and, in most cases, consistently.

To help his readers identify the real place names he had disguised, Hardy produced a map of Wessex complete with 'county' boundaries, natural features, coastal resorts, towns, villages and hamlets. This attempt at lending reality to a fictional world was taken to extreme lengths and became a source of amusement to him.

In a Preface to *The Woodlanders* of April 1912, he says that though honoured by the many inquiries 'for the true name and exact location of the hamlet 'Little Hintock', in which the greater part of the action of this story goes on', he has to confess he does not know himself exactly where it is. However, 'to oblige readers', he once spent 'several hours on a bicycle with a friend in a serious attempt to discover the real spot'; but the search ended in failure, though tourists assured him 'that they have found it without trouble, and that it answers in every particular to the description given'.

EXTENDING THE BOUNDARIES

Despite the amusement he derived from his creation, it is evident that 'Wessex' took on a shape and form that extended the boundaries of his real world.

Once created, the fictional name for a real place in one book was usually carried over to another. The 'Weatherbury' in *Far From The Madding Crowd* appears throughout the Wessex novels as the name of Puddletown, or Piddletown as it was called before the reign of Queen Victoria.

If it all started in a casual way, Hardy soon became identified with his own creation. 'Hardy's Wessex' became popular and the press was quick to cash in on the phrase. By 1895, as Hardy himself says, the public was happy to accept 'the anachronism of a Wessex population living under Queen Victoria; – a modern Wessex of railways, the penny post, mowing and reaping machines, union workhouses, lucifer matches, labourers who could read and write, and National school children'.

'Wessex' both released and harnessed his imagination. Using imagined names gave Hardy greater freedom and saved causing offence to the inhabitants of real-life places. For despite being an imagined world, the Wessex novels contain descriptions of life in the region which are completely authentic. Indeed, Hardy was at pains to impress on his readers the accuracy of his portrait. 'At the date represented in the various narratives things were like that in Wessex', he wrote in his 'General Preface to the Novels and Poems'.

The Wessex depicted in Hardy's novels spans almost the whole of the 19th century – from the Napoleonic Wars at the beginning of the century (the setting of *The Trumpet Major*) to the 1890s of *Jude The Obscure*. Throughout this period the south-west of England, and Dorset in particular, remained relatively remote and, to the visitor from London, old-fashioned. Indeed, there were few visitors to the region from other parts of the country until the last decade of the century. The railway only reached Dorchester in 1847, when Hardy was seven. Hardy's earliest memories were of 'men in the stocks, corn-law agitations, mail-coaches, road-waggons, tinder-boxes and candle-snuffing'.

During Hardy's lifetime the character of the county changed profoundly. The coming of the railways killed

A rural community *(left) The farming seasons bound rural communities together in shared labour – and in the traditional festivities and observances.*

Old Harry Rocks *Dorset's scenic coastline features in many Hardy novels. His fictional place names echo now-forgotten folklore elements.*

off, according to him, 'the orally transmitted ditties of centuries, being slain at a stroke by the London comic songs that were introduced'. But more was to change than the folk songs he so loved.

GRIM REALITY

Condemned, for the most part, to a life of poverty and squalor, the farm labourers of Dorset – among whom Hardy could count close cousins and uncles – were the worst paid and worst housed in the country. In the 1840s the average wage of the Dorset labourer was a pitiful 7s 6d a week – lower than in any other county in England. Hardy grew up acutely aware of the poverty and pain experienced by so many – and witnessed events he was never to forget. 'As a child I knew by sight a sheep-keeping boy who, to my horror, shortly afterwards died of want, the contents of his stomach at the autopsy being raw turnip only.'

While life for those in work was hard – Alexander Somerville in his *The Whistler at the Plough* (1852) recalls 'rising at four in the morning and coming home and supper at seven in the evening' – for those without work, life was a desperate struggle for survival. The workhouse was often the final degrading step.

Finding work was itself a precarious business and depended in many parts of Dorset on the hiring fairs held each year on 14 February. Here the young Hardy saw men standing around dressed in "smock-frocks and gaiters, the shepherds with their crooks, the carters with a zone of whipcord round their hats, thatchers with a straw tucked into the brim . . . in search for a new master". The ruined farmer in *Far From The Madding Crowd,* Gabriel Oak, is forced to seek a master in just such a setting.

To maintain a reasonable family income, the women and children also sought work on the land. A *Royal Commission on the Employment of Children, Young Persons and Women in Agriculture* of 1868, reported that as late as 1867 children under the age of six were working in the fields of Dorset. Sometimes whole families could be found engaged in farm labour. According to the *Victoria County History of Dorset*, 'not only was the labourer expected to work, but his wife, or at least his daughter, were dragged off into full work, and the boys were taken away too early from school'.

The Royal Commission also commented on 'the bad moral effects' on young girls of 'employment in field labour' – an effect Hardy chronicled in the plight of Tess Durbeyfield, "a fieldwoman pure and simple". Her fellow workers are the "dark virago, Car Darch, dubbed Queen of Spades", and "Nancy her sister, nicknamed the Queen of Diamonds". For the innocent Tess they are "a whorage". In real life, coarsened by "starvation, disease, degradation, death", release came in weekly bouts of drunkenness. Illegitimacy was a common result and marriage was too often a contract

Farm Depressions
(below) Though Far From The Madding Crowd *is set in a 'golden' period in English agricultural history, Hardy was well aware of the effects of – and the farmworkers' response to – the agricultural depressions that both preceded and followed it. An essay in* The Dorsetshire Labourer *of 1883 shows his factual knowledge of the state of affairs that led to rick-burning and machine-wrecking or, as depicted here in 1888, the farmers' retaliation.*

between unwilling partners hastily arranged before the birth of a child.

To the Victorian moral conscience the life of the rural poor was shocking. At village social gatherings, such as that reported in *The Times* of 3 August 1846, 'scenes (were) enacted which can at least rival, if not exceed, the disgusting orgies of antiquity'.

CHALLENGING THE IDYLL

Few writers honestly portrayed the countryside and the lives of those who worked on the land. Nostalgia for an idyllic past was the typical attitude of many 19th-century 'country' writers. Alone among the major novelists of his time, Hardy was an unsentimental countryman, who knew from first-hand observation the realities of rural life. He knew the countryside too well to share the picture of 'Merry England' conjured up in London publishing houses and endorsed by people whom he felt should have known better.

Though he lamented the passing of many aspects of traditional rural life, especially the crafts and the folk-tales passed down from generation to generation by word of mouth, he welcomed the improvements in the standard of living of the farm worker achieved in his lifetime. But, though these were 'changes at which we must rejoice', he saw that they also 'brought other changes which [were] not so attractive'. Thus the modern labourer had 'a less intimate and kindly relationship with the land' than that of Gabriel Oak. With the material progress that came later in the century came the values of the town, which for Hardy were in conflict with those of the countryside. Invariably in his novels from *Far From The Madding Crowd* on, it is the arrival of a town-based, or city-educated individual who disrupts and brings misery to the lives of the villagers.

With state education available to all after 1870, the local dialect declined and died. Tess is typical of her generation in speaking "two languages, the dialect at home, more or less; ordinary English abroad and to persons of quality". In its traditional form, local Dorset dialect as spoken by Grammer Oliver in *The Woodlanders* was close to German with expressions such as "ch woll", or "Ich woll", for "I will".

Real rusticity
(right) During Hardy's lifetime, the Dorset countryside was dotted with colourful tradesmen, such as this spar maker of Tolpuddle in the 1880s. Marty South in The Woodlanders *plies a similar trade. Other trades that appear in Hardy's work include 'reddlemen', furze cutters, pole-, peg- and hurdle-makers, heathcroppers, pig killers and a host of casual farm labourers who were able, like ex-farmer Gabriel Oak in* Far From The Madding Crowd, *to turn their hands to most tasks.*

Undisturbed calm
(above) Tranquil scenes such as this capture the atmosphere of the Wessex landscape as dusk approached. But the more distant future cast shadows of a more threatening kind – the traditional way of life was gradually eroded as the outside world encroached on 'anachronistic' Dorset.

Farm buildings
(left) In his novels, Hardy's buildings literally crumble with antiquity. Few, like this tithe barn at Abbotsbury, survive.

By the end of his life Hardy's Wessex had become a tourist attraction, aided by the publication of numerous books of topography of which the most thorough was *Hardy's Wessex* – a work in which Hardy himself had a hand – by his friend Hermann Lea. It was a painstaking reconstruction of every place mentioned in the 'Wessex novels' and contained a large collection of locations and buildings – some of which can still be seen, but many of which no longer stand – that Hardy describes in his text.

But 'Wessex', that region 'bounded on the north side by the Thames, on the south side by the English Channel, on the east by a line running from Hayling Island to Windsor Forest, and on the west by the Cornish coast', as he described it in 1912, was more than a geographical location. It was also 'any and every place' where 'these imperfect little dramas of country life and passions', as he modestly called his novels, were enacted.

ROBERT LOUIS STEVENSON

1850-1894

Robert Louis Stevenson was one of the greatest of all adventure writers. Few have rivalled his gift for telling a rattling yarn, but he also had a powerful moral sense and an acute psychological perception. His own short life was packed with incident, and was strongly motivated by his belief that 'no man is of any use until he has dared everything'. Handsome, witty, generous to a fault, but living always in the shadow of ill health, he was a truly Romantic figure, fit to rank with his most compelling literary creations.

Fragile Adventurer

Undeterred by his physical frailty, Robert Louis Stevenson travelled half-way round the world in pursuit of a dream – he wanted love and adventure, and found them both.

Tall and attractive, with bewitching eyes, Robert Louis Stevenson was a man who made friends easily. Whimsical by nature and outlandish in attire, he never fitted comfortably in the genteel ambience of his birth and from his earliest days was filled with a longing to travel. 'You must understand,' he once wrote to his mother, 'that I shall be a nomad, more or less, until my days be done.'

Stevenson was born on 13 November 1850 in Edinburgh. His father, Thomas, came from the great lighthouse engineering family. His mother Margaret, known as Maggie – with whom Stevenson shared a lung weakness that brought him close to death on many occasions – was the daughter of a clergyman. A wife and mother at barely 20, she was a light-hearted, optimistic woman. But Thomas Stevenson's background of covenanting Presbyterianism left him prey to brooding fits of despair. Nevertheless, he was a kind man, with a soft spot for stray dogs, and in their house at Howard Place he and Maggie doted on their first and only child.

A sick-room atmosphere prevailed in the household. Stevenson's mother was a semi-invalid who was often confined to bed, and Stevenson himself was a sickly, puny child, prone to nightmares. He was affectionately known as 'Smout', a Scots colloquialism meaning 'small fry'. In his early years he saw more of his nurse Alison Cunningham than he did of his mother.

Adoring parents
Youthful and vivacious, Maggie Stevenson doted on her 'wean' (standing by her, right) – and he on her. So struck was she by his precocity that she recorded all his first utterances in an almanack and continued to keep a diary of his sayings throughout his life. Her husband, Thomas Stevenson (inset right), was ten years her senior. A lighthouse engineer and notable inventor, he blended, according to his son's later recollections, 'sterness and softness' in a manner 'that was wholly Scottish'.

Key Dates

1850 born in Edinburgh
1867 enters Edinburgh University
1871 takes up law
1875 meets W. E. Henley
1876 meets Fanny Van de Grift Osbourne
1879 sails for America
1880 marries Fanny
1883 *Treasure Island*
1885 settles in Bournemouth; *A Child's Garden of Verses*
1886 *Dr Jekyll and Mr Hyde* and *Kidnapped*
1888 sails to South Seas
1889 buys Vailima estate in Samoa
1894 dies at Vailima

Beloved Nanny
Alison Cunningham (above right), known as 'Cummie', was Louis' second mother. It was she who sat by his bed through his long nights of sickness, and she to whom he dedicated A Child's Garden of Verses.

Edinburgh's splendours
Stevenson grew up in the genteel elegance of Edinburgh's more affluent city streets, surrounded by the Georgian legacy of crescents, rows of terraces and large, open squares. Although he was to seek out the low life of the city and feel more at home in the 'beggarly slums', this was not what he was born to and was a source of much concern to his parents.

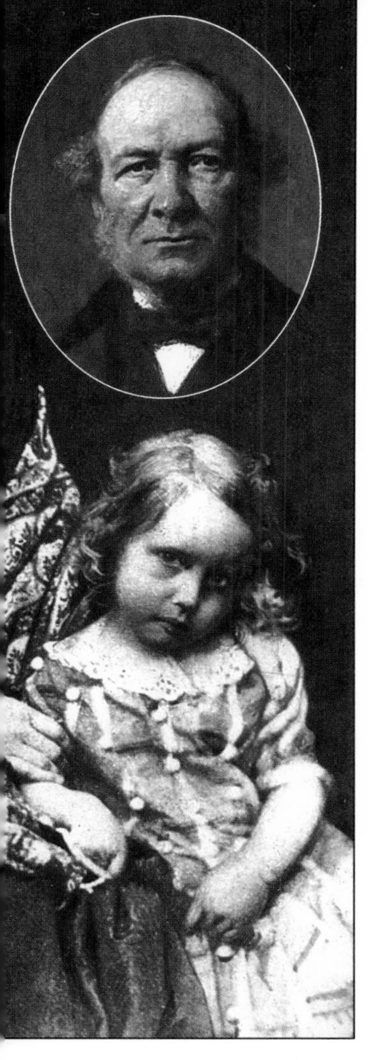

Playroom adventures
Armed with a toy theatre and sets of exciting characters, the young Louis practised his gifts for storytelling.

'Cummie' was a morbidly religious woman who read nothing but devout tracts to her young charge, implanting many 'ecstasies and terrors' in his fevered imagination. His favourite game at this time was 'playing at church', making a pulpit of a chair and sermonizing from it. 'I piped and snivelled over the Bible', he remarked in later life.

The family moved from Howard Place, first to Inverleith Terrace – where Stevenson fell ill with the croup and bronchitis – then, when he was six, to the splendid New Town terrace of Heriot Row. It was on the third floor of this house that he played with the swashbuckling cardboard cut-out figures from the toy theatres called *Skelt's Juvenile Dramas*. This developed the taste for the sort of adventure that was to loom so large in both his tales and his adult life. His enthusiastic playmate then, as in years to come, was his dreamy cousin Bob.

Stevenson attended a local school when he was seven, followed by the Edinburgh Academy. Later, while his mother wintered abroad for her health, he went to a boarding school in Surrey, which he hated. Thomas Stevenson's ambition for his son – that he should enter the family lighthouse business – seemed firmly on course. At 17, he was sent to inspect the harbour works of Fife and Caithness, and in 1867 he entered Edinburgh University to study engineering.

On his own admission Stevenson was an idle student. His 'own private end' at this time was to learn

Literary connections
Six years Louis' senior, Sidney Colvin (above) helped launch Louis into London's literary society. The two had met through Mrs Frances Sitwell, a beautiful and brilliant woman whom Louis revered and called his 'Madonna' (line 3 of letter, above), and whom Colvin also loved. Although she was to marry Colvin, the three remained lifelong friends.

how to become a writer. In his famous phrase he played 'the sedulous ape' to such models as Charles Lamb, William Wordsworth and Daniel Defoe, imitating their work and reading widely. And in 1871 he announced to his long-suffering father that his chosen career was not to be lighthouse engineering, but writing. Thomas Stevenson took this news calmly enough, believing it to be no more than a youthful fad. He merely stipulated that Stevenson should study law to provide a steady occupation should the writing fail.

Stevenson's youthful rebellion against the strict Presbyterian conformity of his childhood reached a peak at this time. With his incorrigible cousin Bob he haunted the brothels of Edinburgh and the port of Leith, and smoked hashish in the lowest taverns, 'the companion of seamen, chimney sweeps and thieves', who called him 'Velvet Coat' because of the bohemian jacket he always wore.

'MADMAN OR FOOL'

In 1873 the aspiring young writer dropped a bombshell that precipitated a crisis in the family. He told Thomas Stevenson he was a non-believer. To his father this was simply not a credible point of view – only a 'madman or a fool' could fail to believe in God. Stevenson's admission poisoned the atmosphere at Heriot Row. It was, he said, 'like a house in which somebody is still waiting burial'. His parents paced about with long faces, and stormy arguments were followed by periods of grim silence.

Finally his parents attempted to cure their son once and for all of his heretical nonsense and packed him off to stay with his cousin Maud, who had married a sensible English clergyman. His stay at Cockfield Rectory near Bury St Edmunds did not have the desired effect, however. Instead, he fell headlong and hopelessly in love with a house guest.

Frances Sitwell – 'Madonna', as he came to call her – was, at 34, 12 years his senior, and the separated wife of a clergyman who had had a not entirely professional interest in choirboys. In no time Stevenson was pour-

Artist friend
John Singer Sargent was a friend of the Stevensons, and a frequent visitor to their house in Bournemouth. He painted them there with Fanny resplendent in Indian garb, and Louis in his familiar velvet jacket.

ing his heart out to 'Madonna' on long country walks. Mrs Sitwell coped gracefully with his youthful ardour. She certainly did not reciprocate his passion, but Stevenson did impress her as a precocious literary talent, and it was through her that he struck up a most fruitful, lasting friendship with the distinguished Cambridge academic Sidney Colvin.

Colvin introduced Stevenson to the refined literary air of the Savile Club in London, and helped set him on a fledgling writing career as a contributor to magazines while he continued to study at the Scottish Bar. At this time too Stevenson met the invalid poet W. E. Henley, with whom he had a turbulent friendship that was to end in mutual bitterness.

For some years, plagued by ill health, Stevenson journeyed restlessly around Scotland and England as well as France, joking in a letter to his mother that she had a tramp and a vagabond for a son. Time had not, however, lessened his determination to be a writer, much to his father's regret. Despite passing his law exams and ceremoniously fixing a brass advocate's plate to the door of number 17 Heriot Row, Stevenson never practised at the Bar. Instead he was soon back in France mixing with the company he liked best – carefree bohemians. When he returned to Edinburgh in the autumn of 1875 he fell into a fit of black depression. He was not to know that on the other side of the bleak Scottish winter waited the fulcrum and love of his life.

A MOMENTOUS MEETING

Stevenson and his cousin Bob had spent a number of summers at Grez, an artists' colony on the edge of the Fontainebleau forest, 60 miles from Paris. Before their next visit word reached them of a stunning addition to the bohemian enclave, a beautiful American woman and her 'bewitching' daughter and son.

Fanny Van de Grift Osbourne had withdrawn to the hotel at Grez after the death of her youngest son in Paris. Her estranged husband had returned to America shortly afterwards. There was much talk of what the 'mad Stevensons' would make of her. Bob Stevenson, the artist and rake, was first on the scene - and he stole her heart. She described him as 'the most beautiful creature I ever saw in my life'. But she had reckoned without Louis (as Robert Louis was known).

Louis Stevenson literally vaulted into Fanny's life in early July 1876. The hotel guests were seated at dinner, with Fanny and her daughter Belle the inevitable centre of chivalrous attention, when there was a noise outside the open window and a shabby figure wearing a hat and carrying a knapsack jumped lightly into the room. 'My cousin Louis Stevenson', announced Bob suavely, like a conjuror. Belle was to claim later that it was love at first sight between the 25-year old Stevenson and her mother.

Over the next two years their love affair deepened and in 1878 Stevenson took his father into his confidence and declared his intention of marrying this woman, who was ten years his senior, still married, and had two children to support. With a resignation that came more easily to him by this time, Thomas Stevenson hardly batted an eyelid – this was just another of his son's whimsical schemes.

Indeed, it seemed to be the case when Fanny and her children abruptly returned to San Francisco. Desolate and confused, Stevenson went to France on his own, hired a donkey called Modestine and tramped around the mountainous countryside of the Cévennes. He could not, however, stop thinking about Fanny.

Back in London and Edinburgh, Stevenson – now a regular magazine contributor – remained gloomy and sickly. His love for Fanny never wavered and he immediately responded to a distraught telegram from her in Monterey, California. He bought a steamship ticket, and, without telling his parents (and against the advice of his literary friends), he set sail from Greenock on 7 August 1879 aboard the SS *Devonia,* bound for New York on the first lap of his journey to California.

The story of his sea voyage and his nightmarish trip West aboard emigrant trains is told in *The Amateur Emigrant,* a tribute to his determination to write and record even amid the most appalling squalor and

Grez, painted by Fanny *(below) By chance, Fanny Osbourne chose to retreat to the French artists' colony at Grez after the death of her youngest son. It was there, in the summer of 1876, that she met the 25-year-old Louis.*

TIGER AND TIGER LILY

Born in Indiana in 1840, Fanny Van de Grift was married at 17 and had three children before she finally left her philandering husband. In the intervening years she had followed him to the most primitive, lawless silver-mining towns of Nevada, had for a time believed him dead (killed by Indians), and had started a new life for herself in San Franscisco.

Unconventional and spirited, she moved with her children to Europe where she met Stevenson (right), who called her his 'tiger and tiger lily'.

Fact or Fiction

WILLIAM ERNEST HENLEY

Stevenson based the turncoat rogue, Long John Silver, on his poet friend and literary collaborator W. E. Henley. Henley, with his bushy hair and red beard was a noisy, argumentative man who enjoyed his whisky. As a boy he had had a foot amputated and Stevenson once wrote to him, 'It was the sight of your maimed strength and masterfulness that begot John Silver.'

despite his own deteriorating health. Nearly dead on his feet, he finally made it to Monterey and his lover's side.

After tribulations of ill health and poverty, the fairy story of Stevenson's love for Fanny had its happy resolution when they were married in San Francisco on 19 May 1880. Their honeymoon was also of a fairy tale quality: a two-month sojourn in an abandoned silver-mining shack on Mount St Helena in the Napa Valley, which Stevenson recaptured in the pages of *The Silverado Squatters*.

The newly-weds returned to Europe, and were reconciled with Stevenson's parents. The new Stevenson family, including Fanny's son Lloyd, now lived in Scotland and spent two winters at the health resort of Davos in the Swiss Alps. During this time Stevenson wrote the book that would ensure his literary fame – the adventure classic *Treasure Island*. He wrote it as much for his father as for his cherished stepson Lloyd. For the book, to his joy and amazement, he was offered 'A hundred jingling, tingling, golden-minted quid'!

After spells in the Highlands and the south of France the Stevensons settled in Bournemouth, where the frail writer was later to liken his life to that of 'a pallid weevil in a biscuit'. Nevertheless, he now entered a most productive phase of his writing career, completing *A Child's Garden of Verses, Kidnapped,* and that Gothic shocker, *The Strange Case of Dr Jekyll and Mr Hyde*. And it was at Bournemouth that Stevenson formed a lasting and mutually admiring friendship with the great American novelist, Henry James.

SOUTH SEAS ADVENTURE

Following the death of his father in May 1887, Stevenson, his mother, Fanny and Lloyd set sail for America on an odyssey that would take them half-way round the world. Now a celebrated writer, Stevenson was abashed by the attention he received in New York. The family settled first at Saranac Lake in the Adirondack Mountains where, as the temperature dropped to 40° below zero, Stevenson put to one side the book he was working on – *The Master of Ballantrae* – and set about turning a long cherished dream into reality; he would hire a boat and venture into the mysterious world of the South Seas.

Samoan sanctuary
When completed, Vailima, painted (top) by Belle, Stevenson's step-daughter, boasted a 50-foot main hall with marble busts and originals by Rodin and Piranesi. Here Stevenson, with his family, spent the happiest days of his life. In the photo Lloyd is standing between Stevenson and his redoubtable mother, with Belle and her son below Fanny. Of her mother-in-law Fanny wrote to Henry James, 'I wish you could but just get a glimpse of that lady taking a moonlight promenade on the beach in the company of a gentleman dressed in a single handkerchief.'

Polynesian paradise
Like Gauguin, a few years later, Stevenson fell in love with Tahiti (above), enchanted by the lushness of the land and the friendliness of the people.

Final days
(Top left) One of many photographs of Stevenson and family in Samoa shows the novelist playing his flageolet in bed at Vailima. When he died, 40 chieftains chopped and axed a path up the steep face of Mount Vaea for Stevenson's grave (above left), knowing that this was the resting place that their cherished storyteller had wanted.

That boat was the schooner *Casco,* which slid out from San Francisco Bay at the end of June 1888 and took the Stevensons to the Marquesas Islands, Tahiti and Honolulu. Stevenson's friends back home – with the honourable exception of Henry James – never really forgave him his self-imposed exile. The fact was he had 'more fun and pleasure of my life these past months than ever before, and more health than any time in ten long years.'

SETTLING DOWN

After more island adventuring and further health crises Stevenson found his final home in December 1889 – at Apia, the capital of Upolu in the Samoan Islands. Here, in several hundred acres of ground, he built a magnificent wooden house called Vailima, filled it with elegant furniture from the family home in faraway Heriot Row, assembled round him a loyal household of Samoan servants, and installed himself, Fanny and her children, and his elderly, redoubtable mother Maggie. And now, amid this subtropical lushness, his thoughts turned to the homeland he would never again set eyes on, and he *"heard again/In my precipitous city beaten bells/Winnow the keen sea wind. And here afar,/ Intent on my own race and place, I wrote . . ."*

The writing in question was *Weir of Hermiston,* an unfinished fragment generally regarded as a masterpiece. Stevenson had been working on this when, on 3 December 1894, he wandered out on to the verandah to talk to Fanny. Suddenly he held his hands to his head, cried out, 'What's that? Do I look strange?', and collapsed on the floor. He never regained consciousness.

Ironically, after the courageous lifelong battle he had fought against his treacherous lung disease, Robert Louis Stevenson died of a brain haemorrhage. He was aged 44, had never been fitter and was on the point of gaining full maturity as a writer.

In accordance with his wishes he was buried on the summit of Mount Vaea. His coffin was draped with the red ensign from the *Casco*. The bronze plaque on his tomb bears these famous lines from his poem *Requiem:*

Here he lies where he longed to be;
Home is the sailor home from the sea,
And the hunter home from the hill.

Edinburgh Life

Cold and austere, colourful and squalid, Edinburgh both repelled and attracted Stevenson. Its climate drove him in search of balmy sunshine, but time and distance only heightened its fascination.

Stevenson spent much of his life travelling for the sake of his health, but the place that most vividly affected his imagination was his native city of Edinburgh. In 1882 he wrote to his friend Charles Baxter from the South of France, recalling their youthful escapades: 'O for ten Edinburgh minutes, sixpence between us and the ever glorious Lothian Road, or dear mysterious Leith Walk.' And even when he was half the globe away in the South Seas he wrote nostalgically of what he called the 'precipitous city'.

Wandering around Edinburgh's steep banks and handsome stone-faced streets today it requires only a small effort of the imagination to be carried back to 1850, the year of Stevenson's birth. In spite of slum clearance and rebuilding, Edinburgh has probably changed less in essentials during the past two centuries than any other capital city in Europe. It is a small place compared with most of the others and (not being a seat of government) more remote from political affairs.

A SPLENDID ERA

Even in the mid-19th century, Edinburgh was a city living on its memory – the memory of the resplendent age in the late 18th century when it had earned the name 'the Athens of the North'. This description referred not only to the Grecian purity of the architecture of the Georgian New Town, but also to the cultural and intellectual flowering that took place at this time. It was the city's heyday in art and literature, when it boasted painters like Allan Ramsay and Sir Henry Raeburn, and

A bustling city
(below and left) The Old Town of Edinburgh was crowded and busy in Stevenson's day, the streets animated by colourful characters. Below left is a square in front of the ancient church of St Giles, but much more typical of this picturesequely squalid area is the tenement scene inset, with washing fluttering from the windows in the manner described by Stevenson in his Edinburgh, Picturesque Notes, *a lively account of the city published in 1878.*

heroes of the Enlightenment such as the philosopher David Hume and the political economist Adam Smith. It was also a time when the English gentry sent their sons to Edinburgh's renowned university.

These things represented only one aspect of Edinburgh, however. As Stevenson wrote, 'Few places, if any, offer a more barbaric display of contrasts to the eye.' He was referring to the remarkable diversity of natural and architectural features that Edinburgh presents within a small compass, from the rugged splendour of the castle on its rock – 'one of the most satisfactory crags in nature' – to the towering tenements, like 'smokey beehives ten stories high', and from the picturesque but squalid Old Town to the New Town's 'open squares and gardens of the wealthy'.

Edinburgh's pleasures
Although Edinburgh was noted for its bad weather and had a reputation for smoky gloom (below), it was a convivial place. Curling, a winter sport associated chiefly with Scotland, drew all classes of society to the ice of Duddingston Loch (above left), and the Advocates' Library (above) was one of several splendid reading rooms that added to the city's attractions.

WINTRY GLOOM

Over the Old Town in Stevenson's day hung the drifting cloud of smoke that gave the city the name of 'Auld Reekie'. Grime attached itself to the stone and added its patina to the blend of innumerable greys for which Edinburgh is famous – grey rock merging in winter with grey watery sky. It can create a lovely sight, but the young, delicate Stevenson shivered in what he called 'one of the vilest climates under the heaven':

'To none but those who have themselves suffered the thing in the body, can the gloom and depression of our Edinburgh winters be brought home. For some constitutions there is something almost physically disgusting in the bleak ugliness of easterly weather; the wind wearies, the sickly sky depresses them . . . The days are so short that a man does much of his business, and certainly all his pleasure, by the haggard glare of gas lamps. The roads are as heavy as a fallow. People go by, so drenched and draggle-tailed that I have often wondered how they found the heart to undress. And meantime the wind whistles through the town as if it were an open window.'

The greyness seemed particularly appropriate on Sundays, for Edinburgh was as conservative and formal a city in its manners as in its architecture. In the New Town, where Stevenson passed his boyhood, the older professions, represented by genteel families from the Church, the Law and the armed services, preserved the old Scottish Sabbath. On this day a harsh discipline kept respectable folk indoors, quiet and immobile behind thick curtains, while church bells moaned their ancient dissonances across empty, windswept streets.

The new rich had left the New Town for the Victorian villas, which in Stevenson's time were stretching in suburbs towards the eastern coast, for although the

Edinburgh fairs
(above and right) Edinburgh is famous for its grey-stoned architectural dignity, but in Stevenson's time a vivid note of colour was supplied by the various fairs that went on in its streets and nearby. Above is a delightful collection of quirky characters at a fair on the outskirts of the city, and on the right is an amazingly energetic scene at the Horse Fair in the Grassmarket, with the Castle in the background.

centre of Edinburgh changed little, there was great expansion in the outlying areas. During the 19th century the population of the city grew from under 100,000 to about 400,000. Essentially that was a native growth, for Edinburgh has never enjoyed the sudden bursts of prosperity that have brought strangers swarming in, nor the sudden economic setbacks that drive people out of a city.

Subject neither to bouts of emigration nor immigration, Edinburgh had, as it has still today, the most indigenous population of any major city in United Kingdom – hence, perhaps, the domesticity of the place, and the tolerant mix of social classes. On the ice of Duddingston Loch it was an everyday event to find minister and judge, poacher and farmhand meeting together in easy familiarity to contest a curling match. By Stevenson's time the division between the classes was no doubt becoming sharper, though it would be rash to accept his verdict that 'social inequality is nowhere more ostentatious than at Edinburgh'.

Just as Georgian Edinburgh had reluctantly aban-

Calton Jail
(right) Edinburgh's most famous prison was the Tolbooth, nicknamed the Heart of Midlothian, but this is the more modern jail at the bottom of Calton Hill. Stevenson was familiar with prison interiors, as he visited his low-life friends when they were in jail.

Fleshmarket Close
(above) Vice was rife in the dingy, decaying streets of Edinburgh's Old Town, and prostitution was a fact of everyday life. In the aptly named Fleshmarket Close, several of the women who stand at doors or appear at windows are probably ladies of easy virtue.

doned the sedan chair for the coach, so Victorian Edinburgh replaced the coach by the horse tram (which first appeared in 1871), but fundamental change was less drastic than elsewhere. Edinburgh escaped the worst consequences of the Industrial Revolution, for its industries were mainly light and clean, its economic importance depending more on its role as the centre of Scottish banking and insurance.

SQUALOR AND VICE

Being free of the 'mass employment' of northern English towns, Edinburgh was also unvisited by 'mass unemployment'. The gulf between master and man, capital and labour, was also less evident than it was in Bolton or Bradford. But the gap between rich and poor widened and became more noticeable. The old convivial life of the tavern, which in an earlier age had been as much a part of Edinburgh as its law courts, churches and assembly rooms, and which had brought together people of all ranks and incomes in a genuinely democratic friendship, was by 1850 a fading institution, conquered by prosperity and Victorian notions of refinement and 'respectability'. The public house was driven morally and socially underground and drinking itself, even the drinking of whisky, was, if not obliterated, transformed into a domestic weakness or a private vice.

In the Old Town of Edinburgh there was squalor as well as vice. The St Giles quarter, washed with rain the year through and bearing a grim and sooty aspect, was a broken-down district of dank arches and dark stairs. Here whole families of the new urban poor huddled in airless one-roomed hovels, washing fluttering from every window. Stevenson wrote of 'an air of sluttishness and dirt' and of 'broken shutters, wry gables, old palsied houses on the brink of ruin, a crumbling human pigsty fit for pigs'. By the Heart of Midlothian (the nickname for Edinburgh's prison), under the ancient Market Cross, fishwives sold oysters and whelks from Newhaven and Musselburgh, and a stray caddie (or messenger) from a grander age might be seen touting for custom among the legal clerks. But drunkenness, thievery and prostitution were the most salient marks of the district, which was now almost entirely segregated from the society of the fashionable New Town.

Dr George Bell, writing in 1850 of his investigations into the health and living conditions of the city's poor, expressed his horror of the scenes he witnessed daily. 'From the toothless infant to the toothless old man, the population of the wynds [narrow alleys] drinks whisky. The drunken drama that is enacted on Satur-

A haunting city
Stevenson had many unpleasant things to say about Edinburgh, but deep in his heart he had an enduring love for the city. This view from the castle hill over the rooftops shows the rugged beauty that haunted his imagination.

day night and Sabbath morning beggars description.'

Overcrowding was at a shocking level and sanitation primitive. Dr H. D. Littlejohn, the city's first Medical Officer of Health, published a *Report on the Sanitary Conditions of the City of Edinburgh* (1865) in which he highlighted such appalling conditions, saying 'that with the possible exception of some districts of Liverpool, in no part of the world does there exist greater overcrowding of population'. Littlejohn's recommendations for improving public health included regular inspection of cow byres (there were still many of these in courts and closes in the city), the lifting of manure every week (instead of every fortnight), and compulsory introduction of water closets into the houses of the poor. During the 1860s the situation was considerably improved by the widespread laying of sewers in the city.

DELIGHTS OF THE FLESH

Away from the ugly, demeaning poverty of St Giles, members of Edinburgh's underworld spent their nights and early mornings among the new Victorian surburbs on the eastern slopes of the city. Indeed, the delights of the flesh gained added piquancy from being stolen at the very heart of the conservative, puritan capital of Scotland. It was those streets which Stevenson had in his mind's eye when he wrote the lines,

I love the night in the City,
The lighted streets and the swinging gait of harlots.

There he sat as a youth, open-eyed, in thieves' kitchens; there were the all-night underground or 'back-of-the-house' supper and drinking rooms; and there, too, the dance halls breathed an intemperate vitality all night long and were a living contradiction of the Glaswegian's taunt (mocking both the prudery and the Anglicized accent of well-to-do Edinburgh) that in the capital sex was what coal was delivered in.

In haunting these disreputable places as a young man, Stevenson was rebelling against the strict values of his upbringing, and his experiences must have had a powerful effect on his imagination, acquainting him with a rich variety of low-life characters. He always carried a note-book with him to record his impressions, and no doubt the low places haunted by Mr Hyde and the coarse-grained villains in *Treasure Island* were at least partly inspired by the sights and sounds of Stevenson's inquisitive youth.

His attitudes towards his native city were summed up in his book *Edinburgh, Picturesque Notes,* published in 1878. Much of what he said was far from complimentary, and he offended some citizens by his remarks about their materialism and ultra-respectability (he noted that the offence was balanced by giving 'a proportionable pleasure to our rivals of Glasgow'). Yet however much he complained about the city of his birth, his most abiding response to it was one of love:

'The weather is raw and boisterous in winter, shifty and ungenial in summer, and downright meteorological purgatory in the spring. The delicate die early, and I, as a survivor, among bleak winds and plumping rain, have been sometimes tempted to envy them their fate. For all who love shelter and the blessings of the sun, who hate dark weather and perpetual tilting against squalls, there could scarcely be found a more unhomely and harassing place of residence. . . They lean over the great bridge which joins the New Town with the Old – and watch the trains smoking out from under them and vanishing into the tunnel on a voyage to brighter skies. Happy the passengers who shake off the dust of Edinburgh, and have heard for the last time the cry of the east wind among her chimney-tops! And yet the place establishes an interest in people's hearts; go where they will, they find no city of the same distinction; go where they will, they take a pride in their old home.'

OSCAR WILDE

1854-1900

'Somehow or other I'll be famous, and if not famous, I'll be notorious,' declared the young Oscar Wilde: he proved to be both. From the moment he burst upon fashionable society he was a celebrity, fêted for his dazzling wit and affectionately mocked for his 'poetic' nature and flamboyant behaviour. His genius as a raconteur and coiner of epigrams made him the most quoted man in London, and when he translated his genius into stories, poems, plays and his sole novel, he was confirmed as one of the most brilliant Victorian writers. But the world in which Wilde moved was riddled with hypocrisy – hypocrisy which Wilde relentlessly exposed. And when his celebrity turned to notoriety, the society that had so flattered him was merciless.

Fame and Infamy

Brilliant, flamboyant and with quicksilver wit, Oscar Wilde was the darling of late Victorian society – until he transgressed its intractable moral laws.

One of the most gifted and most often quoted users of the English language was an Irishman by blood, birth and upbringing. Oscar Wilde lived and conversed much in the style of his writing, alternately shocking and captivating the London society he had chosen for his audience. 'I've put my genius into my life,' he said at the end, 'only my talent into my works.'

Oscar Fingal O'Flahertie Wills Wilde was born on 16 October, 1854 at 21 Westland Row in Dublin, the second son of remarkable parents. His father, Sir William Ralph Wills Wilde, was a leading eye and ear surgeon, a scholar of some repute and a noted archaeologist.

Oscar's mother was even more of a celebrity than his father at the time of their marriage. Under the pen-name 'Speranza', Jane Francesca Elgee, Lady Wilde wrote passionate nationalistic articles for the radical newspaper, *The Nation*, and was an ardent advocate of women's rights. She exerted a powerful influence over her second son's life. 'All poets love their mothers', Wilde later said, 'I worshipped mine.' And she called him 'best and kindest of sons'.

THE FUTURE SCHOLAR

Oscar's childhood was happy and carefree, his parents indulgent and loving. Like most boys of his class, at the age of 10 he was packed off to a public school – Portora Royal, near Enniskillen. Although a bookish boy, Oscar did less well academically than his elder brother Willie, but at the age of 16 he developed a passionate interest in the classics, particularly Greek, at which he excelled. In the autumn of 1871 he entered Trinity College, Dublin, where he

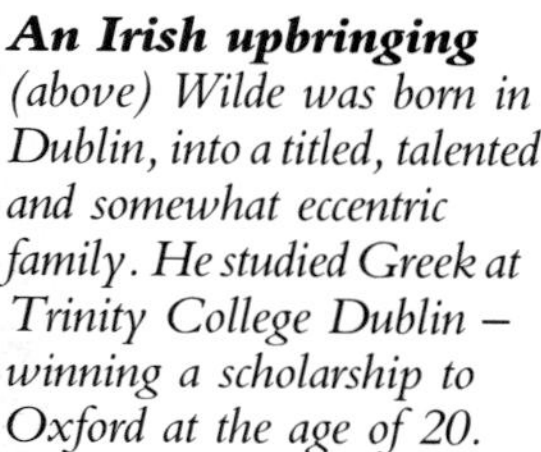

An Irish upbringing
(above) Wilde was born in Dublin, into a titled, talented and somewhat eccentric family. He studied Greek at Trinity College Dublin – winning a scholarship to Oxford at the age of 20.

Dramatic mother
(far left) 'Speranza', Oscar Wilde's mother was a profound influence on her son. She was a well-known Irish Nationalist and poetess (though not a very good one). After marrying in 1851, she became the focal point of Dublin's literary circle. Oscar adored her.

A gifted father
(left) Sir William Wilde, Oscar's father was a famous, gifted surgeon. He had three legitimate children and several illegitimate ones. Like Oscar, he was at the centre of a highly publicized and scandalous trial – when he was accused of molesting one of his patients. (He won the case.) He is seen here exhibiting his notorious and eccentric scruffiness.

won the Berkeley Gold Medal for Greek and in 1874 a scholarship to Magdalen College, Oxford.

'I was the happiest man in the world', exclaimed Wilde, 'when I entered Magdalen for the first time.' He spent four idyllic years at Oxford. Already noted for his brilliant conversation and boldness of dress, Wilde cultivated his taste for the finer things of life. Indeed, as he was to say later, he sometimes felt that his life was one long struggle against stupidity and dullness – vices to which he felt the English were particularly addicted. He left Oxford in 1878. Armed with a double first, the Newdigate Prize for English Verse and the reputation of an eccentric genius, he set out to take London by storm – 'I'll be a poet, a writer, a dramatist. Somehow or other I'll be famous, and if not famous, I'll be notorious'. In the years that were to follow, Oscar Wilde was to be each of these things in turn.

Installing himself in Thames House, Salisbury Street, Wilde began cultivating dandyism and became known as the 'apostle of aestheticism'. During this period of his life, Wilde would do anything to be seen and talked about. "There is only one thing in the world worse than being talked about", he wrote in *The Picture of Dorian Gray*, "and that is not being talked about." He became the talk of the town, his wit, charm and audacity making up for a lack of proven literary accomplishment.

Key Dates

1854 born in Dublin
1871 goes to Trinity College, Dublin
1874 goes to Magdalen College, Oxford
1878 graduates with a double first
1881 *Poems* published
1882 American lecture tour
1884 marries Constance
1891 meets Lord Alfred Douglas. *The Picture of Dorian Gray* published
1895 *The Importance of Being Earnest* performed. Sentenced to two years hard labour at Pentonville and Reading jails
1897 writes *De Profundis*. Goes to live in France
1898 writes *The Ballad of Reading Gaol*
1900 dies in Paris

Roger Viollet

The young Oscar *(left) Wilde, aged two, in a velvet dress. Although some writers have made much of this mode of dress in relation to Oscar's homosexuality, it was customary among the upper classes to dress young boys in what is now considered 'girls' clothing'.*

Magdalen College *(above) Wilde spent four years at Oxford. He was a brilliant classical scholar, gaining a 'double first' (the highest possible grade of degree) and the Newdigate Prize. Armed with academic success, he intended to take London by storm.*

He dressed in a way calculated to shock. His rich velvet coats, knee-breeches, stockings, flowing ties and buckled shoes upset the Victorian gentleman's sense of decorum. His pose was languishing and highly sensitive. Once, asked what he had done all day, he replied, 'I was working on the proof of one of my poems all the morning, and took out a comma. In the afternoon I put it back again.'

SAVED BY PATIENCE

His sayings and doings very soon became the subject of savage satire in *Punch*, but it was Gilbert and Sullivan's comic operetta, *Patience*, that gained him national notoriety. A skit on aestheticism, it was taken to be an attack on Wilde, who nevertheless found it highly amusing. But notoriety did not pay the bills. In an attempt to make some money Wilde published his *Poems* in July 1881. Condemned by critics for their lack of originality, the poet's preoccupation with physical beauty and the bodily grace of boys also raised eyebrows. But happily for Wilde the public showed sufficient interest for the volume to run into five editions.

Ironically, however, it was *Patience* that really saved Wilde from penury. After its success in Britain, the D'Oyly Carte Company decided to take the production across the Atlantic. But for the operetta to be understood it was felt necessary to explain what English 'aestheticism' was. And who better to perform the task than Oscar Wilde himself? Accordingly, on Christmas Eve 1881, Wilde set sail for the New World. Spending almost a year in America, he travelled from coast to coast, and made over 50 personal appearances and a great deal of money.

Returning to Europe, he stayed only briefly in London before moving on to Paris. Here, apart from enjoying café life, he wrote a play, *The Duchess of Padua*, for the American actress Mary Anderson who, on receiving it, promptly turned it down. This set-back forced him to look for another source of income. Back in London in May 1883, Wilde again signed up for a lecture tour – of the English provinces.

Bored by the prospect of lecturing even before the tour began, Wilde nevertheless turned up for the opening night at Wandsworth Town Hall on 24 September and stayed with it to the end at Crystal Palace on 5 March. His repertoire consisted of three talks: 'The House Beautiful', 'The Value of Art in Modern Life', and 'Personal Impressions of America'. As always his physical appearance at first threw his audience – the long locks of earlier years now replaced by a curled 'Neronian coiffure' – but his rich melodious voice and ready wit soon had them all laughing heartily.

Wife and child

(below) Wilde met the beautiful Constance Lloyd in Dublin. They married in 1884, and set up home in Chelsea. The couple had several happy years together, and two children – Cyril (pictured here with his mother) and Vyvyan.

American success

(left) New York was the scene of Wilde's first major public performance. He arrived on 2 January 1882 – ahead of the touring opera Patience, *in order to explain its subject, English aestheticism, to the Americans.*

On arriving in the United States, the customs query 'Have you anything to declare?' gave Wilde the opportunity to reply 'Nothing but my genius'. The Americans could hardly believe what they saw (Oscar in velvet breeches and floppy ties), let alone what they heard. They treated him as a joke, but his lecture tour drew vast crowds and made him a fortune.

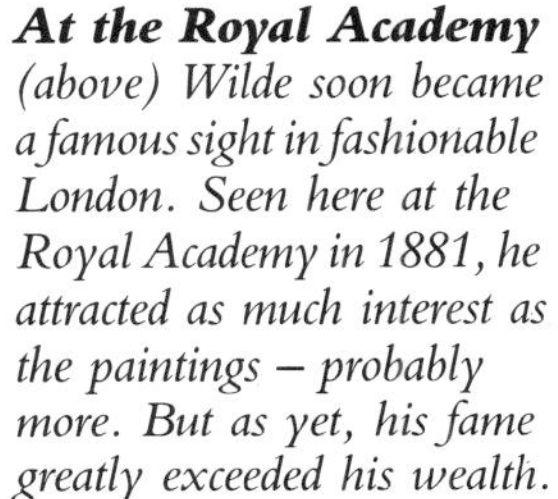

At the Royal Academy *(above) Wilde soon became a famous sight in fashionable London. Seen here at the Royal Academy in 1881, he attracted as much interest as the paintings – probably more. But as yet, his fame greatly exceeded his wealth.*

'The House Beautiful' *Wilde transformed his house in Chelsea into 'The House Beautiful' – with exquisite decorations and works of art.*

In November he was in Dublin where he met and fell in love with Constance Mary Lloyd, who attended his lectures. They had met two years previously and felt a deep attraction for each other. They were married on 29 May 1884. Within a year, a son, Cyril, was born, to be followed by another boy, Vyvyan, the following year. The couple set up home in Tite Street in Chelsea, transforming an ordinary terraced house into 'The House Beautiful'. But Wilde did not have the income to pay for everyday domestic needs, or the extravagant lunches he indulged in at the Café Royal.

Wilde therefore embarked on yet another lecture tour before taking up book reviewing for the *Pall Mall Gazette*. And in June 1887 he became the editor of *The Lady's World*. Changing the title to *The Woman's World*, Wilde enlarged its format, introduced colour on to the front page, and shifted it up-market with articles on literature, art and society. Though circulation increased, Wilde soon tired of it, and his appearances in the office dwindled to a few hours a week, until he resigned in 1889.

If the role of a diligent editor was one which he found irksome, that of family man was even more difficult. After two years of happiness, Wilde grew increasingly bored with his wife and disillusioned with marriage. He developed a close relationship with a 17-year-old ex-Cambridge undergraduate, Robert Ross – a relationship that was to last until Wilde's death.

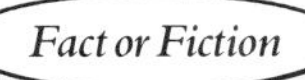

Fact or Fiction

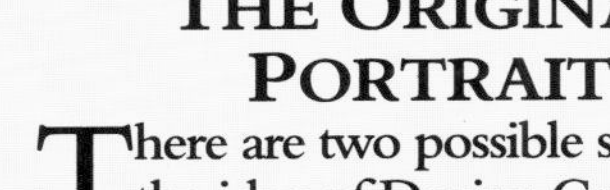

THE ORIGINAL PORTRAIT

There are two possible sources for the idea of Dorian Gray and his portrait. One is that Wilde himself, following a sitting for the artist Frances Richards, looked at his own image and remarked 'What a tragic thing it is! The portrait will never grow older, and I shall. If it was only the other way!'

Another version involves an unknown sitter for the artist Basil Ward. Wilde saw an extremely beautiful young man at his studio and lamented that such a 'glorious creature should ever grow old'. Ward agreed, saying 'How delightful it would be if he could remain exactly as he is while the portrait . . . withered in his stead'.

The original 'Basil' *of the story may have been the artist Basil Ward.*

RISE AND FALL

Wilde's reputation as a major writer rests on the work he produced within a period of seven years, beginning with children's stories including *The Happy Prince* in 1888, and culminating in *The Importance of Being Earnest* in 1895. During these seven years, Wilde experimented with almost every literary form, from short stories to comic drama.

Lady Windermere's Fan, a 'modern drawing-room play with pink lampshades', was first produced at St James's Theatre in February 1892. On the first night Wilde himself appeared on the stage after the performance had ended to rapturous applause. 'Ladies and Gentlemen', he said, 'I congratulate you on the great success of your performance, which persuades me that you think almost as highly of the play as I do.'

By 1895 he had two plays running in the West End and more money coming in than ever before. Wilde was now at the pinnacle of success and good

WILDE VERSUS QUEENSBERRY

The Marquess of Queensberry was out to get Wilde from the day he discovered that he was a close friend of his son, Lord Alfred Douglas. Queensberry even burst into Wilde's home accusing him of 'disgusting conduct'. Shortly after, he accused Wilde of being a sodomite (homosexual). Reckless Oscar immediately took him to court for libel.

The trial became a battle between Queensberry's counsel, Edward Carson, and Wilde. Carson probed; Wilde defended wittily, but he was eventually lacerated by his own cleverness. When asked if he had kissed a certain boy, he replied, 'Oh, dear no. He was a peculiarly ugly boy'. And what, Carson damningly inferred, if he had been beautiful?

Wilde's case was blown. From this moment on events went Queensberry's way. After dropping the case, Wilde himself was arrested on charges of indecency. This trial ended in stalemate; the third resulted in Wilde's prison sentence. It virtually killed him.

fortune. But an incident, in itself insignificant, set in motion a train of events that would bring him ruin.

In 1891 he had developed an obsession for Lord Alfred Douglas, the 21-year-old son of the Marquess of Queensberry. Douglas possessed three qualities which Wilde found irresistible – youth, beauty and a title. In fact, like his 'mad' father, Lord Alfred ('Bosie') was arrogant, wilful, self-indulgent, indiscreet and vengeful. His relationship with Wilde was tempestuous, and soon became common gossip.

Flushed with success, Wilde did little to hide his passion, dining in public and holidaying abroad with Bosie, much to the wrath of Queensberry. Having hounded Wilde for months, threatening to shoot him if he saw him with Bosie in public, on 18 February 1895 Queensberry left his visiting card at Wilde's club, the Albermarle, with the misspelt message 'For Oscar Wilde posing as a somdomite (sic)'.

It would have been safer to ignore the insult, but instead Wilde issued a writ for libel against Queensberry who was duly arrested and charged on 2 March. Assuring counsel that there was no truth in Queensberry's allegation, Wilde was convinced of a favourable verdict. Entering the Old Bailey on 3 April, Wilde played to a packed courtroom. His performance when cross-examined by Sir Edward Carson was masterly.

But on the second day, things did not go so well. Questioned about a certain Alfred Taylor (who kept a disreputable house which Wilde frequently visited), his answers were, as he admitted, 'absurd and silly perjuries'. Pressed by Carson he became evasive and frankly horrified when he realized the amount of evidence Queensberry had amassed against him. He remained self-assured but his answers became damningly revealing.

The feeling of the court was now turning against him, and when it became clear that the Defence had assembled witnesses to prove the justification of Queensberry's claim, Wilde was advised to drop the case. This he did, but instead of leaving the country as everyone advised him to do, he drove to lunch, and on to Bosie's room at the Cadogan Hotel. That evening, Wilde was arrested. The next day he was transferred to Holloway Jail.

Wilde's trial began on 26 April at the Old Bailey. He was charged on 25 counts of gross indecency, and conspiring to procure the commission of acts of indecency. After four days, during which there was a succession of paid witnesses in the box, the jury

Oscar and Bosie
Oscar Wilde met Lord Alfred Douglas (seated) in 1891. Douglas was a striking, spoilt undergraduate who was captivated by Wilde's brilliance. And Wilde, in turn, fell for his 'red rose-leaf lips' and 'slim gilt soul'. The friendship led to Wilde's trial and imprisonment. After, when Wilde had been released and was living in exile, Douglas visited him in France. The always difficult relationship ended when Wilde asked his extremely wealthy friend to lend him some money. The irrational Douglas flew into paroxysms of rage and soon returned to England. They never met again.

retired to consider its verdict. To everyone's surprise, and the judge's obvious irritation, they failed to reach a verdict. On 1 May the case was dismissed and four days later, Wilde was released on bail.

Still, despite the pleading of friends, Wilde refused to flee the country. Consequently on 20 May another trial opened at the Central Criminal Court before Mr Justice Wills. The same ground was covered again, but this time Wilde was found guilty on all but one count and received the sentence of two years hard labour.

Wilde served the whole of his sentence. The first five months were spent at Pentonville in conditions of unrelieved horror. For speaking to another prisoner he was placed in solitary confinement in total darkness for 24 hours. Conditions improved marginally when he was moved to Reading Jail, though he considered he was treated cruelly. His spirit, once so lively and joyous, and his always-precarious health were soon broken.

In the two years he spent in prison, Wilde wrote a long and bitter letter to Lord Alfred accusing him, with good reason, of having caused his downfall. Called *De Profundis* by his literary executor Robert Ross, the letter was only published in its entirety in 1962. Intensely personal, it contains some of the most beautiful of his prose.

Prison drudgery
(below) This contemporary engraving illustrates the appalling degradation and meaningless activity that Wilde endured during his two years' hard labour. He served his full term, and lost his spirit and his health.

EXILE IN FRANCE

After his release on 19 May 1897, Wilde lived out the remainder of his life in France, an exile, 'broken-hearted, ruined, disgraced, a leper and a pariah to men'. In that time, he wrote just one major work, *The Ballad of Reading Gaol*, which was to be his last and finest poem.

After a temporary reconciliation with Bosie, his 'dear boy', the two parted never to meet again. Lack of money and loneliness were his major preoccupations. Constance had divorced him and changed her name before she died prematurely in 1898, and Wilde was forbidden to see either of his sons. He drank heavily. When warned that drinking would kill him, he retorted 'And what have I to live for?' But to a small circle of friends his conversation could be just as lively, good-humoured and witty as ever. Crippled with illness, he continued to joke, saying, 'I am dying, as I have lived, beyond my means'. And of the paper on the wall of his bedroom, he said, 'It is killing me. One of us *has* to go'.

On 30 November 1900 he died of cerebral meningitis, at the age of 46. He had already been received into the Roman Catholic Church and on 3 December was buried at Bagneux.

Fall from grace
(right) With his self-conscious pose and distinctive looks, Wilde had always been a target for caricature. This cruel example shows the once graceful aesthete leaving for France in shame.

Art and Decadence

Worshipping Beauty and cultivating the ideal of 'art for art's sake', the languid young aesthetes of Wilde's set adopted a decadent, sensation-seeking lifestyle that shocked High Victorian morality.

As the 19th century drew to a close, a new mood could be felt among the writers and artists, poets and painters of England – a mood captured perfectly in *The Picture of Dorian Gray*. There was no cohesive 'movement' nor even a common philosophy – just a new spirit, known variously as 'aestheticism', 'decadence' or simply *fin de siecle* (end of century). But the ideas and personalities linked to this mood became, in the popular mind at least, synonymous with anything that was perverse, paradoxical or shocking. And of all the personalities associated with aestheticism, none was seen as more perverse, paradoxical and shocking than Oscar Wilde.

Comic value
(right) Gilbert and Sullivan's comic opera of 1881, Patience, *lampooned Wilde and his ideas. The public delighted in mocking 'aesthetic' poetry, and its practitioners – a trend that publishers of sheet music were quick to cash in on.*

"LANGUID BEAUTY"

Writing in the 1890s on the contemporary aesthete's passion for beautiful things, the writer Max Beerbohm noted in an essay entitled *1880* that 'Beauty had existed long before 1880. It was Mr Oscar Wilde who managed her debut. To study the period is to admit that to him was due no small part of the social vogue Beauty was to enjoy'.

The vogue for 'Beauty' was first seen in the opulent taste in furnishings, fabrics and decor. Dados (elaborate friezes), peacock feathers, willow-pattern blue china, "sinuous draperies and unheard-of greens", all owed something to the aesthetic tastes of Mr Oscar Wilde. But Wilde's influence extended far beyond the home; aesthetes owed him something of their personality too. Beerbohm observed amusedly, 'Into whatever ballroom you went you would find, among the women in tiaras and the fops and the distinguished foreigners, half a score of ragamuffins in velveteen, murmuring sonnets, posturing, waving their hands'.

Wilde, in turn, owed something of his self-conscious posturing to the newly-imported 'dandyism' from France. There it was made fashionable by the fiction of Theophile Gautier, whose *Mademoiselle de Maupin* (1835) came to be known as the 'Bible of the decadents'. The French author J. K. Huysmans' scandalous *A Rebours* is likely to have been the book Dorian Gray receives from Lord Henry Wotton, while Charles Baudelaire's *Les Fleurs du Mal* provided Wilde with a sense of "lurid and languid beauty".

Identifying with disaster
(right) The Decadents were obsessed with tragedy, and were inspired by the deathly beauty of classical, divine disasters. Many were to die tragically young themselves.

Aubrey Beardsley
(left) Emaciated, affected, but a brilliant success at 21, Beardsley personified decadent ideas and behaviour, rivalling Wilde for his notoriety.

The Café Royal set
(below) Ernest Dowson was one of several doomed poets belonging to the 'tragic generation'. A member of Wilde's set and of the Rhymer's Club (which included W. B. Yeats, Lionel Johnson and Richard Le Gallienne) he and his mentors gathered in The Café Royal (bottom), in London's Piccadilly.

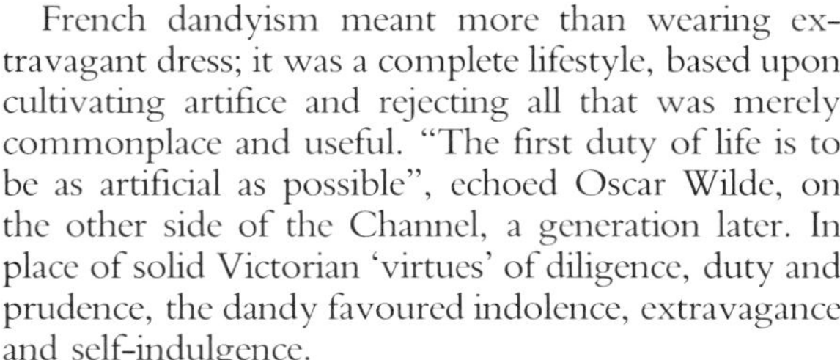

French dandyism meant more than wearing extravagant dress; it was a complete lifestyle, based upon cultivating artifice and rejecting all that was merely commonplace and useful. "The first duty of life is to be as artificial as possible", echoed Oscar Wilde, on the other side of the Channel, a generation later. In place of solid Victorian 'virtues' of diligence, duty and prudence, the dandy favoured indolence, extravagance and self-indulgence.

Life was a perpetual pursuit of new sensations, and the decadent dandy in both France and England – cultivated, affected and refined – experimented with drink, drugs and sex in a way that was frankly shocking to contemporaries. Oscar Wilde may not have paraded down Piccadilly clutching a lily; it was sufficient (as he himself said) for people to believe that he had.

Later, in the late '80s and early '90s, Wilde's innocent lily gave way to an artificially coloured green carnation, the emblem of Parisian homosexuals. By habitually wearing one in his buttonhole, he combined artifice with the hint of forbidden pleasure.

ART AND MORALITY

The aesthete's flagrant disregard for middle-class morality was considered deeply subversive at the time. Their attitude to art was considered especially unsavoury. For most Victorians 'art' was a serious business with a moral purpose. To write as Wilde did in his Preface to *The Picture of Dorian Gray* that "There is no such thing as a moral or an immoral book. Books are well written or badly written. That is all", seemed to be an attack upon the foundations of society itself.

In fact, there was nothing new in this view at all. Gautier had written of *l'art pour l'art* (art for art's sake) more than half a century before *Dorian Gray*. In England, the idea had already been expressed by the painter James Whistler who stated that 'Art should be independent of all clap-trap – should stand alone, and appeal to the artistic sense of eye or ear, without confounding this with emotions entirely foreign to it, as devotion, pity, love, patriotism and the like'. And earlier in the century, the poet John Keats had written *Ode on a Grecian Urn* which contained the line, 'Beauty is truth, truth beauty'.

What Wilde did was to develop the idea into a coherent view of life. To Wilde, "The artist is the creator of beautiful things", and as such above ordinary moral judgements. Since art had nothing to do with morality, the artist was quite literally "beyond good and evil". When Wilde finally appeared in court on charges of homosexuality, it was not just his sexual morals that were being judged but also the idea of 'art for art's sake', and those who subscribed to it.

For the English aesthete, life revolved around the Café Royal in London. Wedged between Piccadilly and Glasshouse Street, it was *the* meeting place of the 'new' artists, writers, poets, musicians and wits. Here Oscar Wilde held court every day from one o'clock onwards and the eager voice of the emaciated painter Aubrey Beardsley could be heard above the general din, disclaiming 'Oh, really! How perfectly sweet!', 'Perfectly enchanting!' or 'Perfectly filthy!'. Beardsley, a success at the age of 21, in some ways rivalled Wilde as the personification of decadence and shared Wilde's

sense of humour, once declaring that he had caught a cold by 'leaving the tassel off his cane'.

To the Café Royal, too, came many more of Wilde's set including the scruffy, tubercular poet Ernest Dowson, who died at the age of just 33. 'Poor wounded wonderful fellow that he was,' wrote Wilde when he died, 'a tragic reproduction of all tragic poetry, like a symbol, or a scene. I hope bay-leaves will be placed on his tomb, and rue, and myrtle too, for he knew what love is.'

Closely associated with the Café Royal set was the Rhymer's Club, whose members included the poet and critic Lionel Johnson who on initially meeting Wilde confessed to a friend, 'I am in love with him'. Also members were Arthur Symons (another poet and critic associated with literary decadence), John Gray (one of Wilde's young, 'precious' poets), and the young Irish poet W. B. Yeats. 'For some years', wrote Yeats, the Rhymer's Club met 'every night in an upper room with a sanded floor in an ancient eating-house in Fleet Street called the Cheshire Cheese.'

The aesthetes, thought Yeats, belonged to a 'tragic generation'. But their decadence was romantic rather than genuinely subversive. Although they wrote about prostitution – a common feature of London streets, but ignored by most 'establishment' writers – their attitude was muted and sentimental, with Symons writing about 'chance romances of the streets' and 'Juliet of the night'. Even homosexuality – a common interest among many members of the Club – was treated demurely, with Lord Alfred Douglas referring to it in a poem as 'The love that dare not speak its name' – a line which Wilde was to defend passionately and eloquently at the Old Bailey.

THE END OF AN ERA

To later generations, the spirit of the decadence was symbolized by *The Yellow Book*. This quarterly review of the arts first appeared in April 1894 with a drawing on the front cover by Beardsley, the quarterly's art editor. At the outset it seemed corrupt and dangerous, but after the first few issues *The Yellow Book* settled down to become a 'safe' publication, with regular contributions from Henry James, Edmund Gosse and George Sainsbury – all conservative writers. And with the trials of Oscar Wilde in 1895, *The Yellow Book's* publishers, The Bodley Head, panicked and sacked Beardsley, the most conspicuous 'decadent' member of staff. When Arthur Symons departed shortly afterwards, the publication became very tame indeed. Wilde himself was dismissive of it, saying that it was 'horrid', 'loathsome' and 'dull'. But since he was not asked to contribute, this criticism may not have been impartial.

Within a year of leaving *The Yellow Book*, Symons and Beardsley brought out a rival publication called *The Savoy*, which stood more courageously for the ideas and art of decadence. It was published by Leonard Smithers, purveyor of erotica, a regular at the Café Royal and a man considered so disreputable by W. B. Yeats, a contributor, that he refused to meet him. *The Savoy* lasted just one year and, apart from articles and drawings from leading 'decadents' (including an ultra-decadent 'romance' written by Aubrey Beardsley called *Under the Hill*), it published pieces from Bernard Shaw,

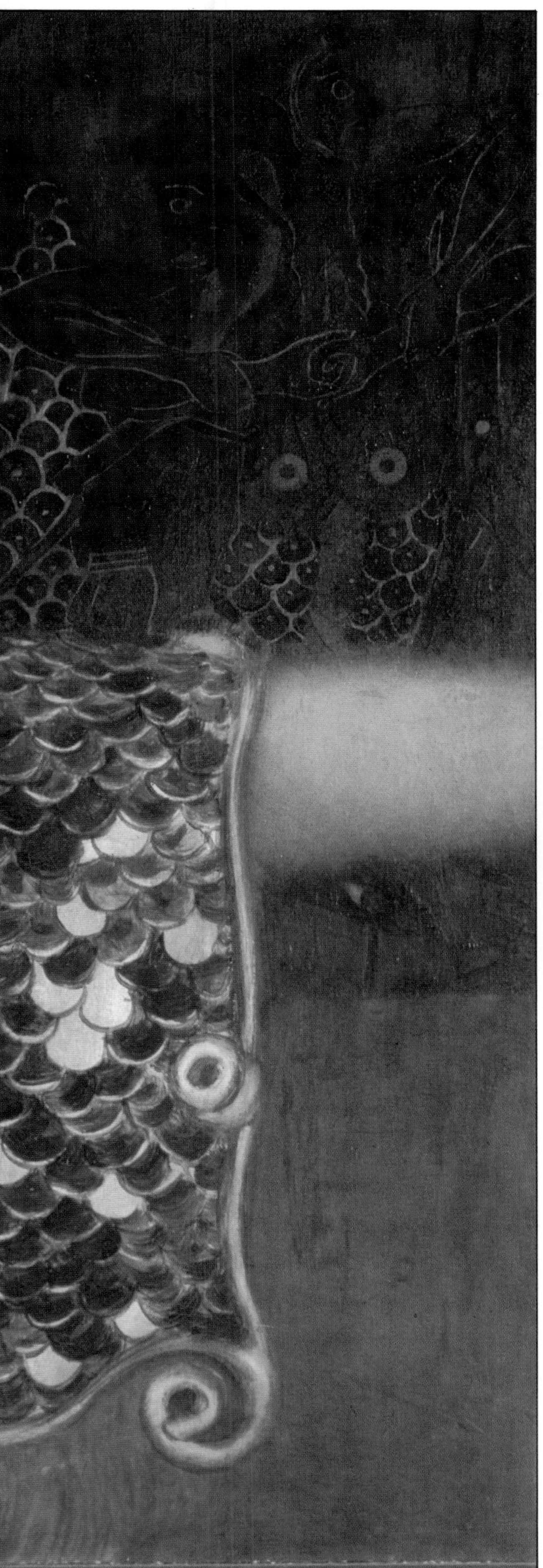

The Yellow Book
An Illustrated Quarterly
Volume I April 1894
London: Elkin Mathews & John Lane
Boston: Copeland & Day
SECOND EDITION
Price 5/- Net

Naughtiness and sin
(above) Beardsley's illustrations were associated with, and came to be used by, the decadent writers of The Café Royal set. His tailpiece to Wilde's play Salomé *typifies his style and the content of many of his drawings – the clean lines depicting sensual nakedness, sinfulness and luxuriousness.*

The Yellow Book
(left) Its art editor and illustrator was Aubrey Beardsley and, at the outset, it seemed to be the mouthpiece for the corrupt ideas of Decadence. But The Yellow Book *– a quarterly arts review published by The Bodley Head – soon degenerated into a safe conservative publication as the 'movement' began to wane.*

Symbolic details
(left) Decadent ideas owed much to European artistic influences, particularly the French and Austrian symbolists. In Gustav Klimt's strangely haunting portrait of the ancient Roman goddess of Wisdom, Pallas Athene, the dense mixture of mysticism, eroticism, classical detail and eerie opulence creates the effect that decadent authors sought to achieve in their writing.

Joseph Conrad, Lionel Johnson and Ford Madox Hueffer (later and better known as Ford Madox Ford).

The Savoy was only half the price of *The Yellow Book*, and was banned by the booksellers W. H. Smith, because it contained in one issue a reproduction of a drawing of a nude by William Blake. But it failed because, with Wilde in prison, 'decadence' was on the wane. The last issue in 1896 was written single-handed by Arthur Symons, who put the magazine's demise down to the fact that 'Comparatively few people care for art at all, and most of these care for it because they mistake it for something else'.

As a group of writers the 'decadents' have not survived. Little of what they produced is read today. Their literary style – following guidelines laid down by Gautier as 'ingenious, complex, learned, full of shades of meaning' – today seems too pretentious and wordy. In the fashion set by the pre-Raphaelite poet and artist Dante Gabriel Rossetti, the decadent writer would spend hours hunting out obscure, archaic and unusual words. His style was stilted, overblown and very artificial – failings not shared by Oscar Wilde.

Decadence did not outlast the death of the old cen-

Languid 'beautiful people'
(left) Maxwell Armfield's homage to the poet Swinburne, depicts the refined elegance and the world-weariness associated with the spirit of 'fin-de-siècle'. The furnishings and decoration in the room are scrupulously detailed in oriental, classical and allegorical imagery – the lily (shown wilting) was one of many flower emblems that came to symbolize the 'foppishness' of the aesthetic movement.

tury, nor did it survive Oscar Wilde's. 'In 1900', wrote W. B. Yeats, 'everybody got off his stilts; henceforth nobody drank absinthe with his black coffee; nobody went mad; nobody committed suicide; nobody joined the Catholic church.'

Yeats' reference to Catholicism is interesting, for among the members of the Rhymer's Club, homosexuality went hand in hand with an almost morbid fascination with 'sin'. Wilde himself shared this fascination, although it was tempered by flippancy and irreverence. Among the young poets, the sense of sin was taken much more seriously. Perhaps because of this, a surprisingly high proportion became converts to Roman Catholicism – which places greater emphasis upon sin and upon its redemption than the Protestant churches.

Dowson, Beardsley, Johnson, Gray all became converts, as did Lord Alfred Douglas, many years later. Even Oscar Wilde was converted to Catholicism on his deathbed (claiming that he had been far too naughty before for the Church to accept him). Nearly all the members of the club died young or comparatively young, and many of the survivors including Symons, went mad.

To the majority of people, as the leader writers of the popular press declared, the whole thing had been a bit of a hoot. For them, the significant event of the 'naughty '90s' – apart from the opportunity to assert their righteous indignation at the fate of Oscar Wilde – was the craze for the 'safety' bicycle (to which Thomas Hardy became devoted) and the 'new' woman seen pedalling through the countryside in her knickerbocker suit. The level of wit served up to the readers of newspapers was a far cry from the polished paradoxes of the decadents. 'The world is divided into two classes', declared one self-congratulatory wag, 'those who ride bicycles and those who don't.' This mania for cycling was behind the success of the music-hall song *Daisy, Daisy, give me your answer do*, which competed in popularity with the nonsense chorus *Ta-ra-ra-boom-de-ay*, which, according to the social historian Holbrook Jackson, 'from 1892 to 1896 . . . affected the country like an epidemic'.

But if the decadents made little impression upon the populace, apart from their scandalous behaviour, Jackson discerned one important trait, which was perhaps common to both. Writing of the 1890s in 1913 he said, 'Life-tasting was the fashion, and the rising generation felt as though it were stepping out of the cages of convention and custom into a freedom full of tremendous possibilities'. A year later World War 1 broke out.

Aesthetic excess
(above) One of numerous popular songs which mocked the vogue for Aestheticism, My Aesthetic Love *was sung and sold 'with immense success'. The cover of the sheet music sums up the popular notion of self-conscious aesthetes – a lady, courted by a fop and cradling a sunflower, contemplates a lily in a room crammed with trendy paraphernalia. Blue china, oriental furniture and furnishings, peacocks' feathers and knick-knacks are prominent – all were available to the fashionable customers who flocked to Liberty's of London. Blue china was, claimed Wilde, something to be 'lived up to'. The craze was not to survive the death of Oscar Wilde or the end of the 19th century.*

JOSEPH CONRAD

1857-1924

Józef Korzeniowski left his native Poland for the tough, adventurous life of a merchant seaman. He survived shipwreck and attempted suicide before coming to England – where he settled to writing of his past experiences in a foreign language for an indifferent public. Despite illness, poverty and a constitutional pessimism, Conrad was true to his new calling and by it achieved fame as the finest foreign ambassador of the English novel.

Home from the Sea

Escaping a bleak childhood for adventure on sunlit seas, Conrad finally settled in a new country to a new career. But he could never outrun the deep pessimism that was his inheritance.

Many aspiring novelists have courted adventure in order to fire their imagination. Joseph Conrad was one lucky exception. He did not start writing until he was 32, or become a full-time writer until he was 39, by which time he had seen more than most people do in a lifetime. He had been involved in gun-running, had tried to kill himself, had left a secure home for a tough life at sea, and had travelled to Europe, Asia, Australia and the Far East. Further voyages of his, particularly to Africa, left his fellow novelist Henry James marvelling, 'No one has *known* . . . the things you know.' Even more impressive was the manner in which Conrad converted these experiences into half-a-dozen brilliant novels, all written in a language he did not learn until he was 20.

Joseph Conrad (or Józef Teodor Konrad Korzeniowski, as he was christened) was born on 3 December 1857 into an aristocratic Polish family. His father Apollo influenced him in three significant ways. As a patriot fighting the Russians, who had annexed Poland, Apollo passed on his hatred of Russia. He also bequeathed to Józef a love for literature – and a profound pessimism.

Being born into an aristocratic Polish family did not mean privilege. In 1861 Apollo was arrested for being politically dangerous and was exiled, with his family, to northern Russia. Here Conrad got his first taste of a deprived, joyless world. Apollo's description of it could have come from one of his son's novels: 'everything [is] rotting and shifting under one's feet . . . The population is a nightmare: disease-ridden corpses'. His wife Eva was the first to succumb to the murderous climate and died four years later. In later life Józef vener-

Exiled and orphaned
Conrad (centre) was born at Berdyczow (below) left), in the part of Poland under Russian domination. When he was three, his parents were exiled to northern Russia for their nationalist activities. Conrad's mother, Eva (top), whom he later revered as 'the ideal of Polish womanhood', died three years later. Father and son were allowed to return to Cracow (below) in 1869, but father Apollo died shortly after and the 11-year-old Józef was left an orphan.

ated her photograph as if it were a religious icon.

For the next three years Apollo, despite his own sickness and poverty, tried to shield Conrad from 'the atmosphere of this place', but it was largely in vain. Conrad grew up 'as though in a monastic cell', repeatedly falling ill. Even worse, Apollo now had terminal consumption and although his sentence was repealed in 1868, enabling them to head south for Cracow, it was too late. Apollo died four months later. According to one biographer, Conrad was in 'inconsolable despair'.

BREAKING FREE

The parental gap was filled by Conrad's uncle Thadeus to whom he 'quickly became devoted.' Thadeus saw education as the key to Conrad's success but he had a difficult task convincing the boy. Another relative wrote that while Conrad 'was intellectually well developed, he hated the rigours of school . . . he used to say that he had a great talent and would become a great writer.'

By the time Conrad was 15, it was getting harder to keep him in school. Prompted by his love of adventure stories and the threat of being conscripted into the Russian army, he pleaded to be allowed to go to sea. For two years Thadeus tried to dissuade him, but at last he relented.

Conrad was based in Marseilles for the next four,

On the waterfront
To escape the threat of military service in the Russian army, and in pursuit of the adventure he had read about, young Conrad (inset) went to Marseilles (above) and became a sailor. Here, difficulty with getting work, abortive attempts at making money and, perhaps, an unhappy love affair reduced Conrad to such despair that he attempted suicide. His faithful Uncle Thadeus redeemed his bad debts, and set the unstable youth on a steadier course – for England and more seafaring.

Key Dates

1857 born in Russian-annexed Poland

1862 family banished to northern Russia

1865 mother dies

1869 father dies

1874 goes to Marseilles

1877 attempts suicide

1878 enters British Merchant Navy

1886 gains British citizenship and Master's certificate

1889 begins writing

1895 goes to Belgian Congo

1896 marries Jessie George

1900 *Lord Jim*

1914 visits Poland

1924 declines knighthood; dies in Kent

wild years. In addition to sailing to the West Indies, he ran through his generous allowance, and further difficulties arose when an irregularity with his work permit ruled out any more voyages. Conrad tried to make a quick fortune by smuggling, but instead lost 3,000 francs in the enterprise. He then borrowed a further 800 which he promptly lost in the gambling rooms at Monte Carlo. In utter despair Conrad attempted suicide. The bullet was aimed at his heart – but missed. This was the first experience of his to be repeatedly used in his novels; he wrote a total of nine fictional suicides, and three of his characters throw their lives away.

Thadeus came to his financial rescue, and 22-year-old Conrad left Marseilles for England, even though he could barely speak six words of the language. From here he continued his seafaring life. Restless and reckless as ever, he repeatedly quarrelled with various captains on trips to the Mediterranean and Australia.

During Conrad's voyages he studied for naval exams and when he was 30 gained his Master's certificate, which enabled him to captain ships. Though he regarded this as a personal triumph – 'vindicating myself' – he was actually growing disillusioned with life at sea, 'sailing for little money and consideration', and was tempted to become a businessman. He was also nearing the point when he would leap into a third, different world – that of the novelist. A lover of all things British – the language, the politics, the freedom – he was naturalized in 1886.

JOURNEY INTO HELL

Conrad had been to the Far East on voyages out of Marseilles, but his first real opportunity to study the area and its people came in 1887, when a back injury forced him into hospital for three months in Singapore. On his recovery, he explored the city, 'riotous with life', and spent four and a half months touring the nearby islands.

Conrad returned to London in 1889. He had had a score of adventures but was penniless and without a real career. Although he had never attempted to write anything longer than a letter, and that usually in French, he began his first novel, *Almayer's Folly*. In 1889 he returned to Poland to visit Thadeus and on the way became involved with Marguerite Poradowska, a woman 10 years older than himself and the widow of his cousin. They struck up an immediate friendship, regularly corresponding with each other over the next few years, often about his writings. It was even rumoured that Conrad proposed to her. She found him a new post and organized his next voyage, which was to prove the most important and difficult of his life – to Africa, up the Congo, into the "heart of darkness".

Shipboard meeting
While first mate of the Torrens *(right), Conrad met John Galsworthy (centre). They spurred each other into writing careers and remained lifelong friends.*

Conrad knew it would be a dangerous journey because he was replacing a young river-steamer captain who had just been murdered by Africans. Even after three months the man was 'still unburied – his hands and feet had been cut off – his clothes taken away . . .' It was a journey into hell. For Conrad, sailing upstream in a 'tin-pot' steamer "was like travelling back to the earliest beginnings of the world, when vegetation rioted on the earth and the big trees were kings . . ." The crew was racked with dysentery and fever, the Europeans suffering the most. The end of the river journey, later brilliantly recaptured in Conrad's masterly novel *Heart of Darkness*, was no Romantic communion with nature, but a terrifying vision of "the vilest scramble for loot". The Europeans were after ivory and no-one was allowed to get in their way.

Conrad went down with acute fever and was prematurely forced back to England. In London he remained in hospital for six weeks, and he was left a prey to malarial gout which intermittently attacked him for the rest of his life, giving him severe pain.

Conrad's pessimism, fuelled by the Congo journey, increased when Thadeus died in 1894. He gave up the sea and turned to writing, his first task being to finish *Almayer's Folly*. The book won good reviews, as did his follow-up, *An Outcast of the Islands*, and this good fortune was matched by an upturn in his personal life.

A MARRIED MAN

In 1896 Conrad married Jessie George, a typist 16 years younger than himself. Though some questioned his choice, the couple complemented each other well, her calm, placid personality offsetting his restless, intense, highly-strung temperament. Married life began in rugged, remote Britanny, where he wrote and she typed out the manuscripts, but malarial gout and depression drove Conrad back to Essex the following year, where he began work on *The Rescuer* and finished

Foreign ports
Conrad sailed all over the world – to Australasia, Martinique, Haiti, Colombia and the West Indies (left), though half his time was spent on shore between voyages.

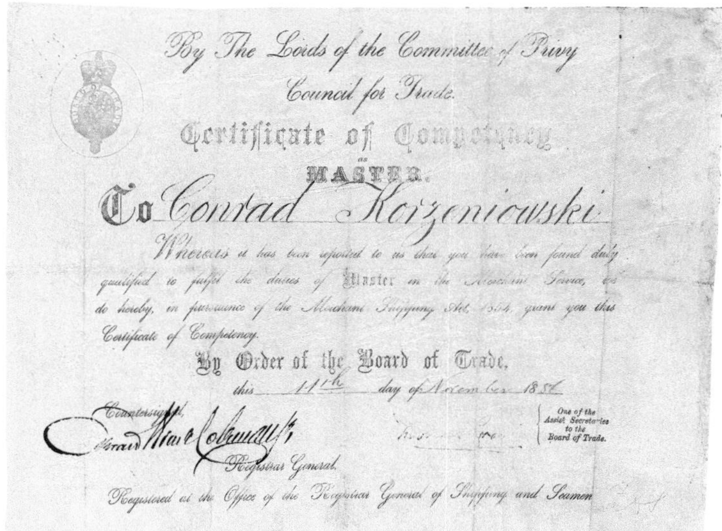

By The Lords of the Committee of Privy Council for Trade.

Certificate of Competency as MASTER.

To Conrad Korzeniowski

Whereas it has been reported to us that you have been found duly qualified to fulfil the duties of Master in the Merchant Service, we do hereby, in pursuance of the Merchant Shipping Act 1854, grant you this Certificate of Competency.

By Order of the Board of Trade, this 11th day of November 18[illegible]

Countersigned, [illegible] Registrar General. [illegible] One of the Assist. Secretaries to the Board of Trade.

Registered at the Office of the Registrar General of Shipping and Seamen

Master mariner
(right) In 1886, at the second attempt, Conrad gained his Master's Certificate, enabling him to captain a ship. His most fateful journey – deep into the Belgian Congo – still awaited him.

GUN-RUNNING TO RUIN

Stranded penniless in Marseilles, young Conrad, in desperation, joined a rebel group intent on returning the deposed monarch, Don Carlos, to the Spanish throne. They were sea-going gun-runners, smuggling weapons to the Royalists. On their last voyage, they were pursued by the coastguard and, to avoid capture, wrecked their boat against the rocky coast. Conrad recounted later how he 'and the other smugglers had hidden for days in a low *posada* [inn], in an underground cellar . . . till the authorities had given up the search'. He wrote many fictionalized accounts of the incident: in *The Mirror of the Sea, The Arrow of Gold* and *The Sisters*. Some suggest he fell in love with the beautiful leader of the group, Doña Rita. She could even have been the real cause of his subsequent suicide bid.

his long seafaring tale, *The Nigger of the 'Narcissus'*.

As a new author, Conrad worked extremely hard wrestling out his narratives. Lack of money was to be an abiding problem for most of his writing life, but such anxieties were tempered by having a quiet, comfortable, rural home and good friends. He rented a farmhouse – Pent Farm in Kent – from fellow writer Ford Madox Ford from 1898 to 1907, and this brought him into contact with a group of major authors including H.G. Wells, Henry James, Rudyard Kipling and Stephen Crane, who lived nearby.

Conrad had stipulated as a condition of his marriage to Jessie that they would have no children – but a son, Borys, was born in 1898. Conrad was not always the dutiful father. On one notorious occasion he disowned the bawling baby and his mother on a train journey, going to sit at the far end of the carriage. But he and Borys came in time to have as close and important a relationship as he had enjoyed with Thadeus. Meanwhile Conrad wrote some of his finest novels at Pent Farm, producing *Lord Jim, Heart of Darkness, Youth,* and many short stories, while continuing to struggle with *The Rescuer,* growling, 'I'm powerless to invent a way out of it'.

PLUNGING FORTUNES

After six good years at the farm, events turned against Conrad. *Nostromo*, the novel on which he had placed enormous financial and literary hopes, got the 'blackest possible frost' from the public. The strain of writing made him ill, while Jessie had her own misfortune, being semi-crippled after injuring her knee. With money already scarce, a banking disaster which lost him part of his savings sent him 'really out of my mind with worry . . . My nerves are all to pieces.' However, a secret government grant of £500 helped alleviate the fearful gloom.

Conrad's next work – *The Secret Agent* (begun in 1905) – was an attempt to hit the best-seller list. But given his complex structuring and weighty prose, it was never likely to be a major success. Conrad despaired when he compared its proceeds with the money being earned by dull, second-rate writers. Moreover his need for financial security had been increased by the birth of a second son. Although his literary agent gave him financial help, he could not prevent Conrad's imminent breakdown. A reporter sent to interview him at this time noted: 'He is abnormally highly strung. He is sensitive, intensely susceptible to any slight jarring influences from outside. His nerves seem to be all on end.'

One symptom of Conrad's worsening state was his increased restlessness. Between 1907 and 1910 the family moved three times. In addition he fell out with his friend Ford Madox Ford, and had such a violent row with his agent that he returned home and collapsed. His wife wrote: 'Months of nervous strain have ended in a complete nervous breakdown. Poor Conrad is very ill . . . [his manuscript is] on a table at the foot of his bed and he lives mixed up in the scenes and holds converse with the characters.'

Inspiring encounters
As a British merchant seaman, Conrad's travels took him to the Far East (above) where he made acquaintance with those exotic characters who would appear later in his novels.

Married life
Though temperamentally Conrad's opposite, Jessie George (left) proved an ideal, placid wife. Despite his wish to be childless, Jessie bore him two sons whom he came to adore. From 1919 the family (right) lived in relative comfort at a house called 'Oswalds' (below), near Canterbury.

AN IRONIC TURN

Gradually he recovered, but his pessimism became awesome. He rejected the possibility of improving the world; it was foolish vanity even to consider it. To him, life was a pointless machine, a 'chaos of scraps of iron' in which nothing mattered because there was only one end, 'cold darkness and silence'. Ironically, at the very time that Conrad's most creative period ended, he won the financial gains he had so longed for. He was paid a good price for his manuscripts, received a Civil Pension,

and *Chance* (which he had deliberately given a more palatable, softened ending) became a hit on both sides of the Atlantic.

In 1914 Conrad made a victorious return to Poland, but the outbreak of World War I forced him and his family back to England. He enthusiastically joined in the war effort, making guest visits to secret naval bases on the East coast, where he stirred the young men to greater resolve by telling stories of danger and glory. But he quickly became disillusioned by this 'nightmare' war. When it was over, he rounded off 23 years of intermittent work on one novel by completing *The Rescuer* (published as *The Rescue*). And he sold the film rights to his works for £4000.

'I AM FINISHED'

When Conrad was 66 he made his first trip to America as one of Britain's most distinguished authors. But he was a reluctant celebrity, shunning 40 press photographers waiting on the quayside. The talks he gave tended to be private ones rather than public lectures; one of the most impressive lasting for nearly three hours. Despite his bad pronunciation ('good' sounded like 'gut', 'blood' like 'blut') the audience was hypnotized as he read of the death of one of his heroines, until his voice broke and he 'was moved to sudden tears'.

Fact or Fiction

ABANDON SHIP!

The steamship *Jeddah* sailed from Singapore in July 1880 carrying over 1,000 Muslim pilgrims. On 8 August, during a storm, it began to take water. Captain Clark set the crew to working the pumps, but rumour spread that the lifeboats were leaving. Chief Officer A.P. Williams, to save his skin, told Clark the passengers meant to murder his wife. Clark took his wife and European officers and boarded the lifeboats. They were picked up and taken to Aden where Clark reported the ship lost. Next day, another steamer towed the *Jeddah* safe into port. Legal judgement called it 'the most extraordinary instance . . . of the abandonment of a disabled and leaking ship'. But Clark's ticket was merely suspended for three years; most blame was put on Williams. Many believe Conrad met Williams – who was certainly one model for Jim in *Lord Jim*. But in Borneo, in 1887, Conrad met young Jim Lingard, known locally as 'Tuan Jim', who fleshed out the fictional hero.

Back in England came two honours. He sat for the great sculptor, Jacob Epstein, and was offered a knighthood, which he rejected. But his end was near. Epstein commented at the time that he 'was crippled with rheumatism, crotchety and ill. He has said to me, "I am finished." ' Years of worry and malarial gout had taken their toll. After a heart attack in June 1924 Conrad confided: 'I begin to feel like a cornered rat'. Shortly after came the second attack. He told his sons, 'You know I am very ill this time'. The next morning, 3 August 1924, he collapsed and died.

The epitaph engraved on the tombstone of one of the greatest 20th-century writers was chosen by the man himself. It was a quotation from the eminently English, Elizabethan poet Edmund Spenser, and it was particularly apt:

Sleep after toyle, port after stormie sea,
Ease after warre, death after life, does greatly please.

The Rape of Africa

What Conrad witnessed in the Belgian Congo – the brutal handiwork of one greedy man – was only the "heart of darkness" beating within a continent similarly threatened from other quarters.

In *Lord Jim*, Conrad writes of the early European traders who went to Borneo in search of pepper, seeing them as heroes suffering for a great cause:

"desire made them defy death in a thousand shapes . . . It made them great! By Heavens! it made them heroic . . . they left their bones to lie bleaching on distant shores, so that wealth might flow to the living at home."

Conrad was bewitched by the romance of adventure, and by dramatic settings where men worked out their moral destiny. But when this spirit of pioneering adventure was overtaken by rank imperialist exploitation, he loathed its brutalities. Even more, he loathed the hypocritical rhetoric that surrounded it.

Conrad spent four months in the Congo in 1890 at the helm of a river-steamer for a Belgian company, and he recorded the horror of what he saw there in *Heart of Darkness*, a savage condemnation of European imperialism at the turn of the century. The great 'scramble for Africa', which Conrad described as "the vilest scramble for loot that ever disfigured the history of human conscience", was completed in the astonishingly short space of 20 years. In 1879 only a small part of Africa was subject to foreign domination. By 1900 virtually the whole of that vast continent had been pillaged and appropriated by imperialist powers.

ONE MAN'S WISH

This was not the work of the missionaries or the explorers, for they had neither territorial nor commerical interest in Africa. It was the combined work of European governments and businessmen who coveted Africa's rich resources. And in the beginning it was the work of one man alone – King Leopold II of Belgium. This ruler of a tiny, confined, European state, sought to satisfy his private greed and yearning for power overseas.

In 1876 Leopold founded, in Brussels, the International Association for the Exploration and Civilisation of Africa. He was its president and he took care to instruct the world in the nobility of his purpose: 'To open to civilisation the only part of the globe where it has not yet penetrated . . . to pierce the shadows which envelope whole peoples is, I dare to say, a crusade worthy of this century of progress.'

Leopold II
Leopold Louis Philippe Marie Victor (right), King of the Belgians from 1865 to 1909, was a man of huge ambition and avarice. He set his sights on an overseas colony in which to expand his sphere of influence and personal profit. The Congo made easy pickings.

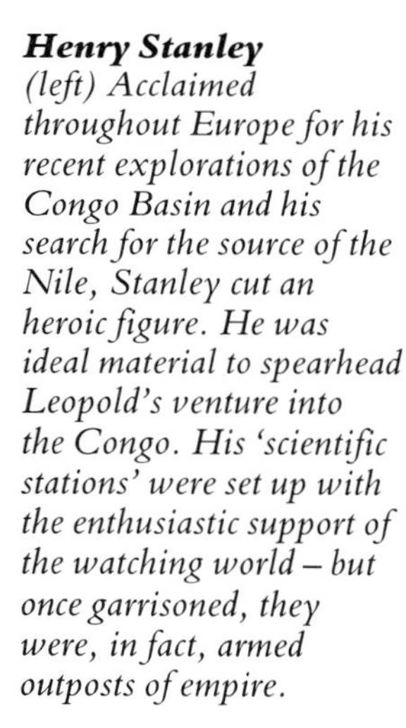

Henry Stanley
(left) Acclaimed throughout Europe for his recent explorations of the Congo Basin and his search for the source of the Nile, Stanley cut an heroic figure. He was ideal material to spearhead Leopold's venture into the Congo. His 'scientific stations' were set up with the enthusiastic support of the watching world – but once garrisoned, they were, in fact, armed outposts of empire.

Henry Stanley, a lion among explorers, who had made a recent historic expedition from Zanzibar to the lower Congo, was appointed Leopold's chief agent. He was charged to create a chain of commercial and scientific stations across the heart of central Africa. He launched steamer routes, signed treaties with tribal chieftains and founded the stations. Each station had a garrison – ostensibly to protect its Christian missions and to lead an assault on Arab slavers, such as the loathsome Tipoo-Tib, who operated in the interior.

But Leopold had private ends in view. He gained control over the Congo and persuaded the European powers, by a clever manipulation of their diplomats, to recognize him as owner as well as ruler of the 'Congo Free State'. Better, he argued, to make the Congo an 'international area of free trade' than to let it fall into the hands of any one of the great powers. So Leopold became the owner of the largest private estate in history, an area almost the size of India and 77 times larger than Belgium. He financed the project almost entirely out of his own pocket.

The booty
The true motives behind the colonization of the Congo were the ivory of elephant tusks (above), and rubber (above right). Every developed country was in the throes of industrialization and was therefore a ready marketplace for rubber – and ill-disposed to criticise Leopold's methods of obtaining it.

The Congo was rich in ivory. It also had something of infinitely greater value to industrial Europe: forest upon forest of rubber trees. With his finances running low, Leopold came up with an easy solution to his shortage of capital. By a decree of 1885, he declared all 'vacant land' in the Congo to be his personal property. It was a simple matter after that to make the land vacant.

HUMAN SACRIFICE

The lives of between five and eight million Congolese were sacrificed to Leopold's greed. He kept for himself the commercial exploitation of the now vacant lands, or granted it to concessionary companies which he nominated, and in many of which he had holdings. The state administrators and the company agents received premiums on the amount of rubber they collected. They were also instructed to exact taxation from the Congolese

The excuse
The King's justification, in the eyes of the civilized world, was the abhorrent slave trade (left) which then blighted the lives of Congolese villagers. Arab slavers often exploited tribal rivalries and used one tribe to attack and capture others. Thorough publicity given to such horrors made Leopold's 'Christian' exploits seem a mission of mercy. His actions did much to suppress Arab slaving profits, but he too used black against black to murder and subjugate the population.

The Berlin Congress *(above) A summit meeting in 1884 to discuss the Congo was convinced by Leopold's arguments. They allowed him to take possession of the Congo rather than expose it to the opportunism of any one super-power.*

Milking for rubber *All stages in the processing of rubber were labour intensive. But when the cost of labour was no more than violence and bullets, the profits to be made were massive.*

who worked the forests for them, and since there was no currency, the taxes were levied in kind – in labour, or in flesh.

If an African worker disobeyed or displeased his master, or if he did not deliver his quota of rubber or ivory, it was commonplace for him to lose a hand. The masters were usually Africans themselves, middlemen in a barbaric trade, who would demonstrate their zeal by presenting to their white bosses whole basketloads of hands. One state official told an American missionary in 1899 that every time a 'forest-guard' or Congolese soldier went out to collect rubber he was given cartridges and required to bring back every unused cartridge or, for every used one, a right hand. The same official claimed that in six months on the Momboyo river 6000 cartridges were used. An account from a state official in the Ubangi region details the 'efficiency' of the system:

'Method of procedure was to arrive in canoes at a village, the inhabitants of which invariably bolted on their arrival; the soldiers were then landed, and commenced looting, taking all the chickens, grain, etc., out of the houses; after this they attacked the natives until able to seize their women; these women were kept as hostages until the Chief of the district brought in the required number of kilogrammes of rubber. The rubber having been brought, the women were sold back to their owners for a couple of goats a-piece, and

Humanitarian champion
The British Consul to the Belgian Free State, Roger Casement (seated, left), appalled by what he saw, began to campaign against Belgian tyranny. After his posting ended, he compiled a report which swung public opinion. He was later hanged as a traitor for pursuing another cause dear to his heart – Irish republicanism.

Congo Railway Company
Leopold gave priority to better communications – to the steamship routes, road-building and, above all, the railway (right). The easy transportation of rubber, ivory and troops facilitated rapid, efficient exploitation of this vast, previously intractable region. To outside observers it seemed, of course, the right arm of civilization reaching deep into Africa's heathen heartlands.

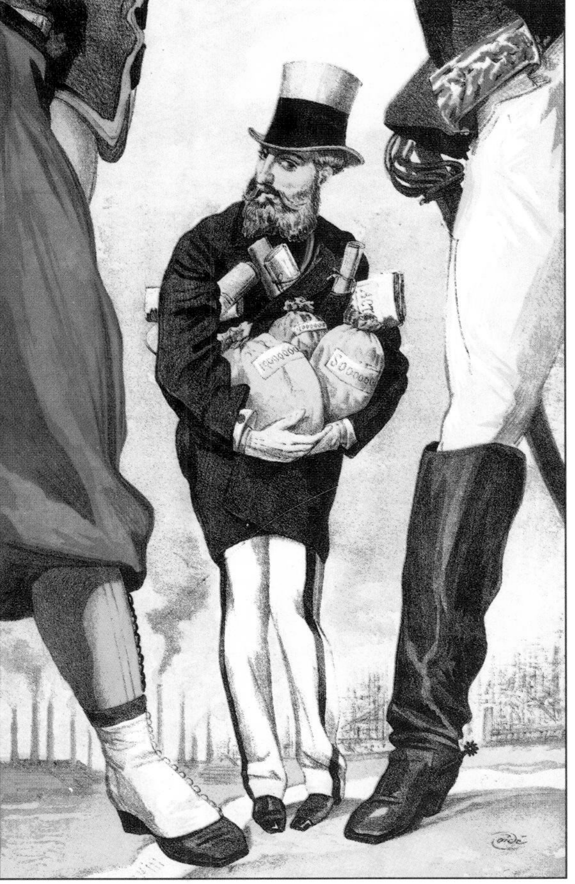

Moneygrubber
When the King's true mercenary motives became clear, the Belgian parliament was shamed by the rest of Europe into taking the reins of power out of the monarch's hands and ousting his instruments of rule from the rubber plantations. Leopold held on grimly to his interests (left), some of which had buttressed his public image as a philanthropist. But before his death in 1909 he lost his 'private estate' in its entirety.

so . . . from village to village until the requisite amount of rubber had been collected.'

An Englishman who worked on the Congo was sitting one evening at Bopoto, smoking with a Belgian official, Lieutenant Blochter. He recalled: 'It was late in the evening when suddenly a force of his [the Lieutenant's] troops returned from an expedition on which he had sent them in the morning. The sergeant held up triumphantly a number of ears fastened together on a string . . . The soldiers were praised for their success, and ordered to return next day and capture the chief.'

No matter how much rubber a worker, or a 'ganger', brought in, the only way that he could please his superiors was to bring in even more the next day. Atrocity heaped upon atrocity. The Congo Railway Company boasted that 'friends of humanity will find that the Congo railway is the means *par excellence* of allowing civilisation to penetrate rapidly and surely into the unknown depths of Africa'. But in *Heart of Darkness* the railway is seen for what it was – an instrument for hastening the mechanism of oppression.

In 1898 Roger Casement, an Irishman and a seasoned servant of the British Consular system, was

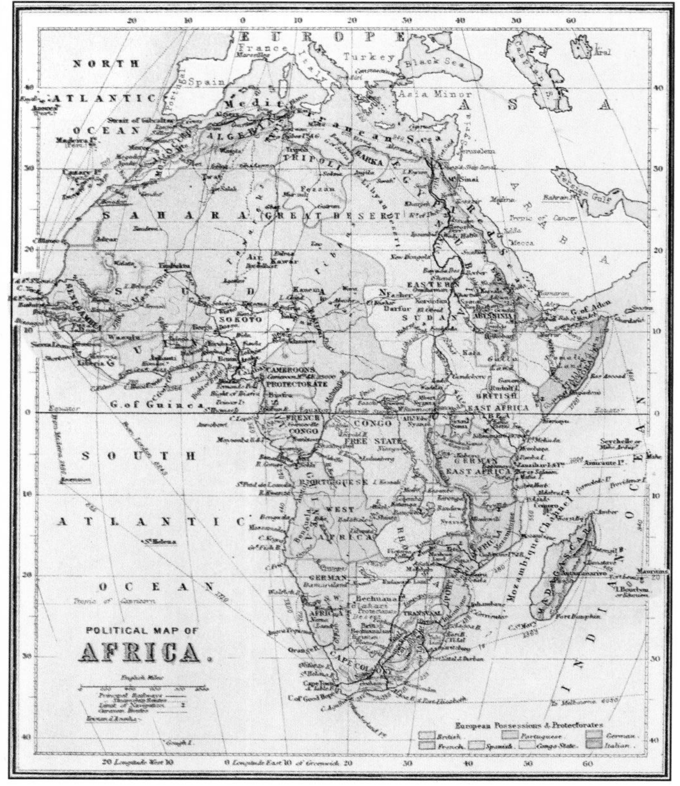

Up for grabs
The rush to condemn Leopold was only surpassed by the rush to imitate him. The entire continent was quickly partitioned into European colonies (above). Rivalry for 'a place in the sun' is thought to have contributed to World War I – a conflict in which borders could be 'adjusted' and 'loot' redistributed among the competing plunderers.

Other kinds of hell
In Lord Jim, *the vile Chester and Robinson contemplate the ultimate colonial project – guano mining (above), in which coolie labour was sweated to death in return for quick, vast profits. This was one of many new variations on a theme springing up worldwide.*

made British Consul for the Congo Free State. He was a fearless opponent of cruelty and exploitation and, between 1901 and 1903, he carried out a thorough investigation of the Congolese barbarities. (In his campaign for change, he tried to enlist the help of Conrad himself.) The report was published in February 1904 and shocked world opinion with the enormity of Leopold's crimes.

In England, E. D. Morel founded the Congo Reform Association to campaign against Leopold. Leopold himself established a commission of inquiry: it found that any miseries to which his African kingdom were subjected were the work of sleeping sickness and smallpox. But the impact of Casement's report forced a change. A more impartial Belgian commission supported Casement's findings and there was a change in the Congo government.

THE CONGO ANNEXED

In return for massive loans of money in 1890 and 1895, Leopold had offered the Belgian government the right to annex the Congo state in 1901, should they wish to. They did not take up the option then, but in 1906, under the pressure of world opinion and their own unease, they voted to annex the Congo Free State. Leopold held out until 1908. He had ruled the Congo for 24 years as his personal commercial monopoly.

The King fought long and hard to retain a profitable source of income. He insisted that Belgium should guarantee the continuation of the *Fondation de la Couronne*, a corporation 'owning' one-tenth of the country and whose revenue from rubber financed the King's acts of public beneficence. The *Fondation* survived for a year before public opinion put a stop to its operations.

During the first ten years of Belgian administration, free trade was wholly restored and the English reformers ceased to clamour for change. There were other areas of the world where other imperialist countries were invading, exploiting and oppressing. Casement, for instance, turned his attention to the atrocities white traders were committing along the Putumayo river in Peru.

'FREE-FOR-ALL'

Leopold's personal coup had long since whetted the appetites of other European governments. When, in 1888, Leopold said that 'the world ought to be our objective' and that 'there are no small nations, there are only small minds', he spoke the kind of rhetoric to fire the mind and heart of every imperialist. In just 18 months (1883-1885), South-West Africa, Togoland, the Cameroons and East Africa all came under German rule. Great Britain, France and Portugal followed Germany's example. By 1900, although Leopold of Belgium was a man disgraced, desperately clinging to his private fiefdom, the great carve-up of Africa was virtually complete.

Everywhere, whether in the Congo, or the East Indies or South America (where Conrad set *Nostromo*), the writer witnessed the same evil. His spokesman-narrator Marlow criticizes all men who would "tear treasure out of the bowels of the land . . . with no more moral purpose at the back of it than there is in burglars breaking into a safe". These were not adventurers:

"They were conquerors, and for that you only want brute force – nothing to boast of . . . They grabbed what they could get for the sake of what was to be got. It was just robbery with violence, aggravated murder on a great scale, and men going at it blind – as is very proper for those who tackle a darkness. The conquest of the earth, which mostly means the taking it away from those who have a different complexion or slightly flatter noses than ourselves, is not a very pretty thing when you look into it too much."

SIR ARTHUR CONAN DOYLE

1859 - 1930

The runaway success of his brain-child Sherlock Holmes propelled Conan Doyle from obscurity as an impoverished doctor into the limelight of public approval. Yet the character was to prove a bane as well as a blessing, and to conflict endlessly with Conan Doyle's self-image as a 'serious' historical novelist. Tireless and outspoken in pursuing his interests – which ranged from patriotism to spiritualism – Conan Doyle was, until his death, one of the most celebrated figures of the Victorian age.

'Steel True, Blade Straight'

Like his fictional heroes, Conan Doyle was a man of action and honour, his personal exploits bringing him as much fame in his lifetime as did his literary creations.

One of the most eminent of all Victorians, Sir Arthur Conan Doyle is known today almost exclusively as the creator of Sherlock Holmes. But in his own day, Conan Doyle was a most celebrated public figure. On the eve of the Boer War, when he called on young men of Britain to support Queen and country he described himself in a letter to his mother as 'the most famous man in England'.

Arthur Conan Doyle was born in Edinburgh on 22 May 1859, the second child of Mary Foley and Charles Doyle. His mother came from a distinguished Scottish military family, and his father was an alcoholic draughtsman. Mary Foley, known as 'The Ma'am', was a formidable personality who had a strong influence over her children. Conan Doyle later described her 'sweet face, her sensitive mouth, her peering, short-sighted eyes, her general suggestion of a plump little hen, who is still on the alert about her chickens.' She brought up her seven children with a strict code of honour and, despite the family's poverty, imbued them with immense pride in their ancestry. Conan Doyle was to turn to her for advice throughout his life.

RIGOROUS SCHOOLING

The Ma'am was determined that he should have a good education and, since the Doyles were a devout Catholic family, sent her son to Stonyhurst, a Jesuit public school in Lancashire. The comforts of home were suddenly replaced by a dour, demanding lifestyle fed by a daily diet of prayers, lessons, stews and sport. Conan Doyle found solace in fiction and became a fervent admirer of Sir Walter Scott, and of Edgar Allan Poe's *The Murders in the Rue Morgue*.

On leaving Stonyhurst, Arthur spent a year at a Jesuit school in Austria before deciding to become a doctor. On the Ma'am's advice he studied medicine at Edinburgh University, graduating when he was 22. Meanwhile, the young student paid his way by working as a clerk for Dr Joseph Bell, a surgeon who later became the model for Sherlock Holmes.

Bell had some of the hallmarks of the great fictional detective, delighting in impressing his students with clever deductions about patients, based on close observation of their clothes, mannerisms and behaviour.

Conan Doyle was still a student when his father, Charles Doyle, was admitted into a nursing home, leav-

The Ma'am
(below left) Conan Doyle remained close to his mother – affectionately known as 'The Ma'am' – until her death. He later recalled her gift for story-telling, and how her voice would sink 'to a horror-stricken whisper when she came to a crisis in her narrative'. He maintained that he was indebted to her for his early love of literature.

Father's fantasies
Epileptic and alcoholic, Conan Doyle's father became increasingly immersed in his own fantasy world – as his self-portrait below suggests – and he finally had to be cared for in a series of homes.

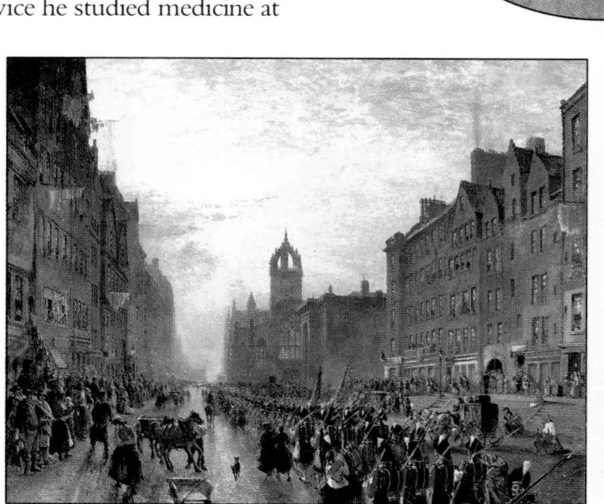

Scottish youth
(right) Edinburgh was the scene of Conan Doyle's early childhood and his days as a medical student. He lived at home to save money, and spent five gruelling years studying subjects which often, he felt, had only 'a very indirect bearing on the art of curing'.

ing the family in difficult financial straits. The following year the young medic began providing for his mother by taking a job as ship's surgeon on the *Hope*, a 400-ton whaler bound for the Arctic. On the seven-month voyage he experienced a completely new world, witnessing the slaughter of Greenland seals, harpooning a whale and nearly drowning in the icy waters. He also made some much-needed money, returning to Edinburgh with 50 gold sovereigns for his mother, and enough to see him through the last year of his course.

DOCTOR AT SEA

The following winter Conan Doyle made a journey of a very different kind aboard the *SS Mayumba*, a cargo and passenger ship bound for West Africa. There was none of the exhilaration of his last voyage, only a sequence of near disasters. Gales in the Bay of Biscay nearly sank the ship; blackwater fever and malaria attacked passengers and crew; Conan Doyle nearly died from typhoid; and on the journey home the ship caught fire – the hull was still smoking when the *Mayumba* docked at Liverpool in January 1882.

That year, a telegram arrived from Plymouth: 'STARTED HERE LAST JUNE. COLOSSAL SUCCESS. COME DOWN BY NEXT TRAIN IF POSSIBLE. PLENTY OF ROOM FOR YOU. SPLENDID OPENING.' It had been sent by an old student friend named George Budd, an energetic if unscrupulous young doctor with countless wild ideas for making a fortune. Conan Doyle joined his friend, but although Budd's new Plymouth practice was indeed crowded with patients, few had any money – and under pressure from his Ma'am, Conan Doyle ended the partnership, wrenching the brass nameplate from the door with his bare hands.

Ship's surgeon
(above) With his father no longer able to keep the family, Conan Doyle, like his sisters, took on the role of family provider. While still a third-year student, he signed up as ship's surgeon on a whaler. The voyage through the ice-packed seas of the Arctic gave him a taste of adventure – and earned him £50 which he later passed on to the Ma'am.

Amusing quackery
(right) Conan Doyle imagined that due application would lead directly to an 'honorary surgeonship'. In the event, the newly-fledged graduate joined the practice of a gifted quack, George Budd. The job was entertaining but far from lucrative, and Conan Doyle was soon supplementing his income by his pen.

Key Dates

1859 born in Edinburgh

1876 studies medicine

1882 sets up practice

1885 marries Louise Hawkins

1887 first Sherlock Holmes story

1891 moves to London

1893 'kills off' Holmes

1896 moves to Surrey

1897 meets Jean Leckie

1900 serves in Boer War

1902 knighted

1903 return of Holmes

1906 Louise dies

1907 marries Jean Leckie

1921 mother dies. Pursues spiritualist activities

1930 dies in Sussex

But Conan Doyle did not return to Edinburgh. Instead, he set up on his own in Southsea, a suburb of Portsmouth, where he was joined by his nine-year-old brother Innes. The boy wrote cheerfully to the Ma'am telling her how 'we have made three bob this week. We have vaxeinated a baby and got hold of a man with consumtion[sic].' But business was very quiet. Had it not been for two crucial developments, it is very unlikely that Conan Doyle would have stayed in Southsea for the next nine years.

The first was his marriage, in August 1885, to Louise Hawkins, the sister of one of his patients. The second was the invention of his master detective Sherlock Holmes. To pass the time and make some money, Arthur had begun writing stories for publication. His notebook records the emergence of his future fictional heroes: 'Ormond Sacker – from Afghanistan. Lived at 221b Upper Baker Street. Sherrinford Holmes – the Laws of Evidence. Reserved, sleepy-eyed young man – philosopher – collector of rare Violins.' By the end of their first adventure, Sacker had become Dr John Watson and Sherrinford had evolved into Sherlock, the two heroes of *A Study in Scarlet*.

First marriage
(above left) Conan Doyle married Louise Hawkins in 1885, when he was a struggling young doctor. But their happiness was to be shattered eight years later, when Louise was diagnosed as having consumption. Believing that country air might help, Conan Doyle built her a large house in Surrey, where he looked after her devotedly until her death.

Interval in Vienna
(above) In search of a speciality, Conan Doyle went to Vienna with Louise, to study eye medicine. But he soon abandoned the lectures because he could not follow them, and wrote a short book instead.

MAKING A NAME

The story was published in *Beeton's Christmas Annuals* in December 1887, earning its author a welcome, if paltry £25. But since Conan Doyle's ambition was to write historical novels, not detective thrillers, he had started *Micah Clarke*, a romance about the 17th-century Monmouth rebellion. When this was first published in 1889, it was an instant success and encouraged him to embark on a medieval tale entitled *The White Company*. Holmes, however, had not been forgotten. *A Study in Scarlet* had slowly been gaining admirers, and a new novel, *The Sign of Four*, was commissioned by an American publisher.

Conan Doyle, now the father of a baby daughter named Mary Louise, had at last earned enough from his writings to escape from the provincial life of Southsea. In 1890, he travelled to Berlin to observe the experiments of a Dr Robert Koch, who had announced a possible cure for tuberculosis. The following year he went – with Louise – to Vienna to study ophthalmics for six months. When they returned to England, they moved to London, and Conan Doyle opened a consulting room in Devonshire Place.

Fact or Fiction

THE REAL SHERLOCK HOLMES

Conan Doyle modelled his famous detective on Dr Joseph Bell, a surgeon and criminal psychologist who lectured at the Edinburgh Infirmary. Bell had the domed forehead, acquiline nose and cool manner that distinguished Holmes, and like him showed remarkable powers of deduction based on close observation.

He deduced, for example, that the bare patch on one patient's corduroy trousers indicated his trade as a cobbler, the patch being worn by constant friction as he hammered shoes. His 'diagnosis' was perfectly correct.

The venture, however, was a complete flop – in six months not a single patient climbed his stairs. So, instead of practising medicine, Conan Doyle started writing full-time in the surgery and, in 1891, published six Sherlock Holmes stories in the new and immensely popular *Strand Magazine*. Ironically, he still regarded the Holmes stories as a distraction from his real vocation as a historical novelist, and resented the amount of time he spent composing them. But they provided an invaluable income, and the editor commissioned a further six stories at £50 a piece.

With the *Strand Magazine's* circulation passing half a million, Conan Doyle's fortunes were transformed. He moved his family to a house in South Norwood and negotiated a cool £1,000 for the 1892 Holmes series. He started mixing in literary circles, and befriended Jerome K. Jerome, author of *Three Men in a Boat*, and J.M. Barrie, the future author of *Peter Pan*. Yet he was still reluctant to tie himself to Holmes, and he and the Ma'am discussed his plans for killing off the detective.

Sporting man of letters
(below) Until well into middle age, Conan Doyle took a vigorous delight in sport of all kinds. Cricket was his great passion – he played for the MCC and scored a century on his first visit to Lord's. He even faced the legendary W.G. Grace, bowling him out on one memorable occasion.

In November 1892, Louise gave birth to a son, Alleyne Kingsley, but there were signs that her health was deteriorating. A journey to Switzerland, with a visit to the spectacular Reichenbach Falls, did nothing to cure her and, when they returned to London, she was diagnosed as suffering from consumption. At the same time Conan Doyle finally decided that he had to put an end to the Holmes saga, dispatching the great detective over the Reichenbach Falls, locked in a fatal struggle with the arch criminal Moriarty in *The Final Problem*. But when the story appeared in December 1893, his readers bombarded the magazine with letters of grief and outrage. Conan Doyle escaped most of the furore. After his father's death in October, he spent a holiday in Switzerland where he sought to relieve his depression by skiing, tobogganing and climbing.

DIVERSE INTERESTS

Since Conan Doyle had by now resolved his financial problems he was free, when he returned to England, to pursue his wide-ranging interests. He was an enthusiastic and capable sportsman – he played cricket and soccer for Portsmouth – and turned out for the MCC on a number of occasions, scoring on his first appearance at Lord's Cricket Ground. He also pursued his interest in psychic phenomena, joining the British Society for Psychical Research. And in 1895, he had a house built in Surrey, so that Louise could escape London's fumes.

At this point Conan Doyle turned to writing drama. His stage play *Waterloo* was a great success in London – so too was a series of comic tales about a dashing Napoleonic cavalry officer entitled *The Exploits of Brigadier Gerard*. But the smooth pattern of the novelist's life was transformed when, in March 1897, he fell in love with Jean Leckie, a young Scotswoman who lived with her parents in Blackheath. She returned his devotion, but he insisted that they should resist the temptation of physical affection while Louise lived. And they both lived by that decision, which committed them to ten years of exhausting self-denial. As usual, Arthur told the Ma'am, but Louise never found out about the 'other woman'.

A long-awaited wedding
(below) A young Scotswoman, Jean Leckie, was Conan Doyle's second bride. The couple were married the year after Louise died, having met ten years previously. They had fallen instantly in love, but agreed on a 'platonic' relationship out of loyalty to Louise. Fourteen years his junior, Jean was to bear Conan Doyle two sons and a daughter.

Conan Doyle reached the age of 40 healthy, wealthy and deeply frustrated. Meanwhile Louise had become a severe invalid, her body wasted by tuberculosis, while arthritis wracked the joints of both hands. Conan Doyle filled his time writing stage plays and stories, riding to hounds, ballooning and holding clay pigeon shoots in the grounds of his house. In 1899, however, the declaration of war against the Boers channelled his energy in another direction. He travelled to the barracks to volunteer in person, only to be rejected as overweight. The following year, however, he was accepted and was sent to South Africa as a senior physician with a private field hospital.

Conan Doyle's war experience transformed him from a celebrity to a pillar of the Establishment. Although he completed only three months of field duty at Bloemfontein, the conditions he saw there – with up to 60 patients a day dying of typhoid – affected him deeply. When he returned to Britain, he found that General Kitchener and the army were under attack for their conduct of the war, and was so incensed that he defended them with a 50,000-word pamphlet on *The War in South Africa*. More than a million copies were sold in Britain. Two years later Conan Doyle was rewarded by a grateful King Edward VII, who knighted him at Buckingham Palace, creating him Deputy Lieutenant of Surrey.

The following year, 1903, saw the revival of Sherlock Holmes. *McClure's Magazine* in New York offered Conan Doyle the then fabulous sum of $5,000 for just six stories, and insisted that Holmes must emerge from the churning foam of Reichenbach, alive and dripping. Conan Doyle duly obliged, and his hero returned in *The Empty House* after a lengthy journey around the world.

Three years later, in July 1906, Louise died after 13 years of illness, and was buried in Surrey. Conan Doyle was too disturbed by her death to continue writing, but, later that year, immersed himself in a real-life detective case. An Indian solicitor named George Edalji had been imprisoned in 1903 for the brutal killing of a horse. He denied any involvement. Alerted to the peculiarities of the case, Conan Doyle studied every scrap of information he could find. Within months he had proved that Edalji had been convicted on grossly flawed evidence and revealed the true identity of the assailant. Edalji was released in 1907.

On 18th September that year, Conan Doyle married Jean Leckie and the two set off for a honeymoon cruise through the eastern Mediterranean, visiting Greece, Egypt and Turkey. On their return they moved into a large new house at Windlesham in Sussex.

Despite his support for the British Empire, Conan Doyle was not uncritical of the Establishment. Though he had stood for Parliament as a Liberal Unionist candidate for Edinburgh, and later for Hardwick, he was ready to oppose injustice wherever he saw it. In 1909 he wrote a pamphlet entitled *The Crime of the Congo*, to expose the cruelties perpetrated on Africans by Belgian colonists. And the following year he devoted himself to the cause of a German Jew named Oscar Slater, who had been falsely convicted of murder.

On this occasion Conan Doyle could achieve no dramatic breakthrough as in the Edalji affair. The legal authorities turned a blind eye to a long campaign conducted through the newspapers, in which Conan Doyle demonstrated that Slater, though an acknowledged pimp and petty criminal, was innocent. The wronged man spent 18 years in jail before being released, suddenly, with no pardon or compensation.

Conan Doyle's campaign urging Britain to prepare for war with Germany, and warning of the U-boat threat, was more effective. His efforts won him the support of the young Winston Churchill. When war did break out, he wrote a pamphlet *To Arms* urging volunteers to enlist, and set up his own local platoon.

At the front
(below) Conan Doyle's patriotism was fired by the outbreak of the Boer War. Although already 40, he wanted to enlist as an example to the 'young athletic sporting men' of England. He joined a hospital unit which followed the advance of General Roberts on Pretoria. The team had to cope with a devastating typhoid outbreak, but Conan Doyle took the opportunity to talk to Boer prisoners, and participants in the British campaign, not least Roberts himself. Later he wrote up his impressions in The Great Boer War.

THE SPIRIT WORLD

Increasingly convinced of physical existence after death, Conan Doyle came to believe that the soul was 'a complete duplicate of the body'. He announced his conversion to spiritualism in 1916, and thereafter channelled his new-found zeal into books, articles and lectures, spending £250,000 on promoting the cause. His enthusiasm even led him to declare a belief in fairies.

The fey and the fake
(left) Photographs of tiny winged female forms, produced by two Yorkshire girls, sparked off Conan Doyle's unflinching belief in fairies. To him they were as 'real' as they appear in this illustration by his uncle (above). The photographs were denounced as fakes, but Conan Doyle, unshakeable in his conviction, went on to state it openly in The Coming of the Fairies. *The ridicule this brought down on his head left Conan Doyle quite unperturbed.*

In defence of a traitor
Sir Roger Casement (right), an Irish nationalist who had supported Germany from the outset of World War One, was, in 1916, under sentence of execution as a traitor. Conan Doyle had been impressed by Casement's exposure of imperialist atrocities in the Belgian Congo, and believed that his recent pro-German activities were proof that the man was mentally unbalanced. Conan Doyle campaigned energetically for a reprieve right up to the last moment, inspired by the injustice of the sentence – but did not succeed.

In 1916 he visited British forces in France and Italy, and like many of his generation, was shattered by the realities of war. In the course of it, he lost his son Kingsley and his brother Innes, as well as several close friends. He was also deeply saddened by the execution of Sir Roger Casement, an Irish nationalist convicted of treasonous conspiracy with the Germans. Conan Doyle was steadfast in his defence of Casement despite the smear campaign against the prisoner.

In the last decade of his life, Conan Doyle continued writing Holmes stories, but devoted his time increasingly to spiritualism. He went on lecture tours to America, Australia, Africa and Europe, spreading the gospel of psychic communications. After the Ma'am died in 1921, Jean became Conan Doyle's spirit medium, whereby he believed he could contact the dead members of his family. Astonishingly, in 1922, he even declared his belief in fairies after seeing some – presumably trick – photographs of two dancing fairies.

For his spiritualist activities he was ridiculed by the world's press, and his cause was not helped by the exposure of numerous fraudulent mediums. But his home life was tranquil and happy. Jean had borne him two sons and a daughter, and his old age was unmarred by ill-health or mental decay. He still enjoyed golf and long walks across the Weald, and he continued to write prolifically. But he also felt the need for greater privacy, and bought another house at Bignell Wood in the New Forest where he could escape the public gaze.

By 1929, however, his health had begun to decline. He was suffering regular heart pains, and was unable to speak on Armistice Day at the Albert Hall. Early in 1930, he was shocked by an internal dispute among colleagues in the Society for Psychical Research and resigned after 37 years of membership. Tired and anxious, he retreated to Windlesham, wrote his will, and tried to rest. The end was not far away. Early in the morning of 7th July 1930, Sir Arthur Conan Doyle died, sitting in his large basket chair, looking out across the garden. He was buried beside the summer-house, and his grave was marked by a simple oak slab on which were carved four words of epitaph: 'Steel True, Blade Straight.'

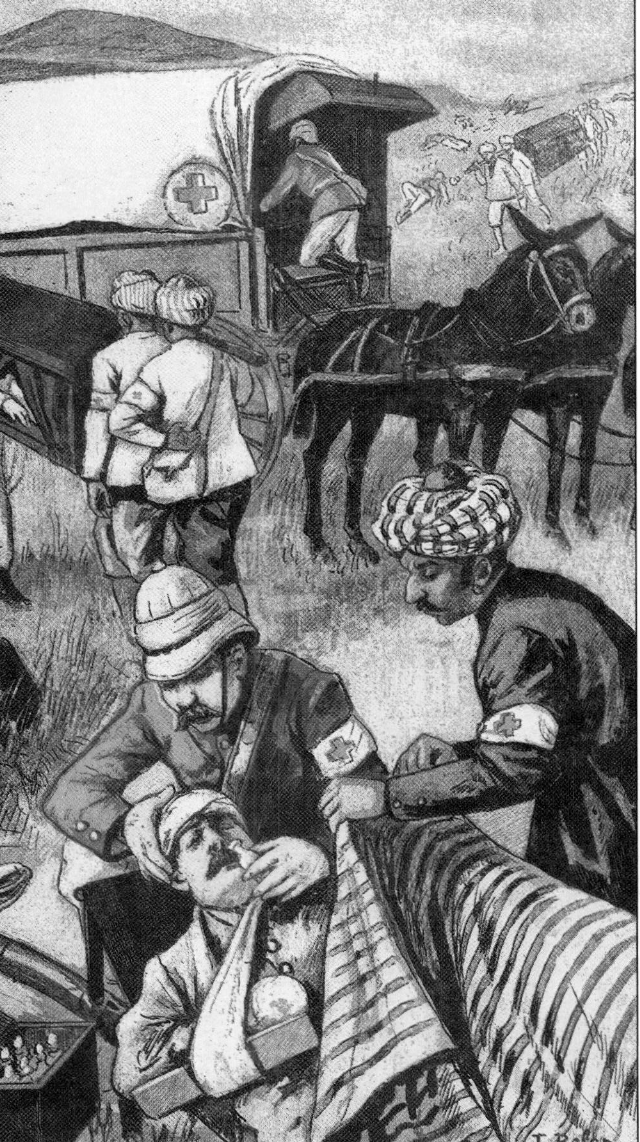

Spreading the word
(below) In later life, Conan Doyle devoted his time and energy increasingly to spiritualism. It influenced both his fiction and his non-fiction, and he travelled widely giving lectures on the subject. This photograph of 1923 shows the entire Doyle family at Victoria Station, en route for a lecture tour of America.

Elementary Detection

Investigative techniques were in their infancy in the Victorian era, but the advent of photography and forensic science gave the law enforcers a fighting chance.

Sherlock Holmes made his fictional debut in *A Study in Scarlet* in 1887; a year later the gruesome Jack the Ripper murders horrified London. There could scarcely be a greater contrast than that between the brilliant investigative feats of the hawk-eyed detective and the bungling attempts of his real-life counterparts to find the savage killer.

The failure to capture the Ripper caused widespread resentment against the police, with protests coming not only from the squalid East End of the capital where the murders were committed, but also from the highest in the land. Some of the more politely worded rebukes came from Queen Victoria herself, who took a keen interest in the case and felt that 'the detective department is not as efficient as it might be'. Others were less tactful, with the satirical magazine *Punch* poking fun at 'the Defective Department'.

Law enforcement as we know it had begun in 1829, when Robert Peel, then Home Secretary, had pushed through the Metropolitan Police Act, creating London's first disciplined police force. Since Peel thought that 'the primary function of an efficient police is the *prevention* of crime', his force consisted mainly of uniformed officers patrolling the streets. While the 'Peelers' were not recruited primarily for their brilliance or education (some could not even read), the Metropolitan Police did set high standards in other ways. And, after initially arousing suspicion and hostility, they gained an enviable reputation for courage and fair play. The degree of public acceptance and administration was clearly shown in 1872, when a threatened police strike was met with newspaper pleas to the force not to abandon the streets to criminals.

GOING UNDERCOVER

In 1842 a small Detective Department consisting of two inspectors and six sergeants was set up, though not everyone approved of the idea. The critics were wary of the growth of underhand 'continental' espionage methods which had come to light in the infamous 1833 Popay case. William Popay, a police sergeant, had passed himself off as a poor artist to infiltrate a subversive movement. When the public found out about Popay's underhand methods, there was an outcry. The police dismissed him. British resistance to an undercover police service was so deeply ingrained that in 1869 the Commissioner of Police reported that a detective system was 'viewed with the greatest suspicion . . . by the majority of Englishmen and is, in fact, entirely

A sea chase
Thinly disguised as father and son, Hawley Crippen and his lover Ethel le Neve were apprehended on board the SS Monrose *when it docked near Quebec. The case made history – it was the first time that a wireless had been used to transmit a vital message across the water. The ensuing sea chase made Chief Inspector Dew into a national hero.*

Police through the ages
The 1750s saw the establishment of the Bow Street Runners (above left), early law enforcers who patrolled the streets of London. One hundred years later Victorian 'Peelers' (left) wore top hats and full uniform, and indeed were respected as much for their uniform as for the duties they performed. The rare attempts by some officers at going undercover were viewed as contemptible – foreign tactics at their worst. Today's Metropolitan Police force was founded in 1829 and the turn-of-the-century scene (above) shows one officer peacefully directing traffic.

foreign to the habits and feelings of the nation'. At this time, there were only 15 detectives in the Metropolitan Police out of a force of 8000.

There were some prominent supporters of the new Detective Department. Charles Dickens considered that it was 'so well-chosen and trained, proceeds so systematically and quietly, does its business in such a workmanlike manner and is always so steadily engaged in the service of the public, that the public really do not know enough of it, to know a tithe of its usefulness.' (Dickens was the first writer to create a fictional detective from the Metropolitan Police – Inspector Bucket in *Bleak House* published 1852-53.)

The picture painted by Dickens was certainly too rosy, for in 1877 three of the four Chief Inspectors in the Department were found guilty of corruption. This prompted a Home Office inquiry and, in 1878, the creation of the newly organized Criminal Investigation Department (CID). There were initially about 250 men attached to the department, but 10 years later, when Jack the Ripper had his brief reign of terror, the number had risen to approximately 800.

Between August and November 1888, Jack the Ripper killed and mutilated five East End prostitutes. While brutal crime was no novelty in this area, these five killings won unprecedented publicity because of their savagery. The public responded with various tip-offs, leading to more than 100 arrests, but the search was hampered because the police had too fixed an idea about the nature of the killer. Anyone 'respectable' (which meant nothing more significant than that they had a decent address) was immediately removed from the list of potential suspects.

The Commissioner of the Metropolitan Police, Sir Charles Warren, handled the case so ineptly that he had to resign even before the final murder was committed. His most incompetent act was to wipe off the murderer's message – chalked on a wall near one of the murder sites – before it could be photographed. His justification for destroying this vital clue was that he was afraid the anti-semitic message would incite trouble in an area with a large Jewish population. Warren also put his faith in a pair of prize bloodhounds – Burgho and Barnaby – who merely succeeded in tracking down entirely innocent people, including a plain-clothes policeman.

Extraordinary means were employed for identifying or trapping the killer. The eyes of one of the victims were photographed in the then popular belief that the last thing they had seen would be imprinted on their eyes. It was even suggested that young, clean-shaven boxers should be disguised as prostitutes to roam the streets at night, wearing steel collars to protect their necks from the Ripper's knife.

The *Sherlock Holmes* stories reinforced the public's image of an inefficient detective force, for Conan Doyle invariably depicts the plodders from the Yard hopelessly trailing several steps behind his crime-solving genius. Fortunately for the police, most of the serious crimes which they had tackled until then had been much less baffling than the Ripper case itself or those solved by Holmes.

For then, as now, most murders were committed either by a relative or associate of the victim, or in the course of another crime (such as a robbery) by someone who already had a criminal record, and whose habits and haunts were well-known to the police. Such crimes were more often solved by patience than by extraordinary mental agility.

In their fight against crime, the Victorian police had few of the aids that are taken for granted today. Foren-

Fingerprints
Although viewed with a mixture of suspicion and derision at the time, the advent of fingerprinting heralded a vast leap forward for crime detection.

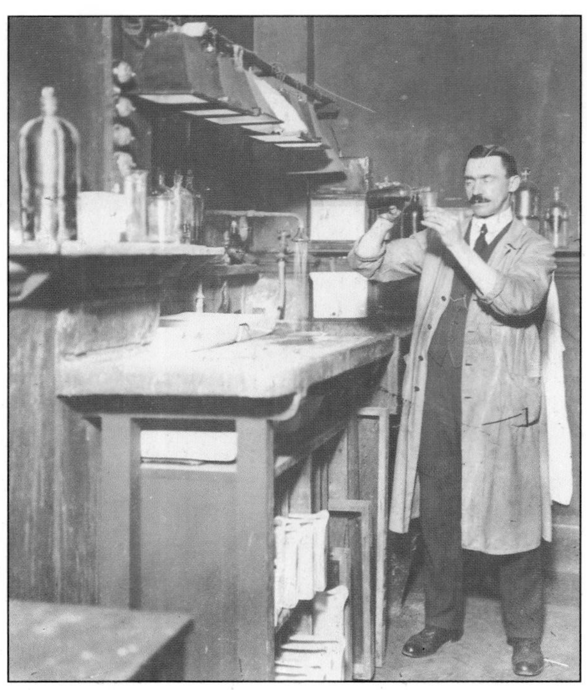

Scotland Yard's Photo Lab
(left) Used to record evidence at the scene of the crime, photography proved to be one more tool in the drive for law enforcement. This first photographic department at New Scotland Yard dates back to 1905.

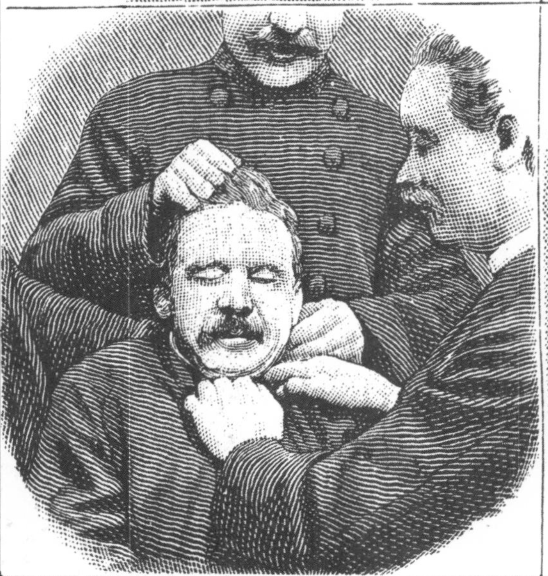

Captured on film
(above) Some forces had a 'Rogues Gallery' – walls plastered with mugshots of suspects. But few prisoners submitted willingly to this, and the likelinesses could be deceptive.

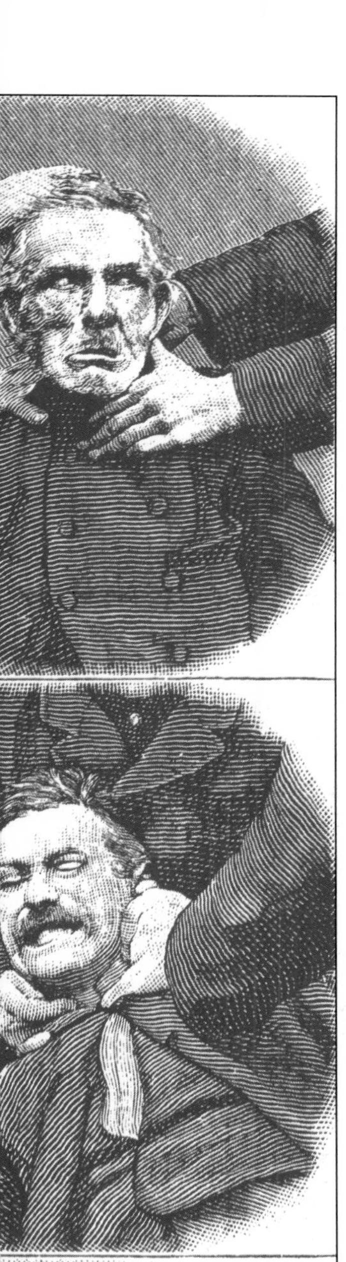

sic science had been used as long ago as 1786, when police trapped a murderer in Kirkcudbrightshire, Scotland by taking plaster casts of his footprints. But forensics had advanced little since then. Consequently, the police were about 10 years behind Sherlock Holmes who, when first introduced to Dr Watson, is overjoyed because he has just discovered an infallible test for identifying bloodstains – "the most practical medico-legal discovery for years." In real life, the biochemical analysis of blood in crime detection was not used until the early 20th century.

Fingerprinting was also introduced in the early 1900s. The idea was brought to England by Sir Edward Henry, who had been Inspector-General of Police in Bengal, where thumb-prints were used to identify illiterate workers. When he became head of the CID in 1901, Henry immediately established Scotland Yard's fingerprint section.

At first there was great resistance to this new-fangled idea, as displayed by a 'disgusted' magistrate who wrote to a national newspaper: 'Scotland Yard, once known as the world's finest police organization, will be the laughing-stock of Europe if it insists on trying to trace criminals by odd ridges on their skins. I, for one, am firmly convinced that no British jury will ever convict a man on "evidence" produced by the half-baked theories some official happened to pick up in India.'

Four years later, however, fingerprint evidence was first used to obtain a murder conviction, when the brothers Alfred and Albert Stratton were found guilty of killing an elderly couple while robbing their shop. Alfred Stratton had left a bloody thumb-print on a cash box, and his defending counsel's contention that the fingerprint system was 'unreliable' and 'savoured more of the French courts than of English justice' was to no avail. The brothers were hanged.

Before the introduction of fingerprinting, criminals had been identified by means of photographs and records, but the system was highly fallible. Eddie Guerin, a French-Irish-American gangster, wrote in his memoirs (1928) that 'on my way to the photographer I picked up a couple of pebbles, put them in my mouth, and screwed up my face until even my own mother would not have recognized me.' The Criminal Records Office (established in 1871) was so inefficient that convicted criminals could beat the system simply by assuming aliases once they had been released from prison.

OUTWITTING THE POLICE

This tactic was used by Charlie Peace, one of the most notorious of Victorian criminals, to try to evade the hangman. Fleeing from Sheffield in 1876, after murdering the husband of a woman with whom he was having an affair, Peace settled in London. He shaved off his beard, dyed his hair, changed his appearance and continued his successful career as a cat burglar. But in 1878, having shot a policeman who caught him breaking into a house, he was captured, tried under his assumed name of John Ward and sentenced to life imprisonment. Unfortunately for him, his current lover decided to claim the £100 reward money for identifying him. Peace was therefore retried under his real name, found guilty in 1879 and sentenced to death by hanging.

The Peace case clearly illustrates the rudimentary communications between regional police forces, of which there were more than 200 in England by the end of the 19th century. The police travelled by public transport, reports were handwritten, and Scotland Yard did not even have a telephone until 1901. With the establishment of a detective training school in 1902, professional standards began to improve at the Yard. But when Scotland Yard detectives were called to help regional police, they often found that they were contending with amateurish police methods as well as with the criminal.

In 1908, for example, Chief Inspector Walter Dew (who had worked on the Jack the Ripper case and later

On the beat
All constables were armed with truncheons, although the Rural Constabulary Act of 1839 permitted the issue of cutlasses. By the 1880s, however, night patrolmen could request revolvers.

Reign of Terror
Jack the Ripper was infamous for his savagery. Not content with simply murdering his victims, he would gut their entrails, dismember them and send specimens to the police.

became famous when he arrested Dr Crippen) investigated the murder of a 12-year-old boy in Salisbury, Wiltshire. When he arrived the day after the killing, he was dismayed to find that the local police had allowed the boy's family to clean up the scene of the crime and have the corpse washed. Dew charged the boy's mother with the murder, but after two trials (the jury in the first were unable to agree on a verdict) she was acquitted.

Chief Inspector Dew was a member of the CID's 'Murder Squad' (never an official title), founded in 1907 to solve difficult murder cases. The Squad made its mark by solving the Dr Crippen case, although flawed investigative techniques nearly enabled Crippen to get off scot-free.

Hawley Harvey Crippen was an American who had settled in England in 1900, with his second wife Cora. Ten years later he poisoned her, cut her up and buried parts of the body in the cellar of his house. A few weeks after the murder, his secretary and lover, Ethel le Neve, moved in with him. Friends, worried about Cora's disappearance, alerted Scotland Yard who sent down Chief Inspector Dew. He interviewed Crippen and searched the house but found nothing suspicious.

A RACE ACROSS THE OCEAN

Crippen, who had told friends that Cora had returned to America and died there, now changed his story. He told Dew that she had left him and that he had invented her death to save face. If Crippen's nerve had held he would have probably got away with it, but he panicked and ran. By the time Dew returned three days later to check a routine point, Crippen and Ethel were fleeing across the Channel. Two days later the remains of Cora Crippen were dug up.

Descriptions of the wanted couple were circulated, and Captain Kendall of the *SS Monrose*, sailing from Antwerp to Canada, thought that he recognized them among his passengers – ineptly disguised as father and son. He sent a wireless message to Dew, who sailed from Liverpool in a faster ship, arriving near Quebec two days before the pair of suspects. They were taken straight back to England where Crippen was found guilty and hanged, and Ethel was acquitted. What made the case so famous was the drama of the sea chase and the fact that a wireless had been used for the first time to catch a murderer. People in England had read about Dew's pursuit – while the fugitives were blissfully unaware that they were being followed. Dew was lionized in the press, and the detective's image was transformed from half-wit to hero.

But Dew's handling of the initial investigation left much to be desired. It had never occurred to him, for example, to ask Crippen why his wife had left behind her expensive collection of dresses if, as he alleged, she had returned permanently to America. And if he had taken the precaution of having Crippen watched, he would never have been able to escape. Sherlock Holmes would never have slipped up in this way. But Conan Doyle could not have bettered the perfect irony of the unsuspecting Crippen, just days away from Canada and freedom, looking at the ship's crackling wireless aerial and remarking, 'What a wonderful invention it is!'

Two faces of the law
The popular image of the police in Victorian times was not simply one of men unswervingly pursuing the guilty, regardless of race, creed or background. All too often the aristocracy was treated with kid gloves, no matter what their crime, while the working classes were subjected to a much more violent enactment of 'justice'. And in the course of duty, police were liable to commit acts of folly and ineptitude – and, at times, even be guilty of corruption.

RUDYARD KIPLING

1865-1936

Rudyard Kipling has always been a controversial figure. He was dubbed by Henry James 'the most complete man of genius I have ever known', and dismissed by George Orwell as 'a jingo-imperialist . . . morally insensitive and aesthetically disgusting'. Yet he has never ceased to delight a vast readership with his brilliant verse and prose, and his stories for children are some of the finest ever written. Kipling's acknowledged masterpiece is an unforgettable portrait of India – *Kim*.

For Love of Empire

Born in India at the height of the British Empire, Kipling championed the virtues of loyalty to Queen and Country to become one of the most eminent Englishmen of his time.

Kipling has become in the public consciousness virtually a personification of the British Empire. He supported and celebrated the Empire with lifelong zeal. But there is much more to Kipling than his imperialism – his love for children and admiration for the 'common man' inspired some of the best-loved stories and verses of all time.

Joseph Rudyard Kipling was born in Bombay on 30 December 1865. His unusual name derived from Lake Rudyard (now Rudyard Reservoir) in Staffordshire, where his parents, John Lockwood Kipling and Alice Macdonald, met on a picnic. In 1865, three months after their marriage, they sailed to India, where John had been appointed Professor of Architectural Sculpture at the newly founded Bombay School of Art.

Although they were not wealthy, the Kiplings had a much better lifestyle than they would have enjoyed in England, with the young Rudyard (or Ruddy as he was sometimes known) being pampered by the household servants. But when he was nearly six Rudyard was abruptly removed from this privileged, exotic world and sent to live with strangers in bleak, blustery Southsea, thousands of miles away on the Sussex coast.

British settlers in India believed that the British way of life was the best, and that children had to be immersed in the culture of their home country and safeguarded from the numerous fatal diseases in India. Children were customarily sent home to live with relations or, failing that, with families who undertook to foster them, for a fee.

CRUEL DESOLATION

Since Rudyard was apparently too difficult for his relations to handle, Alice opted for the Southsea home, which she found in an advertisement. Without explaining what was happening to Rudyard or his younger sister Trix, she took them back to England in 1871. They stayed at Lorne Lodge with 'Uncle Harry' and 'Aunty Rosa' (Captain and Mrs Holloway) for the next six years, estranged from their parents, who could not afford the time and the cost of the journey.

Life was tolerable to begin with, largely because Captain Holloway liked Rudyard and kept a check on his wife's harsh temperament, but when he

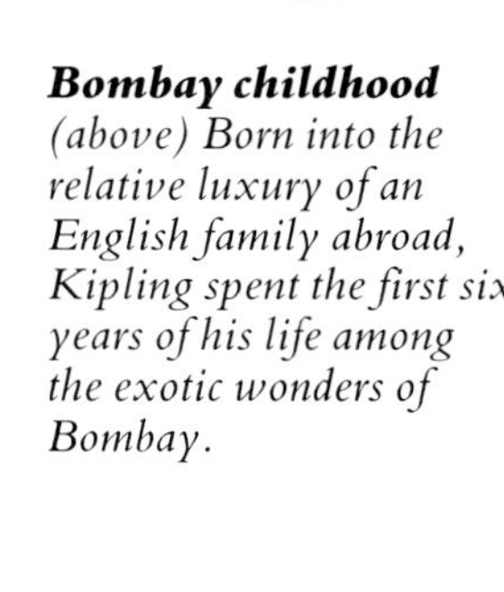

Bombay childhood
(above) Born into the relative luxury of an English family abroad, Kipling spent the first six years of his life among the exotic wonders of Bombay.

Loving parents
Rudyard's father, shown far left in a book-label of his own design, taught at the Bombay School of Art. His talent was put to use in collaboration with his son, for he illustrated Kim *and other works with his low-relief sculptures. Alice, Rudyard's mother, was tender and affectionate, and was also noted for her witty tongue. Kipling loved both parents, and after his father's death he referred to him as 'a great man'.*

died everything changed. Lorne Lodge became Kipling's 'House of Desolation'.

Unlike his sister, Rudyard could do nothing right, and was constantly being punished and locked in his room. There was even a ban on reading, his greatest passion, resulting in furtive sessions in poor light nearly ruining his already weak eyesight. The worst indignity was being sent to school with the placard 'Liar' stitched to his coat. In six years he was reduced from a healthy, robust little boy to a state of constant insecurity. When his mother returned in 1877 to collect him, and bent down for a kiss, his lightning response was to duck as if about to be hit.

DISAPPOINTED SCHOLAR

Years later Kipling recounted the horrors of this period in *The Light That Failed, Baa, Baa, Black Sheep* and his autobiography, *Something of Myself,* though it is hard to discover how much he exaggerated. It is quite possible, however, that the Southsea experience gave him his near mystical love for children, prompting his delight at reading his own stories to them.

Kipling's education continued with a four-year spell at a Devon college, Westward Ho!, which was primarily geared to sending its students into the army. It introduced Kipling to the world of action, which later became a vital ingredient of his literary works, and allowed him to develop a taste for literature. But Rudyard did not stay on for a full upper-class 'English education'. This left him

House of Desolation
Lorne Lodge, Southsea (below), his foster home in England, drove young Rudyard (right) to despair.

Key Dates

1865 born in Bombay

1871 taken to England to 'adoptive' family

1882 returns to India as a journalist

1889 returns to England

1892 marries Caroline Balestier

1892–96 in America

1896–1902 lives on S.E. coast of England

1899 death of daughter, Josephine

1900 first visit to South Africa

1901 *Kim* published

1907 awarded the Nobel Prize

1915–1918 visits naval and army bases

1915 death of son in World War I

1917 invited to work with War Graves Commission

1936 dies in London

EDWARD BURNE-JONES

Apart from his father, Kipling had two uncles who were artists – Sir Edward Burne-Jones and Sir Edward Poynter. Both were highly distinguished in their time and Burne-Jones remains one of the most celebrated of Victorian painters. He was particularly close to his nephew as a youth, when Kipling was lonely as a 'hermit crab'.

Pre-Raphaelite master
Burne-Jones specialized in dreamy evocations of a romantic medieval world – inhabited by beautiful maidens.

with a chip on his shoulder, and he said of his cousin (the future Prime Minister, Stanley Baldwin), 'I'd give anything to be in the Sixth at Harrow as he is, with a university education to follow'. Instead, his father had got Rudyard a job on an English newspaper in India.

Kipling was 16 when he returned to India in 1882. He worked extremely hard at his job, 'never less than 10 hours, and seldom more than 15'. Eventually he wrote weekly articles, most of which were reprinted in his first prose book, *Plain Tales from the Hills* (1888). Around this time Kipling gained his first experience of what it was like to be politically controversial. On entering his club in Lahore (now in Pakistan) the members booed him, though not for anything he had written. In their eyes he was the paper's representative, whose liberal views were not welcome.

TRAVELS IN THE ORIENT

All the while Kipling was rapidly becoming an important literary figure in India, and at the age of 24 he decided it was time to leave his Indian outpost and take on literary London. Save for one visit, this was the last time he saw India, but his time there permanently affected his outlook and his writings. It gave him a landscape and cast of characters for some of his finest works, and the view which became the cornerstone of his political philosophy – that the only force keeping back anarchy was the Empire.

On 9 March 1889 Kipling started a long voyage home, beginning with a three-months' trip to San Francisco via Burma, Malaya, Hong Kong and Japan. The trip gave him a love of cruises, which later became a near-annual palliative against anxiety and ill health. It also sharpened his world view. Not only were the Indians the white man's cultural poor relations, so too were the Chinese, though he treated them more severely, revealing the most unpalatable side of his imperialism. In *From Sea to Sea* (1899), a collection of Kipling's travel letters, he wrote: 'It is justifiable to kill him [the Chinaman]. It would be quite right to wipe the city of Canton off the face of the earth.'

GUNBOAT DIPLOMACY

Kipling's harsh opinions on other countries extended to the United States, and when he sailed into San Francisco he made the infamous remark that there was no need to worry because a couple of British gunboats could easily take the place! His views on the United States soon became ambivalent, however. While he despaired of the inhabitants' clothes, lack of manners, lawlessness, boasting and tendency to spit, he also relished the climate, the free and confident women, and the spectacular scenery.

When Kipling reached England in October 1889 he found his reputation had preceded him. Now he sent it soaring. He wrote consistently well, producing *Barrack-Room Ballads* (offending and delighting many with his ripe vernacular) and some

'Joyous home-coming'
In 1882, not yet 17, Kipling returned to India, this time to Lahore (right), to parents he had barely seen for 11 years: 'the mother proved more delightful than all my imaginings or memories. My father was not only a mine of knowledge and help, but a humorous, tolerant and expert fellow craftsman.' In his new post of journalist, Kipling had a servant, horse, cart and groom. Three times a week, the English of Lahore gathered to play tennis, dance and socialize. Nevertheless, Kipling worked 10 to 15 hours a day, six days a week, he and his boss producing by themselves the only daily paper in the Punjab.

excellent short stories, winning many good reviews, with one in *The Times* crowning him 'the discoverer of India'. His private life was also flourishing: he had recently fallen in love with Caroline 'Carrie' Balestier, his agent's sister.

However, events quickly turned against him. His novel *The Light that Failed* (1890) was a flop, and this, combined with overwork and bad health from various Indian fevers, produced such anxiety that he fled the country after just two years. He made for Australia and the Far East but soon after his departure heard that his agent had died. Kipling dashed back to be with Carrie, arriving on 10 January 1892. They were married eight days later.

Newlyweds' home
After Kipling married Caroline Balestier (right), they set off round the world, ending in Vermont, New England, Carrie's home, where they built a house called Naulakha (above).

Bikanir House
The Kiplings' white bungalow in Lahore was set in its own compound empty of bushes. The family hoped thus to deter insects, which they believed spread disease. Because of this wasteland, neighbours nicknamed the house 'Bikanir', after the Indian desert.

The Kiplings took a round-the-world honeymoon, stopping off in Vermont in the north eastern United States to visit Carrie's parents. Kipling was so excited by the surrounding countryside and its inhabitants that they stayed for four years. They bought some land next to Carrie's family's home, built a house and had a child, Josephine.

FAMILY CONFLICTS

Before they reached the United States, however, they had visited Japan, where Kipling lost his money in a banking collapse, prompting Carrie to take charge of their finances and household management. Kipling benefited from this arrangement in many ways, since it left him free in Vermont to write some of his finest works, including *The Jungle Books*. Yet with Carrie now permanently in charge of their affairs he felt reduced to 'no more than a cork on the water', his life circumscribed by her organization. But if there was a potential for conflict, it never arose; that was saved for the Kiplings' relationship with Carrie's sharp-tongued, penniless, drunken brother Beatty.

Relationships between the two households disintegrated from 1894, culminating in Beatty's threat to kill Kipling. Kipling and Carrie called in the local sheriff, taking Beatty to court. However, according to Carrie, it was Kipling who was left 'a total wreck'. The press had a field day at the great English author's expense and, though a verdict was held over to the next session, the Kiplings had had enough and returned to England.

From 1896 to 1902 they lived briefly in Torquay, then at Rottingdean, a quaint coastal village near Brighton. Kipling was as productive as ever, writing the *Just So* stories and shrewd political items about the threat from Germany and the likelihood of European war. But his life was soon shattered by a more private tragedy.

COLD DEATH

In the winter of 1898-99, the Kiplings went on an American trip to visit Carrie's parents. Despite warnings that the weather was too severe for the children (they now had two girls and a boy) they proceeded with their plan. Sadly the warnings came true. Once in the United States, Kipling went down with severe pneumonia in both lungs, the children with fever. The writer's near-fatal condition became daily front-page news, with reporters besieging his rooms. He even got a 'Get Well' message from the Kaiser.

Kipling eventually recovered, but Josephine did not. Carrie had to keep the news of her death from him until days after the burial, when he was strong enough to take it. Kipling never returned to the United States, and never recovered from this tragedy. Carrie's strength of character pulled him through the following months. *They*, published in 1904, is one of the few works, albeit indirectly, to tackle the heart-rending subject of Josephine's death.

'. . . it's all our own!'
(above) The Jacobean mansion Bateman's, at Burwash in Sussex, was Kipling's home for the last 34 years of his life. Friends found it damp and depressing, but Kipling delighted in its stately grandeur and extensive grounds 'including a mill which was paying taxes in 1296!'

Kipling's time at Rottingdean coincided with the Boer War (1899-1902). Always excited by war, he travelled to South Africa to check the military hospitals and ensure the British troops were being properly cared for. Their condition was woeful. In addition to the fighting they had to contend with typhoid, dysentery and their bungling commanders. Kipling devoted himself to working with the wounded and writing letters home for the most severely disabled. He also produced a newspaper for the troops.

Back home in Rottingdean, he did everything he could to raise the villagers to his own pitch of excitement. He fired a cannon over the cliff's edge to welcome home three local soldiers, and later went through the streets loudly rattling tin cans to celebrate the Relief of Mafeking.

By jingo!
(left) Kipling's popular image is summed up in this cartoon. Champion of vernacular speech, jingoistic patriot, he became almost a caricature of Empire – an image that went against him when the tide of popular opinion later turned away from imperialism.

THE BESIEGED LAUREATE

Kipling was the self-appointed Laureate of the Empire. His friend Cecil Rhodes, the founder of Rhodesia, described him as having 'done more than any other since Disraeli to show the world that the British race is sound at core and that rust and dry rot are strangers to it'. His politics made him a controversial figure and literary critics were often unenthusiastic about his work. But the general reading public adored him. Consequently Kipling's home, all too accessible on the village green, came to be peered at and surrounded by the

Loved and lost
(left inset) Kipling's three children, from left to right, Elsie, John and Josephine, were a source of great, unqualified joy: he spoiled them shamelessly. After Josephine – 'the child that was all to him' – died, he wrote, 'People say that kind of wound heals. It doesn't'. Added to that wound was John's death in World War I, after which Kipling sank into a deep pessimism from which he never recovered.

increasing numbers of curious south-coast tourists.

In 1902 the family moved to Bateman's, a Jacobean house at Burwash, a well-wooded part of the Sussex Weald. The last of his Eastern stories, including *Kim*, were completed at Rottingdean. After the move his fiction took on a wider dimension, partly inspired by the new landscape. In 1907 Kipling won the Nobel Prize for Literature.

Unhappy times were to follow. Many good friends died, Kipling's health began to suffer and, in 1914, as he had been fearing, Europe was plunged into the most horrific war in its history.

King and Trumpeter
By the 1920s, Kipling was a household name – a literary giant and a national figurehead. He is pictured left with King George V, visiting war graves in Belgium in 1922, in his capacity as advisor to the War Graves Commission. The two men became quite friendly, and when they died within a few days of each other – Kipling on his own 44th wedding anniversary – it was said the King had sent his Trumpeter ahead of him.

Fact or Fiction

ZAM-ZAMMAH

***Kim* opens with the hero sitting on the barrel of this great bronze cannon outside the 'Wonder House' – Lahore Museum. Kipling knew the scene well, for his father was curator of the museum.**

Kipling's son John enlisted. Six weeks after he left home the 18-year old went missing in action and Kipling was devastated, undoubtedly feeling partly responsible for his death. Fortunately he never knew that his lines "My son died laughing at some jest, I would I knew/What it were" could not have been further from the truth. John was last seen crying from the pain of a mouth wound.

Kipling's standing after the war was as high as ever. The Prime Minister offered him any honour he wanted, but Kipling was not interested in accepting titles. He turned down the Order of Merit three times and also the poet laureateship, but he was awarded (without his permission) a Companionship of Honour. He continued writing, but his works became increasingly sombre.

PAINFUL ILLNESSES

In his early fifties Kipling began to suffer terrible pains, which went undiagnosed for nearly 20 years, until he was found to have duodenal ulcers. He was well cared for by Carrie, but depressed at the extent to which she over-protected him, and by her parsimonious household management. At its most excessive this extended to switching off the electricity whenever they went away, distributing candles and matches to the unfortunate remaining servants. In 1930, Carrie also fell ill, crippled by rheumatism and attacked by diabetes.

The same year, the Kiplings took a much-needed holiday to Bermuda, and a trip to Egypt. Despite old age the author's mind still teemed with ideas. Also, his belief in the 'English Spirit' was as strong as ever, though he now felt increasingly out of place in the new post-Imperialist world, too right-wing even for the Conservatives. France became the country outside England on which he focused his hopes, and he often holidayed there.

In 1934 Kipling wrote his autobiography *Something of Myself.* Two years later, while setting out for a winter break in Cannes, he had a severe haemorrhage in London. He died four days later, on 18 January 1936. His ashes rest in Poets' Corner, Westminster Abbey.

A Soldier's Life

Kipling was the first writer to take the life of a common soldier as his subject. In India and South Africa he saw at first hand how hard and dangerous the Tommy's life could be.

Kipling never served in the armed forces and he was halfway through his life before he witnessed warfare from the firing line. But his portrayal of the soldier's life in poetry and prose created the popular image of the British Army in late Victorian and Edwardian times. Indeed, many people at the time thought that he influenced not just their public image but the way soldiers saw themselves. Sir George Younghusband, for example, wrote in his book, *A Soldier's Memories in Peace and War* (1917):

'I myself had served for many years with soldiers, but never heard the words or expressions that Rudyard Kipling's soldiers used. Many a time did I ask my brother Officers whether they had heard them. No, never. But sure enough, a few years after, the soldiers thought, and talked, and expressed themselves exactly like Rudyard Kipling had taught them in his stories . . . Rudyard Kipling made the modern soldier.'

Younghusband's comments emphasize that it was essentially the world of the common soldier that Kipling explored. This was a new departure in English literature, for although the rank and file had figured often enough in earlier works (such as Shakespeare's *Henry V*), it had always been in a minor, supporting role. Kipling wrote as much about the barrack-room as the officers' mess.

SWEEPING REFORMS

Great changes were occurring in the British Army in the period when Kipling was growing up, and they were mainly the work of one remarkable man: Edward Cardwell (later Viscount Cardwell), Secretary of State for War from 1868 to 1874. When he took over at the War Office, the Army was notorious for including in its ranks the dregs of the population. (In 1831 the Duke of Wellington had described it as 'composed of the scum of the earth'.) Cardwell wanted a better quality of recruit. He wanted a more efficient army which could match the highly trained Continental forces. (In 1870-71, the Germans crushed France in the Franco-Prussian War with a show of awesome military power.)

One of Cardwell's first reforms was to abolish flogging in peace-time, a move strenuously opposed by most senior officers who regarded it as essential to discipline. By 1881, however, it was also abolished for soldiers on active service. In 1870 Cardwell also succeeded in reducing the minimum length of service from 12 years to six with a regiment and six 'on the reserve' (demobbed but still available for call-up in wartime).

Cardwell's measures stimulated enlistment so successfully that in 1870 he was able to abolish 'bounty money' (a payment made for signing up). But soldiering continued to be a disreputable

'A gentleman in kharki'
(above) This illustration to Kipling's poem 'The Absent-Minded Beggar' (1899) epitomizes the image he helped to create of the staunch British 'Tommy'.

Into battle
(below) The Boer War was the largest conflict the British Army had engaged in since the Napoleonic Wars.

Cultures in conflict
(left) The British in India regarded themselves as the master race, and soldiers were discouraged from fraternizing with the Indians. Thus a soldier could spend a decade in the country and return home almost completely ignorant of its people and cultures.

Pillars of the Empire
(right) In this 1908 cartoon, Kipling is shown alongside Lord Kitchener, the most famous British soldier of his era. Part of the accompanying verse reads: 'When the Empire wants a stitch in her/Send for Kipling and for Kitchener.'

profession. When the future Sir William Robertson gave up a footman's job to join the Army in 1877, his mother told him she 'would rather see him dead than in a red coat'.

Robertson achieved the unprecedented feat of rising from the lowest rank in the army (private) to the highest (field marshal). But although Cardwell had put a stop to the practice of buying commissions and promotions, officers continued to be drawn mainly from the ranks of the aristocracy and gentry. The military establishment was extremely conservative and believed that a system

Family inspiration
(below) Kipling's sculptor father illustrated many of his son's works. This is his portrayal of Mulvaney from Soldiers Three.

Dedicated reformer
(above) Secretary of State for War Edward Cardwell did magnificent work in improving army conditions. He retired exhausted in 1874.

Commander-in-chief
(above) Lord Roberts was the most distinguished soldier in India during Kipling's time. On occasion he consulted Kipling about soldiers' living conditions.

good enough for the Dukes of Marlborough and Wellington should be good enough for anyone else.

Cardwell's reforms also included an important improvement in equipment, with the adoption of the Martini-Henry rifle, the Army's first proper breech-loader, in place of less efficient muzzle-loaders. The result of all these reforms was that the Army, although still lagging behind the military might of Germany and Russia, became a more efficient and up-to-date organization. This was clearly demonstrated in 1882, when the revolt of Arabi Pasha in Egypt was firmly quashed – a far cry from the bungling of the Crimean War.

'BLOOMIN' GOOD PAY'

The basic pay for a private in 1837, when Queen Victoria came to the throne, was indeed the 'Shillin' a day' of which Kipling wrote. By 1890 this had risen to 1s 2d. However, stoppages were made for food, cleaning equipment and other essentials, so that a soldier pocketed much less. The official attitude was that it was pointless paying the men any more, as they would only spend it on drink. Many civilians were worse off, and hunger could be the best recruiting sergeant of all.

Everyday living conditions in garrison towns were improving, with better cooking and bathing facilities (though uninspired food). But a continuing source of misery for the rank and file was the difficulty of leading a satisfactory married life. A soldier had to obtain his commanding officer's permission to marry, but the officer was severely limited in the number of women he was allowed to have living in barracks. If permission was granted, the wife was designated as being 'on the strength'. She moved wherever duty took her husband, or if she had to be left behind was granted a small allowance. A wife married 'off the strength' often faced great hardship, as she would be left to fend for herself (and any children she might have) if her husband happened to be posted elsewhere.

Although one of Cardwell's policies had been to withdraw British troops from the self-governing colonies, the Empire was still so large and far-flung that a soldier was likely to spend much of his term of duty thousands of miles away from home. After the end of the Napoleonic Wars in 1815, Europe enjoyed an unusually peaceful period, but a constant military presence was maintained in overseas territories, where there were frequent skirmishes with rebellious subject peoples. In 1897, the year of Queen Victoria's Diamond Jubilee, the *Daily Mail* called the Victorian era 'emphatically the period of small wars'.

India was by far the biggest drain on manpower. Its territories were then even more vast than they are today, incorporating Pakistan, Bangladesh and part of present-day Burma. The Indian Mutiny of 1857-58, when native troops revolted against British rule, had shaken colonial complacency, and although the Indian Army subsequently proved its loyalty, the British Army kept a very careful watch on it. Generally, about a third of the British Army was stationed in India.

DEADLY WEAPONS

When Kipling was in India as a journalist from 1882 to 1889, the subcontinent was enjoying a period of calm after the end of the Second Afghan War in 1880. For most soldiers, boredom and disease were deadlier enemies than the Afghans.

The most feared disease was cholera, for which there was no known remedy. It struck with horrifying suddenness – all might be well at morning parade, but by nightfall a dozen men could be

Cushy living
(right) When fighting was remote, life in India, especially for officers, could be 'cushy' – the Hindi word for 'pleasant'.

North-West Frontier
India is associated with baking heat, but in the Himalayan north things were far different (photograph taken during the Second Afghan War).

suffering agonizing deaths, enduring acute diarrhoea, vomiting and crippling muscle cramps. It was generally believed that cholera was a kind of deadly, invisible cloud, and the only way to avoid it was to move the battalion or regiment to a temporary camp in a 'clean' area. This 'cholera-dodging' seldom worked. As Kipling wrote:

Since August when it started, it's been stickin' to our tail,
Though they've had us out by marches an' they've 'ad us back by rail;
But it runs as fast as troop trains, and we cannot get away,
An' the sick-list to the colonel makes ten more today.

PRIMITIVE SANITATION

The main cause of cholera was poor sanitation. The bacteria breed in places such as cesspits, and are transmitted by drinking fouled water or eating food contaminated by flies. Florence Nightingale's stress on good hygiene in the Crimea had not gone entirely unheeded, and some of the barracks built in India were airy and pleasant compared with their bleak, cramped equivalents in England. But by today's standards, sanitation was primitive and the stink of the latrines was present day and night. Kipling himself suffered the effects of Calcutta's bad sanitation and his years in India left him a legacy of ill health.

Given the discomfort and monotony of their lives, it is not surprising that soldiers' tempers frayed easily. The phrase 'hot weather shootings' has been used to describe the outbursts of violence that could erupt between comrades-in-arms. The horrible sequel – the military execution – formed the subject for Kipling's 'Danny Deever', which the writer Kingsley Amis has called 'the most harrowing poem in our language'.

Officers and men
The British Army endured primitive living conditions during the Boer War in South Africa (1899-1902). Above is an officers' mess, looking more like a workmen's hut. Right, a drummer boy (the minimum age was 14) writes home. The Army Post Office in South Africa handled 170,000 letters a week.

Sunday was the day most hated by soldiers. The tedium and bullying of the drill square were replaced by Church Parade – which was generally agreed to be even worse and was deeply resented as it took up so much of a 'free' day. Such religious observance remained compulsory until after World War II, but crafty recruits (perhaps tipped off by old hands) could get round it by claiming to belong to some Nonconformist group such as the Plymouth Brethren.

Drinking and sex with prostitutes provided light relief for soldiers in India, as elsewhere. In 1868 commanding officers were empowered to fine soldiers for drunkenness, and in 1876 over a quarter of the whole army was fined. Venereal disease was a scourge, and it has been estimated that at any one time about five per cent of the Army would be unfit for duty because of it. Lord Roberts, commander-in-chief in India from 1885 to 1893, was a member of the Army Temperance Association and one of the many senior officers who frowned on drinking or debauchery.

Despite the great discomforts of life in India, many soldiers preferred to do their service there rather than in England. At times there was little

serious fighting, and if a soldier could come to terms with the climate he had a relatively easy life, for native servants did the worst menial tasks.

In his autobiography, *Something of Myself* (1937), Kipling tells us that he based the soldiers in his Indian stories on real-life characters he had met in Lahore. He obviously loved soldiers' company, but after he left India in 1889, it was not until the Boer War of 1899-1902 that he again came into close, regular contact with the Army. In January 1900 he sailed for Cape Town to combine work as a journalist with convalescence in the sunny climate. His first sight of serious fighting came on 29 March 1900 at the Battle of Karee Siding, an indecisive encounter but one he found thrilling.

WAR IN SOUTH AFRICA

The war against the Boers (descendants of Dutch colonists) was entirely different from any the British Army had experienced. The opponents were not brave but under-equipped native people; they were resourceful guerillas, superb horsemen and crack shots who could exploit the terrain. Winston Churchill wrote in 1899, 'The individual Boer, mounted, in a suitable country is worth four or five regular soldiers.' Against them the skills that looked impressive on the parade ground were useless, and the British suffered a series of humiliating defeats before their sheer weight of numbers turned the tide.

Kipling spent about eight months in South Africa during the war, working on an army newspaper and visiting the wounded. Like many others he was appalled by the conditions endured by the soldiers, among whom typhoid and dysentery were rife. The stench of a camp infected with dysentery could be smelled a mile away.

A fascinating insight into the life of an ordinary British soldier during the war is revealed in the diary kept by Private Frederick Tucker. On 12 March 1900 Tucker wrote: 'We were treated to soft bread again in lieu of biscuits; this was the first

A heroes' welcome
(above) The City Imperial Volunteers are received in splendour in the Guildhall after returning from the Boer War in 1900. Kipling helped to transform the image of the soldier from 'scum of the earth' to source of national pride.

For King and Country
Kipling's son was one of the countless young men to die in the Great War.

G v R I

He whom this scroll commemorates was numbered among those who, at the call of King and Country, left all that was dear to them, endured hardness, faced danger, and finally passed out of the sight of men by the path of duty and self-sacrifice, giving up their own lives that others might live in freedom. Let those who come after see to it that his name be not forgotten.

Lieut. John Kipling
Irish Guards

bread we had tasted since 12 February. We were not sorry for the change, for a month on biscuits of the army type is enough for any man – even if his teeth are like steel.'

In addition, the rain and cold of the winter nights caused much misery. On 28 May 1900 (winter in the southern hemisphere) Tucker wrote: 'It was too cold to sleep and in the morning I found that my top blanket was quite wet and stiff . . . I tried to make some coffee but found my water bottle full of ice.'

The handling of the war (particularly the use of concentration camps for Boer women and children) caused much anti-imperialist and anti-British feeling, but it was also during this war that the British public first really took the common soldier to their hearts. The number of soldiers sent to South Africa was huge – about 450,000 – and almost every town and village in the country contributed its share of men. Thus there was an unprecedented sense of personal involvement. This was heightened by the jingoistic popular Press and Kipling's patriotic verse.

WAR GRAVES COMMISSIONER

Kipling's South African poems include the famous 'Boots' – but generally the verse and stories inspired by the war do not rank high in his literary output. Perhaps close contact with the horrific aspects of warfare cooled some of his patriotic ardour. This process was completed in World War I – particularly after his son was killed in action – when his work reeked of despair.

Kipling kept his sense of duty and loyalty, however, and in 1917 he became one of the War Graves Commissioners. He worked for the Commission for the rest of his life, and it was he who suggested such words as those engraved at the entrance to each war cemetery: 'Their name liveth for evermore'. It is this dignified work that stands as the most fitting memorial to his special relationship with the British soldier.

H. G. WELLS

1866-1946

Born with a brilliant imagination and a consuming intellectual curiosity, Wells made himself famous by foreseeing the danger as well as the potential of science. He achieved equal notoriety by advocating on paper the 'free love' he practised in private. Always impatient for social change, he pursued peace and global unity, quarrelling his way through countless debates and articles, and often shifting ground. Vociferous and energetic in pursuit of his beliefs, he was dubbed the 'great awakener of men'.

Lusty Ambitions

Blessed with a powerful imagination and a thirst for knowledge, Wells escaped a life of insignificant drudgery and set himself forever at odds with the world of smug, repressive respectability.

One of H. G. Wells' most considerable and spectacular achievements is little known – his rise to fame from the humblest beginnings. He was born on 21 September in 1866 in Bromley, Kent, the youngest child of Sarah, a housemaid, and Joseph, a small-time shopkeeper. Wells' childhood betrayed no signs of the enormous success to come, and was probably most notable for loneliness. Sarah tried to stop him playing with other children because she had absorbed some of the snobbery of her employers and regarded his potential playmates as beneath him. To make matters worse, young Herbert George had little contact with his brothers because they were much older than him; while he was still at home, they were at school, and by the time he went to school, they had moved on.

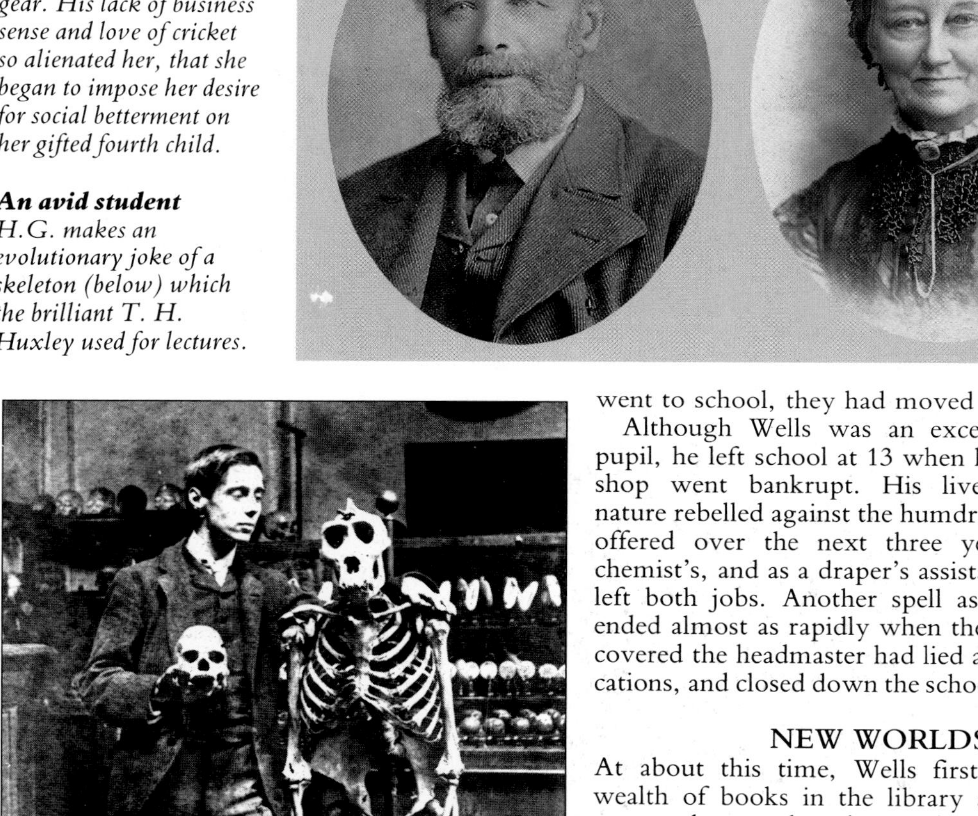

A poor business
Joe and Sarah Wells (right) eked out 'a miserable half living' in a vermin-infested shop selling china and cricket gear. His lack of business sense and love of cricket so alienated her, that she began to impose her desire for social betterment on her gifted fourth child.

An avid student
H.G. makes an evolutionary joke of a skeleton (below) which the brilliant T. H. Huxley used for lectures.

Although Wells was an exceptionally bright pupil, he left school at 13 when his father's china shop went bankrupt. His lively, imaginative nature rebelled against the humdrum work he was offered over the next three years, both as a chemist's, and as a draper's assistant, and he soon left both jobs. Another spell as a pupil-teacher ended almost as rapidly when the authorities discovered the headmaster had lied about his qualifications, and closed down the school.

NEW WORLDS

At about this time, Wells first discovered the wealth of books in the library and attic of the country house where his mother was then working. It sparked off his imagination, making him aware of the extraordinary worlds beyond the real one, waiting to be explored.

But despite this revelation, Wells had no career and was going nowhere until, at the age of 17, he tried to strike out by applying to his first headmaster for a teaching job. He was immediately hired

Key Dates

1866 born in Bromley, Kent

1879 apprentice draper

1891 marries cousin, Isabel Wells

1895 marries 'Jane' Robbins

1898 *The War of the Worlds*

1909 'elopes' with Amber Reeves

1912 meets Rebecca West

1914 birth of their son, Anthony

1934 interviews Stalin and Roosevelt

1946 dies in London

Apprentice draper
'Almost as unquestioning as her belief in Our Father and Our Saviour was her belief in drapers', said H.G. of his mother. When money ran out, she took H.G. (now aged 14) away from school, and apprenticed him at a draper's (below) opposite the gates of Windsor Castle (left).

and thrived in academe, studying science in his spare time. He won a scholarship to the Normal School of Science (now Imperial College) in London, where he was taught by some of the finest minds of his time, notably the biologist Thomas Huxley. Huxley, like Charles Darwin, was one of the leaders of a scientific revolution propelling people out of the Victorian age at a far quicker pace than many could tolerate. Wells, however, devoured Huxley's theories on the origins and purpose of life, although he rapidly lost interest in his studies when allocated less inspiring teachers.

He left college without a degree, but took it externally in 1890, gaining first-class honours in zoology. He had by now acquired three life-long passions: women, social reform and writing. When Wells was 21, he made for London to write his great novel. But when it was finished he was so dissatisfied with his 35,000-word 'magnum opus' that he threw it into the fire. It seemed that he would never rise above a teaching career with its demoralizingly low income, and he spent the next three years in the classroom, although he still continued his writing. Then in 1890 he fell in love with his beautiful young cousin, Isabel Mary Wells, and married her the following June.

The marriage soon disintegrated, however. The two seemed emotionally, sexually, and intellectually incompatible, and Wells, never monogamous by temperament, embarked on a series of affairs. Of these, the most emotionally rewarding was his relationship with one of his students, Amy Catherine 'Jane' Robbins.

It was during the course of this affair that Wells fell ill. He began coughing up blood and went to recuperate from a minor haemorrhage in Eastbourne. Here he dashed off an article for a newspaper and was amazed that not only was it accepted, but they wanted more of the same.

LIBERATION AT LAST

This sudden, minor, literary success did wonders for Wells. He decided to abandon his relationship with Mary for a life with Jane, and this liberation led to an outpouring of brilliant articles and short stories. From 1895, when he married Jane, to 1898, he wrote four of his most popular novels, *The Time Machine, The Island of Dr Moreau, The Invisible Man* and *The War of the Worlds.*

Wells' theory that science afforded infinite possibilities for creating a better world and his daring handling of the new genre of science fiction became instant hits. The critics raved and publishers tripled their advances. But Wells still had one major problem. He had never been healthy (even the earliest descriptions of him depict a timid, weak boy), and had recently suffered a second haemorrhage. In addition he was supporting both his current wife and his ex-wife, and when he decided in 1899 to visit Mary for the first time in five years, the emotional strain proved too much for him. He suffered what could be termed a breakdown and became morbidly aware of his

'Very innocent lovers'
'I was always wanting to board and storm and subjugate her imagination so that it would come out . . . to meet mine', wrote Wells of his first wife, Isabel (right) – but, 'it never came out to meet me.' Nor, apparently, did she delight in sex. Wells quickly felt trapped by this marriage and found the only answer was to replace 'simple honesty . . . by duplicity'. He took lovers. 'I wanted to compensate myself for the humiliation she had so unwittingly put upon me.'

Second marriage
Wells left Isabel for his pupil, 'Jane' Robbins (above). Sexually, Jane was as 'innocent and ignorant' as Isabel, but she was sympathetic to his work and his ideas on personal freedom.

mortality. Yet it was precisely this likelihood of an early death that drove him to write more and better novels.

Another beneficial effect of this setback was that the Royal Literary Fund, worried about his finances, asked several prominent writers to approach him on their behalf to discover whether he needed a loan. Fortunately Wells' books were selling too well for that, but the offer did lead to Wells' friendship with other important writers including Joseph Conrad, Ford Madox Ford, George Gissing, and even Henry James.

Wells' second marriage, however, was by now faring badly. After the birth of two sons, George and Frank, in 1901 and 1903 respectively, Wells lost interest in Jane. They agreed to cease being lovers and, with Jane's consent, Wells looked elsewhere for intellectual and sexual excitement.

A DIFFICULT ROLE

Jane was well aware that there was a hollow core to their marriage, but was nonetheless determined to remain his wife. As she saw it, she still had a crucial role to play in his life, raising their children, keeping the family home for when he chose to return to it and organizing his work. She became an indispensable anchor, and in return enjoyed being the wife of one of the greatest writers of the time. It was a lonely, difficult role, but gradually Jane developed her own life and her own group of friends.

Meanwhile, Wells' interest in sex was extending beyond the physical. Sex, along with religion and science, were the three elements of his furious attack on current morality. He wanted to sweep away the Victorian ethics which he thought were strangling the modern world. Sex should now be

The public image
Given Wells' astonishing beliefs and scandalous lifestyle, the public both laughed and marvelled at him. Punch *pictured him on a flying machine (above). Max Beerbohm drew a cartoon of the older Wells debating with his younger self (left) – indicating how greatly his opinions changed over the years.*

Cocking a snook *(below) A rare secular stained-glass window illustrates the Fabian Society at the time Wells took issue with it. He is seen in the bottom corner, thumbing his nose at the other members. Wells believed in sweeping away the old order, rather than using established channels for political change. He was therefore perpetually at odds with his fellow Fabians – but they always forgave him. George Bernard Shaw wrote that, 'unhindered, unpunished, apparently even undisliked . . . the worse he behaved the more he was indulged, and the more he was indulged the worse he behaved.'*

REBECCA WEST

Although Wells had two wives and countless amours, his most important lover was Rebecca West. Her real name was Cicily Fairfield: at 19 she adopted 'Rebecca', after a fictional heroine. The same year, she met Wells, a man of 46, at the height of his fame. Her own gifts were not immediately apparent to him, but when, in a review of his book *The Passionate Friends,* she endorsed his views on casual sex, he decided an affair might thrive.

They called each other by pet names, she Panther, he Jaguar, denoting their fierce, anti-social mutuality. A son, Anthony, was born in 1914, and Rebecca lived by writing feminist articles, witty, hard-hitting reviews and novels. It was she who finally ended the affair. At 38 she married another man, and went on to produce a mammoth study of Yugoslavia, report the Nuremberg Trials (of war-criminals) and write numerous articles on topical spy scandals. She was made a Dame for her services to literature, and was still writing within months of her death in 1983.

freely discussed and experienced because his vision of a better society was dependent on people leading fulfilled lives, sexually and intellectually. But while the public were excited by Wells' bold descriptions of a new world in which he had welded a poetic vision on to scientific possibilities, few were ready for sexual liberation.

Wells' passionate desire to steer humanity to a better world led to further problems when, in his mid-30s, he joined the Fabian Society. The Fabians also wanted to restructure society, but worked for an intellectual, not a violent revolution. This was much too frustrating for the ever impatient Wells, and in one of the great debates of the time he was challenged by the brilliant Irish playwright George Bernard Shaw to thrash out Fabian policy. Few people could defeat the prodigiously witty and intellectually agile Shaw, let alone Wells, who was not a particularly good speaker or debater. Shaw proclaimed him to be a dreamer of hollow visions who was incapable of working out the complexities of a utopia. Soundly beaten, Wells left the Fabians one year later to found his 'New Republic' through other means. It may be, however, that his decision to quit was also prompted by the fact that he had recently seduced the daughters of two fellow members, one of whom, Amber Reeves, was now pregnant.

Wells ran away with Amber to France, but finding her unequal to the task of looking after him, reverted periodically to Jane, soon suggesting that Amber find herself a husband. Reluctantly she agreed, but Wells continued their affair after her marriage and the birth of his child.

This gave him the material for the novel *Ann Veronica,* in which a liberated young girl rejects convention to become a suffragette, and eventually runs off with an older man. In it Wells refuted the concept of honour, maintaining that not only should a woman yield to any strong sexual temptations, but that she should be proud of having done so. His editors at Macmillans thought it too scandalous to publish, and when it did appear the right-wing critics tore it apart. The fuss died down with his next immensely successful novel, *Mr Polly*, but flared up again with the contentious *New Machiavelli.* Libraries banned the book and Wells left for France to rethink his position, outraged that the world was ignoring his rallying cry.

A MEETING OF MINDS

One person who did understand him, however, was the future novelist Rebecca West. They met in 1912 when Wells, aged 46, was at the height of his fame, and Rebecca West was a radical, attractive 19-year-old. She had written a scathing review of one of his books – which intrigued him – and, after resolving apparent differences, they became lovers. Their affair spanned the next ten years and produced a son, Anthony West, born in 1914. The first four years were among the happiest, most exciting in Wells' life. World War I was looming and to Wells it spelt the promise of a new world – the dead values of the past would be blown away leaving Wells, the self-appointed prophet, to guide his people to the Promised Land.

But before the war had ended, both public and private worlds were collapsing. Rebecca West began to have grave misgivings about sacrificing her career and life to Wells, who was becoming increasingly self-centred and unreliable. And 'The War That Will End War', as Wells had called it, had turned into a mindless slaughter.

On a personal level this was a remarkably hectic time for Wells: he was living at three separate addresses (his private London flat, in Essex with Jane, and wherever Rebecca happened to be); he had had a huge success with *Mr Britling Sees it Through* (reprinted 12 times in the last three months of 1916); and early in 1918 he joined the Department of Propaganda based at Whitehall.

'I AM REALLY FAMOUS'

Because Wells' principal interest was fighting for a new world state which would end wars between individual countries, he soon resigned from his post of Propaganda adviser. To help the world's leading statesmen to realize this aim, as Europe emerged from the end of the war, he researched his massive *Outline of History* to help them better understand their task. Ironically, the very people for whom he had been writing ignored it, and academics scoffed at its eccentricities, gaps and inaccuracies. But Wells' readers loved it, buying over 100,000 copies.

Meanwhile Wells was invited to the United States; his fame preceded him, much to his astonishment and delight. The papers reported everything he did and said, so that Wells had to acknowledge, 'I am really famous here, people turn round in the street and when I went to a play the house stood up and clapped.' He was rapidly turning into an international star and in 1920 went on a visit to Russia where he discussed the future of the world – and particularly of Russia – with the revolutionary Lenin.

From 1920, however, it gradually became clear that Wells was not going to get it all his own way, in private or public. Although Rebecca West regarded him as 'everything one imagines in a genius', she eventually realized that the affair was blotting out her own rich prospects. Wells could neither leave Jane nor marry Rebecca and so, in 1923, as Rebecca later wrote, 'we parted like lovers . . . and you exploded into rage and hate in the afternoon.' Rebecca kept Anthony and Wells agreed to support him.

More trouble followed when Wells reacted to this rejection by throwing himself into an affair with a 30-year old Austrian translator. When he then suddenly abandoned her, she tried to commit suicide in his flat. Any hopes he had of hiding this, or the sham of his marriage to Jane, were ruined when the newspapers headlined the story the following day.

Wells' political life fared little better. It was now certain that despite his immense popularity and meetings with the top politicians of the day his grand design for a new world had come to nothing. He regarded himself as 'a man lit by a vision of the world . . . yet powerless to realise it.' Despite these setbacks, Wells rarely slipped into self-pity, but worked relentlessly for his new world, and still published novels.

In 1927 came another major blow. Wells had been spending an increasing amount of time in France because of ill health, and in June that year

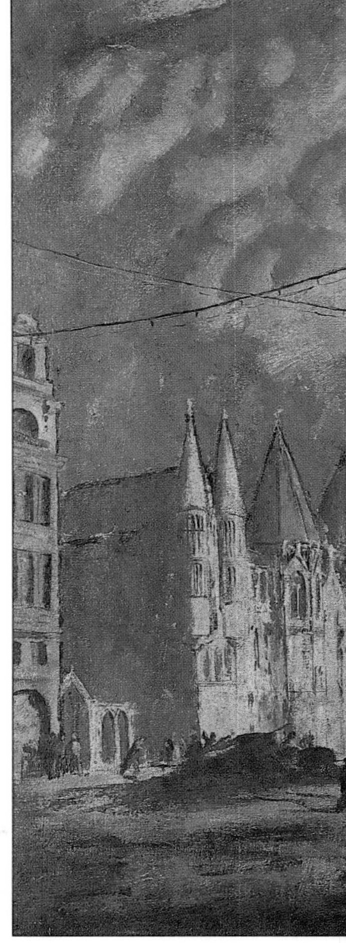

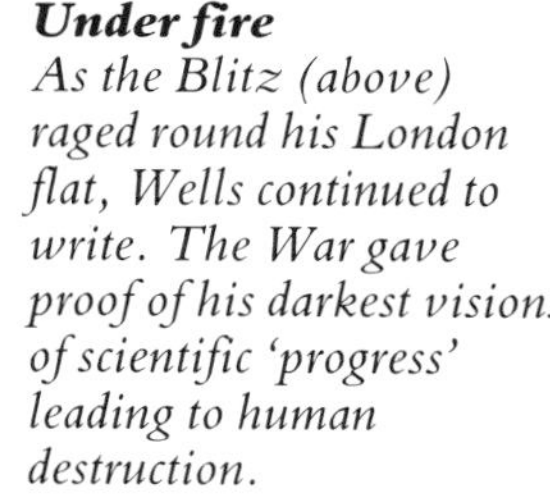

Under fire
As the Blitz (above) raged round his London flat, Wells continued to write. The War gave proof of his darkest visions of scientific 'progress' leading to human destruction.

Meeting with a leader
In 1920 Wells interviewed Lenin (left) for the Sunday Express. *Though Wells had cheered on the 1917 Revolution and considered Lenin 'a very great man', he was sceptical of Lenin's economic plans for Russia. 'Come back and see us in ten years' time', was Lenin's retort. Wells'* Express *articles were sympathetic to the Bolshevik state, and he remained an important interpreter of Russia to the West.*

Fact or Fiction

THE GREAT HOAX

In 1938 Orson Welles made an American radio adaptation of *The War of the Worlds* for transmission on Hallowe'en. Those tuning in late, unwarned, heard fake newscasts followed by 'President Roosevelt' exhorting the nation to remain calm and an 'eye-witness account' of the destruction of New York. All over the country, thousands panicked and fled their homes. Although he denied it, Orson Welles was secretly delighted by the success of his ruse.

was accompanied by Jane when invited to a lecture at the Sorbonne in Paris. Not long after, Jane was diagnosed as having cancer. She died later that year leaving Wells distraught by her loss. In addition, he had to face up to the possibility that his illegitimate son Anthony might also die. Six months later, in 1928, Anthony went down with tuberculosis at the same time that Rebecca became ill with influenza. These catastrophes, as Wells wrote to her, reopen 'all sorts of shut-down tendernesses and I feel like your dear brother and your best friend and your father and your once (and not quite forgetting it) lover.'

But these links with the past were soon ended. Rebecca married in 1930, the same year that Wells sold his old house where he had lived with Jane. Thereafter, until his death, he lived close to Regent's Park in London. Although no longer in the best-selling lists, Wells was by no means forgotten. In 1934 he tackled the world's two most powerful leaders, having interviews with Stalin in Russia and Theodore Roosevelt in America, in order to find common ground that could be the basis of future civilization.

The outbreak of World War II signified the collapse of the core of his life's work. Plans for a peaceful world state were daily blasted as bombs exploded around his flat in central London. And finally, in 1945, one of his earliest fears – the misuse of science – proved all too well founded when the United States dropped two atom bombs on Japan.

By now, Wells was desperately ill, although his mind still forced his ailing body to write. But by midsummer 1946, he was too ill to go on. The man who had enjoyed the affections of so many women died alone in his flat on 13 August.

Wells had risen from a frail, reticent, shabbily dressed shop boy to become the prophet of his generation, and at his funeral, writers, politicians and statesmen assembled together. As Clement Atlee said, the world from now on will seem silent without 'The great awakener of men'.

Renewed fame
Wells' novels won a second lease of life and his celebrity status soared as soon as film techniques were able to do justice to his epic visions. Pictured below arriving at the Leicester Square premiere of The Shape of Things to Come, *Wells revelled in the fame and adulation.*

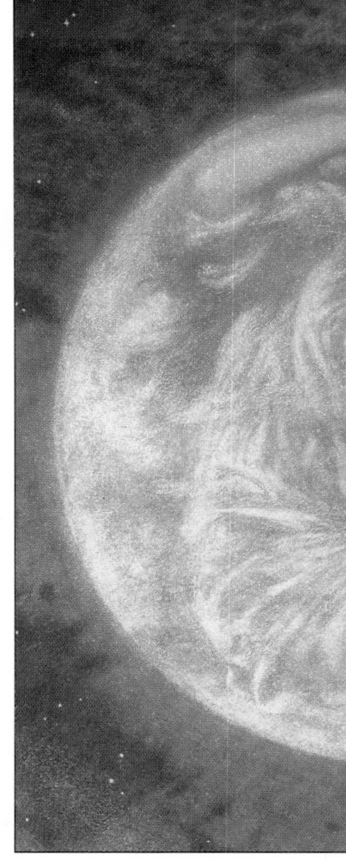

The Dawn of Science Fiction

Victorian notions of science as the key to infinite progress gave birth to a new literary genre. But soon the fiction began to question human competence to control the forces of technology.

The fiction of strange encounters is as old as literature itself, but with the Victorian boom in technology and science came a new kind of story – a genre that explored the seemingly limitless bounds of human knowledge. Victorian self-confidence gave way to doubts, however, and the greatest doubter – and the greatest visionary – was H. G. Wells. Ironically, his anxieties made, and made way for, some of the best science fiction of all.

As a literary form, science fiction has a mixed reputation. It is variously described as futuristic, escapist or visionary, as cheap pulp or prophetic mysticism. This is only natural with a genre that takes so many diverse forms. Some of its elements date back to the dawn of storytelling. The idea of travel far afield and of encounters with strange people and strange customs is even present in Homer's *Odyssey*. This ancient epic poem takes its hero far from known shores where he encounters monsters, suffers supernatural disasters and even quarrels with the gods themselves.

Another common element in science fiction is the 'alternative society' with a better or worse lifestyle than our own. Such fictional societies have often been used as a rich source for satire. Samuel Butler created his distant realm of *Erewhon* to hold 19th-century England up to ridicule. And Jonathan Swift had previously attacked the folly of his age in *Gulliver's Travels* (1726), through his fantastic islands of Lilliput and Brobdingnag, Laputa and Houyhnhnmland.

To the world's end
When the Mediterranean was the centre of the world, the classical journeys of such heroes as Ulysses constituted the ancient equivalent of science fiction. The stories featured strange creatures such as Sirens and storm nymphs in distant and unexplored tracts of ocean (left), born of half-believed sailors' yarns and an amalgam of cultural myths.

Frenchman with panache
Witty satirist and swaggering, stylish romantic, Cyrano de Bergerac (1619-1655) recounted visits to the Sun and Moon in order to make pointed comments about contemporary society.

The Moon, tantalizingly close and yet inscrutable and unexplored, has always been the first resort of fantasy writers. As early as the second century AD, the Greek Lucian of Samosata wrote two extraordinary accounts of journeys to the Moon: *Icaromenippus* and *The True History,* translated into English in 1634.

When, in 1647, the astronomer Hevelius mapped the Moon, he gave rise to a flurry of fiction describing its supposed exploration by travellers. At the time, such stories were about as incredible as the voyages around the world of Ferdinand Magellan and Francis Drake.

Moonshine
Man's fascination with the Moon invested it with strange occupants and magical properties for thousands of years (above left). Hevelius' mapping in 1647 (above) encouraged lively speculation and much satirical fiction. But not until the Victorians envisaged going there was true science fiction born.

FLIGHTS OF FANCY

Cyrano de Bergerac, the French poet, playwright, duellist and soldier, wrote an account of space travel, entitled *A Comical History of the States and Empires of the Moon* (1656). His aim was to satirize contemporary society by a description of lunar communities, but Cyrano also proposed (tongue-in-cheek) seven ways of reaching the Moon. He suggested anointing himself with morning dew and rising on its evaporation; greasing himself with the horn-marrow of beasts sacred to the Moon goddess; building a rocket fuelled with saltpetre; using a smoke-filled balloon; sitting on a metal plate and throwing a magnet repeatedly over his head; sealing up rarefied air in a 20-sided space capsule; and lying, wet-haired, head-on to the moonbeams when the Moon's influence on the sea was at its greatest. Edmond Rostand's play about Cyrano, staged in 1897, and incorporating his anti-gravitational theories, would almost certainly have been known to Wells.

Daniel Defoe (1660-1731), the author of *Robinson Crusoe,* also wrote about 'Worlds in the Moon', with a similarly satirical intent. And the 17th and 18th centuries kept up a steady flow of stories focused on other worlds. They were fiction, but they were not science fiction in the true sense, for there was no attempt at rational or scientific explanations. Travellers were driven off course by storms, borne on wings, or carried to their destination in dreams, like Dante conducted by spirits on a guided tour of the *Inferno* (Hell). Ebenezer Scrooge, that Dickensian traveller through time and space, is within the tradition of Dante and Defoe.

During the 19th century, the phenomenon arose that was vital to the creation of a new literary form: the growth of science and technology. The West's increasing affluence and domination of world trade were aided by new discoveries and technical ingenuity. It seemed that science would soon solve all problems, answer all questions.

Darwin's evolutionary theories also fired the fertile imagination. What if there were beasts which had evolved differently, in isolation, or had not become extinct (as in Conan Doyle's *Lost World* of dinosaurs)? What if Man's evolution took him beyond his present state and into some super-human form? What if Man could interfere

Kingdom of wise men
Jonathan Swift's Gulliver's Travels *includes an encounter with the flying island of Laputa (right). His purpose was not to excite the imagination so much as to provoke debate. His 'alternative society' was a vehicle for social satire.*

Twentieth-century war?
The new century held out the prospect of unprecedented scientific advances. But what form would these take? Writers and artists began to speculate (above) – at a fantasy level.

Danger and derring-do
Author Jules Verne took readers 20,000 leagues under the sea (above), to the centre of the Earth, round the world in 80 days, and to the Moon and back. On every trip, life-threatening dangers beset his heroes. He gave his public well-constructed plots, humour, pace and, above all, detailed and credible futuristic technology – little wonder Verne won such a following among Victorians.

with the natural process of evolution? A new kind of writer awoke to the amazing possibilities.

When Edgar Allan Poe, as a young journalist, began to write a story of a journey to the Moon, he dismissed as fancy the efforts of Cyrano and the rest. His intention was to be as scientific as possible. The object was not satire but plausibility, and it appeared in 1836 under the title *The Unparalleled Adventure of one Hans Pfaall.*

Sir John Herschel set out to observe the southern hemisphere with one of the largest telescopes in the world, and there was every expectation that it would unmask all the Moon's secrets. Not three weeks after Poe's story appeared, a series of articles were printed in *The New York Sun.* They purported to be based on *The Edinburgh Journal of Science*'s coverage of Herschel's discoveries. Later, these articles came to be known as *The Great Lunar Hoax,* for they detailed vegetation, animals, intelligent life forms and cities, all supposedly sighted through Herschel's telescope. They caused a stir similar to that created by Orson Welles' 1938 radio broadcast of *The War of the Worlds.*

VERNE'S VOYAGES

Jules Verne (who hero-worshipped Poe) barely scraped a living writing articles and stories until, in 1863, he began a series called *Voyages Extraordinaires* – accounts of imaginary journeys into the unknown. *Five Weeks in a Balloon* (1863) reads like a factual record, akin to Henry Morton Stanley's dispatches from darkest Africa. Verne was the prime exponent of 'pseudo' scientific fiction. To strengthen his case, he packed his books with elaborate references to facts and figures and the latest scientific discoveries. His readers were enthralled. Verne's journeys took his readers to the North Pole, then to the centre of the Earth, and, having exhausted the Earth's potential, he turned to other worlds.

In *From the Earth to the Moon* (1865), he approached the problem of escaping Earth's gravity with great seriousness, and his novel reaches its climax in the launch of a giant bullet and its voyage around the Moon. He was not so foolish as to allow it to land there. He feared losing his scientific reputation by speculating about the surface of the Moon and then being proved wrong. His characters simply observe that the surface of the Moon is not habitable, and that any life form must inhabit the interior cavities – a theory taken up by H. G. Wells in *The First Men in the Moon* (1901).

Verne laid the foundation of the science fiction genre. His stories were thrilling, informative and optimistic of human progress through scientific advances. He wrote at a time when Victorian self-confidence was at its peak, but there were voices preaching caution even then. The Romantic movement mistrusted the tendency for science and industry to exploit and detach human beings from Nature. Mary Shelley's *Frankenstein* (1818) is the first science fiction story in which the wonders and horrors brought about by technology gallop out of the control and comprehension of the scientist who instigated them.

GLOOMY PREDICTIONS

As time passed, Victorian certitude gave way to the uneasy restlessness of the Edwardians. H. G. Wells, while writing in much the same vein as Jules Verne, added a new (or rather an old) dimension to the genre. He recaptured the element of social criticism present in those early satirical fantasies. An internationalist writing in an age menaced by militarism and jingoism, he told science-based adventure stories but used them to question the accepted values of contemporary society and of science.

Jules Verne
Thrilling, epic and just plausible, the fiction of this brilliant Frenchman captured a young readership brought up in the Age of Science.

His predictions were astounding, leaving aside his merits as a writer or philosopher. He foresaw aerial and chemical warfare, pollution, various machines of war, genetic engineering and the exhaustion of the planet's resources – long before the term 'ecology' was even coined. And he predicted the atom bomb with uncanny accuracy.

Between them, Jules Verne and Wells established a formula for science fiction novels which was aped for many years afterwards. The story would begin with a discourse among gentlemen in which the feasibility of some invention was discussed, and after that the narrative of the adventure would be interspersed with large chunks of theory and/or philosophy.

When the possibility of travel to other planets was originally debated, it was envisaged that the inhabitants would either be like us or comically primitive and exploitable – not unlike those foreign 'savages' the Empire undertook to 'civilize'. It needed the post-Victorian mentality of H. G. Wells to suggest that the Earth could be visited by super-human life-forms and treated with the same disregard as 'civilized' Victorians treated lesser species and primitive cultures.

MARRED MIRACLES

Wells, for all his uncanny foresight, was the product of his time. In him a typically Victorian wonder at science was mixed with Edwardian fear of his fellow men's incompetence to put this science to good use. He chose not to turn his back on the future (as the Romantics had done), nor to reject the past (as the Modernists who dedicated themselves to a new age built on speed, power, design and mechanization did).

Wells' uncomfortable position, straddling the turn of the century, is best expressed in his masterpiece *The Invisible Man* (1897). The story is in the Gothic tradition of Mary Shelley, but is developed as a logical and scientific nightmare. Griffin, the anti-hero who dismisses the common rabble because they cling to their ignorance and do not appreciate the wonders of science, is gradually cut off from that society by his self-made 'miracle'

Art or pulp?
A magazine of the 1930s (left) illustrates the appeal of the gruesome and blood-curdling – elements which damaged the reputation of science fiction as legitimate literature. By contrast, Wells' The Invisible Man *(on the Belgian poster far left), for all its chilling power, has a philosophical element which raises it high above the lurid sci-fi which, at one stage, swamped the market.*

Edgar Rice Burroughs
Burroughs started his writing career on Mars and, after plunging into the African jungle, explored the Earth's centre and the Stone Age. He was a master of Fantasy (left) and one of the first of the American school which made sci-fi pay. His fiction often appeared alongside that of H.G. Wells and Jules Verne, serialized in the earliest specialist magazines.

of invisibility. He loses not just his visible body but his very self, finally cursed, cast out and hunted. Clearly the moral of the tale is that science should not be separated from society, nor trusted as an infallible answer to its problems.

THE SHIFT TO AMERICA

World War I proved Wells' visionary doubts more thoroughly than even he could bear. In the course of it, the tanks and the widespread mechanical destruction he had imagined became a horrible reality. In Britain, the effect was a waning of public interest in science fiction. Immediately after the War, any wish to think about the future gave way to a hedonistic obsession with the present. This was not so in the United States, however, where the public's fascination with and confidence in the future had barely been dented.

In 1919 Harold Hersey edited, in New York, *The Thrill Book,* a magazine which ran for 16 issues, mixing science and adventure. Then, in 1926, the first magazine devoted entirely to science fiction was published by Hugo Gernsback. It was called *Amazing Stories* and drew, at first, on European authors such as Jules Verne and H. G. Wells. But it also gave a creative opportunity to young American authors (and artists), the most notable being Edgar Rice Burroughs, the author of the *Tarzan* stories.

Gernsback relinquished control of *Amazing Stories* and became involved with the twin magazine *Science Wonder Stories* (which popularized the term 'science fiction') and *Air Wonder Stories.* Under the amalgamated titles of *Wonder Stories* these competed for readership with the rival *Astounding Stories.* Unfortunately, in the scramble for higher and higher circulation figures, the style degenerated into the era of the 'bug-eyed monster', the nasty alien. Travellers venturing boldly outwards from Earth invariably encountered strange and grotesque beasts. When, in time, the astronomers proved that no other planet or satellite within the solar system was likely to support the life of earthlings, the pattern changed in favour of extra-terrestrials visiting Earth.

During the 1920s, the United States purveyed a progressive attitude to science; children raised on a diet of the amazing, the astounding and the wonderful, imbibed a notion that human potential was unlimited and invulnerable. Computers would enlarge the brain infinitely. Robots would serve and protect human beings. It took the Wall Street Crash of 1929 to crack American self-confidence, as World War I had undermined that of Europe. Across the Atlantic, the dark image arose of science as a dehumanizing agent; and in Europe, Aldous Huxley was writing the chillingly pessimistic *Brave New World* (1932).

A secondary reaction in literature to dire world events was the expansion of escapist fantasy. *Superman, Flash Gordon* and *Buck Rogers* formed one answer to the public's need to avoid grim reality.

Thus the elements of modern science fiction developed to include superficial, flashy escapism, the prophetic, futuristic vision and social satire. Those who inherited Wells' mantle include Isaac Asimov, Brian Aldiss, Stephen Leacock and George Orwell. And the implications of their writing still need to be taken as seriously as the significance of Wells' *Invisible Man.*

Under a cloud
The menace of The Bomb (below) hung over science fiction for decades. Wells foresaw it, and its eventual use put an end to many writers' hopes that human wisdom would evolve as fast as technology.

JOHN GALSWORTHY

1867-1933

Rebel, social reformer and, finally, an Establishment figure, John Galsworthy was the quintessential English gentleman who became the foremost writer of his day. In his chronicles of the Forsytes, he mirrored both his own family and Victorian and Edwardian conventions and manners. As a moral campaigner, he fought against the injustices of society while remaining fast entrenched inside it. 'He would go to the stake for his opinions but he would go courteously raising his hat.'

Man of Principle

Moulded by the manners of the upper-middle class, Galsworthy was placed 'beyond the pale' by his own behaviour and by his criticism of bourgeois complacency.

John Galsworthy called his fiction 'the criticism of one half of myself by the other'. Though he attacked the class he was born into, he never gave up its formidable privileges, and in time the rebellious young man became the personification of the very society he had condemned.

WEALTH AND STATUS

He was born on 14 August 1867 at Kingston Hill in Surrey, the second of John and Blanche Galsworthy's four children. His mother was by all accounts a rather fussy, narrow-minded woman, tolerated rather than liked by the family. His father, the model for old Jolyon in *The Forsyte Saga,* was a solicitor in the City of London who maintained lucrative business interests. Galsworthy idolized him – 'I was so truly and deeply fond of him that I seemed not to have a fair share of love left to give my mother', he wrote.

The family enjoyed the fruits of 'old' John Galsworthy's wealth in 'that moneymaker's Golden Age, the nineteenth century'. Shortly after Galsworthy's birth they moved to a large private estate at Coombe in Surrey, the original of Soames' grand home, Robin Hill. Galsworthy's father had no fewer than three houses built within the walled gardens of Coombe, and the family lived in them in rotation, while the young Galsworthy had the run of the pastures and woodlands of the estate. It was a privileged and idyllic childhood.

At the age of nine, Galsworthy went to Saugeen prep school in Bournemouth, and five years later, in 1881, to the famous public school Harrow,

Out of town
Old John Galsworthy needed to live near London, but believed in bringing up children in good country air. Near Richmond (right), he built an ugly Gothic mansion called Coombe Warren (below) and two other houses. The family spent time at all three.

Ill-matched parents
Blanche Galsworthy (left), according to her son, 'had no speculation in her soul'. Conscious of having married beneath her, she was soon at odds with husband and family, tolerated rather than liked. John Galsworthy senior, however, inspired admiration and love. He is pictured right with his grandson, Rudolf Sauter, who was to become trustee of the novelist's literary works.

Key Dates

1867 born in Surrey
1890 called to the Bar
1891-94 travels worldwide
1895 affair with Ada
1905 marries Ada
1906 *The Man of Property*
1911 affair with Margaret Morris
1916 serves in French hospital
1932 Nobel Prize
1933 dies, Hampstead

The foreign trips his father sent him on between 1891 and 1894 – to Canada, the South Seas, and Russia – did little to concentrate his mind, or cure him of his love for Sybil Carr, as old John had hoped. Indeed, though Sybil did finally fade from the scene, Galsworthy was now adamant that neither law nor commerce was right for him – 'It does seem to me so beastly dull to go on grinding at a profession or business just to make money', he wrote. It was at this time that his elder sister Lilian began to exert a liberating influence on him.

'WHY DON'T YOU WRITE?'

An intelligent and free-thinking woman, Lilian had grown sharply critical of her parents' values and assumptions. Through her Galsworthy began to question Christianity and to move towards the sort of compassionate, humanistic view of life that came to dominate his thinking. Lilian's marriage in 1894 to the painter Georg Sauter, the son of Bavarian peasants, further influenced him. It brought into the family fold the first person Galsworthy had met whose attitudes had not been shaped by an English upper-middle-class upbringing. For the first time Galsworthy considered the possibility of becoming a writer – a somewhat bohemian profession for someone of his class. 'I do wish I had the gift of writing. I really think that is the nicest way of making money going.'

Galsworthy's future wife, Ada, is credited with hardening this vague hope into a consuming ambition. She claimed that a throwaway remark by her at a Paris railway station 'gave the first impetus towards the literary calling of John Galsworthy'. Certainly Ada's influence – for good and ill – cannot be overestimated.

She and Galsworthy had first met at a family party to celebrate her marriage to Galsworthy's cousin, Arthur. It was a deeply unhappy marriage, one she had agreed to only in order to escape the misery of her unfortunate past (she had been born illegitimate), and she was soon confiding her

where he had 'on the whole a happy time'. According to his headmaster he was 'a quiet, modest, unassuming boy' who 'made his mark both in work and play, without affording any notable promise of distinction in after-life'.

Indeed, when Galsworthy went up to New College, Oxford, in 1886 to read Law, he looked set on the sort of respectable career usually followed by the sons of the upper-middle class. He cared little for intellectual pursuits and was an indifferent student – his favourite pastime at Oxford was gambling on the horses.

FOR LOVE, NOT MONEY

By this time the family had moved into London, to Cambridge Gate on the edge of Regent's Park. Galsworthy divided his college holidays between Cambridge Gate and the country houses of Oxford friends, through whom he met and fell in love with a singing teacher called Sybil Carr. Although he was ardently attached to her, it was not a match that pleased his family.

Galsworthy left Oxford in 1889 with a second class degree in Law and was called to the Bar the following year. He was little suited to the law, however, and pursued it only to please his father – 'I read in various Chambers, practised almost not at all, and disliked my profession thoroughly'.

Harrow's athletic hero
John was head of house and captain of the House Football XI (above). He was rated a capable pupil, although 'weak in composition'.

unhappiness to Galsworthy's sisters, Lilian and Mabel. The harrowing details of her marriage, as related by his sisters, excited first Galsworthy's compassion and, in time, his love. He and Ada began to meet in secret, and in September 1895, when Ada was 30 and Galsworthy 28, they became lovers.

His affair with Ada was to invite the stern censure of the English Establishment, obliging him to resign from his London club and the various directorships secured him by his father. But his love for Ada and his desire to compensate for the miseries of her past were profound. She repaid him with unstinting support for the writing career he decided on after giving up the law for good in 1895.

PERSONAL AND PUBLIC TRIUMPHS

Galsworthy's writing apprenticeship was slow and painful, his early efforts shallow and amateurish – 'For . . . eleven years, I made not one penny out of what I, but practically no others, counted as my profession', he recalled. He was fortunate in having as friend and mentor the influential critic Edward Garnett, then the centre of a group of up-and-coming writers.

It was Galsworthy's burning resentment of the way he and Ada were ostracized for daring to love one another that fuelled his best writing and found its most assured artistic expression in *The Man of Property*, published in March 1906. By this time old John Galsworthy had died, Ada had obtained a divorce from Arthur, and she and Galsworthy had married, after ten long years. The year 1906 marked a peak of artistic achievement for Galsworthy. The enthusiastic reception of *The Man of Property* – 'Book successful . . . excellent reviews', he noted – was followed up by the success of his stage play *The Silver Box*, which closed on a note of triumph in 1907 when the Prince and Princess of Wales attended the last night's performance.

The Galsworthys spent much of their time together on the move, from London to the Devon farmhouse, Wingstone, that Galsworthy loved so much, to Littlehampton and, in the winter, Italy, the south of France or further afield. This itinerant lifestyle was largely for the benefit of Ada's

New College, Oxford
Galsworthy went up to Oxford (above) to read Law in 1886. He was remembered as 'the best dressed man in College . . . withdrawn, saying little, a sensitive amused, somewhat cynical . . . spectator'.

Fact or Fiction

ADA AS IRENE

Irene in *The Forsyte Saga* is modelled on Galsworthy's wife. Ada's attempt to escape her mistaken marriage to Major Arthur Galsworthy is reflected in Irene's doomed love for Bosinney. The author assuaged his sister's worries about fictionalizing this episode by saying, 'who really knows enough or takes enough interest in us . . . to connect A with I, especially as I have changed her hair to gold?' He was wrong, of course. Major Arthur was branded a brutish, Soames-like tyrant – possibly a rapist (as Ada certainly portrayed him). But general opinion knew him for a quiet, pleasant man with a consuming interest in the army.

health. She suffered from asthma and rheumatism and became increasingly sickly after their marriage. Galsworthy nursed her devotedly. They were a very private couple, rather stiff and formal with all but very close friends, and they could not easily forget how society had shunned them.

Nevertheless they were rapidly becoming public figures and Galsworthy began to support a variety of causes in accordance with his passionate beliefs. Always a sensitive soul, distressed by the slightest suffering – whether human or animal – he wrote a flood of articles on issues as diverse as the censorship of plays, women's suffrage, the docking of horses' tails and pigeon shooting.

CAMPAIGNS FOR REFORM

The most successful of these campaigns concerned the practice of solitary confinement in prisons. From his Devon farmhouse Galsworthy made, in 1907, the first of several visits to Dartmoor Gaol and during the next two years completed a rigorous schedule of prison visits throughout the country. His play *Justice,* produced in 1910, was the spearhead of these efforts to effect prison reform. 'It has cost me much peace of mind', he wrote, but his efforts were not in vain. The impact of *Justice* helped force through new legislation that significantly reduced solitary confinement in English prisons.

The philanthropist in Galsworthy was now coming into conflict with the artist. The problem was compounded by Ada's increasingly possessive demands on his time and energies, and brought to crisis point by his affair with a young dancer called Margaret Morris. Margaret was 19 and Galsworthy 43 when he invited her to choreograph and appear in his play *The Little Dream.* At first Ada

Thwarted lover
John's first love did not meet with family approval and he was packed off to Russia (above), partly on family business, partly to forget her. For all the scandal of their premarital 'affair', John and Ada's love had little physical expression. In early middle age (left) his love for the young 'expressive' dancer Margaret Morris (right) shook him to the core. They quickly admitted to the affair, and Ada purported to understand his need for sexual fulfilment. But her 'suffering' persuaded John to break with Margaret entirely. After he had done so, Ada ended all sexual relations.

Seeking distractions
To escape the misery of his broken love affair, Galsworthy sailed with Ada to America (above), there to produce his play, The Pigeon, *and to gratify Ada's continual need for diversion. He later assuaged his guilt at not serving in World War I, by training as a masseur and working in France in Bénévole Hospital, to speed the rehabilitation of wounded soldiers (right). Galsworthy is seated, far left.*

was as taken as her husband with the beautiful and talented dancer, and the Galsworthys helped set her up in her own dance school in London. But slowly, in the course of their professional collaboration, and to the great astonishment of both, Galsworthy and Margaret Morris fell in love.

PASSION SUPPRESSED

The final section of his novel *The Dark Flower* recounts with great frankness the history of their doomed passion. Ada put on a brave face when she found out about it, and for a time Galsworthy and Margaret hoped against hope that Ada might agree to share her husband's love. But Galsworthy knew that his love for Margaret could continue only at the expense of Ada's health and happiness.

The affair was effectively ended by his agonized decision to leave the country with Ada. They went first to Paris, then the south of France, then to America, where he was warmly greeted by his reading public. He and Margaret wrote each other frequent letters which showed that their love burned hotter than ever, but Galsworthy's mind was firmly made up – 'You *must* not be unhappy – do you hear, my dear – you must not, because it makes me unhappier', he chided her.

The affair was over, but its repercussions were not so easily dismissed. The trust between Galsworthy and Ada had been shattered and their marriage would continue on much less intimate terms. In rejecting the youthful passion of Margaret Morris he had also chosen to stifle the emotional side of himself, and his writing suffered.

The outbreak of World War I three years later came as a shattering blow to Galsworthy's belief in the essential goodness of humankind. He felt miserably guilty that at the age of 47 he was too old to fight, so for most of the next four years he wrote at a frantic pace and donated the bulk of his earnings to the war effort. He signed over the family house at Cambridge Gate as a rest home for wounded soldiers and at the end of 1916 he and Ada looked after disabled soldiers in a convalescent hospital in France. Still the guilt was not quite exorcized – 'I'm beginning to feel I'm not pulling my weight', he wrote.

In 1917 he turned down the offer of a knighthood from the Prime Minister, Lloyd George – 'I say Literature is its own reward' – though 12 years later he did accept the Order of Merit. He was now a distinguished man of letters, a pillar of the Establishment of which he had once been so critical. With the purchase of Grove Lodge, an impressive house in Hampstead, and, a few years later, Bury House, a 15-bedroom mansion near Pulborough in Sussex, Galsworthy became truly and ironically a man of property like Soames.

In the early post-War years Galsworthy wrote some of his most commercially successful work, including the second and third novels of *The Forsyte Saga – In Chancery* and *To Let.* The *Saga* was a bestseller on both sides of the Atlantic.

THE PEN CLUB

The international writers' club PEN was inaugurated on 6 October 1921 by Mrs Dawson Scott, and John Galsworthy was its first president. He was the obvious choice: a campaigner on social and ethical issues, and a respected public figure. After World War I, he was anxious to believe once more in the stated aim of PEN: 'friendship and understanding between writers and . . . freedom of expression within and between all nations.' His presidency lasted ten years and he attended eight International Congresses, though it cost him dear to deliver an address; 'for a shy man to be the focus of a crowd is an ordeal', wrote a fellow member, on seeing him there. At the end of his life, Galsworthy donated his Nobel Prize money – £9,000 – to a PEN trust fund to further the cause to which he so firmly adhered.

Artist's immortality
In his last years, honours were heaped on Galsworthy, the man of letters (left). His ashes were scattered by his nephew on the Sussex Downs (below).

Despite this public acclaim, despite the honorary degrees showered on him from Princeton to Oxford, from Dublin to Cambridge, and the constant requests for lectures and public appearances, Galsworthy was increasingly unhappy with his work, afflicted by a gnawing sense of failure – 'I feel absolutely without hope of ever writing anything worth reading again', he wrote in 1920.

COUNTRY SQUIRE

At Bury House, purchased in 1926, he settled down to the sort of life that, like his fiction, harked back to the pre-War era. 'Now nearly bald with a forehead more terrifically domed than ever', he spent his time horseriding on Bury Hill, playing croquet on the lawn and tennis with house guests. He became a benevolent father figure to the local community, paying small weekly pensions to the poorer families and building cottages for his gardeners and domestic staff.

He was already a dying man when he was awarded literature's highest honour, the Nobel Prize, in 1932. For six months he had lived the life of a recluse, struck dumb by attacks of stuttering, shunning the light after a blemish appeared on his nose, yet stubbornly refusing to see a doctor for fear of alarming Ada. He never delivered the speech he drafted for the Nobel award ceremony in Stockholm – by then he was too ill to travel.

John Galsworthy slipped into a coma on the night of 30 January 1933 and died the following morning at home in Hampstead, from a brain tumour. He was 65. He was cremated and his ashes scattered over Bury Hill.

All her married life, the fragile Ada had expected to die first and to be helped through her last days by John. So distraught and enraged was she at his seeming desertion of her that she burned many of his papers. She could not, however, destroy his lasting fame.

The Theatre of Ideas

Edwardian theatre was slow to rise to the challenge of social comment. Then came a new breed of playwrights who drew audiences with realistic controversial drama concerning ordinary people.

In 1906 Galsworthy completed his first play, *The Silver Box*. His friend and mentor, Edward Garnett, immediately recommended it for the Royal Court Theatre in Chelsea. There, J. E. Vedrenne and Harley Granville-Barker were achieving the impossible – attracting large and fashionable audiences to new, daring, experimental plays of the kind formerly confined to small, amateur productions. Granville-Barker was one of the angry young men of the Edwardian theatre, and his work at the Royal Court challenged the Establishment with the new 'Theatre of Ideas', or 'Theatre of the Real'.

During Victoria's reign, the stage was dominated by actor-managers who directed their own companies and usually played the leading parts themselves. The emphasis was on entertainment – this was the heyday of the music hall and burlesque. And even in 'legitimate' theatre the style of acting was mannered and highly artificial. Writers were expected to deliver a regular ration of 'fat' parts and star moments per play, each act ending with a suitably momentous curtain-line and tableau. The more special effects and clichés the better, and any dramatic meaning was drowned out in greasepaint.

There had been no attempt to tackle topical, contentious subjects – no references to the impact of Darwinism, to the struggles of the new trades unions, or to the emerging women's emancipation movement. The serious, even sensational issues

Prophet of gloom
Henrik Ibsen (right) has been called 'the father of modern drama' because he was first to use the stage to debate contemporary social dilemmas, as in his best known play, about a claustrophobic marriage, A Doll's House *(below).*

Fringe to mainstream
Ibsenites – young, enthusiastic intellectuals inspired by Ibsen – seized on the idea of theatre as a political force. But it took a generation of playwrights remarkable for its flair, daring and talent to bring this kind of play from private performance to public platform. A trip to the theatre (above) became both a social event and stimulating opportunity for education and contentious debate.

Diet of froth
Up until the turn of the century, the theatre-going public were accustomed to a diet of light, undemanding entertainment – music hall, burlesque (left), smoking concerts, operettas, melodramas and sitting-room comedies. There was a clear class division between the bawdy, raucous night out for the working classes and the elegant social occasion enjoyed by the furred and bejewelled wealthy. Shakespearian works were the only survivors from a more edifying age, and they were frequently edited and 'improved upon' and made a vehicle for star names mounting 'virtuoso' performances.

addressed in contemporary novels (including Galsworthy's) were simply not the stuff of Victorian theatre, which fed the public on a diet of melodrama and drawing-room, 'cup-and-saucer' comedies.

Harley Granville-Barker was an actor-manager, but one cast in a new mould. He had a very different approach to the plays he directed at the Royal Court. His actors had to unlearn all the florid mannerisms and learn a new, naturalistic technique, with subtlety of movement, facial expression and gesture. The plays had to work without virtuoso set-pieces and, most important, had to have a social message.

Two towering figures dominated the Theatre of Ideas. Their technique for stirring the social conscience could hardly have been more different – one harrowing the very souls of his audiences with bleak, remorseless tragedies, the other more often impaling his audience on shafts of wit and making them laugh their own and society's folly to scorn.

Henrik Ibsen, the great Norwegian playwright, died in the very year of Galsworthy's theatre debut. Ibsen's plays were gloomy masterpieces offering 'Lessons' on the hypocrisy and dual standards of society. He took for his subjects, for example, the role of women in society and the consequences of inherited syphilis. When Ibsen's *A Doll's House* was first performed in London in 1889 it triggered a major debate on the inadequacies of the commerical theatre. 'Ibsenites' – young enthusiasts for the new plays – got together in clubs called Saturday Night Societies to perform works by their hero.

THEATRICAL COLOSSUS

George Bernard Shaw, a fervent apostle of Ibsen's, grew to be the true colossus of the new theatre. By the time of his death, at the age of 94 in 1950, this Irish writer was one of the most famous men in Britain. He began his literary career as a novelist, without success. But he also worked as a critic, of music and drama. In fact, he wrote his first play in collaboration with William Archer,

Granville-Barker
His prodigious talent made him a male lead at 20, a theatre manager before he was 30. He made the Royal Court a rostrum from which a new breed of actor expressed new ideas.

foremost critic of the exaggerated actor-manager style of drama. Archer was responsible for translating Ibsen into English, and it was he who made Shaw an Ibsenite.

Shaw was a highly political animal. He was a leading Fabian socialist who delighted in controversy. He almost teased the media with paradoxical, deliberately shocking comments on matters of public interest. Even without his literary statements, Shaw would have been famous as a personality – everyone knew of the Jaeger suits he wore as an exponent of the 'rational dress movement', and of his vegetarianism. The word 'Shavian' entered the language as an adjective describing ironic wit. But at first, his plays were simply not staged.

THE SILVER BOX

In the 1890s, Shaw earned more money from the foreign rights of his plays than he had from productions in England. Denied the proper outlet for his plays, he published two volumes of them in 1898 under the title *Plays Pleasant and Unpleasant,* including unusually full stage directions, so that the reader could imagine an ideal production. Shaw revelled in dramas dealing with such issues as slum landlordism, prostitution and the archaic marriage laws which enslaved women. In the preface to *Plays Unpleasant* he wrote: 'I must . . . warn my readers that my attacks are directed against themselves, not against my stage figures.'

Granville-Barker established Shaw as a performed playwright in Britain by staging his plays at the Royal Court. In his early twenties he had already played the lead in several of Shaw's plays, and he was still in his twenties when he staged Galsworthy's *The Silver Box.* Galsworthy approved of Shaw, and Shaw approved of *The Silver Box,* but the two men were very different writers and individuals.

Courting success
Harley Granville-Barker, George Bernard Shaw and Galsworthy were united by their work for the Royal Court. They are seen above (left to right) at Galsworthy's farmhouse.

George Bernard Shaw
A shy, eccentric mystic, Shaw (below) ironically cut a flamboyant, provocative figure, with notoriously progressive views. His plays are witty and thought-provoking.

Although not funny, like Shaw's *Pygmalion,* or witty like *Man and Superman,* it is easy to see why *The Silver Box* found favour with the Theatre of Ideas, and why it was accepted by the Royal Court. The valuable box in question belongs in the home of a wealthy Liberal Member of Parliament to which the dissolute young son of the family returns drunk after an evening spent with a prostitute. With him, equally drunk, is Jones, the out-of-work husband of the household's cleaning lady. The embittered Jones, in a spontaneous act of resentment at young Jack Barthwick's opulent lifestyle, removes the silver box. The charwoman is the first to be suspected of theft, and when the box is duly found in Jones' tenement room, the couple are arrested for theft. But it soon becomes clear to the senior Barthwick, the MP, that the legal proceedings may expose his son's scandalous behaviour.

In the last Act, set in a London police court, money, connections and privilege are used to put Jones in prison and muzzle the Press. As Barthwick junior swaggers away, Mrs Jones, who has been left to look after her children alone, appeals to his father's conscience, and is shaken off.

The play's point is that there is one law for the rich and one for the poor. The dissolute Barthwick has absolutely no redeeming qualities. But the most disturbing thing for the Edwardian audience was the depressing, unresolved ending. As one critic wrote, *The Silver Box* was not a cheerful play, 'but if you neglect to see it you will probably miss seeing a play which will continually be quoted when the new school of dramatists has been established.' New repertory companies who were introducing the Theatre of Ideas to other

British cities immediately included Galsworthy's dramas in their repertoires. The Liverpool Rep. began life with a production of *Strife,* Galsworthy's play about industrial relations.

A major obstacle stood in the way of this new school of dramatists: censorship. It was an obstacle which had never hampered the old-style plays, simply because there was rarely any strong meat in them. Shaw's 'unpleasant play', *Mrs Warren's Profession,* on the other hand, revolves around the discovery by a respectable young heiress that her mother is a former prostitute whose fortune derives from a string of continental brothels. It was written and published in the 1890s, but because of censorship could not be professionally produced until 1925.

Then Edward Garnett's play *The Breaking Point* suffered mutilation at the hands of the Lord Chamberlain's officials, in the summer of 1907. A few months later, Granville-Barker's play *Waste* was censored. Their mutual friend Galsworthy was roused to action.

WRITERS AGAINST CENSORSHIP

His status as a leading man of letters meant that he was better placed than many of his fellow dramatists to launch a campaign against insensitive and arbitrary censorship. The first concerted protest took the form of a letter signed by three leading writers of the day: Galsworthy, Gilbert Murray and J. M. Barrie. It was sent to every writer of standing in the country, to elicit their support for a change in the law. When 71 writers had cooperated, the Prime Minister was obliged to take notice – or at least to make a show of doing so. An anti-censorship deputation was received at Downing Street. Optimistically, the writers set about drafting a Parliamentary Bill to reform the mechanism of censorship and to allow some means of appeal. Galsworthy contributed to this campaign a powerfully written pamphlet sarcastically entitled *A Justification of the Censorship of Plays.* When a Parliamentary Committee was set up to investigate the whole question, Galsworthy was a star witness. After elaborate deliberations, this Parliamentary Committee produced a report . . . which had no practical effect whatsoever.

In the long run, the censors' teeth were drawn by time rather than protest. After conventional 'Victorian' society had been shattered by World War I, the arrogant liberties taken by Edwardian Lords Chamberlain became unthinkable.

But, for Galsworthy, the whole protest had been a weary, demoralizing experience. Years later, in 1931, when his support was sought for

Prisoners' plea
Galsworthy campaigned for improved conditions for prisoners (above). Though political agitation achieved little, his 1910 play Justice *had such impact that legislation followed as a direct result. In the play, a fundamentally good man is destroyed pointlessly and unthinkingly by the legal system and by those who enforce it. Routine solitary confinement was the prime target for Galsworthy's scathing attack.*

Contrasting styles
Galsworthy's first play, The Silver Box *(left), is a serious and sober examination of how the law serves the purposes of the rich and crushes the poor beneath its remorseless wheels. Shaw's 1912 play* Androcles and the Lion *(right) claims that in order for life to be worth living, it must contain something worth dying for. Ultimately, Shaw's wit and lightness of touch gave a longer lasting appeal to his plays than the earnestness of other writers, though Galworthy's do warrant revival.*

another campaign against censorship, he replied, 'I have become reconciled to the evil as the least violent form of interference. Therefore if my opinion must be given, I should say leave the matter alone. For nothing anyway will come of a protest.' It was a sad admission of defeat.

Outside the theatre, the pleas of the new playwrights carried little weight. But inside the theatre, as Galsworthy proved himself, it was a different story. He was a great campaigner for prison reform – particularly in the matter of solitary confinement. This was a fact of life for all prisoners at the time. It was imposed for three months on first-time offenders and nine months of the year on habitual offenders. On his repeated visits to prison, particularly Dartmoor and Lewes, Galsworthy saw for himself the pointless and physically devastating effect of this form of punishment. What was the object of driving criminals mad? It was as inhumane as it was counter-productive.

Galsworthy tackled the problem in his most powerful play, *Justice,* a searing account of how one ordinary criminal, a man called Falder, who is guilty of altering a cheque, endures solitary confinement.

CAMPAIGNING FOR JUSTICE

While he wrote, Galsworthy campaigned, too. He used his status to get into the prisons and talk to prisoners. He wrote letters to the Press and initiated a public debate. He lobbied important officials of the prison service as well as leading politicians. With all this activity, he was unintentionally building up the pre-publicity for the play (directed by Granville-Barker in 1910). After enduring the agony of Falder (who commits his crime to help a woman being brutalized by her husband), the audience was stunned. The whole issue of solitary confinement was on the agenda for reform. *Justice*'s impact can be compared with that of the dramatized documentary *Cathy Come Home* on the housing question in the 1960s.

During his campaign, the Home Secretary, Herbert Gladstone, had told Galsworthy that solitary confinement would be reduced to three months for all offenders. After the play, the new Home Secretary, Winston Churchill, told Galsworthy that further reductions were being put into effect.

Gilbert Murray was quick and generous with praise. 'It is a fine thing to have achieved, a really great thing. Does not real life seem a tremendous thing as compared with art when one gets the two together? I mean, how much greater it is to have saved a lot of men and women from two months' solitary confinement than to have sent any number of over-fed audiences into raptures.'

For all Murray's kindly meant sentiments, Galsworthy wanted to be both a great playwright and a successful reformer. When asked whether he would prefer *Justice* to become a theatrical classic without any practical results, or to be forgotten as a play but achieve great reforms, the honest artist in him had to opt for enduring fame.

By the late 1920s, Galsworthy's plays had become perfectly acceptable for commercial theatres in the West End. Avant-garde drama was in the hands of Expressionists, Nihilists, the cult of the Absurd . . . Ironically, its actors had reverted to unrealistic dialogue and stylized techniqes. These new modernists were scornful of the stale, merely 'photographic' Theatre of the Real, forgetting what priceless ground it had won.

New ideas

One well-known survivor of the Theatre of Ideas is Shaw's Pygmalion*; in the 1920s, the celebrated actress Mrs Patrick Campbell made the part of Eliza Doolittle her own (above). Modern audiences, however, have preferred to see didactic drama watered down with glamour and frivolity and to watch* Pygmalion *in the gilded disguise of* My Fair Lady. *As early as the 1930s, a newer, brighter theatre swept aside the Theatre of Ideas, which some critics thought worthy but slow-moving. Bertolt Brecht's* The Threepenny Opera *(above right) was as intellectually stimulating as Galsworthy or Shaw, but it was also extremely colourful, incorporating lively songs. It completely rejected the idea that drama should mirror reality, and Brecht's stylized approach had an enormous influence on the up-and-coming generation of young dramatists.*

W. SOMERSET MAUGHAM

1874 – 1965

A succession of grim early experiences drove Maugham to conclude that Life has no logic to it – no intrinsic meaning. He decided, therefore, to make the most of his talent while enjoying himself to the full. He was medic and bohemian, playwright and novelist, ambulance driver and spy – even his sex life was a search for variety. Although the critics dismissed his work, his readers disagreed, rating him the world over as the supreme storyteller, talented, versatile and engrossing.

Exiled in Splendour

Escaping England's confines and strictures, Maugham settled in the South of France to a life of opulence.

In *The Summing Up*, written in 1938, Somerset Maugham looked back on his life and at the obstacles he had had to overcome. "I had many disabilities. I was small, I had endurance but little physical strength; I stammered; I was shy; I had poor health." But he also "somewhat early . . . made up my mind that, having but one life, I should like to get the most I could out of it." And this he accordingly did, travelling all over the world in search of adventure.

Chère Maman
Renowned for her sweetness and good looks, Edith Maugham (left) had 'an air of romance and tragedy about her', an impression which she unfortunately fulfilled. Always frail, she died of tuberculosis six days after William's eighth birthday. He treasured her memory and kept her portrait in his bedroom until the day he died.

William Somerset Maugham entered the world on 25 January 1874 on the second floor of the British Embassy in Paris. By this quirk of being born on 'British soil', Maugham would be exempt from doing French military service. His father, Robert Ormond Maugham, was a solicitor attached to the Embassy, a man renowned both for his kindness and for his ugliness. Maugham's mother, Edith Mary, was small, over 20 years younger than her husband and as beautiful as he was ugly. They were known, affectionately, as 'Beauty and the Beast', and Maugham's earliest memories of the two of them were almost painfully happy ones.

Born into an upper-middle-class family, Maugham lived in considerable comfort and style. Although he was the fourth son in the family, his brothers were at boarding school much of the time and Maugham often thought of himself as an only child. An imaginative and clever boy, he admired his father, adored his mother, and then suddenly, just after his eighth birthday, his happy world came to an abrupt and traumatic end. His mother, frail from tuberculosis, died after giving birth to a fifth child, who also died. And then two years later, in 1884, Maugham's father died 'of cancer

On British soil
Maugham's life began in relative opulence in Paris (below) on 25 January 1874, born to a lawyer father and society mother; the venue was the second floor of the British Embassy (below left). By being born on what was legally deemed British soil, Maugham and others like him would later be exempted from doing French military service.

Canterbury schooldays
From 1885 to 1889 Maugham was a boarder at King's School in the grounds of Canterbury Cathedral (left). Founded in the fifth century, it was the oldest school in England but its proud history was of little consolation to Maugham. He missed his parents, felt rejected by his uncle, and isolated from the other boys by his stammer. He was a good student, however, and came first in his class in 1886.

and grief'. Like his fictional counterpart in *Of Human Bondage,* the desolate boy was despatched to England to live with an uncle, the Reverend Henry MacDonald Maugham, vicar of Whitstable in Kent, and his German-born wife. According to Maugham his uncle and aunt were a joyless couple, strict, stern and penny-pinching. Already in their fifties when Maugham went to live with them, they were childless and seemingly insensitive to the boy's needs. Maugham spoke little English. He was desperately unhappy and developed a stammer which he was never able to master. Like Philip Carey's club-foot in *Of Human Bondage,* Maugham's speech impediment was a lifelong source of humiliation.

The vicarage
After the warmth and comfort of Paris, the vicarage (below right) in Whitstable, Kent, seemed a harsh substitute. Maugham's aunt and uncle were elderly, childless, set in their ways and ill-equipped as foster-parents. Maugham, then aged ten (below left), was painfully aware of their limitations and petty meannesses.

He escaped from the meanness of the vicarage by becoming a boarder at King's School, Canterbury; but this proved an even worse fate. William hated it. He was bullied mercilessly and mocked for his stammer and his ineptitude at games. Missing his mother, he threw himself into his studies with the hope of going to Cambridge later. But his health was poor. His mother and her sister had both died of tuberculosis, and when, aged 16, it was found that William's lungs were affected, he was sent to the south of France to recover.

IMPROPERLY EDUCATED

The loss of a year's schooling prevented Maugham from going straight to Cambridge, a matter which he later deeply regretted. Because of it, he never considered himself "properly educated". He harboured ambitions to be a writer, but he dared not voice them because writing was not a suitable occupation for a gentleman. Postponing a decision, he went to live for nine months in the German city of Heidelberg, and for the first time "tasted freedom" and "felt myself a man".

Free after eight years of misery, Maugham began to enjoy life. He attended lectures on philosophy and literature at the university. He learned to speak German fluently and was captivated by the cosmopolitan atmosphere of the city, so different from the stuffy, respectable life he had known in England. In Heidelberg he also met Ellingham Brooks, a Cambridge graduate and aspiring poet who was to become a lifelong friend, and with whom Maugham had his first homosexual liaison.

With £150 a year left to him by his father, Maugham felt himself to be independent, although the income was not enough for him to live the life of a gentleman. A career had to be cho-

Key Dates

1873 born in Paris
1882 mother dies
1884 father dies; sent to Whitstable
1892 studies at St. Thomas's Hospital
1914 joins Red Cross; meets Gerald Haxton
1915 Liza born; *Of Human Bondage*
1916 marries Syrie Wellcome
1919-26 world travels
1927 divorces Syrie
1928 buys Villa Mauresque
1940-46 lives in US
1944 Haxton dies
1965 dies at Cap Ferrat

sen. Returning to Whitstable he rejected his uncle's proposal that he enter the Church. He tried accountancy for two months and loathed it. A local doctor suggested medicine. Maugham felt no sense of vocation but agreed, excited by the prospect of living in London. Accordingly, in 1892, he entered St Thomas's Hospital as a medical student.

In his spare time Maugham read extensively, went to the theatre, visited brothels and wrote plays which, in his own words, "delved ruthlessly into the secrets of the human soul". Unable to get his plays performed, he turned his hand to fiction. The very first novel he wrote, *Liza of Lambeth*, was accepted by Fisher Unwin. Published in 1897, it drew on his experiences as an obstetric clerk in the slums of Lambeth. The book was widely reviewed and sold well. Aged 23, Maugham qualified as a doctor, and then, with a £20 advance paid to him by his publishers, he abandoned medicine and began his career as a professional writer.

Spain beckoned. "I settled down in Seville, grew a moustache, smoked Filipino cigars, learnt the guitar, bought a broad-brimmed hat with a flat crown, in which I swaggered down the Sierpes, and hankered for a flowing cape, lined with green and red velvet." After about nine months Maugham returned to London where he continued to write plays, novels and short stories. Several novels were published but none had the impact of *Liza*. Although not well-off, Maugham cultivated the air of a gentleman. He dressed well,

A taste of freedom
Maugham spent a carefree 18 months in Heidelberg (above), discovering literature, ideas, and love – in the person of John Ellingham Brooks. But he needed a profession, and in 1892 he became a medical student at St Thomas's Hospital (left).

travelled widely and socialized with the rich. He spent weekends at the country house of the society hostess Mrs. G. W. Steevens, meeting other writers and artists. He shared a flat in Victoria with his friend Walter Payne, and conducted a number of brief affairs with Payne's discarded girlfriends.

EARLY DISAPPOINTMENTS

In 1903, Maugham's first play, *A Man Of Honour*, was staged in the West End, but it was a flop. He edited a literary magazine, *The Venture*, and when it failed, moved to Paris. There, at Le Chat Blanc restaurant, he met the writers Arnold Bennett, George Moore and Clive Bell. Here too he met the painter Gerald Kelly, an Irish old-Etonian who was later to become President of the Royal Academy and one of Maugham life-long friends.

With the failure of another novel, *The Bishop's Apron,* Maugham seriously considered giving up writing altogether and becoming a ship's doctor. But his fortunes soon turned – in 1907 his play *Lady Frederick* made him the most talked-about playwright in England, and within a year he had four plays running simultaneously in the West End. With his new-found wealth he bought a

house in London's Mayfair, and in 1909 became a member of the prestigious Garrick Club.

Maugham had always craved money and status. Having achieved both he was able to live life as he wished, but there was always a certain ambivalence in his attitude to the society to which he owed his success. Mercilessly exposing the hypocrisy of upper-class English society, Maugham was himself a living example of the double standard. Fastidious, courteous and conventional, he seemed a typical Edwardian man-about-town. He conducted numerous heterosexual love affairs but in private preferred men. With the trial and subsequent vilification of Oscar Wilde still fresh in his mind, Maugham was terrified of prosecution and kept his private life secret.

When War broke out in 1914, Maugham, now aged 40, joined a Red Cross ambulance unit in France. Serving in Flanders, he met a man who was to become the love of his life, the 22-year-old American Gerald Haxton. Haxton was an adventurer, dissipated and unscrupulous. As his relationship with Maugham developed he also revealed himself to be alcoholic, violent, dishonest and unfaithful. But according to Maugham's friend Glenway Wescott, their relationship was "the first completely beautiful, completely appropriate love affair Maugham had ever had". They were to stay together, first as lovers, then Haxton assuming the role of secretary-companion, until Haxton's death in 1944.

Ironically, shortly after meeting Haxton, Maugham learned that he was going to be a father. He had met Syrie Wellcome, an elegant society woman, in 1911. She was married but separated from her husband, and for a while she and Maugham had been constant companions. On 1 September 1915 she gave birth to a daughter, Liza, Maugham's first and only child.

UNWILLING FATHER

Maugham had little desire to assume the responsibilities of a husband and father. When invited by Sir John Wallinger, head of British intelligence in France and Switzerland during World War I, to act as a link between London and agents in the field, Maugham readily agreed. Cited as co-respondent in divorce proceedings brought against Syrie by her husband, Maugham was out of the country before the case came to court.

In 1916 Maugham travelled to New York to arrange the producution of his play *Our Betters*. Pursued by Syrie, he set off for Tahiti with Gerald Haxton to gather material for another novel, based on the life of the French painter Paul Gauguin, published later as *The Moon and Sixpence*. Returning to New York in 1916 he and Syrie married. Neither had any illusions about the other. Syrie knew of his homosexuality, he of her past lovers. Despite his fear of being trapped he felt honour-bound to marry the woman who had borne his child; but Maugham had no intention of being a

War duties
With his knowledge of languages and training as a doctor, Maugham joined the Red Cross Ambulance unit (below) in 1914. He witnessed the ravages of war both in France and in Flanders.

Gerald Haxton
It was while with the Red Cross that Maugham met the handsome extrovert Gerald Haxton (left). A charming, dissolute American, he was to be the love of Maugham's life for the next 30 years.

SYRIE WELLCOME

Born in 1879, Syrie Barnardo was the daughter of the well-known philanthropist Dr Thomas Barnardo, founder of the homes for homeless and orphaned children. At 22 Syrie married the 48-year-old Henry Wellcome of Wellcome pharmaceuticals fame. When Maugham met her in 1911 she was separated from her husband and leading a hectic social life, courted by, among others, Gordon Selfridge of Selfridges department store. She had a child by Maugham – Liza – and was married to him for 11 years while Maugham flitted between her and Gerald Haxton. Although Maugham often maligned her, Syrie was a bright, talented woman who made a brilliant career for herself as an interior decorator.

Dangerous adventures
Maugham's and Haxton's boat capsized when journeying up the Sarawak River in Borneo (right). They nearly drowned, and Haxton suffered a heart attack.

dutiful husband and father. During the eleven years of their marriage Maugham was absent for much of the time, travelling abroad with Gerald Haxton. He felt he had little in common with his wife, regarded her career as an interior designer as socially demeaning and later complained to a friend, Glenway Westcott, that Syrie's "physical demands were intolerable, inexcusable".

After the anticlimax of his marriage, Maugham was again recruited into the ranks of British Intelligence. Armed with a large amount of gold, Maugham's mission was to buy off the Social Democratic government of Alexander Kerensky and keep Russia in the War on the side of the Allies. Maugham met Kerensky and was later to claim that, had he been sent to Russia six months earlier, he might have prevented the Bolshevik uprising. As it was, he was unable to elicit sufficient support to keep Kerensky in power. Soon after his return Maugham, with another bout of tuberculosis, entered Banchory Sanatorium at Kincardine, near Aberdeen in Scotland. During his three-months stay he wrote a play, *Home and Beauty*, and began making notes for his next novel.

FAME AND FORTUNE

With the end of the War Maugham entered into an intensely productive period. The success of *The Moon and Sixpence* in 1919 propelled him into being one of the best-known, most widely read and highly paid authors writing in English. At the end of 1919 he returned to the South Seas with Gerald Haxton, moving on to China, the Malay states and Indo-China before returning to the family home in London for a brief visit.

Throughout the 1920s Maugham's restless globe-trotting continued. In 1922 he visited the South Seas yet again. In 1923 he was in Ceylon and Burma and in 1924 Mexico, where he met D. H. Lawrence at a luncheon party. With a succession of box-office hits running in the West End – including *The Unknown, The Circle, East of Suez* and *Our Betters* – Maugham was now a rich man. In 1927 he and Syrie were officially divorced. Although they were in many ways unsuited to one another, Maugham's continuing relationship with Haxton was at the root of the divorce. Free again, Maugham bought a villa at Cap Ferrat on the French Riviera, where he was to live, apart from the war years, for the rest of his life.

Cap Ferrat is a peninsula which juts into the Mediterranean between Nice and Monte Carlo. In the Villa Mauresque, built by a Belgian King in the 19th century for one of his mistresses, Maugham wrote and entertained in style. In the years before 1939, house guests included the Aga Khan, the Duke and Duchess of Windsor, H. G. Wells, Arnold Bennett, Noël Coward, J. B. Priestley, Lord Beaverbrook, Winston Churchill and

Fact or Fiction

STARVING ARTIST

It is likely that Maugham had his brother Harry in mind when he created Fanny Price in *Of Human Bondage*. She is a starving, unsuccessful artist who finally, in despair, hangs herself and is discovered in her squalid lodgings by Maugham's fictional counterpart, Philip Carey. Similarly Harry was an unsuccessful writer who in July 1904 poisoned himself with nitric acid. He lay in agony for three days before Maugham found him, but it was too late to save him.

Villa Mauresque
Maugham's home for 37 years was the splendid Villa Mauresque near Nice (below left). Here he entertained family, friends and royalty in grand style. Maugham was to sue his daughter (seen below in the swimming pool at the Villa Mauresque with her children) for the return of all the gifts he had given her. Meanwhile, he tried to adopt Alan Searle, his 60-year-old secretary and final companion as his son (below right, dining with Maugham in isolated splendour).

Rudyard Kipling. There was a valet and maid for each guest, excellent food, tennis, bridge and nude bathing. The house was always full of books, flowers and handsome young men. Although mean in many ways – it was not until he was a very old man that he would pay for a taxi when he could use public transport – Maugham was a generous host and employer.

PAINFUL LOSS

Plays, short stories and novels, including *Cakes and Ale*, appeared at regular intervals. Many of Maugham's stories were made into films, and although critics considered the writer old-fashioned and out-of-touch with the times, the reading public continued to buy his work in ever-increasing numbers. Maugham was now 59 but had the energy and stamina of a much younger man. With Haxton at his side, he continued to travel widely.

When war broke out in 1939 Maugham remained at the Villa Mauresque until the Germans invaded France in May 1940. Knowing himself to be on Dr Goebbels' death list because he had helped to secure the release of Lion Feuchtwanger, a German Jew, from French detention, Maugham escaped to England on one of the last boats to leave Nice.

After five months in England, Maugham went to America in October 1940 to join Gerald Haxton. Deprived of his home and the freedom to travel, Maugham was given a modest house by his American publisher, Nelson Doubleday, in the grounds of his estate at Parker's Ferry, South Carolina. Maugham continued writing and toured America giving speeches in support of Britain's war effort. He saw little of Haxton who was working in Washington and drinking heavily. Although their relationship had deteriorated, Maugham remained deeply attached to him and was devastated when he learnt that his friend had TB. He spent a six-month vigil at Haxton's side, writing to another friend: "All the best years of my life were connected with him. . . . They say as one grows older one feels less; I wish it were true." Haxton finally died in November 1944. He was 52 years old – 18 years younger than Maugham.

For Maugham the pain continued. Bereft without Haxton, he wanted to die himself, but gradually, with the help of his nephew Robin and his new secretary Alan Searle, he started to improve. When the war came to an end Maugham returned to the Villa Mauresque accompanied by Searle, who was to remain his constant and faithful companion until Maugham's death.

SAFEGUARDING SECRETS

Known now as the grand old businessman of English letters, Maugham was lionized wherever he went. But public acclaim no longer satisfied him. The man who at 61 had looked "forward to old age" was not enjoying it. Panic-stricken that people should learn secrets about him after his death, he held nightly 'bonfires', destroying volumes of letters and documents relating to his life. In his will he left strict instructions that his executors should do nothing which might aid a would-be biogragher.

Now in his late eighties, Maugham degenerated to the condition of his childhood, utterly dependent on Searle. As his long life drew to a close, he was consumed with bitterness. Never a kind or magnanimous man, his response to the misfortune of others was invariably "what the hell do I care?" In a series of sensational articles published in the *Sunday Express* in 1962, he told all, or almost all – hiding the essential fact of his homosexuality – about his dead wife, whom he portrayed as a malignant shrew. He tried to disinherit his daughter and adopt Alan Searle as a son. Having lost his physical faculties, Maugham finally lost his mind. On 8 December 1965 he fell in his garden at the Villa Mauresque and sank into a coma. On 15 December he died at the Anglo-American Hospital in Nice, six weeks short of his ninety-second birthday.

Secret Agents

Espionage was so unsophisticated at the time of World War I that a gentleman writer such as Maugham could be drafted into the Secret Service for missions of the highest importance.

In the preface to the short stories he based on his experiences as a secret agent Somerset Maugham wrote: "The work of an agent in the Intelligence Department is on the whole extremely monotonous. A lot of it is uncommonly useless." His involvement with espionage in World War I began in 1915, and he thus shared in the germination of British intelligence, which had existed only since 1909. The passage of time has made the true story of 1914-18 espionage hard to unravel. One thing is plain, however: at times it served to change the course of history.

The Secret Service Bureau came into being between August and October 1909. The Home Section, MO5 (later MI5), had a staff of only 19 at the beginning of the War which had risen to 344 by the end. The Foreign Secret Service Bureau (later MI1C, then SIS) was born out of an exaggerated fear of German invasion. Spy scares were rampant – as witnessed by the passing of the Official Secrets Act in 1911. But the FSSB was built of only a handful of part-time agents and vied with the better financed, professional Royal Navy's Intelligence Division, and with spying diplomats. Neither branch could afford to pay staff adequately, so they relied on employing people

Pigeon post
Carrier pigeons – used in espionage since Roman times – were an important means of communication in World War I.

Novelist and spy
Like his friend Maugham, Sir Compton Mackenzie (code-name 'Z') worked for the Secret Service during the War.

with private incomes, rewarding them with immunity from income tax!

Karl Ernst's barber's shop at 402a Caledonian Road, London, had been known by MO5, since 1910, to be the 'letter box' for German spies. So on the day War was declared, all of the 21 known German agents in Britain could be rounded up. During the War several more agents entered the country, purporting to be neutral citizens. But they seldom evaded arrest for more than a few weeks and were shot or hanged according to their military or civilian status.

Although routine counter-espionage began early, everyone thought the War would be over by Christmas. So few countries were geared up for large-scale, long-term espionage. Only as winter saw the unbroken deadlock of trench warfare set in on both Western and Eastern Fronts were spy networks built up.

The French presented the British Intelligence Corps with its first 15 homing pigeons. These would be the prime means of communicating information from behind enemy lines before the advent of portable radios. The pigeons were tolerant of shell fire and did not succumb to poison-gas as readily as human beings. By 1916 three units of pigeon handlers served in the British Courier Service (Royal Engineers), and by the end of the War 20,000 birds had joined the War effort. The security threat to Austro-Germany was so great that any civilian caught in possession of a pigeon ran the risk of being shot.

Britain, France and Belgium agreed to set up a 'joint' intelligence bureau at Folkestone on the English south coast to process agents' reports arriving from occupied Belgium and neutral Holland. The British section was run, until 1917, by a former gunner, Captain Cecil Cameron, from a house on the seafront.

INCOMPETENCE AND BETRAYAL

But Cameron's was not to be the only spy network destined for the Low Countries. Major Walter Kirke, Deputy Head of Intelligence at British Expeditionary Force GHQ established the 'WL' network in April 1915. To organize the network, Kirke picked Major Ernest Wallinger, another gunner. The well-to-do Wallinger set up office in his Knightsbridge flat, near Harrods.

Wallinger, in turn, recruited his elder brother John, an Indian Police captain, who had lost a foot in one of the battles in 1914, to run operations in neutral Switzerland. The first Swiss network collapsed through a mixture of incompetence and betrayal. The British consuls in Swiss cities proved unreliable: closely watched by Swiss police, some were accused of spying and expelled. So in September 1915 John Wallinger recruited Somerset Maugham.

John Wallinger's mistress was a friend of Maugham's own mistress and future wife, Syrie Wellcome. But Maugham had more to recommend him than that. He spoke fluent French and German (in fact he wrote his first play in German). He had private means and, as an unfit 41-year-old, was not likely to be called up. So, after one wartime career driving Red Cross ambulances on the Western Front, Maugham took up a second as a spymaster. Over in Greece, his flamboyant novelist friend Compton Mackenzie, under the code-name 'Z', received lavish funds to report to the fabled 'C' (Captain Mansfield Smith-Cumming RN, first chief of the Secret Services). By contrast, Maugham worked, unpaid, for a shoestring, temporary operation.

ESCAPE LINES

Maugham's first task was to lure into Allied territory an expatriate Englishman living in Lucerne and working for the Germans. To judge from his barely fictional short story 'The Traitor', he was successful. Once a week he crossed Lake Geneva to France to obtain London's instructions. An old woman – a vegetable-seller in the Geneva marketplace – acted as Maugham's courier.

But before December 1916, John Wallinger's Swiss network was closed down. Britain's spy agencies had decided to concentrate entirely on Holland, a nearer neutral country with laxer security. From here the Allies sustained crucial escape lines for prisoners-of-war and reported on train-movements in occupied Belgium. Nurse Edith Cavell, working in Brussels, helped scores of Allied servicemen escape, but was certainly not a spy. Her execution by the Germans on 12 October 1915 sparked worldwide outrage. Ironically, it later saved many genuine Allied female spies from the death sentence, as Germany did not dare risk more damage to its reputation.

By May 1916 the British-run 'Frankignoul' net-

A heroine's death
The nurse Edith Cavell was one of the greatest heroines of World War I – a model of courage and humanity. She was executed by the Germans for helping Allied soldiers to escape from occupied Belgium, and her killing greatly damaged the German reputation. The French illustration (bottom) shows how her death was used for anti-German propaganda.

Miss Edith Cavell

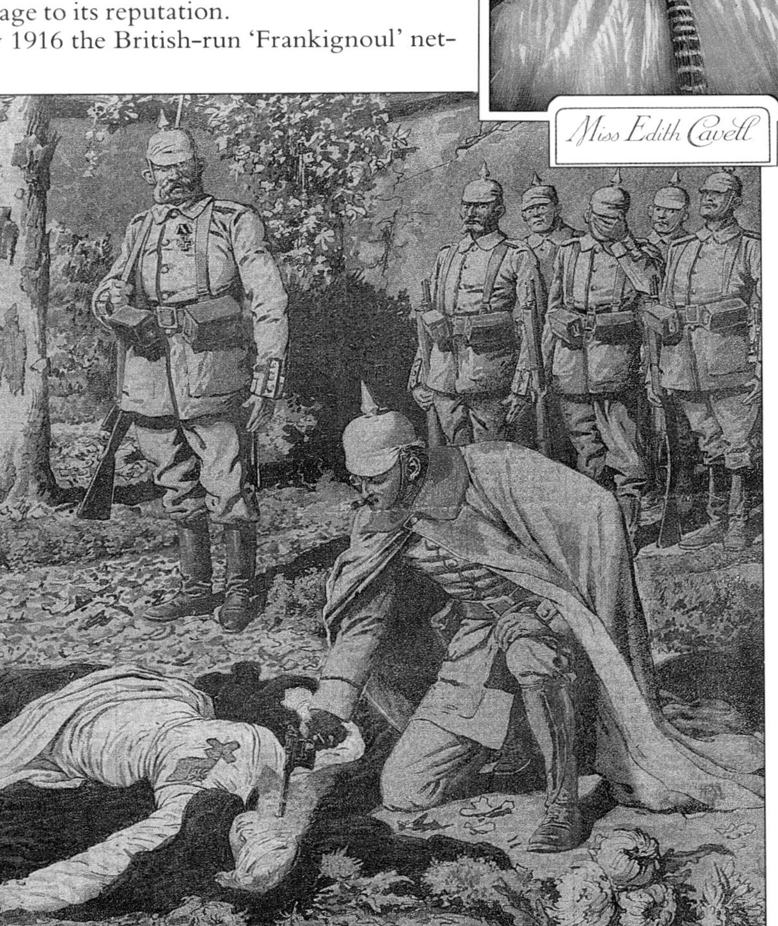

work totalled over 40 train-watching posts. But when reports were captured from the British steamer *Brussels* many arrests followed. The situation was saved by the 'Lux' espionage network organised by Belgian Catholic priests. They smuggled train-watching reports out by barge, past the double electrified fence built by the Germans along the Dutch border. In November 1917 'Lux''s prime-mover, Abbé Buellens, was finally arrested. But by then the even larger 'White Lady' (*La Dame Blanche*) network was in full operation, aided by MI1C. By Armistice, 'White Lady' had 919 agents reporting from 90 observation posts and provided 75 per cent of all Allied intelligence via neutral states.

DOUBLE AGENTS

Backing up 'White Lady', Wallinger had 11 small Belgian networks, three run by double agents. One, called 'Felix', was composed of prostitutes paid in cash and drugs. Thus British intelligence held sway over 5000 Belgian spies (seven times more than French and Belgian Intelligence combined). The Germans convicted 235 Allied agents – only three were British.

From as early as the autumn of 1915 agents were being landed in occupied territory at night by aircraft. Ten British-paid spies were even sent in by balloon early in 1917. The French parachuted agents in to Alsace, and the Allies dropped them into occupied Serbia – as they would do again in World War II. Ingeniously, baskets of carrier pigeons were dropped behind the Western Front too, by parachutes released from a mini-balloon by an alarm-clock timing mechanism. Questionnaires printed in French and Flemish were clipped to the birds' legs in small aluminium containers. At least 40 per cent returned with messages, some within ten hours.

MATA AND MARTHE

German intelligence could never compete with Allied efforts. Mata Hari (literally 'The Eye of the Dawn') was the exotic alias of Dutch dancer Margaret Gertrude Zelle. She has gone down in history as the archetypal spy-seductress, but her career in espionage is obscure and controversial. In 1917 she was arrested in Paris and charged with spying for Germany. She claimed she was a double-agent, working for France against the Germans, but she was found guilty and shot by firing squad. She certainly had many military officers among her lovers, but whether she gained – and passed on – valuable information from them is open to doubt.

By contrast, Marthe Richard, a French war widow, was of inestimable value to the Allies. She volunteered to be an agent only three weeks after her pilot husband Henri's death in action. Multilingual and the owner of a pilot's licence, she became the mistress of the German naval attaché in Madrid reporting to Paris until 1918, as her memoirs, *I Spied for France*, recall.

Meanwhile, over in America, German money was financing a desultory programme of sabotage,

Temptation
Mata Hari (right) and Marthe Richard (below) used their undoubted sex appeal as weapons in the espionage war, but with different results: Mata Hari was executed, Marthe Richard became a national heroine. Before the days of sophisticated electronics, spies used devices such as the hollow bar of chocolate (above) for carrying messages.

which had no effect except to inflame pro-Allied feelings. A mere seven agents operated there after America's entry into the War. The meagre success of German espionage generally is witnessed by the fact that its soldiers knew nothing of tanks, for example, until confronted with them on the battlefield.

THE EASTERN FRONT

It was a different matter in the East. Austro-German code-breakers were keeping effective tabs on Russian troop movements. In order to hasten capitulation of the already demoralized Russians, the German Foreign Office funded revolutionary propaganda. Their master-stroke was to ship Lenin and 32 other revolutionaries in a locked train from Switzerland to Petrograd (now Leningrad) via Sweden in April 1917.

In Petrograd a precarious Provisional Government was attempting to rule after the Tsar's abdication. Its Prime Minister was Alexander Kerensky, a brilliant socialist who had already served as Minister of Justice and War. Unlike Lenin and the Bolsheviks, he wanted to continue the War before transforming Russian society. But his summer offensive failed.

To sustain Kerensky and to prevent the feared Bolshevik coup, MI1C's man in the US, Sir William Wiseman, telephoned an old family friend – Somerset Maugham – then staying in New York. Would he go to Russia and send back information for him. After 48 hours' deliberation Maugham accepted. This time he would be working for the regular British Secret Service, with both London's and Washington's blessing. Wiseman wrung $75,000 out of each for the mission. Maugham received the fabulous sum of $21,000 in salary and expenses, and sailed from San Francisco for Tokyo on 28 July.

A 10-day journey by Trans-Siberian Railway brought Maugham to Petrograd early in September. Through the British Embassy, and in his own secret code, Maugham promptly sent lengthy reports to New York. In them, he was able to name 'the chief German agent in Russia' as Max Warburg, a Hamburg banker.

'Somerville', as Maugham code-named himself, gained speedy access to Kerensky and wined and dined the Prime Minister or other members of government at the luxury Medvied Restaurant. By 24 September, 'Somerville' was reporting that 'Lane' (Kerensky) was losing popularity and changing his mind daily about whether to move to Moscow to avoid the Bolsheviks.

'Russia . . . is just being held together by English agents', wrote the German Foreign Minister on 29 September. He may have had Maugham in mind. On 16 October, Maugham cabled Wise-

Intrigue in Russia

In 1917 Maugham travelled to Russia on an important secret mission. After a journey on the Trans-Siberian Railway (top left) he met Alexander Kerensky (above), the Prime Minister of the second provisional government before the Bolshevik October Revolution, and reported back on the unstable condition of the country. Maugham's path was smoothed by Sasha Kropotkin (inset), whom he had known in London. The daugher of a Russian anarchist prince, she was a formidable woman who became the model for the femme fatale *in one of Maugham's* Ashenden *spy stories.*

man in Washington urging $500,000 a year to be spent on promoting the Menshevik (moderate socialist) cause, and on recruiting Poles, Czechs and Cossacks to counteract 'German plots and propaganda'. The Germans were only 250 miles from Petrograd, which at this time was the Russian capital. Then Lenin returned from Finland on 20 October to persuade his comrades to organize an armed uprising without delay.

MEETING WITH LLOYD GEORGE

On 31 October Kerensky summoned 'Somerville' and gave him a message for Lloyd George. There must be an immediate Allied peace offer 'without annexation or compensation', so that a German refusal would outrage the Russian Army into fighting through another winter. Second, the Allies must regularly supply guns and ammunition. Third, Allied newspapers must be more sympathetic to the new regime. Fourth, the reactionary British Ambassador must be replaced.

Maugham left Petrograd that evening, picking up a Royal Navy destroyer at Oslo for a rough crossing to Scotland. Next morning, having written down Kerensky's message for fear his stutter impair a spoken version, Maugham presented himself at 10 Downing Street. Lloyd George read the account and replied, 'I can't do that', then promptly entered a Cabinet meeting. Forty-eight hours later, Lenin was in power and Maugham's secret service career was over.

As late as 1962 Maugham was still speculating; 'Perhaps if I had been sent to Russia six months sooner, I might have been able to do something . . .' In reality, no amount of money or espionage could have staved off the chaos which ensued. His practical achievements as a spy did not match the spectacular (if embroidered) feats of fellow novelists Compton Mackenzie or A. E. W. Mason. But his experience gave him invaluable material for the 16 *Ashenden* short stories and the 14 others he burnt because they infringed the Official Secrets Act.

Maugham was a conscientious agent, although the *Times Literary Supplement* concluded, upon reviewing his *Ashenden* stories, 'counter-intelligence work consists often of morally indefensible jobs not to be undertaken by the squeamish or the conscience-stricken'. Spy-novelist John Le Carré called Maugham 'the first person to write about espionage in a mood of disenchantment and almost prosaic reality'.

The Russian volcano
Maugham's visit to Russia in 1917 failed in its purposes: to persuade the Russian government to continue the War against Germany, and to prevent the Bolsheviks, led by Lenin (making a speech, above), from winning power. In the West the Russian Revolution seemed like a volcano erupting.

E. M. FORSTER

1879-1970

'One of the most esteemed English novelists of his time', Edward Morgan Forster was a shy, modest man. Brought up in a suburban, middle-class household, dominated by his mother and great-aunt, Forster moved on to the cloistered world of Cambridge intellectuals, before a trip to Italy triggered his first work of fiction. But it was India which inspired the masterpiece that was to be his final novel. He spent the second half of his long life as a critic and campaigner, dying at the age of 91.

Reluctant Outsider

An isolated, lonely man, Forster yearned for love in his private life, but was never at ease with public acclaim. 'I don't like popularity,' he wrote. 'It seems so mad.'

By the age of 31, and the publication of his fourth novel, *Howards End*, Edward Morgan Forster had established himself as one of the great novelists of his time. Yet he always remained a sensitive, timid and modest man for whom friendship and the life of the imagination were more important than fame.

He was born in London on 1 January 1879. His mother, Lily, had been adopted as a child by Marianne Thornton into a wealthy merchant and banking family. Marianne, or 'Monie' as she was called, had encouraged Lily to marry her favourite nephew, Edward Forster, who had taken up architecture after graduating from Cambridge. He was 29 when he married Lily, but just three-and-a-half years later he was dead from consumption, leaving behind a son who was not yet two years old.

IDYLLIC YEARS

Lily moved to a house in Stevenage, Hertfordshire, called Rooksnest. She thought the country air would be good for young Morgan's health, about which she was so obsessive that he was to reach middle age thinking of himself, quite wrongly, as frail. Rooksnest was a large house, complete with tennis court, paddock and orchard. At times Lily found it lonely there, but she and her son soon developed a deep and abiding love for the place.

There were frequent visits to Monie's home in Clapham where little Morgan was the admired and pampered darling of all the women. Talented and precocious, he discovered he could read to himself at the age of four and soon set out to improve the minds of the garden boys whom he befriended in his early years.

What he came to regard as his idyllic years at Rooksnest were spoiled when, at the age of 11, he was sent to Kent House Preparatory School in Eastbourne. The other boys jeered at him, calling him 'Mousie', and he became deeply unhappy. Life did not improve when, at the age of 14, the owner of Rooksnest refused to renew the lease and he and his mother moved to Tonbridge. Here he enrolled as a day-boy at the minor public school and acquired his life-long hatred of the public school system. A fellow pupil remembered him in the 1950s with the following words: 'Forster? . . . A little cissy. We took it out of him, I can tell you.'

At 18, Morgan went to King's College, Cambridge to read Classics and then History. Here he at last came into his own and developed a circle of friends, among them H. O. Meredith, an extremely clever man whom Forster was to later describe as 'my first great love'.

Meredith introduced Forster to the Apostles, the most exclusive intellectual society in Cambridge, which later became the nucleus of the Bloomsbury Group. Its members included Bertrand Russell, John Maynard Keynes, Lytton Strachey, Roger

Key Dates

1879 born in London

1880 father dies

1893 sent to Tonbridge School

1897 becomes student at Cambridge

1901 first trip to Italy

1905 *Where Angels Fear to Tread* published

1906 meets Syed Ross Masood

1910 *Howards End* published; acclaimed as great novelist

1912-13 visits India

1915-19 working in Alexandria

1921 second visit to India

1924 *A Passage to India* published

1930 meets Bob Buckingham

1945 mother dies

1946 moves to Cambridge

1969 awarded Order of Merit

1970 dies in Coventry

Remote father
(left) Edward Forster died before his son reached his second birthday: 'I have never seen myself in him', wrote Forster, 'and letters from him and the photographs have not helped.'

Adoring mother
Forster and his mother (seen together right) enjoyed an extraordinarily close relationship. In later life, he wrote that although she could be 'intermittently tiresome', she provided him with 'a sort of rich subsoil where I have been able to rest and grow'.

Fry, Goldsworthy Lowes Dickinson and Leonard Woolf. They openly attacked the values which Forster had learned to hate at Tonbridge – the snobbery and oppression of English provincial life – and discussed freely and easily such subjects as religion, sex and homosexuality.

This circle regarded Lytton Strachey's nickname for Forster, 'the Taupe', as apt, because 'of his faint physical resemblance to a mole, but principally because he seemed intellectually and emotionally to travel unseen underground and every now and again pop up unexpectedly with some subtle observation or delicate quip which somehow or other he had found in the depths of the earth or of his own soul'.

Forster was probably well aware by now that he was emotionally and sexually drawn to men. But, with his prim upbringing and in the wake of the Oscar Wilde scandal, he tried to contain his dark secret. It was impossible to admit to his friends that he might be homosexual, let alone imagine having physical relations with them.

Forster left Cambridge in 1901 with no definite plans for the future, except for a general hope that he could establish himself as a journalist or writer of fiction. A legacy from Monie had financed

King's College
(above) Forster enjoyed himself immensely at King's College, Cambridge. If he had been 'immature, uninteresting and unphilosophic' before he went up to King's, once there he spread his wings under the liberating influence of 'the Apostles' and others.

Childhood paradise
(right) Forster drew this map of Rooksnest, the house he called 'my childhoood and safety'. With its pond, mysterious attics and neighbouring meadow, Rooksnest was an earthly paradise for a young child. Howards End, the house in the novel of that name, is a lovingly recreated picture of this childhood home. It shares with Rooksnest the magnificent wych-elm 'leaning a little over the house'.

Italian inspiration
(above) 'Charming' San Gimignano, which Forster visited on his first trip to Italy, was the model for Monteriano in Where Angels Fear to Tread.

The Bloomsbury Group
Forster had close contacts with the Bloomsbury Group, the intellectual circle that included Virginia Woolf (centre) and her husband Leonard (right, with pipe).

his education and it now paid for his first trip to Italy, on which he was accompanied by his mother.

It was on the route south, travelling down to Naples and Sicily, that he finally wrote his first successful piece of fiction, a fantasy called *The Story of a Panic*. In writing it he trusted his imagination for the first time and became confident that he was indeed a writer. Forster and his mother had been strictly tourists – 'It was a very timid outing', he said. But the months he spent in Italy had liberated him, and helped him to find his writer's voice.

On returning to England, mother and son moved into a hotel in Bloomsbury so as to be close to the Working Men's College where Forster was to teach Latin once a week. His old friend H. O. Meredith lived nearby and the two re-established a friendship of growing affection and intimacy. For Forster, it was of immense importance – a revelation of the 'greatness' present in the world.

In 1903 Forster, along with other ex-Apostles, began to contribute to *The Independent Review*, a Liberal periodical founded to argue against Tory imperialism, and advocate social reform. The following year, having moved into a flat with his mother, Forster began a series of lectures on Italian art and history. He was kept busy, teaching and writing, and he had the ever-loving, perhaps over-loving, support of his mother. But these were lonely times for him. His friendship with Meredith had ended, and at 25 Forster felt that his life was 'straightening into something rather sad and dull'.

LIBERATING INFLUENCE

A chance of a change came when he took up an appointment in Germany as tutor to the three eldest daughters of Countess von Arnim. At first the Countess – better known as the novelist 'Elizabeth' of the best-seller *Elizabeth and her German Garden* – tried to bully and patronize Forster. But she began to realize that he was not the mousy, undistinguished person she had thought he was. And reading one of his articles in *The Independent Review* confirmed her new opinion. From that point the two got on very well and Forster enjoyed his months in Germany.

He returned to England in time for the publication of *Where Angels Fear to Tread* in October 1905, and it was not long before he met a young, handsome Indian, Syed Ross Masood, who was to become in his own way an extraordinary, liberating, influence for Forster.

Forster had been asked to tutor Masood in Latin

In Egypt . . .
(above) In the liberal atmosphere of Alexandria, where he worked during World War I, Forster at last found love – with a young Egyptian, Mohammed el Adl.

. . . and India
Forster's first trip to India in 1912-13 took in Delhi (below), where he and his friend Masood were obliged to entertain constant streams of visitors.

to prepare his entry to Oxford. He was immediately captivated by his pupil's warmth, spontaneity and effusiveness. Masood was well over six foot tall, and if a lesson bored him, he might pick Forster up bodily and tickle him. The novelist was jolted out of his Englishness, surprised and delighted by Masood's extravagances. Little by little he grew to love him, and though the sexual love was not reciprocated, a bond of genuine friendship developed between the two men.

LITERARY ACCLAIM

In 1908 *A Room With a View* was published and two years later came *Howards End*. His mother was shocked by it, but the press hailed it as the season's great novel, and the shy, reclusive Forster became a reluctant celebrity. As he wrote to Dickinson, 'I don't like popularity. It seems so mad . . . I go about saying I like the money because one is simply bound to be pleased about something on such an occasion. But I don't even like that very much . . . No, It is all insanity.'

He continued his writings, but longed to see Masood, who had recently returned to his home in Aligarh, northern India. In 1912 Forster decided to make his first visit to India. He spent two delightful weeks with Masood, first in Aligarh and then in nearby Delhi, before moving on to Lahore. There he stayed with Malcolm Darling, a former fellow-student at King's, and his wife. Lahore was Anglo-Indian land, and Forster hated it. Although the Darlings were liberal in their attitude to Indians, others were less so. It was here that Forster met the petty-minded 'Turtons and Burtons', whom he was to write about in *A Passage to India*.

Through the Darlings, Forster became the guest and friend of the 24-year-old Maharajah of Dewas State Senior. The Maharajah had a 'clever merry little face in a huge turban', and Forster liked him immediately. The two men met up again later in Delhi, and forged a friendship which was second only to Forster's friendship with Masood.

Eventually it was time to return to England, and Forster made his way back to Weybridge. It was a happy homecoming, and he felt matured and broadened by his experiences. He made several

SYED ROSS MASOOD

Forster dedicated *A Passage to India* to Syed Ross Masood. They met in 1906 and were friends for life. Masood was a striking figure, self-confident, flamboyant and extremely affectionate to all his friends. In Forster's words, he regarded the world 'as a room full of secondary persons with himself feeling intensely in the centre'. He is one of Forster's models for Aziz – just as Fielding shows many of Forster's qualities.

The grandson of the famous Muslim reformer, Sir Syed Ahmed Khan, Masood was a fervent Muslim patriot who loved to tell stories of how he had succeeded in putting down members of the British Raj. But during his years in England he acquired a large circle of English friends and after leaving Oxford he returned to India with much reluctance.

Here he married in 1915 and was given an administrative post by the Nizam of Hyderabad. Following the collapse of his marriage, and then of his finances in the world stock market crash of 1929, he took the post of Vice-Chancellor of the Anglo-Oriental College. Out-manoeuvred by his enemies, he felt forced to resign, a blow from which he never fully recovered. He died from kidney disease in 1937, aged 47.

In Forster's obituary tribute to Masood, he wrote: 'My own debt to him is incalculable. He woke me up out of my suburban and academic life, showed me new horizons and a new civilization . . . Until I met him, India was a vague jumble of rajahs, sahibs, babus and elephants . . .'

pilgrimages to the author Edward Carpenter at the house he shared in Millthorpe in Derbyshire with his working-class lover George Merrill. On one such visit Merrill touched Forster on the backside. It was a casual gesture but remained with Forster for years. 'The sensation was unusual, and I still remember it, as I remember the position of the long vanished tooth . . . It seemed to go straight through the small of my back into my ideas, without involving my thoughts.' Apparently the entire plot of *Maurice*, his novel about homosexual love, rushed into his mind.

With the outbreak of World War I, Forster became depressed and unsettled. He was a pacifist by nature, but wanted to participate at some level. In November 1915 he accordingly left for Alexandria in Egypt, where he was to work as a 'searcher' for the International Red Cross. His duties were not very onerous – they involved gathering information from the wounded in hospital about fellow-soldiers reported missing – and he had plenty of time for his writing.

Lifelong friendships
Forster was devoted to his friends. Above, he is pictured flanked by Bob Buckingham and J. R. Ackerley. Below is his friend and confidante Florence Barger – 'She loves me and I her,' he said.

LOVE AT LAST

In some ways Alexandria suited Forster perfectly. It had a cosmopolitan community of homosexuals and in 1916 he finally 'parted with respectability', embarking on a number of experimental relationships until, in 1917, he fell in love. The recipient of his love was an Egyptian tram conductor called Mohammed el Adl. They made cautious overtures to each other, amused rather than apalled by their different backgrounds, and after a time spent nights as well as days together. For Forster it was joyous. He told a friend, Florence Barger, 'It is awful to think of the thousands who go through youth without ever knowing. I have known in a way before, but never like this. My luck has been amazing.' His 'luck' held for several years, surviving even Mohammed's marriage.

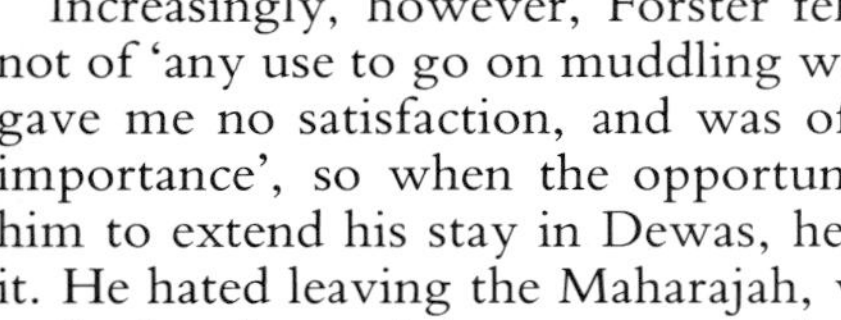

By the end of October 1918, Turkey had surrendered and Forster's work for the Red Cross came to an end. Returning to England in 1919, he worked briefly as literary editor of the Socialist *Daily Herald* and wrote articles and reviews for a variety of periodicals. He also worked on the novel which was to become *A Passage to India*, and when his old friend, the Maharajah of Dewas State Senior, invited him to return to India as private secretary, he accepted gladly.

Relaxing in India
(below) Forster is shown in 1921, playing cards with the Maharajah of Dewas State Senior and his retinue.

Increasingly, however, Forster felt that it was not of 'any use to go on muddling with work that gave me no satisfaction, and was of no essential importance', so when the opportunity arose for him to extend his stay in Dewas, he did not take it. He hated leaving the Maharajah, whom he described as 'one of the sweetest and saintliest men I have ever known', but it was with relief that he left the confusion of Dewas to stay with Masood.

On returning to England in 1922 he started a correspondence with J. R. Ackerley, a then unknown writer. Forster praised his work, Ackerley was flattered and the two became fast friends. Although never lovers, they saw each other regularly, and it was through Ackerley that the 51-year-old Forster met a 26-year-old policeman, Bob Buckingham, in 1930. Buckingham was warm-hearted, genial and eager to better himself. Forster gladly took on his literary education, deriving as much pleasure from the enterprise as did Buckingham. The two men embarked on a relationship which brought Forster great happiness. As he wrote in 1932: 'I have been happy for two years. It mayn't be over yet, but I want to write it down before it gets spoiled by the pain.'

Their close friendship could have been jeopardized by Buckingham's marriage to May Hockey, but May, too, became a valued friend. And Forster even became godfather to their son, whom they named Robert Morgan in his honour. Forster was deeply moved, and through the years he helped with Rob's education and enjoyed being part of the Buckingham family. When Rob died tragically at the age of 29, Forster grieved as though for his own son and provided Rob's young wife and children with a regular allowance.

In 1925 Forster and his mother moved into the only existing house designed by his father – West Hackhurst in Abinger Hammer, near Dorking.

Krishna
The Hindu god (shown in blue) 'sports with the cowherds'.

THE FESTIVAL OF GOKUL ASHTAMI

The last section of *A Passage to India* centres on a festival celebrating the birth of Krishna. According to Forster 'The Krishna festival [in the novel] closely follows the great celebration of Gokul Ashtami, which I attended for nine days in the palace of Dewas State Senior, and which was the strangest and strongest Indian experience ever granted me.' The Festival honours the god Krishna, supposedly born at Gokul, and its aim was to achieve *bhakti* or direct union with the Divine through love.

Much of the ritual had been invented by the Maharajah of Dewas. At its centre was the continual singing of hymns around the altar in the Old Palace, to the accompaniment of cymbals and a harmonium. The festival ended with the announcement of Krishna's birth and a procession from the Old Palace to the Tank, where a clay model of the village of Gokul was ceremoniously thrown into the waters.

Life here went on with a Victorian formality which Forster escaped on visits to the London flat he now maintained for his private life.

Throughout the 1920s and '30s he wrote essays and articles on a wide range of subjects, many of which reflected his devotion to the cause of free speech and his hatred of Nazism and Stalinism. His principles were very much those of the newly founded National Council of Civil Liberties and, in 1934, he agreed to become its first president.

By the time World War II broke out, Lily was crippled by rheumatism and was very demanding. When she died in 1945, at the age of 90, Forster felt drowned by waves of despair and imagined that it would not be long before he died too.

FINAL HONOURS

He made one last trip to India after which he was elected an Honorary Fellow of King's College, with the offer, which he accepted, of a room in college and living quarters nearby. Towards the end of his life Forster reflected, 'Being an important person is a full time job and is bound to generate some inward futility and pretentiousness . . . You need not do any thing – you've arrived . . . And I don't.' But he was far from idle. In his seventies he visited the United States, worked with Eric Crozier on the libretto for Benjamin Britten's opera *Billy Budd*, and wrote two books, one being a biography of his great-aunt and benefactor Marianne Thornton. He continued to write articles until well into his eighties.

In 1953 he was made a Companion of Honour and in 1969, at the age of 90, received the Order of Merit. The following year, at the age of 91, he suffered what was to be a final stroke, and on 7 June he died in the Coventry home of his beloved friends Bob and May Buckingham, holding May's hand. His ashes were scattered in their garden, and five years later, when Bob Buckingham died, his too were scattered over the same rose-bush.

Order of Merit
(right) In the New Year's Honours List of 1969 Forster was awarded the Order of Merit, one of Britain's most prestigious decorations. King's College organized a luncheon in dual celebration of this and his 90th birthday.

Grand old man
(below) Forster stands in his bedroom at King's, where he was made an Honorary Fellow in 1945 – and lionized as 'the greatest living Kingsman'. He suffered his final, fatal stroke there – but Bob Buckingham took him home to Coventry to die.

Sunset of The Raj

British rule in India unified a vast, disparate continent. But inherent in that unification were the seeds of a new and independent nation.

The year before Forster's first visit to India in 1912 saw the third and biggest Great Durbar – an occasion so extravagant, so monumentally self-confident, that it captured, in essence, the nature of the British Raj. It was staged to celebrate the accession to the British throne of George V, and he and Queen Mary travelled to India to see it. Two thousand workers laid 25 square miles of lawn, rose garden and polo pitches.

At the ceremony, the Indian Army paraded in its thousands. Bejewelled maharajahs and elephant-borne princes expressed loyalty to the British Emperor. But such a massive, stage-managed display of sovereignty concealed huge rents in the mantle of British power.

From the middle of the 18th century, India had been called 'the brightest jewel in the royal crown' of Britain. Until the year of the Indian Mutiny – 1857 – the East India Company had looked after the interests of Britain throughout half the subcontinent. The Mutiny was localized, and somewhat confused in origin, but it was carried out with savage commitment. 'Peace' was re-established by the most brutal suppression, but the shock of the revolt had had its impact. On 1 November 1858, Queen Victoria proclaimed that the administration of India had passed from the East India Company to the British Crown, the monarch being represented by a Viceroy.

Queen Victoria took an intense interest in Indian affairs, actively encouraged religious toleration and discouraged 'red-tapeism' ('alas, our great misfortune'). But the aim of this benevolence was clear. Her proclamation stated that 'in their [the Indians'] prosperity will be our strength; in their contentment our security'. The need to heal Anglo-Indian relations was paramount.

So began a second century of domination, and the Victorians were more convinced than ever that their task in India was a sacred duty: 'our work is righteous,' wrote Nathaniel Curzon, one of the most dedicated of the Viceroys.

The reasons why a huge nation of 350 million should allow itself to be subjugated by Britain were various and complex. Firstly, it gained economi-

India's pageant
(right) In A Passage to India, *Adela sees India "always as a frieze, never as a spirit" – a procession of colourful images detached from her experience. For as a member of the British community, she is in a world apart.*

Jewel in the Crown
After the Indian Mutiny in 1857 (below), the East India Company relinquished power to the British Crown. But there were those, even at the height of the Raj, who believed the Queen was risking too much by her intense interest and involvement in Indian affairs. The cartoon (right) refers to the Queen becoming Empress of India.

cally from the British trading network. Secondly, the British brought distinct benefits: they built thousands of miles of railway, irrigated 20 million acres, established universities, schools and hospitals and employed hundreds of thousands of people. But thirdly and most importantly, India did not think of itself as a nation.

Apart from their religious divisions, Indians living in different parts of the vast subcontinent were divided by distance, language and varying economic fortunes. The starvation of a Bengali-speaking peasant could mean little to a flourishing Gujerati-speaking merchant thousands of miles away. But ironically, changes brought about under British rule helped to resolve such divisions.

A COMMON LANGUAGE

Newly built railways and roads made journeys between different regions a matter of days and hours rather than months and weeks. The universal use of English that the Raj insisted upon soon provided a common language in which educated Indians could communicate their problems.

Nationalism itself originated in Europe. It reached India through Indian youth who received a Western education at the universities of Bombay, Bengal and Madras. Here they read the works of the intellectual giants of Victorian England, such as Jeremy Bentham, John Stuart Mill and T. B. Macaulay. They then went on to influential employment in government service, law, journalism or commerce – and to political activity.

The Indian National Congress was formed in 1885, its first meeting being held in Bombay on 28 December. The proceedings specifically included a declaration of loyalty to the British Crown, so it did not begin life seeking independence. Its aim was reforms within the framework of existing British rule. Some members did believe, however, that the British sense of fairness would eventually lead them to concede self-government, and some were in favour of agitation to that end.

The religious divisions of India were reflected in Congress. More than half the Congress participants were Hindus, including members of the strict Jain sect. There were only two Muslims, the rest being Parsees, who were Persian in origin. The Congress was therefore dominated by Hindus, which gave the Muslims cause for suspicion and mistrust.

Among the British themselves opinion was divided as to why they were in India. There was a certain line of thought which argued that the British had generously undertaken to 'civilize' this savage nation until such time as it might be fit for self-government. Another – more honest – outlook

Presumptuous pomp
The Great Durbar of 1911 (below) was a stupendous exercise in public relations, implying universal delight in British domination. But there were already those among a small, educated Indian élite who questioned the new King's right to rule.

said, 'We keep it for the sake of the interests and the honour of England'.

Victorians in England had a distorted view of India. They saw pictures of Hindu widows burned on their husbands' funeral pyres and rejoiced in the thought that the British had put an end to the practice. They heard of famine relief and felt a warm glow of self-righteousness. Meanwhile, the only Indians they actually encountered were the princes and Parsees educated at Oxford and Cambridge – such as 'Ranji', who batted for England in 15 test matches, and Sir M. M. Bhownagree, who held the Tory seat of Bethnal Green.

Those British who lived in India – the Anglo-Indians in Forster's novel – had scarcely a better understanding of the indigenous population. (It is significant that Forster, who wrote with some measure of insight, was not an employee of the Crown, but worked for a Maharajah.) Officials of the Raj, whether soldiers or civil servants, were strenuously

Railway links
(above) The railway transformed communications in India. British engineers and armies of Indian workers laid thousands of miles of track over wildly varying landscapes) across the sub-continent.

Curry, rice and tigers
An illustrated book of the time (left) suggested that Raj life was a mixture of genteel Victorian habits spiced with adventure and novelty. In the hot season, the British would remove to the cooler Himalayan foothills (below). Tiger hunts (right) were often undertaken as family outings, albeit amid a hoard of bearers, beaters, drivers and other servants.

discouraged from fraternizing, and there was no more despised social pariah (outcast) than the Englishman who had 'gone native' and lived with the Indians. Helpful brochures were issued to newcomers instructing them in dealing tactfully with the natives – how not to offend their 'izzat' (self-respect). But this was mere management training and had nothing to do with closing the cultural gap.

Rules of conduct rigidified every aspect of British colonial behaviour. A young government official going out to India would set foot on a social ladder as towering as any caste system. At its base was the common soldier and the 'box wallah' (civilian tradesman); at the top the Viceroy.

The newly recruited civil servant would be expected to remain a bachelor for some years before home-leave enabled him to find a suitable wife. He would work knee-deep in the welter of paperwork which characterized the stupendously bureaucratic Raj. His social life would be restricted and highly formal, the boredom broken only by hunting, polo and the summer removal.

Dazzling Viceroy *George Nathaniel Curzon first saw India as a correspondent for* The Times. *He fell in love with the country and his thrusting ambition took him to the highest rank of all – Viceroy (1898-1905). With an army of 250,000 at his command and more power than most monarchs, he cut a figure larger than life – a writer and explorer as well as a statesman. Proud to the point of arrogance, he made sure always to outdazzle the finest India could offer.*

LITTLE ENGLANDS

In summer the entire mechanism of government moved to the cooler hills, where a succession of little Englands sprang up, complete with hunts, croquet lawns, church, theatre, gymkhanas, newspapers and libraries. By 1903, there were 1400 European-style houses in Simla, the summer capital. Simla's glorious Viceregal lodge housed state balls, and many a romantic liaison began there for wives sent alone to their summer retreats.

Under the Raj, life was empty for British women. Their children were shipped back to England to be educated – providing they had not succumbed to one of the many contagious diseases. Men could spend time at their clubs, offices, barracks or on prolonged business trips; but women had no work to do and had to confine their friendships to whites of their own status – if any lived within visiting distance.

Master and servants *Households of the Raj employed huge numbers of servants – personal attendants, dhobi-wallahs (launderers), punka-wallahs (fan-bearers) and so on. So much servility (below) contributed to the 'sahib's' attitude of superiority. Many Britons would have agreed with Mrs Turton when she told Mrs Moore: "You're superior to everyone in India except one or two of the ranis [princesses], and they're on an equality."*

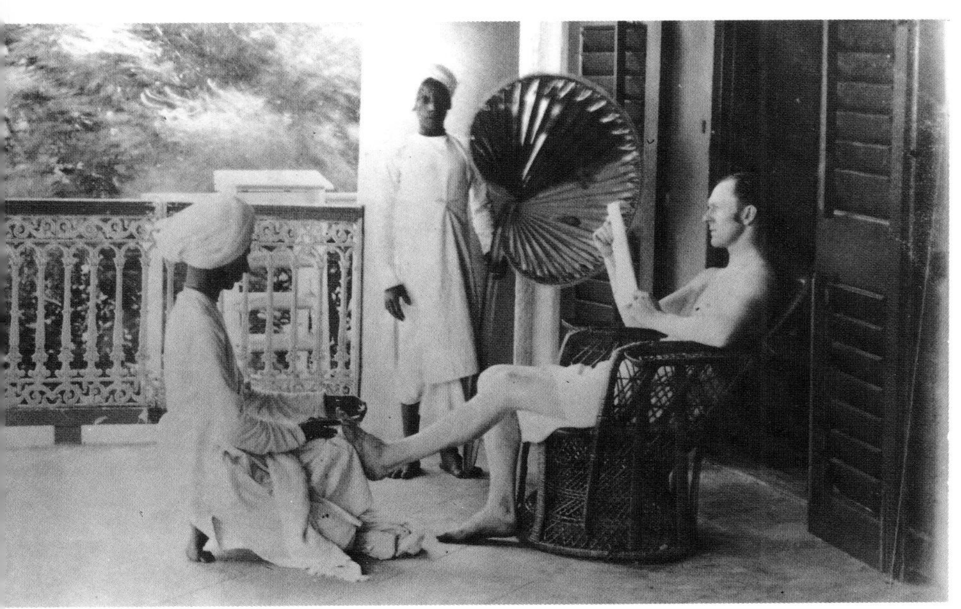

Contempt for inferiors was virtually a rule of etiquette, and contempt for the Indians went without saying. Anglo-Indians never considered that their contempt might be reciprocated.

The future politician Subhas Chandra Bose wrote home from Cambridge University, 'what gives me the greatest joy is to watch the whiteskins serving me and cleaning my shoes.' By 1927, he was a junior member of the National Congress and was advocating direct confrontation with the British Government. His lifetime had seen an irreversible change in Indian thinking.

Japan's victory over Russia in 1905, revolutions in Persia in 1906 and Turkey in 1908 had been an immense stimulus to Asian nationalism. They proved Europeans were not invincible in battle. The Sinn Fein in Ireland had also proved British rule could be challenged by force.

ERROR OF JUDGEMENT

But nothing had a greater impact on the nationalist movement in India than a mistake made by the Viceroy himself. In 1905, Nathaniel Curzon, believing Bengal was too large to be governed efficiently as a single province (it had a population of 80 million), ordered it to be divided. In neither new province were the Bengali-speaking Hindus – the largest single group in the old, undivided province – in the majority. They therefore interpreted Curzon's action as a deliberate move to weaken Hindu-Bengali national feeling. Congress was galvanized into action.

When liberal methods such as petitions and protests failed, Congress resorted to a boycott of British goods. In 1906 it demanded that 'the system of government obtaining in the self-governing British colonies should be extended to India.' This upsurge of Hindu political activity provoked a Muslim reaction. The All-India Muslim League pledged loyalty to British rule, approved the partition of Bengal and condemned the boycott.

The end of an era
British influence was bolstered by India's ruling classes (top), whose fabulous wealth and absolute (local) power depended on no social change. They, too, were the losers when India rejected the Raj. The peaceful resistance of Gandhi and the efforts of last Viceroy Louis Mountbatten (above right) paved the way for India's Independence in 1947.

So, by 1906, there were four major strands of Indian political activity: the moderates within Congress who wanted self-rule by constitutional means; the extremists within Congress who wanted independence through agitation; the Muslims outside Congress who wanted British protection to safeguard their interest; and a small terrorist movement which favoured assassination and sabotage as direct protest against British rule.

The Morley-Minto Reforms (called after the statesmen who devised them) were implemented in 1909, and were an attempt by Britain to make the Raj more of a partnership than a dictatorship. Morley, head of the India Office, said, 'Reforms may not save the Raj, but if they don't, nothing will.' Indian opinion was at least gratified by the re-unification of Bengal in 1911 and the shifting of the capital from Calcutta to Delhi, former site of Mogul imperial splendour.

Any possibility of gradual political change was shattered by the outbreak of war in Europe in 1914. Congress pledged its 'firm resolve to stand by the Empire at all hazards and at all costs', believing that this loyalty would be rewarded in due course. India sent money, supplies and more than a million Indians (of whom 36,000 were killed) served as troops and labourers.

As the war dragged on, however, the spirit of resolve soured. Britain's failure to win an early victory damaged her image of military prowess. Heavy war taxes, inflation and over-recruitment in the Punjab created discontent which outlasted the War. In March 1918, to counteract possible terrorism, the Government passed the Rowlatt Acts, which allowed the authorities to imprison agitators without trial and judges to try cases without juries. In fact, these powers were never used, but the psychological damage done was irreparable. On 13 April, at Amritsar, the local commander, General Dyer, ordered his troops to open fire on a crowd of 10,000 unarmed protesters and pilgrims. No warning was given: 375 people were killed and more than 1200 wounded.

MASSACRE AT AMRITSAR

Indians were horrified at the massacre, and were outraged by the British reaction. Although Dyer was relieved of his command, the Lieutenant Governor of the Punjab approved his action as did a majority in the House of Lords. British newspapers condemned it utterly, but such condemnations came too late to assuage Indian anger.

Too late the British Government outlined an experiment in power-sharing, with the Government of India Act of 1919. A property-owning, educated proportion of the population were to be enfranchized, and their elected representatives were to serve on the Council of State, the State Assembly and Provincial Legislative councils. But the nation was in no mood to be appeased. The first parliament elected under the new system met in Delhi in February 1921. But these first steps towards 'responsible government' coincided with a massive campaign of non-cooperation. Nationalism had become a true mass movement.

Forster wrote *A Passage to India* on the eve of these crucial events. But the novel was restricted in viewpoint, in that the majority of people he came into contact with were members of the ruling classes. He was condemned by the Indians for showing only the white point of view, and by the Anglo-Indians for showing only the Indian point of view. What he showed was the point of view of the ruling classes, both Indian and British. The movement afoot by the time of his second visit (1921) was that of the populace at large.

When Forster returned for the last time to India in 1945, he found the Indians obsessed with 'politics, politics, politics'. The world he had known was ending. Two years later, at midnight on 14 August 1947, India formally gained independence.

VIRGINIA WOOLF

1882-1941

One of the most innovative writers of the 20th century, Virginia Woolf redefined the novel, moving away from conventional narrative to reveal her characters' thought processes and emotional states. The intense sensitivity of her writing reflected an acutely nervous and unstable temperament. She inspired great love from her family and friends, but even their devotion could not keep the terrors of mental illness at bay.

A Fragile Balance

Poised between exuberance and despair, brilliance and the nightmare of madness, Virginia Woolf waged a lifelong battle for clarity, sanity and truthfulness.

Virginia Woolf came from a distinguished and talented family. Her father, Sir Leslie Stephen, was a noted critic and biographer and the first editor of the prestigious *Dictionary of National Biography*. He married twice; his first wife was one of Thackeray's daughters, Minny, and in 1878, three years after Minny's death, he married Julia Duckworth. She was of a similarly illustrious family and the niece of the brilliant Victorian photographer Julia Margaret Cameron. A young widow, she already had three children from her first marriage.

Adeline Virginia Stephen was born on 25 January 1882, the third child after Vanessa and Thoby. The following year, another baby, Adrian, completed the family. Virginia believed that her parents' traditions 'dashed together and flowed confused but not harmonised in her blood'. This rich mix consisted of her mother's fine sensitivity and artistic taste, and her father's equally impressive intellect. In practical terms this meant that from early childhood Virginia was immersed in an exciting and stimulating world in which she was always encouraged to read and study and express her ideas. Her imagination was early sparked into life by the family's annual holidays at St Ives in Cornwall, where Leslie had bought the beautiful Talland House. It was here that young Virginia distinguished herself as a 'demon bowler' at cricket, and indulged in the seaside pleasures of boating, fishing, and long waterfront walks.

Key Dates

1882 born in London

1895 mother dies; first breakdown

1897 half-sister dies

1904 father dies

1905 first Bloomsbury meetings

1906 brother Thoby dies

1912 marries Leonard Woolf

1913 attempts suicide

1915 *The Voyage Out*

1917 starts Hogarth Press

1919 buys Monk's House in Sussex

1922 meets Vita Sackville-West

1927 *To The Lighthouse*

1941 commits suicide

Mother and daughter
When Virginia was 13, 'the greatest disaster that could happen' occurred – her mother Julia died. It brought her happy, secure childhood to an end, and prompted the first of many breakdowns.

Life was a series of adventures for the Stephen children. When Virginia was nine she embarked on a weekly paper – the *Hyde Park Gate News* – with her brother Thoby, and in play sowed the seeds of her life's work. It was not long, however, before this happy, fruitful period of her childhood came to a sudden and painful end.

When Virginia was 13 her beloved mother died. The loss was more than she could bear and caused a nervous collapse in her fragile constitution. 'The greatest disaster that could happen', as she described it, was intensified when Leslie, instead of protecting his children from the terror of Julia's death, inflicted on them his own inconsolable grief. The children's half-sister, Stella, stepped in and looked after the family, but her sudden death two years later undid the good she had done, and caused new anguish.

To make matters worse, Stella's widowed husband Jack started making passionate advances to Vanessa, while Virginia, long terrified by her half-brother George Duckworth's covertly sexual interest in her, retreated into a state of 'frozen and defensive panic'.

From being lively and outgoing, Virginia became painfully introverted and shy. It only

Inspirational summers
The Stephen children spent carefree summers at St Ives in Cornwall and years later Virginia would fondly remember the ocean's 'great plateful of blue water'.

needed one more major shock to send her mad, which is precisely what happened when, in 1904, her father Leslie died from cancer. Virginia's rapidly declining nervous state was signalled, as throughout her life, by severe headaches, followed in this instance by periods of self-accusation, and the nightmarish conviction that birds were speaking to her in Greek, and that King Edward VII was hiding in the garden, muttering unspeakably foul abuse at her.

With due rest and physical care, she recovered, and, with her brothers and sisters, decided to leave behind the past and start a new, freer way of life in Bloomsbury. Yet just as they were finding their feet as young Bohemians, tragedy struck again. In 1906, after a family tour of Greece, both Vanessa and Thoby fell ill. Vanessa recovered, but Thoby, who had contracted typhoid, did not.

BIRTH OF BLOOMSBURY

Although Virginia never entirely got over her brother's death, the Bloomsbury world was starting to take shape. Her sister Vanessa married Thoby's friend, Clive Bell, and their home became a meeting place for a host of ex-Cambridge intellectuals and of talented young artists, politicians and writers. In their midst Virginia started to regain her confidence and find her voice as a writer. She began reviewing for the *Times Literary Supplement* and the *Guardian* and, at the age of 25, tackled her first novel, *The Voyage Out.*

Virginia took her writing most seriously, reworking her novel over and over again from beginning to end, but in company she was fun-loving and witty. When her brother Adrian and his friend Horace Cole devised a hoax on the Royal Navy, she gladly joined in. They informed the Navy that the Emperor of Abyssinia wanted to visit the warship HMS *Dreadnought,* and then blacked their faces and donned exotic robes for the occasion. The Press was there in full force and the elaborate deception received front page coverage complete with a photograph of the '"Abyssinian Princes" who have made all England laugh'.

Almost two years later, in 1911, Virginia and her brother Adrian moved to a four-storeyed house in Brunswick Square and divided it among their friends. The economist Maynard Keynes and the painter Duncan Grant shared the ground floor; Adrian had the second floor and Virginia the third; and Leonard Woolf – the man who was to be the

Kensington vistas
Born at 22 Hyde Park Gate, Virginia inhabited comfortable, fashionable Kensington – a far cry from bohemian Bloomsbury.

Half-sisters
When their mother died, Stella Duckworth (below centre) looked after Vanessa (left) and Virginia – and their grief-stricken father.

mainstay of Virginia's life – took the two rooms at the top. It proved to be a propitious decision. In August 1912, Virginia and Leonard were married.

Captivated by Virginia's beauty and originality, Leonard gladly abandoned a distinguished career in the Colonial Service for her. She loved him devotedly but said with candour: 'I feel no physical attraction to you . . . and yet your caring for me as you do almost overwhelms me', a strange forewarning of the great sacrifice he would have to make. The disruptions in Virginia's childhood and the trauma suffered at the hands of her stepbrother had left ineradicable scars on her. At some deep level she was frightened of men, and even under the tender, patient love of Leonard found herself incapable of any sexual response.

The Woolfs honeymooned on the Continent and returned to their separate writing ventures. Virginia completed *The Voyage Out,* and although the family firm of Duckworth accepted it enthusiastically, the stress of completing it induced a severe period of depression in which she lapsed from headaches to guilt and despair, seeing her nurses as fiends and degenerating into total incoherence and, finally, a coma. Recovery was slow with intermittent periods of relapse over several years

This 1913 attack was one of her worst. She attempted suicide by taking an overdose of sedatives, and while recuperating from that, tried to starve herself to death. Leonard then, as always, played a major part in helping her through. He protected her from the outside world, and sensitively and sincerely praised her work.

Greek tragedy
In 1906 the four Stephen children set off excitedly for Greece (top). They loved it, but the trip had dire consequences – Thoby (above) contracted typhoid fever and never recovered. Virginia was affected by his death for years.

Lytton Strachey
For a heady 24 hours in 1909, Virginia Stephen and the witty, erudite Lytton Strachey (right) were engaged. The engagement was short-lived, however. Strachey panicked at the thought of being intimate with a woman, confessed his fears to Virginia and she, understanding his reluctance and knowing of his male amours, released him. They remained the best of friends, however.

PRINTING VENTURE

Clearly Virginia needed to be distracted from the demons inside her head, and Leonard, in the hope of averting further depressions, bought a small printing press on which he and Virginia began printing their own stories. The success of this venture was less the result of brilliant business decisions than of the Woolfs' store of highly talented friends and contacts, who included T. S. Eliot, D. H. Lawrence, Katherine Mansfield, Lytton Strachey, Sigmund Freud and, later, Vita Sackville-West.

In addition to the press, Virgina was kept fully occupied by her and Leonard's social life and by her varied writings which included a mammoth output of letters, reviews, essays and, from 1915 to 1941, diary entries. However, in 1921, after a relatively peaceful and productive period, she had another severe breakdown.

Virginia's diary entry of 8 August describes how she had 'two whole months rubbed out', 60

Devoted sister
Three years Virginia's senior, the beautiful and talented Vanessa (above) was her sister's constant support and ally.

Sussex Downs
The calm of the Sussex countryside helped assuage the effects of London's hubbub on Virginia's delicate mental state.

LEONARD WOOLF

'I am selfish, jealous, cruel, lustful, a liar and probably worse still' – so the gentle, loving Leonard Woolf described himself in a letter to Virginia asking her to marry him.

Born in 1880, Leonard Woolf joined the Colonial Service after graduating from Cambridge and spent the next seven years in Ceylon, helping to govern the country. In 1911 he returned to England and to his treasured Virginia, and from then on dedicated himself to socialism and to his visionary political philosophy. He believed passionately in a new form of international government and argued his case eloquently.

His extensive literary output included two novels, but he is best remembered for his brilliant five-volume autobiography, which combines an interesting, objective account of the Bloomsbury Group, a touching portrait of life with Virginia, and a record of his fervent aspirations for a better world.

days of 'wearisome headache, jumping pulse, aching back, frets, fidgets . . . all the horrors of the dark cupboard of illness'. Aided by lengthy spells at Monk's House in Rodmell, Sussex (which they had bought in 1919), she gradually made her way out of the 'dark cupboard' and felt well enough to embark on *To the Lighthouse*.

Because of ill health, Virginia was never strong enough to write a series of major novels, and usually followed an important work with a less demanding project, what she termed a 'holiday book'. In this case it was *Orlando* and *A Room of One's Own*. *Orlando* is not just a brilliantly witty novel that transcends conventions of time and gender; it is also a veiled account of her sudden intense relationship with the writer Vita Sackville-West.

The two women had met in 1922, and although Virginia was wary of Vita's reputation as a lesbian, she eventually, after five years, developed an intensely absorbing passion for her. Although there was speculation that Virginia might leave Leonard, she stayed loyal to him, prompting Vita to the angry, incisive, semi-truthful accusation that she liked 'people better through the brain than the heart'.

By now Virginia was an immensely successful writer. *Orlando* soon sold 6000 copies. From 1929 to 1930, she made 'about £1,020 . . . a surprise to me, who was content with £200 for so many years.' *A Room of One's Own* did even better than this, selling 10,000 copies.

New money meant new possessions. The Woolfs bought a car, refurnished the house in Rodmell and began travelling abroad. There was also time off to visit her adored – and adoring – nephews and niece. She always remained in close

Fact or Fiction

LESLIE AND JULIA STEPHEN

Although written some 30 years after their deaths, *To the Lighthouse* was a critical tribute to Virginia Woolf's remarkable and gifted parents, Leslie and Julia Stephen. The fictional Mr and Mrs Ramsay are based on them; indeed Virginia noted in her diary before she embarked on the writing: 'This is going to be fairly short: to have father's character complete in it; and mother's.' She was so successful in her endeavour that her sister Vanessa was moved to comment: 'It is almost painful to have her [their mother] so raised from the dead. You have made one feel the extraordinary beauty of her character, which must be the most difficult thing to do.'

The lure of France
(above) In 1927, some of Virginia and Leonard's intimates began to make an occasional home in Cassis-sur-mer in France. The artist Duncan Grant was the first to move there, followed by Vanessa and her children, then Clive Bell and finally, briefly, Virginia and Leonard themselves. Vanessa and her family settled happily into a house called La Bergère and for three years the Woolfs toyed with the idea of joining them there, tempted by Mediterranean heat, languor and serenity. But the attractions of England and the Hogarth Press proved greater.

contact with Vanessa, who, after Leonard, was the most important person in her life. All the while Virginia and Leonard were part-time publishers, printing the works of the next generation of great writers. This took up so much time that they were eventually forced to employ someone to help run the business.

Virginia's diary entry of 11 October 1929 sums up her position: 'the press is booming – & this celebrity business is quite chronic – & I am richer than I have ever been . . . If I never felt these extraordinarily pervasive strains – of unrest, or rest . . . I should float down into acquiescence. Here is something to fight; and when I wake early I say to myself, Fight, fight."

ANOTHER BREAKDOWN

The 'fight' continued with her highly ambitious revolutionary novel, *The Waves*. But she worked so intensely on it that, tired and weakened, she again had a breakdown. Initial criticism of the book did not help, but the praise which came later helped nurse her back to full health and into the attentions of her second lesbian admirer, the larger-than-life, eccentric composer Dame Ethel Smyth. Virginia wittily described how 'An old woman of seventy-one has fallen in love with me. It's like being caught by a giant crab.' But their friendship lasted just a couple of months before the intensity became too much for Virginia and she retreated into a cautious friendship with her.

Now on the verge of her 50th birthday, Virginia divided her life into two clear parts. In the country she wrote, baked bread, did gardening, and went on long rambling walks, while in London she led a hectic social life, seeing her large number of friends and fêted as the star attraction at countless dinner parties. But she was never long away from her first love, and in 1933 published her next 'holiday' work, *Flush*, a 'biography' of Elizabeth Barrett Browning's spaniel, which she followed with her 'essay-novel' *The Years*.

Sadly, the anxiety and stress of constant rewriting induced her worst breakdown since her suicide attempt of 1913. From 10 April to 10 June 1936 her diary is blank . . . When she took up her pen again she wrote 'at last after 2 months dismal and worse, almost catastrophic illness – never been so near the precipice to my own feelings . . . I'm again on top.' But she was not. On 21 June she referred to a week 'of intense suffering – indeed mornings of torture – & . . . pain in my head – a feeling of complete despair and failure.' And on 23 June she wrote, 'A good day – a bad day – so it goes on. Few people can be so tortured by writing as I am.' Fortunately Virginia was spared further intense suffering by *The Years*' excellent reception both in Britain and in the United States.

Although the late 1930s was a time of great political unrest, Virginia's work betrayed no sign of the alarming rise of European fascism and the Spanish Civil War. She wrote at the other end of the spectrum from writers such as George Orwell and H. G. Wells, whose intent was to design a new and better world. Virginia, instead, wanted to devise a new form for the novel, relentlessly diving inside her characters, asking 'what is it like to be this person, or experience this sensation?' Nothing was real unless she could write about it. As her brother-in-law Clive Bell wrote, 'She lives in a world of fantastic daydreams, half in a world of solid reality, half in a Victorian novel.'

However, both she and Leonard were fully aware that if Hitler were victorious life would be unendurable – and together planned a suicide pact. Increasingly through 1940, as the war appeared to sway towards a Nazi victory, Virginia wondered if the time had not arrived to carry it out.

Strangely, she was exhilarated by the Battle of Britain, fought high over East Sussex and Kent, but appalled when the devastation hit London.

Despite these distractions she wrote on, making rapid progress with *Poyntz Hall* and a history of English literature, *Anon*. As usual, feverish spells of writing were tempered by the calm of village life, but sadly this period was suddenly destroyed in November 1940. Leonard recognized the symptoms of another impending attack.

'TROUGH OF DESPAIR'

In January 1941 her diary entries became preoccupied with death and towards the end of the month she fell into a 'trough of despair'. Unusually, this time it was not connected with finishing a novel. There had been no warning. One moment, at breakfast, she was well; hours later she was violently excited, talking to her mother. Leonard was convinced 'that Virginia's mental condition was more serious than it had been since . . . 1913.' He knew just one wrong word could push her over the brink.

By March 27, Leonard had persuaded Virginia to see her doctor. This lady reassured her that she could survive another attack. But Virginia lost her nerve and the next day she wrote two farewell letters. One, to her sister Vanessa, spelled out that 'I have gone too far this time to come back again. I am certain now that I am going mad again . . . and I know I shan't get over it'. And to Leonard, she explained, 'Dearest, I feel certain I am going mad again. I feel we can't go through another of those terrible times . . . I can't fight any longer . . . I can't go on spoiling your life any longer. I don't think two people could have been happier than we have been.' And, having written her last words to the two people she loved most, she walked out of the house and down to the River Ouse. There, with a large stone in her pocket, she drowned herself.

Vita Sackville-West
Glamorous, aristocratic and gifted, Vita Sackville-West (above) was for a time passionately attached to Virginia. With Virginia's portrait on her desk, she wrote to Clive Bell, 'I would go to the ends of the earth for your sister-in-law.'

A few hours later, panicked by her absence, Leonard ran to the river bank, but found only her walking stick. It was three weeks before her body was sighted in the water. After her cremation, Leonard buried her ashes at the foot of a giant elm in the garden, one of a pair which, with branches intertwining, they had affectionately named after each other. Two years later, as if to underline the tragedy, a gale ripped one of these magnificent trees out of the ground forever.

'All the happiness'
It was from the quiet of Monk's House (above) that Virginia set off one morning, walked down to the river and drowned herself. In her final note to Leonard she wrote: 'Dearest . . . I owe all the happiness of my life to you.' Leonard was to survive her by 28 years.

The Bloomsbury Group

Attracting the most brilliant personalities and advanced thinkers of the day, the Bloomsbury Group broke with Victorian convention in the search for new styles of art, literature and life.

The name of Virginia Woolf is often identified with the group of artists, writers and intellectuals who were her closest friends. This circle of intelligent and gifted people, who came to be called the Bloomsbury Group, included such famous names as Clive Bell, Leonard Woolf, Lytton Strachey and Maynard Keynes. Disparate as they were in personalities and interests, they relied much on each other for social and creative stimulus. Together they sought new ways of thinking and living, and expressed a natural and necessary reaction to Victorian convention and intolerance.

In her own writing, Virginia Woolf certainly drew on the fresh ideas that were discussed in the Bloomsbury heyday. But she, like every other member of the set, developed her own distinctive vision and style. As she became an established writer, so she depended less on the Bloomsbury Group for inspiration, yet their habit of meeting to talk and air views remained a way of life for her. In her early adulthood, however, Bloomsbury gave her the kind of intellectual freedom and interaction that she needed, just as it provided her elder sister Vanessa with the lifestyle she sought to become a fully fledged painter.

EARLY BLOOMSBURY

In 1904, on the death of their father, the Stephen children – Vanessa, Thoby, Virginia and Adrian – moved from the family house in Hyde Park Gate to 46 Gordon Square, London WC1. This move from their stuffy Victorian home to unfashionable Bloomsbury symbolized a rejection of their own social background, and, by implication, its values. It brought down on their heads 'screams' of protest from at least one old family friend, Kitty Maxse.

Thoby had recently graduated from Cambridge, and was now studying to become a barrister. He maintained contact with his university friends, however, and on 16 February 1905, he invited one of them – Saxon Sydney Turner – for an evening chat. On this occasion the only other member of the party was Gurth the sheepdog, but so began the regular Thursday evening gatherings of the Bloomsbury Group. The circle expanded as a matter of course, to include other Cambridge friends of Thoby, in particular the talented Lytton Strachey, Clive Bell and Maynard Keynes.

All of these people were to achieve renown in different fields: Strachey as a critic and biographer, Bell as an art critic, and Maynard Keynes as a political economist of enormous influence. Apart from the fame that awaited them, these men were linked by the intellectual influences of Cambridge, and had all been inspired by the philosophy of G. E. Moore, whose work *Principia Ethica* constituted a rejection of received ideas and conventions. He maintained that: 'By far the most valuable things . . . are . . . the pleasures of human intercourse

Cambridge roots
(above) The Bloomsbury Group developed from student friendships formed at Cambridge University, where several members had belonged to the prestigious, semi-secret Apostles' club.

Leading lights
Apart from being the most influential economic thinker of his generation, Maynard Keynes (above) was renowned for his generosity and energy as a patron of the arts. His interests explicitly refuted the accusation of some critics that the Bloomsbury Group's aesthetic indulgence bypassed all social or political issues. Late in life Keynes became the first chairman of the Arts Council. Other founder members of the Group were Clive Bell and Lytton Strachey (right).

Vanessa Bell
The move to Bloomsbury was largely pioneered by Vanessa Stephen, Virginia's elder sister, who sought a liberated lifestyle in order to paint. Her homes with her husband Clive Bell, and later with Duncan Grant at Charleston, were hives of industry and talk, focal points of Bloomsbury life.

and the enjoyment of beautiful objects . . . it is they . . . that form the rational ultimate end of social progress.'

All the members of the Bloomsbury Group were united by a love of literature and the arts, and, as Clive Bell later wrote, '. . . they shared a taste for discussion in pursuit of truth and a contempt for conventional ways of thinking and feeling, contempt for conventional morals if you will.' Rebellion against Victorian morality and traditional wisdom together with freedom of expression and discussion were therefore the keynotes of the Bloomsbury Group, and these attitudes and ideas were savoured and digested during their evening conversations along with coffee, whisky and buns. One of the most radical aspects of the Group was that women took a central and active part in these discussions.

INVIGORATING TALK

For the first time in their lives, Virginia and Vanessa were not required to be decorative adjuncts at a social gathering, but were expected to contribute to energetic and searching conversation as equals. The two young women who had failed miserably as debutantes now began to shine, and even to startle their male counterparts with glimpses of their originality and wit. It was a heady experience, and Vanessa later wrote, 'You could say what you liked about art, sex or religion; you could also talk freely and very likely dully about the ordinary things of daily life . . . life was exciting, terrible and amusing and one had to explore it thankful that one could do so freely.'

With this relaxation of verbal restraint went a disregard for dress. Virginia and Vanessa, never very fashion-conscious, no longer had to care about what they wore, with the result that old acquaintances were more shocked than ever. Kitty Maxse exclaimed: 'How awful they do look!', and Henry James, an erstwhile friend and admirer of Leslie Stephen, deplored the new company that Virginia and Vanessa kept. But for the young women in question, there was no looking back. Bored and oppressed as they had been by the social requirements of their former life, they took it stoically that they might be – and were – 'cut' by former acquaintances. They were more than compensated by the kind of informal 'education' that they gained from their new associations – an enriching stimulus of which Virginia particularly had felt the lack, when her brothers went off to Cambridge. But now she was their equal. 'Never have I listened so intently to each step and half-step in an argument. Never have I been at such pains to sharpen and launch my own little dart,' she declared.

The structure and development of Bloomsbury altered in 1906 on the tragic and sudden death of Thoby. Soon afterwards, his sister Vanessa married Clive Bell and settled with him at the house in Gordon Square, while Virginia moved with Adrian to nearby Fitzroy Square. Here their

Bloomsbury life
When the Stephens moved to Bloomsbury (right), it was an unfashionable area. Above, Virginia is shown on the roof of 38 Brunswick Square with Leonard and her brother Adrian, in a painting by Duncan Grant.

Influential critic
The self-portrait of Roger Fry (left) shows him as a talented painter, but he was much more important as an art critic. He ardently championed modern French painting, and organized two famous Post-Impressionist exhibitions in London, which introduced the work of artists such as Van Gogh, Gauguin and Cézanne (right) – Fry's favourite painter – to the British public. The initial reaction was mainly one of outrage ('a swindle') and contempt ('a bad joke'), but Fry's advocacy (he was a brilliant lecturer and writer) turned the tide of critical opinion.

neighbour was the painter Duncan Grant. His presence in the group lent greater emphasis to its interest in art, and this was given a dramatic new direction by another connection with an older artist, Roger Fry.

Fry was already a celebrated figure in the art world and had been Curator of Paintings at the Metropolitan Museum in New York. In 1906, he 'discovered' the work of the great French painter Cézanne and, fired with enthusiasm for his work and that of young contemporary French painters, Fry hired the Grafton Galleries in 1910 and gave London its First Post-Impressionist Exhibition. This was the Edwardian public's first taste of an entirely new depiction of reality, and, almost without exception, they hated it.

A PRINCIPLED MINORITY

Roger Fry was soon the object of violent public wrath, and became public enemy number one in the art world. The Bloomsbury Group – and, in particular, Vanessa and Clive Bell and Duncan Grant – rallied to his defence. In so doing, they ranged themselves against a staid but powerful majority, in support of artists now considered to be among the greatest of modern painters. Roger Fry became closely involved with Bloomsbury, and in turn, influenced it enormously, as he did the public's taste – whether they liked it or not. A lover of all things French, he established links between Bloomsbury and the artistic world of Paris, and familiarized them with the work of Picasso, Matisse and Bonnard.

In 1912, Fry mounted the Second Post-Impressionist Exhibition, for which Leonard Woolf, newly returned from Ceylon, acted as secretary. This show was received as badly as the first, and Leonard Woolf recorded with disgust: 'Large numbers of people came to the exhibition,

Omega Workshops
In 1913 Roger Fry founded the Omega Workshops (right), an interior design and furnishing company that attempted to bring modern art into everyday life. The workshops were also meant to provide poor young artists with a regular source of income. Some Omega designs are now highly regarded (the screen far right, painted by Roger Fry himself, is a splendid example), but the Workshops failed commercially and were closed in 1919 amid an undignified scandal.

and nine out of ten of them either roared with laughter at the pictures or were enraged by them . . . The whole business gave me a lamentable view of human nature, its rank stupidity and uncharitableness . . . Hardly any of them made the slightest attempt to look at, let alone understand, the pictures . . .' This blind contempt was the reaction to a roomful of Cézanne watercolours, 'two enormous pictures of more than life-size figures by Matisse and three or four Picassos'.

The following year, Fry founded the Omega Workshops, with a view to applying modernist design to furniture, textiles, pottery and so on, while giving penniless young artists a form of income. Vanessa Bell, Duncan Grant, the artist Wyndham Lewis and Roger Fry were supported in this enterprise by Lady Ottoline Morrell, a flamboyant and sympathetic patroness of the arts. Despite its admirable intentions, however, Omega did not survive, partly because of a smear campaign that was conducted against Roger Fry by Wyndham Lewis. Although his charges of dishonesty and double-dealing were not only answerable but actionable, Fry did not pursue the matter. Omega was finished, and Wyndham Lewis permanently estranged.

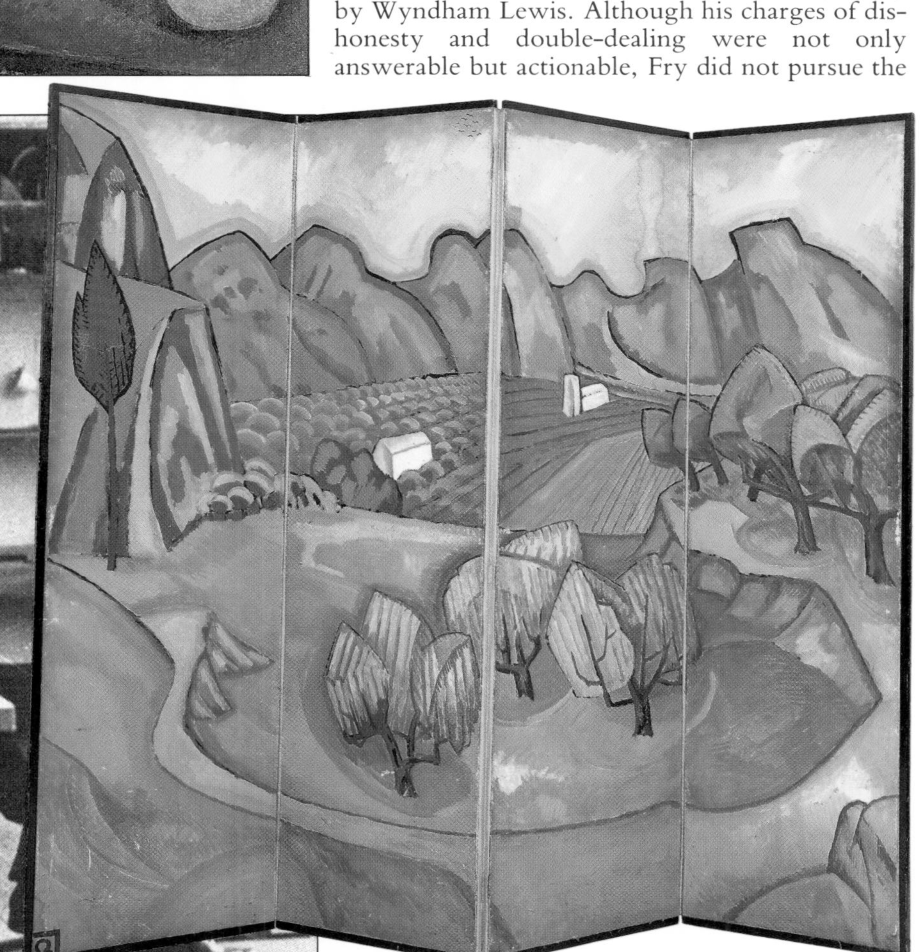

This kind of superior detachment has laid the Bloomsbury Group open to the charge of isolationism and elitism. But they were often pushed into this position by the very rigidity of the Establishment, even if they did 'enjoy' their own sense of superiority.

Duncan Grant
A versatile painter and decorator, Grant was one of the first British artists to be influenced by modern French painting. This self-portrait dates from 1918.

A more constructive and benevolent attitude that was common to Bloomsbury was tolerance. In Virginia Woolf's celebrated book *A Room Of One's Own,* she argues for an alternative kind of women's liberation from the suffragette school of protest. The Emmeline Pankhurst of literature, she says, "will write in a rage when she should write calmly. She will write foolishly where she should write wisely. She will write of herself where she should write of her characters."

Here she is by no means dismissing the suffrage movement, but talking of the problems of writing in protest about anything. Virginia Woolf was typical of Bloomsbury in that she believed ideas should be born of the cross-currents of argument in which there is no conspicuous victor.

During the 1920s, Bloomsbury was very much at the centre of intellectual and literary life in London. This was largely due to the founding of the Woolfs' Hogarth Press, which published many Bloomsbury works as well as those of outside theorists and writers. Among its most influential publications of this period were Lytton Strachey's humane but critical appraisal of the Victorian age, *Eminent Victorians;* Maynard Keynes' analysis of Europe after World War I, *The Economic Consequences of the Peace;* and Roger Fry's *Vision and Design.*

Clive Bell's book *Civilisation* and Leonard Woolf's tract on individual attainment – 'A Civilised Man' – further developed the Bloomsbury quest for social identity and purpose. As in their conversation so in their writing: both men tackled the question of civilization in a

Eccentric patroness
Striking in looks and eccentric in character, Lady Ottoline Morrell (left) played host to the Bloomsbury Group, and to many other writers, artists and intellectuals, in her homes in London and Oxfordshire.

Charleston farmhouse
In 1916 several of the 'Bloomsberries' settled at Charleston (below), which became the Group's favourite country retreat. The studio (below left) was used – and decorated – by Duncan Grant and Vanessa Bell.

rational way, but from totally opposed positions. Leonard Woolf was a socialist who believed that civilization had to be rooted with the masses, rather than imposed by Church or State. Clive Bell was an elitist who, though against violence, believed that civilization was the prerogative solely of a cultured class, whose existence had to be sustained at all costs by the excluded majority.

They were writing in the aftermath of a shattering world war, and their preoccupation was with understanding and so averting the forces of dissolution. Similar ideas underlie Virginia Woolf's work. She invariably sees aggressive threats to a peaceful, fruitful existence as specificially masculine. In *A Room of One's Own* she writes, "I began to envisage an age to come of pure, of self-assertive virility, such as . . . the rules of Italy have already brought into being." In *Orlando*, her ingenious and witty solution to the problem of political and sexual strife is to make the central character a man who wakes up one morning to find himself transformed into a woman.

WAR AND PACIFISM

During World War I, many of the Bloomsbury Group – including Clive Bell, Lytton Strachey and Duncan Grant – were conscientious objectors, and when conscription was introduced in 1916, opted to work on the land. Lady Ottoline Morrell threw open her country estate, Garsington Manor, to such pacifists as these. For the same reason, Vanessa Bell moved with Duncan Grant to Charleston Farmhouse in Sussex. Within walking distance of the Woolfs' home, Charleston continued to be a country retreat and meeting-place for the Bloomsbury Group and many distinguished friends, long after it had served its purpose as a place of political sanctuary.

Charleston was decorated by various members of the Group, including Duncan Grant, who made it his home until his death in 1978 – he was the last of the 'Bloomsberries' to survive. By this time there had been a great revival of interest in the Bloomsbury Group, following a period when they were generally dismissed as elitist, and even accused of being a kind of intellectual mafia, protecting their own interests against outsiders. Opened to the public, Charleston has become a popular place of cultural pilgrimage.

D. H. Lawrence

1885 - 1930

D. H. Lawrence explored previously uncharted areas of human experience. His troubled boyhood and tempestuous marriage, his vulnerability to the powerful forces of sexual passion, all became the raw material of his art. His work outraged many and fell foul of the censors, and Lawrence abandoned England to wander the world in search of a better, truer way of life. He never found rest during his painfully brief career, but his quest enriched modern literature beyond measure.

Prophet or Pornographer?

The critics called his books "sex depravity". His friends called him a visionary. Meanwhile, sick and restless, Lawrence took his burden of passion and talent in search of an earthly paradise.

End-of-terrace
The Lawrences paid an extra sixpence a week for the privilege of renting the end-of-terrace cottage in The Breach (above) in Eastwood. Although a collier's home, it was by no means squalid. Nevertheless, in retrospect, Lawrence found the surrounding industrial landscapes (below) soulless and inhuman – 'visions of pure ugliness'.

With his working-class background and volatile, charismatic personality, D. H. Lawrence cut an unusual figure on the literary scene of the early 1900s. Hailed as a prophet by some and condemned as a pornographer by others, Lawrence was beset by controversy. His short, troubled life was one of stormy relationships and restless wanderings, scarred by bad health and illuminated by a supreme literary talent.

David Herbert Richards Lawrence was born on 11 September 1885 at Eastwood, a little mining town a few miles from Nottingham. His father, Arthur Lawrence, was a hearty, barely literate collier with a taste for the public house that outraged his wife Lydia. Better educated than her husband, Lydia was determined that none of her five children should go 'down t' pit'. Family life was full of rows and tensions, which left their mark on Lawrence and which he was to recapture vividly in one of his most famous novels, *Sons and Lovers*.

The future writer was the Lawrences' fourth child, 'a delicate pale brat with a snuffy nose' whose constitutional frailty was already apparent. His passion for nature and his preference for the company of girls puzzled the rough colliers' sons, but Bert Lawrence was a clever boy who did well enough at the local Board School to be entered for a scholarship to Nottingham High School. He won it – £12 a year – and became one of the very few working-class children to receive a secondary education.

At the end of three years at Nottingham High

Family and friends
The conflict within the Lawrence family (left), with its imposingly handsome father and dauntingly ambitious matriarch, took its toll on Bert (pictured between his parents). He found sanctuary and friendship in the nearby home of Jessie Chambers (above). It was she who first encouraged him to be a writer.

'A damnable time'
Nottingham University College (below) did not live up to the young Lawrence's expectations. 'College gave me nothing,' he wrote, and he left there 'bitten . . . deep with disappointment'.

School, Lawrence, not yet 16, was found a job as a clerk with a surgical goods' firm in the city, and seemed set on a course that was unlikely to alter. But after three months he suffered a severe attack of pneumonia which brought him near to death. His mother, who had just lost her favourite son, nursed Bert devotedly, and a fiercely possessive bond was forged.

But Mrs Lawrence had a rival. As part of his convalescence, Lawrence started visiting the Haggs, a smallholding three miles from Eastwood run by Edmund and Sarah Anne Chambers and their seven children. The happy atmosphere of the farm delighted him, and he fell in love with the whole family. For their part the Chambers brought out the best in Lawrence, whose helpfulness, lively responses and resourcefulness in inventing games brightened their existence. As Mr Chambers declared, 'Work goes like fun when Bert's there'. For several years the Haggs was a second home to Lawrence: 'a new life began in me there'.

TEACHING AND LEARNING

Lawrence never returned to clerking. In 1902 he became a pupil-teacher at the British School in Eastwood, taking classes while himself receiving instruction. After 'three years' teaching of savage collier lads' at £5 a year, he had passed enough examinations and saved enough money to take up a scholarship to Nottingham University College. Although he found college 'mere disillusion, instead of the living contact of men', he did emerge from it a qualified teacher.

Being a student gave Lawrence time for writing. Over the years at the Haggs he had grown very close to one of the Chambers girls, Jessie (the 'Miriam' of *Sons and Lovers*). He was later to describe their relationship as a 'betrothal of six years' standing', though its development was hindered by the jealous hostility of Lawrence's mother. With Jessie, he explored the world of literature, and her encouragement and enthusiasm was vital to his flowering as a writer.

It was this encouragement which was soon to be equally important in getting Lawrence published. In the autumn of 1908 he took up his first official teaching post, at Davidson Road School in Croydon. A few months later, Jessie copied

Key Dates

1885 born at Eastwood

1898 Nottingham High School

1906 Nottingham University College

1908 teacher in Croydon

1909 poems published in *English Review*

1910 mother dies

1911 *The White Peacock*

1912 meets Frieda

1922 visits Ceylon, New Mexico and Australia

1928 *Lady Chatterley's Lover* published in Florence

1930 dies at Vence

out and sent some of his poems to Ford Madox Hueffer, editor of *The English Review*. Hueffer, who had an exceptional flair for recognizing original work, published the poems in his magazine, helped Lawrence to place his first novel, *The White Peacock* published in 1911, and introduced him to London literary life. Lawrence's horizons were widening, though his emotional life was in some confusion – he was involved with Jessie, with another Eastwood woman, Alice Dax, with whom he probably had his first sexual experience, and with Helen Corke, a fellow-teacher at Croydon.

FRIEDA VON RICHTHOFEN

Lawrence's wife was six years older than him – a German aristocrat related to the World War I air ace Baron Manfred von Richthofen, 'the Red Baron'. Her marriage to lecturer Ernest Weekley lasted 12 years, and they had three children. But her provincial life bored her and she had already had several lovers when she met D. H. Lawrence. He wrote, 'She's got a figure like a fine Rubens woman, but her face is almost Greek.' It was he who insisted that an affair was not enough and that Frieda must run away with him. The cost was high: her wronged husband cut her off from her children. After Lawrence's death, Frieda became the lover of his friend John Middleton Murry and later married an Italian, Angelo Ravagli. She died in 1956.

In December 1910 Lawrence's mother died of cancer – a traumatic event that he sought to cope with, or escape from, by becoming engaged to Louie Burrows, 'a glorious girl ... swarthy and ruddy as a pomegranate', with whom he had been friendly since his pupil-teacher days. But 1911 was 'the sick year' – psychologically and eventually physically. In November Lawrence came down with pneumonia again and was told that he would become consumptive if he carried on teaching. The doctor's pronouncement gave him an excuse to break off his by now unwanted engagement, and force him to try his hand at being a full-time professional writer.

The culminating event of this critical period occurred in March 1912, while Lawrence was staying with his sister in Eastwood. He called on his old professor, Ernest Weekley, head of the Department of Modern Languages at Nottingham University College, and met Weekley's German wife, Frieda. Two months later Lawrence and Frieda eloped abroad, and in 1914, after Frieda's divorce, they were married. This was the central relationship of Lawrence's life, explored time and again in his writing. Frieda, a lazy and amoral aristocrat, was quite unlike Lawrence, and sturdily resisted his attempts to dominate or bully her – which was probably just what he needed. Despite infidelities, volcanic rows and furious throwing of plates, the relationship endured.

In 1912 Lawrence and Frieda went to Germany, walked over the Alps into Italy and wintered on Lake Garda. Lawrence was now writing hard, fully launched as a professional. He finished *Sons and Lovers*, which completed his break with Jessie; but more positively, its publication in 1913 brought him new friends in the literary world – most notably the critic John Middleton Murry and the New Zealand born short-story writer Katherine Mansfield, later Murry's wife.

A home in Italy
After a trip through Italy, the Lawrences took a villa in Sicily, at Taormina (above).

Close friendships
Relations between the Murrys (John Middleton Murry and Katherine Mansfield, below) and the Lawrences were intense. Murry resisted Frieda's advances, because of loyalty to his beloved 'Lorenzo', but was often critical of Lawrence's writing.

Most of Lawrence's friendships were fraught, but his relationship with Murry – that of hectoring master and unreliable chief disciple – was particularly strained and tortuous. Among others whom he met during this period were the patron-anthologist Edward Marsh, E.M. Forster, Lady Ottoline Morrell and the philosopher Bertrand Russell, over whom he exercised a remarkable, though temporary, influence.

A NIGHTMARE PERIOD

Newly married, Lawrence was on a walking tour of the Lake District when World War I broke out, trapping him and Frieda in England. Lawrence was quite obviously unfit to serve (though he was twice subjected to military medical examinations). He loathed the war, which he saw as the culmination of soulless mechanization, now applied to mass slaughter. This was a nightmare period, intensified by his first serious clash with British censorship. His novel *The Rainbow*, published in September 1915, was prosecuted for obscenity by the Public Morality Council; the publisher cravenly apologized, pleading that he was unaware of the book's contents, and with a few exceptions (Arnold Bennett was one) its suppression was effected without any protest whatsoever from the literary establishment.

Worse was to follow. The Lawrences settled at Zennor in Cornwall, where their bohemian ways and Frieda's German origin brought them under popular suspicion. The hysterical wartime mood was such that local people even believed the clothes on the Lawrences' washing line to be a semaphore signal intended for lurking U-boats. In 1917, after a police search of their cottage, they were given just three days to pack up and leave Cornwall for an unprohibited area, where they were required to report regularly to the police.

The war completed Lawrence's disenchantment with civilization, intensifying one of his recurrent waking dreams – to set up a colony of like-minded individuals, a utopian community which he named Rananim. In some distant place they could 'live out of the world – make a sort of Garden of Eden of blameless but fulfilled souls'. But when it came to the point, even his closest friends were not keen to leave England and live in too close proximity to a prickly genius such as Lawrence.

The Armistice of November 1918 ended the War, but soon afterwards Lawrence was laid low by the influenza epidemic that was sweeping the world. It was November 1919 before he was able to leave England, which was never again his home. He visited Florence and Capri, meeting the

Villa Mirenda
Lawrence rented the top floor of a hill-top villa in Tuscany for a year. He wrote and painted there – the above view of the Villa Mirenda is painted by him.

Tregarthen Cottage
(below) During the war, Lawrence and Frieda 'hibernated' in the Cornish countryside. But the locals mistrusted them and, branded as spies, the Lawrences were ordered to leave.

novelists Norman Douglas and Compton Mackenzie, before settling in a villa at Taormina in Sicily in March 1920.

Lawrence and Frieda spent two richly creative years at Taormina before his inveterate restlessness drove him to move again. Feeling that Europe was 'finished', he responded favourably to an invitation to Taos in New Mexico from Mabel Dodge Sterne, a much-married American who had set up an artists' colony there. One of its attractions was the local Indian culture; Lawrence was fascinated by primitive peoples, whose 'blood wisdom' seemed to him superior to Western man's 'head consciousness'.

But he was not sure that he would like the formidable Mrs Sterne, and put off a decision while he and Frieda took ship – in the opposite direction. They spent a few weeks at Colombo in Ceylon, enough time to convince Lawrence that he could not live in the tropics. Then they went on to Australia, where Lawrence exercised his uncanny gift for capturing the essence of a place almost at once.

In Western Australia Lawrence met Mollie Skinner, a sometime nurse and sometime novellist whose *The Boy in the Bush* he was later to revise and publish under their joint names. And during a few weeks spent at Thirroul, New South Wales, he wrote his next novel, *Kangaroo*. But Australia could not hold him, and in August 1922 he and Frieda left for San Francisco, Taos and Mabel Sterne.

ROCKY MOUNTAIN HOME

'Taos too much. Mabel Sterne and suppers and motor drives and people dropping in', Lawrence tersely noted of the artists' colony dominated by his hostess, whose designs on him amused and irritated Frieda. But New Mexico was 'the greatest experience from the outside world that I have ever had'. Here Lawrence learned to ride and, as soon as they could, he and Frieda moved out to 'an old brown log cabin' in the Rockies.

The following spring they crossed the border, staying in Mexico City and Chapala while Lawrence began his Mexican novel, *The Plumed Serpent*. But after 3 months they left for New York, intending to sail for England. Frieda was tired of the Mexican heat, and was longing to see her children, who had been kept away from her by her ex-husband but were now grown up. Lawrence went with reluctance ('my soul doesn't want to come to Europe'), and in New York he and Frieda quarrelled violently. Lawrence stayed behind, and for a time it seemed that the marriage was over.

Eventually it was Lawrence who came across the Atlantic to Frieda. But neither enjoyed Europe now, and Lawrence tried – unsuccessfully – to raise recruits to return with him to a New Mexican Rananim. Lawrence and Frieda sailed back to America in March 1924, accompanied on the *Aquitania* by a single disciple – the

Dorothy Brett
This young artist (right), fresh from an affair with John Middleton Murry, devoted herself to Lawrence. She followed him to New Mexico, and painted the above portrait in 1925. But Frieda told her to go, saying 'You are just a beastly nuisance.'

In a new world
'In the magnificent fierce morning of New Mexico one sprang awake . . . the old world gave way to a new,' wrote Lawrence, at first supremely happy in Mabel Sterne's desert community at Taos. He and Dorothy Brett painted and rode together. They both worked on the picture, left, of the ranch. The individual characters are all depictions of Lawrence, Frieda and Brett, occupied in various different daily tasks. But Frieda felt excluded by such intimate shared pastimes as painting.

Hon. Dorothy Brett, a partially deaf, forceful young painter who sported short hair, trousers and an ear trumpet.

The threesome spent spring and summer at Taos and the 'log cabin', now re-named by Lawrence the Kiowa Ranch, which Mabel Sterne generously presented to Frieda. Then they went to Mexico so that Lawrence could finish *The Plumed Serpent* – a disastrous trip during which Frieda insisted on the over-appreciative Brett being sent packing and Lawrence fell desperately ill with malaria at Oaxaca. When he went for a medical examination in Mexico City, a doctor told Lawrence the unpleasant truth – he was consumptive.

In September 1925 Lawrence left the New World – as it turned out, for the last time. He felt 'queer and foreign' in England, and from now onwards lived mainly in Italy. Here he became fascinated by the half-lost civilization of the Etruscans, whom he idealized as a life-loving people destroyed by the power and money-hungry forces of the Romans, a favoured theme of his.

LADY CHATTERLEY

Until the last two years of his life Lawrence remained as prolific as ever, among other works producing no fewer than three versions of the novel *Lady Chatterley's Lover*, his most bluntly expressed advocacy of sexual fulfilment. The book was printed in Florence in 1928, since there was no question of publishing it in England, where vigorous attempts were made to hunt down and destroy copies that had been imported surreptitiously.

Lawrence's notoriety was further increased when his paintings were exhibited at a London gallery in 1929. Twelve thousand people went to see them, including a group of policemen (sent by the Home Secretary) who removed 13 of the paintings. Lawrence's nudes, which now seem inoffensive enough, were judged obscene and narrowly escaped being burnt.

'Goodbye Lorenzo'
'Like a bird we put him away, a few of us who loved him,' wrote Frieda of Lawrence's burial in Vence. Five years later, she and her new husband removed Lawrence's ashes to a chapel built for him at Taos (above), where the ashes were cemented in place to prevent Mabel Sterne stealing them.

"NOT MUCH LEFT OF ME"

By this time, Lawrence was a dying man, having suffered a terrible lung haemorrhage in the summer of 1927. His friend Aldous Huxley described him as 'living by sheer force of will and by nothing else'. On 6 February 1930 Lawrence entered a sanatorium at Vence, in the South of France, where Huxley and H.G. Wells were among the well-wishers who came to see him. He left the sanatorium on 1 March, but died at the nearby Villa Robermond the following day with Frieda beside him.

Lawrence was buried at Vence, but in 1935 his ashes were removed to the Kiowa Ranch in New Mexico, where Frieda placed them in a specially built chapel crowned with Lawrence's personal symbol, the immortal, self-resurrecting, fabulous bird, the phoenix.

Fact or Fiction

MABEL DODGE STERNE

Having buried one husband and divorced two more, Mabel married American Indian Tony Luhan and had predatory designs on Lawrence. Intelligent but spoiled, she liked to dispense largesse to an adoring retinue. She recognized herself as *The Woman Who Rode Away*, a woman who gives herself ritually into the hands of Indians.

Mexican Magic

'The Indian, the Aztec, old Mexico – all that fascinates me and has fascinated me for years. *There* is glamour and magic for me . . . It seems to me my fate.' D. H. LAWRENCE

When D. H. Lawrence visited Mexico in 1923 it captured his imagination as no other country had done or would do. It intrigued and mystified him. It had one reality on the surface and quite another within, and though Lawrence was captivated by both, loving the surface colour, the "brilliant sun . . . on the hibiscus flowers . . . the fluttering yellow and green rags of the banana trees", it was the inner aspect of Mexico, with its darkly mystical people and places, that crept inside him, lodging itself somewhere deep within his being.

Ancient and modern
The Indians were steeped in ritual and mythology, incorporating many ancient beliefs into their own mystical view of life. The carving of the priest (right) dates from around AD *700 and yet has strikingly similar facial features to those of the modern Indian (left).*

GREATER TRUTHS

Throughout his young manhood, Lawrence had been somehow dissatisfied with his surroundings, searching for a greater truth, something to give meaning to the form of everyday things. And Mexico seemed to provide, if not the answer, then certainly a key. The local Indians, with their mixture of magic and ritual, their dances, their closeness to Nature, inspired Lawrence to try to penetrate their 'blood consciousness' and learn the secrets of their ancient, timeless religion. And in the relics of the past – the pyramids and the temples – lay clues to the various civilizations that had tamed and shaped present-day Mexico.

The temples honoured and reflected ancient deities – Aztec, Mayan and Toltec – that were all interlinked. The most celebrated of these deities, Quetzalcoatl, the Plumed Serpent, fascinated Lawrence beyond all the others. Seen all over Mexico in different forms, this deity represented the sort of instinctive life force that Lawrence explored and celebrated in much of his writing.

The Indian population of ancient Mexico was made up of many different tribes and, as Lawrence noted in *The Plumed Serpent,* that variety was still evident in their modern-day descendants, from the "wild, sombre, erect men of the north" to the "quick little Indians, quick as spiders, down in Oaxaca" and the "half-Chinese natives towards Vera Cruz". In Quetzalcoatl they shared a common deity, though their cultural practices and methods of worship differed over time and region.

Like King Arthur, Quetzalcoatl is half-man, half-legend. His historical existence is not disputed, though there is little hard fact to go on. At some time in history – whether before Christ or rather later is not certain – he came among the ancient peoples as a tall, fair-bearded man who was a great civilizer and law-giver, a priest-king of rare compassion and understanding. Both scientist and artist, he introduced the staple diet of maize and, like the Buddha, had a horror of violence towards living things. Subsequent practitioners of his wise and gentle religion took on the name Quetzalcoatl, a confusion that explains the blend of fact and myth surrounding the story of the Plumed Serpent.

Legend has it that as the boy-god grew up, evil magicians tried in vain to tempt him to perform human sacrifices. Chief among these tempters was the malevolent god Tezcatlipoca, who became the Aztec god of war and sacrifice,

Chichén Itzá
The sacred city of Chichén Itzá (below) was the largest centre of Toltec and Mayan civilization. The stepped pyramid was dedicated to Quetzalcoatl, the Plumed Serpent, and serpent imagery in all its forms permeates Mexican culture. The duality between opposed forces, as personified by the Mexican gods, had an irresistible appeal to Lawrence.

Huitzilopochtli. One of his wicked ploys was to deck Quetzalcoatl in finery and to ply him with strong wine. This time he succumbed to temptation, and during a drunken debauch slept with his sister.

Later, when sober, Quetzalcoatl was stricken with horror at what he had done – and knew that penance would have to be paid. Accordingly he and his servants marched to the eastern seashore and there the Plumed Serpent dressed himself in his feathered robes and turquoise mask, built a funeral pyre and threw himself upon it. A flock of birds bore his ashes aloft and he ascended to the heavens as the planet Venus, where, until the date prophesied for his return, he watched over his lands and people. In this story of self-immolation lie the seeds of the later cults of wholesale human sacrifice, cults which Lawrence was to recapture in such stories as *The Woman Who Rode Away*.

Among the earliest of the great pre-Conquest cultures was that of the Mayans. They were based in the jungle city of Chichén Itzá in Yucatán to the east, and the 'City of the Gods', Teotihuacán, situated some 30 miles north-east of modern-day Mexico City. This is the site of the massive Pyramids to the Sun and the Moon, and the famous Temple of Quetzalcoatl, decorated with the sculptures of snarling serpents, that so impressed Lawrence when he went there in 1923.

A FLOURISHING CULTURE

Although human sacrifice was occasionally practised, the religion that dominated these societies still owed something to the gentle and wise ways of the original Quetzalcoatl. For 300 years there was a remarkable flourishing of the arts and sciences. Priests and scholars developed esoteric hieroglyphic scripts and a complex system of time and dates, based on the most precise astronomical calculations.

The Mayans fixed the length of a year (that is, one revolution of the earth round the sun) only a

Sacrificial victim
The Mayans believed that the world could be redeemed only by means of annual sacrifices. To that end Tezcatlipoca, god of all things of this world, donned the human skin of a sacrificial victim, as the Plumed Serpent (below), symbol of the green earth, opened his jaws to receive the body.

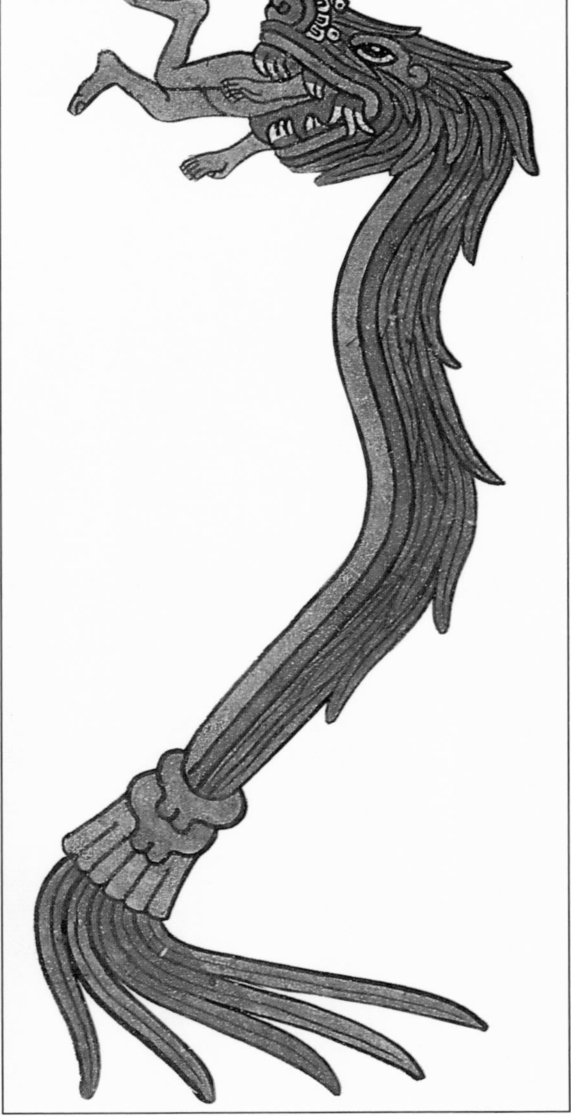

Concepts of time
In Mexican concepts of time, myth and science overlap. The huge calendar stone (left) is Aztec. Carved c. 1503, it represents the present in the centre, with earlier ages surrounding it. Although time was viewed cyclically rather than mathematically, their year was within seconds of our own.

few seconds short of modern calculations. The religious calendar, however, ran to only 260 days (in parts of Mexico and Guatemala the old system is still used and the days are called by their ancient names).

By a complicated calculation involving these two time-spans, a sacred period of 52 years was incorporated into the calendar, during which fires were lit to symbolize the continuation of time. At the end of each of these periods new fires were kindled to ensure that the world did not come to an end.

The ancients' concept of time is fundamental to an understanding of their civilization. In *Mornings in Mexico,* Lawrence says that for the Mexican Indian, "time is a vague, foggy reality", whereas to the Westerner, imagined by Lawrence as representing some form of "white monkey" to the Mexican, "The day is a horrible puzzle of exact spots of time".

The Mexicans' elastic view of time, which can exasperate the European visitor, is rooted very firmly in the old mythology. It is a cyclical rather than a chronological view of the passing of time, a system based on the revolution of the planets in which days, months and years each had their own gods – yesterday could quite easily become tomorrow because all time constantly recurred. This ideology exerted an extraordinary influence over individuals, and dictated, according to the time and day of their birth, their every action – even how and when they would die.

'MASTER CRAFTSMEN'

The so-called Classic period of ancient Mexico came to an abrupt end in about A.D. 900, probably as a result of epidemic, drought and invasion. A tribe called the Toltecs then took over power in the region of Teotihuacán.

Their name means 'Master Craftsmen', and the Toltecs produced some of the most beautiful artefacts of the pre-Hispanic era. Some say that one of their rulers, Topiltzin, was an incarnation of Quetzalcoatl. Certainly the Plumed Serpent was one of their chief deities, together with the wayward and powerful Tezcatlipoca, 'Lord of the Smoking Mirror', to whom they made human sacrifices.

On Tezcatlipoca's feast day, a youth chosen for his presumed likeness to the god would regard it as an honour to give up his life. For twelve months before his sacrifice, he would be the object of great reverence, cherished and accorded the respect normally reserved for gods.

In the uncorrupted teachings and example of Quetzalcoatl, sacrifice had been an ideal only, a symbolic giving up of one's heart as a way to perfect love and understanding. In the Toltec culture, as in those that preceded it, the myth was acted out in real life.

When the heroine of Lawrence's short story *The Woman Who Rode Away* is asked by her Indian captors, "do you bring your heart to the god of Chilchui?", she automatically answers yes – meaning that she is willing to absorb herself in the mystery of their religion and culture. Only later does "An icy pang of fear and certainty" grip her heart as she realizes that their intention is to sacrifice her to their god.

The Aztecs who followed the Toltec culture in the Mexican Valley region, appropriating their deities and adding some of their own, compounded this misconception in the most barbarous way imaginable. In the space of a few

Primitive rituals
As Lawrence wrote, "The Indian is completely embedded in the wonder of his own drama". Even today, Mexicans remain dazzled by their heritage. The 20th-century artist Diego Rivera often drew on this rich past for inspiration, as in the painting above.

hundred years the 'Heron People' – spurred on by their brutish war god Huitzilopochtli ('Left-handed Hummingbird'), who required a constant replenishment of fresh, bleeding hearts – rose from beggarly origins to reign supreme over much of Mexico.

Theirs was a militaristic society. The Aztecs tyrannized their empire, and so feared and hated did they become that at the time of the Spanish Conquest of Mexico in the 16th century, their subject peoples had no hesitation in siding with the Spanish.

Yet the Aztec civilization was one of considerable cultural achievement and interest. The city of Tenochtitlán, built on a lake, was a triumph of engineering and architecture, which to the conquistadors (the conquering Spaniards) appeared as 'an enchanted vision'. Its people were musical and artistic and daily life centred on religious festivals. On their innumerable feast days the populace became divinely drunk on tequila, pulque and mescal, while the priests routinely took massive doses of hallucinatory drugs, derived from mushrooms and cacti, and fell into visionary states.

But the Aztecs' pre-eminence came to depend more and more on the perpetual waging of war – which kept neighbouring tribes in subjection and accrued great riches – and on ceaseless blood-letting to appease Huitzilopochtli. It was a case of a political imperative being justified and encouraged by religious orthodoxy, and it was taken to quite absurd lengths. The 'Xochiyaoyotl', or ritual 'War of the Flowers', was a contest to the death between Aztec warriors and those from subject tribes, which was designed to maintain a steady flow of sacrificial hearts even in 'peacetime'.

Quetzalcoatl
The head of the Plumed Serpent (above and left) juts out on either side of the steps of the temple dedicated to him at Teotihuacán. It dates from AD 700.

Mask of Tezcatlipoca
It was to the fearsome god Tezcatlipoca (left) that human sacrifices were made. On his particular feast day a youth, judged to be the earthly image of the god, was sacrificed in his honour. The boy apparently gave up his life willingly, believing that therein lay a higher form of existence.

Another bizarre rite was the fertility dance dedicated to the god of seed-time and planting, Xipe Totec, the 'Flayed One'. Prisoners from the latest fighting would be sacrificed and the priests would then peel off their skins in a single piece. While the skinless carcase was chopped up and taken away to be feasted on, the priests would don the skins like a body suit and lead a ritual dance from house to house.

HUMAN SACRIFICES

The most notorious of the Aztec rulers was Ahuitzotl, whose name has passed down into the language – 'Qué ahuitzote!', say Mexicans, meaning 'How fierce!' At the dedication ceremony of the Great Temple of Tenochtitlán he ordered the sacrifice of 20,000 prisoners captured in battle. They awaited their fate standing in four lines, more than three miles long.

The victims were spread-eagled over a saddle-shaped stone by four priests holding their arms and legs. The executioner would then stab the obsidian knife into their chests, rummage with his other hand, and wrench free the still-pumping hearts, which he then held aloft, proffering them to the sun. This slaughter at the Great Temple continued for four days until the city stank from the smell of human blood.

Such atrocities were committed in the name of a religion dominated by the mythological figures of Huitzilopochtli and Quetzalcoatl, who represented the opposite forces of war and peace, darkness and light, evil and good.

It was this duality that appealed to Lawrence and found an echo in his own preoccupations with the reconciliation of opposing forces as a way to cosmic understanding. In *The Plumed Serpent* Cipriano "was Huitzilopochtli, Ramon was Quetzalcoatl", intent on purging a people that "took more satisfaction in ultimately destroying their heroes, than . . . raising them high".

THE PLUMED SERPENT'S REVENGE

The bloody Aztec civilization may have destroyed everything that Quetzalcoatl had originally stood for, but he was to have the last laugh. The conquistadors landed in the New World in the very year (1519) when, according to legend, Quetzalcoatl would return to his people and lands. It was a coincidence that struck terror into the hearts of the Aztecs, who believed that the great Plumed Serpent had come back to wreak vengeance on their degenerate culture. Demoralized and fearful, they proved no match for the Spanish leader, Hernán Cortés, and his small army. They easily captured Tenochtitlán (which was rebuilt as Mexico City), despite being overwhelmingly outnumbered, and the Aztec civilization was extinguished forever.

Sacrificial knife
Below is the knife used to gouge out the hearts of the human sacrifices. The handle represents a crouching star god, poised to catch the blood of the victim.

'Saddle-shaped stone'
Although the precise function of the figure at right is in doubt, many believe that it was on this 'saddle-shaped stone' that sacrificial victims had their hearts ripped from their bodies. Pairs of priests would bind the victim's hands and head, and lay him face upwards on the stone, then one priest would plunge the sacrificial knife into his chest before raising the heart upwards in an offering to the sun.

ALDOUS HUXLEY

1894-1963

One of the outstanding intellectual figures of the 20th century, Aldous Huxley was blessed with a mind capable of embracing every field of human knowledge. A witty, acute social commentator, he was hailed as the cynical spokesman of his generation, yet retained a gentleness of character that won him countless friends. He staked his literary reputation on advice and warnings about human progress towards the future, eager to maintain a balanced unity of Science, Nature and Humanity.

Tender-Hearted Pessimist

His prophetic visions seemed doom-laden, but Huxley was a gentle, compassionate man 'in whom wisdom never destroyed innocence'.

Aldous Huxley was not only one of the outstanding writers of his generation, illuminating every subject he touched with a remarkably original intelligence, but also a man whose warmth, humanity, wit and courage in adversity made him a joy and inspiration to a brilliant circle of friends and admirers. His fellow writer Raymond Mortimer said of him: 'Nobody else I know has combined so fine a brain, such encyclopaedic knowledge and so deep a response to all the arts with such sweetness of character.'

A DISTINGUISHED FAMILY

Aldous Leonard Huxley was born on 26 July 1894 at a house called Laleham, near Godalming in Surrey. Socially he belonged to the upper middle class, but in intellectual terms he was born into the aristocracy. His father was Leonard Huxley, a fine classical scholar who was a master at Charterhouse School and later became editor of the *Cornhill Magazine*. His mother was Julia Frances (née Arnold), an exceptional woman who was the driving force of the family. The granddaughter of Dr Thomas Arnold (headmaster of Rugby and a great educational reformer) and niece of the poet and critic Matthew Arnold, she – like her husband – gained a first-class degree at Oxford University. After having four children – Julian (who became an eminent biologist and philosopher), Trevenen, Aldous and Margaret – she established a school for girls at Prior's Field in Surrey. Her sons competed for her love and attention, and Julian later recalled that Aldous in particular loved her 'passionately'.

Aldous came of distinguished lineage on the paternal side, too, for his grandfather was the eminent biologist, Thomas Henry Huxley, a freethinker and champion of Darwinism who gave the word 'agnostic' to the English language. Like his brothers, Aldous was encouraged to read widely from an early age and explore knowledge and ideas. His parents were affectionate and caring, but there was a price to pay for his upbringing: he had to do exceptionally well academically ('Huxleys always get Firsts') and was expected to stifle 'unseemly' emotions. It was this rigidity – characteristic of the repressive formality of Victorian England – against which Aldous, along with many other writers and artists of his generation, reacted. His rebellion was fuelled by three major tragedies in the space of six years: the death of his mother; a chronic eye infection; and the suicide of his brother Trevenen.

The first disaster occurred in November 1908, when Aldous, aged 14, was in his first term at Eton. His mother had cancer and died after a short illness, aged 45. The family was grief-stricken, but Aldous – 'very sensitive and brooding' – largely suppressed his feelings, and after he returned to Eton he distinguished himself academically, particularly in biology. He determined to become a doctor, but his dreams suffered a shattering blow when, in 1911, he suddenly developed a serious infection in both eyes. Sent home from Eton, he

Father and sons
Close-knit and gifted as they were, the Huxleys were dogged by tragedy. The suicide of Trevenen (above right) as a young man shattered his younger brother, Aldous (above).

Key Dates

1894 born in Surrey
1908 mother dies
1914 Trevenen dies
1919 marries Maria Nys
1932 *Brave New World*
1937 settles in the United States
1954 *The Doors of Perception*
1955 Maria dies
1956 marries Laura Archera
1962 elected a Companion of Literature
1963 dies in Los Angeles

Thomas Huxley
Over half a century before Aldous became a student at Balliol College (top), his illustrious grandfather (above) had shaken Oxford's repose with his vigorous and witty support of Darwin's theory of evolution.

Eton College
(left) Excelling at Eton, like his brothers before him, Aldous considered it 'a very good school'.

suffered 18 months of virtual blindness, and his vision was strictly limited for the rest of his life.

Cut off from his friends, his ambitions in shreds, Aldous typically responded by doggedly learning Braille in order to continue his studies. When the infection subsided, he pored painfully over page after page with a huge magnifying glass; and with the help of various tutors, Aldous, like his brothers before him, became a student at Balliol College, Oxford.

Less than a year later, on 23rd August 1914, the 24-year-old Trevenen, who of all the family had done most to encourage his disabled younger brother, committed suicide. Comparatively poor Finals results and a hushed-up affair with the family's parlourmaid have been cited as the causes. For Aldous, however, the reason for Trevenen's death lay deeper. As he wrote to his cousin Gervas, 'It is the highest and best in Trev – his ideals – which have driven him to his death . . . Trev was not strong, but he had the courage to face life with ideals – and his ideals were too much for him.'

TRANSIENCE OF HAPPINESS

The cumulative force of these tragedies impressed upon Aldous a sense of the transience of happiness and the frailty of human life and a belief that high ideals alone were not enough to sustain a person. These impressions were reinforced as he watched many of his Oxford friends go blithely off to die for King and Country in the trenches of World War I. 'The West has plucked its flowers and has thrown/Them fading on the night', he wrote in *The Burning Wheel,* his first collection of poems, published in 1916.

Rejected by the army as totally unfit, he continued his studies, gaining a First in English in June 1916. He wrote triumphantly to his brother Julian: 'I should like to go on for ever learning. I lust for knowledge, as well theoretic and empirical.' The brilliant student cut an unusual figure: immensely tall (six feet four-and-a-half inches) with a pipecleaner frame, his almost sightless eyes emphasizing his charming, rather ethereal air of self-deprecation, he appeared the epitome of the underfed, overbred aesthete. Only his liking for floppy neckwear hinted at a streak of unconventional flamboyance.

After a short spell vainly attempting to do his bit for the war effort at the Air Board, Huxley gained a poorly paid teaching post at Eton. The holidays, however, he spent at Garsington Manor, the Oxfordshire home of Sir Philip and Lady Ottoline Morrell, providers of open house to the Bloomsbury Group of intellectuals, all of whom were opposed to the war. Huxley later recalled: 'The meeting of all these people was of capital importance to me.'

Garsington was a hothouse of culture, new ideas and permissiveness, unlike anything the withdrawn, fledgling writer had encountered before. While staying there in the summer of 1916, however, he met a soulmate in the 16-year-old Belgian refugee Maria Nys. Her innocence, spontaneity

Whitehall wanderings
In 1917, having failed his medical repeatedly because of poor eyesight, Huxley accepted a low-paid clerical job at the Air Board (right), wishing to do his bit for the war effort. But he was, understandably, entirely out of place there. Surrounded by people 'with absolutely no interest in life but making money and gossiping about their hideous homes', he ached from 'the soul-weariness with which this place overcomes one.'

and love of life he found irresistible. The pair fell in love and resolved to marry, but the war, Maria's youth and Aldous' lack of finances seemed insurmountable barriers. Finally after painful years of enforced separation, they were married in Belgium on 10 July 1919.

Maria, loyal, intuitive, loving and sociable, was to have a profound, healing effect on Aldous' life. For 36 years she nursed him through illness after illness, at all times doing everything she could to make his life as tranquil as possible. She was his 'eyes' and later his chauffeur on their countless tours of Europe and America; her sociability and charm brought him the human contact he craved and yet shrank from; she breathed vitality into the sterile, rarefied world of ideas that had threatened to become his prison.

The couple settled in a small flat in Hampstead, north-west London, Huxley having given up teaching and gained an editorial post at the *Athenaeum* magazine. In January 1920 *Limbo,* his first book of short stories, was published; in April, after an alarmingly difficult labour, Maria gave birth to their son Matthew. With a family to support, lack of money was a constant pressure, and Huxley took on extra work, becoming drama and music critic for the *Westminster Gazette,* and then working for *House & Garden.*

By the spring of 1921, they had saved enough to spend the summer in Italy, and it was there in Florence that Huxley completed his first novel, *Crome Yellow.* The critical success it received and also that of a subsequent volume of short stories, *Mortal Coils,* convinced publishers Chatto & Windus that Huxley was worth encouraging. In 1923 they offered him a contract which allowed him to

Nancy Cunard
An outrageous post-war socialite, the beautiful Nancy Cunard (above) was, briefly, the object of Huxley's sudden, passionate, unrequited love. Like one of his characters, he loved her "against reason, against all his ideals and principles, madly . . ."

devote himself from then on to his writing – a long-cherished dream.

Although £500 a year was not a large sum on which to live in London, it would keep his family in relative comfort in Italy, and in early summer of 1923 they moved there, settling in Florence in August. They left England under a cloud, for Huxley had become briefly and passionately involved with the unconventional Twenties socialite Nancy Cunard. The unhappy affair ended as suddenly as it had begun.

The voracious enthusiasm Aldous brought to intellectual pursuits now manifested itself in his desire to see the world. Over the next few years Aldous and Maria toured Italy, France, Holland and Belgium. In September 1925 they were bound for India. Huxley was singularly unimpressed at first by Hindu mysticism and India in general. 'India is depressing as no other country I have ever known. One breathes in it, not air, but dust and hopelessness', he wrote in his diary, published as *Jesting Pilate* in 1926. Interestingly, he was to change his mind profoundly about Indian culture later in life.

After a brief round-the-world trip, the Huxleys returned to England, then went back to Europe. In Florence they became close friends with the ailing D. H. Lawrence and his wife Frieda. The couples continued to meet regularly up to Lawrence's death in 1930. Huxley enjoyed friendships with many famous artists and intellectuals, among them the great violinist Yehudi Menuhin and the art historian Kenneth Clark. Menuhin once said of Huxley, 'his voice was the gentlest melody, ennobled beyond hate, violence and prejudice, yet not without passion.'

In 1930, the Huxleys settled in Sanary-sur-Mer in the South of France. This was to be their home base for the next seven years, where Aldous wrote his chilling view of the future, *Brave New World,* and also *Eyeless in Gaza,* a highly emotional investigation and re-evaluation of his past. The progress of the hero, Anthony Beavis, from misanthropic cynicism to compassion for fellow men mirrors Huxley's own. With the rise of fascism in Europe, Huxley advocated in this book 'positive

Fact or Fiction

GENETIC ENGINEERING

Huxley's alarming prophecy of a world shaped by genetic engineering might have come to pass had Hitler won World War II. The Nazi hierarchy was deeply interested in 'improving' the Aryan race by selective, artificial conception.

Some consider Huxley's vision has been realized – test-tube babies which were once the stuff of science fiction are now a scientific reality. But the author's warning that "in the context of nationalism, eugenics could become an instrument of extraordinary power and extraordinary danger" is still a nightmare possibility worth heeding.

Italian sojourns
Huxley and Maria first travelled to Florence (left) in April 1921. They were captivated, and often returned there, and to the surrounding countryside (below) over the years. Ideally, Huxley would have liked to spend half his time in Italy and half in England – the former for living, the latter for working, two pursuits which he felt he needed to do separately.

The TATLER

MR. AND MRS. ALDOUS HUXLEY AND THEIR SON

High Society
By early 1932, the Huxleys were society figures – front page news for The Tatler. *Huxley, not yet 40, had already made his name with* Point Counter Point *and numerous stories and novels which had appeared almost annually since 1920. He was to lose popularity, however, with his decision to oppose the fascist threat with pacifism.*

Eminent brothers
(left) Julian Huxley, as famous and respected a biologist as Aldous was a man of letters, cherished his meetings with his brother: 'From these encounters, I always returned to my work stimulated and refreshed, my spiritual batteries recharged.'

Impressions of India
(right) In 1925 Huxley saw Indian religion as an evil, commenting: "A little less spirituality, and the Indians would now be free . . . There would be less dirt and more food." Thirty years later, however, he embraced Hindu mysticism, becoming a devotee of Swami Prabhavananda in California.

pacifism', an attempt to fill the prevailing moral vacuum of scepticism and negativity. But the British public were disenchanted by the didactic tone of *Eyeless in Gaza*; and Huxley's pacifism attracted criticism, as did his subsequent departure for the sunshine of California in April 1937.

His reasons for staying in the United States were complex, bound up with his physical and mental state, and the lure of 'easy money' as a Hollywood scriptwriter. Early in 1938, he was hospitalized with bronchitis; full recovery took over a year. He began intensive training in the Bates method, a series of exercises designed to improve eyesight, celebrating the results in *The Art of Seeing*. He also became seriously interested in Indian mysticism, seeking, perhaps, some inner peace at a time when the world was at war.

Later in 1939 Huxley successfully completed his first script for MGM – an adaptation of *Pride and Prejudice* – and was fitfully employed by Hollywood throughout the 1940s, working on *Alice in Wonderland* and on an adaptation of his own short story *The Gioconda Smile* (released in 1948 as *A Woman's Vengeance*). He also investigated spiritualism and homeopathic medicine – the latter a consuming interest since the mid-Thirties, when he had studied with F. M. Alexander, founder of the Alexander Technique, a method of correcting defects in posture to improve mental and physical health. By May 1953, Huxley's researches had led him towards experimenting with hallucinogenic drugs (mescalin and later LSD) and his study of mescalin's mind-enlarging effects, *The Doors of Perception,* remains his most controversial work.

Two years later tragedy struck – Maria, who had done everything in her power to conceal her poor health from Aldous, died of a liver infec-

Hollywood attractions
(below) The glamorous Cocoanut Grove in Hollywood attracted the stars and satellites of the film industry. And here Huxley benefited from lucrative commissions for film scripts – as well as the space and sunshine of California. Among his new friends were Charlie Chaplin, his actress wife Paulette Goddard, and the writer Anita Loos.

HUXLEY AND HALLUCINOGENS

In experimenting with psychedelic or hallucinogenic drugs – mescalin and LSD – Huxley was attempting to extend the frontiers of medical research. His aim was to study their effects on the consciousness. Drugs taken under the right circumstances (and by the right person) Huxley believed could be a force for social good, leading to a "sense of solidarity with the world and its spiritual principle". Although he was distressed by the misuse of drugs, he remained convinced that psychedelic drugs had the power to open doors in the mind that hitherto had been closed. He recorded his findings in the controversial *The Doors of Perception* (1954) and *Heaven and Hell* (1956).

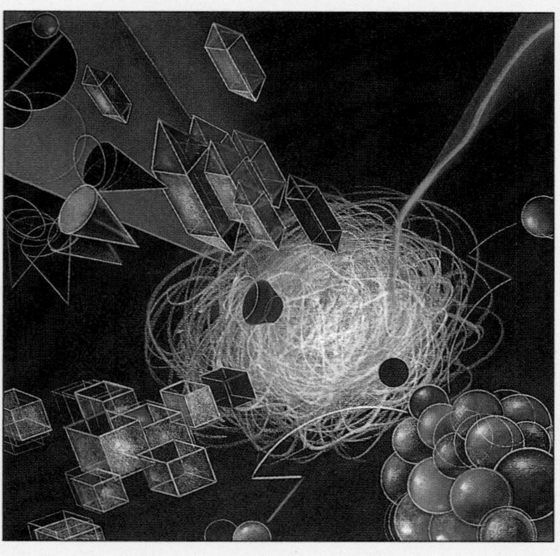

tion. Though friends and family worried that he would be totally helpless without her, Huxley soldiered on through his grief, and found consolation with a friend of his and Maria's, Laura Archera, 20 years his junior. She later recalled: 'I saw then, for the first time, how Aldous applied his philosophy: live here and now . . . He succeeded much of the time. Once in a while he would lapse into a depressed silence. He did not speak much about his pain; he only said, "It is like an amputation."'

The following year Aldous and Laura were quietly married at the Drive-in Wedding Chapel in Yuma, Arizona, on 19 March 1956. His new bride's youthful energy, determination and *joie de vivre* seemed to galvanize Aldous into a further bout of creative activity. He began a long-cherished project, a novel about the possibility of achieving an ideal society (later published as *Island*), re-examined the themes of *Brave New World* in *Brave New World Revisited* and then lectured in Italy.

Menuhin's accolade
To Yehudi Menuhin (below), Huxley was 'as pure in his maturity and ready to respond like a tuned violin in a trained hand'.

In 1959, Huxley embarked on an academic career, becoming Visiting Professor at the University of California and delivering a course of lectures entitled *The Human Condition.* He also accepted an Award of Merit by the American Academy of Arts and Letters. Speedily recovering after treatment for a tumour on his tongue in 1960, he gave further lectures to packed auditoriums all over the US. Some recurrent themes – still relevant today – included the population explosion, human wastefulness with the earth's resources, and the evils of nationalism.

Amid this flurry of recognition by the American literary establishment and the plaudits of a new generation came a cruel blow – his house in Los Angeles was completely gutted by a bushfire. All his books and letters were destroyed. Huxley was soon back at work, however, writing, travelling and lecturing. In June 1962 he at last received acknowledgment of his achievements in Britain, and was elected Companion of Literature by the Royal Society of Literature.

THE FINAL TRAGEDY

A year later in September, tragedy struck for the last time in his life – a malignant tumour was discovered on his neck. He died on 22 November in Los Angeles; eight years later his ashes were returned to England and buried in his parents' grave at Compton in Surrey. Maria Huxley's ashes made the same journey in 1972.

Huxley's novels and essays remain the fascinating creations of one of this century's greatest 'pragmatic dreamers'. As Yehudi Menuhin wrote: 'This was a man in whom wisdom never destroyed innocence. He was a scientist and artist in one – standing for all we most need in a fragmented world . . .'

‘Fordliness’

This farmboy-made-good seemed to promise a future full of affordable luxuries. But as time passed, Henry Ford showed another face to the people who had made him rich.

In Huxley's sterile Utopia of the future, his ‘brave new world’, the place of God is taken by the American car mogul Henry Ford. People swear by the name of Our Ford, and years are counted from the introduction of the Ford Model T motor car. “Ford's in his flivver”, the happy people sigh, “All's well with the world.” Huxley wrote in the early 1930s; he could see all too plainly the seeds of his disturbing vision of the future in the rise of the new consumer society, and deplored its materialism. Few people had done more to bring that society into existence and foster its values than Henry Ford.

Henry Ford himself was something of a hero to many ordinary American people, a man whose rags-to-riches success lay at the heart of the American dream. What he had done, any American with the will and the talent might do too. Ford seemed to have the interests of ‘the little man’ at heart, and his down-to-earth, no-nonsense personality appeared reassuring in a rapidly changing world. When Americans were polled in the 1920s about who they wanted as president, the carmaker from Detroit was far and away the most popular choice, even though he was never a candidate.

Yet Ford was a man of extraordinary contradictions. The Henry Ford who gave his workers the highest wages in America in 1914, was the same Ford who hounded and beat them to despair in the 1930s. The Ford who took on poor immigrants when no other employer would, was also the Ford who became fanatically anti-Jewish in the 1920s.

Rags to riches
A country lad from Michigan, Ford rose to be America's wealthiest industrialist. As pioneer of the world's first cheap car, of mass production and of high wages for shorter hours, he gained a dangerously heady power over the hearts and minds of the people. He had genius, but ultimately lacked wisdom.

The Model T
Ford crusaded for the ‘Tin Lizzie’ (left) with missionary zeal. He aimed to put every hard-working American behind a steering wheel.

Self-advertisement
Ford's belief in his Model T became so absolute that he cancelled advertisements like the one above, believing the car would sell itself. By every post he received letters from farmers enclosing photographs of the 'flivver' pulling ploughs, driving threshing machines, saws and vacuum cleaners, and taking bucolic families on week-end picnics. Why waste money on advertising?

Assembly-line life
The assembly line made Ford a multi-millionaire. The first was built from 'railroad ties, iron slides, and some horses, and they pulled it with a rope'. By the time the Highland Park factory (right) was founded in Detroit in 1913, 'The Ford machinery was the best in the world, everybody knew it.' The assembly line so revolutionized car manufacture that it swiftly took over in Europe (below right) as well as the States. But workers hated it.

The Ford who campaigned for peace in the Great War let his factories be used to churn out arms only months later.

Before Ford came along, motor cars were regarded as rich men's toys, far too expensive and elaborate ever to become everyday means of transport. Ford's dream was to create a car so cheap that even those with modest incomes could afford to buy one.

'I will build a car for the multitude', he earnestly proclaimed. 'It will be large enough for the family but small enough for the individual to run and care for. It will be constructed of the best materials, by the best men to be hired, after the simplest designs that modern engineering can devise. But it will be so low in price that no man making a good salary will be unable to own one – and enjoy with his family the blessings of hours of pleasure in God's great open spaces.'

It was an idea he had cherished ever since he was a boy on his father's farm in Dearborn, Michigan, tinkering with clocks and home-made steam engines in the workshop. 'Hitch your wagon to a star', he had heard the preacher advise one day, and this was his wagon and his star. But for years he could not persuade any of his backers that the idea made business sense. The Ford Motor Company (formed in 1903 when he was 40), grew rich on sales of luxury cars. Ford managed to buy out the opposition with his share of the profits and set to work on his People's Car.

The Model T was created in a tiny room in the Ford Motor Company's Detroit factory. For a year, as the T came gradually to life, Henry Ford would sketch his ideas on a big blackboard, or sit in a rocking chair late into the night, watching the engineers build the car and discussing progress. Ford's little team were fired by his almost childlike enthusiasm. 'God, he could get anything out of us. He'd never say, "I want this done." He'd say, "I wonder if we can do this? I wonder?" Well the men would break their necks to see if they could do it.'

The Model T was finally launched in spring 1908 and its success almost exceeded even Ford's extravagant imagination. Nicknamed affectionately, 'Tin Lizzie' and the 'flivver', this light but rugged little car, perfect for the rough country roads of the day, captured the American imagination and was selling by the thousand within months of its launch. And where America led, Europe soon followed. Before long, Ford's only problem was meeting the enormous demand – and the fact that the price of the car, at over $800, was still much too high for his liking.

MASS PRODUCTION

Ford had argued for years that 'the way to make automobiles is . . . to make them come through the factory just alike, just as one pin is like another when it comes from a pin factory', and the success of the Lizzie gave him the chance to prove it. Standardization opened the way for mass production, and mass production could bring the lower prices Ford craved. Ford's approach was simple but revolutionary: cut prices and you sell more; sell more and you can improve efficiency by mass production, enabling you to cut prices again.

The Ford Company had already tried basic

mass production techniques, with teams of men pulling a part-assembled car through the factory on a rope, while other teams were adding on parts as it moved. Now they built a huge factory at Highland Park in Detroit unlike anything ever seen before.

The Highland Park plant, described by awed visitors as 'the crystal palace' because of its vast windows, was a marvel of organization, with four huge assembly floors, linked together by continuously moving lifts, chutes and conveyor belts, and equipped with some 15,000 specially-designed machines. In its first year of operation (1910), the plant turned out almost 20,000 Model Ts; in 1912 it produced almost four times that number. But Ford's greatest innovation was the assembly line.

'Time loves to be wasted', he often warned, and the assembly line cut wasted time to a minimum, assigning to every worker one simple task which he repeated endlessly and rapidly as components glided past on a moving belt. The acceleration in output was staggering, and in 1913, production of the Model T leaped from 78,000 to almost 250,000. Ford was able to cut the price of the T to $440, noting happily, 'Every time I reduce the charge for our car by one dollar, I get a thousand new buyers.'

But as the Ford company's sales soared to new heights, so the morale of its workers slumped. Henry Ford's personal wealth was huge, but his employees took home a pittance, and the new assembly line with its mindless repetition made them feel like automatons. Few workers could put up with it for more than a couple of months, and turnover of staff at the Highland Park was alarmingly swift.

The company's solution, suggested by Ford's partner James Couzens, was simple but dramatic. They would double average wages to $5 a day and cut the basic working day from 12 to eight hours, converting the factory from two to three shifts. It would be, they claimed, 'the greatest revolution in the matter of rewards for its workers ever known to the industrial world.'

The announcement created a furore, and almost overnight Henry Ford became the most famous industrialist in America. The New York *Globe* was full of praise, saying, 'It has all the advantages and none of the disadvantages of socialism', but the *Wall Street Journal* condemned it as a deeply immoral misapplication of Biblical principles.

Ford was tickled pink by his sudden fame. He had always wanted to be philosopher-inventor like his hero Thomas Edison, not just a rich industrialist, and for years had been jotting down his own pet sayings in little notebooks that he bought by the gross. Now at last he had his chance, and he was in his element casting pearls of wisdom to the eager press. The American public lapped it all up, and his frequent pronouncements on life were looked to almost as the words of a prophet. He won a reputation as a socialist, but his ideas were never more than skin deep.

A moralizing side had always been present in

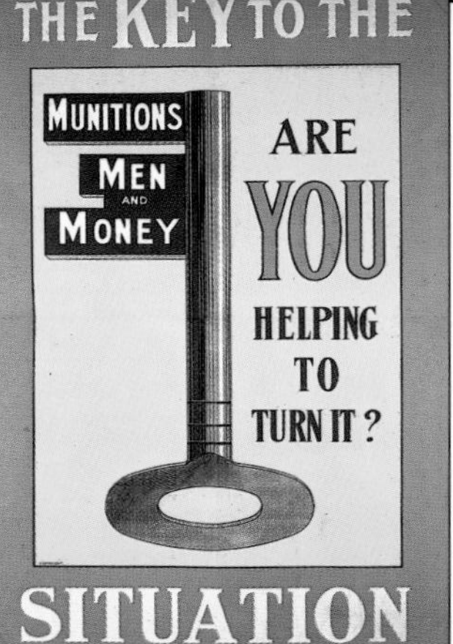

War efforts
Of World War I Ford said to the Press in an unguarded moment, 'I'd give all my money – and my life – to stop it.' The remark committed him to a public show of pacifism which his later manufacture of armaments (above) belied.

Out of step
Some thought it quaint that Ford should hark back to bygone joys (left), old-time dancing (above) and the innocence of a pre-industrial world. But a ruthless egomania accompanied his 'eccentricity', and little by little he fell out of step with family, workers and the modern world.

Ford's apparently simple nature, and now it surfaced with a vengeance. He determined that his workers should not only be paid better, but that they should live better too; the Ford company would turn out better men the way they turned out better cars. So he made the $5 day dependent on a workman's sobriety, decency and self-reliance, and set up a force of company social workers to carry through his ideas.

Many Ford workers understandably resented the frequent intrusion of Ford's Sociological Department into their private lives, but put up with it for the sake of the wages. And there is no doubt that Ford helped the company take on workers that other employers would shun – ex-convicts and immigrants, for example. Firmly believing in the benefits of honest toil, Ford himself would often stop his car to pick up hitch-hikers and tramps to offer them a job at his factory – a chance to 'remake their lives'.

Machine-age man
For all his paternalism, Henry Ford built factories on a principle of repetitive, unremitting labour which reduced workers to mere cogs in the production process. Chaplin's 1936 film Modern Times *(above) lampooned this dehumanizing aspect of the great Industrial Dream. It came out at a time when the Depression had turned Ford employees' unpleasant work into an intolerable, grinding slavery, without even the compensation of high wages. The film touched a raw nerve in Americans who had once hero-worshipped Ford and his imitators.*

FIGHTING FOR PEACE

Ford developed an inspirational belief in his own ability to change the world. When the War in Europe, and America's potential involvement, threatened to ruin all he was working for, he chartered a ship to sail the Atlantic with a group of anti-War activists on a crusade for peace. New York intellectuals ridiculed him mercilessly, but the American public loved him for it. Then, in mid-ocean, Ford seemed to realize that while he was king in Detroit, he was out of his depth in world politics, and soon after the Peace Ship had docked in Europe he abandoned the project and slipped quietly back home.

Both those who dismissed Ford as a mere publicity-seeker and those who saw him as a simpleton were given ammunition by the speed with which his pacifist ideas evaporated. Soon after America had joined the War, Ford conceived a tank based on the Model T and a one-man submarine, nicknamed by journalists the 'U-flivver'. Critics began to snipe at his regular press comments, and on 22 June 1916 the Chicago *Tribune* described him as too ignorant to make any pronouncements to the public at all. Ford immediately sued for libel.

At the trial three years later, Ford was taken apart by the defence lawyer, who argued that Ford was a fraud, too ill-informed to set himself up as an educator of the people. Ford, relying on his epigrams to see him through, was completely floored when the lawyer tested him on his education. During the trial he defined 'chilli con carne' as a large mobile army and 'ballyhoo' as a blackguard, and announced that the American Revolution was in 1812. At one stage he admitted candidly, 'I am ignorant about most things.' Ford won his case, but lost his reputation.

Chastened by the trial and by the failure of his Peace Mission, Ford began to turn inwards. It was as if the challenge of the modern world had become too much for him. From 1920, the cranky side of his nature, always present, began to come to the fore. A golden haze crept over his memories of the boyhood farm he had been so eager to leave, and he started to cherish the past in a way that seemed almost perverse in a man who had done so much to bring the world into the 20th century. Rural America was the real America, he felt: the America of his father, the America fast disappearing in the urbanized, consumerized, hectic world he had helped to create.

The Ford farm at Dearborn he lovingly preserved as it was when he was boy, and often took half-a-dozen boys out there to eat hickory nuts and jump from the hayrick just as he had done all those years ago. He also built up a vast and eccentric collection of artefacts of the real America – it was said that he had one of every kind of shoe ever made in America – and spent billions of dollars building a museum village to preserve the ways of the past. And, to combat the modern tendency for 'sex dancing', he made strenuous efforts to revive the old-time dances of his youth, hiring a dancing master to teach Ford employees how to 'gallop', and painting the steps on the floor of the Engineering Building to help them. None of his top executives dared to miss the weekly dances, where the spritely 60-year-old company head pulled them each in turn around the floor.

THINGS OF THE PAST

Ford's obsession with the past began to spill over into the Motor Company too. Even in 1920, the Tin Lizzie was looking antiquated next to the sleek, sophisticated cars emerging from General Motors and Chrysler. Yet six years later, Ford was still stubbornly resisting any attempts to develop a new Ford car, despite plummeting sales. 'The only thing wrong with that car', he insisted later, 'was that people stopped buying it'.

Some people dismissed all this as harmless eccentricity. But there was something dangerously xenophobic about his retreat into the values of middle America and, in the early 1920s, it

Brakes full on
Ford's overweening confidence in his Model T became a serious stumbling-block in the Thirties. As an old man, nostalgic for the Good Old Days (he is pictured above in his very first car), he no longer saw the need for continual improvement. The joke attributed to him, 'You can have any colour so long as it's black,' summed up his dictatorial attitude towards his customers.

Overtaking
Competitors began bringing out chic, streamlined, stylish cars backed up by image-conscious advertising (above). They swept past the Model T in the outside lane, and left it looking primitive and outmoded. Deaf to the advice of his executives, Henry Ford held on to the reins far too long for the good of his empire.

emerged hideously in an outburst of fanatical anti-Semitism. Convinced that a naturally corrupt conspiracy of Jewish bankers was trying to enslave the honest working man, he hired researchers to find evidence for his belief, and set up a newspaper – which he insisted all Ford customers receive – to expound his views. It is hardly any wonder that in the 1920s Hitler had a picture of Ford on his desk.

FORD AND BENNETT

Ford abandoned his anti-Jewish crusade after losing a libel case, but the nickname of 'Crazy Henry', coined in the days when he was building his first car, began to ring ominously true. Ford had always possessed what people said was his 'mean streak', a livid vein of nastiness which showed itself in cruel practical jokes and, as he grew older, a ruthless obsessiveness.

He had certainly spared no-one in his struggle to achieve total control of the Ford Motor Company, making it by far the largest individually-owned company in the world. And once he was in sole command, Ford's despotic style of management slowly poisoned the positive atmosphere that had made Ford workers proud to be part of the company in better years. A witch-hunt slowly pushed out anyone who would not toe the Ford line, and morale slumped as sharply as sales of Ford cars.

In this cut-throat climate, it was the tough guys who won Ford's praise, and none was tougher than Harry Bennett, an Al Capone-like character whose connections with the gangster world of 1930s America were well-known. Ford doted on Bennett, who flattered him by carrying out even Ford's strangest whims ruthlessly. One day, driving past a Ford-owned garage, Ford asked timidly, 'Why are we in the gas business, Harry?' Later that day, Bennett showed Ford the garage again, now bulldozed flat and covered with turfs and little trees. 'That's nice, Harry', said Ford.

The Great Depression of the 1930s drove down wages throughout the industry and Ford workers suffered more than most. The good times of the $5 day were forgotten and the assembly line was accelerated. At Ford, the regimented nightmare pastiched in Charlie Chaplin's film *Modern Times* was a reality, and men collapsed out of exhaustion and despair: Detroit doctors called it 'Forditis'.

The workers were ripe for unionization but, on Ford's instructions, Bennett organized a huge army of hoods and toughs to carry out 'security' operations, spying on every member of the company in and outside work. Workers suspected of union sympathies were searched regularly for union literature, intimidated, sacked or just beaten up. According to one account, 'There was no sitting, squatting, singing, talking or whistling on the job. Smiling was frowned upon. Workers learned to communicate without moving their lips in what became known as the 'Ford whisper'.

As other motor car companies gradually gave way to the pressure for unionization, Ford held out tenaciously, encouraging Bennett's mobsters to increasingly violent tactics. When in 1937 pictures of bloodied union men and women, brutally beaten by Bennett's men, appeared, splashed across the newspapers, Ford's days as the 'man of the people' were over. Three years later, desperate Ford workers finally went out on strike. With machine guns mounted on the factory walls, Ford and Bennett were ready for a pitched battle, but at the last minute Ford's wife argued for peace.

Ford was now almost 80, irascible and unreasonable. He became more and more reclusive, spending days at a time alone with his wife in their big house at Fairlane. In 1943 his son Edsel died, harried to an early grave, many said, by Ford and Bennett because he had tried to fight his father's worst excesses. Ford was distraught with grief and guilt, consoling himself with his belief in reincarnation, but it was not enough. In 1947 he died a frail, unhappy, lonely old man.

ROBERT GRAVES

1895-1985

Robert Graves' life spanned nearly a century, a century in which he did "the usual storybook things" – he came to manhood, went to war, took life, loved unhappily, married, fathered children, wrote, gained recognition, found love and, essentially, lived happily ever after. Yet behind that list hides a man who only operated by his own rules, in his own time scale, according to his own personal and poetic mythology – a talented man of intense and uncompromising passions.

In Search of a Muse

Never quite at home in the twentieth century, Robert Graves pursued a life true to his poetic principles, searching for a Muse he could serve as man and poet.

Robert von Ranke Graves was a rare individual, an English bohemian of sorts who lived life according to his own rules, not society's. He shunned conventional jobs, social responsibilities (save during the war) and contemporary poetic movements. He was an uncompromising outsider, even as a child, and remained an elusive figure, shrouded in his own poetic myth throughout his life.

The Graves family
Alfred Perceval Graves was a widower with five children when he married Amalie von Ranke. They had five more children: (left to right) Charles, Clarissa, Rosaleen, John and Robert.

Graves was born in London on 24 July 1895, the third of five children. His father was an inspector of schools, the editor of an Irish literary magazine and a minor poet. However, despite these accomplishments he did not, according to Graves, try "to teach me how to write" or show "any understanding of my serious poetry." Nonetheless, the house was always full of books and the two were to share a lifelong passion for literature.

Graves' mother played a less significant role in shaping the future poet. She censored his reading, "believing that innocence was the surest protection against . . . dirtiness and intrigue and lustfulness", as Graves later wrote in his autobiography. Her strong puritan instinct instilled in him a fear of divine retribution which, allied with his own growing sexual fears, created a recurring sense of terror. As an adult, Graves frequently wrestled with this demon, trying to reconcile it with his own innately loving nature.

Unhappy schooldays
"From the moment I arrived at the school [Charterhouse] I suffered an oppression of spirit that I hesitate now to recall in its full intensity . . . My clothes were all wrong . . . My name appeared on the school list as 'R. von R. Graves' . . . 'German' meant 'dirty German' . . . and the legend was put about that I was not only a German but a German-Jew . . . My last resource was to sham insanity . . . It succeeded unexpectedly well. Soon nobody troubled me."

Graves' early schooling was not particularly happy because he was usually regarded as something of an oddity. He went to no less than six prep schools, sometimes for as little as a term; because of his own unhappiness or because of his father's dissatisfaction with the standard of teaching at each place, he was continually moved on. When he was 13, he went to Charterhouse public school which rapidly became, as it had for William Thackeray 70 years before, a psychological 'slaughterhouse'. Even half a century after leaving there, Graves still had nightmares about his wretched experiences. His major problems arose from his abiding love of literature which nobody seemed to understand or to share; from the fact that his name appeared on the school list as 'R. von R. Graves', which his peers seized on as proof of his German allegiance at a time when anti-German prejudice ran high; and from his parents' reluctance to buy him a smart school uniform in an environment noted for its total and unquestioning privilege.

SHAMMING INSANITY

The consequence of his unremitting victimization was that he started to have problems with his heart and nearly suffered a breakdown, after which he decided to "sham insanity", wearing straws in his hair, to ensure that he was left alone. "It succeeded unexpectedly well", he later wrote. Gradually, though, he eased himself out of this role, taking up boxing and developing several strong friendships which made his final school years somewhat more bearable.

When Graves was 19, he put off the opportunity to study English at Oxford, fearing an arid, unimaginative approach to the subject he felt so deeply about. Instead, he enlisted in the army believing, as did so many others, that the war which had just started would soon be over.

Although Graves' army career began slowly, filled with tedious spells guarding German prisoners, he was soon posted to the front line. The hell of no-man's-land, bedecked with a "frozen parade" of corpses, forced him to the conclusion that the only certain means of staying alive involved getting wounded and being sent back home to England. Although he did not actively seek injury, that is precisely what happened to him in July 1916.

Graves was seriously wounded and badly shocked by an explosion, with pieces of shell lodged deep within his chest and thigh. But the army mistakenly informed his parents that 'your son has died of wounds. He was very gallant . . . and is a great loss', later even forwarding them his personal belongings. It was left to Graves to sort out the confusion, which meant requesting *The Times* to announce that his recently printed obituary had been highly premature!

While recuperating in England, Graves became a good friend of the war poet Siegfried Sassoon. Both were so outraged at the mismanagement and calamitous reality of the war that they considered making a formal protest. Sassoon in fact did so, but Graves, anxious for his welfare, persuaded him to be examined by a medical board, who pronounced him shell-shocked and in need of hospital treatment.

When Graves had barely recovered from his physical injuries, he returned to the battlefield in France, where, despite a severe attack of bronchitis and periods of shell shock, he walked up to 12 miles a day through the deep, sucking mud, to and from the front line. Eventually, though, the doctors pronounced him unfit for duty and, in 1917, threatened him with a court martial if he did not return home.

The following year, Graves fell in love with the robust, unconventional Nancy Nicholson, whom he married a year later. Soon after, they had

Harlech countryside
The cool 'indifference' of the terrain around their home in North Wales (above) appealed to Graves: "Once, when I came home on leave from the war (right) I spent about a week of my ten days walking about on these hills to restore my sanity."

Key Dates

1895 born in London
1916 wounded; poems published
1918 marries Nancy Nicholson
1919 moves to Boar's Hill, Oxford
1926 meets Laura Riding
1929 *Goodbye to All That;* settles in Mallorca
1934 *I, Claudius*
1940-46 Vale House Farm, Devon
1946 returns to Deyá, Mallorca
1948 *The White Goddess*
1950 marries Beryl Hodge
1955 *The Greek Myths*
1961-66 Professor of Poetry at Oxford
1985 dies in Deyá

s dispatch,

Miss Nicholson ready to execute an order for any article not in stock. The business is most go-ahead, and no effort is spared to give satisfaction.

The Hon. Mrs. Michael Howard (left) with Miss Nancy Nicholson outside the shop.

Two little customers arrive. Every want is supplied from stock or to order.

The Hon. Mrs. Michael Howard and Miss Nicholson, sister of the famous artist, have opened an "all sorts" shop at Boar's Hill, Oxfordshire, a colony which includes such well-known poets as the Poet Laureate (Dr. Bridges), Mr. John Masefield and others. The sign was painted by Mr. Nicholson.—(*Daily Mirror* photographs.)

Wartime marriage
Not long after their marriage in 1918, Robert and Nancy (above) moved to Boar's Hill near Oxford where, for £3 a month, they rented a cottage from the poet John Masefield. With high expectations, Nancy set up a traditional village shop there (right), where you could 'buy everything from a collar-stud to a saucepan'. However, notwithstanding her willingness 'to execute an order for any article not in stock', the shop was a financial disaster.

their first child and then moved to the rural outskirts of Oxford, as Graves had now decided to commence his university studies. However, this was a fairly unsatisfactory period for him because the marriage started to founder. At first he hoped to be able to renew their love, writing Nancy a poem: "Give then a thought for me/Walking so miserably . . . Swallow your pride, let us be as we used to be." But Nancy regretted their marriage and, as Graves wrote in 1929, wanted "somehow to be dis-married". She did not, however, want to leave him, and over the next three years they had three more children.

Egyptian interlude
In 1926 Graves, Nancy, their children and the newly-arrived Laura Riding sailed to Cairo, where Graves was to be Professor of English. Within a few months, however, they abandoned the venture and returned to England, disenchanted with a 'land where the dead parade the streets'.

Siegfried Sassoon
Dubbed 'Mad Jack' for his recklessness, Siegfried Sassoon met Graves in the trenches of Northern France – two soldier-poets of the Royal Welch Fusiliers. Amid hammering rain, an abundance of rats and the constant sound of shelling, they read each other's poems and formed a powerful friendship. But later they quarrelled bitterly.

Meanwhile, Graves completed his studies and began his lifelong devotion to his Muse, writing eight volumes of poetry between 1920 and 1925. As he later wrote: "Since the age of fifteen poetry has been my ruling passion and I have never intentionally undertaken any task or formed any relationship that seemed inconsistent with poetic principles; which has sometimes won me the reputation of an eccentric." But living out his 'poetic' life was not quite so easy. Graves' problem now, as at various points throughout his life, was to find a woman who could be the human embodiment of his Muse, and whom he could serve as both a man and a poet.

FINDING A GODDESS

Graves could not cast Nancy in this role since she was wholly unlike a Muse, being radical in many of her views and outspoken in her "universal condemnation of men". However, after a difficult period of fruitless searching, he found a woman who did become his incarnate Goddess. In 1926, after a lengthy transatlantic correspondence, Graves finally met the 25-year-old American poet, Laura Riding. He had been offered a teaching post in Cairo and, perennially short of funds, had accepted. Exactly one week after meeting Laura Riding, he set sail with her, his wife Nancy, their four children and a nanny, for Egypt. Laura quickly became the dominant, though not always beneficial force in his life. Initially, their relationship was cemented by their mutal belief in the sanctity of poetry, but gradually their meeting of minds became also a meeting of bodies. Cairo proved less than enthralling, however, and within six months the bizarre 'family' were back on English shores.

Nancy did not seem to object to Graves and Laura's liaison and even attempted to quieten the mounting gossip. By now though, it was evident to all their friends that Graves had found his inspiration. Graves was revitalized by Laura's lively, sympathetic interest in him and what was the most important part of him – his poetry.

Not long after, Graves began living with Laura, falling ever more completely under her influence. She even managed to convince him that she had total control over time and change, and eventually got him to agree to the ludicrous proposition that 'bodies have had their day' when, in 1933, she insisted they became celibate.

One of the main reasons Graves never questioned Laura's role as a 'superior' being, willingly submitting his work to her for approval and subsidising her various literary and non-literary projects, was because, as his Muse, she was both an inspiration and a demanding task master. In short, she appealed to his highly developed sense of Romantic masochism.

However, this 'Holy Trinity', as Graves, his mistress and his wife became known, soon became the 'Four'. This happened in 1929, when the Irishman Geoffrey Phibbs began a literary collaboration with Laura, who gradually fell hopelessly in love with him. Yet this intricate, potentially highly damaging, emotional tangle involving four very different people eventually became too much for Phibbs; he fled from their London home and escaped briefly to France and his abandoned wife Norah. Forced back by the 'Trinity', and in particular by the desperate Laura, he surprised everyone by announcing that from then on he

LAURA RIDING

From 1926 to 1939 Robert Graves had an increasingly demanding and uneasy relationship with the American poet Laura Riding. Born in New York in 1901, she became involved with a group of writers known as the Fugitives before she left America because of their lack of 'complete poetic seriousness'. Graves had the seriousness she was searching for and together they wrote and collaborated on a number of books until, for Laura, more stimulating mentors entered the scene. With the passage of time Riding went from being Graves' Muse to his 'Queen Famine'.

wanted to live with Graves' wife Nancy, not with Laura.

Laura was so devastated by this revelation that she immediately tried to commit suicide. She took a drink of disinfectant and leapt from a fourth-floor window, whereupon Graves dashed down one flight of stairs, and then threw himself out of a third-floor window. Somehow, he survived the fall, and was able to help the badly injured Laura into an ambulance.

As things calmed down over the following weeks, the 'Four' sorted themselves out. The extraordinary incident culminated with Phibbs going to live with Nancy and her children, as he had intended, while Graves and Laura resumed their eccentric partnership.

While Laura was recovering from her fall, Graves wrote the first of his bestsellers, written for no other reason than to make money. Yet though Graves usually, and Laura always, dismissed them as potboilers (because they were written in prose, not poetry), they were in fact, almost without exception, fine works of art. *Goodbye to All That* was the first of these pieces, a brilliant autobiography tackling Graves' experiences at school and in the trenches, and the break-up of his marriage.

MALLORCAN EXILE

With the profits from this book Graves and Laura left England – and the gossip surrounding her suicide bid – for Mallorca. It was this Spanish island which, save for one period of enforced exile, became his home for the rest of his life. Unfortunately life there soon hit problems because their money began to run out, and their relationship was strained by Laura's uncompromising demands. They concentrated on their writing, separately and together, and ran a printing press (an enterprise they had started in England) on which they printed limited editions of their works.

Graves' poems, however, never made him any money. So, in order to build up his dwindling finances, he set about another prose work which he was determined would be a bestseller. In fact *I, Claudius*, published in 1934, turned out to be a greater financial and literary success than he could have imagined, both enabling him to pay for a new house and establishing his reputation as one of the finest writers of the time.

Sadly, Graves' spell of good fortune was temporarily interrupted by the fascist takeover of Mallorca, forcing him and Laura to seek refuge elsewhere from 1936. But though over the next few years they lived in England, Switzerland and America, the turbulence of his everyday life never affected the quality or stability of his writing.

There are few obvious divides in Graves' life, but without doubt one of them occurred in 1939. Laura fell in love with Schuyler Jackson, a married American, who soon assumed Graves' role as her intellectual and loving companion. Fortunately Graves was spared a lengthy period of unhappiness because he too now met a new partner. His relationship with the serene Beryl Hodge provided him with the domestic tranquillity that he had so lacked with Laura.

'Mid-Winter Waking'
After his self-destructive relationship with Laura Riding, growing to know and to love the gentle Beryl Hodge was an extraordinary process of awakening. In a poem inspired by her and aptly titled 'Mid-Winter Waking', he wrote, "Stirring suddenly from long hibernation,/I knew myself once more a poet/ . . . And presently dared open both my eyes." From 1940 to 1946 they lived in a farmhouse (below) in the small village of Galmpton in Devon.

Graves celebrated their union with many tender verses –

"You of your gentleness,
I of my rashness,
Both of despair –
Yet still might share
This happy will."

In another poem he likens his love for Beryl to that of "knowing myself once more a poet". And he did indeed write some of his finest poetry between 1938 and 1945. Meanwhile the atmosphere of his home life radically improved, too, as friends, who had been driven away by the daunting presence of Laura, began to return, and Graves' house filled with the bubbling noises of three children born between 1940 and 1944.

The year 1944 was also momentous for Graves because it was when he began his major poetic

Shared pleasures
Graves and his second family enjoy the Mallorcan sunshine and the relaxed spirit of the island. With Beryl, Graves had four children: William (1940), Lucia (1943), Juan (1944) and Tomas, not shown (1953).

Home sweet home
When Graves was finally able to return to his treasured house, called Canelluñ (below), in Deyá, Mallorca, he was delighted to find everything just as he had left it before the war. As he wrote to his friend and fellow-writer Alan Hodge (Beryl's first husband), 'everything was ten years older but just the same: for example, all my shirts and trousers and socks wearable; and five jars of green tomato chutney, eatable; and cigarette tobacco in my tobacco jar, smokeable.'

statement, *The White Goddess*, shortly after which he returned from his European exile to Mallorca, this time with Beryl. However, while he continued writing poems, essays and prose, one vital element was holding him back: he lacked an incarnate Muse. Beryl never qualified for this role – in fact, had she done so, a long, happy relationship with her might have become impossible – and she does not appear to have objected when, from 1950 to 1952, Graves became very close to yet another woman whom he regarded as his inspiration. Then followed a lean six-year spell as a creative writer – when ironically his fame as a distinguished poet spread to America – until he met his next inspirational Muse.

RULED BY POETRY

Although Graves revered the women whom he cast as his Muses, he was never tempted to leave Beryl for them, though at times she must have felt deeply wounded by his attachments. Furthermore, despite his growing fame he chose never to abandon his spartan lifestyle. He remained "nobody's servant [having] chosen to live on the outskirts of a Majorcan mountain village . . . where life is still ruled by the old agricultural cycle." And poetry remained his "ruling passion".

Yet lack of money forced him to accept several offers to write filmscripts and give lectures, not all of which were disagreeable to him. He also wrote *The Greek Myths*, in which he "connected a lot of mythical patterns which were not connected before". In his mid-sixties, as one of the great writers of his generation, he was offered the CBE (which he declined, not believing in the honours' system), and in 1961 he became Professor of Poetry at Oxford, one of the most popular ever holders of this prestigious post.

Graves kept up his stream of writing until he was 75, and from then on lived quietly in his adopted Mallorcan village of Deyá. He died peacefully, aged 90, on 7 December 1985, among his loved ones and his cherished surroundings. As he would have wished, his gravestone reads simply 'Robert Graves, Poeta'.

Fact or Fiction

I, ROBERT GRAVES . . .

Although *I, Claudius'* hero is clearly the Roman Emperor Claudius I (ruled AD 41-54), there are aspects of his character which are strikingly similar to Graves' view of himself. For example, Graves always saw himself as an outsider, and, like Claudius, he often cultivated that role. While Graves was without stutter or physical deformity, he nevertheless felt himself somehow defective. Long after *I, Claudius* was published, Graves wrote a poem entitled *The Second-Fated* in which he and Claudius merge more pointedly: in it Graves opens with the words "My stutter, my cough, my unfinished sentences . . ."

'Adopted son'
A small fishing village of some 450 inhabitants, Deyá (left) was Graves' spiritual home from 1929. Forty years later the inhabitants paid him an honour which to him matched any literary prize he received in his lifetime: they made him an 'adopted son' of the village – the first and only one ever in the history of Deyá.

Roman Gods and Heroes

The ancient tales of the gods and goddesses of Olympus have haunted the imagination for centuries, inspiring some of Europe's finest art and literature.

When Robert Graves went to Oxford University, he took up the study of English Literature. After 'fourteen years . . . principally at Latin and Greek' he was, he claimed, 'fed up with the Classics'. The Classics had, however, found their way into his blood and throughout his life Graves continued to respond to the imaginative beauties of the ancient world – beauties that are enshrined particularly in the great body of myth and legend that is one of the ancient world's most profound and enduring legacies to Western civilization. Since the Renaissance it has inspired much of Europe's greatest literature and art, just as it coloured much of Graves' own writing.

SUPERHUMAN BEINGS

Ancient myths are varied in origin. There are stories that have some basis in fact (those about the siege of Troy, for example), embroidered through the ages by imperfect recollection and poetic fancy, and others that might be classified as folklore or popular fiction. The type with which we are most familiar, however, are imaginative stories about gods or superhuman beings, often explaining how some custom or natural phenomenon came into being; the Roman god Neptune,

Love on Olympus
Vulcan, the lame god of fire and a great blacksmith (he sits beside his anvil), wooed and married Venus, the goddess of beauty. But later she cuckolded him with Mars, the god of war.

Ruler of the waves
(below) Neptune, the god who ruled the sea and its inhabitants, is drawn through the waves by white seahorses. He was invoked by sailors to give them a safe voyage, but he could also stir up the sea with his trident and cause storms and shipwrecks when he was angry.

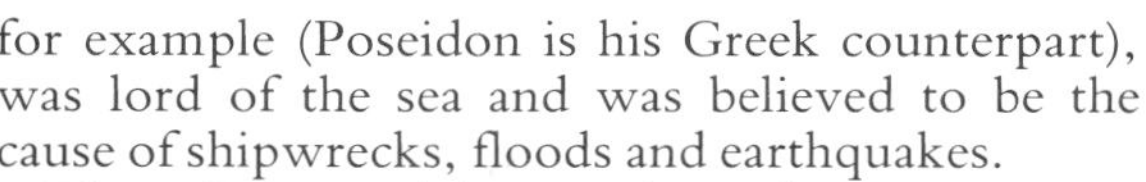

for example (Poseidon is his Greek counterpart), was lord of the sea and was believed to be the cause of shipwrecks, floods and earthquakes.

The religions of the Greeks and Romans were many-layered and differed fundamentally from the chief faiths of the modern world – in fact neither Greek nor Latin has a word that corresponds exactly with the English 'religion' or 'religious'. There was no priestly caste or official creed, no book like the Bible or the Koran to which one can turn for an established body of belief. The Romans in particular borrowed elements freely from the religions of the foreign peoples who formed part of their vast Empire, and there were secret sects and many purely local cults in addition to the 'Establishment' deities. It is not surprising, therefore, that myths often exist in different versions, and that there is much that is confusing or contradictory in classical mythology.

JUPITER'S AMOROUS ADVENTURES

In spite of the varied nature of Roman religion, the major gods and goddesses of the Romans and many of the most famous legends about them were derived directly from the Greeks. It was, however, the Roman poet Ovid (mentioned in *I, Claudius* as going into voluntary exile in Augustus' reign) who was the single most important source for transmitting classical mythology to later ages. His masterpiece, *The Metamorphoses*, is a series of verse tales about mythological characters, linked by the fact that they all deal with the theme of changing shape. The star performer at this trick was undoubtedly Jupiter (Zeus in his Greek form), the king of gods, and his reason for changing shape was usually to escape the jealous attentions of his wife Juno (in Greek Hera) while going about his favourite pursuit of seducing beautiful mortals. In this way he turned himself into a bull to seduce Europa, a swan for Leda, a satyr for Antiope, a shower of gold for Danae and a cloud for Io. Jupiter sometimes took a fancy to boys as well as girls, and he turned himself into an eagle to abduct the beautiful shepherd Ganymede.

Juno did her best to thwart Jupiter's amorous adventures, and their schemes and counterschemes are best illustrated in the story of Io, the daughter of a king of Argos. Jupiter changed himself into a cloud to hide his infidelity, but Juno was not deceived. Changing tack slightly, Jupiter then turned Io into a white heifer, but Juno saw through this ruse, demanded the animal as a present, and set the hundred-eyed giant Argus to guard it. To recover the unfortunate Io/heifer, Jupiter employed his messenger Mercury (Hermes),

King of the gods
The majestic Jupiter is seen in all his remote Olympian splendour, as the nymph Thetis, the mother of the Greek warrior Achilles, seeks favour for her son.

Animal wet nurse
The twins Romulus and Remus, the legendary founders of Rome, were suckled by a wolf and had food brought to them by a woodpecker. Such tales abound in mythology: Jupiter himself was suckled by a goat.

who charmed Argus to sleep with his beautiful playing on the lyre and then cut off his head. Juno took Argus' eyes to decorate the tail of her peacock (a marvellous explanation of how the bird came to have such spectacularly beautifully patterned tail feathers), and in revenge sent a gadfly to torment the hapless Io.

The wranglings of Jupiter and Juno are fairly typical of the escapades of the gods, for although they are represented in Greek, Roman and later art as noble and majestic figures, much of their existence was taken up with lust, jealousy and intrigue in a kind of celestial soap opera. (There was incest, too, for Juno was Jupiter's sister as well as his wife.)

Wisdom and war
Minerva (above, centre) is primarily known as the goddess of wisdom and as the patroness of the arts and learning. She was also, however, associated with war – hence the helmet that she habitually wears. Here she is shown surrounded by philosophers and soldiers – two greatly contrasting professions who came under her protection.

VULCAN'S REVENGE

The most entertaining of the many stories of the tangled love life on Mount Olympus (the home of the gods) concerns Venus (Aphrodite), the goddess of beauty and love, and Mars (Ares), the god of war and son of Jupiter and Juno. Venus was married to Vulcan (Hephaestus), the lame god of fire, but she had an affair with Mars, a brutal character who was otherwise disliked by virtually everyone, including his parents. The sun god Sol (Helios) reported the infidelity to Vulcan, who used his marvellous skills as a blacksmith to take his revenge. He made a net that was so fine it was invisible but so strong it was unbreakable, and secretly fixed it to the adulterers' bed, so next time they made love they were trapped in it. The other gods were called on to witness their shame, although Mercury rather tactlessly remarked that he would not mind being in the same position as Mars.

When, in the narrative of Graves' novel, Claudius is asked to act as a bouncer at a royal brothel, he carries out his duties with such panache that Caligula dubs him Vulcan. Like the god, he has a clumsy, unexpected cunning, and Claudius is not at all displeased by the comparison.

Seduced by a swan
Leda, the wife of King Tyndareus of Sparta, was one of Jupiter's many illicit human lovers. He changed himself into a swan to make love to her, in the hope of avoiding the jealous attentions of his wife Juno.

'TO THE FAIREST'

The theme of the revenge of a thwarted deity had more dire consequences in the story of the Judgement of Paris. Paris was a shepherd who married the daughter of the river god Oeneus. Discordia (Eris), the goddess of strife, was the only one of the gods not invited to the wedding, so to stir up trouble she threw a golden apple inscribed 'To the fairest' among the guests. Juno, Venus and Minerva (Athena), the goddess of wisdom, each claimed the apple, and Jupiter ordered Paris to make the choice. Paris was subjected to outrageous bribery from the three contestants in this celestial beauty competition, and he succumbed to Venus' offer to reward him with the love of any woman in the world. The woman he chose was Helen, the wife of Menelaus, king of Sparta, whose beauty Venus described in the most rapturous terms.

Paris abducted Helen and carried her off to Troy – he had been born the son of Priam, king of Troy, but left to die as a child because his mother had dreamed he would cause the destruction of the city. The dream came true, for the abduction of Helen started the Trojan War, which resulted, after a siege of ten years, in the city being sacked. Two great poems of the ancient world – Homer's *Iliad* and Virgil's *Aeneid* – tell the story of the Trojan War and how the gods took the sides of various warriors and controlled their destinies. Aeneas, a Trojan prince, was under the special protection of Jupiter, and after the destruction of the city he

escaped and eventually founded the colony from which Rome grew. The distinction of founding the city itself is accorded to his descendants Romulus and Remus, twins who were reared by a wolf after they had survived an attempt to drown them at birth. Their mother was a Vestal Virgin who had been ravished by Mars and thrown into prison for being 'unchaste'.

Another famous pair of twins – Castor and Pollux – show that the dividing line between gods and mortals was sometimes a very fine one. According to the best-known account, they were the sons of Leda, a queen of Sparta, and Jupiter, who made love to her in the form of a swan – appropriately they were hatched from an egg. They became famous for their athletic prowess and were among the Argonauts who accompanied Jason on his epic voyage to find the Golden Fleece. After one of the brothers' most celebrated exploits – carrying off the daughters of their uncle Leucippus, who were betrothed to another set of twins – Castor, who was mortal, was killed. Pollux begged Jupiter to allow him and his brother to alternate life and death, one living for a day in the heavens and the other in the underworld, and then exchanging roles the next day. Jupiter agreed and later transformed them into the constellation Gemini (the twins), one of the signs of the Zodiac.

Beauty and the beast
(right) Artists often depict Venus and Mars in various scenes from their extra-marital affair. But here the god and goddess are used rather as timeless symbols expressing the power of beauty and love (Venus) to conquer strife (the brutal Mars).

Labour pains
In one of the fits of madness sent by Juno, Hercules – the product of her husband's extra-marital amours – killed his own children. In penance he had to serve King Eurystheus of Tiryns for twelve years, undertaking any task asked of him. Hercules successfully accomplished the twelve great Labours appointed to him, including slaying the Hydra, a multi-headed monster (left). The vengeful Juno sent a crab to hinder Hercules by biting his foot.

HELPERS OF MANKIND

Castor and Pollux were worshipped as helpers of mankind, and in particular were said to protect sailors in peril at sea. They were also appealed to by soldiers going into battle, and a cult developed for them in Rome, with a large temple dedicated to their worship in the Forum (the great public square) in the 5th century BC.

The attitude of mortals towards the gods was, however, not always one of reverence. In *I, Claudius*, the raving Caligula challenges Neptune to combat, shouting, "you treacherously wrecked my father's fleet". He orders his soldiers to attack the sea with their weapons (rock-hurling catapults as well as arrows and swords). "Neptune made no attempt to defend himself or reply", Graves explains playfully, "except that one man was nipped by a lobster and another stung by a jelly-fish."

In spite of such un-Olympian behaviour, by the time of Claudius the Romans had begun to accord the status of gods to their Emperors, although some people frowned on the practice. In *I, Claudius*, when the deification of the recently deceased Emperor Augustus is being considered, Gallus says, "It was all very well to decree new gods to ignorant Asiatic provincials, but the honourable House [the Senate] ought to pause before ordering educated citizens to worship one of their own number."

GREATEST OF HEROES

The cause of Augustus' deification is supported by Atticus, a senior magistrate, who "solemnly rose to say that when Augustus' corpse had been burned on Mars Field he had seen a cloud descending from heaven and the dead man's spirit then ascending on it, precisely in the way in which tradition relates that the spirits of Romulus and Hercules ascended. He would swear by all the Gods that he was testifying the truth."

The appeal to the example of Hercules (Herakles) was an important one, for he was the most popular of ancient heroes and the only mortal who had been raised after his death to the same status as the supreme Olympian gods. He started life with a great advantage for a hero, for although his mother Alcema was a mortal, his father was Jupiter. It was clear he was cut out for great things when – still a baby in his cradle – he strangled the pair of poisonous snakes that the ever-jealous Juno had sent to kill him.

The rest of Hercules' earthly life was taken up with similar prodigious feats of strength and heroism, triumphing over evil against heavy odds, although he also found time to indulge a sexual appetite that proved him a true son of Jupiter's. He was renowned for his generous, open nature, but he was also subject to fits of madness, when his rage was murderous. At his death (which was brought about by trickery), Jupiter hurled a thunderbolt to consume his funeral pyre and he was carried to Olympus in a chariot by Minerva.

On cloud nine
Jupiter was highly inventive in disguising himself to hide his infidelities with mortals from his wife Juno. Here, changed into a cloud, he is rapturously embraced by Io, but Juno later made her pay for her pleasure.

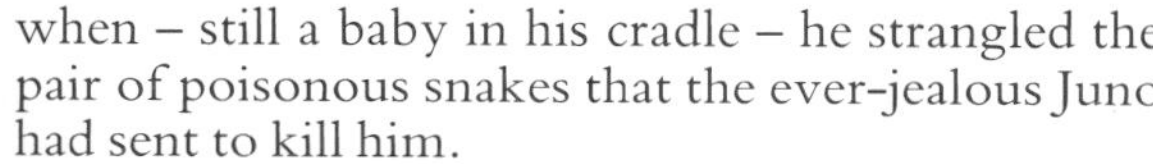

Apple of discord
This divine beauty contest, known as The Judgement of Paris, is one of the most popular mythological subjects in art, not least because it gave painters such a wonderful opportunity of displaying their skill in depicting beautiful female nudes. Paris, the handsomest of mortals, presents the prize of a golden apple to Venus, whom he has declared more beautiful than Juno (left) or Minerva. Venus had bribed him with the offer of the love of Helen of Troy, who Paris later abducted, thus starting the Trojan War.

IMMORTALS OF OLYMPUS

The legends of Hercules are so vivid and so memorable that he has inspired a host of writers and artists, and as he is only one of the immortals of Olympus it is not surprising that classical mythology has continued to haunt the European imagination. To the modern reader, these marvellous stories are often approached through Robert Graves' book *The Greek Myths* (1955), which opens the door to a timeless world of adventure, wonder and enchantment.

EVELYN WAUGH

1903-1966

Evelyn Waugh was a quirky genius who came to revel in his public image of 'eccentric don and testy colonel'. Beneath the mask was a serious artist of great integrity and discipline, a writer who created hilarious anarchy from the most exquisitely precise prose. He made his name as a satirist of upper-class society, while later novels drew on his travel and war experiences. Waugh believed that novelists should not aim to inform or instruct, but to provide entertainment. He did so by crafting novels of timeless comedy that defy you not to laugh out loud.

Against the Tide

Although for a time Waugh entered into the party spirit of the modern age, he was an intensely conservative man, both suspicious and disdainful of the world around him.

Like his fictional self-portrait, Gilbert Pinfold, Evelyn Waugh's "strongest tastes were negative. He abhorred plastics, Picasso, sunbathing, and jazz – everything, in fact, that had happened in his own lifetime." Waugh was a snob and a pessimist, convinced that all change was for the worse. He was also extremely sensitive, prone to self-hatred and despair, a perfectionist who fell short of his own ideals. His renowned rudeness, and the reactionary views he flaunted, were often 'half facetious' – his way of dealing with what seemed an increasingly chaotic world. Waugh purposely made it near impossible for anyone to glimpse the man behind the mask.

He was born in London's West Hampstead on 28 October 1903, the second son of Arthur and Catherine Waugh. Four years later the family moved up the hill to an Edwardian villa called 'Underhill', between Hampstead village and Golders Green. Waugh often expressed regret that he was not born into the aristocracy. Arthur Waugh was a minor literary figure, a reviewer and editor, and managing director of a publishing company. Waugh's mother was descended from the eminent judge Lord Cockburn. He loved her devotedly in childhood, as he did his nurse Lucy Hodges. His father's rather sentimental nature, however, did not find favour with Waugh, and their relationship was often uneasy.

By his own account, Waugh's childhood was unremarkable and 'lyrically happy'. The outbreak of World War I stirred him to early patriotism – he sold jam jars to raise funds for the Red Cross and with friends formed a gang called Pistol Troop for 'the defence of the kingdom'. Artistic as well as typically boyish, he wrote stories, kept diaries and drew pictures.

In 1917 Waugh went to Lancing College on the edge of the South Downs in Sussex. His early days there were 'black misery'. 'That awful little tick, Waugh' was never popular. He was short, plump and bespectacled. The Gothic chapel held more attractions for him than the playing fields, and although he would have liked 'to be accepted as one of this distasteful mob' he found it impossible to conform. He was arrogant and conceited, and to court popularity became a 'Bolshie', playing practical jokes and affecting a generally rebellious air. In the classroom, however, he excelled and came away with many academic prizes.

Lancing College
Waugh flourished academically at school, but was miserably lonely. The school chapel was his 'refuge'.

Happy childhood
(left) Evelyn Waugh's mother, Catherine, 'small, neat, reticent and very active', and (inset, left to right) young Evelyn, his father Arthur, and elder brother, Alec, who also enjoyed a notable career as a novelist. The two brothers got on well. In later years they remembered their childhood at Underhill, Hampstead, as an idyllically happy time.

'War work'
(right) This 1916 diary entry records the young Waugh doing his bit for the war effort, by 'cutting out soles for soldiers' shoes'. 'All the same', he adds, 'I think I shall chuck it soon as it cuts into the holls . . .'

War work.
On the first day of the holls we went to the Golders Green war depot & asked for war work. They received us with open arms & the next day we set to work in cutting out soles for soldiers' shoes.

All the same I think I shall chuck it soon as it cuts into the holls. so frightfully - Dave & Max are of the same opinion. Some of our soles were dreadfully cut out especially Maxwell's

a smart pair

Living it up
(below) Waugh poses on Queensbury, his new motor-bicycle, on Magdalen Bridge, Oxford, in 1925. Though he was no longer a student, he continued the riotous living of his undergraduate days.

Two men – he called them his 'mentors' – exerted great influence on Waugh in his Lancing years. His French teacher J. F. Roxburgh impressed Waugh with his worldly sophistication, while Francis Crease appealed to another side of his character. Crease was 'a neuter, evasive, hypochondriacal recluse' who taught the ancient art of illuminating manuscripts. Though Waugh was quickly to outgrow his admiration of these two figures, they represented contradictory impulses in himself – the man-of-the-world versus the artist – that he never fully resolved.

Key Dates

1903 born in London

1922 goes to Oxford

1928 *Decline and Fall* published. Marries Evelyn Gardner

1930 Divorced. *Vile Bodies* published. Enters Roman Catholic Church

1935 works as war correspondent in Abyssinia

1937 marries Laura Herbert

1940 joins Royal Marines

1941 fights in the battle for Crete

1945 *Brideshead Revisited*

1954 suffers breakdown

1961 *Unconditional Surrender* published

1966 dies at Combe Florey, Somerset

ever with his old Oxford set and with the Bright Young People of the 1920s. On one occasion he was fined 15s 6d for being drunk in charge of a car and his diaries record orgies and pranks with toilet seats.

But he was sickening of such excesses. He began to suffer from the insomnia that was to plague him for the rest of his life. He hated his teaching job and fell into a deep depression over his love for Olivia Plunket Greene 'of the great goo-goo eyes', the sister of an Oxford crony. And when a possible job in Italy fell through he decided on desperate measures – he would kill himself.

TURNING POINT

We have a jellyfish to thank for Waugh's literary legacy. As he swam out to sea under a full moon, intent on drowning, he was stung, literally, back to his senses. In pain, but also very much alive, he returned to the shore. Later he took another teaching post, at what he termed 'a school for backward peers', Aston Clinton, in Buckinghamshire. A typical diary entry reads, 'Taught lunatics. Played rugby football. Drank at Bell.'

He lasted at Aston Clinton until the beginning of 1927, when he was sacked for the combined sins of drinking and trying to seduce a matron. It was then that he decided that life might be better as 'a man of letters.'

Seven months later he was finishing off a biography of the painter Dante Gabriel Rossetti, and his first novel, *Decline and Fall*, was well under way. He was also falling in love with Evelyn

From Lancing, Waugh went on to Hertford College, Oxford, in 1922. His first two terms there were the lull before the storm. There followed a period of riotous, dissipated living that started with his introduction to the Hypocrites Club, a club whose members were notorious for their drunkenness and flamboyance of dress. Waugh held wild dinner parties, had homosexual affairs, drank to excess and made a big show of behaving obnoxiously and rowdily. 'Why do you have to make such a noise?', he was asked. 'Because I'm poor,' he replied. He ran up large debts trying to hold his own with aristocratic and gilded youths like Harold Acton and Hugh Lygon. 'Quite broke and rather stupid and quite incredibly depraved morally', Waugh left Oxford in June 1924 with a poor third class degree in Modern History and little idea of where his life would lead.

His diaries describe the period 1924-28 as 'a record of continuous failure'. Though he had had stories and articles published in university magazines he saw his future in lettering and drawing. But after a disillusioning spell at an art school in London and an aborted plan to become apprenticed to a print maker, financial considerations forced him to take a teaching post in North Wales. He had entered the unhappiest period of his life.

When he could, he drank and partied as much as

He- and She-Evelyn
(above) The breakdown of his first marriage to Evelyn Gardner – after she had fallen in love with another man – came as a complete shock to Waugh. Until then he had thought them a 'serenely happy' couple. For two painful weeks they tried to patch up the marriage, to no avail. 'Evelyn was not an affectionate person. I was', wrote She-Evelyn many years later.

Remote places
(right) Foreign travel inspired much of Waugh's writing. In 1934 he holed himself up in a hotel in Morocco to work on the first half of his fourth novel, A Handful of Dust.

Gardner, a bright and vivacious former debutante. He proposed to her over dinner at the Ritz, and on 27 June 1928 they married quietly and secretly in London. The publication of *Rossetti: His Life and Works* had already signalled Waugh's arrival on the literary scene. *Decline and Fall* came out in September, to great acclaim, as the newlyweds were settling into a small flat in Islington. Waugh could not have been happier.

Just eight months later, however, the marriage had broken down and Waugh's world had fallen apart. 'I did not know it was possible to be so miserable and live', he wrote to Harold Acton. Waugh's divorce, on the grounds of She-Evelyn's adultery with an old Etonian, was granted in June 1930. Three months later Waugh entered the Roman Catholic Church.

FOREIGN TRAVELS

The failure of Waugh's marriage was a watershed in his life and work. It hastened his conversion to Roman Catholicism, a major influence from this time on. It also triggered a new bitterness and misanthropy in him that intensified as he grew older. And it left him, without a domestic anchor, free to travel extensively for the next seven years.

In November 1930, as foreign correspondent for *The Times*, he attended the coronation in Addis Ababa of Emperor Haile Selassie of Ethiopia. He journeyed widely in Africa, a trip that yielded the travel book *Remote People* and his third novel *Black Mischief*. In 1935 he covered the colonial conflict between Italy and Abyssinia for the *Daily Mail*.

CATHOLICISM

For Waugh, the Church of Rome represented tradition, civilized values and good taste – qualities he found increasingly lacking in the world around him. Although he claimed that 'from sixteen to twenty-eight I didn't go to church at all', he was always devout. His decision to convert to Roman Catholicism following the break-up of his first marriage was, typically, based 'on firm intellectual conviction'. But could a man capable of Waugh's unprovoked rudeness and cruelty still be a Christian and a practising Catholic? Nancy Mitford once put the question to him after his jibes had reduced a dinner guest to tears. 'You have no idea', he replied, 'how much nastier I would be if I was not a Catholic.'

Lady Diana Cooper
(above) Lady Diana Cooper, famous society beauty, captivated Waugh with her wit and sophistication, and they developed a warm friendship. She was the model for Mrs Stitch in Scoop *– a portrait that delighted her.*

On his way back to London from this assignment he was granted an interview with the Fascist leader Mussolini in Rome. Waugh always delighted in going against the grain, and paid naïve tribute to Mussolini's brutal imperialism in *Waugh in Abyssinia*. He also found himself in a minority in his support for Franco and the Nationalist cause during the Spanish Civil War.

Many people found such allegiances unpalatable, but his growing celebrity earned him many admirers among the fashionable social

The Hollywood treatment
Waugh would not agree to Brideshead Revisited *being treated as a love story on the big screen – but he and his second wife Laura were entertained lavishly on their visit to California in 1947. He became intrigued by the burial rites at Forest Lawn Cemetery and returned there day after day. It inspired* The Loved One.

Fact or Fiction

ROSA LEWIS

Waugh peopled his novels with many characters drawn from real life. In *Vile Bodies* the owner of Shepheard's Hotel, Lottie Crump, "a fine figure of a woman", is a direct portrait of Rosa Lewis (inset), complete with her two cairn terriers. She ran the Cavendish Hotel (below), one of Waugh's drinking haunts, in London's Jermyn Street. (She also inspired the television series, *The Duchess of Duke Street.)* Waugh also borrowed the name of one of her staff, her aged maître d'hotel, for the vulgar social climber, Archie Schwert. Outraged by her portrayal in *Vile Bodies,* Rosa Lewis barred the 'bastard', 'that little swine Evelyn Waugh' from ever setting foot in the Cavendish Hotel again.

circles. And he was falling in love again. Laura Herbert – ironically, a cousin of his first wife – was 21 when she and Waugh married in London in April 1937. They may have seemed an ill-matched couple – he loud and opinionated, she quiet and reserved – but their marriage, and their six children, brought them great contentment. They lived at Piers Court in Gloucestershire, and later at Combe Florey in Somerset.

Shortly after the outbreak of World War II Waugh joined the Royal Marines as a second lieutenant. He served in Africa and joined the Commandos under Colonel Bob Laycock, with whom he fought in the battle for Crete in 1941. He spent the next two years back in England and saw out the war in Yugoslavia.

The tradition of the officer and gentleman naturally appealed to Waugh, but he made a poor soldier. With his snobbish distaste for those not born to privilege he could not get on with the men in his charge. A fellow officer recorded that 'he bullied them. He bewildered them purposely'. On one occasion his Colonel even placed a sentry outside Waugh's tent to guard against one of his own men trying to kill him while he slept. Waugh's bravery and humour were invaluable assets, however. The terrifying aerial bombardment of the Allied forces on Crete, his first experience of battle, he dismissed with typical composure as being 'like German opera, too long and too loud'.

He completed two novels during the war years, *Put Out More Flags* and *Brideshead Revisited* – the latter an enormous success. In 1947 he and Laura spent a month in Hollywood, courtesy of MGM, to discuss a possible film of *Brideshead*. The film came to nothing, but the trip enabled him to visit Forest Lawn Cemetery where he 'found a deep mine of literary gold' that yielded up his next novel, the gruesomely funny *The Loved One*.

WITHDRAWAL FROM THE WORLD

Waugh had been dismayed by the push for social change signalled by the Labour Party's overwhelming election victory in 1945. He refused to vote in elections on the grounds of what he called 'conscientious objection to parliamentary democracy'. He complemented this intense conservatism by wearing loud check suits in parody of the country squire. From this time on his diaries record a withdrawal from the world.

If Waugh had his critics, he could also command intense loyalty in friends. In those post-war years guests at his West Country 'squiredom', and at his club in London, White's, included the poet John Betjeman and the novelist Graham Greene. With his socialist sympathies, Greene would not seem a natural companion for Waugh, yet their friendship – based largely on their shared religion – lasted until the end of his life.

The first two novels of Waugh's War Trilogy, *Men at Arms* and *Officers and Gentlemen*, were published in 1952 and 1955. By this time Waugh's constant drinking and the use of powerful sleeping draughts had taken their toll. He suffered from deafness and impaired memory and seemed older than his years. Waugh had spent much of his life feeling persecuted, but now such feelings assumed the proportions of persecution mania.

After agreeing to be interviewed for the BBC, he regarded the resultant programme as a malign conspiracy against him. He suspected friends of disloyalty, confused names and events and became alarmed by the state of his mind. As a rest cure, he set sail for Ceylon in January 1954 aboard a small cruise ship, bound, though he did not know it, for a 'sharp but brief attack of insanity'.

A TORMENTED MIND

The letters Laura Waugh received from him during this cruise alarmed her deeply. He claimed he was being plagued day and night by disembodied voices that mocked and abused him. He believed it to be the work of evil spirits. On his return to London he immediately demanded a priest to come and exorcise him of the devils that tormented his mind.

The psychiatrist summoned to his hotel that night diagnosed acute poisoning – Waugh's auditory hallucinations had been brought on by prolonged abuse of sleep-inducing drugs and alcohol. At the suggestion of the psychiatrist he now set to work on *The Ordeal of Gilbert Pinfold.*

The opening chapter of this novel, published in 1957, is a ruthless self-portrait of Waugh in his later years, a blimpish figure, besieged in his country retreat by a rapidly changing world. Waugh himself refused to use the telephone and sported an old-fashioned ear-trumpet that he once ostentatiously lowered when Malcolm Muggeridge rose to speak at a literary luncheon. (Ann Fleming, wife of the novelist Ian, cured him of using this intimidating device, by banging it sharply with a spoon as he held it to his ear.) In May 1959 he was offered the CBE, but turned it down apparently because he believed he was worthy of a higher honour.

He became increasingly melancholic and lethargic. The publication, in 1961, of the concluding volume of the *Sword of Honour, Unconditional Surrender*, marked the end of his career as a novelist. The 'prancing faun', as Harold Acton had described him at Oxford, was now corpulent and florid, worried by his rotting teeth, plagued by insomnia. He spent his mornings breathing on his library window and playing noughts and crosses in the condensation, drinking gin as he did so.

In a letter to his daughter Margaret dated December 1965 Waugh wrote, 'The awful prospect is that I may have more than 20 years ahead . . . Don't let me in my dotage oppress you . . .' But he was not to live another 20 years. On Easter Sunday 1966, after he and his family had celebrated Mass at the nearby Catholic chapel, Evelyn Waugh suffered a sudden and fatal heart attack, releasing him from the ignominy of an empty and unsolicited old age.

Family man
(right) Though he often lost his temper, Waugh the family man was far from the Victorian ogre that he sometimes posed as. He was a loving father to his six children, and fiercely loyal to his wife. For her part, Laura Waugh always coped patiently with her husband's idiosyncrasies.

'Stinkers'
(below) Piers Court, at Stinchcombe in Gloucestershire, was the Waugh family home for 18 years. Well-proportioned and elegant, the 18th-century manor house was a haven from the modern world, and Waugh did much of his work there.

The Roaring Twenties

Following the horrors of the war years, music, razzmatazz and glitter were the order of the day. People partied into the small hours – and loved every minute of it.

The World War of 1914-18 was a cataclysmic event, which changed the world and people's perceptions to such an extent that a grown person looking back at 1913 from the vantage point of 1923 might as easily have been bridging a century as a decade. Today, it is difficult to identify with the world before 1914. The world of *Vile Bodies*, by contrast, seems somehow familiar. In practically every important respect it is the modern world, our world.

Of all the images of the Roaring Twenties, the most striking is that of a pert young woman – free, fun and gamely determined to tackle life as an independent human being. The Sixties Chelsea Girl had a great deal in common with her 'flapper' grandmother. If they were of a mind to do so they both held down a job, took an active interest in politics and viewed their parents as outdated 'fuddy-duddies'. Each lived for the moment and sought pleasure where they could. Slaves to transient fashion, the flappers and the Sixties children changed their attitudes as often as their dress, and seemed to court the disapproval of their elders. If they fancied it, each smoked and drank and maybe even dabbled in drugs with their men friends, and if they wanted to sleep with them they did that too. For both, the term 'Victorian' conveyed their disdain for boring, middle-aged attitudes.

NO TURNING BACK

The 'new woman', as she was described, was a direct product of the First World War. The war had opened up an enormous range of employment opportunities for women, and when it came to an end it was unthinkable that these new working women would all tamely retreat to hearth and home. At the same time, their contribution to the war effort was recognized by all, and in rapid succession a host of male bastions came tumbling down. Women were given the vote and allowed to stand for Parliament. An Act of Parliament in 1918 swept away barriers to most professions, including the Bar, while Cambridge followed Oxford's lead in opening the door to women fellows.

Young women from the middle and upper classes gained the most immediate and direct benefit from these changes, but the effects were felt throughout society. A working-class girl whose mother had spent her life in domestic service could see the wider horizons offered by secretarial work or a job behind the counter of a bustling department store.

Employment of this sort scarcely provided her with affluence, but it took her light years away from the world of 'Upstairs Downstairs'. She

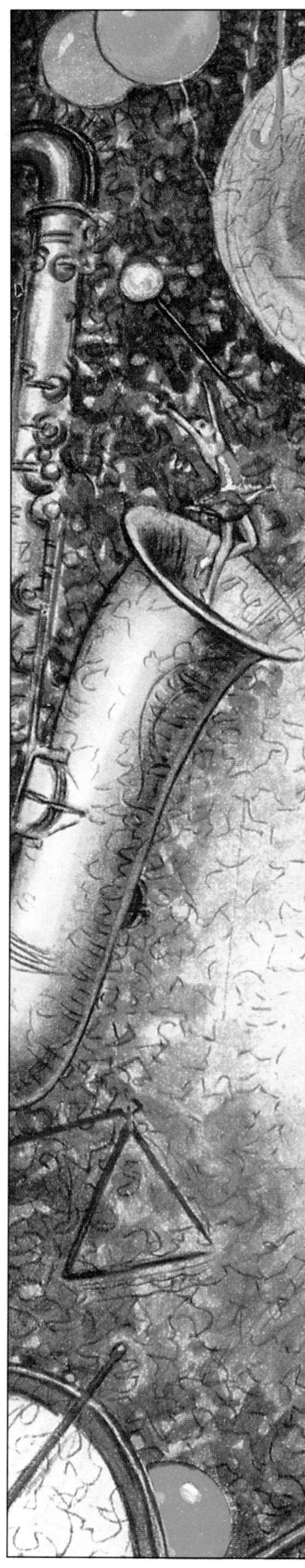

The Jazz Age

After the war, couples boogied as never before. Everything had changed – the Charleston (right) was all the vogue, and black bands (left) could earn more in a single season than the British Prime Minister earned in a year.

could move away from home and perhaps share a flat with other girls. She could go to the pictures, buy gramophone records and keep abreast of the latest dance craze. Also, being able to afford cheap make-up and inexpensive versions of the latest fashions meant that she was able to identify with a particular age group rather than just a particular class. The secretary sharing digs in a drab suburb was a member of the Younger Generation, just as Waugh's 'Bright Young Things' were.

This Younger Generation was bent on having a good time. The slaughter and sacrifice of the war had created almost universal disillusionment. At a philosophical level, this led to a withering assault on the comfortable assumptions of the Victorian Age, in particular on the belief that human beings were rational creatures able to control their own destiny. At an everyday level, this attitude bred cynicism and found expression in a craving for pleasure. Life is short, so make it sweet.

Reckless, defiant gaiety was the hallmark of the Roaring Twenties, and the Bright Young Things led the way. Waugh's bitchy little sketch of the privileged Mayfair set is hilariously funny, but it is right on target: the compulsive flitting from party to party in order to 'be with the action', as a later generation would put it; the wild, boisterous drinking; the infectious sense of irresponsibility; above all the obsession with having fun *all* the time (which was 'just too, *too* divine', as opposed to

Looking to the future
The 'new woman' left behind the trimmings of a former era, happy to display her femininity without props or buttresses. Hair was disarmingly short – like a man's – a symbol of woman's new-found independence and equality.

Changing fashions
In the twenties, to show the knee was considered very daring, but the girl (left) is clearly unrepentant. Rather than lengthen her skirt she decides to tackle the problem from the other angle – raising her garters. And to compound her sins she has cropped hair, defiantly bare arms and a jauntily held cigarette.

anything else, which was 'just too, *too* boring').

The fun began with the music – jazz imported from the progressive and less inhibited United States. With jazz came the new dances – the 'Camel Walk', the 'Shimmy', and then the two really outstanding dance crazes of the decade, the 'Charleston' and the 'Black Bottom'. The music was lively, with pulsing, insistent rhythms and the dance steps caught the energy of the music. Swank hotels hastened to lay out dance floors, while an easing of the strict wartime licensing hours gave birth to a flourishing restaurant and cabaret scene. Drinking as such was curbed at 11 pm, but it was easy to get around that by ordering a sandwich, which extended the period to 12.30 am.

PARTIES AND NIGHT-CLUBS

Another tremendously successful American import was the cocktail, and with it came the cocktail party. The gin-based cocktail encountered stern resistance amongst the older generation, not so much because of its American origin but because of the Victorian association of gin with lower-class drunkenness. The cocktail party too – a brief, early-evening whirl of chattering – seemed odd to those who remembered leisurely Edwardian house parties. Why were the young in so much of a hurry?

Night-clubs dotted London's West End. Some of them were highly respectable and obeyed the law by serving drinks only up to the appointed hour. But essentially night-clubs existed to provide revellers with the chance to enjoy themselves into the small hours, and most night-club owners – and their patrons – were quite prepared to flout the law. Mrs. Kate Meyrick opened the first of her clubs, the notorious '43' in Gerrard St, in 1921 and went on to become the queen of London's night-life. She cheerfully endured raids and fines until in 1924 she was sentenced to – and served – six months in Holloway prison. This 'martyrdom' solidified her social standing, and her three daughters married into the aristocracy.

The private party had nothing to fear from any licensing laws, and at times it appeared as though the Bright Young Things were enjoying a non-stop party, cavorting between their Mayfair heartland and those distant outposts of Knightsbridge and Chelsea. Their most publicized fling was the 'Babies' Ball', where they all rolled up in prams and got wildly drunk prancing around in rompers and pinafores. The innocent sounding Oxford Railway Club was another symptom of this almost calculated high-spiritedness. It was formed to extol the pleasures of drinking through the night on

Sports and pleasure
As women divested themselves of cumbersome clothes, they were able to compete more equally with men in the field of sports. Money helped too, and the fashionable set had time to kill on Europe's tennis courts and golf courses (above). But swimming pools could provide more elaborate entertainment. Fancy-dress parties were in vogue and people went to extraordinary lengths to outdo their friends. Entire baths would be rented for swimming parties and guests could come in colour-coordinated outfits or bearing their own white horse (right).

trains, and its members, who included Evelyn Waugh, would board the Penzance-Aberdeen express at Oxford, attired in full evening dress. They would proceed to drink their way to Leicester, disembark, and catch the southbound train – roistering all the way back to Oxford and the cold light of dawn.

Such innovative and exorbitant ways of getting drunk touched the lives of the pampered few, but there were cheaper crazes which were open to all. Anyone, for instance, could hop about on a Pogo Stick, and in the autumn of 1921 just about everyone did. This curious contraption – a spring-loaded pole with cross-bars for hands and feet – has ever since held a passing attraction for children, but it is hard to imagine grown men and women bouncing along the pavement. It was simply a fad – one more transient phase – as were so many Twenties' pastimes. The Chinese game Mah-Jong was all the rage by mid-decade, and so was the American-imported crossword puzzle.

OUTRAGEOUS EXCESS

Such fads, along with the comings and goings of the fashionable set, were staple fare for the gossip columns of society magazines and popular newspapers. But side by side with the journalistic sensationalism and titillation which features in *Vile Bodies* came a heartfelt condemnation of youthful frivolity. The war had given young people unprecedented respect in the eyes of their elders, but that did not give them *carte blanche* to dress and behave wildly.

Extravagant pleasures
Even the wealthy had felt the pinch of the war years. When it was over they treated themselves to lavish distractions.

There was much fulminating about women's fashions. Women in factories during the war had found it safer and more convenient to cut their hair short and wear trousers. Bobbed hair, trousers and short skirts became badges of the flapper, along with facial make-up, another American import. And it was lamented that the very shape of young women had undergone a dramatic change for the worse in a single generation. Where had those pleasingly ample, fetchingly corsetted Edwardian figures gone? Could those skinny little things whose scanty clothing barely concealed a non-existent bust really be their daughters?

SLEEKER FIGURES

There were, in fact, good reasons for many of these changes. Severe shortages of sugar and butter during the war years had meant that the young had grown into the habit of doing with little. Having become accustomed to imposed slimming, it was then easy for them to slim for fashion. This change in diet was accompanied by other changes too. The enormous gulf between men and women had been narrowed – women could now work, vote, smoke, drive – so it seemed logical that they

The Thirties
(below) The bubble of 1920s gaiety burst with the Depression of the following decade. Driven to action, a throng of unemployed workers from the shipyards and iron and steel works of the North marched on London in protest. Only a lucky few (left) were untouched by these struggles and could look on at the marchers with sublime indifference.

should be able to dress more boyishly too.

Flappers – so called because they sat on the 'flapper-bracket' riding pillion on motorcycles – were easy targets for satire. *Punch* published this biting parody in 1922:

But whether you behold her in her box
Diaphonously clad, with purple locks,
Or jazzing with contortions that outdo
The gestures of a boxing kangaroo . . .
Glorinda holds the centre of the stage,
The most conspicuous monster of our age.

Less trivial than concerns about fashion and frantic dancing was an underlying fear among many that women's new independence and the sexual freedom that everyone seemed to talk about would undermine the hierarchical edifice of family life. Women were at last given the vote on the same terms as men in 1928; Dr. Marie Stopes was making headway in her tireless campaign to spread information on birth control so that women could escape the dangerous burden of excessive pregnancies; divorces were becoming widespread, at least among those above the reach of middle-class morality. Society was changing.

And as the decade drew to a close, so too did the pleasure-obsessed world of *Vile Bodies*. The collapse of the American stock market, the Wall Street Crash of 1929, devastated the economy of the United States and had terrible repercussions in Britain. The glitter of the twenties was replaced by the Depression of the thirties. While the Depression hit the ordinary people (who had no place in Waugh's world) hardest, even for the likes of Adam and Nina, the party was over.

GRAHAM GREENE

1904-1991

One of the most famous modern British novelists, Graham Greene gripped his millions of readers with dramatically conceived narratives of the 20th-century world – a dangerous world in which loyalties are uncertain and everything is at risk. Greene's own life was an eventful one. Above all, he sought relief from his inner tensions through two closely related 'ways of escape' – writing and travelling – which constantly brought him on to 'the dangerous edge of things'.

Courting Danger

Jealous of his privacy and reticent about the contents of his long life, Graham Greene told those who crave an insight into his nature and beliefs: 'Read my books.'

Much of Graham Greene's life remained firmly closed to the public. Although he shunned television appearances and journalistic interviews, he wrote candidly enough about his early years; but his respect for 'the copyright of others' lives' – those closely involved with him – made him doubly reticent to discuss any later events except those on public record. On the other hand, Greene presented his own personality and motives in the starkest terms. He was prone to long, near suicidal depressions and periods of intense boredom from which he broke loose only by taking extreme measures. Much of his life was a search for 'ways of escape' – a phrase that he used as the title of his second volume of autobiography. Among the 'ways of escape' from mundane reality he numbered writing, travel and courting danger – activities in which his pronounced political and religious sympathies were very much in evidence.

Henry Graham Greene was born on 2 October 1904 at Berkhamsted in Hertfordshire, where his father was a housemaster at the public school. As one of six brothers and sisters, with six Greene cousins living only a few hundred yards away, he seems to have had a happy childhood – until at 13 he became a boarder at Berkhamsted School and 'the misery of life started'. The smells, the lack of privacy and the monotony appalled him, and since his father had by this time become headmaster, Greene found himself in a difficult position in relation to the other boys, who gave him his first experiences of betrayal and mental torture.

Over the years, Greene reacted to the horror of school life with successful truancies and occasional, inept attempts at self-destruction. Then, on the last day of the 1920 summer holidays, he took more positive action, leaving his parents a note to say that he would hide out on Berkhamsted Common until they agreed that he need not return to 'prison'. The outcome was anti-climactic, since Greene was found almost at once; but his gesture did persuade his parents that he was in distress, and they arranged for him to undergo psychoanalysis.

The Greene clan
'The Greenes seemed to move as a tribe . . .' (Graham, aged 16, is pictured centre among relations).

Berkhamsted
'. . . a scene of happiness, misery, first love, the attempt to write.'

At the Lancaster Gate home of his analyst, Kenneth Richmond, Greene spent 'perhaps the happiest six months of my life'. The treatment may or may not have worked, but Greene now had two things that he craved – freedom and access to the distractions of London. He returned to the sixth form at Berkhamsted, where, freed from most of the encumbrances of school life, he secured a place at Balliol College, Oxford, to study history. He was already writing 'the most sentimental fantasies in bad poetic prose', one of which, *The Tick of the Clock*, had appeared in his school magazine and was published in a London evening paper.

At Oxford, Greene wrote poetry, edited a magazine, the *Oxford Outlook*, and began his long interest in the cinema. He and his friend Claude Cockburn became members of the Communist Party for a few weeks – mainly, Greene said,

Charles Henry Greene
As headmaster of Berkhamsted School (above right) Graham's father (above) 'was even more distant than our aloof mother'.

Key Dates

1904 born in Berkhamsted

1920 psychoanalysed

1922 Balliol College, Oxford

1926 converts to Catholicism; sub-editor on *The Times*

1927 marries Vivien Dayrell-Browning

1929 publishes first novel

1938 *Brighton Rock*; visits Mexico

1941 intelligence work in Sierra Leone

1943 intelligence work in London

1950s travels in Malaya, Vietnam, Cuba, Kenya, Congo, etc.

1960s travels in Haiti, Chile, Paraguay

1966 settles in Antibes; *The Comedians*

because they hoped it might get them a free holiday to Moscow. One absurd result of this was that for many years – even after he became famous as a 'Catholic novelist' – Greene was allowed only a restricted right of entry to the United States. A more rewarding involvement with politics began when Greene offered his services as a propagandist to the Germans of the Ruhr, who were then – after World War I – suffering under French occupation. This brought him a free holiday down the Rhine and Moselle valleys as an 'observer'. Mysterious visitors continued to frequent his Oxford rooms for some time, but his plans for adopting the role of a double agent were thwarted when the Ruhr problem was solved by international agreement.

DEATH WISH

In spite of such diversions, Greene's Oxford years gave rise to a crisis that reveals a great deal about him. During the long vacation of 1923 he fell obsessively in love with the governess of the youngest Greenes. His lack of success with her evidently contributed to a chronic attack of 'ennui' which persisted until Greene looked in a cupboard and found a revolver belonging to his elder brother – 'a small ladylike object with six chambers'. Having read about Russian roulette, he decided to take the risk on Berkhamsted Common. He put a bullet in one of the chambers, spun the chambers round, then put the revolver to his head and pulled the trigger, knowing that there was a one in six chance of killing himself. Having survived, Greene felt an extraordinary sense of jubilation and a conviction that 'life contained an infinite number of possibilities'. After several more 'games' Russian roulette lost its thrill, but Greene's discovery of danger as a stimulant was to be a permanent influence on his outlook.

After Oxford, Greene was briefly a trainee with the British-American Tobacco Company, worked as a tutor (becoming so bored that he had a perfectly good tooth extracted in order to enjoy a 'holiday' under ether), and secured an unpaid job with *The Nottingham Journal*.

Having become engaged to a Roman Catholic, he felt that he should know something of her beliefs, received instruction, and unexpectedly found himself convinced by the priest's arguments. He was received into the Church in February 1926 – the beginning of a complex, problematical relationship that lasted for well over 60 years.

A FALSE START

In March 1926 Greene was accepted as a sub-editor on *The Times*, where his job was to condense and remodel the news stories sent in by reporters. Thanks to this secure and highly respectable employment he was able to marry Vivien Dayrell-Browning in 1927, eventually becoming the father of two children. Meanwhile he had written two novels that were refused publication, and had begun a third, *The Man Within*, while in hospital with appendicitis. When *The Man Within* was accepted, published in 1929, and sold some 8,000 copies, Greene became convinced that he would be able to live as a professional writer. He

Propaganda aid
Greene wrote for the Germans – and got £25 and a trip to Trier (right) in 1924 for his efforts.

The Times

No. 44263. London Wednesday May 5. 1926 Price 2d.

WEATHER FORECAST. Wind N.E.; fair to dull; risk of local rain.

THE GENERAL STRIKE.

A wide response was made yesterday throughout the country to the call of those Unions which had been ordered by the T.U.C. to bring out their members. Railway workers stopped generally, though at Hull railway clerks are reported to have resumed duty, confining themselves to their ordinary work, and protested against the strike. Commercial road transport was only partially suspended. In London the tramways and the L.G.O.C. services were stopped. The printing industry is practically at a standstill, but lithographers have not been withdrawn, and compositors in London have not received instructions to strike. Large numbers of building operatives, other than those working on housing, came out.

The situation in the engineering trades was confused; men in some districts stopped while in others they continued at work. There was no interference with new construction in the shipbuilding yards, but in one or two districts some of the men engaged on repair work joined in the strike with the dockers.

Food:-Supplies of milk and fish brought into Kings Cross, Euston and Paddington were successfully distributed from the Hyde Park Depot and stations. The Milk & Food Controller expects it will be possible to maintain a satisfactory supply of milk to hospitals, institutions, schools, hotels, restaurants and private consumers. Milk will be 8d. per gallon dearer wholesale and 2d. per quart retail today. Smithfield market has distributed 5,000 tons of meat since Monday.

Mails:- Efforts will be made to forward by means of road transport the mails already shown as due to be dispatched very shortly from London. The position is uncertain and the f... be limited to m... Africa. ...t Bow Stre... required ...

... have to ... India & ... who ... de ...

Liverpool, Leeds, Northampton, Cardiff, Portsmouth, Dover, N.Derbyshire and Monmouthshire.

Evening papers appeared at Bristol, Southampton, several Lancashire towns and Edinburgh, and typescript issues at Manchester, Birmingham and Aberdeen.

The Atlantic Fleet did not sail on its summer cruise at Portsmouth yesterday. The men went on shore duty.

Road & Rail Transport:- There was no railway passenger transport in London yesterday except a few suburban trains. Every available form of private transport was used. A few independent omnibuses were running, but by the evening the railway companies, except the District and Tubes, had an improvised service. Among the railway services to-day will be:- 9.30 a.m., Manchester to Marylebone 9.30 a.m. Marylebone to Manchester; 10.10 a.m Marylebone to Newcastle; 9 a.m Norwich to London; 9 a.m King's Cross to York; 5 p.m. King's Cross to Peterborough; 9 p.m. Peterborough to King's Cross. L.M.S. Electric trains between Watford and Euston and Broad Street will maintain a 40 minutes service. On all sections of the Metropolitan Railway except Moorgate to Finsbury Park, a good service will run to-day from 6.40 a.m. The Underground hope to work a six minute service on the Central London Line to-day from 8 a.m. to 8 p.m. between Wood Lane and Liverpool Street. The following stations only will be open:- Shepherds Bush, Lancaster Gate, Oxford Circus, Tottenham Court Road, Bank, Liverpool Street. A flat fare of 3d will be charged.

The Prime Minister had an audience of the King yesterday morning.

There was no indication last night of any attempt to resume negotiations between the Pri... Minister and the ... rinting an...

The Go... newspap... will ... dis...

Defending **The Times**
In the 1926 General Strike, Greene uncharacteristically pitted himself against the strikers who had, after all, set fire to the building. 'I was emotionally attached to the newspaper' (left).

persuaded his publishers to pay him £200 a year for three years and, against all advice, resigned from *The Times*.

'I left *The Times* the author of a successful first novel. I thought I was a writer already and that the world was at my feet, but life wasn't like that. It was only a false start.' Greene took his family to Chipping Campden in the Cotswolds, where they could live cheaply while he established himself. Instead, he produced two novels that failed commercially and were, in Greene's view, so bad that he has never allowed them to be reprinted. A third, *Stamboul Train,* was to be much more successful, although expensive changes had to be made to the text when the novelist J. B. Priestley threatened to sue for libel.

LONG ROUTE TO *BRIGHTON*

For most of the 1930s, Greene was in debt to his publishers, and could not support his family by his fiction. He survived by writing and reviewing for the *Spectator* and *Night and Day*, among other things contributing regular film criticism for four and a half years. Here too he fell foul of the libel laws (then more stringent than they are today) when he suggested that the child star Shirley Temple 'had a certain adroit coquetry which appealed to middle-aged men'. He was also able to earn some much-needed money by writing film scripts for the producer Alexander Korda, although the results were uninspiring. His film work did not take off until after the war, when Greene wrote *The Fallen Idol* and *The Third Man*.

Greene had already discovered the lure of travel as a 'way of escape'. His most ambitious – and hazardous – pre-war journey was a trip through Liberia and Sierra Leone, made with his 23-year old cousin Barbara. No detailed map of the area existed, and the travellers made do with an American military map that labelled large blank areas with the single word 'cannibals'. The travel book that was to justify the expedition (*Journey Without Maps*, 1936) was suppressed after another threat of a libel action, but Greene managed to clear his debt to his publishers when his first major novel, *Brighton Rock* (1938), enjoyed some success. The same year he visited Mexico, where the Church was being persecuted – an experience which inspired *The Lawless Roads* and his famous novel, *The Power and the Glory*.

Greene also tried, unsuccessfully, to visit Spain during the Civil War in which his sympathies were strongly anti-fascist. The political crises of the 1930s gave him a further motive for travel: 'A restlessness set in then which has never quite been allayed: a desire to be a spectator of history.' But when it became apparent that Britain herself would soon be engulfed by war, Greene raced to make some provision for his family, writing a thriller, *The Confidential Agent*, in six weeks in the mornings (with the help of benzedrine), while going on more slowly in the afternoons with *The Power and the Glory*.

During World War II, Greene's life took on some of the qualities of his fiction. He worked at the Ministry of Information during the Blitz before being recruited into MI6 by his sister Elizabeth. He was sent to West Africa and, after

Journey without mishap
A three-months' trip in 1935 through Liberia (right), walking 15 miles a day, resulted in the book Journey Without Maps. *It was immediately suppressed.*

Sierra Leone
Posted to Freetown (above), from 1942 to 1943 Greene ran a one-man SIS office – inspiration for The Heart of the Matter.

A reckless move
Throwing up his job with The Times, *Greene moved, with his family, to Chipping Campden (left), bent on being a full-time author. Poverty struck.*

Mexican journey
Travelling through the Chiapas mountains (above), Greene was deeply shocked by his first-hand experience of suppression of religion.

three months' training at Lagos (Nigeria), went on to Freetown (Sierra Leone) – supposedly as a member of Special Branch CID – where he established a one-man office. He dismissed his activities there as 'futile efforts to run agents into the Vichy colonies'. In 1943 Greene returned to London and was given responsibility for counter-espionage in Portugal. He worked under Kim Philby, who became a friend; Philby's own secret career, as a Soviet agent, still had a good many years to run before exposure.

It was only after the war that Greene, then in his forties, became a famous and popular writer. *The Heart of the Matter* (1948), a book he later disliked, was 'the start of my success', and the film *The Third Man* became a box-office hit. From this time

DOUBLE AGENT

During World War II, Greene worked for British Intelligence. His superior was Kim Philby (right). In 1951 two British diplomats, Guy Burgess and Donald Maclean, were identified as long-term Soviet agents, but managed to defect before they could be arrested. Clearly they had been tipped off. The insider – the 'third man' – proved to be Kim Philby, who finally disappeared in the Middle East to re-emerge in Moscow as a KGB officer. Greene admired Philby's secret dedication to a cause throughout his long double life: 'Philby really lived out his loyalty.' And when Greene came to write a novel about a double agent (*The Human Factor*), he sent it to Philby for expert comment.

The quiet observer
Four times Greene went to Indo-China (above), once taking tea with Ho Chi Minh in Hanoi. In 1955, he sympathized with both factions in North Vietnam.

onwards, each new Graham Greene novel was an important public event, and the writer's opinions carried increasing weight. His insight into dilemmas of conscience and motive caused him to be consulted by numerous fellow-Catholics, so that he felt himself 'used and exhausted by the victims of religion'.

Ironically, Greene's own religious position had become problematic. By the 1950s he had ceased to be a communicant because his private life was 'not regular', although he continued to express his often unorthodox views on Catholic matters. Later, he ruefully described himself as 'semi-lapsed' but with 'one foot in the door.'

THE HABIT OF DANGER

For Greene the 1950s were 'a period of great unrest', and he travelled more widely than ever. Characteristically he explained that 'it became a habit with me to visit troubled places, not to seek material for novels but to regain the sense of insecurity which I had enjoyed in the three blitzes on London.' Often undertaking journalistic assignments, he spent long periods in Malaya during the Emergency, in Vietnam while the French fought the Viet Minh, in Kenya when the Mau Mau were killing white farmers, and also in Stalinist Poland, pre-Castro Cuba and the Belgian Congo. Although some of his most famous novels emerged from these experiences, Greene also found an escape from the solitude of the fiction writer by beginning a new career as a successful playwright. He greatly relished his involvement in rehearsing and mounting theatrical productions.

In 1966 Greene finally left England and settled at Antibes in the South of France. But despite advancing age he remained an indefatigable traveller, still attracted by novelty and danger, and moved to join the struggle against oppression.

'One of my commitments'
A picture hung on Greene's wall, a gift from Fidel Castro (above). 'I felt very close to the Fidelistas' struggle.

Fact or Fiction

ALEXANDER KORDA

The only character Greene admitted to taking from life was Dreuther, the business tycoon in *Loser Takes All*, modelled on Greene's film-producer friend Alex Korda (right). The expansive Hungarian also gave Greene the plot, by failing to show up at a rendezvous for a Mediterranean cruise, just as Dreuther does – though, unlike his fictional counterpart, Greene did not find consolation by winning a fortune at roulette.

General Torrijos
The left-wing ruler of Panama (above) invited Greene to visit in 1974 and regularly afterwards; they became close friends. 'I fell in love with Panama and its people, just like that, without warning . . . Torrijos knew that I was inclined to take an anti-American attitude.'

Sandinista sympathizer
The Sandinistas in Nicaragua (above) 'asked me to join them as an observer; I refused: Somoza could have had me shot down and put the blame on my friends . . .' Greene (below) felt his fame both freed and hampered him as a political activist.

Some of his actions were public gestures, given added authority by his ever-growing fame: a protest in Prague against repression in Czechoslovakia; resignation from the American Academy of Letters during the Vietnam war; condemnation of British methods of interrogating IRA suspects. But Greene also enjoyed taking a hand in events – carrying a message to Ho Chi Minh, smuggling winter clothing to Castro's rebel followers, meeting Haitian rebels . . . and, apparently in a spirit closer to mischief than to militancy, getting himself deported from Puerto Rico by the Americans, and talking to schoolchildren in right-wing Paraguay on the forbidden subject of Fidel Castro.

BUYING BULLETS

In his seventies Greene became involved with the left-wing ruler of Panama, General Torrijos, whom he supported in Panama's dispute with the United States over the canal. When the matter was resolved in 1977, Greene went to Washington as part of the Panamanian delegation, thoroughly enjoying the irony of his official status in a country which had once been reluctant to grant him entry. More recently still, he was 'a modest help to the Sandinistas in buying bullets which, I hoped, would eventually hit Somoza' (the dictator of Nicaragua, who was eventually overthrown). Of course, as is said in *The Comedians*, "A pen, as well as a silver bullet, can draw blood."

While involved in all these activities, Greene continued to produce books, albeit more slowly than in earlier years. He did not leave the South of France untouched by his pen (in 1982 he published a pamphlet with the title *J'Accuse – The Dark Side of Nice*). But danger did not seek out Graham Greene, and it seems that he spent his last years there without recourse to 'ways of escape'.

Haiti – Nightmare Republic

Colonized by Spain and France, occupied by the US and finally terrorized by its own dictators, Haiti bears the scars in the form of widespread poverty, illiteracy and starvation.

Few major authors have embarked on such extensive or adventurous travels as Graham Greene. His visits to far-flung, troubled countries vividly inspired his most famous writing. One of the most remarkable examples is Haiti, the setting for *The Comedians* – a country with a history of prolonged strife and bloodshed, whose people are even today struggling to establish real democracy.

In December 1492, Christopher Columbus, with a tiny Spanish fleet, landed on the second largest Caribbean island. It was called Aiti – 'mountainous land' – by its indigenous inhabitants, the Arawak Indians, whom Columbus described as 'loveable, tractable, peaceable and praiseworthy'. The Spanish invaders had come for a particular reason: they were looking for gold, which they soon found, on the eastern part of the island.

The 'peaceable' Indians were enslaved by the Spanish invaders and forced to work in the goldmines until near-extinction of the whole tribe. If they managed to survive exhaustion and ill-treatment, they fell victim to diseases imported from Europe, such as smallpox, typhus and influenza. Within 50 years, the native workforce was so depleted that large numbers of African slaves had to be shipped in to replenish the numbers. By now, however, workable gold reserves had become exhausted and the greedy eyes of the conquistadors (Spanish conquerors) had turned to Mexico (1521) and Peru (1532).

FALLING TO THE FRENCH

The Spanish had renamed the island *La Isla Española* (Hispaniola) as it reminded them of home. It remained in Spanish possession, but became a backwater, vulnerable to acquisition by Spain's colonial rivals. In 1586 the city of Santo Domingo was sacked and looted by English forces under Sir Francis Drake, and pirates became increasingly active in the surrounding seas. As Spanish interest in Hispaniola faded, French settlers ensconced themselves on the western part. Their control of this territory, which they named Saint Domingue (the part which today is Haiti), was recognized by the Spanish in 1697.

The French colonists found their 'gold' in the export of sugar, coffee, indigo, cocoa and cotton picked by the slaves. Saint Domingue produced more sugar than all the English Caribbean islands put together, and its overall volume of trade, which required the use of 700 ships, is said to have exceeded that of the thirteen North American colonies. But the planters resented the way in which the mother country creamed off most of the profits. Saint Domingue's sugar had to be refined in French ports and all manufactured goods had to be imported from France. France's stranglehold on Saint Domingue's economic development also encouraged corruption among colonial administrators. For a suitable bribe these officials would turn a blind eye to smuggling, or adjust trading permits causing economic under-development and widespread corruption.

Haiti
This 18th-century map (below) shows Haiti and the focal points of the country's history. Christopher Columbus is seen landing at left, accepting gifts from the natives; slave leader Toussaint L'Ouverture is framed in the lower left corner, and the abolition of slavery is shown centre below.

Labour on tap
The practice of importing African slaves (left) started in the 1520s. Slaves were worked and treated like animals, and when they died were soon replaced. Slavery was to last for more than 250 years, until abolished in 1794.

Slaves uprising
In 1791 the slaves turned against their owners, burning down thousands of coffee estates and sugar plantations. But the death toll was high – 10,000 slaves were killed and 1000 whites. Toussaint L'Ouverture (left), a former slave, joined the struggle and emerged as a brilliant leader.

Caught between the white colonists and the black slaves were their children, mulattos born of white slave-owners and black slave women. In 1791 there were about 28,000 mulattos in Saint Domingue, compared with 40,000 whites and 450,000 blacks. Technically, the mulattos were free and they could own property and even slaves, but apartheid-like measures had been introduced in the 1760s and 1770s to check their influence. Mulattos were, for example, not allowed to marry whites or to reside in France, and certain professions were closed to them. They were also obliged to wear different clothes from whites, to sit in different parts of churches and theatres, and to observe a curfew. Mulatto resentment of such indignities fuelled tensions on the island, but their troubles were slight compared with the appalling treatment that was meted out to the Saint Domingue slaves.

DEATH SENTENCE

Saint Domingue was said to have been 'a mill for crushing negroes as much as for crushing sugar cane'. Any brief description of the conditions endured by the majority of slaves risks being an understatement, for their treatment was nothing less than a protracted death sentence. The slave mortality rate was extremely high, but they were so cheap that their owners, lacking any moral scruples, had no economic incentive to treat them well. Instead of reproducing naturally, the slave population was simply replenished by further shiploads from Africa. The infamous *Code Noir* laid down regulations for their treatment, stipulating, for example, that after one month's absence a caught runaway slave should have his ears cut off and be branded. A longer absence warranted further mutilation, and capture of a runaway after three months justified his death. Notwithstanding these deterrents, and a huge military presence on the island, some slaves – known as maroons – escaped to freedom in the mountains.

The slaves' one solace was voodoo, a religion rooted in West Africa. Because its practices were not understood by the white masters it was also a valuable means of political communication. In August 1791, a voodoo ceremony in the north of the country gave the signal for a well-organized slave uprising under the leadership of the High Priest Boukman. The slaves murdered many of their white oppressors and burned down the plantations. They took advantage of the general confusion sparked off by the French Revolution: this had left whites and mulattos uncertain about their

King Henri I
Ruler of the north of Haiti from 1807 to 1820, Henri Christophe (inset below) had himself crowned in 1811. He indulged himself in erecting spectacular and extravagant castles around the country, including Sans Souci and Citadelle La Ferrière (below).

political rights and the relationship between Saint Domingue and France. The slaves' uprising was to last for twelve years. Boukman was captured and beheaded in its early stages, and then Toussaint L'Ouverture stepped into his place.

Toussaint had been educated by his godfather and taught the medicinal uses of plants by his father, the son of a petty African chieftain who had been captured in war. His skills enabled him to work as a plantation steward, a job normally held by a white man rather than a slave. He was aged about 45 when – despite his privileges – he decided to join the rebels; they seem to have recognized him immediately as their leader. Toussaint perfected the slave army's guerrilla tactics and the art of playing one colonial power off against another. Thus in 1793 he was allied with both Spanish and French royalists. But in 1794, when the French Republic abolished slavery, he reunited with the French revolutionaries to expel the British invaders of Saint Domingue.

LINKS WITH FRANCE

By 1794 Toussaint was acknowledged as the Lieutenant Governor of a colonial state within the French Empire. But after years of war and turmoil it was a predictably authoritarian state. Slavery was replaced by a system of hired labour, and trading arrangements with France became more favourable to the colony. But military men exercised the political power and Toussaint himself controlled government revenue. This was an unhealthy precedent.

Toussaint L'Ouverture trusted in the ideals of the French Revolution. The new Emperor of France, however, Napoleon Bonaparte, was suspicious of Toussaint's independent constitution; and the fabulous profits made in the days of slavery ultimately weighed more with him than the principle of racial equality. In 1801 Napoleon despatched a mammoth French expeditionary force to the Caribbean, and Toussaint, invited to 'negotiate', was ignominously shipped to France. In 1803, aged about 60, he died of debility and maltreatment in a French prison.

American occupation
Plundered by Spain and France, Haiti finally fell prey to American 'protection'.

Exporting art
Brightly coloured, naive painting has become one of the country's most marketable industries.

When they heard of this treachery, Toussaint's lieutenants, Jean-Jacques Dessalines and Henri Christophe, continued the war for Haiti's independence. With American aid, the hard-fighting rebel army vanquished the French, who had already been weakened by yellow fever. The island's independence was declared on 1 January 1804; it was the world's first Black Republic and given its Indian name, Haiti. But the war of independence was followed by civil war. After Dessalines had proclaimed himself Emperor Jacques I, large numbers of whites were massacred, and many more fled the country; tension mounted between mulatto and black citizens. Dessalines himself was killed trying to suppress a mulatto revolt just two years later.

After Dessalines' death, Haiti was temporarily divided. Henri Christophe established a monarchy in the north and proceeded to build a series of castles, the most spectacular of which is Citadelle La Ferriere, which took thirteen years and – reputedly – the lives of 20,000 workers to build. After King Henri I's suicide this kingdom was re-absorbed into Haiti, whose independence France recognized in 1825, on extremely onerous terms. Ninety million gold francs had to be paid to the former mother country, an impossible sum which Haiti could raise only by loans. In 1844 the eastern part of the island seceded as the Dominican Republic. Haiti's history for the rest of the 19th century was

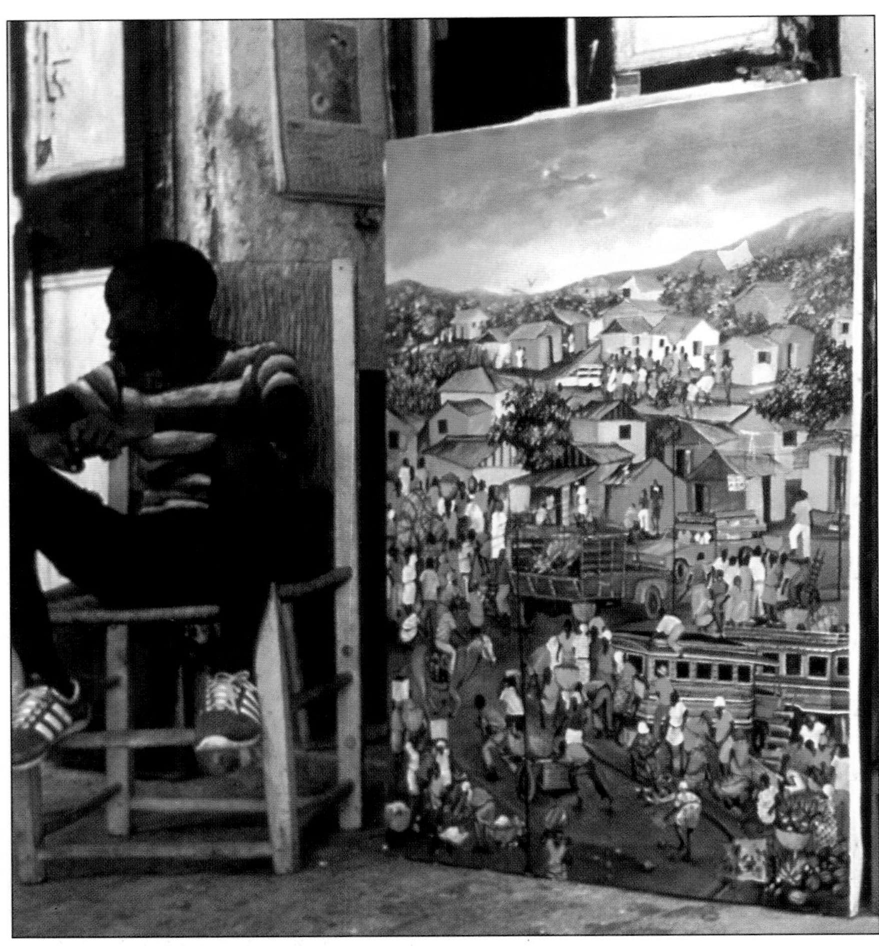

Inescapable poverty
(left) Poverty and unemployment are the bleak realities for most of Haiti's population. With the highest illiteracy, infant mortality and starvation rates, the country is the poorest in the Western hemisphere. The average life expectancy is 48 years.

Fear and loathing
The infamous dictator, Francois Duvalier, known as Papa Doc or Baron Samedi, ruled Haiti with an iron hand – and military backup (right) – from 1957. In 1964 he proclaimed himself Life President, a position he held by reputedly killing tens of thousands of men, women and children until his death in 1971. Even his reign of terror, however, could not suppress the anger of the Haitians (below).

one of constant upheaval, instability and repeated foreign intervention. This, coupled with widespread poverty, particularly in rural areas, led to severe political unrest.

AMERICAN INTERVENTION

Between 1911 and 1915, seven Haitian presidents were overthrown; the last of them, Vilbrun Guillaume Sam, was torn apart by a crowd enraged by a massacre of political prisoners. His death precipitated the American occupation, which lasted from 1915 until 1934. The Americans wished to protect their investments in the railways and ports; and when they left they took the last remaining gold reserves as compensation for Haiti's outstanding debts. Members of the mulatto élite, who

Ruling by force
The 9000 strong Tontons Macoutes propped up Baby Doc's dictatorship, with the assistance of the Army (above), a large presidential guard, and the Leopards – soldiers armed and trained by the US.

Voodoo magic
Baby Doc's face adorns the gate to a voodoo temple (above), symbolizing the marriage of politics and this ancient, primitive religion.

had been sponsored by the Americans at the expense of black Haitians, presided over a country disfigured by corruption, violence and, for the vast majority of its citizens, appalling poverty.

Driven from participation in political life, the black middle class – teachers, doctors, lawyers – developed the *Noiriste* movement. This was an affirmation of Haiti's African roots and of voodoo, and it attracted men like Dr François Duvalier, better known as Papa Doc. In 1946 the first black president since the American occupation, Dumarsais Estimé, was elected. He recognized trade unions, and the mulatto aristocracy's monopoly of political power was broken. François Duvalier was a minister in Estimé's government, and was bitterly opposed to Estimé's successor, Colonel Paul Magloire.

Magloire favoured the old mulatto élite, and was backed by the Army, the Roman Catholic Church and the United States. But he was unsuccessful in trying to prolong his term of office, and, in December 1956, he and his family were forced into exile – leaving behind the traditional hallmark of empty coffers. There was chaos in Haiti until the following year, when François Duvalier was elected president. Although his followers intimidated political rivals during the election, Duvalier's victory was genuine, particularly in the rural areas of Haiti.

PAPA DOC AND BABY DOC

Papa Doc was destined to become the most infamous of Haiti's dictators. No one knows exactly how many people were killed during his regime, but estimates run as high as 50,000. In using terror he was not unusual by Haitian standards: what was unusual was its universality and the fact that prominent people, foreigners and even members of the president's own family were not exempted.

Papa Doc was determined to stay in power, and after the 1964 election had himself proclaimed President for Life. New prayers were published to give him semi-divine status: 'Our Doc who art in the National Palace for life, hallowed be Thy name by present and future generations. Thy will be done at Port-au-Prince and in the provinces. Give us this day our new Haiti . . .' Papa Doc ruled with the aid of his private police, the Tontons Macoutes, the agents of his reign of terror. Within months they liquidated mulattos who had been unable to flee, and they used their position to extort bribes and pay-offs from ordinary citizens.

In addition to political terror, continuing economic havoc and international disapproval, Haiti at this time suffered catastrophic floods, hurricanes and earthquakes. Under Papa Doc, the state was arguably the poorest and unhappiest in the world. Before his death in 1971, Papa Doc named his son, 19-year-old Jean-Claude, as his successor on the same terms. Nicknamed 'Baby Doc' on account of his chubbiness and youth, Jean-Claude Duvalier began his reign with gestures aimed at conciliating world opinion.

OPPOSITION AND EXILE

With an eye to Western financial support, Baby Doc permitted tokens of political opposition and claimed to have abolished the Tontons Macoutes. In reality, however, Baby Doc's regime was simply more selective and discreet in its repression. But since the regime's image had become more palatable, foreign aid began coming to Haiti. The beneficiaries of this were Baby Doc and the mulatto élite with whom he allied himself by his marriage to Michele Bennett. The wedding was financed with two million dollars of Haitian government funds. By the end of 1985, Haiti boiled over and in February 1986 Baby Doc was forced to seek asylum in France. In keeping with the tradition that has leached wealth from Haiti since its colonial beginnings, he took several hundred million dollars with him into exile.

A better tomorrow?
Set in an idyllic location, with miles of golden beaches, an abundance of tropical fruits and breathtaking vistas, Haiti remains a land of contradictions. Perhaps stability lies in the future.

H. E. BATES

1905-1974

One of the great English storytellers, H. E. Bates wove his art from the tiniest and most unlikely shreds of inspiration. He was discovered at the age of 20 and steered towards professionalism by the finest of mentors. His talent withstood ill health and changing fashions, and enabled him to make the leap into the modern world of film and radio. But he remained a countryman first and foremost, immortalizing the particular English landscape he knew so well with his sensuous prose.

A Rural Spirit

Shaped and succoured by the everyday life of a rural community, H. E. Bates found his world abruptly expanded by fame, war and travel. But he always remained true to his English roots.

Bates fondly described his family as 'simple country folk', yet despite his later literary success, he made no serious attempt to leap from their world to a more dazzling one filled with celebrities and literati. Bates' first loves, the countryside and ordinary people, remained the core ingredients of both his life and his fiction.

BOOT BOYS

Herbert Ernest Bates was born on 16 May 1905, at Rushden, in the Nene Valley, Northamptonshire. His formative years were most significantly shaped by his grandfather and father. The latter endowed him with a love for literature and music, the former with a profound feeling for Nature. Both men worked in a local shoe factory, as did Bates' mother, Lucy, who taught him self-reliance and discipline. The family were ardent Methodists and might attend church five times on a Sunday – one consequence of which was that the young Bates grew up with a strong animosity towards organized religion.

In compensation, Rushden had the advantage of beautiful country walks, and Bates also had the chance to join in farm work at harvest time. Such was the pull of the outdoor world that Bates was intensely bored by school, although he was no intellectual slouch. As the brightest in the class, he was given a separate desk and a specially tailored curriculum and, in his own words, he 'soared away' to academic excellence.

In those days, his sights were set on becoming an artist and he took sixpenny lessons from a lady art teacher. His other spare time was filled with football, cricket and reading. Bates' father owned an enormous stock of novels, including those by Sir Arthur Conan Doyle, Rudyard Kipling and J. M. Barrie. And a couple of years before leaving school at 16½, he discovered his true vocation. Asked to write an essay on Shakespeare by an enterprising new teacher, he 'suddenly knew, incontestably that [he] was or was going to be a writer'. From now on he devoured even more books, extending his reading to Milton's prose and the Authorized Version of the Bible.

When he left school, he was 'naïve, extremely gauche and extremely sensitive'. He obtained work as a junior reporter on a local paper, but the daily diet of weddings and rural trivia bored him. Clearly not a budding journalist, Bates resigned and was faced with a bleak future. His next job, unpromising as it seemed, was to prove very useful, for it provided invaluable time.

Now aged 17, Bates began work as a clerk in a leather factory. But there was so little work to do, once the day's orders had been sorted out, that he was free to write. He later described his first effort at a novel as a 'shapeless, amateurish, useless

'Oh! how we walked. *Winter and summer we tramped . . . the footpaths, the blackberry hedges, the river tow-paths, the woodland ridings . . . my father striding out athletically.' Thus Bates grew to love the countryside (above).*

Rushden, Northants *'A palpably dreadful mess of that mixture of blue slate, factory, chapel and that harsh Midland red brick which equally oppresses the heart, soul, eye and senses.' Bates' description of his home town (left) shows less affection than he felt for the 'dry,droll, unshaven independence' of its inhabitants. Most worked at the town's many shoe factories: 'I became very proud of my shoemakers', recalled Bates, who styled his fictional Evensford on Rushden.*

monster'. But with his next, *The Two Sisters,* again written in the warehouse, he struck gold.

A year passed before the third and final draft was ready, in 1925, to send off to London publishers. But before he received their response, he was sacked from the warehouse and, at a time of appalling unemployment, went on the dole. He put his enforced idleness to good use, however, reading the finest short-story writers such as Chekhov, Maupassant, Gorki and Flaubert.

Meanwhile, at a party, Bates met an attractive, quick-witted 17-year-old, Marjorie ('Madge') Cox. Years before, his grandfather had actually saved Madge's life, dashing into her family's cottage one night to save the child when the nearby shoe factory had burst into flames. Bates' joy at meeting her was increased by a generous reply from the publishers Jonathan Cape: they were offering to publish his novel for the then-excellent sum of £25. To his amusement, they assumed the

Summer delights
Young H. E., his mother and baby sister are pictured above at the annual town picnic on Rushden's 'Wesleyan Tea Field'. Harvest found him in the fields (below). (Bates is the child at the foot of the ladder.)

Key Dates

1905 born Rushden, Northamptonshire

1925 first novel, *The Two Sisters*

1931 marries Madge Cox; moves to Kent

1941 joins RAF and writes under the name Flying Officer X

1944 *Fair Stood the Wind for France*

1945 posted to India

1952 *Love for Lydia*

1969-72 three-volume autobiography

1973 awarded CBE

1974 dies at Canterbury

author was a woman, and had addressed the letter to 'Miss Bates'.

The London meeting with Cape's directors and reader was momentous. Not only did it launch Bates' literary career, but it also introduced him to his future advisor and friend Edward Garnett. Garnett gave Bates the tough, incisive criticism that this raw, largely self-taught young man so badly needed, and turned him from a sporadically talented writer into a consistently good one. Garnett also helped Bates through many financial crises, and found ready markets for his short stories among his various literary contacts.

This and subsequent visits to London were the first taste Bates had really had of life beyond the Nene Valley. He was initially delighted by it. By contrast, the world back home suddenly seemed like a 'totally negative wasteland'. But there was worse disillusionment to come: Madge rejected his proposal of marriage.

Bates moved south to London to work in a

A trip to London
At the tender age of 20 (right), Bates was invited up to London (centre) to meet Jonathan Cape, the publisher who had accepted his first novel. At a sophisticated, literary lunch in Soho, Bates felt out of his depth. But his "innocent struggle with the parmesan" paled into insignificance against his next encounter – when his hero, Cape's reader, Edward Garnett entered the restaurant he was overwhelmed.

Fact or Fiction

RUSHDEN HALL

As he wrote *Love for Lydia,* Bates drew on the memory of a visit to Rushden Hall some 30 years before as a reporter. He had 'the strangest feeling that the shaping Divinity had actually sent me there for a purpose'. At about the same time, Bates glimpsed a beautiful girl in a pony-trap. Time fused these events: the girl became Lydia, the Hall the home of the Aspens.

bookshop, heartened afresh by the encouraging reviews of *The Two Sisters* and a new friendship – with the pianist Harriet Cohen. The two almost immediately formed a close bond. Harriet was eager to flirt, but not to take the relationship any further. She filled the void left by Madge and introduced him to the leading artists of the day. But a London lifestyle was not for Bates, and he soon returned to Rushden – to dancing, cricket and football, and to tackling a more ambitious, longer novel: *The Voyagers.* It was a bad point in his life which he later dismissed as a 'literary penal servitude'. He had little money and was terrified that his new novel was not going to shape up.

SHAKEN AWAKE

When Bates finished *The Voyagers,* he was so 'utterly exhausted' that he went to Germany for his first trip abroad. But he did not complete his itinerary because an affectionate letter from Madge sent him hurrying back to England. More than just Madge was waiting for him.

Edward Garnett had read *The Voyagers* and was not pleased. He rejected it as 'an utter absolute disaster'. Bates later recalled how 'that morning [Edward] hit me with everything he'd got'. Though dismayed, Bates knew Garnett was right and was quickly aware that the criticism was aimed at freeing the real artist in him. As Bates wrote in his autobiography, Garnett's attack 'in the finest sense . . . woke me'.

The best of Bates' social life centred on The Cearne, Edward Garnett's stone cottage on the North Downs of Sussex. A typical weekend included a visit from T. E. Lawrence (of Arabia) who biked up from Dorset for tea. Such company was stimulating and, meanwhile, there were trips to London for the theatre and concerts.

Now, in his mid-twenties, Bates married Madge. Once, as a child, glimpsing Kent through a train window, he had been struck by the 'strong impression that somehow this was my second home'. And true to his premonition, Bates now moved to Kent where he and Madge bought a

Man of cultivation
Bates was never so happy as when he was in his garden (above). He wrote several gardening books.

Joining the few
A year after witnessing the Battle of Britain (below), Bates became the official 'voice' of the RAF pilot, writing stories based on the men's tough, courageous lives.

derelict granary. Here, 'while Madge attacked the house and its domestic affairs', Bates began hewing a garden from the wildly overgrown farmyard. It was to be his constant joy and solace, as he created and worked at his vision over the next 40 years.

Meanwhile the Bates lived on £2 a week, and soon they were expecting a first child. Where a lack of money had previously been a problem, it now became a nightmare. Bates worked 'like hell', writing short stories in the morning, articles in the afternoon and reviews in the evening. His remorseless schedule resulted in one alarming blackout when, wandering the streets of London

for an hour or so, he did not know who or where he was.

However, Bates' relentless work did pay off with two successful pieces, *The Mill* and *The Fallow Land.* Throughout the rest of his twenties he struggled to get by financially, and became increasingly prone to severe attacks of abdominal pain and 'always . . . the fear of drying up, of greater debts, of failures and rejections'.

Edward Garnett's death in 1937 devastated Bates, but by now he knew that he had acquired the instincts of a novelist. He was proved right when *Spella Ho,* his next work, was reprinted three times in a year. The money from this work and from the American publishers (who asked him to the United States to serialize it) made him financially secure for the first time in his life. But private success was suddenly countered by public terror. Bates returned to an England on the brink of World War II.

FLYING OFFICER X

Bates and Madge determined to take a last look at Europe before the conflagration: they visited Yugoslavia and Italy, and returned invigorated. Meanwhile, Garnett's son David had taken over as Cape's reader and was waiting to lacerate Bates for spawning a second 'monster' (a novel of 'almost unrelieved melancholy' about a war widow). Fortunately, David also knew how to tinge criticism with encouragement, so that Bates was soon hard at work again, writing more short stories and a survey of the genre.

With a growing family to support, Bates accepted the post of literary editor of the *Spectator* magazine. But he was unsuited to the job and was eventually fired. In 1941 he was given a commission in the RAF's 'Public Relations Department' as a short-story writer. Given the nominal rank of squadron-leader, he was allowed a degree of freedom to observe most aspects of a pilot's life, but was not allowed to risk his own, which meant flying missions were ruled out. Nonetheless, he found no shortage of material. His first piece concerned an officer's awful duty of informing a pilot's relatives that he has been killed in action. Bates' superiors were so impressed with his work that he was given the grand pseudonym of Flying Officer X and, using the name, he now tackled *Fair Stood the Wind for France.*

Bates' spell in the RAF was hallmarked by bouts of stomach pain, and the psychological anguish of watching German doodle bugs (pilotless planes packed with explosives) scream across the Kent skyline towards London. Later he was given the opportunity of travelling to France to inspect the launch sites. He also went further afield – to Malta, Italy, Cairo, Calcutta and Burma. All the while he was storing up incidents and characters for his future fictions.

Bates returned home in 1945 but was at once paralyzed with fear that he could not write. The

Family man
Bates' family is pictured above watching him play cricket: Madge right, his parents and his four children. He revelled in the Kent countryside (above) and its rural pursuits.

Screen success
Film adaptations of such books as The Purple Plain *(below) brought financial comfort to an author already rich in reputation.*

EDWARD GARNETT

Edward Garnett wrote volumes of fiction and non-fiction, but his great contribution to literature lay elsewhere. As reader to the leading publishing house, Jonathan Cape, he discovered and encouraged some of Britain's greatest writers. Bates thought his first meeting with Garnett, in 1925, was a crucial day in his life. The two became close friends, Garnett giving Bates time, constructive (but often savage) criticism, and encouragement. He, his wife, and the son who later took over his post at Cape, lived in spartan rigour at a stone cottage called The Cearne. Here eminent authors often met and talked.

It is impossible to overstate Garnett's importance as a friend and mentor. Bates wrote, 'I have got a monument up to you inside me.' Three years after Garnett's death in 1947, Bates produced a biography of this most distinguished literary figure.

East had a crippling effect, a 'catastrophic impact . . . on his sensitivity' prompted by the 'callous contempt for life' he witnessed there. The only way out was to exorcise everything he had heard and seen by writing about it. The results were two highly successful books: *The Purple Plain* and *The Jacaranda Tree*.

GOING INTO PICTURES

In 1947 Bates' abdominal pains had reached such intensity that his doctors decided he had suffered an internal haemorrhage and operated at last. They had to remove most of his stomach, but he was free of agony for the first time in years.

Three years later came his fine semi-autobiographical novel *Love for Lydia* and a batch of radio plays. Still acutely sensitive to criticism, his writing nearly came to an end after the scathing remarks of a friend on his work, *The Sleepless Moon*. But he was quickly rescued by his love for the short-story form and by the intervention of the film world. Fellow writer A. E. Coppard encouraged him to use 'cinematic' techniques in his writing – fade-outs, cuts and close-ups. The American director Leslie Fenton was so excited by the Flying Officer X stories that he asked Bates to turn them into filmscripts, which he agreed to do, questioning his success in retrospect.

Another great fan of Bates was the director/producer Alexander Korda, who gave him a lavish salary and introduced him to the film director David Lean. Soon afterwards, Lean bought the rights to *Fair Stood the Wind for France* and *The Purple Plain*, giving Gregory Peck the lead role in the latter. He also sent Bates and Madge to Fiji, Samoa and Tahiti in search of inspiration.

When Bates returned to England, however, he launched into a thoroughly British venture, introducing readers to his most memorable creations, the Larkin family, inhabitants of a 'perfick' world. The Larkins achieved best-seller popularity in *The Darling Buds of May* and *A Breath of French Air*. All the while, Bates' imagination was toying with people and incidents and stories from long ago. *The Triple Echo* sprang from an idea he had been nursing for nearly 25 years. Again, Bates' highly cinematic style (perhaps a result of his early love for painting) paid off. The story, published in 1978, was turned into a highly acclaimed film.

In Bates' final years, he turned his mind to an autobiography, issued in three volumes: *The Vanished World, The Blossoming World* and *The World in Ripeness*. By now, he was such an invaluable part of the English story-telling tradition that in 1973 he was awarded the CBE. He died the following year, aged 68, in Canterbury.

Ripe old age
In contrast to many great writers, Bates knew more joy in his old age than his youth. His health was better, and his achievements were crowned by the award of a CBE in 1973. His children and grandchildren he called 'a handsome cornucopia'; the countryside still held its mystical spell, and his talents were undimmed.

Changing Times

Industry's encroachment on the countryside, and the gradual disappearance of age-old farming techniques, transformed more than the landscape: it changed the nature of rural life.

Writing of his grandfather's Northamptonshire smallholding, outside Higham Ferrers, H. E. Bates recalled in *The Vanished World*, "it afforded me the foundation on which all the joys of childhood, together with all my feeling and love of the countryside is based".

Days long gone
When Bates was a boy, the old Coach and Horses inn in Rushden (right) still served "small beer; which, though not strong enough for men, had body enough for boys or . . . 'bwoy-chaps'". But then the bwoy chaps of, say, 10 years old were already labouring half a day in school, half a day in the shoe factory and the evenings and weekends in the fields.

Hand to mouth
At the turn of the century, the seasonal cycle of farm work was done by manual labour (above) and horsepower (below). But as the population grew, old methods could not keep up with its needs.

By contrast, he dismissed nearby Rushden, the shoemaking town where he was born and bred, as a "mixture of blue slate, factory, chapel and that hard Midland red brick which equally oppressed heart, soul, eye and senses."

In Bates' novels real-life Rushden became the unsympathetically viewed town of Evensford. The narrator in *Love for Lydia* is clearly speaking with the author's own voice when he muses "Evensford . . . had taken the pattern of white hawthorn, the gold and the white, the dark steely brown of ploughed earth and the green of corn, and had left us ash-heaps." Bates could not forgive the destruction of the countryside by the encroaching industrial towns.

D. J. Watkins-Pitchford, better known as 'BB', the countryside author and illustrator, was born in 1905, the same year as H. E. Bates, and was also brought up in Northamptonshire. Like Bates he was acutely aware of the changes made to the countryside by the coming of chemical sprays, machinery and motor cars. The sounds and smells as well as the sights of the countryside were transformed: "in the early days of this century England was a *quiet* country. There was no sound of lorries, cars, trains, aeroplanes or even tractors." The sounds of the countryside were the tink-tink of the blacksmith's forge, the clip-clop of horses'

driven by the wheel's rotation, dispersed the seed.

Hand- and horse-power were the order of the day in Bates' youth. Threshing engines, however, might be at work in the rick yard and steam ploughing was catching on: "we imported on to that gut-lugging clay of ours two monsters in the shape of great steam engines, one stationed at one headland of a field, one at the other, the plough being drawn back and forth on a steel coil between." (*The Vanished World*). The last recorded instance of steam-tackle ploughing in Northamptonshire was as late as 1946.

BRINGING IN THE SHEAVES

The intractable five acres of heavy clay which Bates' grandfather farmed in the Nene Valley – land upon which horse after horse fell down dead, wearied from overwork – became the setting for *The Fallow Land*, published in 1932. Though times were hard and the work was unremitting, labour was in good supply and the fields were peopled with a lively cast of characters that were grist to a novelist's mill.

Shoemakers and other industrial workers from the towns worked in the harvest fields in the evenings and at weekends, joining "the great gangs of itinerant Irish labourers who had been seasonally invading England ever since Stuart times." Women and children peopled the harvest field too. After the corn was harvested they would glean the

Grandfather's horses
Bates recalls how his grandfather's farm horses, one by one, "fell down dead. Since their unremitting task was to draw plough, harrow, seed-drill, horse-hoe, trap and a truck . . . this was by no means surprising."

Mechanization was far beyond the means of such small-time farmers. The diesel-driven tractor was slow to catch on, though communally hired 'steam-tackle' was an increasingly familiar sight at ploughing time.

hooves, the barking of dogs and the bleating of sheep. When Bates was a boy, "the cornfield was flowery from end to end", before the use of chemical weed-killers 'ravaged' the countryside. Periwinkles, convolvulus, cowslips, corn-cockles, camomile, cornflower and poppies were abundant in the fields.

LIFE ON THE LAND

Despite the fertility of the land, the period from the late 1870s to 1939 was a time of great stagnation in British agriculture. Farming was in the doldrums (with only brief prosperity during World War I) and Northamptonshire's farmers were particularly badly hit. Between 1872 and 1929, for example, the country lost almost two-thirds of its arable acres as the recession bit deep.

During an era when transport had been revolutionized by the train, the car and the plane, and industry had become heavily mechanized, British agriculture had been left behind. Astonishing as it now seems, the horse was farming's main form of traction right up until 1939. Television and the atom bomb were just around the corner, but the bulk of British farmers had yet to reap the benefit of the petrol engine.

Although the horse-drawn seed drill had been around since the 1850s, in the early 1900s many farmers still walked the fields, broadcasting grain by hand. To sow grass seed the farmer might hand-push a broadcast barrow, which was essentially a long wooden seed hopper mounted on an iron wheelbarrow chassis. Revolving brushes,

Lost arts
Figures central to the 19th-century rural village, such as the smith (above) and the wheelwright (below), virtually disappeared with the coming of motor transport. Their skills were relegated to those of folk crafts, quaintly irrelevant to the fast-moving, mechanized world of the modern farm and village.

fallen corn from the stubble, descending on the "stook-empty fields like flocks of human hens, . . . gleaning frenziedly from dawn to dusk." The grain would produce flour enough to provide bread throughout the winter.

A favourite character of the young Bates was 'Smack'. "Shoemaker by day, he turned into pure peasant countryman by evening, beery, cunning, masterly with whet-stone and scythe." He turned up regularly to lend Bates' grandfather a hand at harvest time. Haymaking is thirsty work, and farmers brewed copious quantities of beer to keep their army of harvest workers happy. Smack, the scythesman, and his father apparently drank 25 pints a day in the hay-field or harvest-field.

The countryside provided a ready source of various kinds of home-brew. Country dwellers of Bates' 'Vanished World' were inveterate winemakers – cowslip and elderberry were great favourites – and Bates recalls that "Old women . . . were still brewing in my boyhood a herb beer, confined solely to summer, made of nettles, . . . dandelions, root ginger and various other wild hedgerow plants." Cottagers also made sloe-gin, as well as blackberry vinegar which was used as a throat-searing remedy for coughs.

HOOTERS AND HYMNS

Set amid the Nene Valley countryside which represented freedom for Bates, was the town of Rushden – a sort of prison. Its "factories, leather, chapels and factory hooters were a world we somehow had to escape from." Rushden, like many provincial towns caught up in the Industrial Revolution, had been a mere village of a few hundred people at the beginning of the 19th century. By the start of the 20th century it was a town of 15,000 people, centred around the shoemaking industry. The gas-lit, terraced streets were dreary, the "pattern of house, factory, bake-house and chapel, with here and there little front-room sweet shops, continued all over town." Children played their games on the street, disturbed occasionally by a bicycle, a tradesman's cart or a horse-drawn dray delivering leather.

Sundays in Rushden were dominated by Sunday School and numerous visits to the chapel, but they were relieved perhaps by the arrival of the water-cress man selling his produce in the streets or by

Smoking short, nose-warming clay pipes, "they lived very largely on kippers, bloaters, tea, beer, cheese, potatoes and plenty of good bread from the coal-ovened bake-houses."

The independent hand-craftsmen worked long hours during the week, often "madly stitching and hammering away until midnight and even into the small hours in pursuit of cash." Come Saturday evening much of the money would be squandered in the pubs and there was a good deal of drunken brawling after hours.

By long tradition they did not go to work on Mondays but would head for the countryside to work on farms or go "rabbiting, coursing, mushrooming, following hounds, walking or riding miles by devious routes to secret hide-outs where bare-fisted bruisers bloodily battered themselves to pulp before crowds of gentry and poor alike."

BAD TIMES, GOOD TIMES

Times were changing in town as well as country. And the days of the hand-craftsman shoemaker, often working at home, were numbered, as machines and factories took over. One-trade towns like Rushden were severely hit in the 1920s by factory closures and short-time working. In *Love for Lydia* Evensford's "streets were melancholy with three-men bands of shuffling heroes with strips of medal ribbons pinned on narrow chests. Back doors were haunted by slow-footed men carrying suitcases . . . that opened to reveal meagre wardrobes of hanging shoelaces and cards of buttons and rolls of cheap pink and blue ribbon for threading through ladies' underwear."

Before the 1920s, entertainment of an organized kind was minimal. There were village fêtes and

Painful nostalgia
"The days in the hayfield were always hot, those in the harvest-field even hotter." But Bates' recollections of childhood summers ache with regret for the lost wild flowers, butterflies and birds which used to co-exist with the farmer's crop of hay (above) or grain. Chemical weedkillers and pesticides eradicated flora and fauna alike. A much greater loss was the wheat customarily gleaned by women and children (right) after hand-reaping and sheaving. With automation, far less grain was scattered. And some needy families had depended on gleanings for their winter bread.

the occasional country ramble. The tenor of weekdays was set by the shoe factories.

The shoemakers themselves were "shag-smoking, snuff-taking, stubble-faced working men, mufflered and capped" who visited the barber only on Wednesdays and Saturdays for a shave.

chapel concerts, but the big day of the year, aside from Christmas, was Feast Sunday. Each of the Midlands' towns had their own, celebrated in July, August or September. "It was truly a business of feasting. It was an occasion for dressing-up, beer-swilling, parading the streets, family reunions, torchlight processions." The fair would come to town, with its "coconut shies, shooting galleries, hoop-las, helter-skelters, gingerbread, round-abouts and spit-rock."

By the 1920s there were shop-outings in charabancs and numerous dances at Parish and Co-op Halls, to which admission was one-and-six. If the dance was some distance away a group of friends might hire a private bus or, as in *Love for Lydia*, an ancient limousine taxi.

NOBLE ESTATES

Any opportunity of getting out of town gave Bates the sense of being let out of prison. It was on journeys by horse-drawn brake with his father's choir, as they travelled to perform at one of the great country houses, that he came to know some of the Halls which crop up so often in his fiction. The serenity and dignity of the noble estates was in marked contrast to the towns and differed also from the farming countryside.

Of the Sanatorium's grounds, in *Love for Lydia*, Richardson comments, "It was possible, up there, above the town . . . to feel, as at the Aspen house, that the town did not exist, that you were far away in clear, undesecrated country." Aspen house itself, of course, was based on Rushden Hall.

In *Spella Ho*, which was published in 1938 and became Bates' first American success, he traces the story of a Great House from 1873 to 1931 and of the uneducated, self-made man who vows to possess it. The house is seen as a remnant of the old pastoral world standing out against the encroaching industrial world.

H. E. Bates' move to Kent in 1931 enabled him to see "with a clearer, far more objective vision the native Midland land I had left." With distance lending perspective, he wrote a spate of Northamptonshire novels – including *The Poacher* and *A House of Women* – with a keen awareness of the changes affecting the countryside he so loved. And the sights, sounds, smells and characters of Bates' youth proved to be a rich seedbed of inspiration and were vividly evoked time and again, most notably in *The Vanished World*. It is of that vanished world, and particularly its countryside, that he writes so lyrically, capturing in painterly words an idyllic, halcyon period when "Always the air in June seems to have been clotted with the intoxication of mown grass, of may-blossom, of moon-daisies."

Sad necessities
The intensification of farming – specialization, mechanization, government intervention, the use of the Land Army in World War II (top) and the never-ending spread of road networks (above) all enhanced productivity. The days recalled so nostalgically by Bates were insecure, inefficient, grindingly hard labour by comparison. But his novels document the vanished beauty of this rural world with a wealth of loving detail.

Selected Reading

In the following listing the date after the work usually refers to the date of publication, when publication was close to the period in which the book was written. When publication followed some time later, both dates are given. Although this book focuses on British writers, a selection of great Irish writers has been included in the Selected Reading, in acknowledgement of the outstanding contribution to English literature by writers of that country.

Geoffrey Chaucer (c. 1340-1400)
The Book of the Duchess (*c.* 1370)
The House of Farne (1370s)
Troilus and Criseyde (*c.* 1385)
The Canterbury Tales (*c.* 1386-1400; printed *c.* 1478 and *c.*1484)

William Shakespeare (1564–1616)
Henry VI Parts One, Two and *Three* (*c.* 1594)
Richard III (*c.* 1594)
Titus Andronicus (1594)
The Two Gentlemen of Verona (*c.* 1594)
The Taming of the Shrew (*c.* 1594)
The Comedy of Errors (*c.* 1594)
Romeo and Juliet (*c.* 1595)
Richard II (*c.* 1595)
Love's Labour's Lost (1598)
Henry IV, Parts One (1598) and *Two* (1600)
Julius Caesar (*c.* 1599)
Henry V (*c.* 1599)
Much Ado About Nothing (1600)
A Midsummer Night's Dream (1600)
The Merchant of Venice (1600)
As You Like It (*c.* 1600)
Twelfth Night (*c.* 1600)
All's Well That Ends Well (*c.* 1602)
The Merry Wives of Windsor (1602)
Troilus and Cressida (*c.* 1602)
Hamlet (*c.* 1602)
Measure for Measure (*c.* 1602)
Othello (*c.* 1603)
Macbeth (*c.* 1605)
King Lear (*c.* 1605)
Antony and Cleopatra (*c.* 1606)
Coriolanus (*c.* 1608)
The Tempest (*c.* 1610)

John Milton (1608-1674)
'Arcades' (*c.* 1630)
'L'Allegro' (*c.* 1631)
'Il Penseroso' (*c.* 1631)
Comus (1634; published 1637)
Lycidas (1637)
Areopagitica (1644)
Paradise Lost (1667)
Paradise Regained (1671)
Samson Agonistes (1671)

John Bunyan (1628-1688)
Grace Abounding (1666)
The Pilgrim's Progress (1676; published (first part) 1678 and 1684)
The Life and Death of Mr Badman (1680)
The Holy War (1682)

Samuel Pepys (1633-1703)
Diary (1660-1669; deciphered 1825; published 1875-1879)
Memoirs of the Navy (1690)

Daniel Defoe (1660-1731)
Robinson Crusoe (1719)
The Further Adventures of Robinson Crusoe (1719)
Captain Singleton (1720)
The Fortunes and Misfortunes of the Famous Moll Flanders (1722)
A History of the Plague Year (1722)
Colonel Jack (1722)
Roxana (1724)

Jonathan Swift (1667-1745)
The Battle of the Books (1697; published 1704)
A Tale of a Tub (1704)
Cadenus and Vanessa (1708)
Gulliver's Travels (1726)
The Grand Question Debated (1729)
A Modest Proposal (1729)

Henry Fielding (1707-1754)
Tom Thumb (1730)
The Adventures of Joseph Andrews (1742)
The Life and Death of Jonathan Wild the Great (1743)
The History of Tom Jones, a Foundling (1749)
Amelia (1751)

Tobias Smollett (1721-1771)
The Adventures of Roderick Random (1748)
The Adventures of Peregrine Pickle (1751)
The Adventures of Ferdinand Count Fathom (1753)
The Life and Adventures of Sir Launcelot Greaves (1762)
Travels through France and Italy (1766)
The Expedition of Humphry Clinker (1771)

William Blake (1757-1827)
An Island in the Moon (*c.* 1784)
Songs of Innocence (1789)
The Marriage of Heaven and Hell (*c.* 1790-1793)
Songs of Experience (1794)
The Everlasting Gospel (1818)

William Wordsworth (1770-1850)
Lyrical Ballads (with Coleridge) (1798)
Michael (1800)
The Excursion ('The Recluse' 1800; 1814)
The Prelude (1805)
Poems in Two Volumes (including 'Resolution and Independence' and 'Intimations of Immortality') (1807)
Peter Bell (1819)
The Waggoner (1819)

Sir Walter Scott (1771-1832)
The Lay of the Last Minstrel (1805)
Marmion (1808)
The Lady of the Lake (1810)
Waverley (1814)
Guy Mannering (1815)
Old Mortality (1816)
Rob Roy (1817)
The Heart of Midlothian (1818)
Ivanhoe (1819)
Kenilworth (1821)
Peveril of the Peak (1822)
Quentin Durward (1823)
Redgauntlet (1824)
The Talisman (1825)
The Fair Maid of Perth (1828)

Samuel Taylor Coleridge (1772-1834)
The Fall of Robespierre (1794)
Lyrical Ballads (with Wordsworth) (1798)
The Rime of the Ancient Mariner (in *Lyrical Ballads*)
Christabel (1797-8; published 1816)
Kubla Khan (1797-8; published 1816)

Jane Austen (1775-1817)
Sense and Sensibility (1811)
Pride and Prejudice (1813)
Mansfield Park (1814)
Emma (1816)
Northanger Abbey (1803; published 1818)
Persuasion (1816; published 1818)

George, Lord Byron (1788-1824)
Childe Harold's Pilgrimage (1812)
The Bride of Abydos (1813)
Giaour (1813)
Lara (1814)
The Corsair (1814)
Don Juan (1819)

Percy Bysshe Shelley (1792-1822)
Queen Mab (1813)
Alastor (1816)
Julian and Maddalo (1818)
Prometheus Unbound (1819; published 1820)
The Cenci (1819)
A Defence of Poetry (1821)

John Keats (1795-1821)
Endymion (1818)
Isabella (1818; published 1820)
Hyperion (1818; published 1820)
The Eve of St Agnes (1819; published 1820)
La Belle Dame sans Merci (1819)

Mary Shelley (1797-1851)
Frankenstein (1818)
Mathilda (*c.* 1820; published 1959)
Valperga (1823)
The Last Man (1826)
Lodore (1835)

Charles Darwin (1809-1882)
The Zoology of the Voyage of HMS Beagle (1838)
On the Origin of Species by Natural Selection (1859)
The Descent of Man, and Selection in Relation to Sex (1871)

Alfred, Lord Tennyson (1809-1892)
Poems (including 'The Lotos Eaters', 'The Lady of Shalott') (1833)
Poems (including 'Locksley Hall', 'Ulysses') (1840; published 1842)
In Memoriam (1833; published 1850)
The Princess (1847)
Maud, and other Poems (1855)
The Idylls of the King (1859)

Elizabeth Gaskell (1810-1865)
Mary Barton (1848)
Cranford (1853)
North and South (1855)
The Life of Charlotte Brontë (1857)
Sylvia's Lovers (1863)
Cousin Phillis (1864)
Wives and Daughters (1866)
Tales of Mystery and Horror (1878)

William Makepeace Thackeray (1811-1863)
The Luck of Barry Lyndon (1844)
Vanity Fair (1847–1848)
The History of Pendennis (1848–1850)
The History of Henry Esmond Esquire (1852)
The Newcomes (1853–1855)
The Rose and the Ring (1855)
The Virginians (1857–1859)

Charles Dickens (1812-1870)
Sketches by 'Boz' (1836–1837)
The Pickwick Papers (1837)
Oliver Twist (1837)
Nicholas Nickleby (1839)
The Old Curiosity Shop (1841)
Barnaby Rudge (1841)
Amercian Notes (1842)
A Christmas Carol (1843)
Martin Chuzzlewit (1844)
Dombey and Son (1848)
David Copperfield (1850)
Bleak House (1853)
A Tale of Two Cities (1859)
Great Expectations (1861)

Robert Browning (1812-1889)
Sordello (1840)
Dramatic Lyrics (including 'My Last Duchess', 'The Pied Piper of Hamelin') (1842)
Dramatic Romances and Lyrics (including 'The Bishop Orders His Tomb . . .') (1845)
Men and Women (including 'Love among the Ruins', 'Andrea del Sarto') (1855)
Dramatis Personae (including 'A Death in the Desert'. 'Caliban Upon Setebos') (1864)
The Ring and the Book (1868–1869)

Anthony Trollope (1815-1882)
The Warden (1855)
Barchester Towers (1857)
The Three Clerks (1857)
Doctor Thorne (1858)
The Bertrams (1859)
Framley Parsonage (1861)
Orley Farm (1862)
The Last Chronicle of Barset (1867)
The Eustace Diamonds (1873)

Charlotte Brontë (1816-1855)
Jane Eyre (1847)
The Professor (1842; published 1857)
Shirley (1849)
Villette (1853)

Emily Brontë (1818-1848)
Wuthering Heights (1847)

Anne Brontë (1820-1849)
Agnes Grey (1847)
The Tenant of Wildfell Hall (1848)

Charles Kingsley (1819-1875)
Alton Locke (1850)
Hypatia (1853)
Westward Ho! (1855)
The Water Babies (1863)
Hereward the Wake (1866)

George Eliot (1819-1880)
Adam Bede (1859)
The Mill on the Floss (1860)
Silas Marner (1861)
Romola (1863)
Felix Holt (1866)
Middlemarch (1871–1872)
Daniel Deronda (1876)

Wilkie Collins (1824-1889)
After Dark (1856)
The Frozen Deep (1857)
The Queen of Hearts (1859)
The Woman in White (1859–1860)
No Name (1862)
Armaldale (1866)
The Moonstone (1868)

Lewis Carroll (1832-1898)
Alice's Adventures in Wonderland (1865)
Through the Looking Glass (1871)
The Hunting of the Snark (1876)

Samuel Butler (1835-1902)
Erewhon (1872)
Life and Habit (1878)
The Authoress of the Odessey (1897)
Erewhon Revisited (1901)
The Way of all Flesh (1903)

Thomas Hardy (1840-1928)
Under the Greenwood Tree (1872)
Far from the Madding Crowd (1874)
The Return of the Native (1878)
The Mayor of Casterbridge (1886)
The Woodlanders (1887)
Tess of the d'Urbervilles (1891)
Jude the Obscure (1896)

Robert Louis Stevenson (1850-1894)
Travels with a Donkey in the Cévennes (1879)
Treasure Island (1883)
A Child's Garden of Verses (1885)
Kidnapped (1886)
The Strange Case of Dr Jekyll and Mr Hyde (1886)
The Master of Ballantrae (1889)
Weir of Hermiston (1896)

Oscar Wilde (1854-1900)
The Happy Prince and Other Tales (1888)
The House of Pomegranates (1891)
The Picture of Dorian Gray (1891)
Lord Arthur Savile's Crime (1891)
Lady Windermere's Fan (1891)
Salomé (1891)
The Importance of Being Earnest (1895)
De Profundis (1897)
The Ballad of Reading Gaol (1898)

George Bernard Shaw (1856-1950)
Widowers' Houses (1893)
Arms and the Man (1894)
Plays Unpleasant (including *Mrs Warren's Profession*) (1898)

Man and Superman (1903)
John Bull's Other Island (1904)
Major Barbara (1905)
Pygmalion (1913)
Heartbreak House (1919)
Back to Methuselah (1921)
Saint Joan (1923)

Joseph Conrad (1857-1924)
An Outcast of the Islands (1896)
The Nigger of the 'Narcissus' (1897)
Heart of Darkness (1899; published 1902)
Lord Jim (1900)
Typhoon (1902)
Youth (1902)
Nostromo (1904)
The Mirror of the Sea (1906)
The Secret Agent (1907)
Under Western Eyes (1911)
Chance (1913)
Victory (1915)
The Shadow Line (1917)
The Rescue (1920)
The Rover (1923)

Sir Arthur Conan Doyle (1859-1930)
A Study in Scarlet (1887)
The White Company (1891)
The Adventures of Sherlock Holmes (1892)
The Final Problem (1893)
The Memoirs of Sherlock Holmes (1894)
The Exploits of Brigadier Gerard (1895)
Rodney Stone (1896)
The Hound of the Baskervilles (1902)
The Lost World (1912)

Rudyard Kipling (1865-1936)
Plain Tales from the Hills (1888)
The Jungle Books (1894, 1895)
The Seven Seas (1896)
Kim (1901)
Just So Stories (1902)
Puck of Pook's Hill (1906)
Rewards and Fairies (including 'The Way Through the Woods' and 'If') (1910)

H. G. Wells (1866-1946)
The Time Machine: An Invention (1895)
The War of the Worlds (1898)
The Island of Dr Moreau (1896)
The Invisible Man (1897)
Love and Mr Lewisham (1900)
Kipps: The Story of a Simple Soul (1905)
Ann Veronica (1909)
The History of Mr Polly (1910)
The Shape of Things to Come (1933)

Arnold Bennett (1867-1931)
Anna of the Five Towns (1902)
The Gates of Wrath (1903)
The Old Wives' Tale (1908)
Clayhanger (1910)
Hilda Lessways (1911)
These Twain (1915)

John Galsworthy (1867-1933)
The Island Pharisees (1904)
The Forsyte Saga (1922)
End of the Chapter (1935)

Ford Madox Ford (1873-1939)
The Shifting of the Fire (1892)
The Inheritors (with Joseph Conrad) (1901)
The Fifth Queen trilogy (1907-1908)
The Good Soldier (1915)

W. Somerset Maugham (1874-1965)
Liza of Lambeth (1897)
Of Human Bondage (1915)
The Moon and Sixpence (1919)
Rain (1921)
The Painted Veil (1925)
Ashenden (1928)
Cakes and Ale (1930)
The Razor's Edge (1944)

E. M. Forster (1879-1970)
Where Angels Fear to Tread (1905)
The Longest Journey (1907)
A Room with a View (1908)
Howard's End (1910)
The Celestial Omnibus (1911)
Maurice (1913-1914; published 1971)
A Passage to India (1924)

James Joyce (1882-1941)
Dubliners (1914)
A Portrait of the Artist as a Young Man (1914-1915)
Ulysses (1922)
Finnegans Wake (1939)

Virginia Woolf (1882-1941)
The Voyage Out (1915)
Night and Day (1919)
Monday or Tuesday (1921)
Jacob's Room (1922)
Mrs Dalloway (1925)
To the Lighthouse (1927)
Orlando: A Biography (1928)
A Room of One's Own (1929)
The Waves (1931)
Flush: A Biography (1933)
The Years (1937)
Between the Acts (1941)
A Haunted House and Other Stories (1943)
Nurse Lugton's Golden Thimble (1966)

Hugh Walpole (1884-1941)
Mr Perrin and Mr Traill (1911)
Fortitude (1913)
The Duchess of Wrexe (1914)
The Dark Forest (1916)
The Secret City (1919)
The Herries Chronicle, including *Rogue Herries* (1930) and *The Bright Pavilions* (1940)

D. H. Lawrence (1885-1930)
The White Peacock (1911)
Sons and Lovers (1913)
The Lost Girl (pre-1914; published 1920)
The Rainbow (1915)
Women in Love (1920)
Aron's Rod (1922)
Kangaroo (1923)
The Plumed Serpent (1926)
Lady Chatterley's Lover (1928; unexpurgated edition 1961)

Siegfried Sassoon (1886-1967)
Counter-Attack (1918)
The Memoirs of a Fox-Hunting Man (1928)
The Old Century (1938)
The Weald of Youth (1942)

T. S. Eliot (1888-1965)
Prufrock and Other Observations (1917)
Poems 1909-1935 (including 'The Waste Land', 'The Hollow Men') (1925)
Murder in the Cathedral (1935)
The Four Quartets (1935-1942)
Collected Poems 1909-1935 (including 'Ash Wednesday') (1936)
Old Possum's Book of Practical Cats (1939)

'Vita' Sackville-West (1892-1962)
Heritage (1919)
The Land (1926)
All Passion Spent (1931)
Collected Poems (1933)

Ivy Compton-Burnett (1884-1969)
Brothers and Sisters (1929)
Daughters and Sons (1937)
Mother and Son (1955)
The Last and the First (1971)

J. R. R. Tolkein (1892-1973)
The Hobbit (1937)
The Lord of the Rings (1954-1955)
The Silmarillon (1977)

Rebecca West (1892-1983)
The Return of the Soldier (1918)
The Judge (1922)
Harriet Hume (1929)
The Thinking Reed (1936)
The Meaning of Treason (1949)
The Fountain Overflows (1956)
The Birds Fall Down (1966)

Aldous Huxley (1894-1963)
Crome Yellow (1921)
Point Counter Point (1928)
Brief Candles (1930)
Brave New World (1932)
Eyeless in Gaza (1936)
After Many a Summer (1939)
Time Must Have a Stop (1944)
The Doors of Perception (1954)

J. B. Priestley (1894-1984)
Benighted (1927)
The Good Companions (1929)
Angel Pavement (1930)

L. P. Hartley (1895-1972)
The Shrimp and the Anemone (1944)
The Sixth Heaven (1946)
Eustace and Hilda (1947)
The Boat (1949)
The Go-Between (1953)

Robert Graves (1895-1985)
The Pier Glass (1921)
Goodbye to All That (1929)
I, Claudius (1934)
Claudius the God (1934)
Antigua, Penny, Puce (1936)
The Long Weekend (1940)
The Story of Mary Powell, Wife to Mr Milton (1943)
The Golden Fleece (1944)
King Jesus (1946)
The White Goddess (1948)
The Greek Myths (1955)
Collected Short Stories (1965)
Poems 1965-1968 (1968)

Richard Hughes (1900-1976)
A Moment of Time (1926)
A High Wind in Jamaica (1929)
The Fox in the Attic (1961)
The Wooden Shepherdess (1973)

George Orwell (1903-1950)
Down and Out in London and Paris (1933)
Keep the Aspidistra Flying (1936)
The Road to Wigan Pier (1937)
Coming Up for Air (1939)
Animal Farm (1945)
Nineteen Eighty-Four (1949)

Evelyn Waugh (1903-1966)
Decline and Fall (1928)
Vile Bodies (1930)
Black Mischief (1932)
A Handful of Dust (1934)
Scoop (1938)
Brideshead Revisited (1945)
The Loved One (1948)
Sword of Honour (1965)

Rosamund Lehmann (1903-1991)
Dusty Answer (1927)
A Note in Music (1930)
The Ballad and the Source (1944)
The Echoing Grove (1953)

Christopher Isherwood (1904-1986)
Mr Norris Changes Trains (1935)
Sally Bowles (1937)
Goodbye to Berlin (1939)
Prater Violet (1945)

Graham Greene (1904-1991)
Babbling April (1925)
Brighton Rock (1938)
The Power and The Glory (1940)
The Heart of the Matter (1948)
The Third Man (1950)
The End of the Affair (1951)
The Quiet American (1955)
Our Man in Havana (1958)
A Burnt Out Case (1961)
The Comedians (1966)
May We Borrow Your Husband? (1967)
Travels with My Aunt (1969)
The Honorary Consul (1973)
Monsignor Quixote (1982)

H. E. Bates (1905-1974)
Charlotte's Row (1931)
The Fallow Land (1932)
The Woman Who Had Imagination (1934)
Fair Stood the Wind for France (1944)
The Scarlet Sword (1950)
Love for Lydia (1952)
The Darling Buds of May (1958)
The Triple Echo (1971)

Anthony Powell (b. 1905)
Afternoon Men (1931)
What's Become of Waring? (1939)
A Dance to the Music of Time (comprising twelve books) (1951-1975)

Mary Renault (1905-1983)
The Charioteer (1953)
The Last of the Wine (1956)
The King Must Die (1958)
The Bull from the Sea (1962)
The Persian Boy (1972)

Samuel Beckett (1906-1991)
Murphy (1938)
Molloy (1951)
Watt (1953)
Malone Dies (1938)
Waiting for Godot (1955)
Krapp's Last Tape (1959)
The Unnamable (1960)

W. H. Auden (1907-1973)
Poems (1930)
The Orators (1932)
Journey to a War (with Christopher Isherwood) (1939)
Another Time (1940)
The Shield of Achilles (1955)
The Dyer's Hand (1962)

William Golding (b. 1911)
Lord of the Flies (1954)
The Inheritors (1955)
Pincher Martin (1956)
The Brass Butterfly (1958)
Free Fall (1959)
Rites of Passage (1980)
The Paper Men (1984)

Mervyn Peake (1911-1968)
Titus Groan (1946)
Gormenghast (1950)
The Glassblowers (1950)
Titus Alone (1959)
The Rhyme of the Flying Bomb (1962)
A Book of Nonsense (1972)

Dylan Thomas (1914-1953)
Deaths and Entrances (1946)
In Country Sleep and Other Poems (1952)
Collected Poems 1934-1952 (1952)
Under Milk Wood: A Play for Voices (1954)

Anthony Burgess (b. 1917)
A Clockwork Orange (1962)
Earthly Powers (1980)
The End of the World News (1982)

Muriel Spark (b. 1918)
The Comforters (1957)
Memento Mori (1959)
The Ballad of Peckham Rye (1960)
The Prime of Miss Jean Brodie (1961)
Collected Poems (1967)
Collected Plays (1967)
The Hothouse by the East River (1972)

Iris Murdoch (b. 1919)
Under the Net (1954)
The Bell (1958)
The Sacred and the Profane Love Machine (1974)
The Sea, The Sea (1978)

Kingsley Amis (b. 1922)
Lucky Jim (1954)
That Uncertain Feeling (1955)
Take a Girl Like You (1960)
The Anti-Death League (1966)
Ending Up (1974)

Edna O'Brien (b. 1932)
The Country Girls (1960)
The Lonely Girl (1962)
Girls in Their Married Bliss (1963)
August is a Wicked Month (1964)
A Pagan Place (1971)
Night (1972)
Johnny I hardly knew you (1977)
Mrs Reinhardt and Other Stories (1978)

Index

Picture Credits

Archiv Für Kunst und Geschichte: 45(bl), 173(l), 266(tr), 322. **Artothek:** 16(t) Staatsgalerie im Hochschloss Füssen, Bayer-Staatsgemäldesammlungen. **Ashmolean Museum, Oxford:** 197(t), 221 Turner of Oxford, Oxford Botley. **Jane Austen Memorial Trust**: 61(t). **BBC Hulton Picture Library**: 101(b), 120, 169(t), 181(t), 197(b), 198(b), 232(l & br), 246, 247(t), 269(b), 273, 281(b), 284(b), 285(t), 293(b), 306(b), 307(t), 309(b), 315(br), 332(t), 333, 334(cr), 335, 339(tl), 343(t&b), 347 Bettman Archive, 361(t), 366(l), 368(b), 370(t), 376(b), 394(b), 395, 403 inset. **Audrey Baker Collection**: 184/5 Christopher Barker. **Courtesy of the Estate of Mrs F. Barger**: 328(c). **Christopher Barker**: 185(b). **Barnaby's Picture Library**: 122(t), 142(t), 156/7. **Barnado's Society**: 127(r). **Bateman's The National Trust**: 280/1. **Courtesy of Mrs H. E. Bates**: 407, 409, 410(t), 412(t). **Beinecke Rare Book & Manuscript Library, Yale University**: 231, 252(c), 255. **Lady Anne Bentinck, on loan to the National Portrait Gallery, London**: 27(b). **Courtesy of Berkhamsted School**: 397(tl & tr). **Bildarchiv Preussischer Kulturbesitz**: 320(tr). **Birmingham Museum & Art Gallery**: 106(b) Ford Madox Brown: The Last of England, 309(t) W. P. Frith: Retribution. **Jan Blencowe/Derek G. Widdicombe**: 224(t). **Bodleian Library, Oxford**: 9(tl), 10(tr), 53(c) Portrait by George Clint, 71 Detail from the miniature of Mary Shelley. **Published by The Bodley Head Ltd**: 'A Variety of Lives: a biography of Sir Hugh Greene' by Michael Tracey: 396(t). **Boston Public Library**: 135(t), 136(b). **Bridgeman Art Library**: 8(b) British Library, 10(tl) Bibliothèque Nationale, Paris, 14(b) British Library, 14/5(b) British Library 17(b), 18(t) British Library, 18(br) Milton Manor Chapel, Oxfordshire, 29(t) John Crowther, White Hart Inn, Southwark, Guildhall Library, 31 Private Collection, 40 Musée de Cluny, Paris, 41(t) British Library, 44(t) Birmingham City Art Gallery, 51(t) David Allan, Roy Miles Fine Paintings, 52/3 Signorini, Gavin Graham Gallery, 56(l) Bertaux: Taking of The Tuileries Palace, Musée de Versailles, 56/7 Grimshaw: River Landscape. Roy Miles Gallery, 57 Millner: An Alpine Lake, Private Collection, 61(cl) Hickman Collection, 64(b) Sir Thomas Lawrence: George IV/Roy Miles Gallery, 65(t) E. B. Leighton: Signing the Register/City of Bristol Museum & Art Gallery, 66/7 J. C. Nattes: Sydney Gardens, Bath/Victoria Art Gallery, Bath, 68(l) Victoria and Albert Museum, 68(r) Cheltenham Art Gallery and Museums, 70(b) Christie's, 74(t) Guildhall Library, 81(r) J. Rosierse: Safe from the Storm (Detail) Christie's, 83 Down House, 84/5 Victoria and Albert Museum, 85(b) T. Eakins: Gross Clinic/Jefferson College Philadelphia, 86(t) George P. Darwin Collection, 92(l) Thorpe Collection, 92(r) British Museum, 96/7 Victoria and Albert Museum, 98/9 Sir Hubert von Herkomer: Hard Times, Manchester City Art Gallery, 100(b), 103(t) Luke Fildes: Homeless and Hungry, Forbes Magazine Collection, New York, 105 Guildhall, London, 109(b) Coram Foundation, 110(b) Rowlandson: The Hazard Room, Victoria and Albert Museum, 110/1 Musée Carnavalet, Paris Lauros-Giraudon, 114/5 David: Napoleon Crossing the Alps, Charlottenburg Castle, Berlin Fabbr, 118(t) Apsley House, London, 123(b) Roy Miles Fine Paintings, 130 Royal Holloway College, 133(t), 134/5 Forbes Magazine Collection, New York, 137, 141(t) De la Rue Co. London, 150/1 F. Holl. The Song of the Shirt Royal Albert Memorial Museum, Exeter, 151 J. W. Haynes: The First and Only One: City of York Art Gallery, 154(t) Forbes Magazine Collection, 162(c) P. Reinagle: The Afternoon Shoot Roy Miles Gallery, 162(b) P. Serusier, The Weaver Musée du Haubergier Senlls, 162/3 Joseph Wright of Derby, Cromford Mill by Moonlight. Private Collection, 163(l) T. Webster, Goodnight. Bristol Museum and Art Gallery, 164 H. B. Parker: Pitmen at Play Copyright National Coal Board, 165 R. B. Martineau: The Christmas Hamper, Private Collection, 166(t) H. Alken Jun: Full Cry, Christie's, 170/1 Oscar & Peter Johnson Ltd, 171(t) Christie's, 172 Guildhall, London, 174 Wolverhampton Art Gallery, 175(t) Christie's 176(t) Walker Art Gallery, 176(b), 177(t) City of York Art Gallery, 180/1 T. F. Collier: Pond at Hampstead. Victoria and Albert Museum, 181(b) W. F. Yeames: Defendant & Counsel, City of Bristol Museum & Art Gallery, 184(t) W. P. Frith. Victoria and Albert Museum, 187(b), 188(t) C. Williams 'Advantages of Modern Education' Victoria and Albert Museum, 188/9 Sir Luke Fildes 'Awaiting Admission to the Casual Ward' Royal Holloway College University of London, Egham Surrey, 201(t) Reverie by D. G. Rosetti Christie's, London, 210/1(t) Private Collection, 211(b) Alexandre Cabanel: Birth of Venus, Louvre Paris/Lauros-Giraudon, 213(t) Jan Van Beers: The Courtesan. Gavin Graham Gallery, 214(b) Adelaide Burgess: 'Begging Girls', Victoria and Albert Museum, 230/1(t) Whitney Museum of American Art, 233(r) 'Ea Haere la Oe' by P. Gauguin, Hermitage, Leningrad, 238 William Daniel, Guildhall Library, 242/3 W. P. Firth: A Private View, Wrackleford House Dorchester, 243(b) Roy Miles Gallery, 250(l) Maxwell Armfield Faustine, Musée d'Orsay, Paris/Giraudon, 253(b) William Callow: Port of Marseilles, Townley Hall Art Gallery & Museums, Burnley, 257(t) W. L. Wyllie: Ebb Tide, Long Reach, Wyllie Gallery, 264(b) Fine Art Society, 264/5 Victoria and Albert Museum, 265(b) F. Holl, Doubtful Hope (detail) Forbes Magazine Collection, 266/7 England v. Australia at Lords 1887/Marylebone Cricket Club, 268(r) British Library, 268(r), 276/7 India Office Library, 278 Sir Edward Burne-Jones: The Mirror of Venus, Gulbenkian Foundation, Lisbon, 278/9 T. Longcroft: Palace at Lahore, Victoria and Albert Museum, 286(t) J. H. F. Bacon: The City Imperial Volunteers, Guildhall Art Gallery, 337(t) Claude Monet: Hyde Park Rhode Island, School of Design, Providence, Rhode Island, USA, 338(b) Dora Carrington, Portrait of Lytton Strachey, Private Collection, 342/3 Albert Goodwin: The Backs, Cambridge, Victoria and Albert Museum, 344/5(t) Paul Cézanne: Still Life, Christie's 348 Charles Longbotham. Sunset and Industry, Victoria and Albert Museum, 360/1 Leigh Simpson: Eton College Christopher Wood Gallery, 362(c) Ambrose McEvoy: Miss Nancy Cunard. Bradford City Art Gallery & Museums, 362/3 Antonetta Brandeis: The Pontevecchio, Florence. Gavin Graham, 364/5 Paul Bremen Collection, 366/7 Victoria and Albert Museum, 368(cl) Private Collection, 379(t) J. A. D. Ingres: Jupiter & Thetis Musée Granet, Aix-en-Provence, 386/7 Tristram Hillier: Village by the sea Morocco 1936/Mayor Gallery, London, 387(b) Ambrose McEvoy: Lady Diana Cooper/Private Collection, 393 Broders: Vichy Comite des Fêtes France 1920 © DACS 1989/Paul Bremen Collection, USA, 410/1 H. E. Tidmarsh: St. Dunstan's Fleet St. 1922/The Guildhall City of London. **British Library**: 11(tl), 12(c), 16(b), 38/9, 63(c), 80(b), 280 Max Beerbohm. Kipling & Britannia. Mrs Eva Reichmann, 328/9, 374(b), 398(t). **British Museum**: 76/7. **The Brontë Society**: 101(t), 145, 146, 147, 148(t), 148/9, 157, 158, 159(c&b), 160(r), 161(l). **Bulloz**: 115(tl). **Sir Philip Burne-Jones**: Portrait of Carrie, Bateman's The National Trust: 279(r). **Ed Buziak**: 168(l), 171(b), 216/7, 223(t&b), 224/5, 226. **Cambridge University Library**: 12(b). **Camera Press**: 316(cl) Freddie Feast, 316/7, 329(b) Study by Cecil Beaton, 405(b). © **Canterbury Heritage Museum**: 251 Joseph Conrad by Dr Kalzimierz Gorski, 254, 256/7. **Castle Museum, Nottingham**: 50(tl). **Cephas Picture Library**: 65(bl). **The Charleston Trust**: 346(bl). **Jean-Loup Charmet**: 18(bl), 104, 265(t), 268/9, 296, 297, 319, 320(b), 402(t&b),

403(tl). **Courtesy of the Headmaster, Charterhouse School**: 372(l). **Christie's**: 372/3 B. W. Leader: Near Harlech, 374/5 H. S. D. Corrodi, An Egyptian Bazaar. **Courtesy of Mrs. A. H. B. Coleridge**: 46(b), 49. **Coventry City Libraries**: 170(t). **Crawford Municipal Art Gallery, Cork**: 321 inset. **Crown Copyright**: 138(t), 142(b). **John Cutten Associates**: 268(l). **DAS Photo**: 354(l). **Daily Telegraph Colour Library**: 413(b) P. Ward. **Deutsche Fotothek**: 380 Rubens Leda Gemäldegalerie: Alte Meisler Dresden. **Dickens House Museum**: 119 R. W. Buss: Dickens' Dream, 122(r), 122/3, 124, 125(tl&tr). **Anthony d'Offay Gallery**: 343(c) Duncan Grant: On the Roof 38 Brunswick Square, 344/5(b), 345(b) Roger Fry: Provençal Valley Screen. **Dodd, Mead & Company Inc**: 257. **Gustave Doré**: 56(r). **Dorset County Museum**: 220/1 MERL Reading. **Dove Cottage Trust**: 45(tl). **Robert Dudley, Earl of Leicester attributed to Steven van der Meulen. Trustees of the Wallace Collection**: 28/9. **By permission of the Governors of Dulwich Picture Gallery**: 30(c). **E. T. Archive:** 9(tr), 93, 113(t) Garrick Club, 126(b), 126/7 Alfred Dunhill Collection, 136/7(t) Garrick Club, 136/7(b) Royal Commonwealth Society, 190(l), 354 inset, 358(tr), 372(t), 374(t). **Edinburgh Booksellers Society:** 38(b). **City of Edinburgh Museums & Art Galleries:** 228 Portrait by G. Fiddes Watt, 228/9(t) Detail from the portrait by Sir George Reid. Scottish National Portrait Gallery, 228/9(b) St Andrew's Square by Carlo Bossoli, 229(l), 229(r) E. Skelt's 'New Smuggler', 230/1(b), 232(tr), 233(tl), 234(l) Style of John Kay: Parliament Close & Public Characters of Edinburgh, 235(tl) The Winning Shot, 236(t) Walter Geike: A Hallow Fair Scene, 236/7 James Hare. **Mary Evans Picture Library:** 9(b), 10/1, 11(tr), 15(tr), 16/7, 17(tr), 20(b), 21(b), 22(b), 23(t) Visscher's view of London 1616, 24 inset, 25(br), 28, 29(c), 70(c), 81(l), 82(t), 84(l), 89(br), 90(t), 92/3, 93(t), 121(l), 127(l), 129(t), 133(b), 149(r) Dulac/J. M. Dent, 150, 164/5, 169(b), 170(b), 177(b), 178(r), 184(b), 186, 188(b), 191(bl), 199(b), 211(t), 214(t), 235(tr&b), 237, 245(l), 252/3, 254/5 A. S. Forrest: Dominica, West Indies, 258, 259, 260, 261(c&l), 262(r), 266(tl), 270, 271, 272(c), 273, 274, 284(t&c), 289 inset, 302(t), 306(t), 308(b), 312/3, 315(bl) Fawcett Library, 316(t), 321(tl), 322 inset, 326(t), 332(bl), 361(c), 366(r), 367, 368(cr), 370(b), 381(b), 390/1, 391, 392(tl), 392(cr) René Vincent Golfing Party © ADAGP 1989, 403(tr). **The Fabian Society:** 290/1. **Fine Art Photographic Library:** 36/7 Alexander Fraser: Loch Katrine, 60, 67(t) J. Pollard: Leaving the White Horse, Piccadilly, 72/3 The Bridge & Castle of Taymouth by A. Nasmyth, 74/5 by courtesy of Schillay & Rehs Inc. New York, 110(t), 116 Baron de Steuben: Napoleon, 116/7 R. C. Woodville: Retreat from Moscow, 117(b) R. A. Hillingford. The Duchess of Richmond's Ball, 128/9, W. P. Frith. The Railway Station, 129, 138(b), 139(t), 148(br), 150/1(b) E. B. Leighton: Prospects, 152(l&r), 153 H. Brooker, The Treasured Volume, 163(r) W. B. Fortescue: Gift House Brethren, 172/3 G. V. Cole Richmond Hill, 182(r) J. A. Grimshaw 'A Moonlit Street', 220(l) Henry John Yeend King. By the Farm Gate, 234(r) Rayner: St. John's St to Canongate, 242(l), 255(b) J. H. Koekkoek. The Shipwreck, 288/9 A. W. Parsons, Windsor from the River, 294(l) Sir E. J. Poynter: The Cave of the Storm Nymphs, 294/5 E. R. Hughes: Radiant Moon, 300/1 E. J. Niemann: Richmond, 303(t) P. L. Bouchard: Moscow, 304/5 H. J. Kinnaird: A Cornfield in Sussex, 306/7 Paul Fischer: An Evening at the Theatre, 312(br) E. G. Grandjean, Paris, Le Boulevard des Italiens, 314/5 James Webb At Heidelberg, 316(b), 326/7 Walter Crane, The Chandni Chowk, Delhi, evening after rain, 330(l) T. J. Barker: The Indian Mutiny, 330/1 R. Mackenzie: An Indian Procession, 338(t) Alfred William Hunt: The Acropolis, 340/1 Pierre Bonnard: A Summer Landscape © ADAGP Paris & DACS London 1989, 350/1 P. S. Kroyer: The Roman Theatre Taormina, 362(t) R. Vicat Cole: Whitehall, 368(t) Alexander Stanhope Forbes: Munitions Girls at Kilnhurst Steelworks © Newlyn Orion, Cornwall, 378 E. K. Brice: Neptune and his Horses, 381(t) S. H. Meteyard: Venus & Mars, 408/9 William Stewart MacGeorge, The Orchard, 416/7 John Clayton Adams: Scything a Meadow. **Fitzwilliam Museum Cambridge:** 123, 179 Portrait of Wilkie Collins by C. A. Collins. **Derek Forss:** 156/7, 192/3. **Fotomas Index:** 12(tl), 12/3(b), 24, 29(b), 30(t,l,b), 41(b), 63(b), 66, 79(c,l,r), 115(tr&b), 117(t), 166(b), 176/7, 187(t), 189, 190(r), 254/5(b) R. Sauter: John Galsworthy, 275 Portrait by William Strang. **Roger Fry:** E. M. Forster/Private Collection: 323. **Kenneth Gay:** 375(b). **Geffrye Museum, London:** 394(t) T. C. Dugdale, Jarrow Marchers. **Gernsheim Collection:** 198, 194(t) Harry Ransom Humanities Research Center, University of Texas at Austin. **Portrait by Margaret Gillies, Dove Cottage Trust:** 47(t). **Giraudon:** 45(tr), 246/7 Gustave Moreau: Les Pretendants. Musée Gustave Moreau, Paris/Lauros, 355 Lauros, 356/7 Diego Rivera: The Totonac Civilisation (detail) INBA/National Palace, Mexico City, 377(r) Louvre, Paris. **Douglass Glass © J. C. C. Glass:** 376(t), 376/7. **Goethemuseum Frankfurt:** 78(r) Ursula Edelmann. **Albert Goodwin:** 325(t) King's College, Cambridge, courtesy of Chris Beetles Ltd., St. James's London. **William Graves:** 377(tl) John Aldridge Canellun, 377(bl). **Greater London Council (Maps & Prints):** 128. **David Hall:** 410(c). **Sonia Halliday Photographs:** 14/5(t). **Sonia Halliday and Laura Lushington:** 15(tl). **Julia Hanson:** 154(b). **Robert Harding Associates:** 124/5, 134(r) Boston Public Library, 216, 217, 218(l), 218/9, 221, 222, 226(t). The Trustees of The Thomas Hardy Memorial Collection in The Dorset County Museum, Dorchester. **Harrow Local Collection:** 132/3. **Hazlitt Gooden & Fox:** 380/1 B. Campi: Minerva with Philosophers, Soldiers and Ladies. **Jim Heimann:** 364(b). **Reproduced by Gracious permission of Her Majesty The Queen**: 21(c) Hans Eworth: Queen Elizabeth I confounding Goddesses (detail), 42(b), 43(t) Benjamin West: Edward III and the Black Prince at the Battle of Crécy, 44(b) Landseer: Victoria & Albert as Queen Phillipa & Edward III at their Bal Costume, 174/5 E. H. Courbold: Dinah Morris Preaching on Hayslope Green, Royal Library Windsor 194/5 Opening of the Great Exhibition by David Roberts, 331 Windsor Castle, Royal Library © Her Majesty the Queen. **Courtesy Highgate Literary and Scientific Institution:** 48(r) Keith Bowden. **John Hillelson Agency:** 341 Gisele Feund. **Michael Holford:** 40/1 British Library, 87(bl), 354/5, 358(l). **Merlin Holland:** 242(r). **The Lady with the Lilacs by Arthur Hughes Art Gallery of Ontario Toronto, Presented in memory of Frances Baines membership Secretary (1951-64) by members of council Women's committee and Staff of the Gallery 1966:** 199(tr). **Hutchinson Library:** 354(r), 357(t), 398/9, 399(t) Liba Taylor, 403(b) and 405(tl) and 406(t) Sarah Errington, 406(c) John Hatt. **By kind permission of Matthew Huxley:** 359, 360, 363(bl), 364(t) W. Suschitzky. **Illustrated London News Picture Library:** 303, 310(l), 363(br), 386, 392(c), 392/3. **Trustees of The Imperial War Museum:** 292/3 Henry Carr. St. Clement Danes on fire after being bombed, 318(b), 320(t), 321(t), 411(b) Paul Nash: Battle of Britain. **India Office Library:** 108 British Library, 282/3 C. J. Cramer-Roberts Jamrud Fort, the Khyber Pass. **Courtesy of Mrs Trevor Jones:** 95, 97(t), 99(b). **Keats House Hampstead:** 55(t) John Varley, 55(b). **The Keystone Collection:** 305, 318(t), 399(b), 400(t&tl), 400/1. **By permission of the Provost and Scholars of King's College Cambridge:** 324(l), 324(r), 325(bl) 328(t&b). **Kipling Society:** 279(tl), 283(b). **James Klugman Collection:** 103(b). **Major and Mrs Edward Knight, Chawton House, Alton:** 61(cr), 62(b). **Kobal Collection:** 82(b), 310(r) UFA, 368/9 NA, 388 inset. **Kunsthistoriches Museum, Vienna:** 89(bl) L. Cranach: Paradise, 382(t) Correggio Jupiter & Io. **Lancing College:** 384/5. **J. G. Lefroy, Carrigglas Manor Longford:** 63(t). **Lenox & Tilden Foundations:** 76 Portrait by Amelia Curran. The Carl H. Pforzheimer Shelley & His Circle Collection, The New York Public Library, Astor. **Stanley Mackenzie Collection:** 264(t). **City of Manchester Art Galleries:** 103(c), 152/3 Eyre Crowe: The Dinner Hour. **Manchester Public Libraries:** 100(t). **Mansell Collection:** 37(b), 59, 61(b), 65(br), 70(t), 97(b), 102, 104/5(t), 106(t), 121(r), 126(c), 131, 134(l), 136(t), 139(t), 140, 144 The Brontë Society, 196(t) Photo by Lewis Carroll, 213(l), 213(br), 215, 233(bl), 243(t), 244/5, 245(b), 249, 263, 269(t), 277(c), 290(c), 291, 294(r), 295(t&b), 305, 308/9, 372(br), 379(b). **The Map House:** 20(tl). **Marylebone Library:** 267 Westminster City Library: Sherlock Holmes collection. **Rodney Matthews:** 296/7, 298(t). **S. & O. Matthews:** 226(b), 241(r). **By kind permission of Mrs Maxwell-Scott, Abbotsford:** 34(l), 35(b), 36(tl), 37(t). **'Memories' Collectors Shop, London:** 396(b). **Metropolitan Police:** 272(l). **Tony Morrison/South American Pictures:** 356, 357(b). **Museen der Stradt Wien:** 248 G. Klimt Pallas Athene. **Museum of the History of Science, Oxford University:** 199(l). **The Museum of London:** 96 Thomas Rowlandson: Cheyne Walk. **Alexander Nasmyth, Princess Street, Private Collection/Phaidon Press:** 35(t). **National Army Museum:** 282/3 George Scott, Royal Horse Artillery, 284/5. **Courtesy National Film Archive:** 412(b). **National Gallery of Ireland:** 135(b), 240(l), 240/1. **National Library of Ireland:** 261(t). **Reproduced by courtesy of the Trustees, The National Gallery, London:** 17(tl) Virgin Panel from Wilton Diptych, 382(b) Rubens: The Judgement of Paris. **Trustees of the National Library of Scotland:** 43(b). **National Maritime Museum:** 87(t). **National Museum of Wales:** 373 Eric Kennington: Capt. Robert Graves. **National Portrait Gallery, London:** 42(t), 45(tc), 45(br), 46(t) Detail from the portrait by Pickersgill, 48(l) portrait by Peter Vandyke, 50/1 portrait by Eliza Trotter, 54(l) Self Portrait, 54(r) Joseph Severn, 73(l) detail from the portrait by Pickersgill, 75(t) detail from the portrait by Opie, 89(t), 98(l), 109(tl), 112(tr), 132, 143, 146/7, 151(r), 155, 161(r), 167, 175(b), 178(l), 180(l), 180(r), 182(l), 183, 191, 192, 193(c), 194(b), 230 portrait by W. Rothenstein, National Library of Scotland, 239, 247(c), 299, 307(b), 338(c), 339(tr) Vanessa Bell, portrait of Leonard Woolf, 340, 342(c&b), 344(t), 346(t) Simon Bussy: portrait of Lady Ottoline Morrell, 365(b), 375(t). **National Trust Photographic Library:** 80(t) portrait by Romney. **By courtesy of The Trustees of the Newdigate Settlement:** 26(l). **Newstead Abbey, Nottingham:** 74(b) detail from the potrait by Amelia Curran. **New York Public Library:** 244 Avents Collection. **New York State Historical Association, Cooperstown:** 141(c). **John Noott:** 218(r). **Norfolk Museums Service (Norwich Castle Museum):** 46/7 J. S. Cotman. **Nottinghamshire County Library Service:** 349(tl), 351(b). **Novosti:** 292. **Nuneaton Museum and Art Gallery:** 168(r) Horace Dudley Studios, 168/9. **From Outlines by Florence Henniker:** 219(l). **Ann & Bury Peerless:** 281(tr).